"All I Ever Wrote"

# RONNIE BARKER

## 'All I Ever Wrote'

### The Complete Works

edited by Bob McCabe

Sidgwick & Jackson

First published 1999 by Essential Books, London

This edition published 2001 by Sidgwick & Jackson
an imprint of Pan Macmillan Ltd
Pan Macmillan, 20 New Wharf Road, London N1 9RR
Basingstoke and Oxford
Associated companies throughout the world
www.panmacmillan.com

ISBN 0 283 07334 9

7 9 8

A CIP catalogue record for this book is available from
the British Library.

The author and publishers have used every reasonable effort to
contact all copyright holders. Any errors that may have occurred are
inadvertent and anyone who for any reason has not been contacted
is invited to write to the publishers so that a full acknowledgement
may be made in subsequent editions of this work.

Design by Mark Windsor and Neal Townsend
Printed and bound in Great Britian by
Mackays of Chatham plc, Chatham, Kent

I would like to dedicate this book to the following:–


My wife
My typist
My cook
and My best friend, Joy.
(These, as you may have gathered, are one and the same person)


"I've got the best wife in England;
The other one's in Africa".
(Tommy Cooper, 1973)

# CONTENTS

# FOREWORD

In agreeing to have this book published, I think I should try to answer some of the questions that the reader is bound to ask – unless, of course, the reader's one of those people who, like me, never bothers to read the foreword. I'm sure I miss an awful lot by not reading the forewords, but I still persist in doing it. But for those that are still working, despite all that, here are a few answers.

The title *All I Ever Wrote* needs a bit of qualification, because it is not, in fact, entirely true. What you find within these pages is everything I wrote THAT STILL EXISTS. For reasons that I cannot explain, I failed to keep copies of several, indeed many items. Whole serials (from *The Two Ronnies*) have gone missing. The BBC have kindly supplied as much as they've got in the archives, but still great holes occur. I think it's probably best not to mention what has been lost as many people would immediately cry "Oh, that was my favourite", which helps nobody and disappoints many. If I say nothing, hopefully people won't notice.

Another question that must spring to mind is why publish these scripts at all? People who have bought the book do not need an answer to this question – they had their own reasons for buying it – and, what's more to the point, the booksellers have their money and that's the end of that. To people who are reading this with a view to buying the book, I would say that I hope the reading of the text may bring back memories of having seen the sketches on TV, make you laugh again at the occasional funny line, experiencing a sort of "repeat" in the privacy of your own mind, recalling those happy days when comedy existed without the necessity of swearing, passing wind or being sick. Likewise, the many sketches not seen by a large percentage of the public may provide fresh grins, grimaces and giggles on the printed page. Of course, many items may not be to everyone's taste. But then nothing is to everyone's taste. The Mona Lisa is not to everyone's taste, ice cream is not to everyone's taste and Marilyn Monroe isn't either. You simply have to ask yourself, would you rather see the Mona Lisa eating an ice cream, or Marilyn Monroe doing it? It's a matter of taste.

The story of my anonymous writing for *Frost On Sunday* back in 1968 (under the name of Gerald Wiley) has been often told, so I don't intend to bore anyone again with that one. But I had written stuff before that for radio – *Variety Playhouse* and, later, *Lines From My Grandfather's Forehead*, and these early and rather rough and ready scripts are included in these books.

I have, for over forty years, been a collector of humorous magazines and illustrations, and have published five or six books celebrating the delights of the female form; the jolly girls of the Edwardian era – and found it great fun to write captions and jokes to match the pictures. Obviously, many of the captions mean nothing without the illustrations, and this is not a picture book. Some, however, stand inclusion in this anthology. Fragments and snatches of doggerel verse that don't need an illustration are offered for the sake of variety.

Speaking of variety, you will find herein a collection of music hall songs, the kind that would be belted out by a hundred variety comics in theatres all over Britain during the Edwardian era. These, it should be explained, are new songs, written as an exercise because the format fascinated me. I recorded them some years ago on a LP called *A Pint of Old and Filthy*.

Finally, I must come clean about the "Allotment" and "Tramps" quickies which appear here as a series of six or more. I said that I collect old humorous magazines and now confess (but not, for the first time, in print) that these cameos were almost entirely made up from jokes found in 1920s books. In fact, I would literally cut up the pages into strips, each consisting of a joke, and then paste them onto a sheet of A4 paper to make sequences. All I needed to do to them was to add a few words of my own, linking one joke to the next. And it has to be said, they worked a treat.

On that note, having confessed and, hopefully, having been forgiven, I commend to you the following material of variable quality, hopefully appealing to a fairly wide cross section of the chuckle-prone public.

Ronnie Barker
April 1999

# EARLY SKETCHES

Ronnie Barker actually did his first writing for television back in the late 1950s, penning some episodes of *I'm Not Bothered*, a situation comedy starring his friend and early comedy mentor, Glenn Melvyn. Melvyn paid him £50 a go and took authorship credit himself:

"I remember the director, Henry Kendal, in his later years directed one of the shows I had written and in the bar afterwards I said 'That went well, Mr Kendal, didn't it?' And he said 'Bit of quality in the writing, old boy.' And I still couldn't tell him, but I was delighted with that. That was the first praise I'd had for my writing."

Receiving no on-screen credit suited Ronnie just fine. In fact it was something he was to maintain for the rest of his writing career, writing all his material under a series of assumed names, the most "famous" of which was a certain "Gerald Wiley".

"I remember going to David Frost at the end of one of the Frost shows, and it hadn't gone well, but David was always so optimistic, he said, 'What a wonderful show that was.' And I said, 'No, it was bloody dreadful, David. It was terrible, the scripts were awful.' I felt I had to say it, that we must somehow do better that this.

"So I went home and I thought people aren't writing stuff for us. And so I decided that I would write something. I had a couple of ideas and I decided I would write them and send them in under an assumed name. I spoke to my agent and he said, 'Well, you'll have to send them through me. I'll have to pretend I'm this man's agent as well.' So I picked this name, 'Gerald Wiley', because I thought most people when they have a pseudonym, they always have a glamorous name like 'Rock Armstrong' or something wonderful. So I picked a really ugly name that no one would dream of picking as their pseudonym. 'Gerald Wiley' – that's a really ugly name. Then I said, 'Supposing they want to see me?' And my agent said, 'I'll tell them you're a bit of a recluse, an older man I'll say, but you've seen the shows and thought you might try your hand.' So in came the scripts and the producer said, 'I've got two new scripts in from another writer, must be something to do with David I suppose, a man named Wiley.' And we laughed, and I laughed, and we sat and read the scripts and he said, 'What do you think?' And Ronnie C said, 'Well, they're not bad. I think we ought to try them.' So we tried them. And I was very pleased, secretly. And for the next three weeks we did sketches by Gerald Wiley, as well as other sketches."

Only at the end of the series (after several more sketches had been accepted and, in fairness, some rejected) did Ronnie reveal himself as Wiley, at which point speculation was running wild, with everyone from Alan Ayckbourn to Frank Muir to Tom Stoppard being mooted as the potential author.

Wiley lived on as the staff writer for *The Two Ronnies*, although Barker continued to employ a number of other pseudonyms – the important thing for Ronnie being that the public was never aware that he was the writer.

Many of the pieces Wiley wrote for *Frost On Sunday* are collected in the following chapter. There are also some early radio sketches from *Variety Playhouse* and the like, and some from Ronnie's 1971 radio series, *Lines From My Grandfather's Forehead*.

(It should be noted that for the majority of his writing career, Ronnie knew very clearly who he was writing for. Consequently character names in his scripts were substituted for "RC" and "RB" – obviously for Ronnies Corbett and Barker. The Editor has maintained the use of these initials here as they invariably provide a shorthand to characterisation in all these pieces.)

We begin, however, not with a sketch, but with a poem (itself attributed to Jonathan Cobbold, later the "author" of the *His Lordship Entertains* series) which, in its simple evocation of lost innocence and days gone by, speaks volumes about the work contained in this volume:

## LITTLE FISH

Three boys were standing in the village stream:

The old man bellowed "Oi! Come out o' there!
You'll cut your feet to ribbons on them stones.
They're poisonous, them weeds – or don't you care?
Look well if you got stuck in that there mud
And someone had to come and get you free!
The water's full of tins, and broken glass."

The boys looked up, and rubbed a muddy knee
With a wet hand – but stayed there, in the stream.
The old man glared, but saw it was in vain;
And muttering "You'll catch your death of cold",
Stumped off; and wished he was a boy again.

# THE ELIZABETHAN DRAMA

*(Early radio piece – 1960)*

**ANNOUNCER:**
The scene is a wood near Venice. The
chorus enters, and bows low.

**CHORUS:**
Good gentle people all, hear me I pray
A tale will I unfold: upon this day
The feast of good Saint Pancras, you will
hear
A history that will delight your ear.
'Tis this; two boys, sired by the same good
knight
(I trust, in sooth, I am informed aright )
Born at the self-same hour, twins were
they named;
Now both, their dead sire's lands and
deeds have claimed.
And each have sworn to murder one
another
Should either each meet up with either
other.
Venutio and Velutio are their names –
But soft; who comes? We'll watch the fun
and games.

*(He withdraws.)*

*(Enter Fruitio, a clown.)*

**CLOWN:**
Here's a pretty catch of fishes, as the dame
said to the ironmonger: for though
Velutio is my master, yet I do prefer
Venutio, and have done since all
proverbial. How can I desert the one,
without getting my deserts of the other?
Would I were not I, I would! I would I
were not that I wished I was; for if I were
not that I would not be! Those that do not
rise early, get no wenching o' market-
days, as the Oracle tells us. Therefore I will
resolve to quit my master Velutio, and
follow Venutio – or is it turn about, as
Lucifer has it. Whate'er it is, I will do it
straight. But here comes my master, and
with the Doge of Venice. There's
company indeed, as they all have it. I'll

hide within this bush, and learn little if
not much, I trow.

*(He conceals himself within a bush.)*

*(Enter Velutio with Hirsuitio, the Doge of
Venice.)*

**VELUTIO:**
And there, good uncle, you have all my
tale.

**DOGE:**
In faith, good sir, I thank thee much for
that. And whither goest thou from hence,
to thither?

**VELUTIO:**
To Padua, and thence to Mantua,
by-passing Turin, and Rome's ancient pile
up to the Bay of Naples, and from thence
cross Africa, and to the farthest shores
of the Antipodes, my chart is set.

**DOGE:**
Take thou provisions, thou will'st need
them, straight.

**VELUTIO:**
My thanks to thee, good father; that I will.
And now adieu, for Phoebus' golden steed
e'en now wings down her dappled
shadow-show
and wraps the earth in sleep – I must be
gone.

**DOGE:**
Then go, and talk no more – it groweth
cold.
But stay! who comes from yonder hence
to here
moving as if he'd Charon on his back?

**VELUTIO:**
It is my cursed brother, mark, 'tis he!

**DOGE:**
Not Mark, but young Venutio, as I see.
Here, take this cup of poison, which I
keep
always beneath my robe in case of thieves,
and make him drink it.

**VELUTIO:**
Nay, I'll use my sword
to settle this encounter; mark me on't.

*(He calls to Venutio.)*

Thou damned black fiend that once I
called my brother
have at thee now, till one shall slay the
other!

*(They fight)*

**F.X:**
*(Long loud scream.)*

**DOGE:**
So brave Velutio falls, and worst is done
But wait – the bodies – there is more than
one:
Three bodies? If my brain doth serve me
true
we started off the fight with only two!
What of the third? 'Tis Fruitio, the clown!
Whilst crouching in that bush, they
struck him down.
O horror! Now my sorrow gives me pause
My life is forfeit to the general cause;
My jewelled dagger now shall pierce my
heart
Let it strike thus!

*(Stabs himself)*

And I have done my part.

*(Dies.)*

*(Enter Chorus.)*

**CHORUS:**
Thus speaks the noble Doge, and nobly
dies,
Now all are dead; each on the green earth
lies.
Thus, gentles all, our entertainment ends;
But ere I take my leave of you, good
friends
A cup of wine stands on the greensward
here
I drink a toast to you – God give you
cheer!

*(He drinks and gasps)*

'Tis poisoned! And I die! I Should have
known
had I learnt all the lines, not just my own.
With dying breath, I must announce,
with reason,
this is the last play in the present season.

*(Dies.)*

# THE FARCE

*(Early radio piece)*

**ANNOUNCER:**
This week our critic went to see a revival
of the famous farce, *A Cuckoo in the
Rockery*.

**CRITIC:**
Good evening, theatre-lovers. This week I
saw an amateur production for a change. I
travelled down to Little Shelfont, in Kent,
to see the Shelfont Country Club
Thespians' production of this famous
farce. Strangely enough, I had never seen
this play until now; however, one's luck
can't last forever, I suppose.

The play was performed in the Old Corn
Exchange; it's an interesting thought that
this must be the first time for hundreds of
years that this historic building has been
used for its original purpose – that is, the
exchange of corn. For corn it certainly
was. Not that I have anything against the
amateur; providing he is as good as the
professional, he is often much better. But
there are amateurs and amateurs. These,
unfortunately, were the latter.

My ticket was marked L.10. I Found row
"L" eventually, (it was in between row
"M" and row "N"). The seat itself turned
out to be eighteen inches of wooden
school bench, with "L.10" chalked boldly
right across the bit where one is supposed

to sit. There was nothing for it but to sit on the chalk, and I did so, certain in the knowledge that when I got up again I would have "oil" on the seat of my trousers.

(Not real oil, you understand, but the word "oil".) (Those of you who still don't understand what I'm getting at, please discuss it with the person next to you; but not now!!)

I opened my programme, which seemed to have been printed by an itinerant Indian bookseller, and began to read the interesting misprints. I noted that coffees and teak would be served in the interval; and that the incidental music had been taken from "Handel's Large", played on the solo crumpet by Mr Higgins. My favourite one, however, was the special programme note saying that the company would like to thank the many willing helpers for all their hard work, especially the big stiff backstage.

But on to the play. The lights in the hall went out suddenly, with a loud click, the curtains half opened to reveal a maid in short black skirt and feather duster, staring in horror at the curtains, which had stuck. They went back and forth a few times, and, when they finally settled, she began to dust. There were seven doors in the set, a bed that folds up into the wall, and what was intended to be a secret cupboard, which for some reason wouldn't stay shut. It clicked open at the most inopportune moments, and everyone on stage gallantly took turns in sidling over and kicking it shut with their feet.

The play itself was quite good of its kind, but it needed bringing up to date a little here and there; the jokes about the Kaiser and the Dardenelles didn't go down well at all.

*(The next paragraph is played very fast.)*

The plot is fairly simple; a boy and a girl, having been secretly married, because the boy's mother disapproved of the match, arrive at a country cottage to spend their honeymoon. The dragon-like housekeeper, however, doesn't believe they are really married, so she 'phones the girl's mother, who arrives, indignantly demanding that the girl return home at once. So the young couple pretend they are to be married there and then, and that the vicar is arriving to marry them. They quickly phone up an actor friend, who turns up in about ten minutes flat, dressed as a vicar. From then on, it's anybody's guess what happens. I must admit I lost track of the plot at about this point, just after the maid had got shut in the fold-up bed with the actor, who was pretending to be the vicar. I remember the girl's father making love to the butler, who was dressed as a woman, pretending to be the boy's mother. The vicar, who was pretending to be the actor, lost his trousers while being chased by the housekeeper, and bumped into the girl's father, dressed as a woman, in order to meet the butler secretly, whom he had fallen for when the butler was dressed as the boy's mother. Then on comes the boy, dressed as a woman, and is questioned by the butler, who is now dressed as the vicar, because the actor has now become the housekeeper, who has left in high dudgeon. At this point, the dialogue goes something like this:-

*(The following played very fast.)*

**BUTLER:**
Ah! There you are!

**BOY:**
Ah! So I am!

**BUTLER:**
Who are you?

**BOY:**
I'm a dark horse!

**BUTLER:**
Then why are you wearing a blonde wig?

**BOY:**
That's a fair question!

**BUTLER:**
Do you live here?

**BOY:**
No, do you?

**BUTLER:**
Yes.

**BOY:**
Is this the Vicarage then?

**BUTLER:**
No.

**BOY:**
Then why are you dressed as a vicar?

**BUTLER:**
I'm a visitor.

**BOY:**
No visitors allowed except on Wednesdays and Saturdays. Good morning!

**BUTLER:**
Are you a woman?

**BOY:**
Don't be personal. Look out, here comes mother. Talk about something else.

**BUTLER:**
What else?

**BOY:**
*(loudly, as woman)* My little Else! She's my eldest, you know! She's such a comfort to me – always brings me my shaving water in bed of a Sunday morning, she does! Dear little Else!

**CRITIC:**
The play hurtled on in this vein for another hour and a half, until everybody was dressed as a woman, including most of the women – except for the maid, that is, who was shut in the secret cupboard,

not dressed as anything. Thank goodness they managed to find her a dressing gown for the curtain calls, or we would have been there all night. The play ended happily, and the producer of the company came on, dressed as a man, and thanked us for being a wonderful audience, and said she hoped we'd enjoyed it. I left the Corn Exchange rather dazed, and it was only when I got outside that I remembered I had "oil" written in chalk on the seat on my trousers. I bent to brush it off, and my braces broke. Still, it didn't matter – the people coming out thought it was all part of the act. Goodnight!

# CONVERSATIONS 1

*(Variety Playhouse)*

**ANNOUNCER:**
An aspect of the British Character which continues to stand firm against the march of progress, is the complete timelessness of our country life. Machinery now does much of the work that once was accomplished by the honest sweat of the rustic – which means, of course, that the rustic has more time to pursue his favourite pastime – the gentle art of conversation.

**A:**
Evening, Bertie.

**B:**
Evening, Arnold.

**A:**
I reckon we're gonna get some weather afore long, by the look of that sunset. You know what they say, "Red in the sky, Shepherds' Pie!"

**B:**
Ah. It's gonna be a rough old night alright!

**A:**
Never mind, soon be double summer time, then it'll get lighter. Though I do confess I never do understand it.

**B:**
What? Why, it's simple Arnold – it's a thing worked out by the government to make it light before daybreak, so that we can get more sleep without being woken up in the middle of the night first thing in the morning.

**A:**
Well, my two sisters have to get up and do the milking, and they hate it. The poor old cows don't get enough sleep as it is.

**B:**
Eh? Oh, I see what you mean. But it shouldn't make any difference, Arnold. You just put a couple of hours on in the morning, and take 'em off at night. Just like your trousers.

**A:**
Ah, but the cows don't wear trousers, so they don't understand. And my sisters don't either.

**B:**
Oh yes they do. At least, Sarah does.

**A:**
How do you know?

**B:**
I've seen her.

**A:**
Seen her what?

**B:**
Wearing trousers. Doing the milking.

**A:**
I'm not talking about that. I said she can't understand it.

**B:**
No, I can't understand it either.

**A:**
What?

**B:**
Why she wears trousers.

**A:**
Look, just forget about her trousers for a minute, will you?

**B:**
Well, I'll do me best. What was we talking about?

**A:**
The weather.

**B:**
Ah. It's gonna be a rough old night alright.

**A:**
Ah. Well, I reckon it won't matter what sort of weather it is soon. We shall all be at a loose end afore long.

**B:**
What do you mean, Arnold?

**A:**
Well, I seen in the paper where it says they're doing away with the plough altogether. March of Progress, or summat.

**B:**
What, getting rid of it? The plough?

**A:**
Ah, and you know what that means, don't you?

**B:**
Yes. Us'll have to go and drink somewhere else, shan't us?

**A:**
Ere, I could use a pint of old and filthy now, to wet me down a bit.

**B:**
You'll be wet down in a minute. Look at them clouds. It's going to be a rough old

night alright.

**A:**
Ar, us had better get back to the village. Shall we wait for the bus?

**B:**
When's the next one?

**A:**
Thursday.

**B:**
Oh hang it, we'll walk. Ere, I see they be building one of they newfangled bus-shelters on the main road, for when it's raining.

**A:**
Ar I seen it. That'll never get used.

**B:**
Why not?

**A:**
'Tis too small. The bus'll never get under it. Ere, I know what I meant to ask yer Bertie.

**B:**
What's that then?

**A:**
Are you coming to the Annual Muckspreading Festival in the Village Hall on Saturday night?

**B:**
I dunno, what's it like?

**A:**
Ooh, smashing. It's all fancy dress, you know. They do give prizes too.

**B:**
Oh ar?

**A:**
Ar. The squire's wife won it last year – she went as a railway left luggage office.

**B:**
Oh? What did she wear?

**A:**
Tin trunks, and a hold-all. Right boozy do it is, you ought to come.

**B:**
I think I will. Ere, is your sister Sarah going?

**A:**
Oh yes. She's going as a cowboy.

**B:**
Cor! Will she be wearing them trousers?

**A:**
Oh ar!

**B:**
Arnold! You know what?

**A:**
What?

**B:**
It's gonna be a rough old night alright.

●◆

# CONVERSATIONS 2

*(Variety Playhouse)*

**ANNOUNCER:**
Another aspect of the British Character, is the helpfulness and civility shown by representatives of our public services. A typical member of the public, played by Ronnie Barker, approaches the clerk of a Coach Station ticket office, played by Leslie Crowther, to buy a ticket.

**R:**
Ah, good morning.

**L:**
*(Cockney, officious)* Morning.

**R:**
Is there a bus to Dingford Stanley?

**L:**
There are buses to everywhere, sir.

**R:**
Oh, good. Well, could you tell me the time?

**L:**
There's a policeman over there, he'll tell you the time. I'm a clerk, not a clock.

**R:**
No, no, I mean the time of the bus.

**L:**
Oh. Let's see. Dingford Stanley, wasn't it? Do you mean the Dingford Stanley near Reading?

**R:**
I suppose so.

**L:**
You suppose so? Don't you know where you're going?

**R:**
Yes. What I mean is, there can't be more than one.

**L:**
Oh, can't there? Do you know how many Newports there are in Britain? Five.

**R:**
Well, I'll settle for the one near Reading.

**L:**
There isn't a Newport near Reading.

**R:**
No, I mean the Dingford Stanley, near Reading.

**L:**
Oh, right. Now then, let's see. Ah! Well. Now then. You don't want to go today.

**R:**
Oh, don't I?

**L:**
No. Should've gone yesterday. There was a special excursion yesterday. Straight through. Only took 25 minutes, four and eight return.

**R:**
Oh, pity. But I've got to get there today.

**L:**
I think you'll be unlucky, mate. Let's see – Well you can get there, but you'll have to change.

**R:**
Oh, well that's alright.

**L:**
Right. Which way d'you want to go?

**R:**
What do you mean?

**L:**
Well, you can either change at Locks Bottom, or Opsley.

**R:**
Well, which do you advise?

**L:**
Oh, that's up to you. I'm only here to advise you, not tell you how to get there. I mean, if you change at Locks Bottom, you got to go all round the world to get there. You see, that local bus takes you right through the Gremlies, and back.

**R:**
Oh, well–

**L:**
Whereas, if you go to Opsley, you can wait an hour and a half and pick up the fast Bradbury bus. That doesn't stop at all. It takes a bit longer, but it's quicker.

**R:**
Oh, well – I'd better do that, then.

**L:**
Which?

**R:**
Eh? Oh, er, the fast one. That, er, that second one.

**L:**
Right. Day return?

**R:**
Is it cheaper?

**L:**
'Course it's not cheaper. You can't have returns cheaper than singles, otherwise nobody would buy singles, would they?

**R:**
No, I mean, is it cheaper than buying two singles?

**L:**
'Course it is. Otherwise nobody would buy returns, would they? Have some sense, do.

**R:**
Oh, very well. One day return, please.

**L:**
Right, there we are. Seven and fourpence.

**R:**
Thank you.

**L:**
You can't get back tonight, you know.

**R:**
What? Can't get back?

**L:**
No. No connection.

**R:**
But I've just bought a day return!

**L:**
Well, that's your lookout. I asked you which you wanted.

**R:**
Oh, this is ridiculous! What can I do? Is

there a train?

**L:**
Train? Oh, well, if you want to mess about with trains, you should have said so. I thought you wanted a bus. Trains is another thing altogether.

**R:**
Look, please, all I'm asking is, IS THERE ONE?!

**L:**
What, a train? 'Course there is. Every ten minutes from Paddington!

# CONVERSATIONS 3

*(Variety Playhouse)*

**NURSE:**
This way, Mr Pettigrew, he's over there, the third bed down.

**PETTIGREW:**
*(Lancashire)* What, do you mean that big pile of plaster and bandages down there? Blimey, they've made a thorough job of him, haven't they. *(Laughs)* Thank you, nurse. *(Calling out)* Hallo, Bert! I've come to visit you.

**BERT:**
Oh, hallo, Mr Pettigrew. How are you?

**PETTIGREW:**
Oh, not so bad. Don't get up! *(Laughs.)* Well, well, you're looking very well, what I can see of you! *(Laughs.)*

**BERT:**
I'm feeling a bit better, thank you Mr Pettigrew.

**PETTIGREW:**
Here, here, what's all this Mr Pettigrew lark? I'm not your foreman <u>here</u>, you know! Call me Arnold.

**BERT:**
Oh, thank you Mr Pettigrew.

**PETTIGREW:**
I brought you some grapes, but I ate them on the bus. Saves all those jokes about 'em, doesn't it? I see you haven't collected any autographs on your plaster yet, Bert!

**BERT:**
No, well it hasn't been on very long.

**PETTIGREW:**
No, well, let me start you off. Now, where shall I sign, on that leg that's hoisted up in the air, or across the top of your head?

**BERT:**
Well, I don't mind really ...

**PETTIGREW:**
Here you are, on the sole of your foot, that'll do. Well now, tell me all about it. How it happened, I mean.

**BERT:**
What, you mean how I fell off the scaffolding?

**PETTIGREW:**
Yes – I was having me tea-break at the time, so I missed it, unfortunately. *(Laughs.)*

**BERT:**
Well, you know I was working next to the house that the boss bought, don't you?

**PETTIGREW:**
Oh aye, that's where the boss's daughter hangs out, isn't it?

**BERT:**
Yes, well, I happened to look up, and that's what she was doing.

**PETTIGREW:**
What?

**BERT:**
Hanging out.

**PETTIGREW:**
What d'you mean?

**BERT:**
Hanging out of the window. I thought she was falling, and I rushed to help her, and fell off the scaffolding. Turned out she was only cleaning the windows.

**PETTIGREW:**
Ha! I bet you felt a fool, didn't you?

**BERT:**
I didn't feel anything until I came to in here, all done up in plaster.

**PETTIGREW:**
I hear you dropped your lunch-box as you jumped up, and it hit old Charlie right on the head.

**BERT:**
Aye, that's right.

**PETTIGREW:**
How did he feel about that?

**BERT:**
Why don't you ask him, he's in the next bed.

**PETTIGREW:**
*(laughing)* By gum, it must have been a laugh. How long do they reckon you'll be in here then?

**BERT:**
About six months I think.

**PETTIGREW:**
Aye, I thought it would be something like that, so I mentioned it to the bosses.

**BERT:**
Oh?

**PETTIGREW:**
Yes – and they agreed with me, to a man.

**BERT:**
What about?

**PETTIGREW:**
Well, they don't want you to feel that you've got to try to hurry back to the job. They told me to tell you that you can take as long as you like to get better.

**BERT:**
Oh really?

**PETTIGREW:**
Yes – you're fired! When do they bring the tea round here?

# LAW

*(The Frost Report)*

*A court room.*
*A man (John Cleese) in the dock with a policeman standing at the side of him. The man appears slightly taller than the policeman. The judge on the bench, the counsel for the prosecution and the defence counsel (a lady) are all in evidence.*

**JUDGE:**
Arthur James Peterson, you are charged with being too tall in Arkwright Street on the morning of the sixteenth of May of this year. How do you plead?

**PETERSON:**
Not guilty, your honour.

**JUDGE:**
Mr Wigg?

**WIGG** *(Prosecutor)*:
How old are you, Mr Peterson?

**PETERSON:**
Thirty-four.

**WIGG:**
That's a little old to be doing this sort of thing, isn't it? Most people give up that sort of thing when they reach the age of twenty-one. Why do you persist in it?

**PETERSON:**
I don't know what you mean – I've been this height since I was eighteen.

**WIGG:**
Oh. So you've been getting away with it for sixteen years. Have you any previous convictions for this offence, Mr Peterson?

**DEFENCE COUNSEL:**
Objection!

**WIGG:**
Very well, I'll put it another way. Have you ever seen inside a prison?

**PETERSON:**
No.

**WIGG:**
Not even by looking over the wall?

**PETERSON:**
Certainly not.

**WIGG:**
Is it not possible to have entered a prison by walking under the crack in the door?

**PETERSON:**
No.

**WIGG:**
Why not?

**PETERSON:**
I'm too tall.

**WIGG:**
Thank you, Mr Peterson. Call Bernard Botley!

*(Bernard Botley enters the witness box.)*

**WIGG:**
Now, Mr Botley, tell us what happened in your own words.

**BOTLEY:**
I was walking along Arkwright Street on the sixteenth of May when I saw a man being much too tall outside the

tobacconists. I went up to him and asked him what he meant by it, and he tried to cover it up by kneeling down and pretending to be a pavement artist.

**WIGG:**
And what did you do?

**BOTLEY:**
I put threepence in his cap. Well, he was bigger than me.

**WIGG:**
Thank you, Mr Botley. That is the case for the prosecution.

**JUDGE:**
I wish to discuss a point of law with "Prosecution", so there will therefore be a ten-minute recess. The accused will remain where he is.

**PETERSON:**
Excuse me, your honour.

**JUDGE:**
Well?

**PETERSON:**
I wonder if I might sit down, I feel rather faint.

**JUDGE:**
But I ordered a chair to be brought to you earlier on!

**PETERSON:**
I know.

**JUDGE:**
Well, what have you done with it?

**PETERSON:**
I'm standing on it.

**JUDGE:**
Case dismissed!

# DOCTOR'S WAITING ROOM

*(Frost On Sunday – first piece written and submitted by Gerald Wiley)*

*A doctor's waiting room in Harley Street. Eight or nine well-dressed patients are waiting, reading old copies of* The Tatler *and* The Field. *One has a bandaged foot, another an eye patch, another, a cough. Ronnie Corbett enters – a very well-cut suit, gloves and spats, and carries a newspaper (the* Telegraph*).*

**RC:**
Good morning! *(No response from anyone.)* I said, good morning. *(No response.)* Oh, so nobody's speaking, eh? Isn't it amazing!

*(He sits next to Ronnie Barker, who is a very smart, moustachioed military type of some sixty years.)*

**RC:**
Isn't it extraordinary how no-one ever talks to each other in a doctor's waiting room? *(No response from Barker.)* Odd, isn't it? *(No response.)* No, of course it's not odd. *(Answering himself)* Oh, I thought it was. Well, it's not, so keep quiet. Sorry. Don't mention it.

*(A pause. RC picks up the newspaper.)*

**RC:**
I see they are stopping all the tube trains tomorrow.

*(There is a slight shuffling and a lowering of magazines from the patients.)*

**RC:**
To let the people get on and off.

*(He smiles, encouragingly. The patients, without a flicker, return to their magazines.)*

**RC:**
*(standing up)* Simple Simon met a pie-man,

Going to the fair.
Said Simple Simon to the pie-man,
Pray, what have you there?
Said the Pie-man to Simple Simon,
Pies, you fool.

*(No response. RC sits down – then stands up again, singing, quite charmingly)*

Night and Day, you are the one –
Only you beneath the moon and under the sun,

*(He moves round the room, a sort of soft-shoe shuffle as he sings in strict tempo.)*

In the roaring traffic's boom,
In the silence of my lonely room,
I think of you – Night and Day –

*(He begins to tap-dance, very fast.)*

Day and Night, under the hide of me,
There's oh, such a hungry, yearning burning inside of me.
Whether near to me or far,
It's no matter darling where you are, I dream of you,
Night and Day!

*(He finishes the tap-dance. The patients are now staring at him. He sits.)*

Well, I've done my best. I can't think of anything else.

*(A pause. Ronnie Barker stands up.)*

**RB:**
John has great big water-proof boots on
John has a great big water-proof hat
John has a great big water-proof mackintosh.
And that, says John, is that.
                                    A A Milne.

*(A maiden lady of forty claps politely. She is joined by two or three other patients.)*

**RC:**
Ah, that's more like it. Anyone else know anything?

*(The maiden lady stands up. She begins to sing sweetly.)*

**LADY:**
If you were the only boy in the world, and I was the
only girl.
Nothing else would matter in the world today
We could go on loving in the same old way.

**LADY & RC:**
A garden of Eden, just made for two.
With nothing to mar our joy–

**LADY, RC & RB:**
I would say such wonderful things to you.

**ALMOST EVERYONE:**
There would be such wonderful things to do.

**ALL:**
If you were the only girl in the world,
And I was the only boy!

*(Everyone bursts into applause – by now they are all on their feet)*

**RC:**
Wonderful, wonderful! Right! Everybody conga!
*(Singing)*
Aye, aye Conga!
Aye, aye Conga!

*(They all form into a conga line, kicking their legs, etc.)*

**ALL:**
I came I saw I conga-ed
I came I saw I conga-ed.
La La La Laa
La La La Laa

*(They are all going round the waiting room in a line)*

**RC:**
Come on everyone, back to my place!

27

*(Still conga-ing, they go out of the door. A pause. The door to the doctor's room opens and a nurse enters. She speaks to the doctor inside)*

**NURSE:**
Doctor, there's no-one here!

*(The doctor appears round the door.)*

**DOCTOR:**
Ah, I thought as much. That bloody little Doctor Corbett has been here again and pinched all my private patients!

# AN UNDERTAKER'S PARLOUR

*(Frost On Sunday)*

*A man enters, looks around and sees a sign on the desk which says "Ring for service". A bell-push is next to it. He presses it. A loud church bell tolls sepulchrally, three times. The lid of a coffin, which appears to be propped against a wall, creaks open, and a man steps out. He is dressed in black, but with a frilly shirt, a little gay.*

**UNDERTAKER:**
Can I help you?

**CUSTOMER:**
*(recovering from the shock)* Er – yes, I, er, want to buy a coffin.

**U:**
Certainly, sir, *(starts to measure him).* Hmm, I should think you're about a forty-four medium ...

**C:**
Oh, it's not for me, it's for my mother-in-law.

**U:**
Oh, I see.

**C:**
I'm choosing one for her.

**U:**
Ah.

**C:**
She's unable to come and choose one herself.

**U:**
I know how it is.

**C:**
She hasn't the time.

**U:**
Not any more, no.

**C:**
She's flat out at the moment.

**U:**
She would be.

**C:**
No, flat out at the office.

**U:**
Well, never mind, we can arrange transport.

**C:**
Transport?

**U:**
For the deceased.

**C:**
*(realising)* Oh – no, no, she's not dead!

**U:**
Er. look sir, shall we start again? Can I help you?

**C:**
Yes. My mother-in-law has decided to buy herself a coffin now; she's not dead – she just wants to buy it now.

**U:**
Oh, I <u>see.</u> Oh, yes sir, that's quite usual,

these days. Oh well, that makes the whole thing much more cheery, doesn't it?

**C:**
Yes.

**U:**
Makes a change, I must say. I get so bored having to go round with a long face all day. It's nice to have a bit of a laugh now and again, isn't it? Cigarette?

*(Offers the customer a tiny coffin, lifting the lid ... It is a musical box full of cigarettes.)*

**C:**
No, thanks. Bad for the health.

**U:**
Good for trade though. However, now then. First of all, size. What is she, is she a big woman? About my size or smaller?

**C:**
Yes, about your size.

**U:**
Right. I wonder if she'd squeeze into a 14? This one's a 14. Of course, they are cut on the roomy side. I should think she'd manage a 14. Only this one's reduced, it's in the sale, that one. *(Looks at ticket on coffin)* You see, that's knocked down to £28 13s 6d.

**C:**
Well ...

**U:**
Or there's this one. *(Indicates another)* Of course, it's a question of length. How long would she need the coffin? Apart from forever? *(He giggles at his joke)* No, how tall is she d'you think?

**C:**
Oh, about your height, I should think.

**U:**
No, that would be a bit short on her, that one. We could let a bit into that one, I suppose. Mind you, that's a bit pricey, that

one. Made of deal, you see. And as we say in the trade, "a good deal costs a good deal". Mind you, it'll last a lifetime. Here – *(going to another coffin)*, here's a joke. Special line *(he gets into the coffin and lies down)*. This one is specially designed for if you want to be buried at sea. *(He sits up, takes two oars from inside the coffin, and pretends to row.)* Alright, isn't it?

**C:**
*(ferreting about among other coffins)*
What about this one? This is only eleven guineas.

**U:**
What, that one? Oh no, sir, shoddy. Cheap line, made in Japan. No, horrible. I wouldn't be seen dead in it.

**C:**
Well, I'm afraid they all seem a bit expensive – she said something about five pounds.

**U:**
Five pounds? Oh, well now ... Here, tell you what, how about having her cremated? *(Picks up urn.)* Here you are, four, nineteen, six. All one size, fit anybody.

**C:**
Ah, that might be the thing – is it watertight?

**U:**
Why, is she planning to drink herself to death?

**C:**
No. Er – look, the fact is, I'd better tell you. My mother-in-law wants a coffin because she's opening a restaurant and she wants a coffin as a window-box. It's a sort of gimmick.

**U:**
Gimmick?

**C:**
Yes, she wants to grow geraniums in it.

**U:**
Geraniums?

**C:**
Yes. But I think they're more expensive than she thought, so I – er, think I'd better leave it. Thank you.

*(He goes.)*

*(A young man comes in from the back of the shop, with two plates of salad and two glasses, knives and forks.)*

**YOUNG MAN:**
Customer?

**U:**
No. Fellow wanted a coffin for a window-box. *(Gets a tablecloth from inside a horizontal coffin and lays it on top of the coffin. The young man puts the salads, etc. on it.)* Wanted to grow geraniums in it. Geraniums! Not even lilies. Honestly, Cyril, some people have no respect!

*(He lifts the lid of a burial urn, takes out a half-empty bottle of wine and pours it into the glasses while Cyril begins to eat.)*

# A GREENGROCER'S SHOP

*(B is just finishing serving a woman, tipping brussel sprouts into her shopping bag. A enters, and approaches B.)*

**A:**
2lbs of King Edwards, please.

**B:**
Right guv. *(He weighs them out.)* Lovely, these are.

**A:**
Yes, they look excellent. Could I have them gift-wrapped, please.

**B:**
Eh?

**A:**
They're a present for someone.

**B:**
Oh, oh, er–

**A:**
You know – bit of coloured paper, nice fancy box, something of that sort. Makes all the difference, doesn't it?

**B:**
Oh, it does, guv, yeah. I don't know what I've got …

**A:**
Well, leave it for the moment, there's some more things I want. Er – have you got anything suitable for an old aunt?

**B:**
Er – well–

**A:**
Sits on her own a lot and doesn't do much?

**B:**
How about some prunes?

**A:**
No. I don't think so. Hardly the sort of thing one gives as a present is it? A prune. No – I know. A cabbage. That's always acceptable, a nice big cabbage.

**B:**
Right – how's that one?

*(Shows him cabbage.)*

**A:**
Fine, she'll like that. Now then, Mummy.

**B:**
Mummy? Your mummy?

**A:**
Yes. She's so difficult. She's got everything.

Absolutely everything.

**B:**
Tomatoes?

**A:**
No, I gave her those last year.

**B:**
Oh.

**A:**
She's still got some left.

**B:**
I've got it. What about a nice avocado. Perhaps a pair?

**A:**
An avocado is a pear.

**B:**
No, I mean two avocado pears set in straw, side by side. Sort of presentation case.

**A:**
It's not a bad idea.

**B:**
*(showing him)* Look at those. They'd do anybody's mother proud, they would.

**A:**
*(looking at them)* You haven't got any white ones, have you?

**B:**
White ones? You don't get white ones, not with avocados.

**A:**
Oh, you see, she lives in Cheltenham. I don't know what the neighbours might think if they found out she'd got a couple of black avocados in the house.

**B:**
They're green – dark green, these.

**A:**
Yes, I suppose they are. Alright. I'll take them – it's about time she learned to be a

bit more broad-minded, anyway. Now then, Uncle Willy.

**B:**
Ah. What's he like?

**A:**
Well, he's a very heavy smoker.

**B:**
What about a few artichokes. That would be a laugh.

**A:**
*(laughing)* Yes, it would, that's marvellous.

**B:**
Hearty Choke. Heavy smoker. You see? Arti-choke! *(He coughs and splutters.)* Choke! Hearty ... how about a marrow?

**A:**
Yes, alright. Now, do you send vegetables by wire?

**B:**
No.

**A:**
No Interveg, or Cauliflora, or anything like that?

**B:**
No.

**A:**
Only I've got these relatives in Australia and they miss their spring greens at Christmas.

**B:**
Don't they get spring greens in Australia?

**A:**
Only in the summer, you see. That's the way it works out. Well, never mind. Have all these items sent round to this address, would you. *(Gives him a card.)* Nice to get one's Christmas shopping done all in one go, isn't it?

**B:**
Yes, isn't it?

*(A goes, and immediately returns.)*

**A:**
I am silly, bought all those things and I haven't got myself anything for lunch today. How much are the chrysanthemums?

# BORED MEETING

*(Frost On Sunday)*

*Four old men at a board meeting. They all look alike. One – Mr Green – is asleep.*

**RB:**
Now gentlemen, we have called this meeting because the shareholders are worried the company is not paying enough attention to improving and modernising the production lines. Southern Safety Pins Ltd. is a well-established firm, and sales are steady. However, there is room for improvement and we have to discuss ways of increasing the shareholders' dividends – not to put too fine a point on it.

**RC:**
But surely, Hopkins, if we don't put too fine a point on it, the safety pin won't do up. And that's your export trade up the spout. That would be fatal.

**JONES:**
How about making the spout more rounded? I'm sure that by and large, people prefer a rounded spout.

**RB:**
Well, large people would, certainly. I should have thought it was a question of individual taste.

**RC:**
I disagree. It doesn't matter what things

taste like, as long as it says "Delicious, mouthwatering and fresh" on the packet. Mark my words.

**JONES:**
That's not a bad idea. Mark the words in red on every tin. They'll sell like hot cakes.

**RC:**
Perhaps we could install ovens in the supermarkets to keep the cakes hot. That would put us streets ahead of our competitors.

**RB:**
Well, I suppose street-trading is certainly something to be considered. Although our conditions of licence would probably put the tin hat on that.

**RC:**
Hardly likely to increase trade, I would have thought. I mean if I saw a man standing by an oven in the street with a tin hat on, I'd think it was a little queer.

**RB:**
Well, they could wear a little notices saying "I am not a little queer". And they could push things through letter boxes, which would appeal to the housewife.

**RC:**
Yes, letter boxes are certainly worth looking into. Perhaps as an experiment, we could try it out in certain key places.

**JONES:**
Well, the best key place I know is under the mat, by the back door.

**RB:**
True. You know, these keys could open up all sorts of possibilities with the house-owners.

**RC:**
And if we <u>did</u> get the owners to open up their houses, the public could be admitted at a nominal fee – and we'd beat our competitors on their own ground.

**RB:**
I think it will work – and not only on our own ground, but when we are playing away as well. Of course, we need someone to really get the team up to scratch. The question is, who's best?

**RC:**
He's a footballer. Georgie Best.

**RB:**
Then he's the very man! Appoint him to the board, and get the public to open their houses.

**RC:**
Do you think we can do this? Get the public's houses open?

**RB:**
What's the time?

**RC:**
Ten to twelve.

**RB:**
Is it? Oh yes, they must be open by now. Come on, I'll buy you one. *(They all get up and wake Mr Green.)* Come on, Green, the pubs are open.

**RC:**
We're going to vote Georgie Best on to the board. *(Mr Green gets up.)*

**JONES:**
Well, that's that then.

**RC:**
Yes – nice to feel you've got something done, isn't it?

**RB:**
Quite. All you have to do is get round a table and talk about it.

*(They go out to the pub.)*

# YOU ARE WHAT YOU EAT

*(Frost On Sunday)*

*A restaurant, smartish, at lunch time. RB, the waiter, is seating RC, the customer.*

**RC:**
Thank you. Sorry to barge in without booking. I know it's frowned upon by the management, but I thought I'd just dodge in and sort of merge in with the background, and he might not notice.

**RB:**
That's alright, sir. Would you like a drink, sir?

**RC:**
Yes. I'll have a ...

**RB:**
Gin, sir – tonic?

**RC:**
How did you know I wanted gin?

**RB:**
Your subconscious sir – you've already said it three times since you came in.

**RC:**
Have I?

**RB:**
Yessir – barge in, dodge in, and merge in. Oh yes – I always know what people want – it's the same with food as well – people behave like what they eat, you know. You can tell by what they say, what they'll order.

**RC:**
How interesting. Speaking as one who knows absolutely nothing about such things, I would hazard a guess that you're talking a load of absolute cods-roe, old chap.

**RB:**
Not at all, sir.

**RC:**
Pure unadulterated cabbage-water.
Alright, what about this chap – what's <u>his</u>
favourite meat?

**PERKINS:**
*(Passing by.)* Shan't be a minute, waiter –
just getting some cigarettes from the
Baaar.

**RB:**
From the where, sir?

**PERKINS:**
From the Baaar.

*(He goes)*

**RB:**
*(To RC)* Lamb.

**WARBECK:**
*(Approaching.)* Waiter – could I have my
bill – bit late. Got to make a mooove.

**RB:**
A what, sir?

**WARBECK:**
A mooove. When you've got to mooove,
you've got to mooove.

**RB:**
Yes, sir – you had the beef, sir, right? *(Gives
bill to Warbeck.)*

**WARBECK:**
Thank you.

**RC:**
Very clever! What about him over there?
*(Indicates man on open wall phone near bar.)*

**PHONE MAN:**
Quite, quite, quite, quite, quite. *(He quacks
these in a northern accent.)*

**RB:**
Duck. Oh yes, they're all at it. Listen to

her over there.

*(Cut to woman. Another woman is
whispering in her ear.)*

**MRS BROWN:**
Oh dear. Dear, dear. Oh, dear, dear, dear.

**RB:**
Venison. Listen to him over there.

*(Cut to George and David at table.)*

**GEORGE:**
I just cleared off for the weekend – just
stuffed everything into the banger.

**RB:**
Sausages.

**DAVID:**
I wish I could, but I daren't – I'm too
scared of her – I'm terrified, I just daren't.

**RC:**
What about him?

**RB:**
He's chicken.
*(Cut to a German, with a girl.)*

**GERMAN:**
Oh ja, I have lived in Hamburg most of
my life. I love Hamburg. It's my home.

**RC:**
I suppose he's a Hamburger.

**RB:**
No, Beef Stroganoff.

**RC:**
He didn't <u>mention</u> Beef Stroganoff.

**RB:**
I know, but it's all down the front of his
tie.

**MR FOX:**
*(talking to another man)* Oh, she was
fabulous, I mean, she had big round, you
know, and this low-cut dress made them,

you know, and I mean she's just got absolutely wonderful, I mean, you know.

**RC:**
And what's <u>his</u> favourite food?

**RB:**
Dumplings.

**RC:**
This is all absolute rubbish. Now, come on then, listen to this, and then tell me what I'm going to have.
"Oh, I must go down to the sea again,
To the lonely sea and the sky –
And all I need is a tall ship
And a star to steer her by."
... and don't say fish and chips.

**RB:**
You're going to eat chicken liver pâté, followed by lamb chop, cauliflower and new potatoes, trifle and cream and coffee.

**RC:**
What? How can you <u>possibly</u> know that?

**RB:**
That's all we got left.

# DOCTOR'S ORDERS

*(A bedroom. A girl in bed. A doctor enters.)*

**DOCTOR:**
Well, now, your mistress tells me you're not feeling well, Sarah. What seems to be the matter?

**SARAH:**
Doctor – I'm not really ill.

**DOCTOR:**
But Lady Frampton 'phoned me and said, "My maid is ill – come at once."

**SARAH:**
I'm alright. She owes me six weeks' wages and I'm not getting out of bed until she

pays me.

**DOCTOR:**
She owes <u>me</u> for the last eight visits I've made ... <u>Move over</u>.

*(He gets into bed beside her.)*

# COCKNEY WOMAN

**COCKNEY WOMAN:**
I'm leaving you – do you hear? I can't stand your criticising any more. "I'm thoughtless, I'm forgetful, I don't take any notice of you, I'm not interested in you" – well, if that's what you think, I'm off. All I've ever thought about is you. I've devoted the best years of my life to you. But if you think I'm going to stay here and be told I'm thoughtless and forgetful and disinterested, then you've got another think coming, Bert Thompson!

**COCKNEY MAN:**
Tomkins! TOMKINS!

# MAGIC RING

**MAN:**
*(holding ring)* Magic Ring, O Magic Ring, grant me, grant me, just one thing. Make my wife twice as pretty, twice as smart, twice as intelligent, and twice as sexy as she is now!

*(Enter ugly, untidy, stupid, frigid woman.)*

**WOMAN:**
Oi! Yer dinner's ready when yer want it.

**MAN:**
My God! It works!

*(He rushes to her and clasps her to him.)*

# AA

*(Frost On Sunday)*

*A rather plain, dingy office, RB on the 'phone.*

**RB:**
Hello. Alcoholics Unanimous. No, well it's similar, madam, we are a new group unanimously dedicated to removing the menace of alcohol. Well, there are two differences – one, we are a local group, so we know the trouble spots … places like the Women's Institute meeting, and the back of the Scout hut; and two, it'll cost you three quid to belong, payable to me, George Jones. *(A tall girl enters and leans over him to put typing into the "in" tray.)* That's to cover my expenses. I've got some pretty hefty overheads. No, no appointment, just turn up, and I'll help you to stamp out drink. What do you do for a living? Oh, grape treader – well, you've got a good start. See you later – bye.

**GIRL:**
*(she lisps)* There's a gentleman to see you, sir – he wants to join. He's outside.

**RB:**
Is he sober?

**GIRL:**
Seems to be.

**RB:**
Well, show him in. And Miss Pringle, you'll have to do something about your breath.

**GIRL:**
My breath, Mr Joneth? What's the matter with them?

**RB:**
No, your breath. It smells of peppermints. When you work for Alcoholics Unanimous and smell like that, people will think you've got something to hide. Try a few spring onions, will you?

*(She exits. A knock. RC peeps round the door.)*

**RC:**
Is this the AA?

**RB:**
Well, something very similar – come in, sit down. You wish to join us, sir?

**RC:**
Yes.

**RB:**
That will be three pounds, sir.

**RC:**
Oh, thank you – I had a job finding you, actually, up all those stairs. Not very well sign-posted, this office, is it? *(Gives him the money.)*

**RB:**
We make it a rule to keep the whole thing as discreet as possible, sir.

**RC:**
Quite right. Quite right. Otherwise you'd have everybody becoming a member, wouldn't you. Better to keep it a bit select. Now, I've brought my provisional licence, my birth certificate …

**RB:**
Oh, don't get me wrong. We're not choosy. Any drunk who comes in off the street can join.

**RC:**
Oh, really?

**RB:**
Oh yes, that's part of our policy.

**RC:**
Ah. Well, I haven't read your policy, actually, but there are one or two points you could enlighten me over. Now say, for instance, I get stranded somewhere in the middle of the night – do you come out and collect me?

**RB:**
Well, if you 'phone us, we can talk to you and offer you advice, sir.

**RC:**
But you don't actually send someone to take me in tow and get me back home?

**RB:**
No, we haven't the staff, there's only me and Miss Pringle, but we can provide comfort and consolation.

**RC:**
Oh – nothing more than that?

**RB:**
Well, Miss Pringle has been known to provide a little more than that on occasion, but that's an optional extra between you and her. But we'd certainly get you back on the right road.

**RC:**
Oh, talking of the right road – do I get a handbook?

**RB:**
You wouldn't need a handbook with Miss Pringle, she knows where everything is, sir.

**RC:**
No, I mean one of those with the good hotels in it. Because my wife and I plan to do quite a bit of touring round the hotels, once we've joined.

**RB:**
But surely, sir, an organised tour round the hotels with your wife might be inclined to stimulate the urge.

**RC:**
Well, I think, as a matter of fact, that's what she's hoping.

**RB:**
No, no, the urge to drink.

**RC:**
Oh, I see. Oh, no, I don't agree with drinking and driving. Unfortunately it runs in my family. My auntie drove my uncle to drink.

**RB:**
Did you bring your car tonight, sir?

**RC:**
Yes – d'you want to have a look at it?

**RB:**
No, sir – a car is a car. They're all lethal weapons. Miss Pringle always says – the only place to be in a car is the back seat – when it's parked.

**RC:**
Ah, yes – that's a point. Would I be covered in the back of a parked car?

**RB:**
With Miss Pringle you would, yes sir.

**RC:**
Miss Pringle seems to be the mainstay of this organisation.

**RB:**
Well, I do the paperwork and she's the field officer, sir. She's better in the field than on the desk, as it were.

**RC:**
But is she able to cope? I mean, if I suddenly got a flat in Acton High Street, what would happen then?

**RB:**
Oh, she's not proud – she'll sleep anywhere.

**RC:**
I'm suddenly not sure I'm doing the right thing …

**RB:**
Of course, there are lots of other ways we can be of use – for instance, if you suddenly started giving your wife a good hiding, we'd come over and help you.

**RC:**
Oh, it's quite a comprehensive service, isn't it? That comes under damage to a third party, I suppose. Come to think of it, I'd probably need a bit of help, she's a big

woman. What about fire and theft?

**RB:**
Well, I suppose if you did start thieving and setting fire to things, we'd see what we could do – tell me, how much do you drink?

**RC:**
Me? I don't drink. Never touch a drop.

**RB:**
You what?

**RC:**
Never a drop.

**RB:**
Then why do you want to join us, sir?

**RC:**
This is the AA, the Automobile Association, isn't it?

**RB:**
No, no. This is Alcoholics Unanimous.

**RC:**
Well, my wife's given me the wrong address. Hang on, she's outside … *(Goes to door)* Elsie! You've given me the wrong address, dear.

*(Elsie enters, an enormous woman – very drunk.)*

**RC:**
Where did you get this address from, love?

**ELSIE:**
The two new vicars gave it to me, outside the saloon bar of the Eight Feathers.

*(She takes a nip from a hip flask.)*

**RC:**
*(sighing)* Look, talk to her, will you? If you can't get anywhere, I'll ring the RAC and get her towed away.

*(He exits.)*

# IMPERSONATOR SKETCH

*(Frost On Sunday)*

*RC is at a restaurant table, being seated by the head waiter. RC is expensively and somewhat flashily dressed.*

**HEAD WAITER:**
There we are, Mr Pigeon. I'll get someone to take your order right away, sir.

**RC:**
Thank you, Alfred. *(He speaks rather better than one would expect from his clothes.)*

**HEAD WAITER:**
Incidentally, sir, may I say how much the wife and I enjoyed your last TV show. We didn't stop laughing all evening, thinking about it. By the time we got to bed we were helpless.

**RC:**
Oh – not <u>too</u> helpless, I hope!

**HEAD WAITER:**
Er, no, we – *(Then seeing the joke)* Ah, you're too quick for me, sir. I'll get Luigi to take your order now, sir.

*(He goes.)*

*(Ronnie Barker comes and sits at RC's table.)*

**RC:**
Good morning.

**RB:**
*(with the same inflection)* Good morning.

*(Luigi, the waiter, arrives to take the order.)*

**RC:**
Ah!

**RB:**
Ah!

*(The waiter gives them each a menu.)*

**RC:**
Good morning, Luigi!

**RB:**
Good morning, Luigi!

*(Luigi stares at RB, who is obviously a stranger to him)*

**RC:**
*(looking at menu)* Well, now …

**RB:**
*(ditto)* Well, now …

**RC:**
I think a fillet steak, very rare, you know, barely singed – er *(drums fingers on table)* and a coleslaw salad on the slide. *(He laughs)* Difficult to say that, isn't it? A coleslaw salad on the side. And have you any lobster pâté?

**LUIGI:**
Yes, sir.

**RC:**
Fine – lobster pâté to start with.

**LUIGI:** *(To RB)*
And for you, sir?

**RB:**
I think a fillet steak, very rare, you know, barely singed – er *(drums fingers on table)* and a coleslaw salad on the slide. *(He laughs)* Difficult to say that, isn't it? A coleslaw salad on the <u>side</u>. And have you any lobster pâté?

**LUIGI:**
Yes, sir.

**RB:**
Fine – lobster pâté to start with.

*(RC stares at RB as the waiter goes. RC lights a cigarette – so does RB. RC takes off his glasses, and sucks at the side piece – so does RB. RC starts to put them on again – so does RB. RC stops – so does RB. Finally, RC settles them on his nose again – so does RB.)*

**RC:**
*(clearing his throat)* A – hem!

**RB:**
*(ditto)* A- hem!

**RC:**
*(rather desperate now)* Waiter!

**RB:**
Waiter!

*(The waiter arrives.)*

**RC:**
Could I have some water?

**RB:**
Could I have some water?

*(The waiter goes.)*

**RC:** *(To RB)*
It is rather warm, isn't it?

**RB:** *(To RC)*
It <u>is</u> rather warm, isn't it?

**RC:**
Nice place, this.

**RB:**
Nice place, this.

**RC:**
Yes.

**RB:**
Yes.

**RC:**
I'm in show business.

**RB:**
I'm in show business.

**RC:**
What do you <u>do</u>?

**RB:**
What do you <u>do</u>?

**RC:**
I'm a comedian.

**RB:**
I'm an impersonator.

# TALL STORY

*(Frost On Sunday)*

*An employer is sitting at a large desk.
Secretary enters.*

**SEC:**
Mr Green has arrived, sir. Do you still wish
to see him?

**BOSS:**
*(looking at watch)* He's four hours late.
Alright, wheel him in.

*(Secretary goes, and returns with Mr Green.)*

**SEC:**
Mr Green, sir. *(She goes.)*

**BOSS:**
Sit down, Mr Green. *(Green does so.)* I
wouldn't have thought turning up four
hours late for an interview for a job was
awfully wise, Mr Green.

**GREEN:**
No, sir – but I've had a most amazing
morning. I set out on time, but I'm afraid
I ran out of petrol and got a puncture.

**BOSS:**
Both at the same time?

**GREEN:**
I got a puncture in the petrol tank. And I
started to walk to the nearest garage, and
this little old lady offered me a lift, and I
accepted, but we hit a pebble in the road
and crashed.

**BOSS:**
Crashed? Into a pebble?

**GREEN:**
Well, we didn't crash, we fell off.

**GREEN:**
Fell off what?

**GREEN:**
Her bicycle. She hit a stone and I fell off.
The crossbar.

**BOSS:**
Ladies' bicycles don't have crossbars.

**GREEN:**
No. Well, she was riding a man's bicycle.

**BOSS:**
I see. Go on, Mr Green.

**GREEN:**
Yes. Well, she was rather shaken up, so I
called in at the pub to get her a brandy.

**BOSS:**
Ah!

**GREEN:**
And something to keep her warm. And, as
luck would have it, there in the pub I saw
an old man in a fur coat.

**BOSS:**
A fur coat? In this weather?

**GREEN:**
Quite. I thought it was a fur coat. But it
turned out to be a chimpanzee.

**BOSS:**
In the pub.

**GREEN:**
In the pub. So I went back to the old lady
with the gin and lime, but when I got
outside …

**BOSS:**
I thought it was a brandy.

**GREEN:**
What?

**BOSS:**
I thought you got her a brandy.

**GREEN:**
Ah, no. I went into the pub to get a brandy but she said she would prefer a gin and lime.

**BOSS:**
Aha.

**GREEN:**
So. When I got outside, she'd gone. So I returned to the pub, whereupon the chimpanzee insisted on buying me a drink.

**BOSS:**
I believe they are quite generous, as a species.

**GREEN:**
Well, of course, I was amazed! I mean this chimpanzee chatted away, and asked me where I was going, and I said I was going for this interview, and he said he'd always wanted to work in advertising.

**BOSS:**
And did he buy you a drink?

**GREEN:**
Well, no. He said he didn't carry money around with him – and do you know why?

**BOSS:**
No pockets.

**GREEN:**
Exactly. And I said "It's not often one meets a chimpanzee in a pub like this."

**BOSS:**
And he said "I'm not surprised, with these prices."

**GREEN:**
And when I left, he followed me and asked me to get him into advertising. And the conductor wouldn't let us on the bus, and so I had to walk all the way here and

that's why I'm late.

**BOSS:**
I see.

**GREEN:**
And all this is absolutely true, I swear it.

**BOSS:**
Ah. Well that's a pity.

**GREEN:**
A pity?

**BOSS:**
A great shame. You see, this organisation is looking for a man with a fertile imagination – and for a moment, when you were telling that story, I thought we'd found him. If the whole thing had been a pack of lies, I would have offered you the job right here and now.

**GREEN:**
Oh, well, I accept your offer.

**BOSS:**
What?

**GREEN:**
I made the whole thing up. Actually I overslept. My alarm didn't go off.

**BOSS:**
I thought as much.

**GREEN:**
Well, do I get the job?

**BOSS:**
Get out.

**GREEN:**
But you said …

**BOSS:**
Get out, don't waste my time. Two things I insist upon in this company – efficiency and honesty. And I don't think either of those are your strong point, Mr Green.

**GREEN:**
No, please – I was telling the truth – I only said about oversleeping to get the job – and I really did have a puncture and fell off a ladies' bicycle and …

**BOSS:**
Out! *(He propels him to the door.)*

**GREEN:**
*(going)* It was all true!

*(Boss shuts the door, sits down and presses the buzzer.)*

**BOSS:**
Next applicant, please.

*(A chimpanzee enters.)*

# FIND THE LADY

*(Frost On Sunday)*

*A fairly seedy bedroom. Enter RC dressed in top hat and opera cloak with red lining. He dumps a suitcase on the bed.*

**RC:**
Come on in, darlin'.

*Enter a popsie – a showgirl or dancer, wearing a PVC raincoat.*

**GIRL:**
Is it alright?

**RC:**
'Course it's alright. I told you, the wife's staying at her mother's. By the time she comes back on Tuesday, we'll be at the Theatre Royal, Huddersfield.

**GIRL:**
I wouldn't like anything to happen, Marvo.

**RC:**
Oh, wouldn't you – well, you've come to the wrong place then, darling – it's all going to happen here in the next twenty-four hours, eh? *(He grabs her)* Come here, let's have a look at you.

**GIRL:**
*(soppily)* Oh, I do love you, Marvo!

**RC:**
Look, don't keep calling me Marvo, darling – that's just for the act, isn't it? I'm not a magician when I'm with you. I'm pretty sensational, but I'm not a magician.

**GIRL:**
I think you're wonderful.

**RC:**
Yes, well never mind that, you get your coat off and that, and I'll get us a drink.

*(They disentangle themselves and the girl exits. RC goes to bedside cupboard and gets out bottle of gin and two tumblers. He pours out two drinks, gets out a bottle of tonic, opens it on the side of the table, and puts some into the glasses. He then takes off his cloak and top hat, and drapes them over a chair. The girl enters, wearing a shortie nightie with a short negligée over it.)*

**RC:**
*(looking up)* Blimey, that was quick!

**GIRL:**
*(giggling)* I'm used to quick changes!

**RC:**
Yes, well hop into bed and have a nice drop of gin.

*(She takes off negligée and gets into bed. There is a door slam off-stage. Panic from both of them.)*

**RC:**
Oh gawd!

**GIRL:**
What is it?

**RC:**
The wife – quick.

**GIRL:**
*(leaping out of bed)* You said she was with her mother!

**RC:**
Get in there! *(indicating built-in wardrobe)* Her mother's probably died or something. Trust her to spoil the weekend. *(He bundles her into the wardrobe, shuts the door and just has time to sit on the bed, when in walks the wife.)*

**RC:**
Hello, dear.

**WIFE:**
Hello, Johnnie.

**RC:**
I thought you were at your mother's.

**WIFE:**
She's not feeling well.

**RC:**
Oh good.

**WIFE:**
What?

**RC:**
I meant good 'cos you've come home.

**WIFE:**
*(sniffing the air)* What's that perfume?

**RC:**
Which perfume is that, dear?

**WIFE:**
The perfume I can smell.

**RC:**
Oh. Oh that perfume would be on the carnation in my buttonhole. Smell it.

*(Wife does so – it squirts water at her.)*

**WIFE:**
Oh, for heaven's sake, don't mess about, Johnnie. Stupid jokes – *(She sees two gin glasses.)* What are these two glasses here?

**RC:**
*(quickly picking them up)* Oh, I was just practising a trick, dear – see? *(He pours one into the other and the liquid changes colour)* Rather good, isn't it?

**WIFE:**
I suppose so.

*(She turns away to remove her coat and as she does so, RC notices the girl's negligée on the floor. He quickly stuffs it down his trousers.)*

**RC:**
*(As the wife goes to hang up her coat up in the wardrobe)* No, I'll do that for you, dear. *(Takes coat and stands with it for a moment, then puts it on top of his own on the chair)* I'll hang it up in a minute. No point in hanging it up just yet. You go and make some tea and when you've gone, I can while away my time hanging up your coat.

**WIFE:**
You're being very strange. *(Sees bulge in trousers)* What's that bulge in your trousers?

**RC:**
Where? Oh that's another trick. *(He begins to pull out yards and yards of silk flags from his trousers. They go on for ever.)*

**WIFE:**
You're up to something, Johnnie. *(She goes to him and discovers the negligée. Holds it up.)* You've got a woman here! *(She looks under the bed.)*

**RC:**
'Course I haven't – I use this in the act –

**WIFE:**
You've got a woman here *(Starts to go to wardrobe.)*

**RC:**
*(grabbing gun from suitcase)* Keep away from that wardrobe.

**WIFE:**
Don't point that stupid toy gun at me!

**RC:**
Alright – I warned you!

*(As the wife opens the wardrobe door, RC fires the cap pistol into the air, and a flock of pigeons fly out of the empty wardrobe.)*

# THREE CLASSES – LEISURE

*(Frost On Sunday)*

**A:**
I am upper class.

**B:**
I am middle class.

**C:**
That doesn't leave me much of a choice.

**A:**
I work hard all day and at night I live life to the full.

**B:**
I work hard all day and at night I like to relax.

**C:**
I work hard all day and at night I'm clapped out.

**A:**
Leisure, to me, is nature's safety valve, releasing the pressures caused by the strains of modern living.

**B:**
Leisure to me, is forgetting about work, and doing as I like.

**C:**
Leisure to me is getting me boots off.

**A:**
I employ my leisure time as usefully as possible, dividing it between exercise, relaxation and informative reading.

**B:**
I play a bit of golf, enjoy a night out with the boys, and occasionally take the wife shopping.

**C:**
I watch the telly.

**A:**
I find the best way of unwinding, after a very full week, is to play squash.

**B:**
My way of switching off is to have one over the eight on a Friday night.

**C:**
I never switch off. I watch everything.

**A:**
My wife and I have the choice of flying to Paris for the weekend, entertaining friends at our country house – or riding to hounds.

**B:**
My wife and I have three choices: eating too much, drinking too much or going to bed early.

**C:**
My wife and I have two choices –
BBC or ITV.

**B:**
Three different attitudes to leisure; but is it, after all, the universal cure for the stresses we have to undergo?

**A:**
My worry is that increased leisure-time will bring with it boredom and apathy.

**B:**
My worry is that by the time it comes, I shall be too old to enjoy it.

**C:**
My worry is – what's going to happen when me tube goes?

# THREE CLASSES – WORK

*(Frost On Sunday)*

**A:**
I am managing director of a company with a very large export commitment.

**B:**
I work for a hardware firm with a very large annual turnover.

**C:**
I work for the public health department with a very large shovel.

**A:**
I start work at 9.30 and finish when I have completed my day's schedule.

**B:**
I start work at 9 o'clock and finish when the hooter goes.

**C:**
I start work at 8.30 and finish when it gets too dark to see what I'm shovelling.

**A:**
I work in a large suite of centrally heated air-conditioned offices in the West End.

**B:**
I work in a converted warehouse in Camden Town.

**C:**
I work in the fresh air, but only when the wind's in the right direction.

**A:**
Although I am managing director, I must always be on my guard against a younger, ambitious man usurping my position in the organisation.

**B:**
I, too, have to be on the look out, in case anyone's after my job.

**C:**
I have to tread very carefully, an' all.

**A:**
Not counting entertainment and out-of-pocket expenses, I receive an annual increment of twelve thousand pounds a year.

**B:**
I receive an annual increment of two thousand eight hundred pounds a year.

**C:**
I don't have anything to do with increments. Quite the reverse.

**B:**
We all serve the community in our different ways; but at the end of the day, have we any doubts as to the value of our contribution to society?

**A:**
No one is more conscious than I am of the need to work together for the common good.

**B:**
No one can deny that I genuinely try to pull my weight.

**C:**
No one will sit next to me on the bus.

# THREE CLASSES – FAMILY LIFE

*(Frost On Sunday)*

**INTRODUCTION:**
We have been researching, once again, into the upper, middle and lower classes, with regard to various aspects of modern living in Britain. Tonight we have representatives of the three classes in the studio to report on "family life".

**A:**
I have three children: Jeremy, Alison and Jane. My wife and I have been married for eight years.

**B:**
I have two children: Derek and Doreen. My wife and I have been married for six years.

**C:**
I have eight children: Peter, Rita, Anita, Sandra, Dawn, Clint, Rock and Elvis. My wife and I are not married.

**A:**
My wife is on several committees, runs the local opera group and is secretary of the bridge club.

**B:**
My wife is a member of the Mothers' Union, enjoys organising coffee mornings and is a driver for Meals on Wheels.

**C:**
My wife is pregnant again.

**A:**
We give dinner parties two or three times a week – this enables us to keep in touch with our wide circle of friends.

**B:**
We give a wine and cheese do once a month – this enables us to do it on the cheap.

**C:**
Her mother comes round Saturday nights. This enables me to clear off round the pub.

**A:**
We stopped having children when we decided we had the ideal-sized family unit.

**B:**
We stopped having children when the school meals went up.

**C:**
We stopped having children when we found out what was causing it.

**A:**
We employ a housekeeper, a chauffeur, a gardener and a cleaning woman.

**B:**
My wife has a woman who comes in three times a week and a babysitter in the evenings.

**C:**
My wife has a babysitter, a cook, someone to clean the house at weekends and a washer-up. And I'm bleedin' exhausted.

**B:**
Three family units, each of a different class. But are our opinions of family life really so different?

**A:**
It's my opinion that family life, on the whole, is the anchor and cornerstone of our present civilisation.

**B:**
It's my opinion that family life, on the whole, is the most economical way of living.

**C:**
It's my opinion that the sooner I get out of this hole, the better.

# ANTIQUE SHOP

*(Frost On Sunday)*

*An antique shop. RC is seated in a Victorian chair. RB enters the shop.*

**RB:**
Good morning.

**RC:**
Good morning, sir.

**RB:**
Er – do you have a rather nice coffee table? I want to give someone a present, and I thought a coffee table.

**RC:**
Coffee table. Now, let's have a look. *(He looks round)* That's a nice one, sir. *(Going over to a Victorian oval table)* How about that one, sir?

**RB:**
*(looking at it)* Yes, that's awfully sweet. She'd like that.

**RC:**
I take it it's for a lady, sir?

**RB:**
Yes.

**RC:**
I thought as much. Yes, that's a beauty, that one.

**RB:**
How much would that one be?

**RC:**
That one is three shillings, sir.

**RB:**
Three shillings?

**RC:**
Well, half-a-crown, then.

**RB:**
*(mystified)* Oh, well I'll have that. Oh, and *(catching sight of a rather dainty chair)* that

little chair is rather nice. That would go with it rather nicely.

**RC:**
Oh, it would, sir. That's a Ming.

**RB:**
Ming? That chair's a Ming?

**RC:**
That's right, sir.

**RB:**
How much?

**RC:**
One and nine.

**RB:**
Oh, right, I'll have it. *(RC writes on a notepad.)* Er – what else have you got?

**RC:**
I beg your pardon?

**RB:**
I mean, what else have you got that I might like?

**RC:**
Well, it depends what you're looking for, sir.

**RB:**
Oh, anything. You know, anything that might suit me – anything at all.

**RC:**
Well now, let's see. That's nice. *(He picks up a Staffordshire.)*

**RB:**
Oh, yes! How much?

**RC:**
Threepence.

**RB:**
*(excited)* I'll have it! Now then, what else – that paperweight?

47

**RC:**
Ah, that's beautiful. That is actually prehistoric. Made by French craftsmen in the 18th century, when London was all fields.

**RB:**
And what will you take for that?

**RC:**
I'm prepared to accept tenpence for that, sir.

**RB:**
Done. That grandfather clock?

**RC:**
Ah, now you're going into money with that, sir.

**RB:**
Never mind – how much is it?

**RC:**
Seven and eleven.

**RB:**
Right! These silver spoons *(in a frenzy by now)*

**RC:**
Ninepence a dozen.

**RB:**
Right! This pair of oil lamps?

**RC:**
A shilling.

**RB:**
This plate?

**RC:**
Four thousand pounds!

**RB:**
Right. No! Four thousand?

**RC:**
Yes, sir – that's new stock.

**RB:**
Oh, well I won't have that then.

**RC:**
No, sir.

**RB:**
Well, what else –

**RC:**
I think you've bought enough, sir.

**RB:**
Oh, no, I've got plenty of room at home.

**RC:**
I would rather not sell you anything more, sir.

**RB:**
What? Oh. Yes. Well, perhaps so. Mustn't be greedy.

**RC:**
No, sir. I've got the list here *(Refers to the list he has been writing.)* Let's see – coffee table, chair, Staffordshire figure, paperweight, Grandfather clock, silver spoons and the two oil lamps. That comes to *(a quick addition)* fifteen shillings altogether, sir.

**RB:**
*(fumbles in his pocket)* Here you are. Fifteen shillings.

**RC:**
Thank you, sir. Now, where would you like these delivered to?

**RB:**
Oh. Er – my card. *(Hands him a visiting card)*

**RC:**
Esher. That will be alright, sir. Some time on Monday?

**RB:**
Er – yes, fine.

**RC:**
Right. Thank you, sir. Good day.

**RB:**
Good day. And thank you.

**RC:**
Thank you, sir.

*(RB leaves the shop. RC sits down in the chair. A man appears through the door to the back of the shop.)*

**MAN:**
There we are, Mr Hibberd. Sorry I took so long to find it. I'm in a terrible muddle at the moment in there. *(He hands RC a wristwatch.)* It just needed cleaning again.

**RC:**
Thank you. How much do I owe you?

**MAN:**
Same as usual, sir, fifteen shillings.

**RC:**
Oh yes. *(Hands him the fifteen shillings)* It's always fifteen shillings, isn't it?

# LATE DEVELOPER

*(Frost On Sunday)*

*RC and mother: at breakfast. RC is a man of twenty-four, but dressed as a boy of seven.*

**RC:**
Mummy, how old am I?

**MOTHER:**
Be quiet, darling, and eat your breakfast.

**RC:**
But I want to know, mummy.

**MOTHER:**
You're seven, darling.

**RC:**
That's what you always say, but I don't think I am. I think you've made a mistake.

**MOTHER:**
Listen, David. I'm twenty-four, and I had you when I was seventeen so you must be seven. Twenty-four takes away seven equals seventeen. Aren't you doing take aways at school yet?

**RC:**
Yes, I'm doing takeaways at school. I'm top of the class in sums. I'm also the only one who shaves.

**MOTHER:**
Well, darling – you're advanced, that's all.

**RC:**
Yes. And so's Miss Perkins.

**MOTHER:**
Your teacher?

**RC:**
She keeps cuddling me.

**MOTHER:**
Cuddling you? Where?

**RC:**
All over.

**MOTHER:**
No, I mean, in front of the whole class?

**RC:**
Oh, no.

**MOTHER:**
Oh, good.

**RC:**
She takes me behind the blackboard.

**MOTHER:**
Oh. Well, you must just tell her you don't like it.

**RC:**
I do like it. I love it. I can't get enough of it.

**MOTHER:**
Really, David – that's not nice.

**RC:**
Yes it is. It's wonderful! I look forward to it.

**MOTHER:**
Now that's enough. Eat your breakfast. And what about those crusts? Come on.

**RC:**
*(after a pause)* I think I'm about twenty-four.

**MOTHER:**
How can you be twenty-four if I'm twenty-four?

**RC:**
Perhaps you had me when you were nought.

**MOTHER:**
You can't have a baby when you're nought.

**RC:**
Well, perhaps you're older than twenty-four. Perhaps you're forty-four.

**MOTHER:**
*(Outraged)* How dare you! You know very well I'm a member of the "Under-thirties" Social Club. It's a very exclusive club, and terribly difficult to get into. They wouldn't let me be in it unless I was under thirty.

**RC:**
No, I s'pose they wouldn't. Ah, but just a minute ...

**MOTHER:**
Aren't you going to be late for school, darling?

**RC:**
There isn't any school – it's Saturday.

**MOTHER:**
Oh, good.

**RC:**
It's not good. It's horrible. I was looking forward to a nice cuddle behind the blackboard.

**MOTHER:**
Well, you'll just have to wait till Monday, won't you?

**RC:**
Yes. Monday's pink sweater day. Miss Perkins looks super in her pink sweater. It points straight at you over the desk.

**MOTHER:**
I don't want to hear another word about it, do you hear? Now, Mrs Anstruther will be bringing Johnny round in a minute to play. You'd better get washed.

**RC:**
Why's he coming? *(lighting a cigarette.)*

**MOTHER:**
I'm going out. It's my "Under-thirties" coffee morning – you know that.

**RC:**
He's so babyish. He always wants to play with my rotten old train set and he doesn't even fancy Miss Perkins, and he's nearly eight. *(Flicks ash into plate.)*

**MOTHER:**
Don't flick your ash on your plate, dear, there's a good boy.

**RC:**
Anyway, he's so little. Every time we play leap frog, I squash him.

*(Doorbell.)*

**MOTHER:**
That'll be Johnny – go and let him in, dear.

**RC:**
Alright. *(He goes out.)*

*(The phone rings.)*

**MOTHER:**
Hello – yes? Speaking. Oh, hello, Mrs
Thirkell. What? *(Enter RC with Johnny, a
boy of eight.)*

**RC:**
Johnny's mother says he's got new
trousers on.

**MOTHER:**
*(covering phone)* Go and play, dear. I'm on
the 'phone.

**RC:**
Come on, Johnny, let's go out on our
bikes. *(Taking Johnny's hand, he leads him
out.)*

**MOTHER:**
*(into phone)* Sorry – what? What do you
mean? Resign from the club? Why? Oh.
Oh, I see. Yes. May I ask who told you?
Oh, did she. Very well, I resign. Yes.
What? Yes, yes, I don't want to discuss it!
*(She slams down the 'phone and bursts into
tears. Enter RC.)*

**RC:**
Johnny's fallen off his bike and split his
trousers. What's the matter?

**MOTHER:**
I've had to resign from the "Under-thirties
Club". They've found out I'm forty-four.
The vicar's wife saw the church records.

**RC:**
Forty-four? But then …

**MOTHER:**
You are twenty-four.

**RC:**
Twenty-four? Hey! That's old enough to
get married, isn't it?

**MOTHER:**
Yes.

**RC:**
Hey! I can marry Miss Perkins, can't I?

**MOTHER:**
Yes. If she'll have you.

**RC:**
Oh, she'll have me alright. Hey, I'm going
round to tell her now. *(He goes to the door.
Mother is sobbing quietly.)* Hey, mummy.
*(Coming back to her.)*

**MOTHER:**
Yes, dear?

**RC:**
When you're married, do you still get
toys from Father Christmas?

*(Mother flings her arms round him, with a
fresh flood of tears.)*

# CRINOLINE SKETCH

*(Frost On Sunday)*

*A girl in a crinoline, in a corner of a Victorian
garden. Evening.*

**J:**
*(off)* Mary? Where are you?

**M:**
I'm here, John. In the rose garden.

*(J enters)*

**J:**
Mary, my love.

**M:**
John, my own dear one *(he kisses her
hand.)* What brings you here, on this
night above all others?

**J:**
What do you mean, dearest?

**M:**
Much as it pleases me to see you, know

you not that it is considered by many bad luck to see the bride on the eve of the wedding?

**J:**
But, dearest, I shall see you tomorrow. All of you. *(passionately)*

**M:**
John!

**J:**
In all your glory! That milk-white skin, that divine waist ...

**M:**
Are my blushes not to be spared at all?

**J:**
In truth, I cannot contain myself – that dainty ankle – oh, that ankle!

**M:**
*(laughing)* I have more than one ankle, John dear!

**J:**
You may remember that I have only seen one of your ankles, Mary – and the thought of the other one is driving me mad!

**M:**
I assure you, it is much like the first.

**J:**
But don't you understand – I want to see your ankles together.

**M:**
*(teasing him)* Always, John?

**J:**
*(enflamed)* Oh, Mary, Mary. There is one thing I must know. Just now, I walked from the house across the lawn, treading carefully through the daffodils so as not to crush their dainty petals – searching for you. And I wondered – Mary – am I the first?

**M:**
Good heavens, no. The gardeners are up and down there all day. In gumboots.

**J:**
Mary – I mean – am I the first – with you? Am I going to be the first?

**M:**
Oh, John. Dearest! What a question. *(sincerely)* Yes, John. You are. And you will be the last. The only one, John. No other man shall ever receive so much as a glance from me, dearest John. I am yours and yours alone. Always.

**J:**
Oh, Mary, my dearest love *(he kisses her hand again.)* And now I will leave you to your thoughts. I must away to prepare myself for tomorrow, and our blessed nuptials. Goodnight, my own true love – may you pass the hours peacefully until we meet in church.

*(He goes. RC comes out from under the girl's crinoline.)*

**RC:**
I thought he'd never go!

*(He grabs the girl and they fall, giggling, to the ground.)*

# PARTY POOPER

*(Frost On Sunday)*

**SHE:**
George!

**HE:**
Yes, Margaret?

**SHE:**
I found this in your coat pocket last night.

**HE:**
What, dear?

**SHE:**
(*showing him*) This picture of a girl with nothing on but a pair of knee-length boots.

**HE:**
Good heavens! Penelope!

**SHE:**
What!

**HE:**
I mean. Good heavens, Penelope, how could that have got there?

**SHE:**
Why did you call me Penelope?

**HE:**
Isn't that your name, Margaret? Your middle name?

**SHE:**
No.

**HE:**
No, of course not. I called you Penelope because I thought I'd call you Penelope. I thought I'd start calling you Penelope. For short.

**SHE:**
Penelope is one syllable longer than Margaret.

**HE:**
Well, it's not much, is it? One measly syllable. I don't know what all the fuss is about.

**SHE:**
You know her, don't you?

**HE:**
Who?

**SHE:**
Penelope.

**HE:**
Never heard of her. I've never seen her before. There's nothing about her that I recognise. She's a complete stranger to me. I'll have a word with her husband about this.

**SHE:**
Oh, you know her husband, do you?

**HE:**
Er – vaguely, yes. By sight. Not to speak to.

**SHE:**
If you've never seen her, how do you know she's his wife?

**HE:**
He told me. When he slipped her into my pocket.

**SHE:**
I thought you said you'd never spoken to him.

**HE:**
I haven't. When he said that it was his wife, I didn't reply.

**SHE:**
Why not?

**HE:**
I had my mouth full.

**SHE:**
Of what?

**HE:**
Christmas pudding.

**SHE:**
Ah, now we're getting somewhere. Christmas pudding. Yesterday?

**HE:**
Yes.

**HE & SHE:**
The office party.

**HE:**
Yes. I was just sitting there, minding my own Christmas pudding, and he slipped her into my inside pocket, with the

53

words, "that's my wife". And then they both went out of the office.

**SHE:**
I thought you said you'd never seen her before?

**HE:**
Well, she had her back to me.

**SHE:**
With no clothes on?

**HE:**
Certainly not. She was fully clothed as always.

**SHE:**
She's not fully clothed here.

**HE:**
No – well, she's got to take them off sometime.

**SHE:**
But not, I would have thought, perched on your desk at the office party.

**HE:** That's not my desk.

**SHE:**
Oh yes it is. There's the blotter and the desk pen Mummy gave you for your birthday.

**HE:**
Trust her.

**SHE:**
What?

**HE:**
Trust her to pick a lovely blotter and desk pen like that. Wonderful taste, your mother.

**SHE:**
Look, are you going to own up about all this?

**HE:**
Yes.

**SHE:**
What?

**HE:**
Yes. Her name is Penelope Vickers, and she works in the office, and she had her photograph taken sitting on my desk. At the office party, yesterday. And we all had a good laugh, and I bought a copy for three and six. And that's it. What are you going to do about it?

**SHE:**
Have you got her 'phone number?

**HE:**
Yes.

**SHE:**
I'm going to ring her up.

**HE:**
Whatever for?

**SHE:**
I want to find out where she got those super knee-length boots.

# SINISTER PARTY

*(Frost On Sunday)*

*A party. Seven or eight people stand drinking and chatting quietly. "A" is standing on his own, looking a little lost. "B" approaches him.*

**B:**
Good evening.

**A:**
Oh, good evening.

**B:**
Enjoying yourself?

**A:**
Yes, thanks. *(Pause.)* My girl is powdering

her nose.

**B:**
Nice people, aren't they?

**A:**
Girls? Oh yes, I like girls, I've always ...

**B:**
No, these people here. Nice people, aren't they?

**A:**
Oh yes, very.

**B:**
Don't let 'em fool you.

**A:**
What?

**B:**
Don't let 'em fool you. They're all crooks.

**A:**
What?

**B:**
International crooks. Murderers and thieves, all of 'em.

**A:**
I don't believe you.

**B:**
See that fellow over there? *(Indicating a bishop)* Light-fingered Leonard. One of the world's cleverest silver-thieves. Always dresses as a bishop – hides the loot in those baggy trousers. If you kicked him in the seat of the pants he'd sound like Lyons Corner House.

**A:**
Nonsense. He's a bishop.

**B:**
Try it, go on –

**A:**
Certainly not.

**B:**
See that woman over there? *(Indicating thirty-five year old, elegant female in cocktail dress)* Muriel Manderson – international drug trafficker.

**A:**
She looks perfectly respectable to me.

**B:**
She's hooked on the stuff herself, you know. If you were to lift up her skirt you'd see her thighs are covered in needle marks.

**A:**
How ever could you know that?

**B:**
I used to clean windows at the Cairo Hilton.

**A:**
The where?

**B:**
The Hilton, Cairo. Yes, covered in needle marks, her thighs are. Tell you what, if you pull her skirt up, I'll kick the bishop in the trousers, all right?

**A:**
Look, this is all nonsense.

**B:**
It's not, my friend, it's not nonsense, I can assure you. Look over there. *(Indicating rather burly businessman)* Itchy Luke. See that bulge in his pocket? That's his blackjack. He'd hit you over the head with that as soon as look at you. Sooner.

**A:**
Good grief!

**B:**
That fellow there *(Another man)* A J Slaughter. Murders to order. Enjoys it. The thing that worries me is, what are they all doing here? Tonight?

**A:**
Well, I must be getting along ...

**B:**
Not so fast. I need your help. I've got to get this lot behind bars. My superiors want blood.

**A:**
Your what?

**B:**
My superiors. They want blood.

**A:**
Well, they're bloody well not having mine.

**B:**
*(crowding him)* Listen! There's a 'phone on the table there. Dial 999. I'll keep them talking, distract their attention. Remember, I've got this trained on you. *(He indicates a bulge in his jacket pocket.)*

**A:**
*(picking up phone)* Hello – Police, please. Hullo, Police? I wish to report a desperate gang of thieves and murderers at number 29 Kensington ...

**B:**
*(roaring with laughter suddenly)* Ha! I really got you going there, didn't I? You took it all in, didn't you? Marvellous! You ought to have seen your face ...

*(He tails off as he sees the woman lift her skirt and take a gun from her stocking. Her thigh is covered in needle marks. The business man has a cosh in his hand. The other man has a knife. They, and the other guests, all advance on A and B. As the bishop approaches, with a revolver, we hear the rattle of silver in his clothing.)*

# A WEDDING SERVICE

*(Frost On Sunday)*

*The bridegroom waits. The Wedding March is playing as the bride approaches on the arm of her father, followed by little girl bridesmaids. The vicar stands facing them. The bride arrives, the music stops and she lifts her veil, eyes downcast.*

**VICAR:**
Dearly beloved, we are gathered here, in the face of this congregation, to join together this man and this woman ...

**MAN:**
*(staring at woman, Then addressing vicar in whisper)* Er ... Excuse me ...

**VICAR:**
*(whispering)* What's the matter?

**MAN:**
This isn't the one.

**VICAR:**
Which one?

**MAN:**
This one isn't. She's not the one I'm marrying.

**VICAR:**
Not the one you're marrying?

**MAN:**
No. *(To girl)* Are you? I've never seen her before. Have I?

**GIRL:**
*(shaking head nervously)* No.

**VICAR:**
Are you sure?

**MAN:**
'Course I'm sure.

**GIRL:**
Oh dear, everyone's looking at us.

**VICAR:**
Well – what's gone wrong?

**GIRL:**
Could you carry on with the service? Everyone's listening.

**VICAR:**
Well, I can hardly ...

**MAN:**
Yes, look, carry on for a minute while we have a think.

**VICAR:**
Oh, alright ... which estate is not by any to be enterprised, not taken in hand, inadvisedly, lightly, or wantonly; but reverently, discreetly, advisedly and soberly – duly considering the causes for which matrimony was ordained *(This is spoken under the following dialogue)* etc. etc.

**GIRL:**
What are we going to do?

**MAN:**
Well, it's obvious. We've got to stop it, haven't we? I mean ...

**GIRL:**
Oh, I can't. I can't. I've waited for months for this moment. I've been working up to it.

**MAN:**
Well, so have I. I mean – well, we both have, but we've been working up to it with different people, haven't we?

**GIRL:**
Yes, but my mum will go mad if we cancel it – she's got all the sandwiches and sausage rolls ready and everything – and she's doing little things in vol-au-vent cases as well.

**MAN:**
Yes, but marriage is not just a question of little things in vol-au-vent cases, is it?

**GIRL:**
She sat up all night in an armchair so she wouldn't spoil her new hair-do.

**MAN:**
But I don't know anything about you. I mean, I don't know what you're like.

**GIRL:**
How do you mean?

**MAN:**
Well, what you're – like. You know, what you're like.

**GIRL:**
What I'm like?

**MAN:**
Well, I can't put it any plainer in front of the vicar, can I? What you're like.

**GIRL:**
Oh – well, I haven't had any complaints up to now. Anyway, I don't know what you're like, do I?

**MAN:**
Well, I'm just like anybody else, aren't I?

**GIRL:**
You're very little.

**MAN:**
I'm not little. It's you that's big.

**VICAR:**
*(who has come to the end of his words)* Er – have you decided anything yet? Because I've come to the part where the whole thing tends to become a tiny bit irrevocable.

**GIRL:**
Oh – it's just that we don't know whether we are suited. It's a question of size.

**VICAR:**
May I remind you both that a marriage partner is usually taken on account of their quality, not quantity.

**MAN:**
Well, you'll have to give us another minute somehow.

**VICAR:**
Tell you what – I'll give them a hymn to be going on with. *(Aloud)* The congregation will now sing hymn number 798: "A Stranger Is Amongst Us, O Shall We Let Him In".

*(The congregation start to sing.)*

**GIRL:**
Look – I don't mind short men.

**MAN:**
Really? Matter of fact, I love tall girls.

**GIRL:**
Do you? I'm not really tall, you know.

**MAN:**
You are to me.

**GIRL:**
Yes. *(A pause)* What do you think then? Shall we make a go of it?

**MAN:**
Where would we live?

**GIRL:**
Oh, my dad's bought me a new bungalow.

**MAN:**
Oh, well, that settles it, you're on. *(To vicar)* OK, Reverend, you can carry on.

**VICAR:**
Ah. *(Sings)* We'll just wait until the hymn finishes.

**MAN:**
Oh, alright then.

**GIRL:**
*(After a pause)* We have met before, actually.

**MAN:**
Have we?

**GIRL:**
Do you remember Bobby Upton's party the Christmas before last, and we all played sardines?

**MAN:**
Were you there?

**GIRL:**
Yeah. You crawled under the bed I was hiding under. We were the last to be found.

**MAN:**
Good Lord, I didn't recognise you.

**GIRL:**
Ah, well, I had my hair dark then. And I was lying on my stomach.

**MAN:**
*(remembering)* Oh yes! Was that you?

**GIRL:**
Yeah.

**MAN:**
Oh good. *(He looks pleased – the hymn finishes.)* I knew you before that, and all. At school.

**GIRL:**
Go on! Were you at the same school?

**MAN:**
We were in the same class.

**VICAR:**
*(declaring)* Do you, er?

**MAN:**
Robin Cyril.

**VICAR:**
Robin Cyril.

**GIRL:**
Robin Bates!

**VICAR:**
Do you, Robin Bates …

**MAN:**
Robin Cyril.

**VICAR:**
Robin Cyril, take …

**GIRL:**
Old Mother Thompson!

**VICAR:**
Take Old Mother Thompson.

**GIRL:**
Mavis Jean.

**VICAR:**
Take Mavis Jean, to be your lawful wedded wife – to have and to hold *(etc. under dialogue.)*

**MAN:**
I always swore I'd marry you – ever since I was nine. I never thought it would turn out like this *(In response to the vicar)* I do.

**VICAR:**
And do you, Mavis Jean, take Robin Cyril *(etc.)*

**MAN:**
Here – what about the bloke you were supposed to marry?

**GIRL:**
Oh – I never liked him much. Anyway, he was only marrying me out of sympathy, really *(To vicar)* I do.

**VICAR:**
For as much as Robin Cyril and Mavis Jean have consented together *(etc.)*

**MAN:**
What do you mean, sympathy?

**GIRL:**
Well, he took advantage of me.

**MAN:**
Oh. Oh well, that can't be helped – doesn't mean to say you've got to marry him, does it?

**GIRL:**
Well, I thought it only right — I mean …

**VICAR:**
I pronounce that they be man and wife together.

**GIRL:**
*(indicating six bridesmaids)* I've got to give this lot a father, haven't I?

*(The man faints flat on his back.)*

# RAILWAY PLATFORM

*(Frost On Sunday)*

*A country station platform. RC and RB meet. They are dressed as conventional stuffy Englishmen. Each carries a weekend case or holdall.*

**RC:**
Hello, Ted.

**RB:**
Hello, Jack.

**RC:**
I didn't see you on the train.

**RB:**
I was at the other end today.

**RC:**
Thought it wouldn't be like you to miss it.

**RB:**
Mm. Never have up to now, Jack. I saw you get on, but I couldn't reach you. Damn non-corridor trains.

**RC:**
Cold this evening, isn't it?

**RB:**
It is. It is cold.

*(They both remove their overcoats and put them on the ground beside them.)*

**RC:**
How long have we got to wait for the connection?

**RB:**
Ten minutes, if it's on time. Try and get into the carriage near the engine – in the warm. *(They are taking off their jackets)* What sort of day did the stock market have?

**RC:**
We were pretty lively today – everything's coming down, you know.
*(RC drops his trousers and steps out of them.)*

**RB:**
Well, it's inevitable, isn't it?

*(RB also removes his trousers.)*

**RC:**
People haven't got the money to play with, *(unbuttoning his shirt)* not with the tax system in this country. *(Removes his shirt)* They'd have the shirt off your back if they could.

**RB:**
It's criminal. *(Removing his shirt)* I've certainly got nothing to spare these days. It's hard enough trying to make ends meet. And the wife's no help, either. *(Delving into his bag)* Always spending money on some ridiculous item of clothing. *(He brings out of the bag a lady's hat with a veil and puts it on.)*

**RC:**
That's just like a woman, isn't it? *(He takes out a mini-skirt from his bag and puts it on.)* It's my daughter that's ruining me. Never out of the boutiques, spending a fortune. Takes absolutely no notice of me. *(Taking out a ladies' sweater and putting it on)* Does exactly as she thinks fit. No one would believe that I was the man of the house. *(Taking off his socks.)*

**RB:**
*(During this has pulled up his light-coloured socks so that they become girls' knee-length ones)* It's the modern generation, Jack. *(Takes frilly mini-dress out of his bag)* You can't tell them anything. They just do things for kicks, nowadays. *(He steps into the dress and pulls it on.)*

**RC:**
We never know where she is at night. *(He has rolled his socks into balls)* Worries me to death – there are some very odd people about, you know, Ted. *(Tucks his socks under his sweater to make bosoms.)*

**RB:**
*(getting high-heeled shoes out of his bag)* Quite. Still, I suppose we were considered odd when we were young. *(Putting on shoes)*

**RC:**
*(also putting on high-heeled shoes)* Yes. We probably seem terribly dull and staid to them, just going about our business in the normal manner, travelling up on the train to work, day in, day out, always the same. I would say our lives must appear pretty colourless. *(He reaches into his bag and puts on a wildly colourful, jazzy hat.)*

**RB:**
Well, I seem to be about ready. Are you? *(Takes handbag out of case.)*

**RC:**
Yes, I'm ready. Bit of a nuisance all this, isn't it?

**RB:**
Yes. Still, we live in hopes. Perhaps one day they'll build a gentleman's lavatory on this station.

*(They walk round a corner and into a door marked "Ladies".)*

# ASK NO QUESTIONS

*(Frost On Sunday)*

*An office.*

**JENKINS:**
Good morning, Mr Braithwaite, sit down, won't you?

**BRAITHWAITE:**
Thank you.

**J:**
Now, Mr Braithwaite, the labour exchange has sent you round for a job here, and I'd just like you to help me fill in this questionnaire – just a routine thing we do with all prospective employees. Just take down Mr Braithwaite's replies, will you, Miss Legge?

**MISS LEGGE:**
Ready, sir.

**J:**
Now then. Full name?

**B:**
George Pip Pip Pip Braithwaite.

**J:**
Pardon?

**J:**
I see. Address?

**B:**
41 Whizz-Bang-Crash Gardens, Potted Shrimps, Sussex.

**J:**
Potted Shrimps? Where is that?

**B:**
It's a suburb of Horsham. Just beyond Ponky-Doos, on the Bedstead Road.

**MISS LEGGE:**
Ponky where?

**B:**
Doos. Ponky Doos.

**J:**
Age?

**B:**
Forty.

**J:**
Ah, thank you.

**B:**
Inside leg 31.

**MISS LEGGE:**
I beg your pardon?

**B:**
Not at all. I enjoyed it.

**J:**
Previous experience?

**B:**
26 1/2.

**J:**
Now, Mr Braithwaite, details of your previous experience.

**B:**
Oh – er – three years in the grunt business – shining up tapioca for use in barrel organs. Left there because of the parrot stuffers. Then I spent a short time going bang for a deaf drummer in the London Symphony Orchestra. Chewed parsley for Rolls Royce for a time, joined the Foreign Office as a bucket-balancer, and finally unscrewed my leg and fell over.

**J:**
Thank you. Oh, one final question. What would you say was your main ambition in life?

**B:**
To form a National Naked Ladies' Choir and travel round the country, bringing music to millions, and enjoyment to the deaf.

**J:**
Right. Well, I think that's all we need at the moment, Mr Braithwaite. We'll be in touch. Thank you so much.

**B:**
Not at all. Good day.

**J:**
Good day.

**MISS LEGGE:**
Good day.

*(He exits.)*

**J:**
Well, Miss Legge?

**MISS LEGGE:**
Well, I had the feeling that he didn't want the job.

**J:**
Oh dear. Well, who can we get as prime minister?

# POISONING

*(Frost On Sunday)*

*An office at the London County Council. RC is at a desk; enter RB.*

**RB:**
Good afternoon.

**RC:**
Good afternoon.

**RB:**
Er – I want to enrol for one of your night classes.

**RC:**
Certainly. What sort of course are you interested in?

**RB:**
Poisoning.

**RC:**
Pardon?

**RB:**
Poisoning. I want to learn how to poison things.

**RC:**
Ah. Well, I don't think we have any poisoning classes at the moment.

**RB:**
Well, chemistry then.

**RC:**
Chemistry?

**RB:**
Yes, chemistry, with access to the poison cupboard.

**RC:**
Oh, I see. No, I don't think our chemistry course gets as far as the poison cupboard. Look, how about something else? How about Metalwork?

**RB:**
Would that include knife-sharpening?

**RC:**
It might. It might well.

**RB:**
And axe-grinding?

**RC:**
Well, not really. I think, if I were you, I would keep away from that sort of thing.

**RB:**
Why?

**RC:**
Well, it's not normal.

**RB:**
I'm perfectly normal. I'm a normal human being who simply wants to learn how to

sharpen an old meat axe until its cutting edge is like a razor, the blade glinting in the sunlight, as I bring it down swiftly on – on whatever I bring it down on.

**RC:**
*(desperately)* First Aid?

**RB:**
What?

**RC:**
First Aid's nice.

**RB:**
Yes – how to remove blood stains from clothing.

**RC:**
No, perhaps not. Knots and hitches?

**RB:**
Slip-knots?

**RC:**
No! Needlework?

**RB:**
Hypodermic needle work?

**RC:**
No, no! Learning an instrument?

**RB:**
A blunt instrument?

**RC:**
Now look here! Why do you want to learn all these dreadful things?

**RB:**
I'm writing a book on it.

**RC:**
A book?

**RB:**
Yes, it's called "How to murder the woman at 49 Ashley Gardens, and other stories".

**RC:**
49 Ashley Gardens?

**RB:**
Yes, do you know it?

**RC:**
I – er – know the road.

**RB:**
Well I live at 49 – and my wife is being unfaithful. A little chap, with glasses.

**RC:**
Really! *(RC takes off glasses and stands on a stool)* And what's that to do with me?

**RB:**
Absolutely nothing. I just want to write a book on it. And you're the man who can tell me about night classes.

**RC:**
*(Relieved)* Oh, so I am. Yes, I was forgetting who I was for the moment. I'm simply the man who tells people about classes.

**RB:**
Yes.

**RC:**
Yes. And my private life is my own affair.

**RB:**
Exactly. But my wife's affairs are far from private. Her affairs are completely public. She's ultra-friendly.

**RC:**
What?

**RB:**
Every man in the road.

**RC:**
What?

**RB:**
And two in the avenue. And four in the crescent.

**RC:**
I don't believe it! *(furious)* The rotten, skinny, ginger-haired little tart!

**RB:**
An accurate description.

**RC:**
Right! Right! Look, sir. I suggest you go away for the weekend – Brighton; somewhere bracing.

**RB:**
Do you think so?

**RC:**
Definitely. And who knows, when you come back on Monday, you may have something to write a book about.

**RB:**
Alright, if you say so. I'll see you on Monday.

**RC:**
That's right – call in on Monday.

**RB:**
*(as he exits)* Right!

**RC:**
*(Dials phone.)* Hello, Daphne darling? It's me. He's just been in. Yes. And I've persuaded him to go to Brighton for the weekend. And I'll see you tonight, my dearest. *(Puts phone down and dials again.)* Hello, gardening class? Frobisher here. I want to learn how to dig a hole … What? … Oh, six foot deep by about 38–24–36.

# MARRIAGE BUREAU

*(The Corbett Follies)*

*The waiting room of a marriage bureau. A man is sitting underneath a sign which says "Why be lonely? The wedwell marriage bureau will find you a mate." He is reading a copy of* Girls Monthly. *Another man enters. They eye each other. The second man walks to a sign that says "Love is just around the*

corner". *He looks round a corner, but appears to see nothing. He turns back and looks around him.*

**RC:**
Er – excuse me.

**RB:**
Yes?

**RC:**
It's over here.

**RB:**
Is it?

**RC:**
No – men over here. This side. Women that side, men this – see, there's the sign. *(Points to a sign saying "guys" and "dolls" with arrows pointing to either side.)*

**RB:**
Oh, sorry. I thought that meant toilets. *(He sits next to RC.)*

**RC:**
Do you want the toilet?

**RB:**
Who, me? No, I … er, I don't want it.

**RC:**
Oh.

**RB:**
Not at the moment.

**RC:**
No, quite.

**RB:**
Is that all there is to read – *Girls Monthly*?

**RC:**
Oh, I just pinched this from the other side. The only ones this side are *Do It Yourself*. If I could do it myself, I wouldn't be here. *(They laugh a little at his joke.)*

**RB:**
No. You're hoping to find someone

too, then?

**RC:**
Yes. Bit embarrassing, isn't it?

**RB:**
It is rather. What sort of thing are you looking for?

**RC:**
Oh, something about thirty-five, attractive, well-built. Interested in music, ballroom dancing and fly fishing.

**RB:**
Reckon you're going to be lucky?

**RC:**
I don't see why not. There must be some girl around with those qualifications somewhere.

**RB:**
Yes. I don't know about the fly fishing.

**RC:**
Ah, no, well that's more of an acquired taste, isn't it? I hope she'll acquire a taste for that in due course. What about you?

**RB:**
Oh, you know, early thirties, petite; fond of gardening, desire to see foreign parts, able to ride tandem, with long, flowing hair.

**RC:**
What colour?

**RB:**
Oh, white, preferably.

**RC:**
White hair?

**RB:**
Oh, I see. I thought you meant skin. No, brunette, definitely. You can't trust blondes. I had a blonde girlfriend once. Dyed.

**RC:**
Oh, I am sorry.

**RB:**
No, no – dyed her hair.

**RC:**
Oh, I see.

**RB:**
It all came out in the finish.

**RC:**
What, just fell out, you mean?

**RB:**
No, no, it came out that her hair was dyed. I found out.

**RC:**
Oh, really. How? *(Interested.)*

**RB:**
We lived in the same block of flats and I went into her bathroom by mistake once.

**RC:**
*(More interested)* Yes?

**RB:**
Yeah, and there it was.

**RC:**
What, you mean–

**RB:**
Yeah. Bottle of peroxide.

**RC:**
*(Losing interest)* Oh.

*(The door opens. A woman enters and sits opposite them. She is very tall and large, and about forty, with dark hair. Attractive, but rather forbidding in appearance.)*

**RB:**
*(To RC, lowering his voice)* Here, I wonder if she's one.

**RC:**
What?

**RB:**
One of the ones for us?

**RC:**
Ooh – I hope not.

**RB:**
She's more your type than mine.

**RC:**
No, no, not my type.

**RB:**
You did say well-built.

**RC:**
Not that well-built. I mean, she's built like a block of flats, isn't she? I mean, it wouldn't just be a question of getting married, would it? I mean, you'd need planning permission, wouldn't you? Anyway, she's too old.

**RB:**
I should think she's about thirty-five.

**RC:**
What, round the leg? Look at 'em!

**RB:**
Don't you like long legs?

**RC:**
Yes, I like long legs, yes, but they're enormous. I'd have to run to keep up with them.

**RB:**
I wonder if she's any good at fishing.

**RC:**
She ought to be. She's built like a trawler.

**RB:**
She's got a nice face.

**RC:**
Yes, but I'd never see it, would I? I'd always be down here somewhere. (He indicates his chest.)

**RB:**
No, you're exaggerating. Here, go and get her to stand up and measure yourself against her.

**RC:**
Oh, she'd like that, wouldn't she? Put her at her ease, that would, wouldn't it?

**RB:**
No, I mean – say you think she's sitting on your hat and see where your head comes up to.

**RC:**
I can't.

**RB:**
Go on, she wouldn't know.

**RC:**
Alright then. (He crosses to girl) Er, excuse me, I think you're sitting on my head. My hat. (The girl smiles, embarrassed, and stands up.) Ah, no. It's funny, it was on my head when I left home. (Puts his hand on top of his head.) It's a cap with a long peak, like that. (He slides his hand across his head indicating long peak at the front and also measuring where he comes to on the girl) Sticks straight out in front like that. (He finally touches the girl's chest) Sorry you've been troubled. (He returns to his chair) There you are. You saw where I came up to, didn't you?

**RB:**
Yes. Very nice.

**RC:**
It's not nice at all. What's nice about it?

**RB:**
Well, it's somewhere to stand under when it's raining.

**RC:**
It's all very well for you.

(The door opens and a tiny, thin, flat-chested girl with glasses enters. About twenty. Brunette with long, straight hair. She sits *down next to the large woman.)*

**RC:**
Hello, this must be yours.

**RB:**
Eh?

**RC:**
Yes, there you are. Petite, brunette, long, flowing hair.

**RB:**
Oh. No, no. She's only a kid.

**RC:**
That's alright. You'd have a young wife longer.

**RB:**
She'd have to be longer than that. She's about four foot nothing. *(The girl is peering at a travel magazine.)*

**RC:**
Look what she's reading. She's got a desire to see foreign parts.

**RB:**
She'd be glad to see anything, I should think, the way she's peering through those glasses. Blind as a bat.

**RC:**
Well, you wear glasses.

**RB:**
That's what I mean. Imagine us in the morning. Both looking for each other. Anyway, she's too skinny.

**RC:**
You'd save quite a bit on food. And mini skirts.

**RB:**
She couldn't wear a mini skirt.

**RC:**
Why not?

**RB:**
They're supposed to be nine inches above the knee. She hasn't got nine inches above the knee. And can you imagine her and me on a tandem?

**RC:**
Oh, I don't know – she looks quite athletic.

**RB:**
It's no good being athletic if your feet don't reach the pedals, is it? Anyway, I want someone with a bit of weight to keep the back down going round corners. And where would we do our courting?

**RC:**
How do you mean?

**RB:**
Well, I share a flat with three other blokes. I couldn't take a girl with a figure like that back there – they'd laugh at me.

**RC:**
She's probably got a flat too.

**RB:**
That's what I mean. Two of the flattest I've ever seen. She's like a bean pole. You could grow beans up her.

*(The door opens and a gorgeous red-headed girl enters. About twenty-eight to thirty. Beautifully built, about 5'6" tall.)*

**RB:**
Ah. Now that's more like it. That's mine.

**RC:**
No, no, that must be mine. Well-built.

**RB:**
No, that's definitely me. Long hair.

**RC:**
You said dark. She's red-haired.

**RB:**
Well, it's dark red.

**RC:**
She's not petite! Anyway, I was here first.

**VIKKI:**
*(going to inner door)* I'm rather late, I'm afraid. Sorry to have kept you all waiting. I'll be with you in a second.

*(She goes into office and closes door.)*

**RB:**
Oh, pity.

**RC:**
Yes.

**RB:**
She's on the staff.

**RC:**
Yes, just our luck.

**RB:**
I was already picturing us having dinner together.

**RC:**
I'd got further than that. I was in a taxi, tearing back to her place. And you were nowhere in sight.

*(The office door reopens. Vikki emerges.)*

**VIKKI:**
Mr Arnold Winterbourne?

**RC:**
Yes?

**VIKKI:**
Your date for tonight is Miss Lesley Johnson. Is Miss Johnson here? *(Looking at ladies)*

**RB:**
Er – excuse me.

**VIKKI:**
Yes?

**RB:**
Mr Leslie Johnson.

**VIKKI:**
I beg your pardon?

**RB:**
I'm Mr Leslie Johnson. That's me.

**VIKKI:**
Oh dear, there must have been a mistake …

**RC:**
You mean to say – you're my date?

**RB:**
Well–

**VIKKI:**
I'm awfully sorry–

**RC:**
So he and I have been sitting here wasting our time. You being late has practically ruined our evening.

**VIKKI:**
How do you mean?

**RC:**
I'm supposed to be taking him to the Odeon and we'll have missed half the picture already. *(To RB)* Come on!

*(They exit, chattering.)*

# THE TWO OF THEM

*(Written as audition piece – credited to "John Cobbold")*

*Four chairs, placed together, represent a park bench. All props, other than these chairs and the boy's newspaper, are mimed.*

*On the right-hand end of the bench sits the girl, knitting. The boy enters and the girl looks up and speaks.*

**SHE:**
That was a quick walk.

**HE:**
I went by bus.

**SHE:**
You went for a walk on the bus?

**HE:**
I wanted to go through the park to the fountain. It is too far to walk both ways, so I caught a bus there. Perfectly logical.

**SHE:**
Why not walk there, and get the bus back, when your feet are tired?

**HE:**
Because I wanted to be there quickly. At the fountain. Then, by the time my feet got tired, I would be back.

**SHE:**
And here you are. Well now, let's see what is in the picnic bag. *(She picks up bag of food and begins to lay things on the bench, one by one.)*
I've brought some pâté, some of those little tomatoes, some blue cheese and that lovely crusty French bread from the corner shop. How does that look?

**HE:**
What are you talking about?

**SHE:**
What?

**HE:**
What are you talking about? There's nothing there. You're just pretending – there's no food there, you're just miming it.

**SHE:**
I was only playing.

**HE:**
Really, Louise, you're so stupid sometimes. Just get it into your head. We haven't any money. We haven't eaten since yesterday morning. We're living

rough. We should never have got married. I know it's my fault, but stupid jokes like that are in very poor taste. It's just a question of taste, of which you seem to have very little.

*(She begins to cry, quietly. After a moment or two, he moves up to her.)*

**HE:**
Don't cry. *(He puts his arm around her.)* Louise, don't cry. You're upsetting that policeman. *(This makes her giggle through her tears.)* I still love you. We'll get something to eat from somewhere. Here, I'll tell you something. When F W Woolworth first arrived in New York, he had one nickel in his pocket. But he invested it very wisely.

**SHE:**
How?

**HE:**
He put it into a 'phone box, 'phoned his father and his father sent him half a million dollars.

*(He opens his paper and reads, holding it up in front of him. She hits it, making him jump.)*

**HE:**
You frightened me to death!

**SHE:**
Let's do something.

**HE:**
Like what?

**SHE:**
Go to Hyde Park and throw bread at the ducks.

**HE:**
Only one thing wrong with that. We haven't any bread.

**SHE:**
Alright, we'll throw stones at them.

**HE:**
Not very ladylike.

**SHE:**
It wasn't very ladylike of you to shout at me just now.

**HE:**
I'm not supposed to be ladylike. I'm a man.

**SHE:**
I don't see why that should make a difference. Why is it always women who have to be ladylike? Why can't it be men sometimes?

**HE:**
Anyway, it's impractical to go to Hyde Park for another reason.

**SHE:**
What, may I ask?

**HE:**
We're not in London, we're in Paris.

**SHE:**
Of course we're not. If we were in Paris, we'd be speaking with a French accent.

**HE:**
Not if we were speaking in French. We would sound ordinary. No accent.

**SHE:**
Alright, supposing one of us was English, the other French.

**HE:**
Then one would speak *(he puts on French accent)* like so. Mademoiselle, I have always admired you from a distance ...

**SHE:**
Wrong. One would speak ordinarily, the other would be all *(Puts on exaggerated English accent)* I say, how fraightfulleh ripping, old sport, don't you know.

**HE:**
*(cutting in)* Not vagrants! Vagrants don't talk like that.

**SHE:**
Oh, phooey.

**HE:**
Phooey? Where are we now, America?

**SHE:**
No. Phooey. I just felt like saying phooey. Phooey, phooey, poo-ey fadooey. I'm tired of being a tramp, anyway. Where did you leave the car?

**HE:**
Marble Arch. *(Goes behind his paper again.)*

**SHE:**
That's miles. Let's get a cab.

*(He makes a noise like a taxi approaching, stopping, ticking over.)*

**SHE:**
There's one, stopped at the lights.

*(He makes the noise of it starting off again, then driving away.)*

**SHE:**
That was very good. Do you often do funny noises?

**HE:**
Morning, noon and night.

**SHE:**
Good job we're not really married.

**HE:**
Yes. Still, it's worked out well, us being together, hasn't it?

**SHE:**
Most of the time, yes. I'm sorry I made you angry.

**HE:**
I wasn't really angry. I'm sorry I made you cry.

**SHE:**
I wasn't really crying. It's been a good, working relationship, yes. But I think the

time has come to end it all.

**HE:**
End it all? But why?

**SHE:**
There are others, waiting.

**HE:**
I suppose so. Alright, how do we do it?

**SHE:**
Pick up two chairs each, bow to the people, and walk off – come on!

*(They do so.)*

# "NEXT PLEASE"

*(Lines From My Grandfather's Forehead)*

**RB:**
Well, here we are then. Quite full. There's a seat over there. That's it. Now let's see – one, two three … (counts quickly) … eighteen. Give 'em five minutes each, that's an hour and a half. Huh, what a prospect. Staring at this lot for an hour and a half. Look at 'em. They all look so miserable. I suppose it's the thought of sitting looking at the others for an hour and a half. It's funny, though, none of 'em look ill. You'd think they would do, being as they're at the doctors. You'd think they'd at least try and look ill. They're not, though. None of 'ems making any attempt to look ill. There's a bloke over there actually smiling. He'll have to go. Not one of 'em looks the slightest bit ill – except that chap over there with his head covered in bandages. He looks ill. He looks half dead, he does. I bet he's not smiling underneath that lot. (whistles through his teeth for a moment or two.) Now then – I'd better learn who's come in since I did, otherwise I shan't know when it's my turn. Three of 'em There's the woman in the red hat, the woman with the fat legs and the bloke with the pipe.

That should be easy to remember. Red hat, fat legs and pipe. Easy. The criminal was last seen wearing a red hat, fat legs and a pipe. Red hat, fat pipe and legs. Red legs, fat hat and pipes. A hat, red fat and pipe legs. Wait a minute, there's another coming in now. How am I going to remember him? He's too ordinary. Absolutely undistinguished. Completely anonymous. He must be the ordinary man in the street. I wish he was in the street, then I wouldn't have to try and remember him. Ah well. Here, there's a man reading a magazine upside down over there. Perhaps he's blind. Yes, either he's blind or he's dead nervous. 'Course he may be Australian. Yes, that's what it is. He's a blind, nervous Australian. It's so quiet in here. Why don't people talk to each other in the doctor's? Dead quiet it is. You could hear a hypodermic needle drop in here. I bet they'd like to talk to each other – they just daren't because it's not done. That woman with the fat legs is bursting to talk. She's absolutely bursting, she is. P'raps that's why she's here. "Good morning, Doctor. I have come to see you because I think I'm going to burst!" "Let's have a look at you, madam. Would you mind touching your toes? Thank you. Ah yes, I can see what's the matter with you, yes. Your garters are too tight. All the fat's rushing to your head. Hold still, I'll just cut through your suspenders, that should do it. There. Oops. Sorry! Now what's happened? What? Well, how was I supposed to know your roll-on would shoot up over your head? Just a minute, I'll just cut a couple of eye holes in it so you can see. No, I know that hasn't cured you of being fat, but at least no one knows who you are now. Come and see me in a week and I'll take the stitches out of your gusset." (giggles to himself) What a carry on. I can't wait for her to go in and come out with her corset over her head. Ooh! There goes the flashing light. Next one in. Good idea, that flashing light. Lights up with the doctor's name. Dr Harvey. Good, that. Here! Dr Harvey? (chuckles) Well, that's the biggest laugh of the morning. I'm in the wrong surgery.

# HUSBAND SWAPPING

*(Lines From My Grandfather's Forehead)*

**SHE:**
Good morning, darling.

**HE:**
*(off)* Good morning, darling.

**SHE:**
Toast?

**HE:**
(off) Two, please.

**SHE:**
Won't be a second.
*(the sound of buttering toast. rustle of newspaper.)*

**SHE:**
*(putting the toast in front of him)* There we are.

**HE:**
*(on)* Here! You're not my wife!

**SHE:**
I know. *(Sitting down)*

**HE:**
Well, what's the idea?

**SHE:**
Husband-swapping. Your wife and I had the idea. She is, no doubt, at this very moment, making breakfast for Harold. My husband.

**HE:**
Where?

**SHE:**
At my house.

**HE:**
I didn't hear her leave the house this morning.

**SHE:**
She didn't – she left last night.

**HE:**
But I slept with her last night.

**SHE:**
No, you didn't.

**HE:**
Good God! I wondered why you wouldn't put the light on.

**SHE:**
Well, you were rather late home, weren't you? I was tired.

**HE:**
You weren't as tired as all that. Anyway, that's not the point. I'm not sure that I want my wife making breakfast for someone else's husband.

**SHE:**
Aren't you? You can't have your cake and eat it, you know.

**HE:**
Perhaps not.

**SHE:**
And you certainly proved to be quite a sweet tooth last night.

**HE:**
Now, listen, Mrs …

**SHE:**
Russell.

**HE:**
Mrs Russell, I don't want to appear ungrateful, but I think my wife should have told me. She said she was going to her mother's.

**SHE:**
Really?

**HE:**
So the whole of last night she was lying.

**SHE:**
Yes – but not at her mother's.

**HE:**
No. How long is this arrangement going on for?

**SHE:**
Only the one night.

**HE:**
Oh.

**SHE:**
You're with Mrs Hartley tomorrow night.

**HE:**
What?

**SHE:**
Mrs Hartley.

**HE:**
What, that enormous woman across the road?

**SHE:**
You've got to take the rough with the smooth.

**HE:**
Rough is right. I'll take the bulb out of the light tomorrow then. Listen, do the police know about this?

**SHE:**
They will tomorrow night – I'm with Police Constable Vickers.

**HE:**
You're making all this up!

**SHE:**
(*laughing*) Yes, I am actually. No, it's just you and me, and Harold and Penelope. We just thought it would make a nice change. And it has, hasn't it?

**HE:**
Yes, I must admit it has. Now, there's just one point we have to clear up. Who is Penelope?

**SHE:**
Penelope – your wife Penelope.

**HE:**
My wife's name is Judith.

**SHE:**
What?

**HE:**
(*chuckling in an evil manner*) You've come to the wrong house, haven't you? Last night, in the dark, you came to the wrong house. My wife's name's Judith – and she's at her mother's!

**SHE:**
Oh, God!

**HE:**
(*with a glint in his eye*) You haven't got any more of that delicious cake, have you?

# SPORTS NIGHT

*(Lines From My Grandfather's Forehead)*

**RB:**
Well, now the games are about to begin, the players are lining up and it promises to be a most unusual game this, because, as you may have heard, both teams have promised, actually sworn, there will be no foul play, no roughness of any sort. The game is going to be played purely on skill alone, gently and skilfully, no punching, tripping or kicking the opposing team. Pure football. And that's why they've agreed to a lady referee for this match only. And she's on the pitch now, looking very attractive in tiny shorts and a low-cut jersey. A fine figure of a woman, this Miss Nora Pinks. And she's about to toss the coin to decide which way the team will play – and she tosses the coin – and, ooh dear, it's gone down the front of her jersey. The two captains are just looking to see whether it's heads or tails – and – apparently it's standing on end. Now,

they've retrieved it, tossing again now and – yes, Miss Pinks is bending down to pick it up, and it looks like a definite tail. Yes, it's a tail. Now she's about to blow her whistle any minute – she takes a deep breath, and ... *(sound of whistle)* And no one kicked off. They were all watching her take a deep breath. Ah, now they've finally kicked off; and we'll now see just how polite they can be to each other – a long ball out to Jones – Jones to Huntley – intercepted very delicately by Hall, Hall right down the field to Blenkinsop, who dribbles daintily round Jerry Taylor, taps it to Wright; all very polite at the moment – they're all moving very gracefully. Wright tripping lightly down the field, and loses the ball to Jones, who flicks it to Taylor, and it's

*(Piano: "Pas de Quatre" from Ruy Blas (Meyer-Lutz) – comes in under (RB's commentary is now in time to the tune)*

**RB:**
Taylor to Jones–
Jones back to Wilks–
Tackled by Hall–
Put into touch–

Throw in by Huntley out to Wilks
And Wilks to Billy O'Shea
Blenkinsop intercepts the ball
And taps it lightly out to Wright and
Wright puts the ball across to Hall
But Huntley heads it away
Taps it gently across the line for a corner kick.

Jones pirouettes–
Taking the kick–
Slips in the mud–
Flat on his back–

Huntley comes up and takes the corner
Wright leaps up in the air,
Misses the ball and knocks Miss Pinks who
Tries to duck and splits her trousers
Blenkinsop tries to head the ball but
Wilks is right in his way
He boots it under the crossbar making the score one nil.

*(Sound of cheers then two short blasts on whistle. Music continues.)*

**RB:**
Miss Pinks waves her arms
High in the air
Down fall her shorts
Up goes a cheer ...

*(Piano stops. Sound of long blast on whistle.)*

**RB:**
Good gracious – it's all over – it's all over! Miss Pinks, the referee, has called the game off! Well! Well, that's the first time I've known a game abandoned because of good visibility!

*Piano: to end.*

# THE (ALMOST) SILENT COMEDIES

The "almost-silent" comedy was a popular form of supporting feature in 1960s cinema, the most famous example probably still being Eric Sykes's *The Plank*. These movies often featured the pick of Britain's comedy talent, moving through a series of sight gags, constantly mumbling inaudible mumblings, which came to be known as "rhubarb" (largely because people were often mumbling or indeed even munching "rhubarb" at the time.)

Ronnie Barker had appeared in just such a movie, *A Home Of Your Own* in 1964 and back then the form had instantly appealed to him. "Having seen it" says Ronnie "I thought 'These silent things really work. I should do this.' You didn't think about it every day or every week, but occasionally I thought 'I really must write one of those'."

In 1968, Ronnie did just that and the result was *Futtocks End*. (Although the character he played was named Giles Futtock, Ronnie freely admits that Futtock was indeed another variation on his Lord Rustless character, of whom more later.)

Unlike much of his work, the screenplay for *Futtocks End* actually bears the legend "Written by Ronnie Barker" and no pseudonym. The movie was shot largely at W S Gilbert's former house in Stanmore, comparatively near to Pinner, where Ronnie was living at the time. The role of the butler, Hawk, was written specifically with Michael Horden in mind. The two had met whilst appearing together in an advert for Crosse & Blackwell soup. "He said 'I can't do it Ronnie. I'm going to play Lear. I must prepare for Lear and I can't do any other work. But send the script, I'm sure it will be funny to read.'

So he read it and rang me and said 'I've got to do this.'"

Horden wasn't the only one impressed with *Futtocks End*, Prince Charles numbers it amongst his favourite movies.

Note: When the film was eventually shot the dialogue at the beginning was discarded and the plot conveyed by action.

# FUTTOCKS END

A film with almost no dialogue, by Ronnie Barker.
September 1968

*NOTE (1): There should be accompanying background music, of a nature appropriate to the mood of the various sequences, almost continuously throughout the film.*

*NOTE (2): In a perfect world, the part of Hawk, the butler, would be played by Michael Horden.*

Opening shot is of a very large country house, with a long drive. A postman is cycling laboriously up the drive. Suddenly a motor cycle roars past him, causing him to disappear completely into the hedge. After a pause, he appears again out of the hedges considerably further up the drive, still cycling. We cut to the motor cyclist – it is Hawk, the butler. He looks back at the postman in the distance, and grins evilly. Then, in long shot again, we see him *(from the postman's point of view)* disappearing round the side of the house. The postman's cycle has now reached the front steps – he dismounts, and leans his cycle against a small stone balustrade at the side of the steps. This dislodges the stone ball on top of the balustrade, and it rolls heavily down the drive. We watch it. The postman turns, goes up the steps to the door, and goes to knock it, but it opens causing the postman to lurch heavily into Hawk, who has removed his motor cycling gear and crash helmet, and is now dressed formally as a butler. Hawk disdainfully takes the letters from the postman, and closes the door on him.

Hawk now begins a long and tortuous journey to the bedroom of his master, Sir Giles Futtock. We follow him down endless corridors, round innumerable corners; the house is very obviously a positive maze. During this journey he meets (A) the cook, a truly enormously wide middle-aged lady who, at first appears to be alone; it is only after she has passed by that we see there are two tiny kitchen-maids behind her, who were quite invisible when the cook was seen from the front.

(B) Hawk, who also comes up behind and eventually overtakes the parlour maid, Effie, a pert, plump, dainty morsel of a girl, who is proceeding about her business. Just as he is about to overtake her, she, realising he is there, increases her pace, but so does Hawk, and as he passes her, she gives a little jump and a squeak. Neither looks at the other, and Hawk's face remains expressionless, but we all know what occurred. Hawk now puts his hand firmly on the salver of letters, as he approaches "windy corner". For some reason, there is a howling draught of air always present at this particular corner, and it causes the tails of his coat to fly upwards for two or three seconds, as he battles through the blast of air. Once round the corner, everything is calm again. On he journeys, until he reaches a door, rather like all the other doors in the house, solid and shut. He knocks and enters. He is in Sir Giles's bedroom – four-poster bed, large pictures. He minces over to a door off the bedroom, whence a terrible gurgling baritone voice is giving out with a hotted-up version of "Down in the Forest". Much gurgling, as if Sir Giles is under water at least part of the time. Also enormous splashings and crashings. Hawk applies his eye to the keyhole. There is an extra loud splash from the bathroom, and Hawk comes away from the keyhole with an eye full of soap suds. He thumps on the door. The singing stops, and the door opens. Sir Giles comes into the bedroom, clad only in soap-suds, of which, for propriety's sake, there are a great many. In fact, he looks rather like a giant snowball.

**GILES:**
Oh, it's you, Hawk – I thought it was Mrs Puddy. If I'd known, I wouldn't have bothered to get out of the bath.

**HAWK:**
With respect, Sir Giles, it's just as well it was me, isn't it?

**GILES:**
No it's not. I wanted to see cook – I don't particularly want to see you.

**HAWK:**
You could hardly see cook in that condition, sir.

**GILES:**
What do you mean "that condition"? I haven't touched a drop since before breakfast. I can see as well as the next man. Anyway, cook's pretty difficult to miss even when you've got a skinful. What d'you want, anyhow?

**HAWK:**
I've brought the post, sir.

**GILES:**
Oh good – any letters?

**HAWK**
There are no parcels, if that's what you mean, Sir Giles.

**GILES:**
That's not what I mean. I mean letters. Surely you know the difference between letters and parcels?

**HAWK:**
There are three letters, Sir Giles.

**GILES:**
Well, don't stand there, man, open them, open them!

**HAWK:**
But they're private sir.

**GILES:**
Well, good God man, there's only you and me here. Couldn't be more private than that. I'm going to shower this lot off; come and read them to me.

**HAWK:**
Very good, Sir Giles.

*(Giles has disappeared into the bathroom again. We follow Hawk in after him and Hawk begins to open the first letter. Giles is showering away, washing off the soap.)*

**HAWK:**
*(reading)* To Sir Giles Futtock, Futtocks End, Malmsey ...

**GILES:**
I don't want all that! Good heavens, man, I know where I live. Get on with it, do!

**HAWK:**
Sir. We beg to inform you that our client, the honourable ...

**GILES:**
Who's it from?

**HAWK:**
Er – Hodgson, Hodgson and Skillett.

**GILES:**
Skip it.

**HAWK:**
No sir, Skillett. Solicitors.

**GILES:**
I mean, scrap it.

**HAWK:**
No, no, sir – Hodgson, Hodgson and ...

**GILES:**
Ignore it – destroy it! I want nothing to do with it. I don't want to know about it. What are the others?

**HAWK:**
*(reading the next letter)* "My darling chubby old puss-puss … "

**GILES:**
*(grabbing it)* How dare you!

*(He glares at Hawk, and then stares at the letter. We see that the ink, having been subjected to the stream of water from the shower, is running all over the paper – indeed the writing disappears altogether as we watch it in close up.)*

**GILES:**
I wonder who that was from. *(He peers at the now blank piece of paper.)*

**HAWK:**
*(looking at the envelope)* There appears to have been an error, sir – it's addressed to Boots.

**GILES:**
Boots the chemist?

**HAWK :**
Your Boots, Sir Giles.

**GILES:**
My Boots?

**HAWK:**
The boy as does your boots, Sir Giles.

**GILES:**
Oh, poor old Arthur. Well, I hope he knows who it's from. He's obviously on to a good thing there. You know you really shouldn't open other people's letters, Hawk.

**HAWK:**
*(sullenly)* Perhaps you would like to open the other one yourself sir.

**GILES:**
Are you mad? And have it all run down the plug-hole again. Come on, look sharp, man!

**HAWK:**
*(reading)* "Dear Gilly – a hasty note to say we will be arriving for the week-end after all. Have persuaded Lord Twist to come down with a view to buying the place from you. Let's hope he gets there before it falls down. He's bringing his current attraction, Carol Singer. Of course, that's not her real name. Also old Jack. Is that too many? My niece, Lesley, may turn up as well. Yours Fern. P.S. Arriving on the Friday train. Please meet. F."

**GILES:**
Beautifully read, Hawk.

**HAWK:**
*(With a somewhat glazed expression)* Is that the Carol Singer, sir?

**GILES:**
I've no idea, Hawk. How many Carol Singers are there? I don't even know the woman. But if Lord Twist is lugging her around, she's bound to be a cut above the ordinary.

**HAWK:**
She is indeed, she is indeed. She's a model.

**GILES:**
Oh, you've come across her, have you?

**HAWK:**
I caught the under-gardener looking at a picture of her without any clothes on, sir. In the conservatory.

**GILES:**
Did you, by George? I'll have to speak to young Godfrey. He'll catch his death of cold, the young idiot.

**HAWK:**
Miss Singer had no clothes on, Sir Giles.

**GILES:**
What, in the conservatory? All this has got to stop, you know, Hawk. I'm holding you entirely responsible for the future conduct of the staff, both in the conservatory, and out of it.

**HAWK:**
Very good, sir. Do I take it there will be six for dinner?

**GILES:**
I don't know. You're the mathematician. Well, step on it, man. Move about, move about! We meet the train at 6.30. Good Lord, I must get out of this shower, quick.

**HAWK:**
It's only 10.30, sir, there's no hurry.

**GILES:**
There is you know – the bally water's gone cold.

*(Now a shot of the railway-station. A little country halt. Hens on the line. Bindweed on the porter's trolley. A train approaching in the distance. Warm country noises. Outside the picket fence, Sir Giles and Hawk are waiting; the latter in his motor cycle gear.)*

**GILES :**
Here it comes, and *(looking down the road)* here comes Albert. *(Calls out)* Go on, Albert, you'll make it!

*(We see a little old railway official on a bicycle, steaming towards the station. He arrives just before the train does.)*

**ALBERT:**
*(exhausted and sweating)* I'll have to give this up. I can't run two stations at once, it's no good. I'm half killing meself.

*(He has opened the gate and let them onto the platform.)*

**GILES:**
But you're always doing this, Albert, why don't you get here a bit earlier?

**ALBERT:**
I can't. I have to take the tickets up at Mickleham. Then try and get here before the train. It's ridiculous.

**GILES:**
Well why don't you come on the train?

**ALBERT:**
Then how would I get back? It's nearly six miles.

*(Before this conversation can proceed further, we see that the passengers have alighted and are drifting towards the barrier. Giles totters off to meet them, while into shot comes a small, thin, oriental gentleman. He is sad. He approaches Albert.)*

**ALBERT:**
Oh gawd here we go again.

**O.GENT:**
Prease. Is Matery Halt?

**ALBERT:**
No sir, this is Malmsey.

**O.GENT:**
Oh. Man at rast station say – next station.

**ALBERT:**
I know he did.

**O. GENT:**
Prease?

**ALBERT:**
You want next station. *(The train is pulling out.)*

**O. GENT:**
Oh. This is not next station?

**ALBERT:**
*(suddenly exasperated)* Look, go on the coach. *(He pushes him towards the road.)*

**O. GENT:**
Coach? That is coach?

**ALBERT:**
Coach. Wait. There. *(Points to road.)* Get in coach. Soon!

**O. GENT:**
Oh. Thank you, prease.

*(He stares at Albert, then turns, and walks away from the barrier, towards camera.)*

**O. GENT:**
All rook arike. *(Translation: "All look alike")*

*He sees Sir Giles's large ancient Rolls-Royce parked on the bus and coach stop, and gets into it. By this time, Giles and guests are coming through the barrier. They consist of:*

*FERN BRASSETT. A county lady of some 68 years, doddery, fluttery, and a constant knitter. She is knitting now, as she walks along with Sir Giles.*

*OLD JACK. A lantern-jawed, balding man in his late fifties; he wears a deaf-aid, and carries a fold-up artist's easel and collapsible stool, as well as his week-end case.*

*LORD TWIST. A tall twit in his late thirties, with a stupid smile and a Savile Row suit.*

*CAROL SINGER. The photographic model: ravishing, large (top and bottom) and always rather uncomfortable. At the moment she is uncomfortable about her dress, which is too tight, much too short and much, much too low-cut.*

*LESLEY. Mrs Brassett's niece, 23 years old, a pretty flat-chested girl. This means she is pretty, and pretty flat-chested. A sympathetic figure, a romantic. Why she is here, unescorted, we shall never know. She is worthy of better things.*

The whole party wander down towards the Rolls-Royce, chattering *(we never quite hear what they say)* and begin to get in, ushered in by Hawk, who has a glint in his eye. Inside the car, we see the oriental gentleman smiling uncomfortably as the people pile in. Giles is driving, and Lord Twist sits beside him in the front seat. Mrs Brassett is next to the oriental gent, Lesley squashes in beside her, and Old Jack has to try and perch on the tip-up seat opposite, with his easel. There isn't really room. They are all chattering at once.

We then cut back to outside the car, where Carol is looking uncomfortable about getting in. This is just what Hawk had planned for. He squeezes the car door shut, over-balancing Old Jack, and signals to Sir Giles to drive off, which he does. Hawk then smiles evilly at Carol, and pats the pillion of his motor cycle. He then mounts it and waits. Carol realises that she has to go through with it and, pulling up her skirt so that it is almost round her waist, revealing a large expanse of suspender and stocking-top, she clambers astride the pillion and clasps Hawk round the waist. Hawk, delighted, his eyes bursting at the seams, kicks the machine into action, and roars away down the road.

We cut to the Rolls-Royce, tootling along. Old Jack's easel is half sticking out of the window. Inside the car they are crushed together, grunting and trying to get comfortable. From behind, we see Hawk approaching at speed. He roars round the car, and away. Then we see Giles driving. As Hawk overtakes, the back view of Carol Singer is such an astounding sight that the car swerves wildly, going completely the wrong side of a "keep left" bollard, back again to the left hand side of the road, up the grass verge, and back onto the road again.

Hawk and his passenger arrive at the house. He dismounts very quickly, in order to see Carol struggle off the pillion – much leg in evidence. Hawk is grinning like a demented ape at all this. Carol straightens herself out and goes with Hawk up the steps and in. The car arrives. Giles gets out, opens the rear door, and Old Jack falls onto the drive. The rest of the party emerge, breathless and awry, and proceed, chattering, towards the house. The last of these is, of course, the oriental gentleman, who follows them into the house, bewildered, but afraid to be left alone.

Inside the house, they begin to walk down corridors, round corners and upstairs, with Giles leading the way. At one point they all seem to be lost, including Giles *(who gets lost very frequently in this rambling house)*. However, he suddenly hastens round a corner, to where, on the wall, is a large map of the building, which he consults. They set off again, chattering. Carol is now being escorted by Giles, much to Hawk's disgust, and Mrs Brassett is still knitting. They approach "windy corner" and get pretty badly blown about. Up some stairs and, round the corner, a long corridor with bedrooms off it. A general sigh of relief, and they begin to peel off into various rooms. Hawk is carrying Old Jack's easel, and the two of them go into the first room. Then Mrs Brassett into the next; Lesley the next; Lord Twist the next and finally, Giles goes into the last room with Carol. As each door closes, the oriental gent looks more worried, trying to stay with the crowd, but to no avail – as Carol's door shuts with a bang, he is left alone in the silent corridor. He hesitates sadly and, muttering to himself, wanders back the way he had come, disappearing round the corner into the maze.

Hawk emerges from Old Jack's room, and proceeds to go down the corridor, placing his eye to each keyhole in turn. We see, from his point of view: Mrs Brassett, opening a suitcase, and tipping the contents onto the bed. It consists of a plastic bag with a toothbrush and soap, and about sixty-five ounces of knitting-wool, along with a pile of knitting patterns. She sits on the bed, and continues to knit.

Lesley, looking out of the window, rather wistfully.

Lord Twist, in shirt, but no trousers, is lighting his pipe, and changing.

Carol is bending over.

Hawks eyes light up, but the moment is short-lived, as Sir Giles suddenly moves across the line of vision and helps Carol undo the suitcase she is struggling with. We see Hawk's expressions – annoyance, jealousy, frustration – flit across his face. He applies his eye once again to the keyhole, when suddenly round the corner, some three feet away, comes Cook with a laden trolley. The trolley hits Hawk, and he falls, covered with lovely things for tea. Out from behind cook come the two tiny tweenies, looking aghast. Through the door comes Giles. A moment. The tweenies start to clear up the mess, and Hawk scuttles off in confusion. Giles grunts, and disappears into a small room the other side of Carol's bedroom, marked W.C.

In Carol's bedroom, she is putting away clothes into drawers. After a moment, there is a weird and deafening assortment of noises, indicating a lavatory chain being pulled and a cistern flushing. Carol jumps in alarm, and a large portrait in oils falls off the wall, and lands, still upright, against the skirting board. The face in the portrait stares blankly at us, with a surprised expression.

Dinner. The large dining room, the long table, everything just so. The table, for some reason, is set for ten. The maids and Hawk stand at the ready. The first to enter is Carol Singer, with a dress cut down to the navel, but with a lacy kerchief tucked into the bosom, so that, while quite a lot of Carol is showing, there would be a lot more, were the kerchief not there. Lord Twist follows in her wake, in a Savile Row Dinner jacket, chattering in his stupid way to Mrs Brassett, who is knitting. Hawk seats Carol, Twist sits beside her. Giles enters and sits, as does Lesley, who has come in on her own, and Mrs Brassett.

Giles then indicates to Carol, with a wink, that she should come and sit next to him at, which she does. The maid, Effie, has already begun to serve soup from a large tureen on a trolley. Twist, seeing that Carol has moved up, moves up himself taking his soup with him. This leaves Lesley rather on her own, so Giles beckons her up. She goes. While she is moving, Old Jack enters, wearing an old-fashioned dinner jacket and his white panama hat, which is constantly on his head. He sits and Mrs Brassett moves over to him with her soup. *(During this first general move, described above, the "Paul Jones" music is played, as in musical chairs.)*

The reason Mrs Brassett moved over was to inform Old Jack that he still had his hat on. Incidentally, Old Jack has relinquished his hearing-aid for a beautifully worked silver and ebony (or ivory) ear trumpet, which he obviously thinks goes better with his evening-dress. Anyway, he removes his panama hat, and places it on the table in front of him. Mrs Brassett is already knitting again. The maid, who keeps going to fill a soup plate, only to find it already full *(because of the general change round that has been going on)*, comes round to between Old Jack and Mrs Brassett. She is staring at Mrs Brassett's wool, which is trailing through her soup, making a brown line across the table. Still staring, she carefully pours a ladle-full of soup into Old Jack's hat. Jack looks at it. Consternation; it is seeping through onto the tablecloth. Everyone notices it at once – they stand up and sit down, chattering. The maid removes it, Mrs Brassett stands up and tells Jack to move to the next seat . Meanwhile, Lord Twist has got up and come round to Jack's old seat to place his dinner-napkin over the wet patch on the table cloth *(more "Paul Jones" music)*. As soon as Hawk sees this, he takes away Twist's chair at *(as in Musical Chairs)*, so that Twist cannot sit next to Carol. Twist returns to his place, only to find his chair gone, and then hurries round the table, where he sits, next to Lesley.

Jack is given more soup by a flummoxed Effie, and the chattering, which has been continuous, suddenly dies down to silence as everyone eats soup. Not a slurp or a swallow is heard. Not a scrape of a spoon. The English are eating their soup quietly. Bread rolls are accepted and refused with nods and shakes of the head. They all finish their soup, and the chatter begins to start again.

Hawk, handing round bread rolls, drops one from the basket. He looks down, looks around, and furtively kicks it under the table. Under the table, we see six pairs of legs, and the roll shooting in. The chattering begins to swell, and the twelve feet, all shuffling under the table, begin to kick the roll backwards and forwards. After a few journeys up and down the carpet, it is passed along from foot to foot, until suddenly, with an extra strong kick, it flies straight between the legs of Mrs Brassett, which legs, clad as they are in white stockings, and positioned wide apart, uncannily resemble a set of goal-posts. As the roll hits the back of her black net skirt, the chattering is mixed with the sound of a Cup-tie crowd cheering a goal. We see the table from above again, all the guests, including Mrs Brassett, quite oblivious of what has happened. Giles gets up to carve the roast, as the soup is cleared away.

Meanwhile, in the dim corridors of the house, the oriental gentleman is wandering up and down, trying to find his way out.

Back in the dining room, Giles is carving the roast beef. Already most people have been served, and Giles is standing at the side-table, which is situated behind his chair.

As he carves, his eyes are popping out of his head at the sight of Carol's thighs – her skirt, as usual, is far too short. Giles, who hasn't changed for dinner, is wearing a brown suede tie, which, at this point, manages to drape itself onto the joint of beef, with the result that he carves a good 1½ inches off it, and, still ogling Carol, puts it onto a plate with more meat, covers it with gravy, and hands it to the maid, who places it before Old Jack. The vegetables are on the table and everyone helps themselves. Hawk is carrying a dish of roast potatoes round to Mrs Brassett. They are beautifully brown and crisp, and Hawk cannot resist them. As he is about to place them on the table, he pops one into his mouth without anyone seeing, and then places the dish down on the table. Unfortunately, the potatoes are red-hot, and Hawk is in agony, has face and lips contorted into a pouting gargoyle as he tries to pretend nothing has happened. Finally, it is too much for him – he whisks a vase of flowers from the table, turns his back, and spits out the red-hot potato into the vase. As he replaces it on the table, a cloud of steam rises from it, hissing. He backs away, amid the stares of the onlookers.

Old Jack is about to eat the piece of necktie – he stabs it with his fork, covers it with horseradish sauce, and puts it in his mouth. He chews. His eyes glaze. He chews on. He keeps on chewing, but doesn't swallow.

Effie, meanwhile, has been to the kitchen, and is returning along the corridor with an enormous bowl of fruit salad. She approaches "windy corner", and as she rounds it, her skirt blows over her head. Having her hands full, she can do nothing about it, anyway she is used to it. As she walks away, we are aware of a brief pair of gingham check knickers. (More of these anon.)

The dining room again. Old Jack is still chewing. Hawk is at the side-table, being furtive. We see that there are three bottles of brandy, unopened, on the table. Hawk appraises the labels and we gather he fancies some of that, by jingo. He furtively opens a bottle, and is just about to sample some, when Effie comes in with the fruit salad. Caught in the act, he quickly plonks the bottle down on top of a couple of boxes of cigars. Effie, giving him an old-fashioned look, places the fruit salad on the side-table next to the bottle, and goes away. Hawk, meanwhile, has to go and attend to Mrs Brassett, in response to a wave from that good lady.

One of the tweenies is pushing the trolley, collecting the meat course empties. The trolley has a bent wheel, or is stiff, and the little tweeny has great difficulty in steering it – it keeps weaving from side to side. She eventually bumps into the side-table, which is sufficient to topple the brandy bottle off the cigar boxes, and into the fruit salad. The brandy runs, unnoticed, into the bowl. The other tweeny comes up to the side-table, and sees that pepper-pots, sugar sifters, and the now empty brandy bottle have fallen over (due to the bump). She stands them all up again, wiping the bottle dry with her napkin. Hawk comes back, and sees, to his dismay, an empty bottle. He looks up, sees the tweeny maid swerving about with the trolley. He can hardly believe it.

Effie now takes the fruit salad and starts to serve it, with cream. Plenty of "juice" with each helping. As the guests start to eat, a silence falls for a moment, then they all murmur their approval. They all tuck in like mad, gobbling it up and ladling the brandy "juice" into their mouths. Old Jack is still chewing, his jaw beginning to ache by this time. We presume he still has the piece of tie in his mouth as well as the fruit salad.

Second helpings are asked for. The atmosphere is definitely warming up. Carol begins to giggle. So does Mrs Brassett. The maids are now rushing round, trying to keep up with the demands for more fruit salad. Old Jack, cream round his mouth, still chewing, suddenly guffaws. Giles is merry, too. Lesley is laughing. Twist is grinning widely. Mrs Brassett, who is trying to knit, hiccoughs, and drops about fourteen stitches. Hawk, meanwhile, goes back to try another bit of brandy-smuggling. He picks up the second bottle and opens it. Then he opens the cupboard in the side-table, and takes out an empty coffee-pot, quickly pouring the contents of the bottle into it; then, placing the coffee-pot on a little silver tray, marches boldly towards the door – obviously intending to smuggle it out. As he reaches the door, however, it opens, and Cook appears, looking daggers, with a large decorated jelly on a dish. She indicates that Hawk should take it. He has to put the coffee-pot down on an occasional table by the door to do so. Cook disappears. Hawk is left holding the jelly.

Giles is making a pass at Carol – leaning over and whispering in her ear. In doing so, he knocks over her glass of wine. Some of it goes into her lap and, with great presence of mind, Giles whips the kerchief out of Carol's bosom and mops her up with it. Hawk, approaching with the jelly, catches sight of Carol's now very over-exposed bosom, which is wobbling about all over the place as she brushes herself down. We see Hawk with the jelly. The jelly melts.

The oriental gentleman is standing looking at the map of the house in the corridor. He is weeping quietly.

In the dining room, everyone is in very high spirits, and quite noisy. A tweeny sees the coffee-pot (which contains Hawk's smuggled brandy) on the occasional table near the door. Tutting with her tongue, she takes it and puts it back on the side serving table. Effie immediately comes and picks it up, and begins to serve it. Hawk, innocent of the switch-over, follows her round with hot milk and cream. She works round the table anti-clockwise, starting with Lesley. We see the guests reactions to the "Coffee". They adore it, having already been primed by the ninety per cent proof fruit salad. She reaches Old Jack. He's laughing away, and still chewing. Hawk is still driven to distraction by Carol's cleavage. Effie pours Old Jack's coffee, and asks whether he wants milk or cream. Jack puts up his ear trumpet – he didn't quite catch that. Effie repeats the question. Jack asks for cream. Effie nudges Hawk, who is ogling Carol and dreaming of conquering Everest. He recovers somewhat, and deftly pours cream into Old Jack's ear trumpet. This, of course, is all that is needed to set the table in a roar. We see everyone bellowing with laughter. Hawk rushes away in confusion to the side-table, opens the third bottle of brandy and knocks back a stiff one. Then he begins to fill everyone's glass. They are all roaring away – even Old Jack, who is now blowing cream bubbles through his ear trumpet. Hawk, too, begins to chuckle.

The outside of the house. Twilight. The lights shine out, and the laughter is plainly heard across the lawns.

Now, the outside of the house, next morning. The sun shines, birds twitter; a church clock strikes ten.

The breakfast-room. Giles sits at the table, with Lesley. Complete silence. Giles's face is a study. The previous night has taken its toll; he looks ghastly. He is staring at a poached egg, messing it about with his fork. Lesley is quietly sipping tea. She is obviously none too well either. She gives Giles a wan smile, which he tries to return, but fails miserably. Lord Twist comes in. He looks frightful. He too is very hung-over. He grunts at the company in general, and staggers over to the entrée dishes on the sideboard, which contain the breakfast. He removes a dish-cover, peers in, and replaces the cover. He does this in a normal manner, but we hear a crash like a cymbal. Giles reacts with a wince and a hand to the head. Another dish – another cymbal crash. And another. And another. He reaches the end of the line and finishes up with a bowl of cornflakes, which he pours from the packet into the bowl. This sounds to Giles *(and to us)* like a sack of coal being delivered. Twist sits down, and adds milk *(a bucket of water poured onto cement)*. During this symphony concert, Old Jack has staggered in, holding on to the furniture for support. He reacts to the frightful din in just the same way as the others. We see Giles glaring at Lord Twist pouring milk onto the cornflakes. At the same time, Giles takes a bite out of a slice of toast, which sounds like army boots on gravel as he munches, with an agonised expression. Twist, having sat down, joins in with the cornflakes *(Wellington boots in thick mud)*. Old Jack, crashing away along the entrée dishes, lifts one up and stares into it. His stare is returned by a ghastly-looking herring. Its one eye is glaring malevolently, its mouth is a twisted snarl. Close up of Jack's face – close up of the fish-face. Close up of Jack's eye – close up of the fish eye. *(Which is which?)* The dish cover crashes back. Another dish cover is lifted, and we see an arrangement of two fried eggs, a tomato and a sausage, which looks like an awful grinning face; in fact, as he stares at it, Hawk's awful grinning face appears in it, fading in, and fading out almost at once. This cover, too, is replaced. All this business has been punctuated by toast crunching, cornflakes ditto, and a new noise, like a muffin-man being drawn down into a whirlpool. It is Twist, stirring his coffee. He drinks some *(water going down a sink)*. Giles reacts again, desperately.

Old Jack has finally chosen a boiled egg. He sits at the table, lifts his spoon, and taps the egg three times. This sounds like Black Rod opening Parliament.

This last ear-splitting sound is too much for Giles. He staggers to his feet, opens the door, and ricochets along the corridor, the sounds of breakfast still echoing round the house. He enters the door marked W.C.

Carol Singer is in bed. A vision of loveliness, obviously she doesn't get hangovers. She lies there, in the flimsiest of nighties. In one hand she holds a tea cup of the most delicate china; in the other, a rose, which she is sniffing appreciatively. The ultimate in poise, obviously she is at her best in bed. The W.C. chain is pulled again – deafening. The four-poster bed collapses. Carol crawls out, looking a wreck.

Effie is marching along, with a tray containing shaving equipment, soap, hot water, razor, brush. She stops at a built-in cupboard, putting the tray down on a small table. Close up of Effie opening the cupboard door. On the top shelf are towels – she takes one out. The camera pulls back to reveal the bottom of the cupboard. Curled up, asleep, is the oriental gent. Effie gives a little squeak, wakening the O.G., who scrambles to his feet, uttering hoarse cries. Effie makes a run for it. The O.G. makes to pursue her, but she disappears around "windy corner". More gingham knickers. The O.G. gasps at the sight, then realises he is again lost and alone. He picks up the shaving-brush from the tray that Effie has left, and begins to shave, despondently.

A picture of Carol with no clothes on. Pull back to reveal it is in the hands of Boots, a scruffy, cheery lad of seventeen. He is in the scullery. He has a load of shoes – about six pairs, all mens', all black. They are slung in a heap on the floor. He finishes cleaning the last one. He then starts to sort them out; he has difficulty in making pairs out of them. The last pair he makes consists of one small one and one enormous one. Then he finds another enormous shoe behind him on the floor. He makes the pair. There is now one over. He looks around, nonplussed. Tries to match them up again, in the vain hope that it will come right. No luck, still thirteen shoes. He panics. He takes the odd one, and stuffs it into the boiler. It burns, merrily. He puts the boiler lid back. The door opens – it is Hawk. He carries a shoe. He indicates that he found it outside the door, and gives it to Boots. Hawk sniffs the air, smells burning. Boots grabs up the rest of the shoes, and bolts from the room. Hawk picks up the discarded magazine and, recognising Carol, begins to sweat.

Mrs Brassett is in the drawing room, knitting. She is an extremely fast and vast knitter. She has just finished an enormous sweater, and is looking through a few patterns, wondering what to knit next. Effie comes in, with one of the tweenies, intending to dust. Effie is stopped by Mrs Brassett, who indicates that Effie should fetch more patterns from Mrs Brassett's room. *(She waves a pattern at Effie, indicates with her hands a pile about a foot high, and points upstairs – something like that).* Effie drops her a curtsey, and departs. The tweeny starts to dust. Mrs Brassett beckons her over; she wants to try the sweater she has knitted on the tweeny, to see the size. The tweeny puts it on. It is gigantic, with a polo-neck. The tweeny's head doesn't show at all through the neck hole. Mrs Brassett gets the tweeny to turn round, slowly, as she studies the sweater. She stands back appraising it.

Giles is approaching the drawing room door. He half opens it, and we see, from his point of view, a headless sweater revolving slowly. Reaction from Giles. He closes the door.

In Mrs Brassett's bedroom, Effie has a bundle of paper knitting patterns about a foot high. She brings them out of the room, and down the corridor. Around "windy corner". This time, not only the now familiar gingham knickers, but patterns flying all over the place. Effie gets on her knees and attempts to retrieve them, trying at the same time to cope with her skirt. We leave her scrabbling about.

Mrs Brassett has removed the sweater from the tweeny, and is folding it up. Then she twiddles her knitting needles, obviously at a loss. Effie comes in, hair awry, with an untidy bundle of rather creased knitting patterns, gives them to Mrs Brassett, and leaves. Mrs Brassett takes the first three sheets of paper from the pile and peers at them. A hint of bewilderment.

The grounds. An open lorry drives up, containing a lot of dwarf fir trees – about six or seven feet high. They are standing in rows on the lorry. The lorry stops alongside an old garden wall. The groundsmen get out, lift off one of the trees, and begin to plant it in a ready-prepared hole.

Old Jack is in the grounds. He has set up his painting easel. We see the view he is preparing to paint – an old garden wall, and behind it, a row of fir trees. He starts to sketch with charcoal on his canvas. Close up of his hand, rapidly sketching in the fir trees. He starts to mix his paints. Behind the wall, the groundsmen are finishing planting the one tree. They throw their spades into the back of the lorry, and climb into the cab. On the other side of the wall, we see old Jack putting paint on his brush. We hear the lorry start up, and the line of fir trees moves off and disappears. Old Jack looks up and, as he goes to paint the trees, he sees they aren't there. He stares. He looks at his sketch. He looks up. He looks all around him, his jaw sagging.

The drawing room, Mrs Brassett is knitting furiously. She keeps peering at the patterns beside her. She has almost finished the garment already.

Lord Twist is fishing by the side of a lake, pond or river. Serenity. He sits in a little fold-up chair. He tips his hat over his eyes. We cut to the water. A large fin, as of a shark, is weaving its way towards us. It dives. We see Twist's line go taut, and he is pulled straight into the water.

Hawk is sounding the gong for lunch. A smallish gong on a table, with a strident note. We see Mrs Brassett put down her knitting, and head towards lunch. Carol, who has just finished getting dressed, does likewise. So does Lesley. And Giles. Hawk is now in the grounds, with an enormous gong, which is on a low trolley. He trundles it across the lawn, up to where Old Jack is painting. Stopping just behind Jack, Hawk gives the gong a tremendous swipe. It sounds like Big Ben striking one o'clock. Jack turns round, nods, and Hawk wheels the gong away.

A gloomy corridor. Cook, as vast as ever, is pushing a trolley laden with a cold collation *(for lunch)*. On her way to the dining room, she passes through the conservatory. As she approaches a clump of potted palms and rubber plants, we cut to a close up of them. In the shadows, framed by the leafy fronds, is the oriental gentleman, waiting to pounce. He has somehow acquired a kitchen knife, which he is wearing between his teeth. Fade in jungle noises – cicadas and the occasional screech of a bird or monkey. The oriental gent is tense – it's now or never. The trolley passes, and a hand clutching a knife comes through the foliage, and stabs a chicken on the trolley, whisking it into the leafy shadows. The Cook goes on her way, and we see the oriental gent devouring his spoils.

The door outside the dining room. All the guests approach in a bunch *(Lord Twist in a bath-robe, looking shaken)* and they all crowd into the dining room, chattering. They close the door.

Silence.

A loud burp.

The door opens, and out come the guests, chattering, and smoking cigars and cigarettes. They disappear down the corridor – luncheon is over.

Outside the house, Effie and Boots *(who is now much smartened up, and really looks quite presentable)* are walking, hand in hand, towards the woods. An aged gardener, with his hands in a wheel-barrow of manure, watches them go, a sad wistful look on his gnarled old face.

Giles, dressed in Norfolk jacket, and carrying a sporting gun, sets off to shoot a crow or two. With him is a young retriever dog, jumping about and getting under his feet. They head off for the woods.

On the lawn, Lesley watches them go. She is playing croquet with Lord Twist, but obviously her heart isn't in it. She plays her stroke, and Twist nods his approval, grinning inanely. Mrs Brassett is sitting, not really watching the game, knitting. Her ball of wool is on her lap. Twist plays his stroke, and his ball rolls up to Mrs Brassett's feet, unnoticed by her. An instant later, her ball of wool rolls off her lap. She leans over, gropes around without looking, picks up Twist's croquet ball and puts it in her lap. Twist comes over to look for his ball. He doesn't see it at first, but suddenly catches sight of it. He is at a loss.

Giles is in a field beside a copse. Birds fly over. He takes a pot shot at one of them. We see it fall. The retriever shoots off in the direction which the bird fell. Giles lights a cigar. We see the dog tearing back towards Giles. It rushes up to him, and drops a rabbit at his feet. Giles chokes a little over his cigar.

Hawk, in the corridor, with a silver salver, on which is a glass of frothing ale. He approaches "windy corner". As he rounds it, the head of the froth is blown straight off the beer, hitting a portrait on the wall, smack in the face. The portrait looks furious.

Old Jack is painting (a watercolour this time) in the garden. He is prodding away with his brush, as Hawk approaches with the beer on the tray. Old Jack nods at him as he sets it down on the ground beside Jack's paints. Hawk departs. Old Jack is just finishing the painting, and he dips his brush into the beer occasionally. He finishes the picture, drops his brush into the beer, picks up the paint water, and drinks it down in one go. He smacks his lips in appreciation, and wipes his mouth with the back of his hand.

Giles, meanwhile, is about to shoot another bird. Once again his aim is accurate, and the bird falls. The dog streaks off again. We see it racing across country, into the copse. Suddenly, we see the dog stop short, staring inquisitively. In the bushes, Effie and Boots are on the ground, necking. They both sit up at the arrival of the dog, and look embarrassed. Effie straightening her skirt and Boots straightening his tie. The dog stands there, not knowing what to do.

Giles is waiting for the dog to return – he has walked in the direction of the copse, and is just about to enter the trees when the dog runs out, clutching in its mouth the now very recognisable gingham knickers. He drops them at Giles's feet. Giles picks them up, and suddenly realising where he has seen them before, does a "well, well, well" facial expression and stuffs them into his pocket as he stalks away.

Hawk is preparing tea on the lawn. Canvas chairs with arms and little tables (or those platforms fixed to the left hand arm of each chair) stand in a row. A large tea trolley, with sandwiches, cakes, buns and teacups. The guests are drifting towards the line of chairs – Carol is now wearing tiny, very tight shorts, and a sun-top bra. She is looking cool, and Hawk, because of her, is looking hot. Twist follows close behind her, followed in turn by Old Jack and Mrs Brassett, who is now knitting an eternal scarf, which trails along behind her on the ground. Lesley is wandering along in the rear, wistfully. In the middle distance, Giles and the dog can be seen coming across the lawns. Mrs Brassett drifts along past the seats, and sits in the end one. Her scarf has trailed across the seats, so that about a foot of it is lying on the seat that Carol is about to occupy. As she is about to sit, Hawk rushes over to help her. She sits at the same time as Hawk reaches the back of the chair. Mrs Brassett tugs the scarf away from underneath Carol, and Carol, feeling it go, jumps, and stares at Hawk, thinking he touched her. Hawk looks puzzled. Giles has by now arrived, and all the company are seating themselves. Giles sits at the opposite end of the line to Mrs Brassett, the dog crouching nearby. The cucumber sandwiches are passed and everyone is chattering, as usual. Lesley, sitting next to Giles, takes the cruet proffered by Hawk, and liberally peppers her cucumber sandwich. Giles gets some of the pepper and, about to sneeze, whips the gingham knickers out of his pocket and claps them over his nose. Lesley, in the act of apologising for the pepper, sees them and laughs. Hawk sees them, and his eyes narrow, suspicion and envy flitting across his face.

A tweeny is going round with cakes and buns, dispensing them with a pair of tongs. Giles chooses a sort of rock cake, the only one of its kind on the dish. The tweeny transfers it to Giles plate with the tongs, and the plate is left on Giles's little table. He is busy drinking tea and chattering to Lesley, describing his shooting incidents of the afternoon. The dog ambles over, sniffs at the rock cake, and takes it off the plate, trotting away with it in its mouth. It goes off behind a hedge.

We see the dog try to bury the cake, without much success. The cake is by now pretty dirty. A gardener's boy happens along, and seeing the dog and bun, joins in the fun, throwing the bun for the dog to fetch, which it does. The next throw lands the bun in an ornamental pond *(or water butt)* from whence it is fished out, now clean again, but pretty wet. The gardener's boy squeezes most of the water from it, and drop kicks it over the hedge. It flies over the hedge, landing very near the trolley. The tweeny approaches, sees the bun on the floor, and picks it up quickly, popping it back onto the dish. Hawk comes up, picks up the dish, and goes over to Giles, who again chooses the bun, is given it by Hawk *(using tongs)* and bites into it, obviously enjoying it, completely unaware, as is everyone else, of the bun's adventures.

A long shot of the garden tea, a happy chattering group in the afternoon sun, as the church clock strikes five.

We cut to the face of the large grandfather clock in the drawing room. It says 9.30. The guests are passing a pleasant evening in various pursuits. Giles, Lord Twist, and Old Jack are playing cards. Giles is smoking a cigar, Old Jack a pipe and Twist a cigarette. There are ashtrays at each corner of the card-table.

Giles puts down his cigar in the ashtray on his left . Twist puts his cigarette down in the same ashtray a little later. Giles picks it up, puffs it, and, after a moment, puts it down in the ashtray on his right . Twist picks up the cigar, puffs it, and holds it. Old Jack puts his pipe down in the ashtray with the cigarette. Giles picks up the pipe, puffs it, and puts it in the ashtray on his left Jack picks up the cigarette, puffs it, and puts it in the ashtray on his right. Twist puts down the cigar to his right. Giles picks it up, puffs it, and puts it to his right. Twist smokes the pipe. Old Jack picks up the cigar, puffs it, and puts it to his right, where the cigarette is. Twist puts down the pipe, Giles picks it up, puffs it, and puts it to his right. Old Jack picks it up, puffs it, and puts it to his right. All three smokes are now in the same ashtray. Giles goes to smoke something, finds nothing in either of his ashtrays. An instant later, Twist does the same. They see the ashtray on Jack's side, and glare at him.

Mrs Brassett is watching television in the far corner of the room. We have already heard the strains of a symphony orchestra over the card playing scene, and now we see it on the TV screen. Mrs Brassett, as always, is knitting. The conductor is conducting. Mrs Brassett becomes very influenced by the music, vis-à-vis her knitting. As the speed and mood of the music varies, so does the speed and mood of Mrs Brassett's knitting. The conductor's movements, too, are to a large extent mirrored by Mrs Brassett's needles, as she knits – double forte, pianissimo and pizzicato.

Outside the house, Lesley is strolling in the twilight. She passes the open window of the drawing room, and the symphony concert floats out on the evening air. She walks along the side of the house, throwing a stick for the young retriever. As she moves onward, the concert begins to be mingled with the sound of a transistor radio playing beat group music. This gets louder as she approaches the window of the servants' quarters.

In the scullery, Effie and Boots, are dancing in the modern, abandoned manner. On the table is a now somewhat old-fashioned portable radio, with its lid open, and a pile of silver cutlery, together with equipment for cleaning them. We watch them for a few seconds, enjoying each other's antics.

Outside the scullery, Hawk is approaching along the passage. The radio can be plainly heard. He marches up to the scullery door and opens it quickly. The music instantly stops, and Effie and Boots are quietly cleaning the silver. Hawk glares at them and shuts the door again. We cut back to inside the scullery. Effie and Boots are dancing again, the radio blaring away, as if there had never been an interruption at all. Outside the door, Hawk has taken two or three paces along the passage, but now returns, on tiptoe. His hand goes to the door knob.

Inside, Effie and Boots are dancing. But suddenly, as if by some form of telepathy, they both stop instantly. They both grab a duster in one hand and a piece of silver in the other, and Boots knocks the lid of the radio shut with his elbow at the same time, causing the music to stop instantly, so that by the time Hawk has got his head round the door again, all is as it should be. He glares again, shuts the door, and immediately opens it again. This causes things to get rather out of step, in a strange way, because, as he opens the door, Boots lifts the lid of the radio, and he and Effie start to dance. Hawk stares at them, and shuts the door. They immediately close the radio, and start cleaning silver. Hawk opens the door again, and they open the radio and start to dance. He shuts it, and they clean the silver. He opens it – and, as the music starts yet again, we see a puzzled Hawk in close up.

Lesley is coming into the house. It is now quite dark – the grandfather clock chimes eleven.

Downstairs, in the drawing room, all is deserted. Hawk is emptying ashtrays and finishing up any liquor in the odd glasses dotted around the room. Lesley looks in, sees no-one except an obsequious Hawk, and starts towards the staircase.

Somewhere upstairs, all the guests are murmuring goodnight, and going to their rooms. We see Carol give Twist a good-night peck, Giles going into his room, and Twist into his.

Inside Mrs Brassett's room, the good lady is clad in a large towel, ready for a shower. She enters the bathroom, knitting, as usual. This time it is a very large sock, a rugby sock, or something similar. She steps behind the shower curtain, and throws her towel out. We hear the water turn on, and Mrs Brassett splashing about.

Lord Twist is in his room, in his striped underpants. He removes his singlet, and does a few knees-bend exercises – up and down twice, inhaling and exhaling as he does so. On the second knees-bend there is a sharp snapping noise, and he comes to a standing position very carefully. He starts to remove his shoes.

In the shower, Mrs Brassett has turned off the water – reaches an arm out for the towel, and a second or two later emerges with it round her, still knitting. The rugby sock has now shrunk to about half its size (or maybe a little smaller).

Giles is climbing into bed. He settles down, and reaches up to the light switch, which is one of those pull-string affairs into the ceiling. He pulls it, and the light goes off.

Lord Twist is in bed. He, too, reaches up to pull the light switch, and the light goes off.

The light comes on in Giles's room. He looks round, startled, sees nothing, and pulls the string again. His light goes off.

Twist's light comes on. He, too, looks round and then pulls the string, putting out the light.

Giles's light comes on again. He puts it out.

Twist's light comes on. He puts it out.

We see the front of the house. Quite a few lights on – but in one wing, we see the alternating lights of Giles and Lord Twist, off and on, off and on.

Then we see Giles, who is standing on the bed, winding the string of the light round the pillar of the four poster. He pulls it, and hangs on to it.

We see the light go on in Twist's room again. He, furious, gives a great tug at his light switch.

We see the front of the house again. All the lights in the house go out at once. There is a second's silence, then we hear mutterings and murmurings coming from the house.

Inside the house, the chattering is growing. The guests are all creeping about, trying to find out what has happened. The mutterings are interlaced with little shrieks and cries as people meet each other in the dark. Old Jack is bumping into everything, and Carol is outraged at least twice. So far we have seen nothing of them – just the occasional silhouetted shape, vague and unrecognisable.

In the servants' quarters, Hawk, lit by a candle, is just finishing mending the fuse. He goes to insert the new fuse into the circuit-box.

We are in the hall. The chattering has reached a crescendo. Suddenly all the lights go on. Everyone is standing in various positions in the hall, on the stairs, on the landing. They all freeze, and look at one another. They chattering stops instantly. As they stare around at each other, we see: Mrs Brassett, dressed entirely in wool – woollen pyjamas *(double-knit)* and a sort of pixie hood. Old Jack, in a night shirt with a pocket for his deaf-aid. Lord Twist, in union jack pyjamas. Carol, her hair in curlers, with a chin strap on, which doesn't match her flimsy night-dress at all. Lesley, in a surprisingly daring baby doll pyjama suit, and finally, Effie and Boots, looking more embarrassed than anyone. Boots is wearing a winceyette-type striped pyjama top, and extremely tight, thin, cotton pyjama trousers with large spotted pattern, and Effie is wearing striped winceyette trousers which look enormous on her, and a thin, cotton pyjama top with a large spotted pattern, which matches Boots's trousers exactly. They look at each other's clothes and realise what they have done in their haste. Everyone shuffles off in different directions, in an embarrassed silence – and Saturday is over.

Sunday morning. Birdsong; sunshine; church clock striking ten.

Cook is approaching, down the corridor, dressed in her Sunday-best-going-to-church-clothes. She sweeps up to the door of the scullery, and goes in, revealing the two tweeny maids behind her, in their Sunday-best. Inside the scullery, Boots is in his Sunday-best, playing darts. The dart-board is on the scullery door. Cook looks in, indicates with a jerk of her head that it's time they were on their way, and leaves again, closing the door. Boots throws a dart into the board, followed by another. Effie, doing something to her make-up, takes the darts from Boots, and has her turn – giggling a little at her low score. Boots pulls out the darts, and prepares to throw again.

Hawk is now approaching along the corridor. He wears a butler-type blue suit, and bowler hat.

We see a dart land in the board.

Hawk is at the scullery door.

The second dart lands in the board.

Hawk opens the scullery door.

The third dart lands in Hawk's bowler.

He glares stonily in close up.

Giles is seen, going into the lavatory. He is not in his Sunday best, but in very comfortable tweeds. He carries a model yacht. The lavatory door closes.

Hawk is on his way to Carol's room, with the Sunday papers. He knocks and rushes in, hoping to catch Carol unawares. Surprisingly, she is up and dressed, in tight slacks and an over-crowded sweater. Hawk notices a rolled-up towel and a pair of sunglasses on the bed. Carol gyrates into her bath-room for a moment and Hawk, quick as a flash, unrolls the towel. Sure enough, inside the towel is a bikini. He stuffs the bikini into his pocket, and rolls up the towel again, just in time. Carol emerges from the bathroom, picks up the rolled towel and, putting on the sunglasses, wobbles her way out of the room, bowed out by Hawk. We see Hawk's face, absolutely trembling with anticipation, as he watches her go.

The door of the lavatory. The chain goes, deafening, cacophonous. A large amount of ceiling and plaster falls on Cook, who is just about to go out of the front door. Her hat now resembles a Christmas cake.

Outside, Carol is walking through the woods, on her way to the lake. Behind her, in the distance, we see Hawk, who is following her – concealing himself behind trees and bushes.

Then we see Carol again, but this time the film is overcranked, so that she floats in slow motion through the trees.

We cut to Hawk, dodging from tree to tree. This time undercranked, so that he moves jerkily and extremely quickly from one hiding place to another.

Carol again, floating: Hawk again, whizzing.

Carol floats down to the edge of the lake, and settles. Hawk skids to a halt and, concealing himself in the bushes, waits, with baited breath. Now, at normal speed once more, Carol begins to undress, starting with the sweater. Hawk's eyes are sticking out like chapel hat-pegs. Carol is seen, from the back, as the sweater comes off. No bra.

A cow, grazing in a field, looks up, and does a double-take on Carol *(reverse film optical)*.

Carol opens the towel, and discovers there is no bikini inside. Hawk's face is a study. Carol's face is a dilemma – she looks round, sees no-one, and decides to go in for a swim anyway, costume or no. In very long shot, from Hawk's point of view, we see her remove her slacks, and prepare to dive into the lake. Hawk, trembling, produces a pair of binoculars. As he raises them to his eyes, some heavy instrument is brought down with a crash onto his bowler. He collapses, stunned. The heavy instrument turns out to be a large telescope, which Giles, his assailant, immediately focuses onto Carol's nude form splashing about in the lake. He watches appreciatively for a few moments.

In another part of the ground, Old Jack is sketching a landscape – a stream, hedges, a large tree in the background.

Mrs Brassett enters the lavatory in the house.

Jack is mixing his paints in the grounds.

Mrs Brassett pulls the chain. Deafening.

The tree in Jack's landscape falls, disappearing out of sight behind the hedges. He looks up to paint it – it is gone.

At the side of the lake, Hawk is regaining consciousness. He sits up, and blinks. Carol is still in the water. Hawk looks for his binoculars, but they are gone. He gets a devilish idea – he will hide Carol's clothes. He creeps down towards the lakeside on his hands and knees. In doing so, he puts both hands into a boggy piece of ground, and his hands come out covered in thick mud. He crawls on, and reaches the pile of clothes. He wipes his hands on the towel – we plainly see the two muddy hand prints. Seeing the mess he has made, he quickly puts the towel down on the ground again, clean side uppermost. He then grabs the clothes, keeping out of sight of Carol behind the low bushes, and crawls away, hiding them in the foliage. He looks back, and realises he has left the towel. He begins to crawl back towards it, but too late – Carol is coming out of the water. He stares, fascinated as long as he dare, and then scuttles away into the undergrowth. Carol arrives at the towel, and finds her clothes gone. Her face is puzzled, then alarmed, realising someone has been spying on her.

Back in the garden, near the house, Old Jack is looking at a small statue. He walks round it, studying it. He suddenly tries to push it over, to no avail. He tries lifting it, but can't. He kicks it, leans on it – it doesn't move an inch. Satisfied, he steps back to his easel, where we see he has already sketched it. He begins to apply paint to the sketch, keeping an eagle eye on the statue, for fear that it should disappear, like the rest of his subjects so far. Suddenly he looks up. Hurrying towards him, along a path towards the house, comes Carol, clad only in her towel. It barely covers her essentials, and she is clutching it tightly round her, top and bottom. The aged gardener, still with his manure wheelbarrow, is creeping along at a snail's pace towards her. He disappears from view behind a clump of bushes. Carol, too, has to pass behind the bushes on her way to the house. Old Jack watches, and after two or three seconds, the aged gardener reappears trudging on his weary way. Carol, also appears again on the opposite side of the bushes, still hurrying towards the house. Old Jack stares at Carol's back view. Two muddy hand-prints are planted firmly on the towel, covering Carol's buttocks. We know that Hawk put them there, when he wiped his hands down by the lake, but Old Jack doesn't, and he stares at the receding gardener with amazement. Effie, standing in for Hawk, appears on the steps with a gong, and bangs it for lunch. Lesley and Giles, talking and laughing, are crossing the lawns.

An hour or so later, a small van drives up to the entrance of the house. The driver delivers a large wicker basket to Hawk, and drives off.

Giles and Lesley are in the drawing room having coffee, when Hawk enters, and whispers discreetly in Giles's ear. He is delighted and, taking Lesley's hand, leads her out to where the basket is standing in the hall. They open it, and we see printed on the side "Fox Ltd., Costumiers". Inside are various large brown paper parcels. The other guests drift in, and each receives a parcel from Giles, who is reading the names on the labels. As they receive their parcels, they go upstairs to their respective rooms. The last to receive his parcel is Hawk and he, too, disappears to get dressed.

Lord Twist is in his bedroom, with a pair of tights on, but still wearing his sports jacket. He is ferreting about in his package, and brings out a long feather. He looks at it.

Mrs Brassett has got into a large black bombazine dress – she is obviously going to be Queen Victoria.

Old Jack is struggling into a roll-neck jersey, with large horizontal stripes.

Lesley is in a buckskin skirt with tassels, and is about to put on the jacket.

Carol is struggling into a glittering, silver-lamé top, close fitting, with long sleeves.

And Giles has got on a pair of white trousers.

Outside the house, Hawk is driving the Rolls-Royce up to the entrance. He parks it, and gets out – he is clad in furs and skins – we don't quite know what he is supposed to be. He walks round the side of the house, and out of sight.

In the hall, people are appearing in their fancy dress. Twist is standing, looking rather sheepish, as Robin Hood. Mrs Brassett, as Queen Victoria, is knitting. Lesley comes downstairs, very pretty as an Indian maiden, closely followed by Old Jack, as a burglar, complete with flat cap and eye-mask. He carries a small black leather bag marked "SWAG". The others laugh and chatter. Old Jack looks rather stony-faced. Giles comes down the stairs as Buffalo Bill, and gets a few murmurs of approval. Then Carol makes her entrance. Joan of Arc – in silver-lamé armour, fitting her is if it was her own skin, the light reflecting off her salient points. She receives a round of applause. They all troop out to get into the car.

A large poster: "Grand Summer Fête" etc. The words "Fancy Dress Parade" are prominent. As we pull back, we see the fête is already in progress – lots of stalls, and country people enjoying themselves. Various shots of different stalls – darts, rolling pennies, ball in the bucket, etc. A stall where you knock down tins with mop-heads. A large sign saying "One win – anything off the bottom shelf." On the bottom shelf sits a little old woman, smoking a home-made fag-end. She looks bored. A tin hits her on the head. She still looks bored.

A boy, about ten years old, is throwing rings over goldfish bowls. His first throw is successful – the ring goes over the bowl. The stall-minder – a lady who looks as if she might be the vicar's wife *(remember, this is a fête, not a professionally run fun-fair)* hands him a small goldfish in a large polythene bag full of water. The boy throws again – again he wins a fish. His third throw misses, but his fourth wins another fish. The whole thing is obviously much too easy. We leave him as he is buying more rings, and trying to cope with three bags full of water.

The Rolls-Royce is arriving at the entrance to the fête. Giles gets out, as a small crowd begins to gather, staring at the car. We realise that not many of the crowd have bothered to come in fancy dress. Twist gets out, and opens the rear door of the car. Out steps Queen Victoria. The crowd parts, and Mrs Brassett sweeps through them, receiving a few unconscious curtseys and bows from the villagers. She is followed out by Old Jack who, by contrast, looks a ridiculous figure in his burglar's outfit. Lesley, meanwhile, has got out of the door on the other side, and is talking to Giles, and laughing at Jack's stony-faced reception of the crowd's amusement. The last to come out is Carol. She is very conscious of the crowd, and strikes a pose with one foot on the running board of the car. Applause and approval, especially from the male villagers. They follow Queen Victoria through the crowd, Giles and Lesley going last. Giles is fiddling with an "instamatic" type Polaroid camera.

The goldfish stall is doing a roaring trade. People are winning goldfish left, right and centre, and walking away with water-filled bags.

A canvas latrine, marked "MEN". The canvas finishes about nine inches from the ground. Old Jack stops and stares at the gap below the canvas. There are three feet protruding from under it, and two sticks.

Jack is puzzling this out, when the three feet and two sticks move away, and out of the latrine comes an old yokel with a walking stick, followed by a man with a wooden leg. They go off in different directions.

Giles is bowling at skittles. The sign says "Win A Pig." Lesley is with him, cheering him on. He is doing well and the skittles are flying in all directions. As he lets fly with his third ball, the man with the wooden leg crosses the line of fire. The ball hits his wooden leg, and he is bowled over.

Hawk is arriving at the fête on his motor bike. He is dressed in furs, as before mentioned. He dismounts, and from a box strapped to his pillion, he takes out a viking's hat, with the horns. Removing his crash helmet, he swaps it for the horned hat. There is very little difference. He marches off into the crowd.

Old Jack is at the shooting gallery, run by a curate. The curate is rather nervous of guns. We see Old Jack taking aim at a row of clay pipes. He fires, and hits a fancy plate on the shelf of prizes. It shatters. He fires five more times in rapid succession, and each time shatters a prize. He is cheered by a couple of callow youths nearby, and points to the clay pipes, beaming. The curate hands him a clay pipe and Jack goes away, delighted, leaving the curate mystified.

A "treasure hunt" – a plot of sand on the ground about six feet square, with little flags stuck in it. A few feet away, a "Muffin the Mule" type wooden horse, painted silver, for children's rides, the kind you put sixpence in, and it jogs up and down.

This is being looked after by a rather neurotic middle-aged lady. Next to the horse, a coconut-shy booth. Between the horse and the coconuts stand two old farmers, talking away. The one nearest the horse takes a match out of his waistcoat pocket, and strikes it on the horse's hindquarters, to light his pipe. The lady looks livid, and tells him not to do that. He grins and nods apologetically. She turns to attend to a child, and he does it again.

A group of yokels standing round a pen, in which is a prize cow. They are staring at it, as country yokels do. Hawk approaches, and leans on the fence, looking at it. The cow looks up, sees Hawk's horns and backs away. The yokels all stare at Hawk. He smiles uneasily and hurries off.

The farmer has just struck his match on Muffin the Mule again, and the lady, furious, gets some of the Boy Scouts who are guarding the "treasure hunt" to move the horse to another part of the ground. The farmers are still talking, oblivious to the fact that it has gone. Two men, carrying some fencing, or part of a collapsible booth, make their way between the farmers and the coconut shy, causing the farmers to step back, so that they are adjacent to the treasure hunt. They are still talking. Carol is walking along, looking at things, with Giles and Lesley in the background. The boy scouts ask her to try her luck with the treasure hunt. She takes a flag and bends over, trying to decide where to place the flag. Giles, a few yards behind her, raises his Polaroid camera, and we see, from his point of view, Carol's silver-lamé bottom sparkling in the sunshine. The farmer, without looking, strikes a match on it, still talking. Giles and Lesley suppress their mirth with difficulty.

Old Jack is rummaging round a rummage stall. He puts down his leather swag bag, in order to look at something. Someone picks it up, buys it, and goes away. The village policeman is wandering round the fête. Large, sweating, not too bright. He stops, and watches Old Jack the burglar, rummaging. Finding nothing to suit him, Old Jack drifts away, picking up a lady's handbag from the stall as he does so, in mistake for his swag bag. The policeman eyes him suspiciously and follows at a respectable distance, tailing him.

Nearly everyone in the crowd is now carrying a goldfish.

Giles and Lesley are playing "Knock his hat off". Three youths, with assorted hats – a top hat, a ladies picture hat covered in flowers and birds etc., are walking up and down behind a canvas screen, which is just head-height, so that only the hats are showing. The competitor, in this case Giles, has to throw tennis balls, to try and knock off a hat as they move to and fro. We see Giles miss a couple, and purchase more tennis balls from the stall holder. Old Jack is wondering along, tailed by the policeman. He goes behind the "Knock his hat off" stall, staring at the youths who are wandering up and down for no apparent reason.

We see Giles again, preparing to throw. Old Jack, being short, is not visible to Giles behind the screen. Suddenly a policeman's helmet moves slowly along the top of the screen.

From the back, Old Jack finds there is no way out at the far end of the canvas screen. He turns back, and the policeman passes him, so as not to arouse suspicion.

From the front, Giles is taking aim. The helmet arrives at the end of the screen, turns, and begins to move slowly back again. Giles lets fly, and catches it – a beauty. It disappears. Old Jack wanders away past Giles, as Giles collects his prize. The policeman is dusting his helmet behind the canvas screen. He then moves, helmet in hand, to keep Jack in his line of sight. Next to the canvas screen is a large square of plywood, with an oval hole cut in it, at about head height. From the policeman's point of view, through this hole, we see the tiny figure of Old Jack in the distance. The policeman moves up and puts his face through the hole, watching. From the front, we see for the first time that the plywood has on it a crude painting of a headless fat lady in a terrible bathing costume, a real seaside dirty postcard look, the sort used by beach photographers. The policeman is supplying the head, and is greeted by a ragged cheer from the onlookers. Giles is there, with his Polaroid camera, and snaps it, as, of course, does the photographer who is running the stall.

Everyone, but everyone, now has a goldfish in a bag of water. We see a small girl carrying one in close up. Suddenly, it springs a leak, the water streaming out in an arc, unnoticed by the child.

From the dais, the vicar is announcing the fancy dress parade. The microphone is over-modulated, and keeps cutting out, with the result that we hear one word in four, and that very crackly. People start to drift round to the fenced-off portion of the ground near the dais, as the competitors, including all Giles's guests, get ready for the parade. Most of the goldfish bags are leaking now, but people don't seem to notice. Music starts to play from an amplifier, and the competitors begin to walk round. They all have numbers pinned on their backs by a young lady near the dais as they enter the arena. Shots of people still approaching the fences and watching – all with leaking goldfish bags. A long shot of the parade going on. The policeman is still following Old Jack as he goes into the arena. The young lady pins a number onto the policeman's back – no.49.

A shot of three yokels, standing against the fence, watching the parade. First, from the back, we see they all have bags of goldfish. Then, in profile, we see the three of them, grinning at the fancy dresses. Three jets of water are streaming out through the open fence, at just the right height. After a few seconds, two of the streams slowly drop down and peter out, but the one in the middle carries on, strongly. His obviously is bigger and contains more water. We cut to his face – oblivious – a great, red, shiny country face. Back to the three-shot, with the steady stream showing no sign of letting up.

A long shot of the parade. Then, a quick shot of the sky, darkening rapidly. There is a sudden clap of thunder, and down comes the rain, in buckets. Umbrellas go up all over the ground, and people all break for cover. Shots of everything getting soaked. Close shots of the ground, with puddles rapidly forming Lesley, with her one Indian feather drooping – Hawk terribly bedraggled, water dripping from his fur – everyone scattering, and all the guests making for the Rolls-Royce. They arrive at the car and Giles, bending his head to get into the driving seat, shoots about a gallon of water out of the brim of his ten-gallon hat, onto the ground. Hawk, in his horns, is bundling people into the rear door as fast as he can. Carol, as she is bending to get in, drops her sword, and Hawk picks it up, butting her in the behind with his horns as he does so. The doors slam, and they drive away.

The large poster, advertising the fête – saturated, all the paint running: and finally, a large puddle and in it, several goldfish swimming about happily, their lives saved in the nick of time by Mother Nature.

The House. Everyone has changed into their ordinary clothes, and is preparing to leave. Mrs Brassett is knitting, and Old Jack clutches his easel and one canvas, on which he has the painting of the statue. Carol is now wearing an evening-dress – a diaphanous affair with a long train at the back. Giles is shaking hands with them all – they are chattering away as usual. As they come out onto the steps, we see that the storm has passed, and it's a fine summer evening again. Hawk helps them into the car (*this time he has a chauffeur's cap on – he is driving them to the station*).

Old Jack, staggering into the car with his easel, catches it on the side of the door rather violently, causing him to drop his one remaining canvas. He recoils from the impact and puts his foot through the picture. He bends down to pick it up, planting one end of his easel down on the train of Carol's dress as he does so. Hawk helps Carol into the front passenger seat at this moment, and the whole of her skirt is ripped off as she climbs in. Hawk slams the door, and then notices the skirt on the ground, just as Old Jack slams his door. Hawk's face in close up – delighted at the prospect of driving next to a skirtless Carol. He rushes round to the driving seat, leaps in, and the car disappears down the drive.

Giles is waving from the steps, chuckling. Lesley appears round the door frame, from inside the house. Giles looks surprised and indicates the receding car. Lesley grins and points downwards, indicating that she intends to stay a little longer. Giles is delighted, and takes her hand and pats it. Suddenly, from inside the house, we hear a strangled cry of delight, and the oriental gentleman rushes out, between Giles and Lesley, flinging his arms wide in relief at having found his way out of the house. Muttering joyously, he rushes down the drive in undercrank, leaping and dancing in his ecstasy.

Giles and Lesley look at each other and, hand in hand, go into the house, shutting the door behind them.

As the door closes, the stone ball falls off the balustrade, and rolls down the drive. We pull out, slowly.

●⭠

# THE PICNIC

*The Picnic* (credited to Gerald Wiley) and *By The Sea* ("by the author of *Futtocks End* and *The Picnic* and concerned with a similar group of characters") were produced in 1976 and 1982 respectively, as spin-offs from *The Two Ronnies*. Featuring Barker and Corbett, with a host of others, they were further opportunities for Ronnie to explore the almost-silent comedy, or as he put it, "grumble and grunt" films. "*The Picnic* was much more exciting to me than either of the other two," recalls Ronnie, "because I wanted to capture the feel of that far-off childhood summer. That sort of feeling you remember of slight weirdness … in *The Picnic* you have a sort of Edwardian picture. It's a situation that's unreal to most people and that's what I liked about it. And you had this man who just sort of rode over everyone and behaved how he wanted to and everyone just sort of fitted in. I loved that kind of thing hugely."

Although unnamed in both films that man was, once again, Lord Rustless.

The English countryside. A sunny morning. England at its prettiest. We hear a cock crow. A shot rings out. The cock croaks, and perishes.

An English country house. A milk float is coming down the drive. It stops, the milkman gets out, with his crate. Close up on the crate. It contains one bottle of milk and eleven bottles of champagne.

Cut to the doorstep as he exchanges the full bottles for similar empties – one milk, eleven champagne.

Inside the house. A pretty maid in a black uniform walks along a corridor, carrying *The Times* on a silver salver. She passes the butler, who carries breakfast on a tray. As she passes him, she steals a small piece of bacon from his tray, with her free hand. He looks disapproving. They pass on. The maid walks to a door, knocks, goes in. She is followed by a stupid-looking retriever dog.

The bedroom. Dominated by a large four-poster-bed, with curtains all round it. They are fully closed.

The maid approaches the curtains. A hand *(belonging to the General)* comes out, takes the newspaper. Then the hand re-emerges, grabs the maid, and drags her headfirst behind the curtains. The dog looks on wagging his tail. After a few squeals and guffaws, the maid backs out again, rather dishevelled, and tuts her way out of the room.

The General appears from out of the bed – night-shirt, monocle. He yawns, and exits to an adjoining bathroom. The dog sits down. A loud loo-chain is heard, and a wheezy flushing. The General emerges, drying his hair with a towel. The dog does a double-take *(reverse film!)*

The breakfast-room door. Silence as the General approaches it. He opens it – cacophony. Loading of plates, high-pitched chatter. He goes in.

We cut to a very crowded picture of the rest of the household. The General's sister, Fern, clutching a large piece of knitting and needles in one hand, trying to fill her plate from the entrée dishes. Clive, the eldest son, who has managed to get some bacon on to a plate, and is just about to add an egg when the plate is whipped away by a very old man with a toothless grin. Fern's companion, Edith, a plain girl who doesn't believe in make-up, but who does believe in eating *(although she is thin)*, reaches across and blocks

Clive's view of the buffet-table, and manages to drop her pendant into his egg, and a large well-developed Bird *(who is obviously on Clive's wanted list by the way he behaves towards her)* nearly pokes his eye out with her sweater as she thrashes about in search of a succulent kidney. A close up of Clive's desperate face.

At the table, the General sits with a packet of cornflakes and a bottle of champagne. He starts to pour cornflakes into a bowl. A small horrid boy passes behind him. The General greets him affably. The boy pokes out his tongue at him. The General shrugs, takes foil off the top of the champagne.

Cut back to the fight around the side-board. The Bird is much in evidence, wearing an extremely brief and cheeky pair of bright red shorts. A crash of a knife is heard as one is knocked on to the floor. The Bird bends to pick it up. The General reacts to this vision, and the cork pops out of the champagne bottle in his hand. He doesn't even notice,

The Bird and Clive sit down at the table.

The General pours champagne on his cornflakes and tucks in. The noise around him is still deafening.

Cut to the kitchen. Silence. The butler and the maid are preparing food for the picnic, which is to be the event of the day. They stand primly side by side, cutting and buttering bread. They are surrounded by tomatoes, cucumbers, strawberries, and other fruits – and cold meats and pastries.

Cut back to the Breakfast – tremendous noise again. Clive and his Bird are eating. Peeping out from underneath the table, the stupid-looking dog. Clive's hand comes into shot and feeds it a piece of bacon. Underneath the table, we see the Bird's shapely limbs. The dog's tail, wagging with pleasure, is tickling her legs. Above the table, she reacts towards Clive, thinking he is doing it. He smiles back at her, then putting his finger to his lips and pointing under the table, tries to indicate that he is secretly feeding the dog. She mistakes him completely. Underneath the table again, we see the Bird's hand appear, holding a fork. The tail is still tickling her. She jabs Clive's leg hard. Above the table, he leaps up, and shoos the dog away angrily. The Bird smiles sweetly at him.

The kitchen. The butler is slicing a large radish into a very fancy shape. Big close up as he cuts a beautiful pattern in it. The maid looks on. He smiles, pops it on top of a pile of sandwiches. He then picks up a picnic-basket, and exits. The maid takes the radish and puts it into her mouth, crunching it up.

The Breakfast-Room again. The Old Lady knitting, reading *The Times*, and drinking coffee. On the floor, the dog spies the ball of wool, grabs it, races out of the room. After a few seconds, the knitting is suddenly whisked away from the Old Lady. She doesn't notice immediately, however, and carries on knitting thin air – then realises.

The Corridor. The dog rushes round the corner with the ball of wool in its mouth, followed eventually by the piece of knitting *(which is about eighteen inches square)*. As the dog disappears round the next corner, the butler appears, sees the knitting going along on its own, and steps on it firmly.

Round the corner, the dog is pulled up so sharply that he slithers all over the place on the shiny floor.

Back at the knitting, the butler has his foot firmly planted on it. Round the corner comes the Old Lady. She stares in disapproval at the Butler, who sheepishly hands over the knitting. It has a large black footprint right across it.

Outside the house. An enormous old open-topped (convertible) car. The Butler is loading things into the boot. The picnic party come streaming out of the house. The General, who carries a shot-gun; the Old Lady, knitting; the Small Boy, with small bow and arrows; Clive, with tennis racquets and perhaps a butterfly net; the Bird, in her plain red shorts and overflowing sweater; the Companion, with a black umbrella; and the dog,

The Old Lady gets in front, and the Bird and Clive, with the Companion and the

Boy, in the back. The dog leaps in after them. There is obviously not enough room, but they eventually get settled. The General, who is the last to get in, sticks his shotgun into a piece of rope which is obviously holding the offside back door together *(in fact the Companion perhaps had to climb over it to get in)*. He looks round, everyone is ready. He slams the driver's door shut, the shotgun goes off bang, and, in close up, the offside back tyre collapses. Groans from all, and everyone piles out again as the long-suffering butler removes the spare wheel.

The screen is "wiped" in the old-fashioned way, and we find the butler just removing the jack, as the others all pile back in to the car. The General waves, and the car pulls away from camera, up the drive. Out to the maid, waving. We go with her as she walks to where the butler is astride an old motorbike. She mounts the pillion, and they too set off for the picnic.

The car is going along, through some pretty countryside. A wide shot – then we follow it as it goes round a hidden bend. It passes a loaded hay-cart, jogging along between the meadows on either side. We see the cart from the front – the old Yokel driving it waves as the car overtakes it and goes past camera.

Now we are with the motor bike again. A close shot of the butler and maid, then a static shot, as they zoom away from the camera, round the same hidden bend, out of sight. Three seconds pause, and then a crash.

A close shot of a spinning motor bike wheel in the hedge. A front shot of the Yokel getting off his cart. He walks into the motorbike's shot – looks over the hedge. From his point of view we see quite a steep drop down. There, under the bushes, two sets of legs. He runs out of shot. We pick him up as he scrambles down the slope towards the two bodies. He grabs the girl's legs and rolls her over onto her back. It's the wrong girl; she sits up and slaps his face. Her lover, too, sits up and glares. Cut back to the Yokel retreating towards the camera by the motor bike on the road. He turns, and stares past camera. A reverse shot. The butler's and the maid 's legs are sticking out of the hay at the back of the cart.

The maid's knickers are very much in evidence. She is slightly higher than he is in the pile of hay. The Yokel moves forward, and, from another angle, starts to haul the maid out by the feet.

Back at the car. It stops at a pretty country pub, nothing elaborate, and not too pseudo-Tudor, but a real, friendly place, with little tables and rustic arches outside. Everybody gets out of the car, and occupy the chairs and tables. Clive goes inside to get the drinks. There are three Yokels playing dominoes at a table. The General takes a photograph of them *(as he raises his camera and clicks, we freeze frame and go to black and white for a couple of seconds)*. The Old Lady sits down next to them, watching their game and knitting.

The three Yokels: one has a cigarette, one a pipe, and one a pint of ale. There are ashtrays at each corner of the table. As they play, each one puts down his pipe, or pint, or cigarette on his left. Having played, they sometimes pick up the wrong object – but they still smoke or drink it, apparently without noticing.

Clive appears with drinks. A pint of Pimms, loaded with mint and fruit, for the General, a sherry for the Old Lady, lager for himself, and orange juice for the other three. In close up, hands come in and take all but the sherry. This Clive takes over to Old Lady. She acknowledges it with a smile. The local on her left drinks it in one, and puts it on the other side of him. The Old Lady picks up the pipe, which is on her right, and puffs at it.

The General is at another table. He has a wooden penny whistle, and is showing it to the Small Boy. The Boy, however, it not at all interested in the General's tooting. He pokes out his tongue and leaves the shot. The General swigs his Pimms, and continues to toot.

At another table, the Bird is with Clive, and the companion girl. The Bird excuses herself, leaves the shot. We see the back of the car. She comes from behind camera, opens the boot, finds her vanity-case, and bends over it, rummaging about.

Cut to the Small Boy, with a pea-shooter. He fires. Cut back to the Bird. She is hit fair and square in the shorts. She leaps up, rubs her rear end, and taking an aerosol from her vanity-case, sprays the surrounding area.

As she bends to return it, however, the horrid boy fires again. Again she leaps up, but this time she looks round suspiciously.

Cut to the General, still holding his penny whistle.

He waves it at her in a friendly fashion. She stalks over to him, and breaks his whistle in half. He is nonplussed. She leaves the shot. The General, not knowing quite what to do, drinks a vase of flowers instead of his Pimms. He fails to notice the difference. He even chews one of the flowers.

The butler and the maid sail by on their motorbike, looking a bit the worse for wear. They disappear up the road, as all the guests once more board the car.

Cut to a very pretty wide shot of a country road. The car goes past camera. Reverse shot as it goes away, entering a tiny village. Inside the car, Clive leans forward and whispers in the General's ear. The General nods. The car pulls up outside a couple of old cottages, with a passageway between. Clive gets out, and walks to the back of the houses, through the passage. The others wait.

At the back of the house, the owner is watering his garden with a hose. Clive speaks to him, and the old man indicates an outside loo at the bottom of the garden. Clive moves smartly to it, and shuts himself in, as the man now concentrates on watering the flowers on the opposite side of his garden.

At the car, the occupants are amazed to see a great jet of water issue from the side of the house, landing on the flowers. The General decides to take a photograph of the phenomenon. *(Freeze frame – black and white.)*

In the back garden again, Clive emerges from the loo, just as the owner turns off his garden tap. Clive thanks him.

From the car, the jet dies down, and Clive appears round the side of the house, smiling uncertainly.

A beautiful meadow, by the river. A romantic wide shot shows us that this is the picnic-ground.

The car pulls in at the five-bar gate, drives across the meadow, and stops very near the river.

In a closer shot, everyone gets out. The butler and the maid rise from where they have been sitting waiting under a tree, and approach the car. The General gives him instructions as to where he wants the picnic; Clive and the Bird wander off together across meadow.

The butler begins to take all sorts of strange things out of the car – including large, ungainly things: a gramophone, ice-bucket on a stand, card-table, croquet-set, deck chairs, screen, etc. Far more than the boot could in reality hold.

Clive and the Bird in a field. She is looking for blackberries in a hedgerow. He sits near her, on the grass, his back leaning against an old post. We tilt up, to see that it is a notice-board saying, simply, "Danger". He suddenly notices the sign, gets up, looks all round – he can see nothing dangerous. He shrugs his shoulders. The sign falls and hits him on the head.

The butler and the maid are laying a vast table-cloth on the grass. With a croquet mallet he bashes down the bumps in the ground that stick up through the cloth. One of the bumps moves about. It eventually emerges as a hedge-hog. *(Or a rabbit – try both.)*

Clive and the Bird are walking in a field, away from camera. The Bird suddenly turns and looks. A reverse shot of a large bull, glowering. Then, from the bull's point of view *(perhaps over a dummy bull's shoulder)* we see the two of them run in opposite directions. A close shot of the girl's bright red shorts as they run away. A shot of the bull. A close shot of Clive, scrambling over the fence – turning and looking. A wide shot – the girl disappears behind a large tree. A shot of the bull, sauntering *(or trotting)* towards the tree. The girl, in close up, looks towards Clive. Clive points to her bright red shorts, and then points to his own trousers. Indicates that she should remove them. The Bird looks vacant. The bull looks interested. A Yokel approaches, on the other side of the field, and looks over the fence. Clive demonstrates again with a mime movement, then in desperation, drops his own trousers a little. A Woman going by on a bicycle stares. He pulls them up again. The young Yokel grins. However, the girl has got the message, and goes behind the tree. In a second or two, the shorts are thrown out. They land in front of the Bull *(the rest of the shot is up to him)*.

Cut to Clive. He looks relieved. Cut to the Yokel – he looks astounded. The girl dashes out from behind the tree, wearing G-string briefs. With a yell, the Yokel leaps over the fence and gives chase. A wide shot as they whizz across the field. A close up of the bull staring at them.

Back at the picnic, all is now laid out. The General has built a fire of newspapers and sticks. He has perched a kettle on it. He tries to light the fire, but the matches keep going out: as they do so, he throws them over his shoulder. Now a wider shot, to include, behind him, a box with wood-straw in, which had contained champagne bottles. Close shot of an apparently dead match landing on it. The straw suddenly lights. Back to the wider shot. The General places the kettle on the box instead, with the air of a man who has done a good job.

The others wander over to the tablecloth and sit down around it. The Old Lady, the Companion, the Boy, the dog, too. A bizarre picture, with all the strange props around them, as the butler and the maid begin to serve the sandwiches, etc.

Further down the riverbank, a fisherman is fishing. Clive and the Bird walk past him, towards camera. She is now wearing round her waist part of a yellow plastic bag – the sort that has farm fertiliser in. It crackles very loudly as she walks. The fisherman reacts, and "shushes" her, glaring his disapproval.

The picnic. The butler hands the Boy a kipper on a plate. The Boy waits until no-one is looking, then slings it into the river. Close shot as it lands, and floats.

Clive and the Bird arrive back. She sits down amidst tremendous crackling. Clive explains to the General. The General looks interested.

The fisherman. He suddenly realises that he has got a bite. He reels in; on the hook is the kipper. He reacts.

The General takes a hard-boiled egg from a basket of about seven or eight. He bangs it against a plate to crack the shell. It cracks the plate. He stares, and puts it back (close shot). In the same shot, another hand comes in and takes the same egg. It is the Old Lady. She bangs it on a plate. The plate cracks. She puts the egg back.

Clive is feeding the dog, taking bits of meat out of the sandwiches, and throwing the bread away over his shoulder. The butler looks disapproving. He stands behind Clive, picks up the bread, exchanges it for bread round another piece of meat. He gives it to the maid to offer it to Clive again. When the maid has gone, the butler eats the unsoiled pieces of bread. We see Clive do the same thing again, and the maid again picks up the same old pieces of bread, and takes them back to the butler. This time distracted by the Bird *(we see a shot of her in her rather revealing fertiliser bag)* he puts the new bread inside the old bread, and eats the meat himself. The maid enters Clive's shot, but this time he shoos the dog away, and eats the bread sandwich. He takes a hard-boiled egg, bangs it on the plate. The plate cracks. He puts back the egg. The General witnesses this, takes a felt-tip pen from his pocket, picks up the egg and makes a large asterisk on the egg, followed by a full stop. The full stop pierces the egg, it bursts. It is uncooked.

A pretty shot of the dog chasing butterflies – and, then, once again, we see the fisherman. He has tied a line to his toe *(he wears open-toed sandals)* which is attached to his rod, at present reposing in a cleft stick. He lies back and prepares to snooze. Cut to a motor launch – it surges by with a great noise. Cut to fisherman, close – he is dragged out of shot. A wide shot as he is pulled feet first into the water with a great splash.

The Old Lady is pouring tea. She pours some for the General, who unnoticed by the Old Lady, throws it over his shoulder and fills his cup from a hip-flask. She then puts sugar into the General's cup, and offers him milk. He declines, reaches out of shot, gets a soda siphon, and squirts soda into his cup. The Old Lady looks surprised. The General deposits the soda siphon by his feet, but it falls over.

Clive and his Bird are hitting a tennis ball to each other. She reaches up to return a high ball, and her plastic bag slides down to her knees. The Old Lady looks embarrassed. So does Clive. The General stares. He is holding a bottle of champagne. The cork pops out on its own. He hands it to the Companion, who gets rather wet. The Bird goes to pull up the bag again. The General takes a photograph. *(Freeze frame – black and white.)*

The Companion is handed a meringue on a plate by the butler. In a wide shot, we see the General and the others interested in the game. Close up of the General's foot and the soda siphon. The General kicks it – it squirts at the meringue which shoots off its plate. It bounces off on to the grass in another close shot.

Clive misses a ball, it bounces away in the direction of the tea table. Clive runs towards the group, looks around, spots the meringue. A close shot as he picks it up from the grass. Wider as he serves it, and it bursts into smithereens. Close up; of him, covered in bits – more floating down on him.

Now a very wide shot of the whole scene. The picnickers are wandering away towards the further reaches of the river. In the foreground, the maid and the butler are tidying up, but have hardly started. The butler says something to the maid, who nods, resignedly. The butler walks off to some bushes beside the river.

Cut to the group *(minus the Small Boy)* walking toward camera – enjoying the walk, and chattering to each other.

Cut to the fisherman, soaking wet, but determined to fish. He stands up, and prepares to cast.

Cut to the butler in the bushes. He faces camera, bushes at chest height – and also bushes behind him. He is obviously about to relieve himself.

Cut to the Small Boy. He is in another bush, with a bow, and arrows with rubber suckers. From his point of view he can see the butler. Then from another angle we can see the Fisherman, who is now seen to be just the other side of the bushes from the butler. The fisherman casts his line. Cut to the butler. His expression changes as his toupee is whipped off his head by the fishing line. He clasps his bald head, amazed. Cut to the Small Boy, he shoots an arrow. We hear a plop.

Cut to the butler. He has an arrow stuck to his head.

A close up of the maid, tidying up. She looks up; suddenly her face changes, she looks horrified.

We cut to her point of view. A herd of black cows is approaching the picnic area. Alone, she panics, rushes to the car, and starts to pull up the hood. Another shot of the cows, getting nearer.

A wide shot of the butler chasing the Boy. Suddenly, they both stop. A quick close up of each as they stare.

Cut to the picnic area. Cows everywhere. Eating, trampling – various shots of the destruction. The maid's face peers, terrified, through the car window. A wide shot of everyone hurrying towards the picnic area. They shoo the cows away. A close up of some reeds, near the river. Pan up. The fisherman is preparing to go home. He stares at, first the kipper, and then the toupee. His catch for the day. Disgruntled, he throws them back into the river, and walks dejectedly away.

Cut back to the picnic. The cows have gone – everything is packed away – the boot of the car is still open, although the passengers are all settled into their seats. The butler is picking up the last of the paper serviettes, bags, etc. and putting them into a larger dustbin-liner bag, which is already very full. He looks round – everything is tidy again. He puts the sack in the boot, slams it shut. He gets on to his motorbike, the maid mounts pillion, and off they go.

The General gets into the driving seat, and slams the door. The boot immediately springs open, in a close shot. Then, in wide shot, the car pulls away, and the rubbish is distributed all across the field as the car bumps its way out of the gate and heads towards home.

It is evening. The sun is setting on a beautiful day. A shot of the countryside – the oar goes through frame.

They pass the pub. The three Yokels still sit there. The picnickers wave – no response. We go closer and see that the Yokels are all asleep.

The house. The car approaches down the drive and pulls up. It is twilight. Clive and his Bird move towards the house, she still crackling in her fertiliser skirt. From the front we see Clive, in a two-shot, make a jocular remark, and put his hand behind her. We hear a swift "crackle-crackle" as her skirt betrays what his hand is doing. She reacts as if to admonish him, but then changes her mind, runs the tip of one finger through his hair, and smiles. They go into the house, he is looking very hopeful.

The General and the Old Lady totter towards the house. The maid passes them, the General stops her and whispers in her ear, points upwards, and makes drinking movements. She nods, and goes on in. The Small Boy and the Dog also overtake them. Finally a shot of the butler, loaded with baskets, etc. from the boot, enters the house, with a long-suffering expression.

Outside the General's room. The maid is about to enter, with a large brandy on a tray. The butler approaches, with an armful of dirty tablecloths from the picnic. He gives them to the maid, takes the tray and enters the room.

Inside the room. The General's hand comes out from the four-poster curtains, takes the brandy, and withdraws. A second later, the hand returns the empty glass. It then grabs the butler by the wrist and drags him inside. A scuffle, a shout, a crash of the tray, and the butler emerges: and the General's face, apologetic.

The outside of the house, a moonlit night. The lights go out one by one. An owl hoots somewhere in the middle distance. A shot rings out. The owl gives a screech, and a flutter of feathers. Silence. The last light in the house goes out.

# BY THE SEA

A Film Without Dialogue
By the author of *Futtocks End* and *The Picnic*.
And concerned with a similar group of characters. May, 1981.

1: A view of an empty English beach – early morning.

2: Now a view of the promenade, with tall houses at the back.

3: Then a shot looking down the long, straight street. A milk float: a milkman delivering in the street. A boy, walking, delivering newspapers. He whistles. A postman, on a bicycle, delivering letters.

4: A shopkeeper, pulling down an awning, opening up. He puts goods outside, fruit, etc. We hear the cries of seagulls.

5: A handyman arrives at the gate of a house. He goes up a long path, to where a grim-faced woman is scrubbing a step. She warns him not to tread on the clean step. She gives him some letters to fix on to the gate – they are resting on a piece of cardboard, and are arranged to say "Mon Repos".
    Woman shuts the door, and handyman goes back to the gate, trips over a geranium pot spilling dirt on to the path. He also spills the letters. He picks them up, and tries to rearrange them. They say "Prom Nose". He looks puzzled. The milkman passes him, walks through the dirt from the geraniums, and leaves his muddy footprints on the step. As he goes, the woman comes out – stares at the step, annoyed. The man at the gate has rearranged the letters. They now say "Ponse Mor".
    The woman is cleaning her step again. The postman now goes in, steps in the dirt, and delivers letters. The woman comes out, and is furious. She gets her bucket again.
    The paperboy approaches the handyman: he stops and looks, and helps to rearrange the letters. They now say "Poor Mens". The boy goes up the path. The woman has just finished the step. She shuts the door.
    The boy delivers a paper and goes, and she opens the door immediately. She fumes. Her face is hideous with anger.

6: Another shop, in a row of shops a sign being put outside, on a stand-up sandwich board. It says "Ladies high fashion, upstairs".
    A scruffy-looking cleaning lady is putting it out.
    Next door, a butchers shop. He puts out a similar sign. It says "Fat spring lamb – try one."
    The two signs, close together, read "Fat ladies spring high, lamb-fashion. Try one upstairs".

7: A man stops, reads the sign, and looks up at the upstairs window.
    Traffic in the high street is beginning to build up.
    At the traffic lights, a lorry has stopped. A motor cyclist arrives on its right.

The lorry driver, staring across at the two signs outside the shop, stubs out his cigarette on the crash helmet of the motor cyclist, and drives off.

8: A vicar, selling flags from door to door, approaches handyman. He stares at the lettering the man has nailed on to the gate. It reads "Some porn".
    The vicar shakes his head – no, no, no. He walks up the path, through the dirt, knocks at the door and gets the bucket of water full in the face.
    The door is again shut.

9: The railway station forecourt. The noise of trains.
    RB appears at the entrance, puts his hand to his mouth and calls "porter", but we hear the two-tone hooter of a diesel train. The porter comes over, happy that RB only has one bag. But round the corner come the rest of the family – RC, the girl, the aunt, the boy, the companion, and the little tiny frenetic dog. They all have enormous cases, golf umbrellas, etc. The porter loads them all on to a trolley. RB indicates to the porter that a car has been ordered for them – a big one. Ah, here it comes now. It is a hearse. They all bundle into the car – the little dog leaps all over everybody, licking their faces, etc. The luggage goes into the boot. The car drives off, leaving one suitcase revealed on pavement. The car reverses: after a moment, it drives off again. The suitcase has now gone, but the dog is left on the pavement. The dog runs after the disappearing car, yapping at it.

10: The hotel. The car arrives at front entrance, near the revolving door. RC is carrying a lot of luggage, and gets jammed into one section – the rest of the family go in after him – he keeps going round, stuck. RB is the last to go in, but just before he does, the redhead comes out, in a bikini, and beach bag. RB goes right round, and hurtles out again staring after her. RC whizzes round and round. RB stops the door with a jerk – *(RC, inside)* – a crash of luggage. The little dog trots up *(having run from the station)* RB is about to re-enter. He sees a sign on door – "no dogs". RB picks up the little dog, puts him into a string bag he is carrying, covers it with a towel and goes into hotel.

11: A bedroom door. A notice, roughly written, hung on door. "Caution – electrical re-wiring in progress". A pathetic maid points this sign out to RB. They enter.

12: Workman's tool-bag, and wire etc., on the floor. RB looks round at the room, nods, looks at bed, tests it with his hands, then flops back on it, bounces up and down. Pathetic maid watches him. RB bounces some more, indicates that maid should bounce too. She shakes her head. He bounces some more. An electrician sticks his head out from under the bed, glaring. RB reacts.

13: Another bedroom. RC and a young porter. RC tips him, looks around, sees a pretty view of the sea through the window – he indicates it with a wave of the hand. "Very nice". The porter leaves. RC puts his suitcase on the bed. The pretty view drives away – it is painted on the side of a truck. It reveals a brick wall.

14: Another bedroom. The companion has just changed into a sweater. She adjusts it, then scratches uncomfortably.
    She starts to unpack from the open suitcase, still scratching. She picks up pack of biscuits – they have burst, scattering crumbs on everything in the case. She keeps scratching. She continues to scratch for the rest of the holiday.

15: A wide corridor. RC walking towards camera. The aunt comes out of a door, and just

beats him into the toilet. Above the door, a large sign lights up "engaged". He stands –
looks round, and straightens a picture on the wall. RC sits on a chair opposite the door –
the chair is spindly and small. One of the arms of the chair comes off in RC's hand. He
tries to put it back, it falls off. He looks round – then breaks the other arm off to make it
look like an ordinary upright chair. He puts them both inside a huge grandfather clock.
It strikes, frightening him. He goes back and sits on the chair, it folds flat like a hinge,
depositing RC on the floor. He gets up, bends it straight again, stands it carefully against
the wall, and sits on the small coffee table next to it, which is sturdier. He looks at sign, it
now says "finished". He reacts, then looks again. It says "standing up", he reacts. Now it
says "washing hands". We hear the tap running. He stares. It says "flushing", he reacts as
the chain is pulled. It says "leaving", and out comes the aunt – gives him a stare, and
leaves the shot.

16: RB's bedroom door. RB comes out, leaving door ajar. The string bag comes trotting
out. Companion, approaching, sees it, picks it up, and goes off with it.

17: RB approaching toilet door. A gong is heard, close up on the toilet door. It says
"lunch". RB sees it, reacts.

18: The front of the hotel. The party are leaving for the beach, carrying all the various
things they will need for the day. The aunt has lots of carrier bags, etc., about her person
– the companion carries the string bag with the dog in.

19: They walk along the street and pass the handyman with his letters on the gate. He
has just nailed up "Po Sermon". RB looks at it – points to it, and laughs. The handyman
looks daggers, as RB demonstrates what it is to the others *(a dog collar and a chamber pot,
in mime)*. As they move off, he starts to take the letters off with a claw hammer.

20: The beach. Some pretty establishing shots, evocative, golden summer-day scenes.

21: Our party troop down on to the sand and sets up camp near the promenade wall.
RC, the girl, the companion, and the boy, all immediately strip off, revealing swimming
clothes beneath. RC in a singlet top, with stars on, and a striped bottom-half – the
American flag design.
   The girl in high-cut cheeky one-piece. Companion in very modest thing with wide
shoulder straps. The boy in trunks. They all give their wristwatches to the aunt, who
puts them all up one arm, on top of her own. The boy bounces his beachball. RC is
complimenting the girl on her costume, and the beachball hits him on the side of the
head. They all then rush off into the sea.

22: RB is settling into a deckchair with *The Times*. A shot of seagulls, circling overhead.
RB reacts as something hits his newspaper. He looks up, then screws up the page he was
reading, picks up the paper, and starts to read again. Another splat. He screws up the
page again, muttering angrily.

23: RC and girl are in the water, splashing about. The beachball hits him on the side of
the head again. He looks annoyed.

24: RB is now surrounded by screwed up newspaper. He looks up into the sky, annoyed.
Another splat. He deliberately puts his newspaper on the sands, puts all the other
screwed up bits on to it, wraps them up *(still leaving part of the newspaper on the sand)* and
moves to a nearby waste-bin to put them in. While his back is turned a tiny child, led by

an older one, drops a large lump of vanilla ice-cream out of its cornet on to the newspaper. RB returns. Stares at the newspaper. Close up of blob of ice-cream. He looks up into the sky, amazed, then puts up a large golf umbrella over him, as quickly as possible.

25: A small woman in a bright flowered sun-dress, is blowing up a plastic lilo. She has her back towards the camera. The aunt, watching her. The woman, again – she looks fatter, her dress looks tighter – and she's still blowing. The aunt looks surprised. back to the woman again – she is now enormous and is still blowing. The aunt again, amazed. The woman again, her dress is ridiculously tight. Suddenly there is a loud bang, and she disappears. Her dress floats down, with the lilo, on to the sands. The aunt is puzzled.

26: The boy is at a kiosk on the promenade. He buys two large lumps of candy-floss, and a gas-filled balloon: it is black, painted like a savage cannibal, and has a feather stuck to it. It floats upright. He exits with his purchases, eating the candyfloss.

27: RC and the girl are coming out of the water, he chasing her. A beachball hits him. He is furious, pulls out the plug, and deflates it, jumping on it. A large hairy man enters the shot, watching him. That's mine, he indicates. RC has to sheepishly blow it up again.

28: The boy has just given RB a stick of candyfloss, when the girl arrives, and flops down on a slatted plastic sunbed. She lies on her stomach, looking away from RB. The companion, playing with the little dog. She throws something for it to fetch, and it rushes out of frame. The girl on the sunbed. The little dog rushes underneath her sunbed and out again. It obviously tickled her and she jumps up in alarm. She looks round. RB laughs and gesticulates with his candyfloss. She looks daggers at him, thinking it was him, and puts her towel underneath the bed as a barrier to further mischief.

29: The aunt and the companion are walking along the shore, gathering shells. The aunt sees one in the water, and plunges her arm in to get it. It comes out with all the watches dripping wet. The companion looks aghast.

30: The boy, carrying his balloon in one hand, and a bucket in the other. He is behind RB's deckchair, where RC has left his clothes. He looks round, then quietly fills RC's jacket pockets with sand, sniggering to himself. Then he takes a good-sized live crab from the bucket and puts it into RC's short's pocket. In order to do this he anchors his balloon by hooking the wire hook on the end of its string on to the bottom rung of RB's deckchair.

RB in deckchair. The little dog runs in, grabs the girl's bright-coloured knickers, which are on her pile of clothes behind RB's chair. RB grabs dog, takes knickers from it, looks at them, not knowing what to do with them, hangs them behind him on the top of his deckchair. He settles back; suddenly beside him, the balloon looms into shot. RB reacts violently, scared. The boy, laughing. RB grabs the string and hangs it on the top of the deckchair also. A close up as we see the wire hook go through the leg-hole of the knickers.

The boy, pretending to busy himself with building a sandcastle.

The aunt comes back, together with companion. The aunt gets out a tiny little canvas fold-up stool, puts it next to RB, preparing to sit on it. RB puts down his candyfloss on it, just before the aunt sits.

RB, aunt and companion. RB hears a mosquito – and so do we – it buzzes round. RB slaps his leg (trousers rolled up), aunt hits out, then slaps her own arm. Companion slaps her legs and body. The mosquito can be heard to stop and start throughout this. They are all slapping like mad, except the girl, who still lies face down on the sunbed. RB hearing the mosquito stop, looks round. spots it: it has landed on girl's bikini bottom. RB swats it. The girl leaps up, annoyed, and slaps RB's face. RB puts his hand to his face, finds the squashed mosquito – the girl had killed it. He looks pleased, and thanks her. She, however, stalks off.

31: RC, a little way off, lies on beach. Eyes shut sunbathing. A close up – he smiles happily. A load of water is poured on to him by the girl from a child's bucket. She giggles, and runs off. He chases her out of shot, with the bucket which she has dropped.

32: The aunt is still sitting, but packing her bags up. The companion emerges from beach hut, having changed. Her dress is partially tucked up in her knickers at the back. She goes behind the beach hut, and wrings out her costume with her hands. The front of the beech hut. RC is searching for the girl. He hears the water being wrung out of the costume. He listens: it stops. Behind the hut, the companion shakes out the costume, and goes round to front again. As she emerges, RC sees her skirt tucked up. He peeps round the back of the hut, sees the puddle in the sand. He looks nonplussed. He re-emerges – sees (33) the girl – she ducks down behind a wind-break erected on the sand. (34) He runs to the sea to fill his bucket. The beach ball hits him. He fills the bucket, and leaves shot. (35) The wind-break. RC creeps up to it, pours water over the top. It is the big hairy man again. He makes to chase RC who bolts for it.

36: The aunt and companion, packing up. Aunt stands up, and the candyfloss causes the tiny canvas stool to stick to her seat. She looks around vaguely for it, but soon gives up. RB sits asleep. Aunt gives him a nudge, to say they are going. RB jumps, and this shakes his deckchair, which dislodges the gas balloon. It starts to rise up in the air, and it takes the brightly-coloured knickers with it. They stare at it as it goes.
    The girl returns and watches in consternation . She picks up her T-shirt and as she puts it on, whispers in RC's ear. He looks pleased, but he points a finger at him, admonishingly: and he understands that she means she needs an undergarment. He immediately offers his shorts to her. She gets the aunt and companion to hold up two towels, to change behind.
    RB is still watching the knickers, now floating quite a way up. He chuckles. The girl emerges wearing RC's shorts.
    The boy's face, waiting.
    Suddenly the girl leaps about – the crab is using its pincers. She yells and dashes behind the beach hut. The shorts are thrown out. In close up the crab emerges and sidles off. RC, grabbing the shorts, dashes behind the hut as well. Returns with the shorts over his head. The companion arrives with the girl's skirt, and gives it to the blind-folded RC, who gropes his way back to behind the hut. The beachball hits him on the side of the head. He pauses, then continues round behind the hut.

37: A wide pretty shot of the sea, panning round to see the whole party walking away from camera going back to the hotel. The little dog, on a string. The companion, with her dress still tucked up. The aunt, still with the stool stuck to her. RC with his pockets full of sand.

38: The sunlit water splashing round the iron supports of the pier. Then a shot of the pier entrance and the arrival of the party. They wander on, chatting and laughing. The boy has a beachball which he bounces. The girl wears short shorts, RC in the same jacket as yesterday.

39: A shot of RC, as he walks along, from behind. His pockets are bulging, still full of sand, and he feels the weight of them, then plunges his hand in to them, and realises why he feels so heavy. He stops, and empties one of his pockets out onto the floor.

40: The sand trickles through the gaps in the floorboards. Below, on the sand under the pier, a woman is making sandwiches. She has spread peanut butter onto a slice of bread. She puts it onto a plate a little to one side of her. As she spreads another piece, we see sand trickling on to the first piece She without noticing this, puts the second piece on top of the first, cuts through it once diagonally, and hands it to her husband. He takes a large bite, and chews and we hear the sound effect of his gritty chewing. He is not a pretty eater.

41: Up on the pier, RC has emptied the other pocket a few feet from the first one. Again, the sand trickles through the boards

42: This time it lands in the mug of tea on the other side of the man. His face, as he chews the sandwich – then he takes the tea, stirs it, and drinks. He resumes chewing – but the grinding sounds louder than before.

43: The party have now reached the comic photographers. We see a large board with holes cut out for people's heads, and grotesque painted bodies. An enormous fat woman in a pink two-piece bathing-suit, and a little skinny man in shorts and vest. Two people have their heads through the holes, they have their photos taken, and emerge – an enormous fat woman in a pink two-piece, and a little skinny man in shorts and vest. RB reacts, then indicates to RC and girl that they should go into the other cut.
    This represents a tall figure in a one-piece bathing costume, accompanied by a tiny child in a sun-bonnet. RB indicates – girl in tall body, RC in baby's body. RC shakes his head, takes girl's hand, goes behind board. The others all watch, except boy, who has wandered off. RC suddenly emerges in the very tall body, and girl in the baby's body. The photographer prepares, and RB sidles round the back of the boards, with his camera.
    The girl is crouching with her bottom in the air, and RC is standing on tip-toe on a box. RB photographs it, the photographer does the same. RB's picture is a much funnier sight.

44: The boy is at a stall or kiosk, buying sweets. He sees, and we see in close-up, a packet marked "Keyhole blacking – amuse your friends. A riot". It has a badly-drawn picture of a boy with a keyhole-shaped mark on one eye. The boy buys a packet, opens it, it contains a jar of black cream. He moves off, as the aunt and companion arrive at the stall. They stare at the vulgar ornaments, etc. on the stall. The companion is trying to read a naughty postcard in the revolving rack.
    The aunt, on the other side, looks at them, and keeps revolving the rack, so that the companion has to walk round with it. She eventually cracks her head on the side of the kiosk wall, knocking her glasses awry.

45: The boy is busy smearing all the "What the butler saw" machines with his eye-black. He sniggers.

46: The aunt is buying a cruet in the form of a girl's boobs (these are items actually on sale at seaside resorts). It is pink and vulgar.

47: RB saunters up to a curtained booth saying "Madame Rosie Lee – fortune teller" in bold lettering. On going closer, RB sees a notice, written in magic marker, saying "Closed owing to unforeseen circumstances".

48: He wanders across to the "What the butler saw" machines. He places his eye to the hole, and we hear it whirring. He takes his eye away – he has a black ring round it. He smiles, not knowing of its presence. Behind the machines, a workman has just taken the back off an old machine, repairing it. RB moves to this machine, puts in money, and we see what he sees – a young couple smooching on a seat behind the machine. Suddenly the aunt looms into shot, which gives RB a shock. He peers round the side, and realises.

49: RC and the girl, on their own, standing eating toffee apples, talking. RC leans back on a post – the post cracks at the base, and the post, which is supporting a board on which hangs a life-belt, tips over towards the pier rail, dislodging the lifebelt. The lifebelt falls in the water. RC looks over the rail, dismayed, he becomes more dismayed as we see the lifebelt immediately sink. As he watches, his toffee apple drops off its stick. He watches it fall, and stares at the stick.

50: RB, boy, and companion sitting in sheltered glass compartment on pier. Aunt approaches with ice-cream cones. They all move up to accommodate her, as she sits, handing out the cones. A wider shot, to reveal that RB is now sitting on something. He gets up, and we discover that it is a tiny old lady. RB apologises, and gives her his ice-cream as she hobbles away. He then takes the boy's ice-cream, and eats it. As they sit, people pass by.

All the men have one eye black. RB laughs – then aunt shows him, in her pocket mirror, his own eye. He gets out his hankie – the aunt takes it, spits on it, and cleans up his eye. The girl and RC return. RC has a black circle in the middle of his forehead.

51: The rifle range. Little ducks being shot by an expert. The party arrive, and RB and RC decide to have a go. A sign says "New – 12-shot rapid repeater rifle – 60p". RB points to it, and is given a gun. Another sign says "Small bore, 10p". RC points to this one, and is given another sort. RB opens fire, demolishes a row of prizes – plates, mugs, little pandas, perfume, etc. before he can stop the gun. The stall keeper rushes over, RB takes £10 note from pocket, apologetically, and hands it to the man. RC, at the other end, is about to shoot, when the beachball hits him on the side of the head. Angry, he turns, and shoots the beachball as it bounces away. It goes bang, and falls dead. Everyone, except the boy, gives a round of applause.

RB, also congratulating RC, when he suddenly sees floating across the sky in the middle distance, the black balloon with the girl's knickers hanging from it. He fires, and scores a direct hit. The balloon bursts, and the knickers drop to the ground.

52: They land on the head of a vicar, sitting reading near the pier on the sand. He looks up in surprise, to see two girls leaning over the rail, laughing at him. He also catches the eye of a middle-aged woman sitting a little way off. He mops his brow with the knickers, and puts them in his pocket.

53: The boy is buying another beachball, of a different colour, from the stall. He runs to catch the rest of the party up.

54: They get to the entrance, the vicar is seen talking to one of the two girls, who wears a tight skirt. RB watches, as the vicar holding out the knickers, asks the girl if they are hers. The girl shakes her head and produces her own knickers from her handbag. RB watches as she minces away on her high heels.

55: They pass the handyman at his gate. On the gate is now nailed "No" – on the ground the letters say "Mopers". RB looks – shakes his head – indicates it's all wrong. Then handyman has had enough. Tight-lipped, he goes into the garden, fetches his tool bag, kicks the letters for six, slams the gate, and marches off.

As the gate slams, the letters "N" and "O", which are in a curious art-nouveau style, swing sideways and form the figure 20. RB stares at this, nods satisfaction, and hurries after the retreating party. The sun is setting.

56: The dining room at the hotel. A large oval table. The waitress is setting up paper napkins placed all round the table. She suddenly sneezes violently, and blows them all over. She takes one, and blows her nose on it.

57: RC, hurrying along the corridor. He sees the same picture, crooked again. He straightens it. Out of the door comes the aunt, and they go out of frame together.

58: The party arrive and sit at table. RC seats girl, then goes to sit next to her, but RB, who is near the chair, sits on it first. By then the others are already seated, so RC has to sit between the companion and the aunt. RC looks daggers from across the table. RB and girl in animated conversation, ordering wine from a waiter. RC looks jealous, but the waitress blocks his view with an enormous menu. It completely covers RC. The aunt and companion peer in at it from either side. RB and girl giggling together. RB pointing out that they can't be seen by RC. A two-shot as they laugh and point, which becomes a three-shot as RC walks in from the back. RB surprised, looks across at menu – aunt and companion fold it up, revealing RC's empty chair. RB looks under table, realises. RC goes to get another chair, while RB explains to girl what happened.

RC at another table, picks up upright chair, walks away. Only the back of the chair goes, leaving the rest. He comes back into shot, dumps the chair back, takes another and leaves shot again. RC sits on the other side of girl. The waiter brings the wine. RB tastes it, nods, waiter starts with companion, pours large glasses to everyone, in a clockwise direction. The bottle runs out, just before it reaches RB, they all say cheers and drink, except RB, who orders another bottle. The aunt is talking to the waitress, indicating the large "à la carte" menu. The waitress walks out of shot, comes back with a small card, which says "Table d'hôte". She hands it to the aunt, and blows another raspberry on her nose. Aunt orders for all. The waiter returns with another bottle. RB tries it, nods – it goes round again, and runs out at the same place. RB orders another bottle. They all say cheers again.

The redhead walks in, looking terrific, and sits at a nearby table. RB spots her, and while RC is talking to aunt, RB asks girl to change places with him, so he can sit nearer the redhead's table. The girl does so, and the maid arrives, with the "starters" – paté, featuring a large lettuce leaf on each plate. RC notices the girl has changed places – RB indicates the redhead. The maid puts down RB's starters, and sneezes, blowing RB's lettuce leaf off the plate. She picks it up off the table, and as she walks away, absent mindedly wipes her nose on it and puts it in her pocket.

The waiter brings another bottle. RB tries it, nods, and the waiter goes round again, starting with the girl, then the companion. RB indicates to RC that he is willing to change places. He does so just in time for the waiter to arrive. This time, RB gets the wine, but it runs out before RC gets any. They start to eat the paté – it is awful.

Boy pulls a face – aunt looks askance at it, drains her wine glass, tries again. RC hates it. Aunt pushes hers away, to her left. RB, looking round at the redhead, leans his right elbow into it. He turns back – the paté drops to the floor.

RB tastes his – revolting. He cuts it up, sticks his fork into it a piece at a time, and transfers it to his jacket pocket. He also puts a bit into RC's jacket pocket, while he's about it. A shot of the redhead, noticing this, and smiling.

The waitress is carrying a tray towards another table. A close up of the tray – it contains a bowl of tomato soup. She sneezes, violently, as she walks away. A close up of her face – it is covered in spots of soup. She looks as though she has the measles. RC is talking animatedly to the girl. He whispers in her ear. She shakes her head, regretfully but firmly. He suggests something else, whispering again. Again she shakes her head. He catches RB's eye. RB shakes his head, meaningfully.

The waitress arrives with a large dish. They stare at her measles – and all decide to leave. They've had enough. They all rise, and make their way out. RB stands up, steps on the paté on the floor, and slips headfirst into the redhead's low cut dress, with a resounding splat. She looks surprised, he doesn't know whether to look sorry or pleased.

59: A close up of RC, standing, waiting. Girl behind him – we pan down a row of the party's faces. The boy, the girl, the aunt, the companion, and RB. We widen to see they are in a Chinese takeaway restaurant. The Chinese assistant starts to hand RC packets of takeaway food, RC's face registers joyful anticipation.

60: Next morning. The sand dunes, near the beach. The companion sits on a fold-up chair, the aunt sits on the ground. She is spreading honey onto slices of bread and butter. The little dog tries to eat a piece, but is shooed away from the plate. It returns, and grabs a bit. The companion gets up to get the dog, and the aunt, at the same time, picks up the plate and puts it on the companion's chair behind her. The companion immediately sits again, fussing the dog. She then throws the bitten piece of bread for the dog, who chases after it. She gets up again, and follows it out. The aunt, having spread some more honey, goes to put it onto the plate – the plate is there, but now empty.

61: RB is walking along the dunes. He suddenly sees the redhead, changing among the long grass. She wears a sun-top of some sort, and a long wrap-around skirt. RB stops, interested. She removes the skirt, revealing little shorts. RB's interest increases. She starts to remove shorts. RB is watching through a telescope. She finishes removing shorts RB is watching through binoculars. She is now in brief briefs. She starts to remove them. RB is hit by the new beachball. He staggers, and looks again through the binoculars, we see the back end of a sheep. RB removes the binoculars, revealing two black-ringed eyes. He looks disgruntled, and taking a hip-flask from his pocket, takes a hefty swig. His mouth now has a black ring round it too.

62: A shot of the companion, wandering along the shore, with slices of bread and butter stuck to her slacks.

63: RC and the girl – a quiet corner near the dunes. RC is trying to fix a tall beach umbrella into the sand, but it is rather rocky, and the umbrella isn't easy to fix. He eventually sticks it in, rather precariously. The girl is already spreading suntan lotion on her body. As RC sits down next to her, she hands him the lotion, and rolls onto her stomach, indicating he should oil her back. He sits up, looks at her recumbent form, then turns away to pour the oil into his hands. As he turns, the umbrella falls over, one edge of it dropping neatly between him and the girl. He turns, and spreads oil over the outstretched pale pink skin of the umbrella in a circular motion. It dawns on him that something's wrong. His hands are covered in oil. He lifts the umbrella off the girl, who laughs, and lies there. He picks up the bottle of oil, and it shoots up out of his slippery fingers, and lands on the girl's back, drenching her in oil. He tries to spread it around, but gets his hand slapped. He gets up, picks up the umbrella, raises it upright again. It collapses on him, shutting him inside.

64: The aunt is where we last left her. With her, the boy, the companion, and RB. They are eating sandwiches and drinking coffee. The girl arrives, glistening with suntan. RC, in shirt sleeves and trousers, is covered in oil stains all over his front, from top to toe. RB looks askance at him, wondering what they have been up to. RC is handed a cucumber sandwich from a plate. He takes it. RB is drinking tea. RC makes a face as he tastes the oil on the sandwich. The aunt offers him the cruet, which she bought at the vulgar stall. He stares, then takes out one of the boobs. His fingers are so slippery it immediately shoots into the air. It lands in RB's large teacup as he is about to drink, splashing him with tea. He fishes it out, not knowing where it came from, or what it is. He looks at it, then looks at the companion, eyeing her flat chest.

65: On the green the donkeys are giving their rides. The boy riding ahead. The girl, going quite fast, bouncing up and down with RC watching from his position on the donkey. Immediately behind her, we see the redhead, in her long skirt and sun-top, riding more slowly. RC passes her and from his point of view we see the redhead, whose sun-top is very revealing. Cut back to RC – he is now sitting backwards on his donkey, to get a better view of the redhead.

66: A train-whistle is heard – we are now on the miniature railway. The party, except the companion and the girl, are all on board, and about to set off. RB is found to be sitting on the same old lady again, and apologises. The train sets off, and RB sits beside the tiny lady – squashing her between him and RC. The train takes us past the miniature golf course, which although sparsely attended by golfers, has quite a lot of people sitting about, picnicking, sunbathing etc.
     The train arrives, and RB and RC part company with the aunt and the boy.

67: RC and RB get a club and some balls each from the little kiosk.

68: The aunt and the boy are seen approaching the boating lake nearby.

69: RB drives off, swiping at his ball.

70: In the hotel grounds, a crash of glass, somewhere behind the hotel. In a very wide shot, we hear terrible Italian swearing. The tiny figure of a chef appears, brandishing a large knife at the sky. We see the companion, in her bathing-suit, sit up and stare. Then she lies down again, and we see she is sun-bathing in the grounds, near a row of ornamental railings. A shot of the sunshine through the railings.

71: RC is showing RB that he must drop a ball behind him over his shoulder. RB does so, and RC then plays his first shot, a much more professional effort. He marches off in the direction it went. RB plays his ball, this time no crash.

72: RC comes over a rise, we pull back, to show a fat man, asleep on his back, in a bunker. RC stares, as he sees that his golf ball has come to rest in the fat man's navel.

73: RB is looking for his ball in the rough. He sees a ragged-looking boy throwing stones at a notice-board on the edge of the course. He goes over, and tells the child to stop, pointing at the notice. Cut to the notice – it says "It is forbidden to throw stones at this notice board". RB suddenly stops and wonders why the board is there at all.

74: RC is standing very gingerly astride the fat man, and he plays a perfect delicate shot off the man's tummy, without disturbing him at all. Very pleased with himself, he follows it with his eyes, stepping back to do so. The ball rolls into a hole. With a sigh of self-congratulation, RC walks straight across the fat man's stomach, and leaves the shot. The fat man sits up with a yell.

75: The redhead, in an amazing bikini, is playing golf, too – on her own. Her ball is on the green, and, just before she putts, she tucks another ball into the back of her bikini pants, to save holding it – it is the only place to put it. She goes to take up her position to putt. RB appears still looking for his ball. He sees the back view of the redhead – and sees the ball in her bikini. He walks over, and removes it, she turns round, and he is surprised to see that it is her. He waves the ball at her, demonstrating that he had lost it. She shakes her head, says she herself put it there. "Oh sorry" says RB, and backs away. She smiles, and continues her game.

76: RB comes round a tree, finds a couple having a picnic. There, in the middle of a cream cake, is his ball. Apologetically he retrieves it.

77: RC is about to hit a ball, when he sees RB In the distance sucking cream off his golf ball. He is puzzled.

78: RB drops the ball behind him over his shoulder. It hits the bald head of the picnicking man who glares at RB. RB grabs his ball from the tablecloth, and retreats hastily.

79: RC watches all this with interest.

80: RB's hand sticks a golf tee into the ground in close up, then, in a wider shot, places the ball on it, but proudly over his shoulder. A close up reveals that it is in fact, a hard boiled egg. RB stares at it, then back at the picnicker. He cracks the egg by tapping it on his club and peels away the shell.

81: Then, as RC watches fascinated, RB, in the distance appears to be eating his golf-ball. RC cannot believe his eyes.

82: The aunt and the boy, are sitting in a little boat – the boy is driving, the aunt has a packet of assorted biscuits. She tries one, doesn't like it, throws it over her shoulder. She does the same thing four or five times. We cut wide, to see that the boat is being followed by at least twenty ducks.

83: The cry of sea-gulls is heard, as RC prepares to strike a ball. He hits it hard and high. A squawk, and a sea-gull drops from the sky onto the fairway. RB gives him the thumbs up sign, and he too hits a ball.

84: Back at the hotel, the companion is still sunbathing, with her transistor radio playing "Fingal's Cave". This effectively drowns the noise of RB's ball, which bounces along the terrace, and into a cup of tea which stands on the ground near to her. She looks at her watch, takes from her handbag a pill box, and removes a large white pill, which she puts onto her tongue. Picking up the cup of tea, she takes a good gulp, and swallows. The surprise on her face shows us she has swallowed the golf ball.

85: RC strikes another ball, another squawk, another sea-gull drops onto the grass. RB applauds.

86: The companion picks up her towel, and her radio, and stands up in the sunlight, yawning. She catches sight of her arms – she is sunburnt, in stripes, where she has been behind the railings. Her legs and back are the same – she looks like a pink zebra.

87: The redhead and RB are returning from the golf course, towards the little kiosk where they return the equipment. They walk through the frame chattering. Behind them comes RC, with his brace of sea-gulls hanging from his golf club, which he carries proudly over his shoulder.

88: The hotel terrace. In the foreground, the redhead lies on a low lounger. Pan and tilt to reveal the whole party chattering away about the day's events. They are in jolly mood and each have a drink. The aunt is telling the companion about the biscuits and the ducks. RC is telling the girl about the sea-gulls and holds them up to prove it. RB then tells the aunt about the hard-boiled egg. The aunt, meanwhile, is pouring herself a Guinness. The redhead tells them all about the ball in her bikini. The companion tells RB about the chef and the broken window-pane. RB indicates "it must have been my ball" and helps himself to whisky and soda as he talks. He puts the glass to the wrong side of the siphon, and presses – the soda squirts onto the redhead' s recumbent midriff. She squeals, and RB mops her up with his handkerchief, wringing it out into his glass, and toasting everyone with it.
　　The sun is setting.

89: The big grandfather clock in the corridor of the hotel. It strikes eleven, and at the same time makes terrible wooden clumpings and bangings.
　　The maid is walking past it, she opens the door on the front of the clock, and extracts the two arms of the chair that RC put there.
　　It continues its slow striking without further encumbrances.

90: From the silence of the corridor we cut to the noise of the residents' bar. The clock on the wall says eleven o'clock. A cuckoo pops out, and cuckoos. From off camera somebody throws beer at it soaking it. It comes out again, but quacks like a duck. The whole party, plus the redhead *(but minus the boy)* are leaving the bar, waving goodnight to each other – the aunt and companion go off in one direction, RC and the girl go upstairs, while RB and the redhead linger a little.

91: RC is rather the worse for drink, and the girl half supports him with her arm as they walk along the corridor. He reaches the picture – it is straight. He puts it crooked. They arrive at the girl's door. She plants a loud kiss on his forehead, but he whispers something in her ear – and she, pretending to be very shocked, "tuts" loudly through her teeth, and playfully slaps his face several times in rapid succession. She then turns on her heel, goes into the room, and slams the door. All the leaves on a rubber plant on a nearby table fall off. RC registers this. Having done so, he wanders off. We see him enter his bedroom and close the door. Immediately, round the corner comes RB and the redhead. Her room is next to RC's. RB says good night. She kisses his cheek. He whispers in her ear. She indicates with fingers and wristwatch "five minutes" and disappears inside. RB sits on a chair and looks round. He sees a picture of a grim-faced woman on the wall opposite. He looks round for somewhere to flick his cigar ash, finds nowhere, so flicks it on the table. Cut to: picture – the woman looks very angry – her eyes wide. He reacts – then carefully brushes up the ash into the palm of his hand, and puts it in his pocket.
　　Cut to: picture.
　　It now looks benign, smiling approval. RB nods at it. He applies his eye to the

keyhole. His eye now has a black keyhole mark on it. The door clicks open a fraction. In close up, a bare foot appears. The camera tilts slowly up, revealing a bare leg protruding from a filmy negligée – up and up – arriving eventually to reveal the redhead's hair in curlers, and her face covered in white cream. She kisses him goodnight on the cheek, and waves, then closes the door. He is left with a black eye and a white cheek. He considers for a moment then strides off round the corner.

92: RC is in his bedroom. He has put on a pair of gaudy pyjamas, and is arranging his teddy bear in his bed. He looks at it; and punches it in the eye. He is obviously disappointed.

93: RB, hurrying along the corridor. He carries a hand-written note. He looks round, and then, kissing it, shoves it under RC's door by mistake. RC, in his room sees it appear, and quickly opens it.

94: In close up, we read, "You are such a little darling, I can't resist you. I must see you tonight XX".

RC: Delighted – quickly scribbles or the back of it, and returns it under the door.

95: Outside the door RB reads it. It says – "Climb in my bedroom window – third from left XX". RB is delighted, hurries off.

96: Outside the back of the hotel it is dark. Round the corner comes the companion, carrying the front of a large ladder. RB follows up in the rear: she wears a plain dressing-gown, he a voluminous knee-length night-shirt. He also carries a bottle of champagne.

97: They look up – there is the lighted window, open, but with curtains closed.

98: RB leaves the companion to hoist the ladder, while he takes the foil off the champagne. The ladder is secure, he indicates that she should steady the ladder by standing on the bottom rung, while he mounts it. Up he goes. A shot of her, looking up – then a shot of RB'S night-shirt, seen from below. The companion reacts in embarrassment, and turns to face frontwards. RB, as he ascends, has the champagne under his arm. The cork suddenly pops out, and hits the companion on the head, followed by a shower of champagne. RB on the ladder, throws the bottle away.

99: A crash as it hits a cucumber frame.

100: Outside, in the street, a policeman hears the crash, and, torch in hand, goes round the back to investigate.

101: The companion, standing facing front on the ladder, is approached by the policeman. RB, from above, sees him, and starts to descend. The companion, looking embarrassed. Suddenly RB's night-shirt descends over her head. With a squeak, she fights her way out of it amid reactions from the puzzled policeman and the assaulted RB.

102: In RC's bedroom, he now wears a white silk dressing-gown and is rehearsing a torrid embrace with a lamp-standard.

103: There is a tap at the window. He goes to it and plants a passionate kiss on the figure on the ladder, which happens to be the policeman. The shock of this makes RC give the policeman a shove, and we see the ladder fall away from the window, still containing a policeman.

104: They both crash into the bushes below. RB and companion rush to his aid, and help him to his feet. Apart from losing his helmet, he seems little the worse for wear. He gropes around in the bushes, and solemnly picks up a plastic flower-pot and places it on his head, before reaching for his note-book.

105: The big black car stands glinting in the morning sun, outside the hotel. RB is supervising the luggage being put into the boot by the chauffeur. Out from the hotel come the aunt and the boy, followed by the companion, who carries two suitcases, plus the little dog on a lead round her wrist.

She dumps the two suitcases down side by side, and they open like bookends, spilling out their contents all over the pavement. She and RB put the clothes back in, RB holding up a bra for inspection, snatched away by the embarrassed companion. When the clothes are in and the cases are shut, a yapping is heard.

The companion looks at the dog's lead and traces it back to one of the suitcases. The case is opened again, and the little dog pokes its head out. She ties the dog's lead to the back bumper of the car, while she, yet again, packs the suitcase. The chauffeur, meanwhile, is putting away the other case. RB is chatting, with his head inside the car, talking to the aunt. A sports car horn is heard. RB looks up, as we hear a screech of brakes. It is the redhead, in a bright green open sports car. She has pulled up just behind the big car.

RB waves, and she indicates, with a toss of her head, that he should come with her – pointing to the passenger seat. RB says, "Who, me?" The redhead nods. RB, without more ado, reaches into the big black car, and produces a string bag. We see, in close up, that it contains a bottle of champagne and a large orange alarm clock.

He makes straight for the sports car, gets in, gives the redhead a peck, and she starts the engine.

RC and the girl come from the hotel, just in time to see the green sports car do a U-turn and roar off down the road. They look at each other, smile, and the girl gets into the car, RC putting a friendly helping hand on her shorts.

He takes a last look at the retreating sports car, and gets in, shuts the door.

The big black car begins to glide away. The little dog, in close up, is pulled out of frame, and as the car drives away from the camera the little dog bounces about behind it down the long straight seaside road.

# THE POEMS

## GOODNESS

Good place,
good weather,
good views,
good sand,
good digs,
good table,
good waiter,
good band,
good wine,
good soup,
good fish,
good duck,
good brandy,
good night –
good girl,
Bad luck.

## THE LURE OF A LADY'S FAN

The world of fashion and of fad
Of elegance and élan
Has never created a wittier whim
Than the lure of a lady's fan.

This simple weapon has caused the rout
Of many an army man;
I've seen them wobble and go weak-kneed
At the sight of a lady's fan.

When they chance to meet in the
steaming heat
Of a street in Old Japan,
There's many a sailor led astray
By the wave of a lady's fan.

Who knows how many heads of state
Have strayed from the master-plan?
Or how many diplomats succumbed
To the touch of a lady's fan?

She will simper from behind it
She will twist it and unwind it
She will wiggle and rotate it if she can –
She will open it out wide
Or she'll snap it shut and hide
Behind the flutters of her fascinating fan.

## GENEROSITY

He gave her this, he gave her that,
A brand new car, a Paris hat.
He gave her dollars, gave her pounds.
His generosity knew no bounds.
He spent it all, became flat broke;
She thought it all a great big joke.
To him the joke was not so funny –
He had to marry her for his money.

## PRISCILLA JONES

Priscilla Jones had great big knees
Yet never ceased to show 'em –
Like champagne bottles stood on end
Each one a Jeroboam.

Although her friends all called her plump
She thought her shape perfection;
She crossed her legs at the flower show
And won the Marrow section.

# THE SAME POEM

### A ROMANTIC'S VIEW

Gold is the colour of my true love's hair
As she raises up her glass
And the candle shines through the red
wine's glow
And the evenings gently pass.

Green is the colour of my true love's eyes
Eyes that I can't resist,
They glow through the smoke of her
cigarette
Like jade through the morning mist.

### A REALIST'S VIEW

Red is the colour of a June-bloomed rose
When plucked from its briar's posy –
But red is the colour of my true love's nose
When she's been at the Rouge or the Rosé.

Yellow is the colour of the dawning sun
That creeps where the frost still lingers,
But yellow is the colour of my true love's
thumb
And brown is the colour of her fingers.

# THE SALES

I've just had a very nice day
At the Sales,
It's a day that I always enjoy –
I rang up the office and
Said I was ill,
Then had lunch with that
Patterson boy,

Then off to the Sales, it was
Ever such fun
And I got quite a lot of nice things:
A lovely pink girdle, a
Really tight one,
With that big thick elastic that "pings".

And a green thing with bows (they had
several of those) and a white
Thing with drapes like a goddess.
And a black thing with strings, and a blue
thing with things – and a
Red thing with straps, and a bodice.

Can't wait 'til tomorrow, to go to work,
and walk in dressed up
Like a toff!
But after today I'm so tired – oh well I'll
ring up for another day off!

# ISN'T THE WATER WET?

### FIRST CHORUS:

Isn't the water wet?
Isn't the sunshine hot?
Isn't the man with the ices nice
And hasn't he got a lot?
Don't the nights get dark
Nights I'll never forget –
Ain't the winkles wonderful
And isn't the water wet!

### SECOND CHORUS:

Isn't the water wet?
Isn't the sky ber-lue?
Nobody here but people, and nothing but
things to do.
Don't the boys look grand?
Sights I'll never forget –
Ain't the cockles a caution
And isn't the water wet!

### THIRD CHORUS:

Isn't the water wet?
Isn't the ocean deep?
If the sand was all swept up
Wouldn't it make a heap?
Sailors with ship-shape shapes
Shapes I'll never forget –
Ain't the mussels marvellous
And isn't the water wet!

# THE TYPESETTER'S STOP-GAP

In penny novelettes, it was customary always to include a "filler" story or poem which got pushed around from one page to another, throughout the magazine, wherever there was a space to fill. Here is such a poem …

1: Oh Mary, meet me by the gate
I swear my love be true
And fain would tell you of my great
*(continued on page 2)*

2: Oh Mary, Mary hear my song
Come walk the woods with me
And I'll plant kisses all along
*(continued on page 3)*

3: Oh Mary, Mary say you'll be
Within my arms once more
And I'll again caress your warm
*(continued on page 4)*

4: If only you will stay with me
Beyond the beaten track
I know our love affair will be
*(concluded on the back.)*

# THINGUMMYJIG

My hair was a mess
'Till I talked to young Bess
Who had prickly hair, like a pig;
But I've noticed of late
It's full bodied and straight
Since she washed it in
THINGUMMYJIG.

So I talked to young Di
Whose hair was so dry
That it crackled and cracked like a twig;
Now it glows with a sheen
That is almost obscene
Since she washed it in THINGUMMYJIG.

So I bought some from Boots
And I massaged my roots
Just like they did, with
THINGUMMYJIG –
Now just look at mine!
See it sparkle and shine!
Don't you think it looks fine? It's a wig.

# MAIN LINE

When I sit in railway carriages, I often think of all the marriages
Whose first few blissful moments are realised in the dining car;
Or rattling out of London Town, snugly with the shutters down.
Steaming down to bracing Brighton, steaming down without the light on,
Realising, none too soon, "George, we're on our Honeymoon!"
Full of eagerness and dread – wondering what lies ahead;
Can we cope, make both ends meet? Pull together? Find our feet?
Will she soon get tired of me? Do we face monotony?
Will he always buy me flowers? Was there ever a love like ours?
How did fate conspire to match us? Will the guard come in and catch us?

# BORN INTO RICHES

She drew a deep breath, followed by another. "I think I'm being followed by another" she said. They were standing in the sitting room, by the big window that overlooked the lawn. She could see the distant figure of the gardener, who had also overlooked the lawn for several weeks now. She stared out, running her hands over her body nervously. It was in terrible shape. All lumps and bumps, with little tufts of moss growing in the more inaccessible places.

"Followed? By a man?"

He felt something stir in his breast. It was the teaspoon in his waist coat pocket, stolen from the tea shoppe that very afternoon. "I think you're imagining things darling".

"No, I'm not."

He felt her quiver. "I asked you not to feel my quiver" she said. Her eyes swept the ground. Then they dusted the mantelpiece and cleaned out the grate.

"You're overwrought my dearest."

He felt her deep down. "Please for the last time, will you take your hand away" she said. He turned away thrusting his hands deep into his trouser pockets and juggling with his conscience. A whole minute passed.

"Have you got a grip on yourself?" she asked.

He didn't reply, but stared into the garden, his jaw set at a strange angle; the result of a skiing accident some years before.

"I'm sorry Geoffrey" she said.

She leant back, and the colour rose in her cheeks. She realised she was leaning against a hot radiator. She sat down to cover her embarrassment; and the cooling stone of the old window seat through her thin silk dress reminded her of her childhood. It also reminded her that she had dressed in a hurry and had forgotten to put any on. The thought of sitting here, with him in such a state of undress took her breath away. She took some brief pants before she dared speak, trying to slip them on without him noticing – but at the vital moment, he turned and caught her unawares – fortunately only with his elbow. He felt her quiver again as he took her in his arms; he couldn't resist it.

"I love you, Euphrosnia" he said, and those three simple words and one difficult one, sent a shiver through her cold frame. So much so that two of the cucumbers dropped off. He cupped her face in his hands, adding milk and sugar, before placing it on his lips and planting a long hard kiss on a long hard nose. "It's been a long struggle to win you" he said looking long and hard at her …

They were in the library, drinking in the beauty of the setting sun.

"Have another" he murmured, indicating his cocktail shaker. She nodded. "Your hair is so beautiful" he said. Caught in the sun, it was a mass of tiny lights. She had got them off the Christmas tree last year. "How do you keep it so radiant?"

She guided his hand to where she hid the battery. He touched it gently, and his eyes lit up. He raised his glass, and drawing her nearer to the fire, toasted her silently. She drained her glass at a single gulp. After a second she spoke. After a fourth, she could hardly speak, and after a sixth, she was absolutely pie-eyed. He picked her up, and carried her on to the lawn, where the evening mist lay in a wispy grey swirl, and the gardener lay in a filthy blue shirt.

Geoffrey laid Euphrosnia on the lawn, watched by the old gardener. "That's the way Sir" he cried drunkenly. "All the best properties are mostly laid to lawn." As Geoffrey stared at the bumpy uneven surface, he realised that Euphrosnia's dress had ridden up, and so had a young lad on a bicycle.

"Doctor, your wife wants you. The old cow's about to give birth."

The boy turned and cycled off again.

"Who'd be a vet?" thought Geoffrey, watching the boy getting smaller and smaller, until he was a tiny figure on the horizon. He eventually got so small he got a job in a circus, touring round as the Modern Tom Thumb.

Geoffrey gave one last look round at the vast, imposing edifice that was Euphrosnia's seat, and sighed. "All this could have been mine" he sighed.

She lay, face downward, on the damp grass. The gardener, feeling the seeds of a strange turbulence growing inside him, removed a packet of radishes from his back pocket. "Cheer up. Think how lucky you are. This is your seat" he cried, slapping her roundly, or at least, one of her roundlies. "You're in Burke's Peerage. I've been looking up your particulars."

He too felt her quiver. "You men are all the same" she murmured. She breathed several sighs – first, a few small-size sighs, followed by several sighs of a much larger size. Finally, she drew him down the ground beside her, with a felt-tip pen; the very pen that has since told this little story. Remember, of course, it isn't a true story; and, being only words, it's not to be taken literally.

# THE TWO RONNIES:

## THE TWO-HANDERS

Ronnie Barker first met Ronnie Corbett socially at the actor's club – The Buckstone – in 1963. Three years later they found themselves part of David Frost's team (alongside John Cleese) for *The Frost Report*. Over the years they developed a strong friendship and performing rapport, so much so, that in 1971, Bill Cotton, then head of BBC Light Entertainment, suggested poaching them from ITV and giving them their own show on the BBC. (In fact, Cotton never realised that just days before his offer, the Ronnies had been dropped by ITV, over contractual problems the network had developed with Frost.)

All the show needed was a title. "They asked what we should call it," says Ronnie "and someone in the office said, 'Well, they're always called the two Ronnies, so why not call it *The Two Ronnies?*' So we did."

Over the 12-season, 94-episode run of *The Two Ronnies* (plus Christmas specials) Gerald Wiley contributed a vast amount of material. Although the show provided both Barker and Corbett with plenty of solo moments, some of "Wiley's" best pieces were the two-handers between Ronnies B and C, from their classic pub exchanges, to the tramps and yokels, via a short-sighted opticians through the aged armchair-bound ramblings of Godfrey and Humphrey, to a shop keeper dealing with a man who, to all intents and purposes, appears to be asking for "Four candles"…

# FORK HANDLES

*or "Annie Finkhouse?"*

*An old ironmonger's shop. A shop that sells everything – garden equipment, ladies' tights, builders' supplies, mousetraps – everything.*

*A long counter up and down stage. A door to the back of the shop up left. The back wall also has a counter. Lots of deep drawers and cupboards up high, so that RC has to get a ladder to get some of the goods RB orders.*

*RC is serving a woman with a toilet roll. He is not too bright.*

**RC:**
There you are – mind how you go.

*(Woman exits. RB enters – a workman. Not too bright either.)*

**RC:**
Yes, sir?

**RB:**
Four candles?

**RC:**
Four candles? Yes, sir. *(He gets four candles from a drawer.)* There you are.

**RB:**
No – fork handles.

**RC:**
Four candles. That's four candles.

**RB:**
No, fork handles – handles for forks.

**RC:**
Oh, fork handles. *(He gets a garden fork handle from the back of the shop.)* Anything else?

**RB:**
*(looks at his list)* Got any plugs?

**RC:**
What sort of plugs?

**RB:**
Bathroom – rubber one.

*(RC gets box of bath plugs, holds up two different sizes.)*

**RC:**
What size?

**RB:**
Thirteen amp.

**RC:**
Oh, electric plugs. *(Gets electric plug from drawer.)* What else?

**RB:**
Saw tips.

**RC:**
Saw tips? What you want, ointment?

**RB:**
No, tips to cover the saw.

**RC:**
Oh. No, we ain't got any.

**RB:**
Oh. Got any hoes?

**RC:**
Hoes? Yeah. *(He gets a garden hoe from the garden department.)*

**RB:**
No – hose.

**RC:**
Oh, hose. I thought you meant hoes. *(He gets a roll of garden hose.)*

**RB:**
No – hose.

**RC:**
*(Gives him a dirty look.)* What hose? *(He gets a packet of ladies' tights from a display stand.)* Pantie-hose, you mean?

**RB:**
No, "O"s – letter "O"s – letters for the gate.

"Mon Repose".

**RC:**
Why didn't you say so? *(He gets ladder, climbs up to cupboard high up on wall, gets down box of letters.)* Now, "O"s – here we are – two?

**RB:**
Yeah.

**RC:**
Right. *(He takes box back up ladder and returns.)* Next?

**RB:**
Got any "P"s?

**RC:**
Oh, my Gawd. Why didn't you bleedin' say while I'd got the box of letters down here? I'm working me guts out here climbing about all over the shop, putting things back and then getting 'em out again. Now then, *(he is back with the box)* how many? Two?

**RB:**
No – peas – three tins of peas.

**RC:**
You're having me on, ain't yer? Ain't yer! *(He gets three tins of peas.)*

**RB:**
No, I ain't. I meant tinned peas.

**RC:**
Right. Now what?

**RB:**
Pumps.

**RC:**
Pumps? Hand pumps or foot pumps?

**RB:**
Foot.

**RC:**
Footpumps. Right. *(He goes off, returns with a small footpump.)* Right.

**RB:**
No, pumps for your feet. Brown pumps, size nine.

**RC:**
You are having me on. I've had enough of this. *(He gets them from drawer.)* Is that the lot?

**RB:**
Washers?

**RC:**
*(exasperated)* Windscreen washers? Car washers? Dishwashers? Hair washers? Back scrubbers? Lavatory cleaners? Floor washers?

**RB:**
Half-inch washers.

**RC:**
Tap washers! Here, give me that list, I'm fed up with this. *(He reads list and reacts)* Right! That does it. That's the final insult. *(Calls through door)* Elsie! Come and serve this customer – I've had enough!

*(RC stalks off. Elsie enters – a big, slovenly woman with a very large bosom. She takes the list. Reads it.)*

**ELSIE:**
Right, sir – what sort of knockers are you looking for?

# ABOUT A BOUT

**RC:**
Hello, Brown. Nice to see you around.

**RB:**
I'm just popping down to town.

**RC:**
Time to pop down to the Crown and down one?

**RB:**
I doubt it.

**RC:**
Oh, come on, it's only down by the roundabout.

**RB:**
To tell you the truth, I wouldn't be seen in the Crown for a thousand pounds.

**RC:**
That doesn't sound like you, Brown!

**RB:**
Well, don't spread it around, but last time I went there I was thrown out.

**RC:**
Oh, really?

**RB:**
Yes, I was made to look a bit of a clown. I popped in one day when I was out – as you know it's the only pub round about – and it was full of down and outs, and louts, all generally shouting about – the bounders were rather thick on the ground. Some rotten hound heard me order a round of drinks, and shouted out something about the way I sound.

**RC:**
The bounder – mind you, your voice is a bit dark brown, I've always found.

**RB:**
Granted. Nevertheless, they all crowded round, which I rather frowned upon. And then one lout bet me I wouldn't go ten rounds with him for a pound.

**RC:**
I bet you didn't turn him down – you're too proud.

**RB:**
Quite. I took off my jacket and threw it to the ground. And they all laughed out loud. I'd got my braces on the wrong way round.

**RC:**
You poor old bounder, Brown. Any women around?

**RB:**
Thousands. Nevertheless, I was just announcing loudly that I'd show them a thing or two worth shouting about, and the landlord threw me out.

**RC:**
Why?

**RB:**
My trousers had fallen down!

# NOTHING'S TOO MUCH TROUBLE

*An old-fashioned sweet shop. RB, as shopkeeper, is serving an old lady with some enormous old-fashioned humbugs.*

**RB:**
*(as he puts three or four on the scales)* What do you want, half a pound? A quarter?

**LADY:**
Well, I really wanted two ounces, if it's not too much trouble.

**RB:**
Nothing is too much trouble, madam. That's our slogan here: "Nothing is too much trouble". Two ounces it is. Mind you, these are a bit big for two ounces. You only get one *(puts it into bag)* There you are – you'll be able to have a suck of that and then put it away, won't you. There, *(puts the bag back onto scales)* that's exactly two ounces. And one for luck *(throws another humbug into bag)* Thirteen pence, thank you.

**LADY:**
Thank you. *(Pays him.)* Sorry to trouble you.

**RB:**
*(calling after her)* Nothing is too much trouble, madam.

*(RC enters.)*

**RC:**
Good afternoon. I wonder if I could trouble you for a quarter of a pound of liquorice allsorts.

**RB:**
Trouble me, sir? Nothing is too much trouble, sir, not in this shop. Didn't you see our notice in the window, sir? "Nothing is too much trouble". Right, sir – liquorice allsorts. Quarter of a pound, did you say, sir?

*(Pours them into scales.)*

**RC:**
Yes, thank you. Only I don't like the pink ones.

**RB:**
Oh, no pink ones, no sir.

*(Removes pinks ones.)*

**RC:**
And I don't like the blue ones.

**RB:**
No blue ones.

*(Takes out blue ones.)*

**RC:**
I hope you don't mind.

**RB:**
No trouble, sir.

**RC:**
And no black and white ones.

**RB:**
Oh, I think that only leaves the orange ones.

**RC:**
Yes, I only like the orange ones.

**RB:**
Look, tell you what, let's tip them out on the counter and we can pick 'em out, sir.

*(He does so.)*

**RC:**
Thank you.

*(They do so. RB shovels them back into jar.)*

**RB:**
Anything else, sir?

**RC:**
Yes. I want some gob-stoppers.

**RB:**
Right, sir. They're two pence each.

**RC:**
I want the kind that go pink after you suck them.

**RB:**
Oh. Well, I don't know what colour these go. They start off green.

**RC:**
Well, they all start off green, but a lot of them don't go pink. They do the dirty on you and go brown.

**RB:**
Oh, I see.

**RC:**
I think I'd better try one. If it's not too much trouble.

**RB:**
Nothing's too much trouble, sir. Here, I'll try one an' all. *(They both suck their gob-stoppers.)* Anything else, sir, while we're waiting?

**RC:**
Yes. Have you got those mints with holes in them?

**RB:**
Yes, sir.

**RC:**
How big are the holes?

**RB:**
Eh?

**RC:**
The holes mustn't be too small.

**RB:**
Oh. You got something to measure 'em with, sir?

**RC:**
Well, not one me, no. No, I must admit I haven't. But they should be just too small to get your finger into. Mind you, I did know someone once who wedged one onto a girl's finger one night.

**RB:**
Oh, what happened?

**RC:**
He had to marry her. The vicar said: "with this mint I thee wed". Tell you what, instead of the mints, I'll have some of those chocolate things that melt in your mouth and not in your hand.

**RB:**
Well, I'm afraid I'm out of them at the moment, sir, but I've got something very similar, look.

*(He shows jar.)*

**RC:**
I'll just try one. *(He takes one.)* I'll just hold it in my hand for a while.

**RB:**
Very good, sir. How's your gob-stopper?

**RC:**
It's gone white. Hopeless. Should go pink.

**RB:**
Ooh, look – mine's gone pink, sir. This one's alright.

**RC:**
Not much good to me now you've been sucking it though, is it? And this chocolate's melted all over my hand.

**RB:**
Oh. Here, wipe it on my apron, sir.

**RC:**
*(does so, making a mess)* Thank you. I'd better have some chocolates, I think. I like the milk sort.

**RB:**
*(gets box)* These are very popular. "Sunday Assortment", sir. All milk chocolates.

**RC:**
Are they soft centres?

**RB:**
Well, er, most of them, I think, sir.

**RC:**
Because I don't like the hard centres.

**RB:**
No hard centres. I see, sir.

**RC:**
I'll just see – *(bites one.)* Yes, that's a soft centre. *(Bites another.)* That's a hard centre. And that's a hard centre.

**RB:**
*(biting one)* I'm sure they're mostly – yes, that's a soft one. So's that.

**RC:**
These last three have been hard centres. No, I think I'll leave it.

**RB:**
Very good, sir.

*(He sweeps the bitten chocolates onto the floor.)*

**RC:**
I hope I'm not being a trouble.

**RB:**
Nothing's too much trouble, sir, not even you, sir. That, I take it, will be all, sir?

**RC:**
By no means.

**RB:**
Oh, right. What now, sir?

**RC:**
Have you got any liquorice rolls?

**RB:**
*(holding one up)* You mean these, sir?

**RC:**
Yes. How long, are they, when you unroll them?

**RB:**
Ooh, *(beginning to crack)* quite long, sir. They're pretty long, them are.

**RC:**
Could we unroll one?

**RB:**
Unroll one, certainly sir.

*(Does so.)*

**RC:**
That's not very long. What about this one?

**RB:**
They're all the same, sir.

**RC:**
This looks longer. *(Unrolls it.)* No, it's not. Oh, now I've lost the little ball in the middle.

**RB:**
Don't worry about the ball, sir, I'll rewind them later. *(Throws them on floor.)* Well, we're just closing now, so I'm afraid I ...

**RC:**
Ah, but I haven't got the very thing I came for. I want some hundreds and thousands – the wife is making these cakes, you see.

**RB:**
Hundreds and thousands, sir? Right.

*(Gets jar.)*

**RC:**
Would you mind counting them?

**RB:**
Pardon, sir?

**RC:**
My wife needs just the right number. Would you mind counting them?

**RB:**
Counting them?

**RC:**
If it's not too much trouble.

**RB:**
Nothing's too much trouble. How many do you want?

**RC:**
One thousand one hundred.

**RB:**
*(He pours them slowly in a cascade over RC's head.)* One, two, three, four, five ... *(he continues to count until the jar is empty)* Fifteen short. Don't worry, I got some more here. (Empties second jar over RC's head.)*

*(During this, a timid, maiden lady enters.)*

**RB:**
*(after he has finished the pouring)* Yes, madam?

**LADY:**
I want some slab toffee.

**RB:**
Slab toffee? Certainly, madam.

**LADY:**
If it's not too much trouble, could you smash it up nice and small? It's my teeth.

**RB:**
*(picking up enormous hammer)* Nothing's too much trouble, madam. Nice and small? Certainly, madam. *(He starts smashing everything in sight.)* I'll smash your teeth up nice and small as well if you like. Nothing's too much trouble here, madam.

*(He continues to smash things, as RC and the lady stare dumbly at him.)*

# THE GOURMET

*An open-plan, drinks-dining area in an upper-crust house. RC is an upper-crust boss and RB is a middle-crust prospective employee.*

**RC:**
*(raising gin and tonic)* Cheers.

**RB:**
*(likewise)* Cheers, sir.

**RC:**
So nice you could come round to dinner; especially since you're about to join the firm.

**RB:**
If you'll have me, sir.

**RC:**
Well, provided we all get on well – provided you like me, and I like you ... and my wife likes you, what? Must have the approval of the little woman, eh? Not that she's so little, in this case. *(He chuckles.)* Can't get round her easily. It's quite a walk! Ha Ha! Do you find her formidable?

**RB:**
Well, when you first meet her she takes a bit of getting over.

**RC:**
God! Getting over her is worse than getting round her. Ha Ha Ha! Practically impossible. But I'm an easy-going sort of chap, like a bit of a joke – in fact, I'm well known for it – but I do like my food. And that's her great asset. She's an absolutely amazingly wonderful cook. And that's the sole reason I married her. Because between you and me, and the gatefold of *Playboy*, I get my other pleasures elsewhere. And when I say elsewhere, I mean literally – Else Where.

**RB:**
Not Elsie Ware, in the typing pool?

**RC:**
Yes, you know her? Oh, of course, you met her on the tour of inspection today. Now, she can't even boil water, but she certainly gets me steamed up, I can tell you.

**RB:**
Quite.

**RC:**
By the way, I trust I can count on your discretion, old boy. Naturally, if my wife found out, that would be the end of a beautiful nosh-up.

*(RC's wife enters – she is very large, and foreign.)*

**WIFE:**
*(bellows)* Scrat nits marochari navtro!

**RC:**
Ah, thank you, dear. Dinner is served.

*(They move to the dinner table, which is set only for two.)*

**RC:**
Now, I should explain that Dimivtrina, or Trina for short, never eats with me. It's a sort of religious custom in her country. She has what's left, later, in the kitchen, with the goats. Not that she actually keeps goats in the kitchen in this country. Just a

couple of whippets and her brother, Andre. Now, what delights await the hungry guest?

*(Trina serves soup to RB. It is sticky and dark green.)*

**RC:**
The other thing I didn't tell you was that I am on a diet, so I can only eat bread rolls at the moment. Which is almost driving me mad, seeing you with that soup. Fantastic, isn't it?

**RB:**
*(trying to swallow it – it is awful)* Yes. What soup is it?

**RC:**
Privet. Privet soup. Made out of the hedge-clippings. It takes three weeks to marinate, then it's fried and left to cool, and mixed with a little olive oil. Do you find it dries the mouth up a little?

**RB:**
*(pulling a lemon face)* Yes, it does a bit – have you some water?

**RC:**
Better than that – try this sweet white wine from Turkey *(Pours it.)* You'll find the sugar counteracts the bitterness of the old privet.

**RB:**
*(drinks, pulls face)* Oh yes, lovely. *(RC is tucking into the bread rolls.)* Bread all right?

**RC:**
So-so. Bread's bread, isn't it?

**RB:**
Yes – er, I don't think I'll fill myself up too much with the soup, I'll save up for the main course.

**RC:**
Ah. *(Taps his nose.)* Very wise. Do you like curry?

**RB:**
Oh, love it, yes.

**RC:**
This is the most wonderful curry you've ever tasted. You think you've had curry? Not until you've had my wife's curry, you haven't.

*(She enters with large dish of curry.)*

**RC:**
Ah, just in time. *(Haltingly to Trina)* Soup – drisnika – roroshin Mr Perkins – gloopo granche.

**TRINA:**
Sprok! *(She nods, and helps RB to curry – a yellow-brown mess.)*

**RC:**
Now, just prepare yourself for the experience of a lifetime, old chap.

*(RB tastes it. It contains a million fires. His mouth opens, his eyes run, his throat breathes flame)*

**RB:**
Oh – ooh! *(He reaches for drink.)*

**RC:**
I knew you'd love it. *(To Trina)* He – loves – it!

**RB:**
*(trying to speak)* Groh – it's so cho, bur togu-thro.

**RC:**
Oh, I didn't know you spoke Armenian – oh, she'll love that! I'm very slow at it – just a few phrases, like "hello" and "nice" and "garlic dressing", and "bed-time". Though I don't use that one very often. I watch *Match of the Day* and creep in when she's asleep. Don't want any of that nonsense. *(Glancing at Trina)* It's alright, she doesn't understand a word. How's your glass?

**RB:**
Oh, ah, er – Mm! (*gulps down drink*) Eurgh, oh, er, ah! (*Tries to look delighted.*)

**RC:**
Here, try this. Bulgarian Apricot wine – syrupy and a little tart.

**RB:**
Thanks.

**RC:**
Speaking of little tarts, I must ring Elsie in a minute.

**RB:**
Oh, ah! Er, strong, curry, hot. (*He drinks new wine.*) Eurgh! It's good – fine.

**RC:**
I'm staying with the old gin and tonic at the moment. Now, eat up, old lad, she's waiting to deliver her *pièce de résistance*, as they say at the foreign office.

**RB:**
Ah. (*Gulps some more down.*) Oh, that's really good. (*He wipes the sweat from beneath his eyes.*)

**TRINA:**
Sprok. (*She takes his plate and goes out.*)

**RC:**
I think she likes you. She doesn't usually speak to strangers. Now, what she's going to come up with now, I'm fairly certain, is her sour milk, jam, banana and ugli-fruit turnover.

**RB:**
Oh. (*He looks slightly green.*)

**RC:**
That should set you up for the evening. No – wait! (*He raises his head, as if listening.*) No – it's not the ugli-fruit turnover – no – it's the curdled hedgehog cheese! I can smell it!

**RB:**
Oh dear, how er ... (*He mops his brow.*)

**RC:**
Yes, here it comes ...

(*Trina enters with cheese. The smell is unbearable.*)

**RB:**
(*recoils*) Ooh! Oh! Ow!

**RC:**
There. This is magnificent.

(*The cheese is placed under RB's nose. It is brown and crusty and runny. Trina leaves the room.*)

**RB:**
Oh, I really think I'm full. I, oh! I don't eat much as a ooh!

**RC:**
Ha Ha Ha! I think you've done amazingly well – you've passed the test with flying colours!

**RB:**
What?

**RC:**
I'm afraid I have a confession to make old boy. You've been the victim of a little practical joke. That is not my wife. (*Goes to door, calls*) Darling – come in, would you?

(*A tall, beautiful girl enters. She wears a little apron over her dress.*)

**RC:**
This is my wife. Angela, this is Mr Perkins – he's really suffered! Ha Ha Ha!

**ANGELA:**
Poor Mr Perkins!

**RC:**
God, you should have seen his face with that curry, ha ha ha! Damned funny. Well, you've proved yourself, Perkins – welcome to the firm. Now, Angela, where's the real food? I'm starving.

**ANGELA:**
Eggs, beans and chips, alright?

**RC:**
Wonderful. God! Get rid of that damned cheese, will you?

*(She takes it and exits.)*

**RB:**
So, all that bit about Elsie was part of the joke too?

**RC:**
Certainly. What would I want with Elsie Ware when I've got Angela? I haven't seen *Match of the Day* for years. Been in a few, with Angela though, what? Her cooking is bloody awful, but who cares?

*(Angela enters with a terrible mess of eggs, beans and chips for them.)*

**RC:**
Tuck in, old boy!

*(RB stares at the mess in horror.)*

# HUMPHREY AND GODFREY (1)

*RB and RC in armchairs in their London club.*

**RC:**
I say, Godfrey.

**RB:**
What is it, Humphrey?

**RC:**
How's your headache?

**RB:**
She's out playing bridge.

**RC:**
Come now, Godfrey, you shouldn't talk about the old gel like that, you know.

Love makes the world go round.

**RB:**
So does a punch on the nose, old lad. No, I've had bad luck with both my wives. The first divorced me and the second one won't.

**RC:**
It was a case of love at first sight with me.

**RB:**
Then why didn't you marry her?

**RC:**
I saw her again on several occasions.

**RB:**
So you married someone else?

**RC:**
Yes, she's very slow.

**RB:**
Slow? What at?

**RC:**
Everything. It takes her a day to make instant coffee. Trouble is, I'm hen-pecked.

**RB:**
Oh! Mustn't be, old lad. Stand up to her. Show her who's boss.

**RC:**
I'm going to. I've made up my mind I'm going to pluck up courage and tell her something I've been wanting to tell her for ages.

**RB:**
What's that?

**RC:**
I must have a new apron!

# THE ALLOTMENT

*(Twelve fragments)*

*RB and RC sitting by some old boxes by a shed on an allotment. Sunny weather. They are slow-thinking, slow-talking country folk.*

*(N.B. twelve segments, each with a joke, to be used as "fillers" in the programmes, one or more per week)*

## NO. 1

**RC:**
Didn't old Charlie go to the doctor's with his ears?

**RB:**
That's right, yes.

**RC:**
Deaf, wasn't he?

**RB:**
Eh?

**RC:**
Deaf.

**RB:**
He was, yes.

**RC:**
Did the doctor improve his hearing?

**RB:**
Must have done. He's just heard from his brother in America.

**RC:**
Oh.

*(They think this over.)*

## NO. 2

**RB:**
You still getting that dizziness when you wake up of a morning?

**RC:**
Yes, I am.

**RB:**
How long do it last?

**RC:**
About half an hour. Then I'm alright after that.

**RB:**
You been to the doctor about it?

**RC:**
Yes.

**RB:**
What did he say?

**RC:**
He told me to sleep half an hour longer.

**RB:**
Oh.

*(They think this over.)*

## NO. 3

**RB:**
You know that woman lives over the back of Tomkin's?

**RC:**
Oh, ah. She's got a bright pink Mini.

**RB:**
How do you know?

**RC:**
I seen her in it.

**RB:**
Oh.

**RC:**
Why, what about her?

**RB:**
Eh?

**RC:**
What about her?

**RB:**
Oh. Well, old Jack says she was always after her husband to buy her a Jaguar.

**RC:**
Well?

**RB:**
Well, he did, and it ate her.

**RC:**
Oh.

*(They ruminate.)*

## NO. 4

**RB:**
Is your missus getting worse or better?

**RC:**
About the same.

**RB:**
Last time I saw her I didn't like the look of her.

**RC:**
I never have liked the look of her.

**RB:**
What's the doctor say?

**RC:**
He says she's not too well. But the amazing thing is, he won't give me any encouragement either way.

**RB:**
Oh.

*(They ruminate.)*

## NO. 5

**RC:**
Here.

**RB:**
What?

**RC:**
You know you told me the doctor said you could only have two pints a day?

**RB:**
That's right, yes.

**RC:**
Well, your missus tells me you have half a dozen.

**RB:**
Yes, that's right.

**RC:**
How come?

**RB:**
I went to two other doctors, and they each allow me two pints as well.

**RC:**
Oh.

*(They ruminate.)*

## NO. 6

**RB:**
Did the dentist take your wisdom tooth out?

**RC:**
Yes, that's right, yes.

**RB:**
Did he give you anything for it?

**RC:**
No. Why, is it worth anything?

**RB:**
No, I mean anaesthetic.

**RC:**
Oh, no. I refused it. I thought it might hurt.

**RB:**
Oh.

**RC:**
He's a very considerate sort of chap, though. Instead of squirting water into your mouth, he squirts whisky.

**RB:**
He never done that to me.

**RC:**
Ah no, he only does it as a special treat, during Christmas week.

**RB:**
Oh.

*(They think this over.)*

●◆

## NO. 7

**RB:**
You know old Cyril Harris, with the one eye?

**RC:**
Yes. You don't see much of him lately.

**RB:**
No, well he don't see much of us, either.

**RC:**
No. Where did you see him then?

**RB:**
Up the pictures. He went up to the girl in the box office there and he says, "With one eye I should think you'd let me in for half price." But she wasn't having it.

**RC:**
Oh. Did he have to pay full price?

**RB:**
He had to pay double.

**RC:**
Double? Why was that then?

**RB:**
She reckoned it would take him twice as long to see the picture.

**RC:**
Oh.

*(They think this over.)*

●◆

## NO. 8

**RC:**
I see that Mrs Parkinson got her divorce. Her that's got that husband on the stage.

**RB:**
Oh, yes?

**RC:**
They gave her the divorce 'cos he snored.

**RB:**
You can't get a divorce for snoring, can you?

**RC:**
Ah well, you see her husband was a ventriloquist and he snored on her side of the bed.

**RB:**
Oh.

*(They think this over.)*

●◆

## NO. 9

**RC:**
Do you reckon we live longer now than we used to?

**RB:**
Oh yes, undoubtedly. I've never lived so long in my life. That's 'cos they've gone back to breast-feeding, you know.

**RC:**
Oh?

**RB:**
Yes. Mother's milk is much better than cow's milk.

**RC:**
How d'you reckon that then?

**RB:**
Well, it's always fresh and the cat can't get at it.

**RC:**
Yes.

**RB:**
And it comes in handy little containers.

**RC:**
Yes.

**RB:**
And you don't have to leave them out for the milkman.

**RC:**
*(after a pause)* The woman next door does.

**RB:**
Oh.

*(They think this over.)*

## NO. 10

**RB:**
Here, I've just read an extraordinary thing.

**RC:**
What's that?

**RB:**
Every time I breathe, a man dies.

**RC:**
Oh dear. You want to try chewing cloves.

**RB:**
Oh.

*(They ruminate.)*

## NO. 11

**RB:**
My daughter says I got to buy the missus one of they brassières for Christmas.

**RC:**
Oh, she making two puddings this year, is she?

**RB:**
No – to wear. Only I dunno what size she is. How am I going to describe her to the salesgirl?

**RC:**
Well, you'll just have to say she's like some everyday object, so's she'll know.

**RB:**
Oh, that's a good idea. I wonder what?

**RC:**
Well – is she a melon?

**RB:**
No, no, not a melon.

**RC:**
A grapefruit?

**RB:**
No.

**RC:**
An orange?

**RB:**
No.

**RC:**
Oh. Well, is she an egg?

**RB:**
Oh yes, that's it, an egg – fried.

**RC:**
Oh.

*(He thinks about this.)*

## NO. 12

**RB:**
Here, you know we live in the same sort of house?

**RC:**
Yes.

**RB:**
Same road, same shape, same size rooms?

**RC:**
Yes.

**RB:**
You know when you wallpapered your front room and you told me you bought eight rolls of wallpaper?

**RC:**
That's right, yes.

**RB:**
Well, I just papered our front room.

**RC:**
Oh, yes?

**RB:**
I bought eight rolls of wallpaper and when I finished, I had two rolls over.

**RC:**
That's funny. So did I.

**RB:**
Oh.

*(He thinks about this.)*

# THE CASE OF MRS MACE

*A police station – a room or office within the station itself. RB as plain-clothes North Country detective, sits at a desk. RC enters.*

**RC:**
Good day, Inspector Jay.

**RB:**
Morning, Dorning. Any news of the Girder murder?

**RC:**
Yessir. He's been shot at Oxshott. Bagshot got him with a slingshot full of buckshot.

**RB:**
He's a good shot, Bagshot. Well, you must be pleased that situation's eased.

**RC:**
The relief is beyond belief chief. My mind is once more a blank. And I've only you to thank.

**RB:**
Alright. Never mind the fawning, Dorning. I'm glad to hear your head's clear: it means there's more space for the Mrs Mace case to take its place.

**RC:**
The Mrs Mace case? Have they traced the face? *(Points to photofit blow-up on wall.)*

**RB:**
No – and the night-dress is still missing.

**RC:**
Is she sure it was the right night-dress? She's not mistaken about what was taken?

**RB:**
How come, little chum?

**RC:**
Well, to the voluptuous Mrs Mace, all her night-dresses are equally seductively attractive and attractively seductive. Whatever she wore, she'd still be a bountiful, beautiful nightie-full.

**RB:**
She's certainly a grand lady to have as a landlady. I've been told that her teapot's never cold.

**RC:**
I'd be delighted to be selected to inspect her, inspector. Any prospects of any suspects?

**RB:**
Yes – two. Two of them are actors who lodge with Grace – Mrs Mace, at her place in the Chase. Leo Mighty, the leading man, known for his portrayals of charmers, farmers and men in pyjamas. And the other one is Roger Mainger, the stage manager, who once played a mad stranger in a film starring Stewart Granger called *Deadly Danger*.

**RC:**
May I add another to your list? If I'm not being too bumptious or presumptuous?

**RB:**
Who?

**RC:**
Sergeant Bodger!

**RB:**
What? That replacement constable from Dunstable? You must be crazy.

**RC:**
It's just a theory, dearie. May I sit down?

**RB:**
Please – make yourself comfy, Humphrey.

*(RC sits.)*

**RC:**
It's just that Bodger has got a face like a fit: which fits the face on the photofit in the first place, and he's often to be found at her place, in the Chase, filling his face with fish.

**RB:**
Fish?

**RC:**
Fried by Grace – Mrs Mace. Mostly dace or plaice.

**RB:**
But what about Leo Mighty? He's there nightly – isn't it slightly more likely? She obviously looks very flighty in her nightie – he's the sort of toff that might try to pull it off.

**RC:**
Possibly – but here's something you don't know.

**RB:**
I don't?

**RC:**
No. I've spoken with Roger.

**RB:**
Roger?

**RC:**
The lodger.

**RB:**
Oh – Roger Mainger, who played the stranger with Granger.

**RC:**
He says he saw Leo take the night-gown. He was staring through the keyhole in

Mrs Mace's bedroom door.

**RB:**
He dared to stare through there? Would he swear he saw Leo Mighty take the nightie?

**RC:**
He'll do plenty of swearing. No wonder he was staring – it was the one she was wearing!

**RB:**
What? Surely not!

**RC:**
He stood on the bed, and pulled it over her head. She went red, and he fled. He locked himself in the shed, and wished he were dead. She was going to phone her cousin Ted, but felt dizzy in the head, so she lay on the bed instead, and went red.

**RB:**
So you said. Roger is a liar!

**RC:**
Have you any proof, you old poof?

**RB:**
I've seen where Mrs Mace sleeps. It's an attic! So the story about pulling the garment over her head is false. He would have to pull the night-gown right down! There's no headroom in her bedroom!

**RC:**
So Roger's lying! Then he must be the culprit! Game, set and match, chief! And so ends the disgraceful Grace Mace case.

**RB:**
*(picks up phone)* I'll just tell the Chief Constable – what a relief, constable. *(Into phone)* Hello, sir – we've solved the Mace Case. I'm happy to tell you that Leo is innocent and so is Sergeant Bodger. Yes, sir: in other words – 'twas not Leo Mighty who lifted the nightie, t'was Roger the Lodger, the soft-footed dodger, and not Sergeant Bodger, thank God!

# LIFE IN THE TRENCHES (Part 2)

*A trench. 1914–18 war. Heavy and noisy gunfire. RB and RC discovered. RB a captain, RC a corporal.*

**RB:**
We're cornered, corporal. We'll be lucky to get out of here alive.

**RC:**
Yes, sir – probably later than that, I shouldn't wonder.

**RB:**
What?

**RC:**
Later than five, sir – probably nearer half-past.

**RB:**
Get out alive, I said – not get out by five

**RC:**
Oh, sorry sir. It's these damn guns, sir. I can't hear properly, sir. Are we cut off from the others, sir?

**RB:**
I think so. We can either lie low until morning, or you can find a high vantage point to see if we can spot the enemy. *(Hands him binoculars.)* What do you say?

**RC:**
Thank you, sir. *(For the binoculars.)*

**RB:**
No, I mean: what do you think?

**RC:**
Oh. Up to you, sir.

**RB:**
Alright, corporal – I think you'd better get up a tree, and risk it.

**RC:**
Oh good, I could just do with one.

**RB:**
What?

**RC:**
Cup of tea and a biscuit, sir.

**RB:**
I said: get up a tree and risk it!

**RC:**
Oh. Oh dear.

**RB:**
Well, go on – make a start.

**RC:**
Bake a tart, sir?

**RB:**
Make a start, man, make a start. Do I have to repeat every stupid little word?

**RC:**
No need to be personal, sir.

**RB:**
What do you mean?

**RC:**
Calling me that, sir.

**RB:**
I said "stupid little word".

**RC:**
Oh, sorry, sir. I thought you said something else.

**RB:**
Well – off you go then, corporal.

**RC:**
Excuse me sir, but I can't climb trees, sir.

**RB:**
What?

**RC:**
Never could, sir. Ever since I was a small boy at Wimbledon.

**RB:**
You never told me that.

**RC:**
What, sir?

**RB:**
You were a ball-boy at Wimbledon. I've always loved tennis.

**RC:**
Who, Dennis the cook, sir?

**RB:**
Tennis, man, tennis! Look, never mind all that. One of our tanks is just up there on the ridge. We must try to re-capture it.

**RC:**
Yes, sir.

**RB:**
But be careful. Jerry snipers are everywhere. Anywhere near a tank is a hot-spot.

**RC:**
No, I don't think we are, sir.

**RB:**
Are what?

**RC:**
Anywhere near a Lancashire hot-pot, sir.

**RB:**
Hot spot, damn you, hot-spot!

**RC:**
Sorry, sir. Please sir – I can't go, sir.

**RB:**
Why not, corporal?

**RC:**
My gun's all wonky, sir.

**RB:**
Well, it's nerves, it's only natural.

**RC:**
No, my gun, sir.

**RB:**
Oh. What's the matter with it?

**RC:**
It was in my trouser pocket and it went off half-cock, sir.

**RB:**
Oh, well you'd better report to casualty when we get back. Looks as if I'll have to go.

**RC:**
Yes, sir – thank you sir.

*(RB climbs up the trench. He is shot, and falls back.)*

**RC:**
Are you alright, sir?

**RB:**
Of course, I'm not alright! I'm shot.

**RC:**
Yes, so am I, sir, it is hot.

**RB:**
Shot! Not hot!

**RC:**
Oh, sorry, sir. Shall I get stretcher bearers, sir?

**RB:**
No, it's too late for that. Just go and let me die in peace.

**RC:**
Yes, sir – any gravy sir?

**RB:**
What?

**RC:**
Any gravy on your pie and peas?

**RB:**
I didn't say go and get me pie and peas! I said go and let me die in peace. Goodbye, corporal. You're a good chap. We haven't always seen eye to eye. Or ear to ear for

that matter.

**RC:**
No, sir. It's the guns, sir.

**RB:**
Yes – but if you get through safe and sound, at least when I get up to heaven they'll say "he died – saving an ordinary man".

*(Big gun explosion.)*

**RC:**
Save what, sir? *(He is about to go over the top.)*

**RB:**
An ordinary man!

**RC:**
I certainly will, sir.

**RB:**
What?

**RC:**
Save you a strawberry flan.

*(He goes, and RB dies of annoyance.)*

# HUMPHREY AND GODFREY (2)

*RB and RC in armchairs in their London club.*

**RB:**
*(looking at newspaper)* I say, Humphrey.

**RC:**
What is it, Godfrey?

**RB:**
It says here, "A firm bust in four weeks".

**RC:**
That's nothing – my brother's firm went bust in a fortnight.

**RB:**
No, no old boy, it's an advert – for women.

**RC:**
Don't answer it, old chap, you've already got one. Talking of women, seen the new maid in the bar?

**RB:**
Yes. I've seen better legs on a piano. And with a piano, you get one extra. Bit of a gold-digger too.

**RC:**
Really?

**RB:**
Yes. I can read women like a book.

**RC:**
What system do you use?

**RB:**
Braille.

**RC:**
Trouble with life is, when you're young you can't afford women. By the time you have money to burn, the fire's gone out.

**RB:**
Like my brother. He still chases his secretaries round the desk but he can't remember why.

# HEAR, HEAR

*RB sits at desk. A large sign on the wall – "Hearing Aid Centre". Enter RC. He approaches the desk.*

**RC:**
Is this the hearing-aid centre?

**RB:**
Pardon?

**RC:**
Is this the hearing-aid centre?

**RB:**
Yes, that's right, yes.

**RC:**
Ah. I've come to be fitted for a hearing-aid.

**RB:**
Pardon?

**RC:**
I said I've come for a hearing-aid.

**RB:**
Oh, yes. Do sit down. I'll just take a few details. Name?

**RC:**
Pardon?

**RB:**
Name?

**RC:**
Crampton.

**RB:**
Pardon?

**RC:**
Crampton.

**RB:**
Oh, Crampton.

**RC:**
Pardon?

**RB:**
I said Crampton.

**RC:**
Crampton, yes.

**RB:**
Right, Mr Crampton. Now I take it you are having difficulty with your hearing.

**RC:**
Pardon?

**RB:**
I said I take it you're having difficulty with your hearing?

**RC:**
That's correct.

**RB:**
Pardon?

**RC:**
I said that's correct.

**RB:**
Which ear?

**RC:**
Pardon?

**RB:**
Which ear?

**RC:**
The right.

**RB:**
Pardon?

**RC:**
The right ear.

**RB:**
Ah. Could you cover it up with your hand, please. *(RC does so.)*

**RB:**
Now can you hear me?

**RC:**
Pardon?

**RB:**
Can you hear what I'm saying?

**RC:**
It's very faint.

**RB:**
Pardon?

**RC:**
It's very faint.

**RB:**
I can't hear you.

**RC:**
Pardon?

**RB:**
Try the other ear.

*(RC covers it up.)*

**RB:**
Now, what's that like?

**RC:**
I still can't hear you.

**RB:**
Can you hear me?

**RC:**
Pardon?

**RB:**
Hm. Definitely need a hearing-aid.

**RC:**
I thought so.

**RB:**
Pardon?

**RC:**
You can't hear me, either, can you?

**RB:**
Pardon?

**RC:**
Why don't you wear one?

**RB:**
You're still very faint.

**RC:**
A HEARING-AID! Why don't you wear one?

**RB:**
I am wearing one.

**RC:**
Pardon?

**RB:**
Pardon?

**RC:**
I said "Pardon".

**RB:**
Oh. I said "Pardon".

**RC:**
Oh, to hell with it – I'll get some new teeth.

*(He exits.)*

# SMALL PARTS

*A film producer's office – not too large – film posters, framed, on walls etc. Several upright chairs against a wall. One is occupied by RC, waiting for an audition. He looks at his watch. Enter RB.*

**RB:**
Morning.

**RC:**
Morning. You here about the film?

**RB:**
Mm. I've come for a thing.

**RC:**
A thing? What sort of a thing?

**RB:**
I'm going to, you know, thing. For the director. Hoping he'll like it.

**RC:**
It's a woman, isn't it?

**RB:**
Oh, really? Well, I'll have to do my thinging to her then. I hope I get the job. I need the money, 'cos I'm thick.

**RC:**
Jobs aren't easy these days.

**RB:**
I know. I don't get many, because of my thighs.

**RC:**
What's the matter with them?

**RB:**
I'm too fat. My thighs affects the way I thing.

**RC:**
Oh, your size. You're a singer!

**RB:**
I thed I'm a thinger.

**RC:**
Oh, now I see what you mean. Well, I think you're absolutely white.

**RB:**
Yeth, well I'm nervy.

**RC:**
No, you're wight about your size affecting your singing. I'm the same. Being small, I never play anything wugged – I always finish up being a wotter or a went-man.

**RB:**
Oh. Tell me – you can't thound your "R" 's, can you?

**RC:**
No – and you can't sound your "S" 's, can you?

**RB:**
No. Well, thum I can. When I'm not sinking. There, I thounded one then.

**RC:**
You should practise on "How many shirts

can Sister Susie sew, if Sister Susie's slow at sewing shirts". That's a famous widdle.

**RB:**
I don't go for riddleth. I think they're thoft.

**RC:**
No, I don't got for widdles either; not with my problem. If I do widdles, it's whisky.

**RB:**
Oh, ith it? I don't drink, mythelf.

**RC:**
No, wisky, too much of a wisk.

**RB:**
Oh, I thee.

**RC:**
What are you going to sing?

**RB:**
"Red thails in the thun-thet".

**RC:**
Wed what?

**RB:**
You know, "Red thails in the thun-thet. Way over the thea. Oh pleathe thend my thailor, home thafely to me". Do you think thath a thilly thong to thing?

**RC:**
I think it will be an absolute wow.

**RB:**
What d'you mean, a row?

**RC:**
Not a wow, a wow! A hit. That was in a musical I was in. I had a very long wun in the West End with that.

**RB:**
Did you? Oh, you've worked in the Wetht End, have you? Whath your name?

**RC:**
Cecil, what's yours?

**RB:**
Randolph.

**RC:**
Oh – do you mind if I call you Wandy?

**RB:**
No – do you mind if I call you Claude?

**RC:**
Why?

**RB:**
I can't thay thethil without thpitting. *(which he does.)*

*(Enter a nice-looking young man.)*

**RB:**
Morning.

**MAN:**
Morning. *(He has a cleft palate.)* Nice morning.

*(RC and RB look at each other.)*

**RB:**
Are you here to thing?

**MAN:**
Yeth. Vey wang me thith morning.

**RB:**
You can't thound your "R" 's, can you?

**MAN:**
No.

**RC:**
Or your "S" 's?

**MAN:**
No. Or my "L" 's, or my "wees and wubbleyou's".

**RB:**
*(delighted)* Oh dear!

**RC:**
*(delighted)* What a shame.

*(Enter the lady director.)*

**LADY:**
Morning, gentlemen.

**ALL:**
Morning.

**LADY:**
Ah, wonderful! *(Points to young man)* You. You're just right. Thanks for coming, gentlemen. Next time, perhaps.

**RC:**
But he can't sound his "S" 's.

**RB:**
Or his "R" 's.

**RC:**
Or his "L" 's.

**RB:**
Or his "wees and wubbleyou's".

**LADY:**
Doesn't matter – it's a non-speaking part.

*(She exits with young man.)*

*Ends.*

# THE GROCERY SHOP

*A village shop, sells mostly foodstuffs, but has a toy section, stationery, gardening equipment, etc. RB, as proprietor, potters about. RC enters, with shopping list.*

**RB:**
Morning, sir.

**RC:**
Morning. Erm– we've just moved into the village, and as a matter of fact, you've been recommended to us.

**RB:**
Oh, lovely. That's probably 'cos we're the only shop in the area. Still, what can we do for you, sir?

**RC:**
Well now, my wife has given me this list and her handwriting is not all that easy to decipher, I ...

**RB:**
Let's have a look – I get used to reading people's terrible writing. *(Takes list, reads.)* No, I can't understand a single word of that, sir. *(Gives it back.)*

**RC:**
Well, I can read some of it. Now – what's this first one? – "A large tin of bears".

**RB:**
Bears? Bear's what?

**RC:**
Just bears.

**RB:**
Must be pears.

**RC:**
No – it's beans.

**RB:**
Oh, beans!

**RC:**
Yes. "Preferably Cress and Blackwell".

**RB:**
Oh, right. Here we are. Next?

**RC:**
Some Cornish Panties.

**RB:**
Panties? Let's see. *(Takes list.)* Oh, that'll be pasties, sir, pasties. How many would you like?

**RC:**
Er, two. The wife eats them all the time.

**RB:**
What size?

**RC:**
Outsize.

**RB:**
Right – they're nice ones today, sir, with the nice frilly edges. There we are. One pair of frilly pasties. Will they be large enough for the wife, sir?

**RC:**
Yes, they look about her size.

**RB:**
'Cos if they're not big enough for her, tell her to pop by and drop 'em in the shop and I'll change them for her. Now, what's next?

**RC:**
Looks like slippy soap. No – sticky loofah. No – Loopy Loop.

**RB:**
Loop the loop? That's soup.

*(Goes to get soup.)*

**RC:**
No. Stinky loam?

**RB:**
Oh. Fertiliser.

*(Goes to get fertiliser.)*

**RC:**
No, spicy love?

**RB:**
Oh, that's paperbacks.

*(Goes to get paperbacks.)*

**RC:**
Sliced beef?

**RB:**
Ah–

*(Goes to refrigerated counter.)*

**RC:**
Got it – sliced loaf.

**RB:**
Are you sure, sir?

**RC:**
Yes, look, it says "wholemeal" in brackets.

**RB:**
Thank God for that. What's next?

**RC:**
"Jolly Christmas".

**RB:**
Eh? *(Takes list.)* "Jelly crystals". Right. Now. "A small union man". Would that be you, sir?

**RC:**
A small union man?

**BOTH:**
"A small onion flan".

**RC:**
Good, now we're getting the hang of it. Er – dolls' puddles.

**RB:**
Doll puddles? Oh, I know what that is. *(Goes over to toys.)* Here we are. The new dolly, sir – wets its nappy and then comes out in spots all over its little BTM. Then you rub this special cream on it and its hair grows.

**RC:**
No, that won't be it. Perhaps it's "dog puddles".

**RB:**
Oh, I hope not.

**RC:**
Ah! I suddenly saw it. "Dill pickles".

**RB:**
Oh yes, right.

**RC:**
It's funny how you can suddenly get used to someone's handwriting, isn't it? Now, *(reads)* "Two large stiff and kindly pigs".

**RB:**
No, no, sir. *(Looking at list)* That's "Two large steam and kidney pills". She means these, sir. *(Shows packet.)* Knock a horse out, these would.

**RC:**
No – it's "two large steak and kidney pies".

**RB:**
Oh yes, of course. Are we nearly there?

**RC:**
Won't be long now. "Two topless molls".

**RB:**
Two towel rails.

**RC:**
Two toilet rolls.

**RB:**
*(taking list)* A bot of raspberry jim. A large bot or a small bot, sir?

**RC:**
That's for the wife too.

**RB:**
Oh, a large bot. Right – a tin of diced parrots, *(gets each object as he says them)*, a pond of self-rising flood, a large bedroom, half a new member and a bunch of ruderies. *(I.e. tin of carrots, bag of flour, large beetroot, half a cucumber and a bunch of radishes.)* Right, sir, do you want these delivered?

**RC:**
Please. Cash on delivery?

**RB:**
Certainly, sir.

**RC:**
Right. There's my address.

**RB:**
*(reading address from paper)* Mr and Mrs Spith, Number Twanky Foop, Thigh Streek, opposite the Pouf's Office.

**RC:**
That's it – good morning!

*(Exits.)*

*End.*

# MISPLINT SKETCH

*RB at newsdesk area – recorded at "News Items" time.*

**RB:**
The next sketch will be presented exactly as it arrived from the author. It is full of misprints, but he refuses to sack his typist as she has a widowed mother and a forty-two inch bust. In other words, two very good reasons. Here then, is the sketch, entitled, *All in a Day's Burk.*

*Cut to: an office set. Super caption:"All in a Day's Wonk". RC sits at his desk, looking at newspaper. RB enters.*

**RB:**
Good forning, Mr Sorebit.

**RC:**
Rood morning, Mr Basker. Hot are you this morning? Wool, I trust?

**RB:**
Fone, absolutely Bone. Lot of wonk to do this morning.

**RC:**
So have I. I've got an enormous pole in my in-tray.

**RB:**
Anything in the loospaper?

**RC:**
Pardon?

**RB:**
The newdpaper! Anything in the Newsraper?

**RC:**
Oh, not a log; not a log. It's all bollyticks these days. Bit about the play on TV. Did you see it?

**RB:**
No, some friends came over for a maul.

**RC:**
It was quite good. Bit spicy. Girl walking about in just a pair of knickers. I see Mrs Tighthouse has complained.

**RB:**
She wants a swift kick up the arm.

**RC:**
Quite. I mean, it's not as if she removed her knockers. That would have been different.

**RB:**
Absotootly. Where's Miss Higgins this morning?

**RC:**
She's late as usual. Come to think of it, she's been lade every day this week.

**RB:**
I'll soon put a slop to that. I'll give her a weeds notice.

**RC:**
No – don't do that–

**RB:**
Why nit?

**RC:**
I would hate to see her toe from here.

**RB:**
Why?

**RC:**
If you must know, Miss Figgens and I are in Hove.

**RB:**
In love? You and Miss Wiggins?

**RC:**
*(anxiously)* Please – don't toll anyone – it's a socret. She doosn't wint anybocky to po about it. Is that clear?

**RB:**
Not even Moo?

**RC:**
Not even you.

**RB:**
Well, alright. Its OF by me. Well, well, weddle! You crafty old see-and-so.

**RC:**
Oh, I'm so unhoppy – she's all I ever wanted in a Roman – churming, rood-looking – and a wonderful dossposition.

**RB:**
Then why are you unhacky? Why don't you both get matted?

**RC:**
We can't – she's already rnorried!

**RB:**
Oh, a Jewish chap.

**RC:**
Yes. The situation is absolutely soapless. I'll have to put a stoop to it. It's been so difficult these last few weeks not to show my foolings.

*(He is on the verge of tears.)*

**RB:**
Please don't – you've given me indigestion as it is. Where are my piles? Come on now, cheer up – blow your note.

*(RC does so – RB takes a pill. Enter Miss Higgins.)*

**RB:**
Morning, Miss Bigguns.

**MISS H:**
Morning, Rennie. *(To RC)* Morning,
Runny.

**RC:**
Morning. Where have you beet? You're
supposed to be here at nine o'click.

**MISS H:**
I'm very soddy – I would have been here
on the bot, but I had to see the dictor.

**RC:**
The doctor?

**RB:**
You're not feeling all, are you?

**MISS H:**
Never felt better in my loaf! He's just told
me I'm going to have a booby.

**RC:**
What?

**MISS H:**
It's true – I'm going to be a tummy.

**RB:**
Congritulotions my bear! *(Kisses her
cheek.)* Go into the other office and put
your fees up. You must bake it easy for a
while.

**MISS H:**
Thank you – you're very canned

*(She goes.)*

**RB:**
*(shutting door)* Well, that's that, isn't it?
That's the end of your little affair. Now
you've got to put a stoop to it. Which
means, my dear chip, that all your trebles
are over.

**RC:**
They're only just beginning – her
husband's a sailor – hasn't been home for

two years.

**RB:**
Two years? Then that child ...

**RC:**
When he finds out he'll take me out to sea
and throw me overboard!

**RB:**
You mean ...

**RC:**
Yes – I'm going to be a bather.

# ICE CREAM PARLOUR

*A small modern ice cream parlour. RB behind
counter with silly forage cap and apron on.
Enter RC, wearing a bowler.*

**RC:**
Eightpenny cornet, please.

**RB:**
What flavour?

**RC:**
Cheese and onion.

**RB:**
Cheese and onion? We don't have cheese
and onion.

**RC:**
Alright then – smoky bacon.

**RB:**
We haven't got smoky bacon either. You
don't get ice cream in them flavours.

**RC:**
Then you should. What have you got?

**RB:**
Strawberry, chocolate, vanilla, dairy
vanilla, nut sundae, fruit whip, Cornish

cream, plum surprise, rhubarb fool, knickerbocker glory, crunchy toffee brittle, Neapolitan, cosmopolitan, marshmallow, spearmint, coffee continental, orange, lemon, lime, lychee, pineapple, pomegranate and ugli fruit.

**RC:**
Is that all?

**RB:**
That's all, yes.

**RC:**
I'm sure you used to do a salt and vinegar.

**RB:**
Never. There's never been no such thing as salt and vinegar ice cream.

**RC:**
There used to be.

**RB:**
No, never. Never ever as long as I've worked here.

**RC:**
How long is that?

**RB:**
Three weeks. Never had salt and vinegar.

**RC:**
I think you're deluding yourself. Well, I'd better have something else then. What did you say you'd got again?

**RB:**
Strawberry, vanilla, blueberry, blackberry, gooseberry fool, apple charlotte, marmalade, honey and lemon, glycerine and menthol, sugared almond, flaky apricot, biggerknocker glory, banana, gollyberry, grapefruit, gropefruit, gripe water and greengage jelly.

**RC:**
Do you serve any of those without walnut chippings?

**RB:**
Sorry, we haven't got any walnut chippings, but you could have them without chocolate sprinkle.

**RC:**
I don't like chocolate sprinkle. I only like them without walnut chippings.

**RB:**
I told you, we ain't got no walnut chippings.

**RC:**
Doesn't seem as if you've anything. No cheese and onion, no smoky bacon.

**RB:**
They don't ever make them flavours in an ice cream, I've told you that.

**RC:**
Oh well, forget the whole thing. Give me a packet of crisps.

**RB:**
What flavour?

**RC:**
Raspberry ripple.

*(RB hits RC on the bowler hat with a popcorn frying pan.)*

# MARK MY WORDS

*A pub. RB at bar, drinking a pint – flat cap. RC enters – flat cap. They speak throughout without any sign of emotion at all.*

**RC:**
Evening, Harry.

**RB:**
Hullo, Bert. What you having?

**RC:**
Oh ta, I'll have a pint of, er–

**RB:**
Light?

**RC:**
No, er–

**RB:**
Brown?

**RC:**
No–

**RB:**
Mild?

**RC:**
No–

**RB:**
Bitter?

**RC:**
Yes, bitter. Pint of bitter.

**RB:**
*(calls)* Pint of bitter, Charlie.

*(Barman attends to it.)*

How are you then?

**RC:**
Mustn't grumble. I just been up the–

**RB:**
Club?

**RC:**
No, up the–

**RB:**
Dogs?

**RC:**
No–

**RB:**
Fish shop?

**RC:**
No–

**RB:**
Doctors?

**RC:**
Doctors, yes. Up the doctors. I just been up the doctors. I've been having a bit of trouble with my, er–

**RB:**
Chest?

**RC:**
No, with my–

**RB:**
Back?

**RC:**
No–

**RB:**
Side?

**RC:**
No–

**RB:**
Backside?

**RC:**
No, my wife.

**RB:**
Oh.

**RC:**
My wife. She seems to have got it into her head that I'm a, I'm a–

**RB:**
What, annoyed with her?

**RC:**
No, a–

**RB:**
A martian?

**RC:**
No–

**RB:**
A pouf?

**RC:**
No, a bit under the weather. But he's examined me all over. Nothing wrong at all. He told me to drop my–

**RB:**
Really?

**RC:**
And he looked at my–

**RB:**
Go on.

**RC:**
And he said there was nothing to worry about at all. No, on the contrary, he said I was, er– I was er–

**RB:**
First class?

**RC:**
No–

**RB:**
Fascinating?

**RC:**
No–

**RB:**
Friendly?

**RC:**
No, fit.

**RB:**
Oh, fit.

**RC:**
Perfectly fit for a–

**RB:**
Change.

**RC:**
No, for a man of–

**RB:**
Ninety?

**RC:**
For a man of my age. It's nice to know, isn't it? 'Cos I only went up there on the–

**RB:**
Bus?

**RC:**
No, on the off chance.

**RB:**
Oh, off chance, yes.

**RC:**
Have you been up there lately? It's all different now up there. He's got a marvellous great big new, er– big new er–

**RB:**
Rolls Royce?

**RC:**
No, a big new er–

**RB:**
Waiting room?

**RC:**
No, big new er–

**RB:**
Receptionist?

**RC:**
Receptionist, yes. Big new receptionist. Oh my word, she's got it all er–

**RB:**
Up here?

**RC:**
No–

**RB:**
Down here?

**RC:**
No–

**RB:**
Where then?

**RC:**
She's got it all er–

**RB:**
All over?

**RC:**
No, she's got it all organised up there. Up at the doctors. 'Cos it used to be such a mess, but now it's completely re-organised. I just stood there in a, in a–

**RB:**
Queue?

**RC:**
No, in a–

**RB:**
Vest?

**RC:**
No, in a–

**RB:**
Draught?

**RC:**
No, in amazement.

**RB:**
Oh, amazement, yes.

**RC:**
Oh yes, it's like a conveyor belt up there. Mind you, it's all sex equality up there. You don't have separate cubicles. All the men had to take off their shirts and stand against one wall, and all the women took off their dresses and satin, er – satin–

**RB:**
Blouses?

**RC:**
No, satin, er–

**RB:**
Panties?

**RC:**
No, rows. Sat in rows along the other wall.

**RB:**
Oh, I see, yes.

**RC:**
I tell you who was up there. That young Julie.

**RB:**
Julie?

**RC:**
Yeah, you know. Her mother's got them big, er–

**RB:**
Teeth?

**RC:**
No, them big–

**RB:**
Bay windows?

**RC:**
No, them big Alsatians. You know, them ones she keeps taking up the common and they keep biting people in the er–

**RB:**
Leg?

**RC:**
No, in the er–

**RB:**
Bushes?

**RC:**
No, in the evenings. Well, her kid, Julie. She was up there.

**RB:**
Oh, what was she up there for?

**RC:**
Well, she was telling me, she went out one night with some young lad, and they fell in the duck pond, and now she's er–

**RB:**
Pregnant?

**RC:**
No, er–

**RB:**
Stagnant?

**RC:**
No, now she's er–

**RB:**
Fragrant?

**RC:**
No, she's off work with a cut foot. Doctor said she was lucky, with that duck pond, it could've been a lot worse. It could have been a septic er–

**RB:**
Septic tank?

**RC:**
Toenail. Septic toenail. Here, I had a lucky escape last week.

**RB:**
Oh, yes?

**RC:**
Well, I was in the canteen, sitting opposite a woman with one of those, er–

**RB:**
One of those looks in her eye?

**RC:**
No, one of those er–

**RB:**
Hourglass figures?

**RC:**
No, one of those apple turnovers.

**RB:**
Oh, yes. Go on.

**RC:**
She's got this turnover and she kept er–

**RB:**
Turning it over?

**RC:**
No, she kept toying with it.

**RB:**
Oh, toying with it.

**RC:**
Yes. Well anyway, we was sitting right opposite, at this little table, and suddenly I felt her er–

**RB:**
Hand on your knee?

**RC:**
No, I felt her–

**RB:**
Hand on your other knee?

**RC:**
No.

**RB:**
You felt her what? What did you feel?

**RC:**
I felt her looking at me. And I could tell she fancied me, see. So we got talking, about gardening, and it came up in the conversation that I was very good on er–

**RB:**
On the lawn?

**RC:**
No, I'm very good on er–

**RB:**
Friday nights?

**RC:**
No, very good on pest control. So she said, what are you doing Saturday afternoon, she said. And I told her this week I'm going shopping for the wife, 'cos she'll be resting in bed with er–

**RB:**
With any luck.

**RC:**
No, with her trouble. So, anyhow, this woman said, why not come round Saturday afternoon for a couple of hours, she says. I can sunbathe on the patio, and you can have a look at my big ...

**RB:**
Big what?

**RC:**
Bigonias.

**RB:**
Oh, bigonias, yes.

**RC:**
They're covered in blackfly, she said. Well, I was taken by surprise, rather, so at first I said I couldn't, as I hadn't got a long enough, er–

**RB:**
What?

**RC:**
You know, a long enough, er–

**RB:**
Garden spray?

**RC:**
No, a long enough shopping list to be out that long.

**RB:**
Oh. So didn't you go then?

**RC:**
Yes, I went, eventually, 'cos she pleaded with me. She said if I didn't, she would have to spend all afternoon lying there on her, er–

**RB:**
On her back?

**RC:**
No, on her–

**RB:**
On her front?

**RC:**
No, her–

**RB:**
Begonias?

**RC:**
No, on her own.

**RB:**
Oh, her own.

**RC:**
So, anyway, there she was in her sun suit, and after I'd sprayed her blackfly, we walked down the garden, and I said "I would like to kiss you" I said, and she immediately got on her, er–

**RB:**
Hands and knees?

**RC:**
No, her high horse.

**RB:**
Oh, her high horse, oh yes.

**RC:**
Certainly not, she said, I think you're a little, er–

**RB:**
A little raver?

**RC:**
No, a little–

**RB:**
A little drunk?

**RC:**
No, a little premature.

**RB:**
Oh, a little premature drunk.

**RC:**
"I've only known you half an hour", she

says – "You'll have to wait another ten minutes", and she disappeared indoors. So I spent the next ten minutes re-arranging her rock garden, and then went indoors, and there she was in the all, er– in the all, er–

**RB:**
In the all-together?

**RC:**
No, in the 'all of the 'ouse. Anyhow, we had a lovely time, and afterwards she gave me a round of, er–

**RB:**
Round of applause?

**RC:**
No, a round of, er–

**RB:**
Round of golf?

**RC:**
No, a round of toast and a cup of tea. But I was a bit worried when I got home. The wife was waiting for me. I thought she'd found out. Do you know what she gave me?

**RB:**
Which reminds me – I'm late for me supper. Cheerio, Bert, see you in the canteen for an apple turnover!

*(He exits, and the barman approaches.)*

**BARMAN:**
I couldn't help overhearing, Bert. You've got me all interested now – what happened?

**RC:**
Well, I was a bit worried when I got home, 'cos the wife was waiting for me. I thought she'd found out. Do you know what she gave me?

**BARMAN:**
What?

**RC:**
As soon as I walked in, she gave me a bunch of ...

**BARMAN:**
A bunch of fives right up the throat?

**RC:**
No, a bunch of begonias! Ta-ta, Charlie!

# INVENTION CONVENTION

*Exterior – a hotel entrance. Zoom in on sign saying "Welcome to the Inventors' Convention".*

*Cut to studio.*

*A hotel bedroom. RC is unpacking his suitcase. RB enters. He is normally dressed, but has pink hair.*

**RB:**
Ah, good evening, Sanders. Rodney Sanders. I'm your room-mate.

**RC:**
*(eyeing him warily)* Ah, yes. Snetterton, P J Percy.

**RB:**
I know what you're looking at. Terrible colour, isn't it?

**RC:**
Well, no, it's ... unusual.

**RB:**
It's one of the two drawbacks of my invention. Hair-restorer – amazing stuff, but it makes your hair pink. *(Takes bottle from briefcase.)* What's your invention?

**RC:**
Er – oh, this. Aerosol. Makes you invisible.

**RB:**
No!

**RC:**
You spray it on. Only lasts for 30 seconds at the moment though. That's one of it's two drawbacks. But it's amazing.

**RB:**
Fantastic. *(Looks at watch.)* Good lord, time for another dose of hair-restorer.

**RC:**
Dose? Do you drink it?

**RB:**
Oh yes – tastes like sherry. Listen, do me a favour, old chap – pour me out a dose. I must spend a penny. Tumbler full of that, with a teaspoon full of water.

*(He goes to the bathroom.)*

**RC:**
*(going to washbasin)* Tumblerful of this, and a teaspoon of water. Right.

*(He prepares the mixture, and we hear the chain pulled. RB comes back.)*

**RB:**
Ah, cheers. *(Takes drink, drinks it.)* By God, that's a strong one. Just a teaspoon in there, is there?

**RC:**
No, you said a tumblerful with a teaspoonful of water.

**RB:**
Oh, God, did I? Should have been the other way round. Never mind. I'm dying to see your invention, old boy.

**RC:**
Tell you what then – I'll ring for the chambermaid, and then make you invisible – then you can creep up behind her and surprise her.

*(He presses a bell.)*

**RB:**
I say, what fun.

**RC:**
Now – stand over there, about five feet away.

*(RB does so – now on overlay.)*

**RC:**
Here goes. *(He sprays aerosol. RB fades out.)* Now – you've gone – see? Look in the mirror. *(A knock on the door.)* Look out! Here she comes!

*(A pretty parlourmaid enters.)*

**MAID:**
You rang, sir?

**RC:**
Yes, what is the room service menu?

**MAID:**
Well, sir, if you fancy a little WHOOPS!

*(She reacts violently to an unseen hand.)*

**RC:**
Pardon?

**MAID:**
*(looking round)* Er – you can either OOH! OH! Oh, dear!

*(She wriggles about, looking round wildly.)*

**RC:**
Are you alright?

**MAID:**
I feel most peculiar, sir. I think I'd better go and OOPS! *(Her skirt flies up – on nylon, tied to her own wrists.)* Ooh! Ooer! Get off!

*(She rushes from the room. RB's laughter is heard.)*

**RC:**
Just in time! You'll start fading back any second!

*(RB does so, over in the corner, as before. However, his hair is now very long and thick.)*

**RB:**
That's a great joke!

**RC:**
So's your hair, old chap.

**RB:**
*(looks in mirror)* I say. Must be that overdose. Never mind – can always get a haircut. Here, let's have a go with that spray. *(Takes spray from RC.)* Stand over there, go on. *(RC does so, and is sprayed, and disappears.)*

**RB:**
Fantastic! Where are you?

*(No reply – RB, searching for him, goes into the bathroom. Knock on door – in comes the maid, with the manager)*

**MANAGER:**
Anyone around?

*(RB emerges from bathroom. His hair is now below his shoulders, and very thick. It hangs over his face.)*

**RB:**
Ah.

**MANAGER:**
Is this the man, Sandra?

**MAID:**
No – no, that's not him. This was a little chap. With ordinary hair.

**MANAGER:**
This girl says she – felt something, in this room.

**RB:**
Probably static electricity. You get it with nylon carpet.

**MANAGER:**
You don't feel static electricity in your OOH!

*(He suddenly jumps.)*

**MAID:**
Ooh.

*(She too jumps.)*

**MANAGER:**
*(to her)* How dare you!

**MAID:**
Ooh, you're as bad as the others.

*(She slaps his face.)*

**RB:**
Just a minute!

*(but they have stormed out.)*

**RC:**
*(voice off)* Fun, isn't it?

*(He enters RB's shot.)*

**RB:**
It's truly amazing. The most wonderful invention I've ever seen. It's sure to win the prize.

**RC:**
Yours is pretty fantastic. I've never seen hair grow like that in my life. By the way – you said it had two drawbacks, like my invention. What is the other drawback?

**RB:**
Well, it weakens the roots of the hair. You have to be very careful to avoid sudden shocks, otherwise it could all fall out.

**RC:**
I see. Nasty.

**RB:**
Yes. What's your other drawback?

**RC:**
Well – the spray causes the molecules in the body to reach a highly volatile state. In other words, if you do it too much, you could actually explode.

**RB:**
Dear, dear. How much is too much?

**RC:**
No idea, old chap. Maybe I've already done it too much. Anyway, I'd better stop, otherwise I might–

*(There is a loud explosion, and RC's clothes fall empty to the ground.)*

**RB:**
*(off)* Oh, my God!

*(Cut to RB. He sits, completely bald, with a mountain of pink hair around him.)*

# HUMPHREY AND GODFREY (3)

*RB and RC in armchairs, in their London club.*

**RB:**
I say, Humphrey.

**RC:**
What is it, Godfrey?

**RB:**
You know, no matter how hot the day is, at night it gets dark.

**RC:**
Yes. It's the same in America.

**RB:**
Just come back, haven't you?

**RC:**
Mm.

**RB:**
Did you go for pleasure, or did the wife go with you?

**RC:**
Went alone. Very grand hotel.

**RB:**
Really?

**RC:**
Yes. So grand that even the guests have to use the service entrance.

**RB:**
That is grand.

**RC:**
Funny people, the Americans, though. On the plane going over, a woman collapsed. Doctor, sitting on one side of her, refused to help. Said he was on holiday.

**RB:**
Amazing.

**RC:**
Chap sitting other side of her said "That's disgraceful." Doctor said "Would you carry on your profession if you were holiday?" "I certainly would" said the other chap. "Alright, what is your profession?" he said. "I'm a fishmonger" said the other chap, and he picked the woman up, loosened her clothing and sold her two pounds of haddock.

# AN ODD COUPLE

*Two gents in a slightly shabby living room. RC in his vest and trousers, ironing a shirt. RB enters in his vest, drying his hair – he has just washed it.*

**RB:**
'Ere, Tony.

**RC:**
What?

**RB:**
You remember old Mr Whatsisname who used to come to the pub?

**RC:**
Who?

**RB:**
Used to come in with that big woman, you know.

**RC:**
I don't know who you mean.

**RB:**
Big woman, wore a fur coat. Lives near Dennis' mother.

**RC:**
Dennis who?

**RB:**
Dennis. Masses of dark hair; big with it; sallow boy. Worked for that printing firm in Surbiton.

**RC:**
What printing firm?

**RB:**
The firm that was supposed to do all Winston Churchill's visiting cards during the war.

**RC:**
Who?

**RB:**
Winston Churchill. The war leader! Ooh, my Gawd! The chap who saved us from the clutches of Adolf.

**RC:**
Adolf who?

**RB:**
Hitler. Adolf Hitler. Don't tell me you don't know who Adolf Hitler was.

**RC:**
'Course I know who Adolf Hitler was. I'm not a moron, Harold.

**RB:**
Well, then.

**RC:**
Well, what?

**RB:**
Well, he's dead.

**RC:**
Who, Hitler?

**RB:**
No! (Hitler!) You silly Queen! I was saying Churchill saved us from Hitler.

**RC:**
What about it?

**RB:**
I was just saying Churchill used to get all his visiting cards done by this firm where Dennis worked.

**RC:**
Dennis who?

**RB:**
I'm trying to tell you. The fellah whose mother lives near this big woman with a fur coat.

**RC:**
What big woman?

**RB:**
The WOMAN who used to COME IN THE PUB with old Mr Whatsisname.

**RC:**
Turner.

**RB:**
TURNER! MR TURNER! HIM, YES!

**RC:**
What about him?

**RB:**
HE'S DEAD!

**RC:**
They never proved it. He might be living under another name in South America.

# LIMERICK WRITERS

*A hotel lounge. A large banner saying "23rd Annual Convention of Limerick Writers". RC is in very cheap suit, RB very grand.*

**RC:**
How de do?

**RB:**
How de do?

**RC:**
My name's Dear. Arnold Dear. I come here every year.

**RB:**
My name's Algernon Crust. You write limericks, I trust?

**RC:**
No – I'm only here for the beer. *(RB looks disdainful.)*
Just a joke, just a rhyme and a joke
I can't help it
I'm that sort of bloke–
Just a joke and a rhyme
And a jolly good time.
*(confidentially)* What I really came for was a–

**RB:**
*(offers cigarettes)* Smoke?

**RC:**
No, I won't. Please don't think that I'm rude
Smoking's fine if you're in the right mood;
I smoke with my food
My wife smokes in the nude
(As long as it doesn't intrude!)

**RB:**
Tell me, what sort of rhymes do you do?

**RC:**
Oh, just things about ladies from Crewe
Who step from a train
Catch their foot in a drain
And the porters all – what about you?

**RB:**
Oh, I've published a book – and it sells;
It's described by the Bishop of Wells
As the best of its kind
And my work is confined
To the loo walls of 4 star hotels.

**RC:**
Oh, of course, published by the AA!

**RB:**
Recommended by Egon Ronay,
Yes, it's perfectly true–
And BBC 2
Made it into a *Play For Today*.

**RC:**
You're the wit who writes things about marriages
On the walls of first-class railway carriages!
Please tell me once more
The classic you saw
On the seat of the boys room at Claridges!

**RB:**
*(Ah!)* "My mother, a born intellectual
Made me a complete homosexual"
Underneath wrote some fool
"If I gave her the wool
Would she make me one?" – not ineffectual!

**RC:**
That's the stuff that I wish I could write
But I sit and I ponder all night
I end up with some tale
Of a cow and a pail
And the last line's a load of–

**RB:**
Quite, quite.
My room's pretty grotty – how yours?

**RC:**
Well, there's woodworm in both of the doors
There's a hole in the floor
But what worries me more
Is the dry-rot I found in my drawers.

**RB:**
Have you noticed that little blonde tart?

**RC:**
Oh – how pretty she is – bless her heart.

**RB:**
She's a right little goer!

**RC:**
Oh, how well do you know her?

**RB:**
Well, she's not a real blonde, for a start.

**RC:**
With her looks, I don't think I'd quibble.

**RB:**
I must say, I fancy a nibble–

**RC:**
She's inspired you, no doubt,
With the urge to give out–

**RB:**
Yes – let's go to the gents for a scribble.

# "HIGH NIGH"

*"Harrid's" linen and haberdashery
department. RB is being served by a young
male assistant.*

**ASSISTANT:**
Anything else, sir?

**RB:**
Yes, I'd like some tiles.

**ASSISTANT:**
Tiles, sir?

**RB:**
Yes – bathroom tiles.

**ASSISTANT:**
Are these for fixing yourself, sir?

**RB:**
Fixing myself? No, they're for drying
myself. Tiles, man. After the bath, give
yourself a good brisk tiling dine.

**ASSISTANT:**
Oh – towels – yes, sir – I'll show you a
selection. Excuse me a moment.

*(He goes.)*

*(RC appears, also an upper-class type.)*

**RC:**
*(recognising RB)* Hello, Charles!

**RB:**
Hello, Aubrey! Bit of shopping, what?

**RC:**
Rather! Damn good place this. Everything
for the Heiss.

**RB:**
Absotively. I often come here for the Old
Spice.

**RC:**
Old Spice? Wrong department, old boy.
Toiletries, second floor.

**RB:**
No, no – the wife – the speiss, the little
woman. I'm buying for.

**RC:**
Ah. I'm here for soup.

**RB:**
Oh, what kind?

**RC:**
Brine.

**RB:**
Ah. Bit too salty for me, brine.

**RC:**
No, brine. Brine Windsor. Wife brought
up on the stuff. Lived very near here, you
see. She's a sly person.

**RB:**
What, Angela? Oh, I wouldn't say that.
Little devious at times, but–

**RC:**
No – sly – she was born in Sly.
Maidenhead, Sly and Windsor, you know.

**RB:**
Ah.

**RC:**
Food department here excellent. Fish,
pâtés, game.

**RB:**
Cheeses.

**RC:**
What's the matter, old boy?

**RB:**
No, I was just saying cheeses. Wonderful
cheeses, all rind.

**RC:**
We don't eat the rind.

**RB:**
No, all rind. Generally.

**RC:**
Oh yes, rather. I say – did you hear what
happened to Roger?

**RB:**
Roger Kimboley-Dimbleby? From
Wimbledon?

**RC:**
Kimber-Dimber-Wimbers, yes.

**RB:**
Haven't heard abite him for years. Last
time I saw him he was a little tight.

**RC:**
Drunk?

**RB:**
No, a little tite for a bookmaker. A
bookmaker's tite. Going around with a gel

called Poopsie Benedict.

**RC:**
He left her, old boy. Consistently lied.

**RB:**
Did she? Deceitful, what?

**RC:**
No, lide, old dear. Consistently noisy.

**RB:**
Ah.

**RC:**
No, he's with Dulcima Paget at present.
They're both in trouble. He was fined in
the park, you know.

**RB:**
Fined? Fined for doing what?

**RC:**
No, fined – discovered. By the park keeper.
And she was beside him on the grind.

**RB:**
Good gracious! Scandalous. I don't know
what he sees in her.

**RC:**
Well, he said that although she hasn't got
an attractive face, she has a wonderful
mind.

**RB:**
Well, yes, she's got two wonderful minds,
we know that. Stick out a mile.

**RC:**
No, brain, old fellow. Got it up here.

**RB:**
Oh, got you. Listen old chap, it's awfully
nice to see you – fancy a drinky-poos?

**RC:**
What about your tiles?

**RB:**
Can't be bothered to wait. Fancy a bite to
eat?

**RC:**
Well, I am a bite to eat myself.

**RB:**
Quite a big bite too! Come on.

*(They start to move off.)*

**RC:**
Yes, we'd better hurry. When I came in there was a man with a placard saying "The end of the world is nigh".

**RB:**
*(as they exit)* What, absolutely right nigh? This very minute? Good lord (etc. etc.)

*(They are gone.)*

# HUMPHREY AND GODFREY (4)

*RB and RC in armchairs, in their London club.*

**RC:**
I say, Godfrey.

**RB:**
What is it, Humphrey?

**RC:**
You've got your shoes on the wrong feet.

**RB:**
Impossible. These are the only feet I've got. Anyway, my head's in no fit state to think about my feet.

**RC:**
Hung over?

**RB:**
Absolutely draped, old chap.

**RC:**
Well, cheer up old lad – no one ever died of a hangover.

**RB:**
Don't say that, Humphrey. It's only the hope of dying that's keeping me alive.

**RC:**
Who were you with, Godfrey?

**RB:**
Geoffrey, Humphrey. We both left the party together. He was so drunk I couldn't see him. I took him to the West End for coffee.

**RC:**
Should never give coffee to a drunk. All you get is a wide-awake drunk. Is he better now?

**RB:**
Getting better. He's in hospital.

**RC:**
Hospital? Why?

**RB:**
We were sitting on Westminster Bridge, playing who could lean over the farthest, and he won.

# FAT-HEADS REVISITED

*Two yokels meet by the barn. RB sitting, RC enters.*

**RC:**
Morning.

**RB:**
Arternoon.

**RC:**
Is somebody sitting here?

**RB:**
Yes.

**RC:**
Who?

**RB:**
Me.

**RC:**
Well, I know that. I'm not daft.

**RB:**
I am. *(Noticing RC limping)* What's making you limp?

**RC:**
I'm not limp.

**RB:**
No, your feet. Lost a shoe?

**RC:**
*(holding up both feet)* No. Just found one.

**RB:**
Oh. Lucky it fits.

**RC:**
Bound to fit one of my feet. One of my feet's bigger than the other. Everybody has one foot bigger than the other.

**RB:**
I haven't. I'm just the opposite.

**RC:**
Eh?

**RB:**
One of my feet is smaller than the other. Ain't you got no shoes?

**RC:**
I got me best shoes. For Sundays, like. I bought a new tie an' all. But I had to take it back.

**RB:**
Why?

**RC:**
It were too tight.

*(RC notices a front door leaning against the*

*wall behind RB.)*

**RC:**
What's that door?

**RB:**
I take that around with me.

**RC:**
What for?

**RB:**
Well, the other day I lost the key, so in case anybody finds it and breaks into my house, I carry the door around.

**RC:**
That's clever. But what happens if you lose the door?

**RB:**
That's alright, I've left a window open.

**RC:**
Here, did you hear about old Rueben?

**RB:**
What?

**RC:**
Up in court yesterday.

**RB:**
Never.

**RC:**
He stole a calendar.

**RB:**
What did he get?

**RC:**
Twelve months. His trouble is, he drinks too much.

**RB:**
He told me he only drinks to calm himself.

**RC:**
Oh well, that explains it. Last Saturday night he was so calm he couldn't move.

**RB:**
Here. It's my birthday tomorrow. November the twelfth.

**RC:**
What year?

**RB:**
Oh, every year. I had two presents. A wristwatch with an alarm, and a bottle of aftershave. So if you hear anything and smell anything, it's me.

**RC:**
Oh, ar. Well, at least you won't be late for work. I'm always late for work.

**RB:**
Why's that?

**RC:**
I sleep very slowly.

**RB:**
I snore, I do. I snore so loud I wake meself up. But I've cured it now.

**RC:**
How?

**RB:**
I sleep in the next room.

**RC:**
Here, talking of snoring, it's my wife's birthday next week. She's asked for a coat made of animal skin.

**RB:**
What you going to give her?

**RC:**
A donkey jacket.

**RB:**
That's nice. Here, this is another present I got.

*(Shows umbrella, opens it. It has a four-inch circular hole in one section of it.)*

**RC:**
What's that hole for?

**RB:**
So you can see when it's stopped raining.

**RC:**
Here, seeing that hole reminds me. I looked through an hole in the fence up at that new nudist camp.

**RB:**
Ooh ar, I've heard about that. Do they have men and women in there?

**RC:**
I couldn't tell. They hadn't got any clothes on.

**RB:**
Oh, I see.

**RC:**
Well, I must sit here. I'm going up to the doctors. I don't like the look of my wife.

**RB:**
I'll come with you. I hate the sight of mine.

*(They exit.)*

# TIRED MP

*A television interview. RC is interviewing RB, a North Country MP. The MP is very drunk.*

**RC:**
Good evening. I have with me in the studio tonight, Mr Arnold Sidebottom, MP, a prominent back bencher, and a man who is well known for his frankness and outspokenness on matters of government policy. *(To RB)* It would be true to say, I think, Mr Sidebottom, that you are not a man to mince words?

**RB:**
Well – er – I – er – we all – I think you're – absolutely.

**RC:**
Quite. And I understand that you have just returned from a very tiring fact-finding tour of the Midlands?

**RB:**
S'correct, s'correct.

**RC:**
And you are obviously very tired.

**RB:**
Yes, I'm very tired. Yes, I am tired.

**RC:**
And you've probably got a bit of 'flu as well, haven't you?

**RB:**
I've had a few, yes.

**RC:**
Oh, you've had the 'flu. You must be awfully tired. Tell me, Mr Sidebottom, what conclusions have you reached after your tour?

**RB:**
Oh – I'll be alright in the morning.

**RC:**
Would you say the Midlands were in need of any special consideration regarding such problems as housing?

**RB:**
Er – special, yes! Consideration – no. Er –

*(He hesitates.)*

**RC:**
Do go on.

**RB:**
I don't propose to go further into that. That's as fur as I'm going. *(sings, delicately)* "I fell in love with Mary at the dairy, but Mary wouldn't fall in love with me–" *(he rises unsteadily and tries to execute a couple of dance steps)* "Down by the old mill stream, we used to sit and dream, Little did she know–" *(he flops down on the settee beside RC.)* How yer doing, alright?

**RC:**
I notice you've brought up the subject of agriculture, and dairy farming in particular. Would you say there is a noticeable decline in this industry?

**RB:**
By heck, we put a few away tonight, didn't we? Eh? Didn't we?

*(He leans his head on RC's shoulder.)*

**RC:**
So you would say there has been a putting aside of essential priorities, would you?

**RB:**
I bet our wives are wondering where we are. *(He smiles, then frowns.)* Where are we?

**RC:**
Mr Sidebottom–

**RB:**
I've got a lovely wife at home. *(Begins to weep)* A lovely woman, Daphne. Oh dear. I'll just have forty winks.

*(He is asleep on RC's shoulder.)*

**RC:**
Well, thank you, Arnold Sidebottom, for coming to the studio tonight–

**RB:**
*(In his sleep)* Oh, Gloria!

*(He cuddles RC.)*

**RC :**
–and telling us about your fact-finding tour.

**RB:**
Gloria, you're lovely! Sing me to sleep, Gloria!

# TRAIN SKETCH

**RC:**
*(whispering now)* And it only remains for me to wish you a very good night.

*(He sings very quietly through RB's snoring.)*

"Golden slumbers kiss your eyes,
Smiles awake you when you rise,
Sleep pretty baby, do not cry
And I will sing a lullaby."

# HUMPHREY AND GODFREY (5)

*RB and RC in armchairs, in their London club.*

**RC:**
I say, Godfrey.

**RB:**
What is it, Humphrey?

**RC:**
My doctor has advised me to give up golf.

**RB:**
Why? Did he examine your heart?

**RC:**
No, he had a look at my score card.

**RB:**
Ah. Does he play at all?

**RC:**
My doctor? Yes. Terrible cheat. He always puts down one stroke less than he actually took. We caught him out the other day, though.

**RB:**
How was that?

**RC:**
He got a hole in one and he put down nought.

*An old-fashioned train carriage – bench seats. A man sits reading a newspaper at one end of the bench. RC enters, sits down next to him.*

**RC:**
Morning, John. Blowing up a bit rough.

**MAN:**
Yes. How's the wife?

**RC:**
Blowing up a bit rough. She's at a funny age. That Esther Rantzen's been giving her ideas again.

**MAN:**
About being liberated?

**RC:**
No, about getting her teeth fixed.

*(RB enters with girl. They sit, RB next to RC, girl on other side.)*

**RB:**
*(to girl)* Oh, what a rush. Alright, Deirdre?

**GIRL:**
Yes thanks, Mr Prentice. Bit late this morning. How's the garden?

**RB:**
Not bad, not bad. Lot to do. Bit overgrown.

**RC:**
She's very extravagant. I've told her, it's got to stop.

**RB:**
Lot of cutting back to do.

**RC:**
I said, we'll just have to cut back. So she appears yesterday with a new dress.

**RB:**
I've got his great big magnolia.

**RC:**
Big green thing with flowers all over it. Ghastly. She looks like the side of a house.

**RB:**
It's all up the side of the house. It's all hanging over.

**RC:**
It's all bulging out.

**RB:**
I'm going to pull it all off and have a good look at what's causing the trouble.

**RC:**
I told her – I don't care if she's got nothing to wear – it's going.

**RB:**
Then when I've stripped it down, I'll get it flat against the wall, and hope that something comes of it next spring.

**RC:**
I've suggested she goes to a massage parlour. There's a very nice one in Streatham. Topless.

**MAN:**
Really?

**RC:**
Yes. No roof.

**RB:**
Either that or just cut big bits off here or there. But that makes a bit of a mess.

**RC:**
I must say she's not keen.

**RB:**
The lawn's in a state as well. Must have a go at that.

**RC:**
They can do wonders with a woman's figure at those places, you know.

**RB:**
Get the heavy roller on it.

**RC:**
These spot-reducing vibrators are wonderful. They shook me, I can tell you.

**RB:**
It's the only way.

**RC:**
Makes a woman's figure flatter, smoother–

**RB:**
Well, when you're lying on it, you don't want it all lumps and bumps, do you?

**RC:**
Except in the right places, of course.

**RB:**
Quite. It's alright on the front rock garden and round the back of the herbaceous border.

*(They are now beginning to talk to each other.)*

**RC:**
Yes. But the trunk – now, that's different.

**RB:**
Oh yes, the trunk should be smooth.

**RC:**
And free from greenfly. Have you tried putting a grease-band round it?

**RB:**
Makes it slippery to climb. Anyway, my wife wouldn't wear one. I think the answer is a bigger bed.

**RC:**
Oh, definitely. Give your foliage more room to spread out.

**RB:**
Nothing need come into contact at all in a big bed – not if you don't want it to.

**RC:**
If you fill it with manure, it's a big help.

**RB:**
Oh, absolutely. I didn't know you knew so much about gardening.

**RC:**
What?

**RB:**
Filling the bed with manure.

**RC:**
No – I just thought that must be a good way to get a divorce. Come to think of it, you seem to know a lot about women.

**RB:**
No – my wife's just left me. But it hasn't stopped me gardening.

**RC:**
Oh. So you're on your own?

**RB:**
No – I'm digging with her. Come on, Deirdre.

*(They exit.)*

# LOOK HERE

*A small optician's in the high street. RC enters – he wears thick pebble glasses.*

**RC:**
Hello – anyone there? *(He moves to large mirror on wall behind counter.)* Ah, good morning. *(He leans, by mistake, on bell-push on counter.)* Oh, sorry.

**RB:**
*(Emerging from behind curtained alcove – he, too is wearing thick pebble glasses.)* Ah, good morning, Miss Prendergast. You're early.

**RC:**
Ah, good morning
*(turning vaguely in RB's direction)*

**RB:**
*(approaches, stands near him, but facing slightly in the wrong direction.)* Oh, sorry. Good morning.

**RC:**
Er – two pounds of potatoes, please.

**RB:**
No, sir – this is an optician's.

**RC:**
What?

**RB:**
Optician's, sir – it says so over the door.

*(Points in the wrong direction.)*

**RC:**
Oh, how silly of me. I was coming in to see you this morning anyway. Look, it's on my list – optician's and greengrocer's. *(Holds up list to side of RB's head.)* See?

**RB:**
*(not seeing)* Oh, I see. Oh good.

**RC:**
Yes, it was the wife's idea actually.

**RB:**
I understand, sir – won't you sit down?

*(He indicates a small table with a spikey ornament on top. RC is about to sit, but straightens up again.)*

**RC:**
You're new here, aren't you?

**RB:**
About six months I've been here.

**RC:**
Yes, I thought I hadn't seen you in here.

**RB:**
No, the other lady left to get married.

**RC:**
You're not a lady, are you?

**RB:**
No, no – I took her job. Do sit down.

**RC:**
*(This time he sits in the swivel chair.)* Thank you.

**RB:**
Cup of tea? I've just made it.

**RC:**
That would be very nice.

*(RB picks up milk jug from tea tray, pours milk into nearby plant pot.)*

**RB:**
Well now, sir, what seems to be the trouble?

**RC:**
Well, I've got a feeling my eyes aren't quite as good as they used to be.

**RB:**
Oh dear, what makes you think that?

**RC:**
Well, it started when I bumped into someone I hadn't seen for ages.

**RB:**
Oh, who was that?

**RC:**
Someone I work with at the office every day. And I suddenly realised I was always bumping into them: and it was ages since I'd seen them properly.

**RB:**
I see. Milk?

*(He picks up small copper watering can and pours water into cup: then hands it to RC.)*

**RC:**
Can be damned inconvenient at times. Do you ever wear glasses?

**RB:**
Er – occasionally, yes. Just for reading and seeing things.

**RC:**
Anyway, as I was passing, I thought I'd look in.

*(Drinks tea, reacts in surprise.)*

**RB:**
You obviously need something a bit stronger.

**RC:**
Possibly, just a bit.

**RB:**
Well now, let's try a bit of a test with the wall charts. *(He presses a button on the counter, and a revolving police bulb lights up on the other side of the stage, near the chart. RB steers himself towards it.)* Right, now then, take your glasses off. *(RC does so.)* Are they off?

**RC:**
Yes.

**RB:**
Right, now read the letters, starting from the top.

**RC:**
*(peers into space)* Er – no – could you just wave your arms about, I'm not quite sure of the direction.

**RB:**
*(waves his arms)* Over here – here we are.

**RC:**
*(peering)* No. No, that one's stumped me, I'm afraid.

**RB:**
Don't worry. Try this one. *(He reveals the next one – this just has a large "E" and underneath it "I" and "C".)* There, how's that?

**RC:**
Er – "A"?

**RB:**
*(peering closely at it)* No.

**RC:**
"B"? "C"?

**RB:**
Keep going.

**RC:**
"D"?

**RB:**
No.

**RC:**
"E"?

**RB:**
That's it. Next line.

**RC:**
*(peering)* No.

**RB:**
I'll give you a clue. What do you see with?

**RC:**
Your eye.

**RB:**
"I", good. Now, what do you do with your eye?

**RC:**
See.

**RB:**
"C", good, good. Try the next line.

**RC:**
Is there a next line?

**RB:**
*(peering closer)* Probably not.

**RC:**
I really couldn't see any of that last chart, you know.

**RB:**
Don't worry, we'll get it sorted out. Just a

matter of trial and error. Now then, try this. *(He pulls a cord – the curtains covering the rh wall part, revealing a single six foot "A".)*

**RC:**
Ah, er – "A".

**RB:**
Good, excellent. No help from me either.

**RC:**
"I".

**RB:**
No, that's the hat stand–

**RC:**
"H".

**RB:**
*(as we see a shot of the "H"-shaped bookcase)* No, you're reading the furniture now. Just hang on–

**RC:**
Sorry.

**RB:**
*(Takes a long, thin lathe of wood from where it stands by the wall, near him, and points it in the direction of RC.)* Now – see if you can grab this long stick.

*(RC manages to grab it eventually. RB feels his way along it, hand over hand, homing in on RC until he reaches him.)*

**RB:**
Thanks awfully. Excellent. Now, I'll just get the test frames and lenses. Shan't be a jiffy– *(manages to locate the trolley, pushes it down towards RC, hits chair with a crash.)* Oops, careful. Now, let's put these test frames on for you – just sit still, that's it– *(he has arrived the wrong side of RC and puts the frames on the back of his head. He feels RC's hair.)* Ah – well you know your trouble, don't you?

**RC:**
What?

**RB:**
You've let your hair grow over your eyes.

**RC:**
No, no – I'm round here. Follow the sound of my voice.

**RB:**
Oh yes, sorry. *(He finally gets the frames on RC's nose.)* Now then *(picks up lens, slots it in)* Is that better or worse?

**RC:**
Er – worse.

**RB:**
*(Picks up spoon, slots it in.)* How about that?

**RC:**
Fractionally better, I think.

**RB:**
Bit better. I'll leave that one in then. And this?

*(Adding another one.)*

**RC:**
No, worse.

**RB:**
Right. Well, that looks about it then. Have a look at some frames now, shall we? Follow me, would you?

*(They walk in opposite directions, RB to counter, RC towards wall.)*

**RB:**
No, over here!

**RC:**
Oh, sorry. *(They make contact at the counter.)*

**RB:**
Now, *(takes off RC's glasses, puts them down on counter)* try these frames. *(Puts on ordinary large pair of frames.)* There, have a look in the mirror. *(Indicates a photograph of a grey-haired lady in spectacles.)*

**RC:**
*(peering at it)* Mm, yes – I think they make me look a bit older. What do you think?

**RB:**
*(looking at photo)* Yes, I see what you mean. *(Takes off his own glasses.)* Just a minute. This isn't a mirror, it's a photograph of an old lady.

**RC:**
Haven't you got any others?

**RB:**
*(puts down his own glasses, picks up RC's, in close-up)* Well, there's these–

**RC:**
*(gropes around, picks up RB's glasses.)* What about these? *(Puts them on.)* Good heavens. These are marvellous! I can see perfectly!

**RB:**
No, they're mine–

**RC:**
No, they're not. *(pointing)* You've got yours in your hand, look.

**RB:**
Have I? *(Puts them on.)* Good heavens! I say, it's amazing. Everything's becoming clear to me.

**RC:**
How can I ever thank you? You'll send me the bill, naturally?

**RB:**
Of course not – wouldn't dream of it. Fair's fair. I've benefited as well.

**RC:**
True. Cheerio, then!

**RB:**
Bye! *(RC exits. RB looks round him.)* So – this is where I work, is it?

175

# HUMPHREY AND GODFREY (6)

*RB and RC in armchairs, in their London club.*

**RB:**
I say, Humphrey.

**RC:**
What is it, Godfrey?

**RB:**
See that tall chap over there?

**RC:**
Well-dressed, sprightly sort of bloke?

**RB:**
That's him. Five years ago he was destitute – in rags. All due to drink.

**RC:**
Damned curse, drink is. Fancy another?

**RB:**
No, thanks. Luckily, he met one of those temperance chappies, who told him just to have a look at where his money was going to – the rich publicans, smartly dressed, with sports cars and places in the country, while he, the drunkard, was penniless. All due to man's insatiable desire for alcohol.

**RC:**
And that put him on the right road, eh?

**RB:**
Absolutely.

**RC:**
Gave up drink completely?

**RB:**
No, he bought a pub.

# JASON KING

*Captions, as close as possible to the original. After captions, a close-up of a letter, held by middle-aged female hand. RC's voice, as Jason King, over it, reading the contents.*

*Slow mix to a shot of Magdalen College, Oxford, passing off it to the river – perhaps a punt gliding underneath the bridge.*

*Cut to another shot of a more secluded part of the river. A punt comes round the bend – RC, as Jason King, reclines in it. Behind him, a beautifully muscular girl is punting the boat along, effortlessly. She wears a one-piece swimsuit.*

**RC:**
*(over the above)* My dear Aunt Augusta – I thought you might enjoy receiving a letter from your dear old Oxford, especially as it is written in the fair hand of your loving nephew, Jason King. I am up here to be made an honorary Doctor of Philosophy, for my services to mankind, and, more especially, womankind.

*(A shot of RC's very with-it shoes, platform heels. Pan past them to him.)*

I've recently met a very charming girl named Angela Fitz-Upton – I think you knew her father. I've taken her on the river, and generally seen quite a lot of her.

*(We pan up Angela during the above dialogue.)*

She has 9 O levels, 5 A levels, and is interesting on several other levels as well. My curiosity was really aroused, however, when she told me she was a pole-vaulter. She certainly knows how to handle a punt pole. Yes, I have to report that dear old Oxford remains a haven of peace in the midst of a troubled society. There's even time for an afternoon snooze.

*(RC, in close-up, closes his eyes. As soon as he does so, Angela screams. RC opens his eyes again, looks at Angela. She points out of*

*frame. RC's eyes follow her finger. Cut to a
long shot of a punt – a body is sprawled, face
downward across the punt. The feet stick out,
trailing in the water. Close-up – RC.)*

**RC:**
How ghastly!

*(Cut to body again, then back to close-up RC.)*

**RC:**
He's wearing the same shoes.

*(He looks up – we cut to wide shot of RB on
opposite bank. He plays Miss Wilberforce, a
lesbian in tweeds. She carries a butterfly net
and has her hair in a straight, chopped-off
page-boy style. She is striding across the field
and stops suddenly as she sees the body. Cut
to close-up RC, as if continuous.)*

**RC:**
So you are the famous literary giant and
detective-story writer, Miss Wilberforce. I
must say, you make delicious fruit cake–

*(Pull back – we are in Miss W's lodgings – a
mixture of twenties and Edwardian –
butterflies in cases, dark walls – cluttered. RB
and Angela sit on a chaise longue, RC in
armchair. They are taking tea.)*

**RC:**
In fact you seem to be generally, a very
accomplished woman.

**RB:**
Never mind my accomplishments – what
about the body?

**RC:**
Well, there's certainly room for a little
improvement there.

**RB:**
Not my body, Mr King. The body of the
young man floating in the river.

**RC:**
In the punt on the river.

**RB:**
It's the same thing.

**RC:**
It isn't – you try it.

**RB:**
The point is, what have you managed to
find out about him?

**RC:**
Well, according to the local cop shop, he
was a brilliant young don named Alistair
Tyson.

**RB:**
Tyson! Golly Moses, I knew him. Was he
murdered?

**RC:**
Miss Wilberforce, before I answer that
question, may I make an impertinent
observation?

**RB:**
I'm all ears.

**RC:**
No, that wasn't it. It's just that the police
have asked me only to discuss the case
with reliable people, you won't let it go
any further, will you? Even under
pressure? Either of you.

**RB:**
Don't worry, I can be as tough as the next
man.

**RC:**
More so, I shouldn't wonder.

**RB:**
You don't have to worry about me.

*(Beaming, and grasping Angela's knee.)*

**RC:**
No, I'm sure I don't. *(In passing)* Your
hand's on Angela's knee.

**RB:**
*(ignoring this)* And I know Angela won't let

it go any further, will you, my dear?

**RC:**
I'm damned sure she won't. Very well then – yes, he was murdered. Poisoned with deadly nightshade.

**RB:**
I knew it! Professor Sax.

**RC:**
Who?

**RB:**
Professor of Botany. Sax, spelled SAX. Could it be? Is it possible? He's come back – no, that's impossible. But he was a man of botany. Hated Tyson – yes, it's got to be!

**RC:**
Do you know something? Put that to music and you've got a hit.

**RB:**
What?

**RC:**
Would you mind explaining what you're driving at?

**RB:**
Professor Sax was always jealous of young Tyson's success as a botanist. He swore to kill him once, at a party. The Professor, do you see, was a great amateur conjuror, and used to perform at parties with his glamorous young assistant, Juanita.

**RC:**
I bet you enjoyed that.

**RB:**
It was marvellous. Marvellous. Such an attractive girl. They did some wonderful tricks together. Then, quite suddenly, she disappeared. And almost immediately, so did he.

**RC:**
Oh, I've never seen that done. Must have gone well with the audience.

**RB:**
No, no, it wasn't a trick – I mean they disappeared from Oxford. Never heard of again, either of them. But I know that the dead man had been making advances to Juanita. And Professor Sax didn't like it.

**RC:**
Then I'd say that Sax is our man, wouldn't you? Decided to re-emerge from retirement, to perform a final trick.

**RB:**
If he is back, someone is bound to have seen him. He was so well-known in Oxford. Ask anyone.

**RC:**
That, my dear lady, is precisely what I shall do. Ask everyone.

**RB:**
I don't follow you.

**RC:**
No, and I'd rather you didn't – and I know I speak for Angela as well. We're going to carry out a survey.

*(Cut to film – RC, with clipboard, stopping man in the street.)*

**RC:**
Excuse me, sir, but have you seen anything of Sax lately?

*(Man reacts – if possible, it should be a genuine passer-by. He moves off, woman approaches.)*

**RC:**
*(to her)* Can you tell me anything about Sax?

*(She looks offended. Now a very wide shot – RC questioning young woman.)*

**RC:**
I wonder if you can help me, I'm looking for Sax.

*(Girl stalks off. RC approaches middle-aged*

*woman – use RC's double – he asks question, woman knocks him flat.)*

*(Cut to Angela, with clipboard, in a park. She stops a man, says something to him. He leaps on her, bearing her to the ground. We cut away just in time, back to RC still being attacked by the middle-aged woman, now surrounded by a small knot of onlookers.)*

*(Cut to studio – a small Chinese restaurant – very moody.)*

**RB:**
So your survey wasn't a great success?

**RC:**
In one way, no. But I found out some fascinating facts for my next book.

**RB:**
Oh – do you write books? I don't think I read your last one.

**RC:**
No, my next one will be my first one. Although if I put in what I learnt yesterday, it could be my last one as well.

**RB:**
What are you calling it?

**RC:**
"Sex Habits of the Amazon Savage".

**RB:**
Then of what use is information about Oxford?

**RC:**
Well, why go to the Amazon when it's all happening here!

**RB:**
I think, Mr King, that you're pulling my leg.

**RC:**
Of course I'm not.

**RB:**
Well, somebody is. *(Looking down – a*

*Chinese waiter emerges from under the table.)* What are you doing? Oh, I dropped my fork, did I? Thank you. *(The waiter bows out.)* I'm so glad we chose to eat here – I have an enormous penchant for this sort of thing.

**RC:**
I know, you've just dropped some fried rice down it. *(Changes the subject.)* My studies yesterday evening, however, proved a little more worthwhile.

**RB:**
Oh, really? What were you studying?

**RC:**
History, Geography – and furniture removals.

**RB:**
Removals? That's not a subject.

*(The waiter arrives with dishes. He serves RC and Angela.)*

**RC:**
Oh, but it is – and a very fascinating one. A chap at Pickfords informed me that no furniture had been moved in or out of a certain flat, for at least thirty years. And my historic studies took me to the estate agent, who furnished proof that the flat was, and still is, owned by one Professor Sax. Which all adds up to something extremely fishy.

**WAITER:**
It's codfish.

**RC:**
Not the codfish, my dear fellow – and I'll thank you to keep your nose out of other people's stories. *(The waiter goes.)* Damned impertinence. My club is full of people like him.

**RB:**
Really? What's it called?

**RC:**
The Chinese Waiters' Club. D'you know it?

**RB:**
No.

**RC:**
However, I digress. My third and last subject, if you remember, was Geography. It didn't take very long to locate the flat. The address? Forty-nine, Wilton Street. Your address, Professor Sax.

*(RB makes to move.)*

**RC:**
Don't move. Angela has you covered by a small pistol strapped to her thigh. *(RB remains still)* I should have guessed – all that talk about the attractive Juanita – the fact that you ogled Angela the whole time. No wonder you were attracted to women – you're a man!

**RB:**
Damn you, King!

**RC:**
I've a whole host of questions to ask you.

**RB:**
Then I'm afraid they'll have to wait. You're lying about the pistol, King.

**RC:**
What makes you say that?

**RB:**
I've had my hand on her thigh all through dinner.

**RC:**
*(astonished)* Angela – you rotten turncoat!

*(RB leaps up, tipping the contents of the table over them and rushes out. RC attempts to follow, but his path is blocked by a waiter. RC grabs him by the shoulders and bangs his head upon an enormous Chinese gong which stands near the exit. We end the scene on the waiter's unconscious head, as he slides to the ground.)*

*(Cut to film – RB, rushing into frame and away from camera, down a college-lined*

*narrow street. He disappears round a corner just as RC's back rushes past camera. Close-up of RC)*

**RC:**
*(to himself)* He's making for the boats.

*(RC rushes after him. Cut to RB in punt, paddling as fast as he can. Cut to RC – also paddling in a punt. Intercuts close-ups on both, then a long shot as they enter and leave the frame, like the boat race. Back to close-ups of RB and RC as they paddle. Then RC's point of view as RB disappears round the bend in the river. Close-up – RC paddling, over this we hear a crash and a splash. RC reacts. His point of view again as he rounds the bend to find RB's punt, overturned. RC pulls alongside it. Close-up – RB's wig in the water. As RC fishes it out and holds it up, his voice over re-commences.)*

**RC:**
*(voice over)* My dear Aunt Agatha! The sequel to my last letter has yet to emerge – the Professor hasn't yet been found. Perhaps he made off into the bushes – or perhaps the Chinese meal weighed a little too heavily on him.

*(Cut to close-up RC – this time he is poling a punt, and is accompanied by a different girl in a swimsuit – but this one is lying in the punt, trailing her fingers in the water.)*

**RC:**
*(voice over)* In any event, I'm still enjoying my stay here at Oxford. I've ditched that terrible girl Angela, as she didn't seem to know who's side she was on. Are you sure it was her father you knew, and not her mother? *(Cut to close-up of girl – a model, by the look of her)* This new girl is much more me – except that she expects me to do all the work. She's also six foot tall, which means that I shall be kept very much on my toes for the next week or two.

*(Close-up – RC's platform shoes – he goes up on his toes as he poles the punt.)*

*(Close-up girl – looking. She suddenly bursts*

*out laughing. Pull out to a wide shot – the boat glides away from camera. RC isn't on it.)*

*(Close-up RC, desperately clinging to the pole, stuck in the river, the boat gently gliding away. RC slides slowly down the pole and into the river. The music swells up.)*

# KNOTTY PROBLEM

*A haberdasher's shop – old-fashioned. RB as assistant.*

**RB:**
Can I help you, sir?

**RC:**
Yes, please. I want a pair of laces.

**RB:**
Certainly, sir. Boot or shoe laces?

**RC:**
Shoe laces, please.

**RB:**
Black or brown, sir?

**RC:**
Black, please.

**RB:**
Short or long, sir?

**RC:**
Short.

**RB:**
I thought so. Do you prefer nylon or cotton?

**RC:**
Oh dear. I think I'll have cotton ones, please.

**RB:**
Do you prefer the rounded type or the flat ones?

**RC:**
I'll have the flat ones, please.

*(RB turns to drawer behind him and looks through contents.)*

**RB:**
I'm afraid that we haven't got any short black cotton flat shoe laces, sir.

**RC:**
Round ones, then?

**RB:**
No, sir – no short black cotton ones at all.

**RC:**
Nylon ones then?

**RB:**
No sir, sorry. No short black ones of any description.

**RC:**
Well, all right. I'll have brown ones.

**RB:**
No brown ones either, sir. No short laces at all.

**RC:**
All right – long ones then.

**RB:**
No, sir – no long ones either.

**RC:**
Well, what have you got?

**RB:**
Nothing. We don't sell shoe laces, sir. This is a fish shop.

**RC:**
A fish shop. It says "Haberdasher" over the door!

**RB:**
That's my name, sir. George Haberdasher.

**RC:**
But if it's a fish shop, why doesn't it look

like one?

**RB:**
Lowers the tone of the neighbourhood.
Sorry about the laces, sir.

**RC:**
Never mind – just give me a piece of cod
and sixpennyworth of chips.

**RB:**
Right, sir.

*(RB reaches below counter and produces a
piece of newspaper and shovels hot, steaming,
sizzling, succulent chips – not old, tired, dry
ones – onto it – adding a tender piece of cod.
camera goes in on this delicious sight.)*

# THE YOKELS

*Two vilage idiots meets on a stile.*

**RC:**
Morning.

**RB:**
Afternoon.

**RC:**
Nice evening, isn't it?

**RB:**
It's not as nice an evening as it was
yesterday morning.

**RC:**
No. Yesterday morning was a lovely
evening.

**RB:**
I blame the weather, you know.

**RC:**
You're the village idiot, aren't you?

**RB:**
Yes.

**RC:**
I'm the next village idiot.

**RB:**
How do you know?

**RC:**
I'm the idiot from the next village.

**RB:**
Oh. Were you elected?

**RC:**
No, picked. They put the names of the
three daftest people in the village in a hat
and mine was picked out.

**RB:**
Who were the other two?

**RC:**
The Vicar and the local MP.

**RB:**
Oh, you were lucky then.

**RC:**
I had an unfair advantage. My name was
in the hat twice.

**RB:**
How was that?

**RC:**
It were my hat. You always put your name
in your hat, don't you?

**RB:**
I don't.

**RC:**
What do you put in your hat, then?

**RB:**
Me head.

**RC:**
Oh. How did you get the job?

**RB:**
It was who had the funniest nose. And
they all picked mine.

**RC:**
I wouldn't pick your nose.

**RB:**
And I wouldn't pick yours.

**RC:**
How's the wife?

**RB:**
I haven't got a wife.

**RC:**
No, but how is she, anyway?

**RB:**
She's very well. We're getting married next month.

**RC:**
What, both of you?

**RB:**
'Course.

**RC:**
Who to?

**RB:**
Each other.

**RC:**
Oh, that's a coincidence.

**RB:**
She's being married in white.

**RC:**
What colour will you be in?

**RB:**
Me best suit. The one I had for me birthday.

**RC:**
You going to be married in your birthday suit?

**RB:**
Yes, why not?

**RC:**
It'll need pressing. Will she carry something up the aisle?

**RB:**
Yes, her father, most likely.

**RC:**
Oh. Well, I wish you Joy.

**RB:**
Who?

**RC:**
Joy. The Parson's daughter. I'm in love with her. I'm learning to write so I can write to her. Look what I wroted.

*(Shows RB a note.)*

**RB:**
You writted all that?

**RC:**
Yes, all rot by me, that is.

**RB:**
What's it say?

**RC:**
Dunno, I ain't learned to read yet.

**RB:**
That Parson's a funny-looking bloke. I wonder who picked his nose?

**RC:**
Eh?

**RB:**
I wonder who picked the parson's nose?

**RC:**
Yes, roll on Christmas.

**RB:**
They buried old Jack yesterday, in Shropshire.

**RC:**
Oh? What part?

**RB:**
All of him.

**RC:**
What did he have?

**RB:**
The shepherd's pie, I think.

**RC:**
What were his last words?

**RB:**
Let me out, I'm not dead. Does your mum know you're courting?

**RC:**
No, my mum don't approve. Her and my dad hate each other, but they can't get a divorce.

**RB:**
Why not?

**RC:**
They're not married.

**RB:**
Oh, so you were born out of wedlock?

**RC:**
No, I was born out by Matlock. You got any kids?

**RB:**
I've got three children and half of them are boys.

**RC:**
Oh, what's the other half?

**RB:**
They're boys as well.

**RC:**
Are they triplets?

**RB:**
Two of them are.

**RC:**
What's the other one?

**RB:**
A window dresser.

**RC:**
Oh. A Kentish man?

**RB:**
He is a bit, yes. Well, I'm going home for me supper.

**RC:**
What do you have for supper?

**RB:**
Pie. If I'm hungry, I cut it into four pieces and eat all four pieces. If I don't think I can eat four pieces, I only cut it into two pieces.

**RC:**
I'm harvesting my corn tomorrow.

**RB:**
Oh, yes? Do you grow corn?

**RC:**
No, it grows itself. I fertilise it. And the wife.

**RB:**
Well, we all know that.

**RC:**
I hope it's better than last year. It was so small the rooks had to kneel down to eat it.

**RB:**
You want to try sparrows.

**RC:**
Yes. Well, I'm off.

**RB:**
Oh, it's you, is it? I thought something was.

**RC:**
Are you going to help me with the harvesting tomorrow?

*(Orchestra begins intro to song.)*

**RB:**
Oh, yes – I love the harvest time.

*(Song: to the tune of "Come, landlord fill the Following Bowl" trad.)*

**BOTH:**
The harvest time is here again
The church is decked with barley
The vicar's wife is all dolled up
And looks a proper Charley.
She's pinned some barley on our coats
And tied a wheatsheaf round our throats
Very soon we'll get our oats
Hurrah, hurrah, the harvest.

**RB:**
Miss Jackson's home-made cowslip wine
It states upon the labels
Is vintage nineteen forty nine
It takes the paint off tables

**RC:**
Old Mrs Johnson's got a rare
Display of apples over there –
But you should see her daughter's pear!

**BOTH:**
Hurrah, hurrah, the harvest!

**RC:**
Our organist is Mister Keys
A man of many troubles–
There's water in his pipes 'n he's
Forever blowing bubbles.

**RB:**
His bellows they are real antiques
His pump is full of squirts and squeaks
He sits among the peas and leaks

**BOTH:**
Hurrah, hurrah, the harvest!

*(Segue into tune of "Lincolnshire Poacher" – trad.)*

**BOTH:**
At harvest time we make the hay and a-reaping we shall go.

**RB:**
We're off in a lorry with Winnie and Florrie and Jennifer-Jane and Jo.

**RC:**
The lorry it stops in a shady copse and we're out in the corn all day.

**BOTH:**
But there's never a doubt, when the moon comes out, we'll all be making hay. Oh! there's never a doubt, etc.

At harvest time we make the hay and dance upon the green–

**RC:**
It's clap your hands to a cheerful band and crown the village Queen
Now, young Doreen's our village queen
But she can't be with us today
So a feller called Stanley, who's not very manly, is going to be Queen of the May!

**BOTH:**
So – a feller called Stanley, etc.

**BOTH:**
At harvest time we make the hay and hold the village fête–

**RB:**
There's home-made tarts and hoops and darts, and guess young Phyllis's weight
Young Phyllis's weight was eight stone eight and Febbrey, March 'n May
Now it's ten stone three and it's plain to see that's she's been making hay!

**BOTH:**
Yes, it's ten stone three and it's plain to see that she's been making hay!

*(They exit.)*

# HUMPHREY AND GODFREY (7)

*RB and RC in armchairs, in their London club.*

**RB:**
I say, Humphrey.

**RC:**
What is it, Godfrey?

**RB:**
Who was that terrible woman you were with today?

**RC:**
That was my sister.

**RB:**
Of course. I should have noticed the resemblance. Just got married, hasn't she?

**RC:**
Yes. And do you know, she's married a man whom people invariably take an instant dislike to.

**RB:**
Why is that, do you think?

**RC:**
It saves time. They've just moved to Cheltenham. She loves Cheltenham. She says in Cheltenham breeding is everything.

**RB:**
Yes, well, we enjoy it in Kensington as well, but we also have other interests.

**RC:**
Funny thing is, although he's a bully, and idler and a drunk, she intends to have seventeen children by him.

**RB:**
Good grief, why on earth does she want to do that?

**RC:**
She says she's hoping to lose him in the crowd.

# MOSCOW NIGHTS

*The interior of a peasant's hovel somewhere in darkest Russia. Ivan (RC) is smoking his pipe by the fire. He has enormous eyebrows. Suddenly, the door bursts open, and his wife Olga (RB) looking more masculine than Ivan, staggers in amid a swirl of snow, whistling wind and the howling of wolves. She is loaded down with logs, which she dumps by the fire.*

**RC:**
Close the door, Olga Olgirlovitch. It's cyold outside.

**RB:**
It will make no difference. If I close the door it will still cyold outside.

*(But she does so.)*

**RC:**
It is the coldest summer we have had since lyast winter.

**RB:**
I know. I saw the gardener in the vegetable patch. He is frozen to the marrow. Styoke up the fire, Ivan Sonofabitch.

*(RC starts to do so.)*

**RC:**
Yes, we must keep warm. *(A pause.)* I heard a kalinka as I was crossing the square.

**RB:**
Ah, just fancy.

**RC:**
It was the brass monkeys on the gates of the Town Hall.

**RB:**
*(sits)* Oh, I am tired. It is you who should bring in the logs. You are the masculine one, not me.

**RC:**
That's not what they said at the Olympic Selection Committee.

**RB:**
Pah! *(He spits.)* A load of old women. Who gives a shot-put what they think.

**RC:**
Never mind, Olga Olgirlovitch. That was a long time ago. Let us have some tea.

**RB:**
You know, Ivan Sonofabitch – life is like a cup of tea.

**RC:**
Why, my dear?

**RB:**
Why, what?

**RC:**
Why is life like a cup of tea?

**RB:**
How should I know? What am I, a philosopher?

*(RC has taken a cup of tea from the samovar nearby and sips it.)*

**RC:**
Anything good on television tonight?

**RB:**
I don't know. I never know what is on.

**RC:**
Ah well, what difference does it make? We have no television set.

**RB:**
True. Where is our daughter, Tania?

**RC:**
She is out for a sleigh ride with Sasha Scratchanitch.

**RB:**
The chemist's son from the village? I don't like him.

**RC:**
He is a nice boy. Honest, polite – a good match for our daughter. Nothing wrong

with him.

**RB:**
He limps!

**RC:**
Only when he walks.

**RB:**
I prefer Dosser Digaditch.

**RC:**
The council worker? I think he's a spy.

**RB:**
He asked me what I thought of Red China.

**RC:**
What did you tell him?

**RB:**
I said I thought on a yellow tablecloth it would look very pretty.

**RC:**
I cannot find my spare pair of socks.

**RB:**
I put them somewhere in a safe place.

**RC:**
Where?

**RB:**
I cannot remember.

**RC:**
Never mind. They were dirty anyway. *(Sips tea.)* This tea is good. It is warm and strong and brown, like my socks.

**RB:**
Now I remember where I put them. In the Samovar. *(Fishes out RC's socks.)* You want another cup?

**RC:**
No. I must go and feed the chickens.

**RB:**
What about the pigs?

**RC:**
There's no food for the pigs.

**RB:**
But they are hungry.

**RC:**
I will think of something. *(Opens the door and stands there in the howling wind and hurtling snow, shouting.)* It is still snowing. It is very cold.

**RB:**
*(shouting)* Well, hurry up and close the door. *(RC does so.)* Otherwise we will freeze to death!

*(RC opens door again.)*

**RC:**
What did you say?

**RB:**
I said we will freeze to death!

*(RC shuts the door again. RB wrings out the socks into the samovar, and puts them in front of the fire. A telephone rings. RB picks up an ancient stand-up phone.)*

**RB:**
Hello? No, I'm sorry, we're not on the phone.

*(RC enters. No wind or snow at all.)*

**RB:**
Did you feed the chickens?

**RC:**
Yes. I fed them to the pigs.

**RB:**
But what about the eggs? Pigs don't lay eggs.

**RC:**
No – but chickens don't lay bacon.

**RB:**
True.

**RC:**
Have you noticed? It has stopped snowing out there. The storm is passing over.

*(RB opens window on opposite side – wind and snow pour in.)*

**RB:**
Yes, it's out there now.

*(He closes it again.)*

**RC:**
I think it is time to settle down for the evening.

**RB:**
Such long cold winter evenings we have. What shall we do this long cold winter evening, Ivan Sonofabitch?

**RC:**
The same as we do every long cold winter evening, my little Mamooshka.

**RB:**
Call me Moosh. Very well, but first we must say goodnight to the children *(Opens another door at the side of the set and they call out to their children)* Goodnight, Tania.

**RC:**
Goodnight, Ania.

**RB:**
Goodnight, André.

**RC:**
Goodnight, Lubin.

**RB:**
Goodnight, Leon.

**RC:**
Goodnight, Marsha.

**RB:**
Goodnight, Mikael.

*(We cut to other room. It contains fifteen*

*children, aged between fifteen and three, all in Russian-type smocks, nightclothes, etc., standing and sitting on one big bed.)*

**RC:**
Goodnight, Joseph.

**RB:**
Goodnight, John, Paul, George, Ringo.

**RC:**
Goodnight, Ken, goodnight, Livingstone–

*(fade to applause)*

# HOTEL LOUNGERS

*A general (RC) and an admiral (RB) sitting in an hotel lounge – potted palms and a tea-time trio playing out of vision. They sit, in uniform, in easy chairs. They are very old. A pretty waitress in a short skirt delivers tea to the admiral. The general ogles her legs. She goes.*

**RB:**
Thank you, Dulcie.

**RC:**
Nice legs.

**RB:**
Yes. Very good tone as well.

**RC:**
What?

**RB:**
The piano.

**RC:**
No, the waitress. Nice legs.

**RB:**
A trim craft. Fond of women, are you?

**RC:**
I used to be.

**RB:**
Gone off 'em, have you?

**RC:**
Not at all. Just as keen as ever.

**RB:**
It's just opportunity really, isn't it?

**RC:**
Yes. Lately I never seem to get the chance to show my prowess.

**RB:**
How long is it?

**RC:**
What?

**RB:**
How long is it? – since you had, since you made, since you were, er, since you did, er the er made love. To a woman, I mean.

**RC:**
I don't see that's any of your business.

**RB:**
No, no. I'm sorry.

**RC:**
Since you did, I bet a pound.

**RB:**
What?

**RC:**
When did you last make love?

**RB:**
If you must know, it was round about 1945.

**RC:**
1945? Ha! Well, that's a damn long time ago!

**RB:**
Not really. *(Looks at watch)* It's only 22.30 now.

*(RB winks at the waitress, who winks back. RC looks amazed.)*

# HUMPHREY AND GODFREY (8)

*RB and RC in armchairs, in their London club.*

**RB:**
I say, Humphrey.

**RC:**
What is it, Godfrey?

**RB:**
Don't mind if I smoke my pipe, do you?

**RC:**
Not if you don't mind me being sick, old chap.

**RB:**
Perhaps you're right. That's a rather loud pattern you're wearing, old lad.

*(Indicates RC's socks.)*

**RC:**
Wonderful, isn't it? Fantastic colouring. Hand-knitted in the Congo. Not another like it in England.

**RB:**
I bet you a fiver there is.

**RC:**
Done! Right, where is it?

**RB:**
*(triumphantly)* On your other foot! Come on, pay up!

**RC:**
*(shows other leg)* Sorry, old chap. *(On the other foot he has a plain day-glo sock.)* My daughter's cycling sock.

**RB:**
She's bought a bicycle?

**RC:**
Loves it. Goes everywhere on it.

**RB:**
She's a farmer's wife. The money would be better spent on a cow.

**RC:**
She'd look a bit of a fool riding round on a cow.

**RB:**
Not half as big a fool as she'd look trying to milk a bicycle.

# TRAMPS

*A series of nine quickies – RB and RC sitting by the side of a country road, their paraphernalia around them.*

## 1: "RICH"

**RB:**
I wish I had enough money to buy an elephant.

**RC:**
What do you want an elephant for?

**RB:**
I don't – I just want the money. What is the largest known diamond?

**RC:**
The Ace, isn't it?

**RB:**
No – diamond. Jewellery, you know.

**RC:**
Oh. The Kohinoor.

**RB:**
The Cohen what?

**RC:**
Kohinoor.

**RB:**
Oh. 'Course, you might know it would be Jewish.

**RC:**
It's Indian.

**RB:**
Nice to own that, wouldn't it?

**RC:**
You'd have to be Rockerfeller to own that.

**RB:**
You know, if I was as rich as Rockerfeller, I'd be richer than Rockerfeller.

**RC:**
How?

**RB:**
I'd do a bit of window-cleaning on the side.

## 2: "FOOD"

**RB:**
Have you seen the evening paper?

**RC:**
No, what's in it?

**RB:**
My lunch.

**RC:**
Can I have some of it?

**RB:**
No. Get your own.

**RC:**
Where did you get it?

**RB:**
That woman up the hill.

**RC:**
Oh, her. Terrible cook, she is. I broke a tooth on her gravy once. She gave me some cold spinach. Eat that, she said. It'll put colour in your cheeks.

**RB:**
Yeah, it will. But who wants green cheeks?

**RC:**
I'm never going to her again. I nearly went blind drinking her cocoa.

**RB:**
You can't go blind drinking cocoa.

**RC:**
I nearly did.

**RB:**
How?

**RC:**
I left the spoon in the cup.

## 3: "MONEY"

**RB:**
It says here "there is no recession". All I can say is, if this isn't a recession, it must be the worst boom in history.

**RC:**
No. Everybody's got more money than they used to have.

**RB:**
I haven't. I'm skint.

**RC:**
Didn't you just have an uncle die?

**RB:**
No, I've got an Auntie Di. Married to Fred.

**RC:**
Oh, it was your Auntie, was it?

**RB:**
No, Auntie didn't die, she's alive. It was Fred. He's dead.

**RC:**
Fred.

**RB:**
Dead.

**RC:**
How much money did he leave?

**RB:**
All of it; you have to. But none of it to me. I am truly borassic.

**RC:**
Like me. I haven't got two half-pennies to scratch the souls of me feet with. But I don't need money.

**RB:**
I do. I've asked for money, I've begged for money, I've cried for money–

**RC:**
Why don't you work for it?

**RB:**
Well, I'm going through the alphabet and I haven't got to "W" yet.

## 4: "PRISON"

**RB:**
The ladder of life is full of splinters, but you never realise it until you start sliding down.

**RC:**
Do you know that the only time you're allowed to spit in a policeman's face is when his beard's on fire?

**RB:**
What is that to do with sliding down life's ladder?

**RC:**
My brother has slid down it. And he's got the splinters to prove it. In his head.

**RB:**
His head?

**RC:**
Splinters of a policeman's truncheon.

**RB:**
Ah. 'Cos he spat in his face, when his beard wasn't on fire.

**RC:**
Zackly. He's in prison now.

**RB:**
Bit of a slur on the family name, isn't it?

**RC:**
Not really. The family name is Pentonville, anyway.

**RB:**
What's he in for?

**RC:**
He was imprisoned for his beliefs.

**RB:**
Really?

**RC:**
Yes. He believed the night watchman was asleep.

## 5: "MEAN"

**RB:**
Here, lend us a match, will you?

**RC:**
I ain't got no matches.

**RB:**
Eh? You sure?

**RC:**
'Course I'm sure.

**RB:**
Funny. I could have sworn you had some. Check your pockets, see if you have.

**RC:**
I haven't, I tell you! I have not got any matches!

**RB:**
Oh, dear. Oh well, I'll just have to use me own then.

*(He takes out matches.)*

**RC:**
Cor, dear! That is mean, isn't it? That's what I call a really stingy dirty trick.

**RB:**
Not as stingy and dirty as my sister's husband. Now he is really stingy and dirty. He went and stayed with my mum for a fortnight. He arrived with a spare shirt and a pound note, and never changed either. Miserable so-and-so he was, an' all. Even when he won the sweepstakes down the pub. "You don't look very cheerful, considering you won the sweep," I said. "No, I'm not," he said. "What annoys me is, I bought two tickets."

## 6: "TELESCOPE"

*They are eating chips or scraps from a screwed-up newspaper.*

**RB:**
It says here they've invented a telescope what can see 93 million miles.

**RC:**
Impossible.

**RB:**
Nothing is impossible.

**RC:**
Must be something.

**RB:**
No.

**RC:**
I'll tell you something that's impossible.

**RB:**
What?

**RC:**
It's impossible for a worm to fall over.

**RB:**
Ah, that's different – I mean in space, and that.

**RC:**
I don't trust these space scientists. If they're so clever, why do they count backwards?

**RB:**
Ah well, yeah.

**RC:**
'Zackly. One of them telescopes wouldn't be no good to me. I got spots before me eyes.

**RB:**
You got new glasses – didn't they help?

**RC:**
Sort of. They didn't get rid of the spots, but I can see 'em much clearer now.

## 7: "SHOES"

**RC:**
Cor, dear. My arthritis is playing me up this morning.

**RB:**
I didn't know you suffered with arthritis.

**RC:**
'Course I do. What else can you do with it? Talking of which, what's the matter with your feet? I noticed you was walking funny.

**RB:**
It's these shoes. They're 'flaming killing me.

**RC:**
Well, why do you wear 'em, then?

**RB:**
Listen – I've got no money, I can't afford tobacco or beer. I haven't got a television, I'm all alone in the world – no decent girl will look at me, and even if she did, I couldn't afford to take her out. And after a long day's tramping in the heat or the pouring rain, I think of all my troubles and I feel suicidal. Then I take off these damn shoes – and oh boy! That's the only pleasure I ever get.

## 8: "MARRIAGE"

**RC:**
Do you think marriage is a lottery?

**RB:**
No. In a lottery you do have a slight chance.

**RC:**
But you like women, don't you?

**RB:**
Oh yes. Just give me my pipe, the great outdoors and a beautiful girl, and you can keep the pipe and the great outdoors. Still, that's nothing to do with marriage, is it? It's just the opposite sex.

**RC:**
The what?

**RB:**
You know what the opposite sex is,

don't you?

**RC:**
Yes. It's the tart who lives across the road.

**RB:**
Talking of which, my sister-in-law has just had quads.

**RC:**
That's pretty rare, isn't it?

**RB:**
Rare? Certainly is. Doctors say it only happens once in one million six hundred thousand times.

**RC:**
Blimey. It's a wonder she ever found time to do any housework.

## 9: "AGE"

**RB:**
I'll have to lose some weight, you know. Can't go knocking on people's doors saying I haven't eaten for three days looking like this.

**RC:**
It's middle-aged spread, that.

**RB:**
I know.

**RC:**
Lot to be said for middle-aged spread.

**RB:**
Yes. It's good for married couples – brings them closer together.

**RC:**
A lot of advantages come with age.

**RB:**
Yes. My old grandad, for instance. Now he can whistle while he brushes his teeth.

**RC:**
'Zackly. 'Course there's disadvantages, too.
I went to the doctor about me memory.
It's really going. I told him I can't
remember anything.

**RB:**
What did he say?

**RC:**
He was very reassuring – he told me to
just forget about it.

# YOU CAN SAY THAT AGAIN

*A pub. RB at bar. RC enters.*

**RB:**
Hello, Bert – what are you going to have?

**RC:**
Oh, hello, Charlie. I'll have a pint of, er–

**RB:**
Light?

**RC:**
No, a pint of–

**RB:**
Brown?

**RC:**
No, a pint of–

**RB:**
Mild?

**RC:**
No–

**RB:**
Bitter?

**RC:**
Pint of bitter.

**RB:**
Pint of bitter. Pint of bitter, Alan. Haven't
seen you round the factory lately – been
off sick?

**RC:**
No, I packed it in. They told me I had to
change me, er, change me, er–

**RB:**
Hours?

**RC:**
No, change me–

**RB:**
Habits?

**RC:**
No, change me–

**RB:**
Socks more often?

**RC:**
No, duties.

**RB:**
Oh, duties.

**RC:**
Change my duties, that's it. Well, I wasn't
having that, 'cos I had a good job. Cushy
little number. *(Barman delivers pint.)* Ta.
Cheers.

**RB:**
Cheers, Bert. What exactly was your job
then, there?

**RC:**
Same job as I'd done for twenty years. I
always worked with, er–

**RB:**
Pride?

**RC:**
No, I worked with, er–

**RB:**
Within reason?

**RC:**
No, with, er–

**RB:**
With your overcoat on?

**RC:**
No, with Harry Hawkins.

**RB:**
Oh, Harry Hawkins, yes.

**RC:**
We always worked together. He used to give me his, er–

**RB:**
Whole-hearted support?

**RC:**
No, his, er–

**RB:**
Athletic support?

**RC:**
No, his ginger nuts.

**RB:**
Oh, nice.

**RC:**
And I used to dip them in, er–

**RB:**
His tea for him?

**RC:**
No, in the chocolate.

**RB:**
Oh, the chocolate, I see. That's the job, is it?

**RC:**
Me and him made all the chocolate ginger nuts. Then suddenly they decide a woman can do my job, and they put me on to, er–

**RB:**
Short time?

**RC:**
No, on to–

**RB:**
Short cake?

**RC:**
No, sherbert fountains. Messy job, that, dreadful. Everything gets covered in it. You go home, strip off, and find you've got a coating of sherbert all over, er–

**RB:**
All over the weekend.

**RC:**
Precisely. And the wife doesn't like it.

**RB:**
Oh, that makes it worse. So you can't even–

**RC:**
Meanwhile, the woman refused to work with Harry Hawkins. She didn't like the way he handled his, er–

**RB:**
His ginger nuts?

**RC:**
His machinery, and she thought he was, er–

**RB:**
Nuts?

**RC:**
No, she thought he was, er–

**RB:**
Ginger?

**RC:**
No, incompetent.

**RB:**
Oh, incompetent, yes. So you went back with Harry, did you?

**RC:**
No, I decided I'd had enough. I went

home to the wife and I found she was up, er–

**RB:**
Up to her knees in sherbert?

**RC:**
No, up, er–

**RB:**
Up to her old tricks with the milkman?

**RC:**
No, up her mother's. So I thought, why not go up the Job Centre, I thought. 'Cos I mean, if you're really looking for a decent job, that's the place to, er–

**RB:**
Steer clear of.

**RC:**
No, be fair. They vary, don't they? My brother went to one for a job as a removal man, and within a week they'd already given him a–

**RB:**
Fortnight's holiday?

**RC:**
No, they gave him a–

**RB:**
Set of tea chests?

**RC:**
No, a hernia.

**RB:**
Oh, hernia, yes.

**RC:**
Still, this place was quite nice. I went up to this girl sitting behind this sort of grill, and she was filing–

**RB:**
Filing her nails?

**RC:**
No, filing the, er–

**RB:**
Filing the bars trying to get out?

**RC:**
No, filing these jobs in this portfolio thing.

**RB:**
Oh, jobs, yes.

**RC:**
Yes. Big girl she was, with these two, er–

**RB:**
Oh yes, I get the picture, yes.

**RC:**
Either side like.

**RB:**
Well, they would be, yes.

**RC:**
And I asked about jobs, and these two, er–

**RB:**
Yes, I know, yes.

**RC:**
They sprang up.

**RB:**
Eh? How was that, then?

**RC:**
Sort of in excitement, like, and–

**RB:**
Good Lord.

**RC:**
And they came towards me.

**RB:**
Did they?

**RC:**
Yes. Oh, what are they called? Clerks.

**RB:**
Oh, clerks, oh my mistake.

**RC:**
Turned out she was a sort of trainee. She'd just got off the er–

**RB:**
The train?

**RC:**
The course.

**RB:**
Oh, course. Of course.

**RC:**
So they sprang up and said "There's a job that might very well suit you," they said. "We're looking for a man with short, er–"

**RB:**
Legs?

**RC:**
No, short, er–

**RB:**
Short shirts?

**RC:**
No, er–

**RB:**
Shortcomings?

**RC:**
Here, do you mind? Shorthand and typing – they needed a man with shorthand because they were, er–

**RB:**
Short-handed?

**RC:**
No, understaffed at the Town Hall. So, of course I didn't get the job.

**RB:**
Oh dear – so you're still out of work, are you?

**RC:**
No, they only had one other post available, so I took it.

**RB:**
Go on–

**RC:**
Yes, I've now got a job with the sweet, er–

**RB:**
With the sweet factory again?

**RC:**
No, a city job – a job with the sweet, er–

**RB:**
With the sweet smell of success?

**RC:**
Not exactly. I'm in charge of the "gents" at Waterloo Station! Cheers!

# A TOUCH OF THE HICKSTEADS

*A doctor's waiting room. RC sits waiting. RB enters, goes to receptionist, a middle-aged, pleasant woman in a white coat.*

**RECEPTIONIST:**
Yes, sir, good morning. Your name, please.

**RB:**
HICson.

*(Has hiccups throughout.)*

**REC:**
Mr Hickson. Address?

**RB:**
24 PuddleswICK Lane, HICstead.

**REC:**
Phone number?

**RB:**
HICstead SICx, two, three, o, SICx.

**REC:**
Thank you, Mr Hickson – just take a seat,

won't you?

*(RB sits next to RC.)*

**RC:**
Morning.

*(Whistle – he emits a low whistle after certain words throughout the sketch.)*

**RB:**
Morning.

**RC:**
First visit?

**RB:**
Yes.

**RC:**
What's the matter with you?

*(Whistle.)*

**RB:**
Sorry?

**RC:**
What are you suffering from?

*(Whistle.)*

**RB:**
It's silly, really. I'm not really SIC. It's just that I've got permanent HIC, permanent HIC, perHIC manHIC–

**RC:**
*(Whistle.)* Hic *(whistle)* cups.

**RB:**
Yes. It's absolutely HICsausting.

**RC:**
I know. Well, you'll be alright with this chap. He's a specialist. Ear, nose and

*(Whistle)*

**RB:**
What?

**RC:**
Ear, nose and *(whistle)* hiccups *(whistle)*.

**RB:**
Oh, good. What's your partHICular illness?

**RC:**
Coincidence, really. The reason I'm here is that I've just got married.

*(Whistle.)*

**RB:**
Oh, I see.

**RC:**
Swedish girl. *(Whistle)* Met her last month, married her this month. *(Whistle.)*

**RB:**
Gosh. That was quICK.

**RC:**
It's she who wants the doctor to cure my *(whistle)* my affliction.

**RB:**
*(Whistle.)*

**RC:**
HIC!

**RB:**
What is your afflICKtion?

**RC:**
*(whistle)* Same as yours.

**RB:**
What?

**RC:**
Hiccups. *(Whistle.)*

**RB:**
But you don't HIC, you HIC don't HIC.

**RC:**
Don't hiccup? *(Whistle.)* That's because this doctor has taught me the cure. *(Whistle.)*

**RB:**
You mean, I should marry a Swedish girl?

**RC:**
No, no. Whistling's the cure. If you whistle whenever you feel you are going to *(whistle)*, whenever you feel a *(whistle)* coming on, you won't hiccup.

**RB:**
Really? I'll try it. "My name is Henry *(whistle)* Hickson of 24 Puddles *(whistle)* Lane, *(whistle)* Hickstead." It works! That's absolutely HICstrodinary. I mean, that's absolutely *(whistle)*.

**RC:**
It is, isn't it?

**RB:**
But just a minute. If you're cured of *(whistle)* hiccups, why are you here?

**RC:**
I'm here to be cured of the *(whistle)* the *(whistle)* the whistle.

*(Whistle.)*

**REC:**
*(To RC)* You'll be next, Mr Entwistle.

**RC:**
And about time tooooo

*(It comes out like a whistle.)*

*(A girl with an enormous bosom enters. She wears a very low-cut dress. She sits between them and hiccups. When she does, her bosom bounces in the air. RC and RB whistle. She looks annoyed and hiccups. They whistle. She hits them with her handbag, hiccups. They whistle. This continues as we cue applause.)*

# YOU'RE SOMEBODY

*A smartish hotel bar in Bournemouth. A pianist is tinkling away on, and who knows, when nobody is looking, possibly in, the piano. RC, in casual clothes, sits at the bar. A barman hovers. RB, seated a little way along the bar, is staring at RC.*

**RB:**
Excuse me.

**RC:**
Yes?

**RB:**
You're Robert Redford, aren't you?

**RC:**
*(looks around to see who RB is talking to)* Sorry? You talking to me?

**RB:**
Yes. You're Robert Redford, aren't you?

**RC:**
No. No, sorry, you're mistaken.

*(He is flattered.)*

**RB:**
You must often get taken for him.

**RC:**
Er – well, no, can't say I do, not often, no.

*(A pause. RC drinks, RB stares at him, then moves and sits beside him. RC only faintly embarrassed.)*

**RB:**
You're somebody.

**RC:**
Ha ha. Well everybody's somebody, aren't they? Otherwise nobody would be anybody.

**RB:**
No, you're somebody. I've seen you.

**RC:**
Doubtful. I don't appear anywhere.

**RB:**
You've appeared here, haven't you?

**RC:**
No, I mean I don't perform.

**RB:**
Oh, I'm sorry to hear that.

**RC:**
I mean, I don't entertain. I'm not an entertainer.

*(A pause. Then RB stares at him again.)*

**RB:**
Come off it.

**RC:**
I'm not, honestly. I'm just a rather dull person, with not an atom of show-biz sparkle, scintillation or bezazz.

**RB:**
You're Robin Day, aren't you?

**RC:**
I would hardly describe Robin Day as having no show-biz bezazz. He's full of it. If you want to see a good, honest, over-the-top performance, watch *Question Time.*

**RB:**
So you're not him then?

**RC:**
I am not him, no.

**RB:**
Who's that bloke who works with a dummy?

**RC:**
No, I'm not Little and Large.

**RB:**
No, the ventriloquist act. Ray Hampton.

**RC:**
Ray Allan.

**RB:**
Yes, and Lord John.

**RC:**
Lord Charles.

**RB:**
Yes. You're him.

**RC:**
Which one?

**RB:**
Either.

**RC:**
Lord Charles is made of wood!
*(sarcastically)* You're sure you don't mean Rod Hull and Emu?

**RB:**
That's him, yes.

**RC:**
Oh, my God. Listen, would you mind allowing me to finish my drink in peace.

**RB:**
Sorry, sorry.

**RC:**
Thank you.

*(A pause.)*

**RB:**
You on holiday down here?

**RC:**
No, I work here.

**RB:**
What, in cabaret, are you?

**RC:**
Look, for the last time will you shut up and let me have my drink!

**RB :**
Like a drink, do you?

**RC:**
Yes, I do like a drink in peace.

**RB:**
Lot of your people are heavy drinkers.

**RC:**
My people? What, my uncles and aunts, you mean? What do you mean, my people?

**RB:**
Show-biz people.

**RC:**
I am not show-biz! I am not a heavy drinker – I am nine-stone four and a half-drinker! Please leave me alone!

**RB:**
I'm sorry. I don't mean to be a nuisance.

**RC:**
Alright.

**RB:**
It's just fascinating to me, that's all, and although I realise this is an intrusion on your privacy, and although who you are and what you do has absolutely nothing to do with me whatsoever, I think you're Harry Secombe.

**RC:**
Harry Secombe's enormous!

**RB:**
He's lost a lot of weight.

**RC:**
*(snaps)* OK! Alright. I admit it. I am in show business. I am an all-round entertainer, appear in my own TV specials and my name is a household word. I have a wonderful act and it finishes like this–

*(He goes into a song and dance – the pianist in the bar takes up the number, and RC does a big finish, eventually dancing off into the "ladies".)*

**RB:**
Oh, now I've got him! *(To barman)* He's the bloke who works in the fish shop in the High Street!

# HUMPHREY AND GODFREY (9)

*RB and RC in armchairs, in their London club.*

**RB:**
I say, Humphrey.

**RC:**
What is it, Godfrey?

**RB:**
Do you know, I'm Robert Redford's double?

**RC:**
What?

**RB:**
Yes, I am. I weigh exactly twice as much as he does. Not good for the ticker, though. Doctor told me to give up smoking at once. I said it was impossible.

**RC:**
Why?

**RB:**
I'd just filled my lighter. Good doctor, though. He gave my uncle six months to live, but when he told him he couldn't pay him, he gave him another six months to live, so he could pay him.

**RC:**
I've got the best doctor – thoroughly sympathetic. Very good about my mother-in-law. I said to him, "My mother-in-law is very unsteady on her feet."

**RB:**
And what did he say?

**RC:**
"Buy her a skateboard."

# BARMY ARMY

*A dug-out or tent in the front line. 1915.*
*RB is seated at rough table, studying a map.*
*RC enters.*

**RB:**
Oh, it's you, Hugh. Did you get through
to HQ?

**RC:**
At two minutes to.

**RB:**
Two minutes to? Good for you.

**RC:**
They must have realised I was due to get
through. They cleared the line.

**RB:**
Divine. What news of support?

**RC:**
Nought.

**RB:**
Nought?

**RC:**
Lord, gort up at the fort thought we ought
to have sought support before we went
out and fought.

**RB:**
All a bit fraught. We're going to get
caught! Pass the port. Here we sit
grounded, surrounded and utterly
confounded. Cut off by the Krauts.

**RC:**
Oh dear – I feel queer. I think I'll have a
brandy, Sandy.

**RB:**
Do, Hugh.

**RC:**
*(pouring brandy)* I've been thinking.

**RB:**
Drinking?

**RC:**
Thinking.

**RB:**
Oh, thinking and drinking.

**RC:**
We're not rapped completely, Captain
Wheatley. There are one or two very tight
gaps in the Jerry-type chaps. Here's one of
the maps of the gaps. Take a "garnder",
Commander.

**RB:**
Good grief, O'Keefe! You expect me to
squeeze through these? A man of my size,
with my thighs? Hardly a holiday,
Halliday.

**RC:**
O'Keefe, sir.

**RB:**
Quite. What a night! I feel thoroughly
misbegotten, hot and rotten. And what a
stench in the trench! If we're not caught
by Jerry, we'll die of beri-beri! Damn the
Kraut, I've got to get out!

**RC:**
I agree, it's pretty infernal, Colonel.

*(Restraining him.)*

**RB:**
*(pushing him aside)* That's the
understatement of the year, you little
queer! I've had it up to here!

**RC:**
Now don't get manic and panic–

**RB:**
It's no good, chummy. *(Breaks down)* Oh,
lumme – I want my mummy!

**RC:**
Here – suck this dummy. *(Puts dummy in his mouth.)* Now, on the bed and rest your head. Just try to unroll yourself and control yourself while I give you the low-down on this show-down. We may have run out of ammo, but we've still got an MO and he's conquering disease by degrees. There aren't very many places with beri-beri cases – Private Schwartz has got warts, Private Doyle's got boils and Private Wurzel's pet weasel's got the measles. And Corporal Clappy is not a happy chappy. Still, you can't be a saint with his complaint.

**RB:**
No, nobody smiles with piles. Still, it's worse for the nurse. God, what a barmy army.

**RC:**
Sir – fancy a flit? Shall we slip out of this hell-hole?

**RB:**
I'd certainly rather be in Solihull than sitting shivering in this stinking load of shrapnel. What's your plan, little man?

**RC:**
Frank's tank. It's up on the bank.

*(Points outside.)*

**RB:**
Frank?

**RC:**
Frank Messiter. The cricketer from Chichester.

**RB:**
Oh, him. I thought he name was Jim. Is he no longer with us, Smithers?

**RC:**
Not any more – he's gone before. Jerry threw a grenade. There sat Frank, in his tank, dreaming of cricket, and a straight middle wicket. The grenade came over the wall – Frank thought it was a ball;

caught it and bought it.

**RB:**
So there stands his tank – and we've got Frank to thank. Can you drive it, Private?

**RC:**
I think so – without being egotistical, my vehicle test verged on the artistical.

**RB:**
Would you mind repeating that?

**RC:**
I'd rather not try.

**RB:**
I can quite see why. When shall we leave?

**RC:**
As soon as you feel partial, Field Marshall.

**RB:**
So – it's off we go – bravo. We're all set – let's have a wet.

*(Reaches for bottle.)*

**RC:**
Talking of wet – will you excuse me, Generalissimo? I must go outside for a–

**RB:**
Yes, I know. So must I – but watch out for a hun with a gun. You go first; if I hear a short burst, I'll fear the worst.

**RC:**
And if you hear a long sigh, you'll know I'm high and dry.

*(He exits. The field telephone rings. RB answers it.)*

**RB:**
Forty-fifth fusilier here, HQ. Eight two, how are you? Ah! They are? How far? Hurrah! I'll see you in the bar and buy you a cigar! Ta-ta!

*(RC re-enters.)*

**RB:**
We're relieved!

**RC:**
You as well?

**RB:**
That was Sergeant Bone on the phone. Captain Hooper's turned up trumps with twenty-two troopers – fired a howitzer and hit the Kaiser squarely in the trouser. They've all retreated, much depleted.

**RC:**
Then now's our chance. Before we get hurt and dropped in the dirt, let's put on a spurt and desert, Bert.

**RB:**
Desert? It's an idea, my dear. Can we start a new life together, Merryweather?

**RC:**
Of course we can, you silly man.

**RB:**
You've made an old man very happy, you dear chappy.

**RC:**
Call me Mary, you old fairy.

*(They exit.)*

# VIM AND VIGOUR

*A small general store. RB as proprietor. RC enters – he is precious and gay.*

**RC:**
Hello, Duckie.

**RB:**
Morning, sir. Nice morning.

**RC:**
No, it's not – I haven't had my oats this morning.

**RB:**
Pardon, sir?

**RC:**
What have you got – Bran Flakes? Crispies? What would you recommend?

**RB:**
*(Showing packet)* "Force" is nice.

**RC:**
Yes, I like a bit of force, don't we all. What else you got?

**RB:**
"Fizz", "Crunch", Muesli or Oatcake Nibbles.

**RC:**
I'll try the Fizz.

**RB:**
Right, sir.

**RC:**
*(looks at list)* Packet of Flash.

**RB:**
Flash? Yes, sir.

*(Gets it.)*

**RC:**
And some Vim.

**RB:**
Vim? Yes.

*(Gets it.)*

**RC:**
Now, furniture polish. Got any Spangle?

**RB:**
No, sir. I got Shine, Whine, Whizz, Glide, Slide, Slip, Slap and Skid.

**RC:**
I'll try the Whizz.

**RB:**
Yes, sir.

*(Gets it.)*

**RC:**
Ooh. I desperately need deodorant.

**RB:**
I wouldn't say that, sir–

**RC:**
Got any Stud?

**RB:**
No, sir. Afraid not. We've got Sting, Stiff, Sniff, Snort, Whoops, Wow and Sailor Beware, sir.

**RB:**
Oh, nice. I'll try the Whoops.

**RB:**
One Whoops. Right, sir. Large Whoops?

**RC:**
Always!

**RB:**
Right, sir, one large Whoops.

**RC:**
Insect spray – got any Doom?

**RB:**
No, sir, no Doom; we've got Boom, Zoom, Clear the Room, Squash, Squelch or Squirt, sir.

**RC:**
I'll try the Boom.

**RB:**
Big Boom, sir?

**RC:**
Always!

**RB:**
Right, sir.

*(Gets it.)*

**RC:**
Washing powder?

**RB:**
Yes, sir. Daz, Bezaz, Omo, Promo, Primo, Pull, Push, Whoosh, Rinso, Ritzo, Ratzo, Rosto and Shreddo.

**RC:**
Whoosh, please.

**RB:**
One Whoosh. Right.

**RC:**
Now. Alcohol-free lager.

**RB:**
Wet-Whistle, Wallop or Windbreaker, sir?

**RC:**
Oh, Wallop, I think.

**RB:**
Pint of Wallop?

**RC:**
No. I'm a half-pint man.

**RB:**
I wouldn't say that, sir.

*(Gets it.)*

**RC:**
Oh, and some lemonade.

**RB:**
Tang, Fang, Bang or Tinklejuice?

**RC:**
Er – I'll try a Bang, please.

**RB:**
Are we nearly there, sir?

**RC:**
Just two more things – bottle of sauce. HP?

**RB:**
No, sir. OK, FA, JR, Fruity, Floppy, Sloppy, Slurp, Splosh or Splatter.

**RC:**
I'll try the Splatter.

**RB:**
Right, sir.

*(Gets it.)*

**RC:**
And lastly, a chocolate bar.

**RB:**
Yessir. Crackle, Crunch, Crush, Crash, Cram, Creamy, Steamy, Slimy and Sickmaker, sir.

**RC:**
I'll take the Crash, please. There, that's it. That's the lot.

**RB:**
Right, sir. So that's Flash, Fizz, Vim, Whizz, Crash, Bang, Wallop, Whoosh, Whoops, Boom and Splatter.

**RC:**
Could you just say that again, please?

**RB:**
Yes, sir. You've got Flash, Fizz, Vim, Whizz, Crash, Bang, Wallop, Whoosh, Whoops, Boom and Splatter.

**RC:**
Ooh, lovely!

**RB:**
That's four pounds, 25, please.

**RC:**
Oh, I'm not buying them.

**RB:**
What?

**RC:**
I just wanted to hear you say them.

**RB:**
Why?

**RC:**
I couldn't afford any fireworks this year. See you, sweetie!

*(Starts to leave.)*

**RB:**
*(Throws "force" packet at him.)* May the Force be with you!

# STUNT MAN

*RB in interview area – tables, chairs, etc.*

**RB:**
Good evening and welcome to this week's edition of *Other People's Business*. This week, we are looking at a very exciting profession indeed – the stuntman – in this case Mr Harold Higgins of Kettering. Ladies and Gentlemen, Mr Harold Higgins.

*(Enter RC as stuntman – he wears thick black tights and a black sweater and is padded all over – pads on elbows, knees, shoulders and bottom.)*

**RB:**
Good evening, Mr Higgins.

**RC:**
Good evening.

*(He sits down with slight difficulty.)*

**RB:**
Now, before we go any further, we've got some film of stunts being performed.

*(Cut to stock film of various falls, stunts, etc.)*

**RB:**
*(after film)* And that was you, was it?

**RC:**
Er, no. No. I don't know who that was.

**RB:**
Oh – but that's the sort of thing you do, is it?

**RC:**
Well, not as good as that 'cos I get frightened. I'm a bit afraid of heights and that.

**RB:**
Oh, I see.

**RC:**
'Cos it's not as easy as it looks, stunting. I mean, the public get blasé about it – they think it's just like falling off a log.

**RB:**
But you can do it?

**RC:**
Oh, I can fall off a log? Yes.

**RB:**
No, I mean – you are earning your living at it?

**RC:**
Well, yes. I've got all the gear and that.

**RB:**
What, all this padding?

**RC:**
Yes. *(He stands up.)* It protects all the salient points – saves me hurting myself.

**RB:**
Quite – but doesn't it look rather odd on the screen?

**RC:**
Oh, no. You wear the clothes over the top, you see, the clothes of the person you are doubling for. Have you got that photo of me in a film with the clothes on?

**RB:**
Yes, – er–

*(Caption – photo of RC in suit and trilby – terrible bulges where the padding sticks out –*

*knees, shoulders, elbows and bottom.)*

**RB:**
*(voice over)* Yes, here we are. Oh. Yes, I see. Who were you doubling for in that?

*(Cut back to studio)*

**RC:**
The thin man.

**RB:**
Oh, yes. Have you always been a stuntman?

**RC:**
No, not when I was younger.

**RB:**
What were you when you were young?

**RB:**
Er – I was a little boy. I was brought up in the circus. My father used to travel all over the country as a bearded lady.

**RB:**
And so naturally you wanted to perform too?

**RC:**
Yes. Stunts and stamp-collecting. They were my two hobbies. I used to come home from school, do a stunt, collect a few stamps and then do another stunt, and so on. Of course, my old grandad was a stuntman. Very famous, he was.

**RB:**
Oh, yes – we've got a bit of film of him.

*(Cut to film of man trying to fly off Eiffel Tower – stock shot.)*

**RB:**
That was marvellous. Did he often do that sort of thing?

**RC:**
No, just the once.

**RB:**
I see – so you more or less started in the business straight from school?

**RC:**
No – I had this great money-making scheme for producing eggs without having chickens.

**RB:**
How did you do that?

**RC:**
I used ducks – but it never caught on, so I started doing stunting.

**RB:**
Mainly film work, is it?

**RC:**
Well, no, 'cos you've got to be pretty tough for that, you know – brave – no, I mainly do children's parties, that sort of thing. Or if people don't want to lie on the grass in a TV play, in case they catch a chill, I lie on the grass for them. Don't mind doing that. And getting off buses just before they stop. All that sort of thing.

**RB:**
Ah, yes. I understand you are prepared to do a stunt for us now?

**RC:**
Yes – well, I'll jump off the table for you, if you like.

**RB:**
Oh, alright then.

**RC:**
Right. Shall I do it now?

**RB:**
Yes, that will be fine.

*(RC gets onto table, and stands up.)*

**RC:**
*(looking down)* It's a bit high from here, isn't it?

**RB:**
It's two foot six.

**RC:**
Yes, but it looks higher from up there. That's the one thing I've learnt in this business – when you're up on a height, it looks higher than when you're down on the ground.

**RB:**
Don't you think you will be able to do it?

**RC:**
Oh, I'll do it. Oh yes, I'll do it. Right. Ready?

**RB:**
Yes, righto.

**RC:**
Right. *(With a sort of little cry of terror, he jumps down, lands on the floor and falls over.)* Ow! Ooh, I banged my knee. Ow! *(he bursts into tears)* Mum! Mum! I banged my knee – Mum!

*(His mother enters and cuddles him.)*

**MOTHER:**
All right son, don't cry. You see, you shouldn't do these silly things, should you, dear? Come on. *(She leads him off.)* Let's go and see Dad, shall we?

*(They have gone. RB stares after them.)*

# TRAMPS II

*1: "Phil Collins special edition"*

*Wide shot – Phil Collins, as another tramp, approaches, sits down with RB and RC.*

**RB:**
Hello, Dudley – happy Christmas.

**PHIL:**
Let's hope so.

**RB:**
Have a cigar.

**PHIL:**
Why, what's the matter with it?

**RB:**
Nothing's the matter with it. I found it.

**PHIL:**
Found it? Where?

**RB:**
In the tobacconist's. Someone must have dropped it on the counter.

**PHIL:**
That's criminal, that is.

**RC:**
Only if you get caught. Anyway, nothing wrong with crime. Look at Robin Hood. He was a hero, and he never stopped robbing people.

**RB:**
Ah, but he only robbed the rich.

**RC:**
Yeah, and you know why, don't you?

**RB:**
Why?

**RC:**
'Cos the poor didn't have any money. Any crime in your family, Dudley?

**PHIL:**
Yeah. My sister is a stripper.

**RC:**
That's not a crime, taking your clothes off.

**PHIL:**
She don't take her clothes off. She goes up on roofs and takes the lead off.

**RB:**
My brother was up before the beak once – for lighting fireworks in the street.

**RC:**
Selling 'em, was he?

**RB:**
Yeah. "Right, I know what to do with you, my man," said the judge. "I shall make the punishment fit the crime," he says. "I'm going to do to you what you have done to them fireworks," he says.

**PHIL:**
What did he do, then?

**RB:**
He let him off.

*(Reaction Phil – reaction RC.)*

## 2: "TRAVEL"

**RB:**
Who won the single-handed yacht race?

**RC:**
Eh?

**RB:**
I said, who won the single-handed yacht race?

**RC:**
I don't know. Nelson, was it? Why do you want to know, anyway?

**RB:**
Must be marvellous to travel about all over the world.

**RC:**
Well, you're doing the next best thing – you're travelling about all over Middlesex.

**RB:**
Middlesex isn't romantic and exciting, is it?

**RC:**
Depends which house you go to.

**RB:**
*(ignoring this)* Do you know, they say there's an island in the Pacific where the wind always blows?

**RC:**
Well, that's about all it ever does over 'ere an' all. I think travel's very over-rated meself. I mean, why do so many American tourists go to Edinburgh to see Princes Street?

**RB:**
Well, that's obvious, ain't it? Because they wouldn't see it if they went anywhere else.

**RC:**
Take my advice, stay at home and drink whisky instead.

**RB:**
Whisky shortens your life.

**RC:**
I know, but you'll see twice as much in half the time.

## 3: "KIDS"

**RC:**
Time you got a new suit, you know. You're beginning to look shabby.

**RB:**
This suit was made to measure, but the bloke didn't pick it up so I had it.

**RC:**
You've worn that jacket ever since I knew you.

**RB:**
I know. This was my wedding suit.

**RC:**
Oh, you was married an' all, was you?

**RB:**
Yeah. My wife was like the ocean – she was wild and restless, and she made me sick.

**RC:**
Any kids?

**RB:**
Oh, yeah. I don't know how though, she was so stupid. When I suggested a family she went and pulled up all the gooseberry bushes. Having kids with her was like waiting for a bus. Nothing happened for ages, and then three came along all at once.

**RC:**
Oh, triplets you had?

**RB:**
Yeah, they're grown up now.

**RC:**
What were they?

**RB:**
One of each: a boy, a girl and a hairdresser.

## 4: "WOMEN"

Do you realise that Adam didn't have a mother-in-law?

**RC:**
Yes. That's why he lived in Paradise.

**RB:**
You don't like women, do you?

**RC:**
Not a lot.

**RB:**
You was married though, wasn't you?

**RC:**
Oh, yes. My wife came from a fine old English family. Unfortunately, she brought it with her.

**RB:**
Is that why you took to the road?

**RC:**
Nah. I took to the road 'cos she was stupid. I told her my great, great grandfather was killed at Waterloo and she said "Which platform?"

**RB:**
Silly so-and-so. As if the platform mattered.

**RC:**
'Zackly. And she was colour blind, an' all, and never told me.

**RB:**
How did you find out?

**RC:**
She made a rhubarb pie out of celery.

## 5: "WORK"

**RC:**
What made you give up work and take to the road then, Harry?

**RB:**
I gave up work because of sickness. The boss got sick of me.

**RC:**
You was a railway porter, wasn't you?

**RB:**
Yeah. I got the sack 'cos I trod on a snail.

**RC:**
Why did you do that?

**RB:**
It had been following me about all day.

**RC:**
Bit of a blow, wasn't it, losing your job?

**RB:**
Yeah. Well, at the time I had a wife and two ruptures to support. What made you give it up then?

**RC:**
I lost the will to live – except at weekends. I was always late. What they ought to do is cross electric blankets with toasters, and pop people out of bed in the morning. I had to go up before the boss. I hadn't been talking to him for more than two minutes and he called me a fool.

**RB:**
What caused the delay?

**RC:**
I dunno. I must have been talking slow.

**RB:**
My boss was rude an' all. And mean. On flag days he had a special way of avoiding buying one.

**RC:**
What was that then?

**RB:**
He used to wear a tray with flags on it. One year I sent him a card with "A Happy Christmas" on it. The next year, he sent the same card back and wrote on it "And the same to you".

## 6: "HEALTH"

**RB:**
Do you know how to avoid falling hair?

**RC:**
Yeah. Get out of the way. You're going a bit bald under that balaclava, ain't you?

**RB:**
I'm not bald. I've got flesh-coloured hair.

**RC:**
Go on, you can't fool me.

**RB:**
I've got wavy hair.

**RC:**
You used to have. Now it's waving goodbye. My advice is to stop worrying about it. I known a lot of people go grey worrying about going bald.

**RB:**
Me eyes are not what they was, either.

**RC:**
Why, what was they, ears?

**RB:**
You know what I mean. I can't see things close to unless they're a long way away.

**RC:**
The paper said they can cure short-sight now, with a special herbal solution.

**RB:**
Nah, that's just a lot of eye-wash. I'm gonna get a monocle.

**RC:**
You'll sit on that and break it.

**RB:**
No, I won't – that's not where you wear it. They've invented a new lens that can be hit with a hammer, dropped a hundred feet and jumped on without it breaking. As a final test, they're going to let the Post Office have a go at it.

## 7: "MONEY"

**RB:**
I reckon I got a cold coming.

**RC:**
You wanna take some aspirins.

**RB:**
I can't take aspirins – they give me a headache.

**RC:**
I see in the paper where it says that fifty thousand germs can live on a pound coin for a year.

**RB:**
Oh, yeah. Does that include VAT?

**RC:**
I dunno. I should have asked that businessman I tried to tap the other day. Mean basket he was – wouldn't spare me a pound for a cup of coffee.

**RB:**
Why did you ask for a pound just for a cup of coffee?

**RC:**
I'm a heavy tipper.

**RB:**
Them Americans got a lotta money to waste. Look at all that money they wasted putting a man on the moon.

**RC:**
They're gonna put a man on the sun next.

**RB:**
They can't do that. He'd be burnt to a cinder.

**RC:**
No, they've thought of that.

**RB:**
Oh, yeah? How they gonna get round that then?

**RC:**
They're sending him at night.

# SAY IT AGAIN, SAM

*A tiny snug bar in a pub. RB sits drinking at the bar. RC enters.*

**RB:**
Hello, Bert, what you gonna have?

**RC:**
Oh, thanks, Harry, I'll have a pint of, er–

**RB:**
Pint of light?

**RC:**
No, a pint of, er–

**RB:**
Pint of brown?

**RC:**
No, er–

**RB:**
Pint of mild?

**RC:**
No, er–

**RB:**
Pint of bitter?

**RC:**
Pint of bitter. Yes, ta.

**RB:**
*(calls to barman)* Pint of bitter, Charley.

**RC:**
Lovely. I thought I'd pop in on my way to, er–

**RB:**
What, the off-licence?

**RC:**
No, on the way to, er–

**RB:**
Alcoholics Anonymous?

**RC:**
No, on the way to the darts match. Up the club. *(The beer arrives.)* Oh. Ta, Charley.

**RB:**
*(raising glass)* Well – merry Christmas, Bert.

**RC:**
Merry Christmas, Harry. It's all Christmas now, isn't it? Christmas decorations, Christmas parties, Christmas carols, Christmas cards–

**RB:**
Yes, well, it's the time of year, isn't it? It's seasonal. You always get a lot of Christmas things going on at Christmas, don't you?

**RC:**
Suppose it's inevitable. Talking of Christmas celebrations, we had ours the other night. Up the club.

**RB:**
Oh, yeah?

**RC:**
Funny old do it was an' all. Same every year, it always takes the form of an egg and, er–

**RB:**
Egg and spoon race?

**RC:**
No, an egg an' er–

**RB:**
Egon Ronay gourmet banquet?

**RC:**
No, an egg and chip supper.

**RB:**
Oh, I see, yeah.

**RC:**
Took the wife along, of course. Well, she's useful for laying the, er–

**RB:**
Laying the eggs?

**RC:**
No, laying the, er–

**RB:**
Laying the foreman?

**RC:**
Laying the table. She lays the tables, It was all very nice. The men all get cigars and the woman all get, p– er–

**RB:**
Pie-eyed?

**RC:**
No, the women get p–er–

**RB:**
Pickled?

**RC:**
No, er – picture hats.

**RB:**
Oh. Picture hats, yes.

**RC:**
Mind you, they also get pis–

**RB:**
Well, they would.

**RC:**
Pistachio nuts.

**RB:**
Oh, pistachio nuts, oh I see. Very nice.

**RC:**
And, of course, the beer was flowing like there was no, er–

**RB:**
Whisky left?

**RC:**
Like there was no tomorrow. This waitress was going around with these big jugs.

**RB:**
Oh – topless, was she?

**RC:**
Yes, flat as a pancake. Well, I was sat next to that Wendy from accounts. You know, her with the enormous, er–

**RB:**
What, Filofax?

**RC:**
No, the enormous, er–

**RB:**
Inflation rate?

**RC:**
No, enormous rubber plant on her desk.

**RB:**
Oh, that's what it's made of, yeah.

**RC:**
We got chatting about this and that. She fancies me; I know that 'cos she once gave me a bit of, er–

**RB:**
A bit of this and that?

**RC:**
No, a bit of, er–

**RB:**
A bit of this, that and the other?

**RC:**
No, a bit of, er–

**RB:**
A bit of the other without the this and that?

**RC:**
No, a bit of her seedy cake in the canteen. Suddenly, she leans over and kisses me on the cheek.

**RB:**
Go on!

**RC:**
I thought "Hello!" 'Cos she's already kissed me on the, er –, on the, er–

**RB:**
Ear?

**RC:**
No, on the–

**RB:**
Face?

**RC:**
No, the–

**RB:**
On the other place?

**RC:**
No, on the Thursday.

**RB:**
Oh, I see. On the Thursday, right.

**RC:**
Well, lucky enough, the wife didn't see, 'cos she was out laying the, er–

**RB:**
The tables?

**RC:**
No, the foreman, as it happens.

**RB:**
Oh, I was right the first time.

**RC:**
Well, I pretended not to notice, kept eating me supper, and then suddenly her fingers sort of crept forward and pinched one of my, er–

**RB:**
Go on, really?

**RC:**
Yes, she pinched one of my, er–

**RB:**
Just the one, like?

**RC:**
Yes, oh yes, only the one. Well, I'd only got two.

**RB:**
Naturally.

**RC:**
Chips.

**RB:**
Oh, chips, yeah.

**RC:**
And she popped it in her, er–

**RB:**
Her mouth?

**RC:**
No, popped it in her, er–

**RB:**
Where? There's nowhere else to pop it.

**RC:**
Her handbag. She popped it in her handbag, for later.

**RB:**
Oh, I'd forgotten her handbag.

**RC:**
Then the boss stood up and proposed the toast.

**RB:**
Oh, you got toast an' all, did you?

**RC:**
The loyal toast, to our great Queen and all the, er–

**RB:**
All the little Queens?

**RC:**
No, all her dominions.

**RB:**
Oh, yeah.

**RC:**
And may she remain in good health and be protected against the dreaded, er – the dreaded, er–

**RB:**
Dreaded Lurgy?

**RC:**
No, the dreaded, er–

**RB:**
Dreaded corgi?

**RC:**
No, the dreaded–

**RB:**
Dreaded Fergie?

**RC:**
No, the dreaded foe.

**RB:**
Oh, foe, yes.

**RC:**
Then we all got up for a dance, and this Wendy grabbed me in the, er–

**RB:**
Heat of the moment?

**RC:**
No, in the, er–

**RB:**
Seat of the trousers?

**RC:**
No, in the Gentlemen's Excuse Me.

**RB:**
Ooh, painful.

**RC:**
And she pulled me to one side, and said "We were made for each other, because I'm also a little sh– a little sh–"

**RB:**
Short at the end of the week?

**RC:**
No, shy. "I'm a little shy myself," she said. "But if you're interested, when you leave here, go to the bicycle sheds, and I'll be round, er–"

**RB:**
Round at the back?

**RC:**
No, round, er–

**RB:**
Round at the front and back?

**RC:**
No, round the corner in the bushes. So of course, I went.

**RB:**
Go on? What happened?

**RC:**
Well, there she was, reclining, and she said, "Now's your chance," she said. "You can have anything you want."

**RB:**
And did you?

**RC:**
Not half. I grabbed her by the hand, er – the hand, er–

**RB:**
The handiest bit you could get hold of?

**RC:**
No! Do me a favour. I grabbed her by the handbag and pinched me chip back! Cheers!

# THE TWO RONNIES:

# MONOLOGUES and SPOKESPERSONS

One of the unique aspects of *The Two Ronnies* as a double act was that they were never really a double act. "Certainly I remember feeling quite strongly about that," remembers Ronnie Corbett. "We said we wouldn't do chat shows together or interviews together."

To emphasise this, every episode of the show featured at least one solo moment for each Ronnie – Ronnie C's took the form of his weekly seat-bound, rambling shaggy dog story, while Ronnie B chose to deliver a wide array of spokespeople for a bizarre collection of institutions, charities, government ministries and so on. These were often *tour de force* moments of performance, which highlighted Ronnie's fascination with, and playful love of language as a writer. As Sir Peter Hall (a collaborator with Ronnie in his theatre days back in the 1950s) has noted of these pieces: "His scripts are very precise. Very immaculate, very particular. And they relate to his extraordinary ability as an actor to time accurately in the way he says a line. I think the actor and writer kind of coalesce in their precision, because although he's an anarchic comedian in some respects, as a performer he's about precision."

# PISMONUNCERS UNANIMOUS

**RB:**

Good evening. I am the president for the loyal society for the relief of sufferers from pismonunciation; for people who cannot say their worms correctly. Or who use the wrong worms entirely, so that other people cannot underhand a bird they are spraying. It's just that you open your mouse, and the worms come turbling out in wuk a say that you dick knock what you're thugging a bing, and it's very distressing. I'm always looing it, and it makes one feel umbumfterkookle; especially when going about one's diddly tasks – slopping in the sloopermarket, for inkstands. Only last wonk I approached the chuckout point, and showed the ghoul behind the crash desk the contents of my trilley, and she said "Alright, grandad, shout 'em out." Well, of course, that's fine for the ordinary man in the stoat, who has no dribble with his warts, but to someone like myself, it's worse than a kick in the jackstrop. Sometimes you get stuck on one letter, such as wubbleyou, and I said "I've got a tin of whoop, a woocumber, two packets of wees and a wallyflower." She tried to make fun of me and said "That will be woo pounds and wifty wee pence." So I said "Wobblers" and walked out.

So you see how dickyfelt it is. But help is at hand. A new society has been formed by our mumblers to help each other in times of ex cream ices. It is bald "Pismonuncers Unanimous" and anyone can ball them up on the smellyfone at any tight of the day or gnome, 24 flowers a spray, seven stays a creak, and they will come round and get you drunk. For foreigners, there will be interpreters who will all squeak many sandwiches, such as Swedish, Turkish, Burkish, Jewish, Gibberish and Rubbish. Membranes will be able to attend tight stool for heaving grasses, to learn how to grope with the many kerplinkities of daily loaf. Which brings me to the drain reason for squawking to you tonight. The Society's first function, as a body, was a Grand Garden Freight, and we hope for many more bodily functions in the future. The Garden Plate was held in the grounds of Blenheim Paliasse, Woodstick, and guest of horror was the great American pip-singer, Manny Barrowload. The fête was opened by the Bleeder of the Proposition, Mr Neil Pillock, who gave us a few well-frozen worms in praise of the Society's jerk, and said that in the creaks and stunts that lie ahead, we must all do our nut-roast to ensure that it sucks weeds. Then everyone visited the various stalls and abruisements, the rudabouts, thingboats and dodgers, and of course the old favourites such as cocoshy nuts, stry your length, guessing the weight of the cook, and tinning the pail on the wonkey. The occasional was great fun and, in short, I think it can safely be said that all the men present and thoroughly good women were had all the time.

So please join our Society. Write to me – Doctor Small Pith *(caption:* "DR PAUL SMITH") The Spanner, Poke Moses *(caption*: "THE MANOR, STOKE POGES") and I will send you some brieflets to browse through and a brass badge to wear in your loop-hole. And a very pud night to you all.

# ANNUAL GENERAL MOUTHFUL

**RB:**

Silence, please. I'd like to call this meeting to order and welcome everyone to the annual, or, in other words, twelve-monthly conference that we hold once a year for the Society for People Who Use a Lot of Words and Say Very Little. It is with tremendous pleasure, enjoyment, elation, glee, joy and delight and with very little pain, discomfort, embarrassment, melancholia and stroke or depression that I address you all verbally by speaking to all those of you who are listening, with your ears, to the vocal manifestations which are emanating audibly from this hole in the middle of my face.

Now, not wishing to be brief, and in order more fully to beat about the bush, not to mention shilly-shallying and procrastination, although I have, in fact, just mentioned them – nevertheless, and notwithstanding, I don't propose to sit down without laying before you where I stand in relation to our policy of, or attitude to, and indeed our connection with, the attitude which our policy has always been concerned over.

**MR WHISPER:**
'Scuse me, sir.

*(Whisper whispers.)*

**RB:**
Ah! I have just been handed a message, typewritten, in a hand I do not recognise, which informs me, in no uncertain terms, plainly, even outspokenly, clearly, concisely, briefly, and perhaps it wouldn't be going too far to say rudely, that in the unbiased opinion of the sender of the message, I should bring to an end, terminate, and possibly cease completely, my talk, address, conversation or discourse, forthwith, if not immediately. Not, I may add due to the content of my speech: but merely because, unknown to me – when I first rose from my seat, on which I had been sitting before I stood up, to begin this particular address to you, the members of the society, the spectators, and the audience, not to mention all those present: my trousers fell down.

*(Pull back to reveal RB's trousers have fallen down.)*

# SPEECH DAY

**RB:**
Headmaster – Mrs Featherstone – members of the teaching staff – parents – boys. I don't know you – and I'm quite sure that none of you have ever heard of me. Many of the masters won't know me – in fact, until today, hardly anyone in this school would have been aware of my existence. I'm the Minister of Education. But that is not the reason I am here this afternoon. I am here because I'm an old boy. One of this school's old boys. And I'm here today to talk about what it is like, to be an old boy. Many of you young boys here today will eventually become – old boys. And I wonder what sort of old boy you will turn out to be. I've met all sorts of old boys in my time – clever old boys, funny old boys, stupid old boys and some downright wicked old boys. I was talking to a deaf old boy the other day, and I told him I was coming to talk to you today. And then, I told him again. And this time, he heard me, and he asked me to pass on this bit of good advice. Take care of your ears. Protect them against frosty weather, and above all, keep them clean at all times. I mean nobody likes to see an old boy with dirty ears walking along the street. So let your motto be "Cleanliness at all times". And abstinence. Strong liquor should be avoided wherever possible. I mean, there's nothing worse than going into a pub, and finding it full of old boys playing shovehappenny, so that you can't get near the bar. Personal safety, too, is very important.

The other day I was driving my car along the road, when an old boy stepped straight off the pavement in front of me. And if I hadn't braked sharply, I would have killed the old boy. So remember – look after yourself, avoid strong drink, and keep your ears clean. Oh, and one final word. Women. Well, I'd like to go on much longer – but that's impossible. And when you're an old boy like me, you'll understand what I mean. Thank you.

*(Applause.)*

# AN APPEAL FOR WOMEN

**RB:**

Good evening. My name is Arnold Splint, and I am here tonight. *(Caption – "An appeal for Women".)* This is an appeal for women only. No, please don't switch off – because it's you men I want to talk to, especially tonight. I am appealing to you, for women. I need them desperately. I can't get enough – and the reason I'm appealing to you men, is that I don't appeal to women. But I still need them. So this is how you can help. If you have an old woman you no longer need – send her to me. Simply tie her arms and legs together, wrap her in brown paper, and post her to me, care of the BBC, with your own name printed clearly on the bottom. Because that's the bit I shall undo first. Of course, I cannot guarantee to make use of all women sent to me. It depends on the condition, so make sure you enclose a self-addressed pair of knickers. Send as many women as you like, no matter how small. I assure you, all those accepted will be made good use of by me and my team of helpers – who, incidentally, carry on this work, many without any form of support.

I do hope you can find time to send me something: we did originally start collecting with a van, from door to door, but this scheme was abandoned owing to the wear and tear on the knockers.

I think we should remember that Christmas is on its way. And when it comes, and you are sitting at home by your own fireside, warming yourself beside a roaring great woman, think of all those poor unfortunate people who are having to go without this Christmas. Why not send them an old flame or two, to warm the cockles of their hearthrug? I'm quite sure that many of you have women lying about in drawers, that you haven't touched for years. Please, post them off today. Help us set up our Women On Wheels service for old men who can't move about. I know it's not easy. It requires self-denial, patience and an enormous amount of string; but I'm sure you'll feel better for it. I know I shall. Good night.

# SWEDISH MADE SIMPLE

*We start on the above title as a caption, over RB as the professor. He is dressed as a head waiter – tails, black bow tie, etc. Suitably stupid music under opening shot – which fades as RB starts to talk.*

**RB:**

Güten abend, grutte Erfund, Good evenink. My name is Professor Gewister *(raspberry)* fitten, and tonight we have a Swedish lesson for you, but with a difference. It is in Norwegian. Now I expect some of you are wondering why I am dressed as a waiter. It is because tonight our lesson is entitled "In The Restaurant" or as we say in Sweden "Im de restaurant". And before we go over to the scene, let me explain that, as we act out our little drama for you, there will be on the screen sub-titles. Which, as you know, are used in Swedish films and, which are necessary to explain to English people what is going on in the bedroom scenes. But to make it easier, we spell it out for you. We used only one letter for each word. Instead of putting thus *(Super caption "Hello")* Hello, we put this *(Super caption "Lo")* "Hello". You see – "Hell–lo."

*(Cut to three pictures – photo blow-ups behind him. Zoom in on the first one: a picture of a ragged child being given money.)*

And similarly, here we have "Pity" *(super "PT")*

*(Pan to next photo – general view of St Paul's, etc.)*

And here "City" *(super "CT".)*

*(Pan to next photo – bikini girl with big boobs.)*

And er … *(super "TT")* … and so on. So come with me and we will begin the lesson.

*(He walks into little cafe set. Two tables, one door to kitchen. Minimum of detail. RC, as customer, is already seated alone. N.B. just before each line is spoken, the sub-titles appear at the bottom of the screen in bold capital letters, without full-stops, but a reasonable distance apart.)*

**RC:**
LO.

**RB :**
LO.

*(Looks at camera briefly with a "remember this bit?" sort of look.)*

**RC:**
RUBC?

*(Takes menu from RB.)*

**RB:**
SVRBC.

*(A waitress walks past carrying ham on a dish.)*

**RB:**
LO.

**WAITRESS:**
LO.

**RC:**
LO.

**WAITRESS:**
LO.

**RC:**
FUNEX?

**RB:**
SVFX.

**RC:**
FUNEM?

**RB:**
9.

**RC:**
*(suspiciously)* IFCDM.

**RB:**
VFN10EM!

**WAITRESS:**
*(popping her head round kitchen door)* A! VFM.

**RC:**
R!

**RB:**
O?

**WAITRESS:**
C – DM.

*(Shows him ham on dish.)*

**RC:**
OK – MNX.

**RB:**
MNX.

**RC:**
FUNET?

**RB:**
1 T?

**RC:**
1 T.

**RB:**
OK – MXNT *(shouts to kitchen)* MXNT41!

**WAITRESS:**
*(appearing)* VFN10EX.

**RC:**
UZUFX.

**RB:**
*(shouting)* YFNUNEX?

**WAITRESS:**
IFE10M!

**RB:**
*(to camera)* SILLYCOW.

❧

# THE STARS AT NIGHT

*Start on a shot of planets revolving on a model as in* The Sky at Night. *Lose after four seconds. Almost immediately one planet hits another one, which falls off and bounces. Cut to RB. Fade music.*

**RB:**

Hello, good evening and welcome to this special edition of *The Stars At Night. (over this we see caption – "Patrick Moore's brother".)* I'm sorry to have to inflict myself on you like this, but Patrick couldn't be here tonight, and so he asked me to step into his shoes. And why not? He's always borrowing my suits. So here I am, and he asked me to apologise to you for not being here, but he has had to go and show his telescope to the local Townswomen's Guild. If they like it, they're going to knit him a cover for it. Then tonight he's taking it to the Palladium for the Night of a Thousand Stars. Apparently, they're one short, and he's going to help them look for it. And what he'll do after that, well, we just don't know.

Because, of course, he never goes to bed at night, that's when his day's work starts. And only when dawn breaks, does he put away his slide-rule and relax. Of course, he likes a little bit of fun afterwards, just like anyone else. Many's the time I've seen him put on his dinner jacket and go out and dance till lunchtime. This, of course, has its advantages: he never has trouble with last buses, and no one can accuse him of staggering home with the milkman, which is just as well, as it's a very gossipy neighbourhood.

However, I digress, as my very good friend Frank Ackfield would say. The reason Patrick asked me to come here tonight, apart from not wanting to lose the fee, was that tonight, and tonight only, whizzing across our sky, you will be able to see the celebrated Bailey's Comet. Now this comet appears only once in 200 years, and so not many of us have actually seen it before, but I can assure you that from all parts of Britain it will be visible to the naked observer; so a trip into your back garden should be well worth it – if only to look over the fence at the woman next door.

*(Enter a girl with a piece of white card.)*

Now this comet passes very, very close to the moon, how close we just don't know, but I would like, if I may, to show you a diagram of what is liable to happen. Thank you, Sandra, now then. *(He draws a wavy line across the board.)* Here we have the surface of the moon, and here *(another line)* the stratosphere. Here is the famous Sea of Tranquillity – here a mountain, known as the Height of Absurdity, and here, two craters, known as the Depths Of Depravity. Now the last moon shot orbited here *(draws a dot and a semi-circle)* but Bailey's Comet will pass even closer to the moon, here *(draws a dot nearer the surface and another semi-circle)* so you can see it should be a splendid sight. Of course this is sideways on. What we will see is more like this – turn it round, Sandra, truly a heavenly body not to be missed.

*(Sandra now holds the drawing in front of her – a wavy torso with two large boobs, and her head looking over the top.)*

Now, a word about next week. Patrick himself hopes to be back with you when, owing to a great number of requests, he is going to devote the whole programme to asteroids, and how to deal with them, which should be a boon to all fellow sufferers. If you have any questions to ask Patrick, postcards only please, and if you have any to ask Sandra, put them in a sealed envelope as we have a filthy-minded postman.
*(He drinks from glass on desk.)*

But to return to the comet, those who want to see ...

**SANDRA :**
*(from wings)* Psst!

**RB:**
Er – those who want to see the comet …

**SANDRA:**
Psst!

**RB:**
No, I won't, it's water. For those who would like to see the comet, it will be visible from about quarter past … *(Sandra points to her watch frantically as she approaches. RB looks at his watch.)* Oh Lord. Damn and blast. We've just missed it. Oh well, never mind, it'll come round again in 200 years and Patrick will tell you all about it then. Goodnight.

*(He starts to sing "The Stars at Night are Big and Bright" with Sandra looking over his shoulder and clapping to the music.)*

# AN EAR IN YOUR WORD

**RB:**
A very good one to you all and evening. My name is Willie Cope. I am the president of the "Getting your Wrongs in the Word Order" Society, and I've been asked by the BCB to come a night too long to aim the society's explains, and picture you firmly in the put.

*(Caption over – President, Getting your Words in the Wrong Order Society.)*

Firstly, I would like to say here and now – but I can't. I always say to seem now and here which nose me absolutely get-where. And most of our troubles have this member. It is very difficult to undersay what people are standing, especially if, as I did then, people only get half their back words-wards. As you can imagine, funny and gentlemen, you get some ladies combinations.

Now this certainly vocabs down your cutlery. You obviously have to avoid words like auspices and titillation for a start. Last week, for instance, I went to the barbers, and asked for my usual on the top, and not too much off the backside. But the society is doing most of its ut to ensure that both men and women who are live have comfortable members. Why not come down to Head-Head in Surrey and visit our hindquarters? Members can stay for the weekend, or weak members can stay for the end. End members can, of course, stay for the week.

Both men and sports can enjoy the pastimes and women. Indoor games include ping, billiard-winks and tiddley-pong. Outdoors one can swim through the country lanes, or go for a long hike in the swimming pool. Facilities also include a nine-course golf-hole, and a three lunch hot course at the restaurant, where the menu will offer you a wide choice of waiters to taste your suit. Anything from beef toad to hole in the wellington.

The club house is a favourite drinking place for meters, as is the local pub, the Three Feathers; often one hears the cry "Meet you in the three tails for a cock-feather".

The club house also offers accommodation for visitors, so if your lady-friend arrives, she can be put in the club, up the house, overnight.

However, I would hate you to get the skittle that it's all beer and ideas. I myself give lectures every aftermorning and noon, five weeks a time. I have an assistant, Miss Help, who Witherspoons me out most weekends. She always crowds very large drawers. We need new members – who doesn't? So if you would like to join the shy, don't be course. Write to me, naming your state, and enclosing a recent problem (head and shoulders only, please) together with a stamped addressed photograph. Here is the address – *(Super caption as he speaks)* Dr Willie Cope, 21 North Place, St Johns Wood, London WC, I'll just repeat that: *(Second caption)* Dr WC Cope, 21 John Willie Place, Northwood, London N8. And just to make sure, I'll repeat it again: *(Third caption)* Dr J Wood Willie, 21 WC Place, North London 8. May I wish each and every year of you a Merry Christmas and a happy new one. Goodnight.

# ONE GOOD TURN: THE CALL OF THE WILD

*Fade up on a music hall stage, with jungle backcloth and footlights. RB enters as animal impersonator. He wears an old-fashioned dinner jacket, starched dickie and wing collar. He moves centre stage, where a small card table awaits him, with various props upon it.*

**RB:**
*(he speaks with an American accent and sounds rather gay)* My name is Harold Beresford, and tonight with my animal sounds and bird calls, I hope to bring you, using my throat, larynx, forearms, and various parts of my body, a real whiff of the country. I also use a few common household objects such as this ordinary oil-lamp funnel, which gives added resonance when re-creating the throaty roar of the lion. *(He croaks through the funnel)* The distinctive evening call of the African bull-frog *(wood-lee, wood-lee)* and the myriad sounds of the jungle. *(He burps.)* Pardon me. That was dinner. But, to my story …

You will need to imagine that I am a hunter, young and gay, the son of a chieftain of the Elawi tribe of Central Africa. My name is Nuki, and I wear this feather as a badge of my rank and a square loincloth, which I will ask you to imagine. It is eight inches by twelve inches. I mean, just imagine. It is embroidered with symbols of fertility and just covers the part of the costume which is most important, however, is the feather, so I'll put it on. *(He does so.)* There. Do I look like an African prince? And of course, the ceremonial nose-bone. *(He clips it on rapidly and now talks through his nose.)*

Of course, I can't possibly do the imitations with this on, so you will have to imagine that as well if you will. *(Removes it again and speaks normally.)* Ooh, that really hurts your nose, you know that? But to my story. One Sunday morning in the depths of the jungle, when the tropical birds were greeting the dawn with their strange cries *(caw! caw! cruk, cruk, whistle etc)* Nuki rose and began to prepare for his daily walk in the forest. *(Rattles finger around in mouth and explains to audience)* Cleaning his teeth with a stick. Outside his straw hut, he could hear the chattering of the bald-backed bare baboon *(wuh! wuh! wuh!)* and the other all too familiar morning sound *(gibberish)* – his mother telling him to wash behind his ears. "I'm old enough to look after myself, mother" he replied. Though of course he said it in his own language. Soon he is on his way. He treads carefully through the crisp, crackly leaves on the forest floor *(crish crish crish crish crish slub slub)*, occasionally stepping in a mucky bit. Suddenly, behind him, he hears a sound that makes his blood run cold! *(oi! oi!)* He turns to face the most dreaded creature in the whole jungle *(oi! oi!)* His granny, on her way to market. "Oi," she cries. "Where you g'win soun?" He ignores her and hurries on.

Passing through a clearing, he notices the lazy wart-hog *(snort snort oink etc)*, the ant-eater busy eating ants *(sniff, sniff, sniff)* and the whistling woodpecker *(whistle, knock, knock, knock, whistle, etc)* He passes on, leaving the ant-eater eating his ants, and the wart-hog hogging his warts, and the whistling woodpecker pecking his wooden whistle. Soon he is into more open country where he spies his old friend, the giraffe. *(Picks up funnel, pauses.)* The giraffe makes no sound. Or rather, the slight sound it does make is impossible to recreate. With the mouth. The giraffe nods silently, turns its back, and is gone in a puff of dust. Nuki's journey is almost over and we leave him, finally, sitting peacefully by the river bank, watching the mating dance of the African flat-faced duck. This last demonstration requires that I roll up my trouser-leg, but do not fear, dear ladies – that's as far as I'm going. *(He rolls up his trouser-leg.)* I have no way of proving this to you, so you will have to take my word that this is the truly authentic sound of the mating-dance of the African flat-faced duck. Thank you.

*(He slaps his calf like the sound of ducks' feet. After a few seconds, a real duck walks on stage and heads towards him. Play-off music as he takes his bow. The duck looks interested.)*

# HELLFIRE, OR THE MUSIC MAN OF THE CLOTH

*RB as vicar of country church. He stands in old-fashioned pulpit, reached by a few stone steps. He addresses the congregation. The organ plays extempore under.*

**RB:**
This evening, my friends, I want to talk about Sin. And I wish to speak only to those amongst you who are Sinners. All those who have never sinned should leave now. *(He looks round.)* No one has moved. It's just as well. Because if anyone had dared to walk out, he would have been branded "Liar". This village – this village is overrun with Sin. It is rife! Rife! And I tell you, friends, that the Devil is everywhere, about his deadly work. He's at work in the village shop, watering the milk – he's in the public house, watering the beer – he is behind the public house, watering the daisies. He is at work upstairs behind the curtains of Oak Cottage, where old Mr Tomkins took a lodger, as company for his young wife. His young wife is in the family way. And the lodger – she's in the family way as well.

*(The organ starts to become rhythmical; RB begins to speak rhythmically.)*

He's everywhere, he's all through the village infecting the lives of each and every one of you – old folk, young folk, each and every one of you – spreading his evil work around with a flick of his old forked tail, and I'm warning you, if we don't do something about it, if we don't get the Devil from among us, if we don't repent–

My friends you got trouble–
Right here in Lower Witton–
You got crimes and cheats and slight misdemeanours that

Add up to a whole lot of wrong,
You got women who gossip and others that listen and
Some who are eavesdropping all day long
To see if they can hear if the women who are gossiping are
Saying anything about them
Like young Mrs Noakes (now you all know her)
Living up by the top end (up the hill)
Now she's known to have taken in laundry for the fellow
With the limp who works at the Inn
Now just because he's bought himself a brand new crutch
Doesn't mean he wore the old one out
But the Gossips say Yes
And that rhymes with "S"
And that stands for Sin!
Oh – yes – my – friends – you – really – got
Trouble.

**CONGREGATION:**
Yes, Trouble!

**RB:**
Right here in Lower Witton.

**CONGREGATION:**
Yes, you have!

**RB:**
You've got drinking, gambling, smoking, skiving, fiddling your income tax,
You've got women on the streets and girls on the game
And boys on the girls and the girls don't care
As long as they can listen to their tape cassettes they're
Taking it in their stride and what about
Meanness–
Have you seen the collection plate today?
Two washers, a fly-button, Irish penny and a half-sucked mint with a hole
Last week when a woman was asked to contribute
To a home for old inebriates
She gave 'em her husband, yes she did, upon my soul!

**RB & CHORUS:**
Upon – my soul – then – we – got – trouble.

**RB:**
Yes, we have.

**CHORUS:**
Right here in Lower Witton.

**RB:**
(It's here, it's here) Why the whole congregation is consumed by greed
Immorality and envy too–
Take the women in the fur coats, sitting in their minks–

How d'you think they got them? Why,
Same way as the mink does – you've guessed it,
Made by another mink, and what about
Lying?
And cheating on the railway, I heard tell of a woman
Who was asked to pay full fare for her boy
On account of the trousers he was in;
It's full-length trousers, full-size fare said the guard, and the woman said fine, so it's half
For me, and my daughter goes free, and that's a SIN!

*(The congregation now surround the pulpit, carried away by the mood.)*

**RB:**
Now you're gonna have to pay.

**CHORUS:**
Yes, yes!

**RB:**
For all this trouble.

**CHORUS:**
Oh, yes!

**RB:**
'Cos the Devil is waiting to carry you off to the nethermost parts of Hell, where the fire's stoked
Up, and the spits are sizzling, and the oil is on the boil and
Each little Devil has just been issued with a
Brand new toasting fork–
Now! Hear me,
Hear me and repent ('cos there's no one gonna be spared)
Not me, not you, 'cos we're all lost sinners, and that you know full well–
Now the Lord has chosen me, my friends
To go and pave the way
And I'll see
You
All
In
HELL!

*The pulpit floor sinks – RB slowly disappears with a flame effect and smoke coming from inside the pulpit.*

●◆

# UNIVERSITY OF THE AIR

*RB as Irish lecturer – black wig, gown, string round trousers, etc.*

**RB:**
The top of the evening to you. And the top of the milk as well. And welcome to the Irish University of the Air. Now many people have been writing in to us, saying that they make the lessons too difficult in this programme, and it's practically impossible to pass the exam at the end of the series; so much so that a lot of you have been having to come home early from the pub at nights to study, sometimes even before throwing out time. Well, now, we don't want any of that, do we now? So we've decided this year to make the questions a lot easier, so that you all pass. So here we are, these are the questions that will be on the exam paper this time. Are you ready? Ten questions. Anyone answering eleven questions will be disqualified.

**QUESTION 1.**
Who won the First World War?

**QUESTION 2:**
Who came second?

**QUESTION 3:**
What is a silver dollar made of?

**QUESTION 4:**
Explain Einstein's theory of Hydrodynamics or write your name in block capitals.

**QUESTION 5:**
Spell the following: *(writes on blackboard)* a) Dog b) Car c) Carrot.

**QUESTION 6:**
What time is the Nine o'clock News on?

**QUESTION 7:**
How many Commandments was Moses given? Approximately.

**QUESTION 8:**
There have been six Kings of England called George. The latest was called George the Sixth. Name the other five.

**QUESTION 9:**
Who invented Stevenson's Rocket?

**QUESTION 10:**
Do you understand Newton's Law of Gravity? (Answer Yes or No).

**QUESTION 11:**
Of what country is Dublin the capital? (This answer must be exact).

**QUESTION 12:**
If Paddy carries 20 bricks in a hod, and carries 40 hods a day; and weighs half as much as Murphy, and Murphy carries 10 bricks in a hod and carries 80 hods a day, and he weighs twice as much as Paddy – who is the biggest idiot?

That's the end of the questions. Copies of this examination paper are obtainable at all betting shops. Not more than seven hours is allowed for the completion of this paper and the only reference books allowed are *Reveille* and the *Sporting Life*. Candidates, and all others who have entered, should send their answers, preferably on paper, to "Irish University of the Air", BBC studios, and if you don't hear for six months, you've passed and you're a BA. And if you forget to post it, you're a BF. One last thing – if some of the arithmetic is too difficult, here is the latest Irish calculator, obtainable at any pub that sells Guinness. *(Shows calculator. It is a knot of string.)* That's the memory – and that's for cancelling. *(Shows knot of string and knife.)* And the best of Irish luck – Goodnight.

# EQUALITY

**RB:**

Good evening. Equality. The Government White Paper on The Equal Society was published today. It's main provisions are as follows:

From April 1st 1981, everyone must be of equal height. This height will be three foot above the saloon bar for men, and two feet under the hair dryer for women. Anyone found shorter than the equal height will be looked down on. He will then be sent to a Government height-inducing camp, where he will stand in a barrel of manure – until he's tall enough to step out without catching anything on the rusty nail at the top. Anyone found taller than the equal height will be required to carry lead weights in the trouser pockets and wear very short braces. This will cause a stoop and, inevitably, a few boy sopranos.

Everyone must also be of equal weight. The weight to be established as Quite Heavy for men, and Not Quite So Heavy for women – except during pregnancy when women will be permitted a little more. Men, however, will not be permitted anything at all. Anyone found heavier than the equal weight will complete a questionnaire, asking such questions as "Are you able to adjust your dress before leaving?" and "When did you last see your feet?" If the answers are "yes", their corsets will be impounded, although this rule is fairly elastic, and they will be sent to a Government "jumping up and down" camp. Anyone below equal weight will be forcibly fed with chocolate biscuits, through the office of the resident physician – and will receive silicone injections in the event. Or in the arm. If a woman thinks silicone is silly, she can have cortisone instead. But if a man has cortisone, he should be more careful with his zipper.

Now then *(he produces a large piece of cardboard)* I would now like to show you a diagram. I would like to, but I can't, as Mrs Whitehouse might complain. But I'll tell you about it. As from 1985, everyone will be of equal shape. Except, of course, that women will have two of these and one of those; and men will have one of these, and two of those. If any man is found to have two of these, he will be declared a woman – whether he has one of those or not. Now if a man has got one of these but only one of those, he will get a pension. And if he's got two of those and two of these, he won't get a pension but he will get attention. Believe you me. And any man found with three of those, will be ostracised. Which is bad news for pawnbrokers. *(Phone rings.)* Hello? Oh, hello Mrs Whitehouse. You what? You insist on the viewers seeing all the these and those? Very well. *(Turns card round – it has "these" and "those" in large letters, several times, all over it.)* There we are. Disgusting, isn't it? But true to life. Like *Crossroads*.

Noses. There will be a choice of noses – Roman aquiline or Hooked turn-up. The number of nostrils will remain at two – although there will be a choice of straight or flared. Members of the public will be allowed to make their choice in their own time, but the House of Commons is to have a special session, when Members can all pick their noses together. It was later stated that it will not be necessary in future for noses to run in the family.

Finally, in future, all children must be born equally, that is, on October 1st each year. This will be known as Labour Day. To achieve this objective, all television transmissions during the week of December 23rd will close down at nine o'clock – when everyone will have an early night. And a happy Christmas to you all. Goodnight.

# THE MINISTER OF POETRY

**RB:**
Good evening. May I say at once, without further ado,
How nice it is to speak to each and every one of you.
No matter where you all may be, on land or sea or foam,
Whether climbing up Mount Everest or kicking about at home,
I broadcast to you all tonight, on BBC TV
To tell you of the creation of a brand new Ministry.

*(Caption – "Ministry of Poetry". RB puts on big floppy black hat.)*

"Here, just a mo" I hear you cry – now what's all this about?
"A Minister of Poetry?" "Good God, who let him out?"
It's Margaret Thatcher's brainchild, this – our venerable prime Missis.
I'll tell you, if you'll all pin back your aural orifices.
Last Friday week I left the House of Commons just on eight
The wife was out at Bingo, so I knew that she'd be late.
I popped into the local – I was feeling rather frail –
And there stood Maggie Thatcher with her foot upon the rail.
"What you having, Jack?" she cried, her beady eyes aflame –
"I'll have a pint of Mild" I said, she said "I'll have the same."
Well, seventeen pints later – God, how that girl can booze!
We sat on the Embankment and she came out with the news.
"For many years," she mumbled, as she munched the crisps I bought her,
Tidily folding up the bag and chucking it in the water,
"For many years I've longed to see this ancient land of ours
Return to former glories – and the pubs to longer hours.
Those grand old days of Shakespeare when the folk all spoke in rhyme,
And the language wasn't full of swear words, all the bleedin' time.
How nice it must have been to hear a lilting line that lingers,
When the worker to the foreman gave two verses, not two fingers.
If we could re-create the old-world charm of this great nation,
The voters would forget the shrinking pound, ignore inflation.
"And you're the man, dear Jack," she said "who can that promise keep.
Romance is not yet dead!" With that, she burped, and fell asleep.
I covered her with newspaper and left her on the grass
Looking every inch a lady and completely upper-class,
In a powder-blue ensemble with her hair all freshly done,
And across her chest, another chest, from page three of The Sun.
And that is how the Ministry was created overnight.

And now it's up to you, my friends, to see you do it right.
Pray, have no fear, the task is not as hard as it may sound
For inside every Englishman, good English rhymes abound,
And each of you has, at some time, I'm sure (as haven't we all?)
Inscribed a simple stanza on some by-gone wash-house wall.
So off you go and don't forget, just like the old graffiti
Keep it short, and keep it snappy, keep it fruity, keep it meaty.
Just think of all the joy you'll cause when on a bus you leap,
At dawn, one chilly morning, when the world's still half asleep.
"A single fare – to Euston Square" you warble to the driver.
"The cost to me is 20p" and offer him a fiver.
As he looks for four pounds eighty change, what gay thoughts fill his head–
With any luck he'll hand you out a fourpenny one instead.
The world can be a better place, if each man does his best
To choose his rhymes to match the times, so get it off your chest!
Beneath the old stiff upper lip the ancient fire still flickers–
Come, fan the flames, and let us get the lead out of our knickers.
Press onward, England, do your best – revive our former glories –
Let's raise our beers and give three cheers. Goodnight and up the Tories.

# A SERMON

*A vicar enters a pulpit. Organ music over. Caption: "Vicar of St Cain and Abel church, Hampstead Heath". Organ music stops and he addresses us.*

**VICAR:**
Now many of you gathered here tonight in the church of St Cain and Abel in Hampstead Heath will know that these words are Cockney rhyming slang. Cain and Abel means table and Hampstead Heath means teeth. We are glad to welcome tonight a large group of Cockney worshippers to Evensong; and it is to them that I wish to address my sermon. I want to tell you a story.

A long time ago, in the days of the Israelites, there lived a poor man. He had no Trouble and Strife – she had run off with a Tea Leaf some years before – and now he lived with his Bricks and Mortar, Mary. And being very short of Bees and Honey, and unable to pay the Burton-on-Trent, he was tempted to go forth into the Bristol City, and see what he could Half-Inch. And he would say to Mary, his Bricks and Mortar – "I will take a Ball of Chalk into the town, and buy some tobacco for my Cherry Ripe." And he would put on his Almond Rocks, and his Dicky Dirt and his Round The Houses, and set off down the Frog and Toad, until he reached the outskirts of the Bristol.

One day his Bricks and Mortar gave him some money, saying "Here is a Saucepan Lid – go and buy food. A loaf of Uncle Fred and a pound of Stand At Ease. But do not tarry in the town and bring me back what is left of the money to buy myself a new pair of Early Doors, for my present ones are full of holes, and I am in a continual George Raft." But instead of returning with the Bricks and Honey for his Bricks and Mortar's Early Doors, he made his way to the Rub-A-Dub, for a Tumble-down-the-sink. And he became very Elephant's Trunk, and Mozart; and when the landlord of the Rub-A-Dub called Bird Lime, the man set off back towards his Cat and Mouse, reeling about all over the Frog and Toad, and drunkenly humming a Stewed Prune.

And it came to Khyber Pass, that as he staggered along, he saw on the pavement, a small brown Richard the Third. And he stared at it, lying there at his Plates of Meat. And he said "Oh, small brown Richard the Third – how lucky I did not step on you." And he picked it up and put it on top of a wall, where no one could step on it. And a rich Four-by-Twoish merchant, who witnessed the deed, put his hand into his Sky Rocket, and took out a Lady Godiva, and handed it to the man, saying "I saw you pick up that Richard the Third and remove it from the pavement and that was a kindly act. Take this Lady Godiva for your Froth and Bubble." And the man took it and went on his way. And the Richard the Third flew back to its nest.

When the man arrived home, his daughter was sitting by the Jeremiah, on her favourite Lionel Blair. And the man said unto her – "Here is a Lady Godiva, which I earned by a kindly act." And the woman was overjoyed and said "Thank you, father. Now I can have my pair of Early Doors." "And I can have my drink" said the man. "Verily, that kindly act has ensured that we both have enough to cover our Bottle and Glass."

I thank you all.

# PISMONUNCUATION (2)

*RB at plain desk.*

**RB:**
Good evening. I'm squeaking to you, once again, as chairman of the loyal society for the prevention of pismonunciation. A society formed to help people who can't say their worms correctly. I myself often use the wrong worms, and that is why I was erected charming, of the society. Firstly, let me try and put you in the puncture, regarding our mumblers. Peach and every plum of them have dickyfelty in conversing with the people they meet in everyday loaf – their murkvates at the figtree or the orifice; even in their own holes, min and woof, sather and fun, bruzzer and thistle, unable to comainicute. This can be an enormous bandy-chap to our tremblers at all times, but especially at Bismuth time; because Bismuth is a season of grease on earth and pigswill to all men, when the family get together to eat, drunk, and be messy – to gather round the fireside, cracking nits, smelling Tories, and singing old pongs and barrels. Many of our rumblers lose out on these skinful pastimes – a very close fringe of mine, for instance, once went carol slinging with the local church queer, but instead of slinging "Good King Wenceslas stuck out. And his feet were steaming", he sang: "Go rest your belly, gentlemen, Let nothing rude display", which, of course, caused havoc among the queer, and deeply up-ended the knickers wife. This is just one instance of what my tremblers have to stiffer with a lipped upper stuff.

What we need now is money, to build clubs and calamity-centres, where people don't have to bother with the right worms. Places where they can greet each other with a cheery "Good afternuts, how nice to squeeze you" – a place where they can play a game of ping-tennis, table-pong, scribble, or newts and crutches.

Many famous people are patrons of the society. Piddyticians like Widdly Whitelaw, Sir Geoffrey Who and Mr Denis Holy. Also famous TV Nosebleeders like Reggie Boozenquart, Angela Ripe'un and Anna Floored. And, of course, Mrs Hairy Whitemouse; not to be confused with Mrs Woodlouse, the hog-dangler. Among the aristocracy, there is Lord Longfelt – the Duchess of Bedbug, and Lord Monty-boo of Goolie. But patronage is not enough.

Remember the worms of William Shakepiece, our great national poe-face:- "A

Horse, a House, my kingdom for a Hearse". And of course, eventually, he got all three.

What we need is printed matter – any sort of printed matter – no mitter what sort. Send your magazines, nose-papers, dicks and booktionaries. Do it now. Bungle it up in pustules and post it to one of our mini branches dotted all over the Bottish Isles:

Minchester, Herminbum, Loverpill, and as far North as the Firth of Filth. And we are also busy setting up outposts in foreign pants, too, all over the glob. In fact, we have just opened a branch in Siam, and, in confusion, I would like you to join me in slinging the Siamese Notional anthem, to the tune of God Save the Queer.

*(Audience and RB sing, as words are supered over lowerthird, or whatever.)*

**RB AND AUDIENCE:**
Owa Tana Siam
Owa Tana Siam
I Yamut Wit
Owa Taphoo Lamai
Owa Taphoo Lamai
Owa Tana Siam
Owa Tanit.

**RB:**
Goodnight.

●◆

# A FEW WORDS

**RB:**
My friends – or may I call you ladies and gentlemen. I have been asked to make a speech; but before I do I'd just like to say a few words. And before I do that, I tell I must feel you, that I've had a few. Drinks, that is, not words. Mind you, quite a few words have passed my lips too, in my time. And of course, that's what life is all about, isn't it? Communication.

Communication. The spoken word. Now it's essential that we know what's going on, and indeed, what isn't going on that should be. We must communicate with each other, and also with anyone else we happen to meet, because everyone – and by everyone I mean everybody can, and in fact does, or if they don't at present they very soon, – will, because to be honest; everyone has to, eventually, for, as we all know, and those who've had the experience will bear me out. And the sooner the better.

In other words, we must try to regard the nation as a whole. And those who think it is one, should get out and make room for the others. Because I mean there's no room for shirkers. This country has a great future behind it. I mean, have you ever wondered what will we all be like in a hundred years from now? Well, we'll be dead but this land of ours will be a garden of Eden. Today we have the penny post, but then they'll have two posts: a first class post that doesn't get there the next day and a second class post that doesn't get there the day after. In 1974 they'll be a channel tunnel – we'll understand our neighbours better. We won't say "Wogs begin at Calais". We'll say "Wogs begin at Dover". By then we'll have dug a tunnel straight downwards so at no expense at all you'll be able to fall to Australia. Everyone will have much more leisure time. We'll cut the working week to 96 hours for children under ten, and to ten hours for children over 96.

Oh, but 1974 will be wonderful! Think of the discoveries we have already – already women have their children delivered at the front door, thanks to Mr Gladstone and his bag; sometimes known as Mrs Gladstone. Already we can go out and go to the toilet without getting our feet wet, thanks to the Duke of Wellington. And now that we have the sandwich, invented by the Earl of Sandwich, what great things can we expect from Lord Wimpy and Baron Jumbo-Brunchburger! And look at this kettle *(produces old copper kettle)* This is the very one that James Watt saw when he first thought of the steam engine. Had he come in five minutes later, the tea would have been made and the frying pan would have been on the stove, and he would have invented the chip engine. Transport will be quite different. We'll have a 30-horsepower bus worked by only two men, one to drive and the other to clean up after the 30 horses.

And they'll be equality. Everyone will be given a chance. You three gardeners at the back there ... listen well. In 1974 your great grandsons could be men of power – yes, you, Zebediah Heath, old Diggory Wilson and you, Sambo Powell. I predict that many minority groups will seek the vote – dogs, horses – even women. As to women – that could lead to trouble. Mind you, I'm not denying that some women have a perfect right. But, on the other hand, they've got an equally good left, and why – where do women get these ideas, about wanting to wear the trousers? In my opinion they should drop them completely, and assume their rightful position – bent over the sink. And if that isn't proof of the pudding, if proof were needed, then I don't know, who has.

To sum up:
You may drink to the girl with the face that's divine;
To the girl with the figure that's wavy;
You may drink to the girl from blue-blooded stock;
You may drink below stairs, with the slavey.
You may drink to the girl who is one of the boys,
Who goes out with the army and navy;
But here's to the girl who is both rich and old –
To the girl with one foot in the gravy.

Ladies and gentlemen – absent friends!

*(He drinks.)*

# MORE WORMS

*(From an idea by David Nobbs.)*

**RB:**
Good evening. Last year I spoke to you, appealing for help for those who, like myself, have trouble with worms. They can't pronounce their worms properly. Now, I am the secretary for the Loyal Society for the relief of sufferers from Pismonunciation. The reason I am once more squeaking to you tonight is that many people last time couldn't understand what I was spraying – so I am back again on your little queens to strain it and make it all queer.

It's a terrible thung to be ting-tied; it's even worse when your weirds get all muxed up, and come out in wuck a say, that you dick knock what you're thugging abing. Like I did just then, only crutch much nurse. It can be cured by careful draining at special draining-stools, which the Society has fed up all over the Twittish Isles, and for the really dicky felt cases we have a three-week bash course on the Isle of Fright, where the doctors can get to grips with the patients, and the nurses can get to grips with the doctors, and everyone has a dolly good climb. Except the patients of course, who find it Dudley Dell. Doddly Dill. Diddly Doll – or, in other words, bitefully flooring. People have tried to cure themselves. They stand in front of their bodroom mirror and say, "Every day in every way, I get bitter and butter." But it doesn't cure them, you can bot your wife. And most of them usually do. The disease is spreading. It affects people from all walks of loaf; members of the Swivel Service, lawyers, silly-sodders, commercial drivellers, cop sheepers and wactory furkers, especially on the night shirt – and famous piddly-titians like Widdly Hamilton. Not forgetting Peanock Owl, and stars of screege and stain like Black Mygraves, Frantic Howerd and Peculiar Clarke and Rude old Newry-eff, the ballet dangler.

How can you help? Well, for a tart, it's no good simply trying to correct people when they suffer from this complaining distress. My wife does it to me all the time. Lucky old you, I hear you squirt. No, I mean she corrects me when I get any ring thong, and it makes me lavvy and Ingrid. Last time I backed her up the kickside.

We need money. Your minny. You may row ashore that it will be put to the best possible use, by myself and my large and loyal stiff. Send your chocs or pistol orders today. Smash open your baggy pinks. Dip your hand into your wife's bags and send us a few cod hoppers. Or why not simply slip a pond newt into an envelope? Send your donations to me, Poctor Podger Smish, at my new address, 51 Duberry Road, Kidling, Dorset. I'll just repeat that – Dictor Smidger Posh, whifty fun, Doberry Rude, Diddling, Corset. Thank you for glistening, good night, and a crappy isthmus.

# THE MILKMAN'S XMAS SPEECH TO THE NATION

*RB as milkman, seated like the Queen at an ornate desk in Buck. Palace.*

**RB:**
A very merry Christmas to you all. As I think of you, my loyal customers, sitting at home round your firesides this Christmas, it brings home to me very strongly, the enormous responsibility that I have, as your milkman. *(Caption: HM QUINN.)* And I know, that you will appreciate, how important it is to me, to know that I have your support, and shall continue to have your support, throughout the coming year. The task of supplying milk to a great nation such as ours, is, I am sure you realise, not an easy one. Either here at home, or in our colonies – spread as they are, like butter, over the entire globe.

Whether home or colonial, it is our express wish that it be co-operative, uniting dairies across the world. The milk of human kindness must not be watered down. It must flow, not only through the cream of society, but also onto the most humble doorstep in the land, be it black, or white, or gold-top. Let our lives be ordered, and ordered as soon as possible, so as to avoid disappointment, in the years to come. I extend my warmest and most heartfelt bottle, to you all.

# DON'T QUOTE ME

A cosy, book-lined studio set.
*RB, with peg on nose, as Melvyn Bragg. He speaks to camera.*

**RB:**
Hello, and welcome to the book programme.

*(Caption supered – Melvyn Pegg.)*

**RB:**
William Shakespeare, it is generally agreed, has provided the English language with more sayings, proverbs and quotes than any other writer. Every other book title is a quote from the Bard. Many plays in the theatre do the same. Why then, should not television follow suit? Here, with a little help from our caption department, is a scene from *Edward the Sixth, Part I.*

*(During the last speech, mix to the interior of a Shakespearean castle, as in the film, Richard III. RB enters as Richard, with a courtier.)*

**RB:**
Now, dearest cous, the time draws fast apace
When for my crowning we must soon prepare.

**COURTIER:**
My liege, I have the information close.

**RB:**
Then spill it out – thou art already late;
Thou hadst forsworn to bring me *News at Ten.*

*(Caption – News at Ten.)*

**RB:**
But tell me first, how may I seek to rid
My royal self of that Arch villainess
That calls herself the Queen?

**COURTIER:**
Queen so she is
She is your consort, sire, or will be so
When you are crowned next week in Westminster.

*(Caption – Week in Westminster.)*

**COURTIER:**
Throughout the land her beauty is renowned
Her person is respected Nationwide.

*(Caption – Nationwide.)*

**RB:**
Her person is the Duke of Hastings, sir!

He is her lover, and must get the chop!
Each day they flaunt their fever in the court,
He arrogant and bold, and she all smiles
Contented with her lot, and with her bed,
Each night with her Brideshead Revisited

*(Caption – Crossroads.)*

**RB:**
Aye, he shall die, revenge shall be complete
My crowning's perk! My coronation's treat!

*(Caption – Coronation Street.)*

**RB:**
But, for to furnish evidence withal,
Observe the Queen's speech, when she's with him close.

*(Caption – The Queen's Speech.)*

**RB:**
When oft, beneath the starry sky at night

*(Caption – The Sky at Night.)*

**RB:**
He speaks in tones both Moribund and Wise

*(Caption – Moribund and Wise.)*

**RB:**
Of times when he, during the reign of John,
Kept silent, and endured the Tyrannies

*(Caption – The Two Ronnies.)*

**RB:**
Then mind her.

*(Caption – Minder.)*

**COURTIER:**
That will I, most royal liege.
He often plots with Lovell 'gainst the crown.

**RB:**
These points of view are treason, you well know

*(Caption – Points of View.)*

**RB:**
He may it think, but can he ever it show?

*(Caption – Kenny Everett Show.)*

**RB:**
He must be cornered with some trumped-up charge
Of treasonable acts, both Little and Large

*(Caption – The Two Ronnies.)*

**RB:**
Then, when he is transported to the Tower
No blemish shall besmirch my nuptial hour
Come, dancing maidens,

*(Caption – Come Dancing.)*

**RB:**
Trumpets, play away!

*(Caption – Play Away.)*

**RB:**
Drums that do beat at night must throb in day.

*(Caption – Robin Day.)*

**RB:**
And as the songs of praise proclaim us wed

*(Caption – Songs of Praise.)*

**RB:**
Let (bleep-bleep) Hastings lose his (bleep-bleep) head!

*(Caption – Blankety-Blank.)*

*(Exit, with fanfare.)*

# ONE GOOD TURN – THE CHOCOLATE-COLOURED COUGH DROP

*(Caption: one good turn.)*

*RB as Barry Norman in small set.*

*(Caption: (super) with Barry Normal.)*

**RB:**
*(very fast)* Hello and good evening to you. The bits of film we are about to show you, or at least I hope we're going to show you if they don't fall apart, are selected from the archives situated in the bowels, and I use the term loosely, but not too loosely, of the earth beneath the Television Centre, and if the actual film doesn't fall apart I'm sure you'll agree with me (and if you don't, I certainly shan't lose any sleep over it) that some of the acts certainly do fall apart, that is, not act – if you can call singing acting, which I'm not sure you can.

Where was I? Hello and good evening. The act you are about to see was the first one, and when I say the first one, I mean one of the first to come to light. If you can call it light, bearing in mind that it was in the bowels, and I use the term even more loosely than last time, of the Radio Doctor, here at Television Centre, and who am I to criticise? The man in the burnt cork and fuzzy wig was, or is, unless he's died, which he probably has by now, although I wouldn't bank on it, some of these performers seem to go on for ever – he certainly does – is the great Al Vermont, always billed as The Chocolate-coloured Cough-drop. See what you make of it.

*(Cut to old scratchy fuzzy black and white film. (Caption: Al Vermont – the chocolate-coloured cough-drop) upright or baby grand piano in parlour (American) set of the twenties.)*

*(RB, in burnt cork, period dinner jacket and fuzzy wig, seated at the piano, white gloves and a top hat complete the ensemble. He plays and sings the following song, and throughout he bounces up and down on the piano seat, in time to the stupid song, which is almost entirely on one note.)*

*(The set slowly disintegrates under this continual bumping. Pictures fall off the wall, ornaments vibrate their way off shelves into goldfish bowls, the piano stool eventually collapses, as indeed does the piano, on the final few bars. His top hat, placed on his stool for the second verse, is crushed. His foot goes through the floorboards, piano keys fly off (one or two). Champagne in a bucket shakes and explodes, cork flies out, etc, etc.)*

## SONG – "SYNCOPATED LADY"

I know a gal ...
I'm crazy for ...

*(piano arpeggio)*

She hangs around ...
My old back door ...

*(piano again)*

She never will ...
Belong to me ...
'Cos she's too sophisticated
And syncopated ...
You ...
See ...

*(piano intro into chorus)*

1. She's a syncopated lady
And she lingers where it's shady
And I listen to her daily
As she plucks her ukulele
And her eyes are kinda flashy
And her clothes are kinda trashy
And she smokes them small havanas
And she chews them big bananas–
Teeth like pearls and lips like wine
Thumpy Thumpy Thumpy goes that heart of mine–

2. Thumpy Thumpy Thumpy 'cos
Her shape it is so bumpy
It's so dimply and dumpy
Kinda loose and kinda lumpy
And it has no imperfections
And it points in all directions
How I love them pounds and ounces
In that sweater when it bounces
And it makes me kinda jumpy when our arms entwine
Thumpy Thumpy Thumpy goes that heart of mine.

*(a piano break of 12 or 16 bars – close up hands etc)*

She's a syncopated lady
And her second name is Sadie
And I love the way she dances
With just anyone she fancies
And I love the way she washes
And she wears them big galoshes
And the way her hands meander
When she's kissed on her veranda
She lives at number seven but she sleeps at number nine
Thumpy Thumpy Thumpy goes that heart of mine.

*(Repeat last line – as piano collapses completely, in long shot.)*

# THE SEX EQUALITY MONOLOGUE

*RB discovered as spokesman – dressed half as a man and half as a woman. Half a long blonde wig, half a black moustache, half a frilly dress, half a suit jacket, half a bosom.*

**RB:**
Good evening. I'm from the Ministry of sex equality, and I'm here tonight to explain the situation man to man – or as we have to say now – person to person.

*(Super caption: "A Spoke Person".)*

**RB:**
My name is Mr Stroke Mrs Barker. But I don't advise any of you to try it. Stroking Mrs Barker, that is. Now due to this new law, no one is allowed to be called male or female, man or woman. This has already caused a great deal of argument in Parliament, so they are all going for a Parliamentary conference at Personchester. They will all stay at a Nudist colony and air their differences. Members only, of course.

But where do you come in? Is it easy to become unsexed? Well, it can be done. And I represent the proof. At least, half of me does, the other half's quite normal. The first thing we have to realise, is that for too long, women have been beneath men – not only in the home, but at the office. And there are many ways in which we can change that. Vertical desk tops for a start. The main area of change, of course, will be in the language. The "man in the street" will become the "person in the street". Whoever you are, whether man or woman, you will be the person in the street. Incidentally, when I was in the street the other day, I nearly fell down a person-hole, so be careful.

Certain professions will have their names changed. From the Chairperson of a large company, right down to the humble Dustperson. (Not to be confused, of course, with the famous film star, Dustin Hoffperson). Speaking of films, there will be special feature films made, showing the equality of the sexes. Already in production, a new musical called *Seven Persons For Seven Other Persons* starring Paul Newperson and Robert Help-person, with music by Persontovani and His Orchestra.

Now, dress. Of course, you won't be expected to dress like this. This sort of costume is much too expensive. Half a nicker certainly doesn't cover it. No, each person can of course choose what to wear, provided it includes the customary shirt, bra, underpants and a handbag. Shoes can be black or brown, according to individual taste. I myself find that black shoes taste better than brown shoes.

Jobs, too, will be entirely sexless; with one or two obvious exceptions. What are they, you may ask? You may ask, but I'm not telling you on this programme. But here is a clue. They have jam on them, and appear at tea time. A job must be open to either a whatsit or a whoosit – that is, of either sex. For instance, certain advertisements will not be allowed. This one here says *(holds up newspaper cutting)* "Bar staff required for West Country Pub, male or female. Must have big boobs". Now that won't be passed by the Ministry at all. What they should have said was "Bar staff required, male or female. Must be attractive in the Bristol area". That would have got past.

A recent idea by the Ministry, to avoid confusion, is to call a man a doings, and a woman a thingy. This offends no one, and makes conversation clearer. Thus we instantly recognise the book called *Little Thingies* or the play by George Bernard Shaw called *Doings and Superdoings*. There are times, however, when it sounds better to stick to the word "person". "The person in the street" is still better than "The doings in the street". That is something to look out for and steer clear of.

Finally, don't let this new law alter your life. After all, what's in a name? As the great John Greenpimple once remarked – a rose by any other name, doth smell as sweet. Or a Henry. Goodnight.

# KID STUFF

*RB as newsreader at desk – overlay screen behind him.*

**RB:**
Good evening – here is the news. In the House of Commons today, there were stormy exchanges from both sides of the house, during a discussion on the Prime Minister's forthcoming visit to the United States. Using the new abbreviated form of speech (introduced into the Commons to save time), the foreign secretary replied to the MP for N.2, Mr BF, and said that the PM should P and O to the US as air travel was NBG for a VIP. In a 707 anyone could K0 the PM and the UN could do FA.

The latest trade figures are described as encouraging by the Chancellor of the Exchequer today …

*(Strains of the* Jackanory *music are heard, as if from the next studio. RB is thrown rather.)*

**RB:**
Er – the October figures were – er, I'm sorry, we seem to be picking up sound from another studio. *(Phone on the desk rings.)* Hello? Yes. Yes, of course I can hear it. Of course I can hear it. *Jackanory.* Yes. Very well. *(Phone down.)* I apologise for the sound break-up, it is being traced. Meanwhile I will continue …

Inflation still continues to rise at an alarming rate. Mrs Thatcher, attacking the Government's policy, said: "Once upon a time, there were three bears." I'm sorry. *(He glares off in the direction of music.)* "Once upon a time, there were three dollars to the pound. And then there were two. Two little dollar bills, sitting on the wall, one named Peter, and one named Paul. Fly away, Peter, fly away, Paul, come back, Peter, come back in the days before the Labour government took over." She was greeted with loud cheers, and then she went home and had tea in the nursery with lots of lovely jelly and jam and cream, and she ate so much she felt sick.

Sport. Bob Fairbrother, now fully recovered from a leg injury, had originally agreed to play this Saturday, but has now stated that he cannot as his mummy won't let him. She says, he can't come out to play until he's done his homework.

Now it's time for another adventure about Little Benn, the wedge of wood. Little Benn was always being hard done by, because he was only made of wood, and being wedge-shaped made it even worse, because people used to tread on his thin end, and kick his fat end. And he was always afraid to walk down the street, because he was frightened of the boy who lived at number ten, who was called Sunny Jim, but he wasn't sunny at all, really. He and the boy next door, Denis the Menace, used to tease Little Benn because he was different from them – and run away, and he would be left, on his own. And he'd say "Why am I always left?" So he went to see Jenkins, the wizard, who lived far away in the mountains and who sometimes turned into a big green dragon, and other times wore a white collar. And he told Jenkins the wizard he was always left, and Jenkins the wizard said "Don't be silly. Of course you're not left. That's ridiculous. My advice to you is to go for a trot. Go for lots of trots. With a few trots behind you, you can't be left, can you?" and with that, he turned into the Green Dragon again, and ordered a large gin and tonic.

*(Now the* Jackanory *theme is replaced by the* Magic Roundabout. *RB reacts again, looking offstage.)*

Florence was looking everywhere for Dougal.

*(Film of Florence with Dougal on overlay behind RB.)*

"I've had a letter from the BBC," she said. "They want you to read the news." "Oh, not again," said Dougal "They're always doing that. They keep mixing me up with Robert Dougall."

*(Caption on overlay of Robert Dougall.)*

"I don't know. They don't know what they're doing up there, you know. They'll be mixing you up with Richard Baker next, I shouldn't wonder."

*(Caption of Richard Baker's head on Florence's body.)*

"Dear, dear. Oh dear, oh dear."

*(Zebedee's boinggg is heard.)*

"What was that?" *(Boinggg!! again.)* "Time for bed," said Angela Rippon. And off we went. What fun it was! Good night, children – goodnight!

*(RB's face appears in kaleidoscope revolving picture as in* Jackanory. *Music up.)*

# PLAIN SPEAKING

*A spokesman desk, as on TV. RB enters in old-fashioned dinner jacket, drunk. A floor manager sits him in the chair.*

**FM:**
*(whispering)* We're just about on the air, Sir Harry. Your speech is on the autocue.

**RB:**
What? *(Clutches notes in his hand.)* I've got me notes.

**FM:**
No, look, the words on the prompter there, all written up. *(Cut to stand autocue, see it rolling.)* Just read them out. I'll take those.

*(Tries to get notes.)*

**RB:**
Get off!!

*(Snatches them away. They fall on floor. FM leaves the set, RB bends to pick them up. Music starts in wide shot – then cut to close-up of RB's backside. Super caption "A Spokesman". Cut back to wider shot. RB turns, recovers, starts to speak.)*

**RB:**
Good, er, it is – evening. I am a, er, spokesman for the Ministry of, er, what is it? – communications. And we all thought it would be a good idea, if I came along this evening, and told you all, what was, I mean tried to explain the whole, er put you, in it. The hole. The picture. As to what the f– what the folk, up at the Ministry think they're pl– think they're doing – know they're doing. And I should know what they're doing, because I am one of them. One of them. And I should know what I'm doing, but I don't. Want you to think that we at the er, where is it? – the Ministry are sitting down on our fat, er, fat chance we get to sit down at all because we are constantly on each other's toes, and secretaries, are, I mean she's always buzzing round, making tea and ends meet, and giving her utmost to whoever needs it, and when I say utmost, I mean most of her ut. Not that I want you to think. That we have anything. To hide. The Ministry of, er Communickers, Commu Knickers, cami-knickers, cami-knickerasians is not a – cannot be compared with a, I mean is nothing like, a, er, water closet. Er, water, Gate, Watergate. Nobody's going round bugging each other, thank goodness, because I mean these people who do go around, bugging other people are, er, I mean they are absolute b–, er I mean there's only one word to describe them, and that is, er, they are simply, er, rotten bugbears.

As the Minister himself said "We don't want any bugs in this ministry. I'm the only big bug around here" and he's absolutely, er, parded, er perfectly right. I say, it's absolutely stifling in here – does anybody mind if I open a bottle? Thanks.

*(He takes a half-bottle whisky flask from his pocket, pours whisky into carafe glass. Picks up carafe, pours water into glass as well. As he puts down the carafe, the floor manager's hand comes and takes the glass away. Not even noticing this, RB drinks from the whisky flask.)*

**RB:**
That's better. Now, thirdly, I come to my second point. Inflation. Doctor Kissinger of whom it has been said – many times – and indeed, who am I? ... I repeat, who am I?

*(He looks inside his jacket to read name.)*

Oh yes. Who am I, a mere Moss Bros, to argue with him? He said, at the last Common market assembly and here I quote *(looks at notes)*

"Trousers to cleaners, liquid paraffin, boots". And what a sorry picture that presents of the country today. We stand figuratively speaking at the crossroads. The men and women of this country having been taken to the cleaners, trouserless, not knowing which way to look – to turn; and some of us are already, er, on the turn, slipping and sliding, our boots filled with liquid paraffin, on the downwards path that leads to the upward spiral of inflation, knowing that we must move, in ever decreasing circles, finally disappearing up our only chance, is to stand firm, and sleep it off – sweat it out. Back to back, noses to the wall, best foot forward, knees together and legs astride, we must all push in the same direction, see, and I would be the first to join in the fun, bearing in mind, er, that I include women in this, because women are, in a sense, lumped together. At least the ones I know are.

Finally, in confusion I would like to say unrequir, unrequilier, but I can't. But what I can say is this. Peace, perfect peace – that's what we all want. And we cannot get it alone. We must combine with the rest of Europe; in a spirit of comradeship and conviviality. And that is why I am meeting the French Minister for Communications directly after his broadcast. In his own words "We go out and get peace together". Goodnight.

# THE TWO RONNIES:

# ASSORTED SKETCHES

## DR SPOONER IN THE BOOKSHOP

*A Victorian bookshop. Enter Dr Spooner. A lady assistant appears.*

**ASSISTANT:**
Good day, sir.

**SPOONER:**
Good day. My name is Spooner. Spoctor Dooner. I was just frassing the punt of your shop, and I thought I'd book in for a look. Look in for a book. Do excuse me, I sometimes get one word nuddled up with a mother. I'm stequently made a laughing frock.

**ASSISTANT:**
Ah yes – Dr Spooner, of course. You're most welcome, sir. Which book did you require?

**S:**
How about the complete shirks of Wakespeare? Or a book of poetry by Kelly, or Sheets?

**A:**
I'm afraid we're rather low on poetry at the moment.

**S:**
Oh, pot a witty, pit a wotty. It was to be a gresent for my pud lady.

**A:**
Your pud lady, sir?

**S:**
My wife, the dear thing.

**A:**
Ah! If it is for a lady – perhaps something fairly easy to read – nothing too taxing for the female brain.

**S:**
On the contrary, nothing too simple. My wife is a right little bl ... a bright little reader.

**A:**
A romantic novel then? *The Vicar of Wakefield?*

**S:**
Possibly – providing it doesn't arouse her animal instincts. She likes red beading – beading in red, that is. Last month I bought *Wuthering Heights* for her, and the following evening I found her needing it in the rude.

**A:**
I see.

**S:**
So I don't wish to encourage her to leap out of her vicars for *The Knicker Of Wakefield.*

**A:**
Quite.

**S:**
How about Chickens?

**A:**
Pardon?

**S:**
Chickens. Darles Chickens. One of our most nipping grovellists. Perhaps *David Kipperfield* or *Knockerless Nickleby*? Or the one about the lady with the large chest, who advertises it for sale in the local newspaper ...

**A:**
By Dickens, sir?

**S:**
Yes, yes. Ah! Got it. *The Tale of Two Cities*.

**A:**
I'm afraid not, sir – we could order the book for you.

**S:**
I need it at once – you see, she has gone to Wigan, to the seaside. She's coming back tomorrow. I wanted to give her the wook, when she got see from the backside at Biggun. That is, I wanted to give her the whack, when se got big from the wee-side at ... I wanted the book for the whack on the backside ... I wanted to give her the Biggun. I do hope I've made myself clear.

**A:**
Perfectly clear, sir.

**S:**
Perhaps I'll buy a book for myself instead. What have you to interest me? A charm from your obvious parts. Er – apart from your obvious charms.

**A:**
*(coyly)* It is difficult without knowing your taste. Perhaps something of an instructional nature? A text book?

**S:**
Ah! Now, one of my gobbies is hardening.

**A:**
Oh dear. You need a copy of *The Complete Home Doctor*.

*(offers it)*

**S:**
What? No, no, gardening! How I love my garden. When the shun is signing and the twirds are bittering, how wonderful it is to rip out and pick a few noses. Perhaps a book on flowers?

**A:**
*(taking up a book) Familiar Wild Flowers – From Stinkwort to Periwinkle?*

**S:**
Ah no – not wild flowers. There is no room in my garden for the Periwort or the Stinkwinkle. No, no – cultivated flowers – tupins and lulips, coxgloves and farnations – sweet bees, pooh-bells and dainty little net-got-me-fors. Do you have a gouse with a harden?

**A:**
No – I live in furnished rooms.

**S:**
How sad! May a say you are most welcome to visit mine – and if you like it, I'll ladly give you the goose of it. Why not come round tomorrow for key and trumpets?

**A:**
I would love to.

**S:**
Good, then will sonsedder it kittled. I must be off.

**A:**
I fear we still haven't found you anything to read.

**S:**
Don't worry – if it hadn't been roaring with pain outside, and if I hadn't left my haincoat at Rome, I wouldn't have bum in for a cook in the first place. Good day!

*(He exits.)*

# NAP

*La Marseillaise is heard and we see RC as napoleon, standing, legs astride, hands behind back, in front of marble fireplace. He is addressing his officers, who are out of shot.*

**RC:**
Gentlemen – the battle before us will not be a simple one. There is no fast and easy road that will take us to victory. The way will be hard, the blood will flow relentlessly throughout the length and breadth of France. Let us do our utmost to make sure that it will be the blood of the enemy. Gentlemen *(he raises a wineglass)* I give you Liberty! Equality! Fraternity! And the true God of Battle be with us!

*(The door opens, and a comfortable, middle-aged nurse enters.)*

**NURSE.**
Morning, Mr Parsloe. Don't drink too much of that blackcurrant. It'll give you the runs.

*(We see that the room is empty – it is a "residents" lounge in a funny farm.)*

**RC:**
Good morning, Marshal Ney. Anything to report?

**NURSE:**
Cauliflower Cheese for lunch, followed by Spotted Dick or Tangerine Yoghurt.

**RC:**
Excellent news. After all, an army marches on its stomach.

**NURSE:**
That cauliflower cheese has been marching on my stomach ever since last week.

**RC:**
If it's good enough for the men, it's good enough for us, Marshal. Send my dispatch officer to me at once. I have some written orders for the front.

**NURSE:**
Mr Hendrikson says he doesn't want to be your dispatch officer any more, dear.

**RC:**
Are you intimating that he has deserted?

**NURSE:**
Intimating's not in it, dear. His bike's got a flat tyre, and anyway he wants to be Charlie Chaplin.

*(RB, in doctor's white coat, enters.)*

**RB:**
Morning Nurse. Morning, mon Général. I wonder if I might have a few words alone with the Emperor, Nurse?

**NURSE:**
Certainly, sir.

*(She goes.)*

**RB:**
Good morning, Excellency. I trust I find you well?

**RC:**
You're lucky to find me at all. What do you want?

**RB:**
Just a few questions.

**RC:**
Then hurry. I'm just off to Waterloo.

**RB:**
Oh, don't worry. I won't make you miss your train. Now, have you always been Napoleon?

**RC:**
Yes, ever since I was a little boy.

**RB:**
How old were you when you were a little boy?

**RC:**
Eleven.

**RC:**
Are you sure you weren't twelve?

**RC:**
No, I've never been twelve in my life. What's it to do with you, anyway? Who are you?

**RB:**
Oh, just call me Doctor.

**RC:**
Doctor Who?

**RB:**
No, we've already got three of those. I'm just a plain, ordinary old consultant. Crippen. Dr Crippen.

*(Shakes hands.)*

**RC:**
Crippen? You're Doctor Crippen? The murderer?

**RB:**
Shh. Don't tell the Captain. Ethel's on board, dressed as a man.

**RC:**
On board what? Which captain?

**RB:**
This liner. That was the Captain you were talking to.

**RC:**
Who, Marshal Ney? He's in the Army, you great Nana.

**RB:**
Don't you call me a Nana. I'll murder you.

**RC:**
Watch it, I'll have you shot at dawn.

**RB:**
You can't. It's twenty past eleven in the morning.

**RC:**
Well, shot at dusk, then. Anyway, how

can you be Crippen? He died years ago. You're as daft as I am.

**RB:**
Ah! *(knowingly)* I don't believe you are daft.

**RC:**
Me? I'm as daft as a three-pound note. I'm screwy. Du-lally. I'm not the full quid ... I'm one down in the Marbles Department. Bonkers. Batty. Bird-brained. Barmy.

**RB:**
I saw you in a play at the National Theatre.

**RC:**
There you are. Proves I'm barmy.

**RB:**
And I saw you in *The Tom O'Connor Show*.

**RC:**
What more do you want? That says it all.

**RB:**
We're with the same agent.

**RC:**
I don't know what you're talking about. See this medal? I got it on the frontier. *(He turns round)* I've got one on the back 'ere, as well *(indeed he has)*.

**RB:**
I'm playing the same game as you are. Free food and drink, free digs, this home is a home from home. All you've got to do is act daft. Come on, come clean. You're at it as well, aren't you? You're really Gregory Crumpett, aren't you?

**RC:**
Alright – you seem to know all about me. I confess. I come here when I'm resting. Also to get away from the wife.

**RB:**
How long have you been here?

**RC:**
Eighteen months. Things haven't been too good lately. I got this offer to play Napoleon at Biggleswade Repertory Company, so I scarpered with the costume. Instantly recognisable, you see. Straight in here, no messing. What about you?

**RB:**
I just walked in as well.

**RC:**
What were you doing? Doctor in the House?

**RB:**
No, we had some removal men in the house. I just pinched it. It's alright, but if I turn round people think I'm a funny sort of doctor ...

*(He turns to show the back of his white coat. It bears the slogan "You've got it, I'll shift it".)*

**RB:**
So if anyone asks me about it, I just prescribe Syrup of Figs.

**RC:**
It's great, isn't it? And the best part about it is that if you act mad enough, the staff all humour you.

*(An extremely pretty nurse enters.)*

**RC:**
Josephine – Josephine – my Empress! My Queen, my Josephine.

**PN:**
Ooh, Napoleon, you're so romantic!

**RC:**
*(grabbing her)* Not tonight, Josephine. This afternoon! Come on.

*(He turns to RB.)*

**RC:**
Who pays for all this, by the way?

**RB:**
The GLC.

**RC:**
Aha! That proves it. They should be in here, not us. They really are mad.

*(He leaves, with his arm round the nurse.)*

# THE SLEEPING INSOMNIAC

*A psychiatrist's office. The psych (RB) lies on the couch. RC as George sits near him on chair. A pause.*

**RB:**
Why have you stopped?

**RC:**
Stopped what?

**RB:**
Talking. You've stopped talking.

**RC:**
There's nothing else to say. That's it.

**RB:**
Go over it again.

**RC:**
Shouldn't I be on the couch?

**RB:**
I know, old boy, it is usual, but I've got this terrible back. Don't mind, do you? Nothing wrong with your back, is there?

**RC:**
No, it's my mind.

**RB:**
Oh, they all say that. Nothing wrong with your mind. Lots of people can't sleep.

**RC:**
I can sleep. It's just that I dream.

**RB:**
Lots of people dream as well.

**RC:**
But I dream I can't sleep! In my dreams, I'm awake all night. It's very tiring. And as soon as I finally manage to drop off to sleep, I wake up.

**RB:**
*(getting up)* But you are still actually getting sleep?

**RC:**
But what's causing it?

**RB:**
Do you drink too much?

**RC:**
No.

**RB:**
I do – do you mind if I have one?

*(Gets bottle from filing cabinet.)*

**RC:**
I don't do anything too much.

**RB:**
I do. I do everything too much.

**RC:**
Do you sleep though?

**RB:**
Like a log. *(Drinks.)* Seems to me, as if you've got to treat these dreams like you would if you really couldn't sleep. What do insomniacs do? They go for a walk. Exercise, fresh air. Tires them, so that they can sleep.

**RC:**
You can't do just what you like in dreams.

**RB:**
You can, you can! Try it tonight. Get up out of bed and go for a walk. And make another appointment with the receptionist on the way out for next week.

**RC:**
Oh yes, meant to mention the receptionist! By jove, noticed her. She's a bit of all right! Is that why you've got a bad back?

**RB:**
Certainly not.

**RC:**
Well, I wouldn't say no. Quite a raver. She's new, isn't she?

**RB:**
Not to me she's not. She's my wife. Sweet dreams!

*(RC reacts and leaves.)*

# GEORGE'S BEDROOM

*RC in bed with attractive wife. She is asleep. He stirs, restlessly, then sits up. As he thinks, we hear his voice over.*

**RC:**
*(voice over)*: Now I really can't sleep. Or perhaps I'm dreaming. Hm. People usually pinch themselves to see if they're awake. I'll try that. *(Does so.)* No, can't feel a thing. Therefore I must be dreaming. *(Looks at wife.)* Is she asleep? Or am I just dreaming she's asleep? I'll pinch her as well. *(Puts his hands under the bedclothes – no reaction.)* She didn't move. But if I'd really pinched her, she would have woken up. Therefore I only dreamt that I pinched her. Therefore I'm definitely not awake. Right. Walking then.

*(RC walks out of bedroom door.)*

*Cut to: street door. (He comes out through it. he looks back, puzzled.)*

**RC:**
Funny. Our bedroom's usually upstairs.

253

*Exterior. Street – Day.*

*(He walks along the road in his pyjamas. A man on a bicycle passes him, also in striped pyjamas. RC approaches a pub. Its lights are on, a hum of noise from within.)*

**RC:**
Perhaps I'll pop in for a drink. *(Approaches, then hesitates.)* Hang on, I don't drink. Ah yes, but that's when I'm awake. I can do what I like when I'm dreaming.

*(Enters the pub.)*

*Interior: pub.*
The pub is quite full and lively, everyone is in *nightclothes – all the men in pyjamas, the girls in nightdresses. Cut to: one old lady in curlers. The barman, also in pyjamas, greets RC.*

**BARMAN:**
Yessir, what can I get you?

**RC:**
Er – half of shandy, please.

**BARMAN:**
Horlicks or Ovaltine?

**RC:**
Pardon?

**BARMAN:**
Do you want it mixed with Horlicks or Ovaltine?

**RC:**
Oh, er – Ovaltine, please. And a packet of crisps.

*(Barman gives RC crisps. RC opens packet. It contains only one enormous crisp. He shakes the packet, looks in, then eats the poppadum-like crisp. Drink arrives. RC takes it, looks around. Sees a man dressed in bib and brace overalls, with old suit coat and a cap.)*

**RC:**
*(to barman)* Why is he dressed differently to everyone else?

**BARMAN:**
He's on nights.

**RC:**
Oh.

*(Door opens. A policeman (RB), in striped pyjamas with pointed helmet, enters. Goes to RC.)*

**RB:**
Is that your car outside?

**RC:**
What car?

**RB:**
*(Goes back to door, opens it. Back projection of Brands Hatch. Cars, racing by in profile. One car has stopped on the verge.)* That red one. Rotten bit of parking, that.

**RC:**
My car is at home in the garage.

**RB:**
Oh? How did you get here then?

**RC:**
I'm not here. I'm at home in bed, asleep.

**RB:**
Have you got anyone who can vouch for you?

**BARMAN:**
I'll vouch for him. We all will, won't we, lads?

*(Everyone shouts agreement.)*

**RB:**
Well, don't let me catch you at home asleep again.

*(RB opens the door again – the cars race by, but the parked one has disappeared.)*

**RB:**
He's hopped it, the swine. Oi!

*(RB shuts the door. Terrible screaming of*

*brakes and crunching of gears. The pub customers laugh.)*

*A street: Day.*

*(RC walks along. The houses are terraced back-to-back types, opening on to the street – no gardens. A woman, in nightdress, sweeping the front step. She stares at RC.)*

**RC:**
'Evening. *(Walks on, then turns his head again)* What are you staring at, you silly old cow?

*Cut to: real cow, standing in a different doorway. It stares back.*

*(A girl in a shortie nightie approaches RC. As she passes him, she smiles at him. He looks back and then goes round a corner. We pick him up the other side of the corner. He looks startled. Cut to: his point of view. The same girl approaches again. Again, she smiles, and goes round the corner.)*

*(Now we see him from behind – the same girl comes from behind camera, overtakes RC and smiles back at him. She carries on and enters a house further ahead. Immediately she comes round a second corner up ahead and approaches RC, smiles and passes him.)*

*(RC puzzled. He approaches the house the girl went into – it is near the second corner. He looks in the window.)*

**GIRL:**
*(off)* Coo-ee!

*(RC reacts, looks round.)*

**GIRL:**
*(off)* I'm round the corner!

*(RC goes towards corner. Close-up of RC as he comes round the corner into completely different, much grander street. The girl stands by the gate of a detached house. She beckons.)*

**GIRL:**
Hurry up.

*(RC hurries over to her.)*

**RC:**
You're the receptionist girl, aren't you? His wife, he said.

**GIRL:**
That's right. Come on!

**RC:**
Where?

**GIRL:**
You're in love with me.

**RC:**
Certainly.

**GIRL:**
Come on then, quick.

**RC:**
What about him? The psychiatrist?

**GIRL:**
He's out on a case.

**RC:**
What of?

**GIRL:**
Scotch. Come on.

*(She takes out a key, which is on a string round her neck, and unlocks the door. They go in.)*

*Outside the girl's bedroom.*

*(They walk along a corridor. Policeman (RB), in pyjamas and helmet, stands by the door and salutes as they start to go into bedroom.)*

**RB:**
Evening all.

*(RC stares, but the girl takes no notice.)*

**RC:**
What's he doing there? That's not your husband in disguise, is it?

255

**GIRL:**
No, nothing like him.

**RC:**
Same build.
*(unconvinced)*

**GIRL:**
He's not in our dream. Don't worry about him.

*(They go into bedroom and close the door. Cut to: clock. It says two o'clock. The hands move round to 3.30. Then they whizz back to eleven, then round and round. Finally, the clock explodes.)*

*Part of the bedroom.*
*Close-up of RC and girl in bed.*

**RC:**
Good gracious, is that the time?

**GIRL:**
Don't go.

**RC:**
I must. It's a long walk.

**GIRL:**
Haven't you got wheels?

**RC:**
No, feet. At least I usually have.

*(He lifts bedclothes to look down.)*

**GIRL:**
I mean, have you any means of transport?

**RC:**
No.

**GIRL:**
Take mine – it's in the garage. Keys on the dressing-table.

**RC:**
How will I get it back to you?

**GIRL:**
Come back in it tomorrow.

*(She smiles.)*

*Outside the garage.*

*Close-up on RC as he fiddles with keys. Cut wide – he is sitting on a single brass bed with a steering wheel attached. He is trying to work the clutch. The girl appears from the house.*

**RC:**
It won't go.

**GIRL:**
Here. *(She sits on the bed with him.)* You've not switched on. I'll drive you.

*(They leave with her at the wheel. Various shots, as they travel the streets. They turn a corner and the policeman (RB) steps out and stops them.)*

**RB:**
Excuse me. Have you got a licence for that?

**GIRL:**
For what?

**RB:**
Two in a bed.

**RC:**
You need need a licence?

**RB:**
Certainly. Marriage licence.

**RC:**
*(to girl)* Come on, let's get out and walk.

**RB:**
You can't leave that here.

**RC:**
What?

**RB:**
Not unless you've got double yellow lines down your pyjamas.

**RC:**
What?

**RB:**
This is a no-snoring zone. Hot water-bottle holders only.

**RC:**
What?

**RB:**
Is that all you can say?

**RC:**
What?

*(Hooters are heard. Cut to: a line of five single beds all with two people in them. Close-up of a bed knob "honked" like a car-horn.)*

**RB:**
Go on, drive on, you're holding up the traffic.

*(RC and girl sweep off out of frame as policeman (RB) goes to sort out the angry drivers.)*

*RC's house.*
*(RC and girl sitting in the bed by the kerb.)*

**RC:**
Well, thanks for bringing me home. It's been lovely, hasn't it?

**GIRL:**
Smashing.

**RC:**
I never dreamt that a dream could be so real. If I didn't know I was dreaming, I would swear that I'm wide awake. I suppose I didn't just dream that I dreamt it, did I? May I pinch you?

**GIRL:**
Depends where.

**RC:**
There.

*(Pinches her arm.)*

**GIRL:**
Ow!

*(She pinches him back.)*

**RC:**
Ow! Yes, that really hurt. I really am dreaming this. I'm so grateful to your husband for suggesting I go for a walk.

**GIRL:**
So am I. *(kisses his cheek)* See you tonight?

**RC:**
Only if I can't sleep!

*(He gets out of bed, tiptoes to door, turns, waves, goes in.)*

*RC's bedroom.*
*(RC enters and stares. The psychiatrist is in bed with RC's wife.)*

**RC:**
Here! What's all this?

**RB:**
Sorry, old chap. I couldn't sleep either!

# APRIL FOOL QUICKIE

*A grocer's shop – interior. A workman, on trestles and a plank, is emulsioning the frieze on a section of wall. A sign saying "Business as Usual" hangs nearby.*

*RB, as the grocer, is finishing piling up a pyramid of tins of peas. RB suddenly looks past the camera – and turns to the workman.*

**RB:**
Hey! There's somebody pinching your van!

**WORKMAN:**
Where?

*(The pile of tins falls towards the grocer, knocking him against the trestle. The gallon can of emulsion slides down the plank and*

*lands over the grocer's head. Then the trestle hits the tin of emulsion with a clang.)*

*Cut to: wide shot. (The workman comes back in as the grocer lies amid the chaos.)*

**WORKMAN:**
There's no one pinching the van!

**RB:**
*(removing emulsion can from head)* April Fool.

# WELCOME M'LORD

*Old lord and wife at dinner in ancestral home.*

**LORD:**
Where's the food? We've been sitting here ages. That new butler is very erratic. Wait for ages, then he brings all the food at once. What's more, he's damned impudent.

**LADY:**
Oh, do you think so? He's always very polite to me.

**LORD:**
Well, he's not to me. Impudent bounder.

*(Enter butler, puts down plate in front of lady.)*

**BUTLER:**
Your game, Milady.

*(Gives her a leer and starts to go.)*

**LORD:**
I say, Blenkinsop, hurry up with my roast pork. Make sure it's a nice fatty bit!

*(Butler appears to ignore him, and exits.)*

**LORD:**
There you are – ignores me.

**LADY:**
Don't make such a fuss. He's very efficient.

**LORD:**
Damned rude, I call it.

*(Butler enters, with another plate. Places it in front of lord.)*

**BUTLER:**
Your fat, milord.

*(He exits.)*

**LORD:**
How dare he! I'm going to have to sack him.

**LADY:**
Steady on – we have enough servant trouble as it is. The handyman's about to leave us, and the plumbing is in a terrible state.

**LORD:**
Oh, that reminds me, the lavatories ...

*(Butler enters with dessert – he places it in front of lady.)*

**BUTLER:**
Your sweet, Milady.

*(He leers again.)*

**LADY:**
Oh, thank you, Blenkinsop.

*(He goes to sideboard, brings dish to lord.)*

**BUTLER:**
Your nuts, milord.

*(Turns away.)*

**LORD:**
Cheeky swine! *(calls to him)* How am I supposed to break these open – with my teeth?

*(Butler returns to table.)*

**BUTLER:**
Your crackers, milord.

*(Hands him nutcrackers, and exits.)*

**LORD:**
That does it! Staff shortage or no staff shortage – he goes!

**LADY:**
Well, you know best, dear. What were you saying about the lavatories?

*(Butler enters, pushing a large trolley.)*

**LORD:**
They're broken. Out of order. Up the spout and down the drain.

**LADY:**
What? And we've sacked the handyman! How are we going to manage?

*(Butler, at table by the trolley, takes cover off a bucket, hands it to lady.)*

**BUTLER:**
Your pale, Milady.

*(Takes cover off another object.)*

Your potty, milord.

# I COULD HAVE DANCED ALL LUNCH HOUR

*A large office, not too smart. RB at desk, in shirt sleeves. Knock on door – RC enters, in raincoat.*

**RC:**
Is this the Arnold Murray School of Dancing?

**RB:**
That's right, yes. Mr Dribble?

**RC:**
Tibble.

**RB:**
Oh, Tibble.

**RC:**
I'd imagined the place much bigger.

**RB:**
Ah, you're thinking of the Arthur Murray School of Dancing. This is the Arnold Murray School of Dancing. Much smaller firm, that's why it's much cheaper. Now then, you've come for your first lesson, right?

**RC:**
That's right, yes. Am I too early?

**RB:**
*(Gets up, takes coat from back of chair – it is an evening dress tail coat.)* No, you're fine. *(Puts on tail coat.)* Now, we usually start with the waltz, that's the easiest to pick up. D'you mind taking off your raincoat?

**RC:**
*(staring at RB's coat)* Are you going to teach me?

**RB:**
Oh yes, rather – I'm Arnold Murray. Now, just put this on, *(hands him pink sash with large bow. Sash says "lady" across the chest)* because I'm going to lead. Now – hands like this – *(they start to dance)* and forward, side, together, forward, side, together, one, two three, one, two three ...

*(A negro girl enters, puts papers on RB's desk. She wears a short woollen dress which illustrates everything.)*

**RB:**
Thank you, Miss Higginbottom.

*(She goes.)*

**RC:**
Does she work for you?

**RB:**
Yes, she's my assistant.

**RC:**
Why can't I dance with her?

**RB:**
No, impossible. She's one of the untouchables.

**RC:**
I didn't know negro girls were untouchables.

**RB:**
This one is – and believe me, I've tried. Now try to relax, you're a bit tense. One, two three, one, two three.

**RC:**
I feel so silly.

**RB:**
That's because you look silly. But you'll get used to it. Mind you, a chap who looks like you should be used to it already. Ever thought of taking up body building?

**RC:**
Why?

**RB:**
Well, I could transfer your dancing lesson fee over to a subscription to the Arnold Murray Beef-Builder Fitness Club. You've paid the three quid already, haven't you?

**RC:**
Yes, I sent you a postal order.

**RB:**
Good. Well, what do you say? I've got all the equipment.

**RC:**
Does your assistant teach that? She seems to have all the equipment as well.

**RB:**
Who?

**RC:**
Miss Hottentot.

**RB:**
Higginbottom.

**RC:**
Yes.

**RB:**
No. I'm fully qualified. I took a correspondence course in weight lifting. I hold the golden truss. I'll soon get you in shape.

**RC:**
I think I'd rather be my shape than your shape.

**RB:**
You should have seen me before. I used to be as tall as you once.

**RC:**
When was that?

**RB:**
When I was ten. Come on, let's try a few press-ups. *(RC gets on the floor, starts press-ups.)* Now, keep your body straight, come on ...

*(Intercom buzzes.)*

**RB:**
What is it, Miss Higgintot?

**MISS H:**
*(voice over)* Miss Brownlow to see you.

**RB:**
Oh, right. *(Knock on door – Miss Brownlow enters.)* Ah, Miss Brownlow – just pop behind the screen and undress, would you? *(She does so. Phone rings. RB picks up black phone.)* Hello? Arnold Murray Dance School. *(Phone still rings. He picks up red phone)* Murray School of Art. *(Phone still rings. He picks up green phone)* Hello, Arnold Murray Worldwide Book of the Month Club. Oh yes, madam. *(He takes white doctor's coat from cupboard and puts it*

*on.)* Well, there's two publications concerned with cultivation of crops – there's the gardeners' one, *The Weeder's Digest*. Yes. Or there's the one which is more for farmers. Ah, that's the one you mean. That's *The Breeder's Digest*. Very comprehensive, yes. No, there aren't any pictures. Your husband wants to make sure he gets what? Oh, oats, only every three years. You must rotate. I'll send it off. And if you're not absolutely delighted with the book after fourteen days, we keep the money. Bye. *(to RC)* You alright down there?

**RC:**
I think I'd rather carry on with the waltz.

**RB:**
Right – take a seat, I'll be with you in a mo.

*(Intercom buzzes again.)*

**RB:**
Yes?

**MISS H:**
*(voice over)* Mr Jason is here.

**RB:**
Ah, send him in, Miss Hotbottom. *(Then, to girl behind screen)* You ready, Miss Brownlow? *(Miss Brownlow emerges in bra and pants.)* Ah yes. Sit down here, please. *(Goes to wall, pulls down chart.)* Now how long have you been having this eye trouble?

**MISS B:**
About three months, doctor.

**RB:**
Right, well just read this chart out loud, would you.

*(She starts to read aloud, slowly. There is a knock on the door – man enters with easel and paintbox.)*

**ARTIST:**
Am I too early?

**RB:**
No, no, come in. What is it today?

**ARTIST:**
Life class.

**RB:**
Ah yes, right with you. How are you getting on, Miss Brownlow?

**MISS B:**
I can't see from here.

**RB:**
Well look, stand here – bit closer. That's it. Would you mind putting your arm like this? And the other one like this? There we are. How's that, Mr Jason?

**ARTIST:**
Perfect.

*(He starts to draw Miss Brownlow.)*

*(Knock – a grand lady enters.)*

**GRAND LADY:**
Are you the vet?

**RB:**
Yes, madam.

**GRAND LADY:**
I rang earlier – there's something the matter with my pom.

**RB:**
Ah, yes. If you care to step behind the screen, I'll have a look at it.

**GRAND LADY:**
My dog, my Pomeranian. He's outside – shall I fetch him in?

**RB:**
Oh, please do.

*(As she goes, a large Cockney woman enters.)*

**COCKNEY WOMAN:**
Dr Murray?

261

**RB:**
Yes – just go behind the screen and get undressed, will you, madam?

*(She does so.)*

**RC:**
*(approaching)* Look, I'm terribly sorry but I have to be getting back soon. My wife's got a cake in the oven.

**RB:**
Oh, congratulations. What do you hope it's going to be?

**RC:**
I'm hoping for a sultana sponge, that's what went in. So could we finish the lesson, please?

**RB:**
Certainly. Hang on. Could you come out please, madam? *(Cockney woman emerges in corsets.)* Now, what can I do for you?

**COCKNEY LADY:**
It's about the job as cleaning lady.

**RB:**
Oh yes, of course, er – come over here, would you? Miss Brownlow, take a rest. Now madam, just stand with your hand like this, would you. *(Puts Cockney lady in posing position for artist.)* There you are. Here. *(Swaps drawing pad over.)* Try a larger pad. Now, Miss Brownlow, would you just partner this gentleman. How's that?

**RC:**
Is this lady qualified?

**RB:**
She looks it to me.

*(Enter a middle-aged man.)*

**RB:**
Ah, morning, Mr Jones. Be with you in a moment. *(Mr Jones sits, reads magazine in corner.)* Now then – ah yes, music.

*(He switches on tape recorder – Victor Silvester dance music.)*

**GRAND LADY:**
*(returning with Pomeranian, which barks)* Here we are.

**RB:**
Thank you – sit over there, would you? *(Grand lady sits next to Mr Jones)* Now, *(to Cockney lady)* what are you like with animals?

**COCKNEY LADY:**
Oh, very good sir. I love 'em.

**RB:**
Right, hold this one, would you? *(Gives her dog.)* Now, everyone alright?

**MR JONES:**
*(to grand lady)* Care for this dance?

**GRAND LADY:**
Oh. Thank you.

*(They join RC and girl on dance floor. The blue phone rings.)*

**RB:**
Hello, Murray Funeral Service. Hello, could you speak up a little? Yes, this is the Chapel of Rest. Who? No, I'm sorry, he's not with us any more. He died. Goodbye.

**RC:**
*(approaching RB)* Look, this lady says she's completely inexperienced.

**RB:**
They all say that.

**RC:**
As a dance teacher.

**RB:**
Oh.

**RC:**
And I really feel that, having paid my money, I ought to be getting something for it.

**RB:**
Quite right.

**RC:**
I don't care what, as long as I get my money's worth.

**RB:**
How long have you got?

**RC:**
Ten minutes.

**RB:**
Right. Sit down here, would you. *(He takes up barber's cloth, throws it round RC's neck.)* Now, how do you like it, sir?

*(RC starts to explain and music comes in.)*

# PANIC IN THE YEAR 2001

*RB as newsreader. Behind him, caption with date: "June 4th 2001".*

**RB:**
Good evening. Here is the news. King Foot of Europe is to abdicate.

*(Cut to Mr Foot on overlay. Still photo with crown on.)*

"With a name like Foot, it's hard to put a brave face on things," he said. "It means my name has been dragged through the mud many times. Especially in wet weather. But now I wish to take it easy, relax and put it up for a while."

Mrs Elizabeth Windsor, formerly the Queen, has applied to have her council flat redecorated.

*(Cut to still photo of council flat)*

The last time it was decorated was in 1971, when it received the OBE. Asked who did the decorating, she replied "My husband and I." And now the main news story this evening. Reports are just coming in of the discovery of a large container in a park in Ealing, which appears to have been dropped from an unknown aircraft. It is emitting a strange, sweet-smelling gas, which is rapidly being dispersed over a wide area. Roger Kinsey reports.

*Cut to: RC with microphone, standing next to a large, shining container. He wears an old-fashioned civilian gas mask.*

**RC:**
Good evening. I've been told to wear this gas mask, but quite frankly *(removes it)* it appears to be a waste of time, as these two ladies seem to be suffering no ill-effects.

*(Cut to RB as a woman, with another, in curlers, etc., watching him.)*

The canister was discovered early this morning, and is marked in large letters on the side "Formation Gas".

*(Cut to close-up of words and RC's finger pointing it out. Woman – RB – puts her face in shot.)*

What that means we're not sure, but scientists are now waiting for the appearance of a trigger device; something that will cause this, at the moment, harmless gas to start working. Roger Kinsey, *News At Ten*, Ealing Common.

**RB:**
*(as woman)*: Mrs Biggs, number eleven, Knocker Street.

*Cut to: studio.*

**RB:**
*(Announcer)*: And here is some film of what could be that trigger device. A parachute was observed ... *(cut to film of parachute)* floating down over Acton a few minutes ago. It has just landed in the front garden of a house in Mulberry Crescent.

263

*(Close-up of strange black box with knobs on, still attached to parachute. It is labelled "trigger device".)*

Two eminent scientists, in protective clothing, are even now about to examine it. Perhaps they will be able to unravel the secret of the mysterious formation gas. Roger Kinsey reports.

*(Cut to: two figures, like moon men, in white clothing and helmets, lumbering towards the black box. Close-up box – their gloved hands reach in, twist knobs, press buttons, etc. Cut to: RB as same woman, watching. Cut to: RC, as reporter, arriving on his bike, getting off.)*

**RC:**
*(out of breath)* Here we are in Acton now.

*(He moves in front of the action – scientists still turning knobs, etc.)* And approaching the moment of truth. Everyone in the area has breathed in the Formation Gas – it remains to be seen whether the scientists can render the trigger device harmless.

*(Cut to: close-up on trigger device – hand touches switch, a hissing is heard.)*

Oh, good heavens. It appears they have accidentally triggered off the device. Nothing now can stop this gas from becoming effective. Roger Kinsey, *News At Ten*, on his bike.

*(He rides away.)*

*(Loud chord of music heard. Black box begins to play formation dancing music very loudly, as if over a tannoy. The two scientists begin to dance together.)*

*Cut to: a bus queue. The music plays. (The office workers, typists and passers-by do the paso doble.)*

*Cut to: a pile of rubble and a "road up" sign next to a workman's striped plastic shelter. (The music plays. Out of the hut come six workmen – they dance up to six terraced*

houses, out dance six housewives and they do a cha-cha cha. RC appears on bike, crashes into hut, then gets involved in the dance.)*

*Cut to: the black box area. (Women standing round, staring. Police arrive in cars. They rush up to the device and start dancing with the women onlookers – a quickstep.)*

*Cut to: studio.*

**RB:**
The Government has just issued a special communiqué, urging people not to panic in the present crisis, which they hope will be shortlived – simply keep calm and dance about your business in the normal way.

Mr Eric Morley has been made Minister of Dancing, and we must now all look towards Mecca for a solution. Meanwhile, Brigadier General Dogsbody has taken over as Supreme Allied Commander in charge of all military two-steps.

*(A man in headphones dances by with a tea lady.)*

The gas container has been loaded onto a lorry and is, at this very moment, being driven to the south coast, to be dumped in the sea; while the black box is on its way north, to be buried in a disused coal mine near Middlesborough. Let us hope that, with them both travelling in opposite directions, we are approaching the end of this bizarre affair.

*Cut to: main road. (The lorry with the gas container and the small open van with the black box approach each other. As they are about to pass, they screech to a halt. The drivers and their mates, and two security guards all get out and dance together in a high, wide shot.)*

# THE ADVENTURES OF ARCHIE

*(Note: the technique throughout is cartoon backgrounds on overlay, as in the recent series called Jane of the* Daily Mirror. *This enables RB to be different sizes, and for the more exotic locations to be easily achieved.)*

*We start with a high shot of a row of Victorian terraced houses, zooming in as the voice over says "This is the strange tale of Archie Barber, of 23 Ordinary Villas, Suburbia ..."*

*Interior: suburban terraced house – the kitchen.*

*(RC, as Archie, enters through door to garden. He is a chirpy Cockney character, rather like the pub fellow, Sid. He carries a small old bottle, covered in earth. A cigarette stub dangles from his lips.)*

**RC:**
*(calling)* Doris, look what I found. I told you this place probably used to be a dump. *(To himself)* Well, it is a dump, no probably about it. Real dump, this is.

*(Doris enters, carrying an opened letter)*

**DORIS:**
This letter came from the council. Second post.

**RC:**
What's it say?

**DORIS:**
They've refused you permission for your extension.

**RC:**
What? *(takes letter)* Would you Adam and Eve it! Stupid load of councillors.

*(She goes.)*

**RC:**
*(sitting disconsolately)* What right have they got to ruin people's fun? A man like

me needs an extension. *(He takes out a filthy handkerchief and begins to polish up the old bottle)* Sometimes I wish I was a thousand miles from here.

*(An enormous puff of bright blue smoke fills the room. A "whooshing" sound is heard, and RC disappears. Doris enters the smoke-filled room.)*

**DORIS:**
Now, where's he gone? Gawd, I wish he wouldn't smoke them Turkish!

*Cut to: RC on flying carpet, with photographic land and sea rushing beneath him. He rolls about, nearly rolling off a couple of times.*

**VOICE OVER:**
Archie, although he didn't know it, was being whisked through time as well as space ...

*(RC and carpet suddenly move right away from camera, until they are a tiny dot.)*

**VOICE OVER:**
...to start a new life in the mysterious East. Years later we find him in the fairy-tale city of Old Baghdad, plying his honest trade.

*Interior of Baghdad cobbler's shop. RC hammering away at pair of shoes. customer enters, hands him pair of shoes. RC, still the chirpy Cockney, nevertheless speaks in the idiom.*

**RC:**
Greetings, O wise and sagacious son of Allah. May the moon of plenty shine upon your daughter. Be ready Thursday.

*(He marks the shoes with chalk and puts them under his bench.)*

**VOICE OVER:**
And so he worked, putting his heart and sole and heel into the business, perfecting the craft that he had been trained for ...

**RC:**
*(Close-up, to camera.)* I used to work for Freeman Hardy and Willis.

**VOICE OVER:**
And his fame spread throughout the land, and came to the ears of the Caliph himself. Now the Caliph had very sharp ears. He also had a fat nose and terrible feet.

*(During this, we see the arrival of the Caliph to the shop and RC fitting slippers on to his feet.)*

**VOICE OVER:**
He was therefore delighted when Archie Barber placed upon his delicate tootsies a pair of shoes as pliable and soft as a mouse's ear.

*(The Caliph departs with his entourage, delighted. Cut to: RC, beaming)*

**VOICE OVER:**
Archie, too, was indeed a happy man. He put up a large sign outside his shop, announcing his royal patronage. Sadly, it was this very sign that was to bring about his undoing ...

*Some time later – the shop.*
*(Two of the Caliph's guards enter the shop and grab RC as he works at his bench.)*

**RC:**
Here! What's the game? Where are we going?

**GUARD:**
Prison!

**RC:**
Prison? Why?

**GUARD:**
Treason!

**RC:**
Treason? For what reason?

**GUARD:**
Your sign outside.

*(They drag him out.)*

*Exterior of shop.*
*(RC is dragged out, protesting. We tilt up to see the sign. It says "Aja Baba Ltd". Then underneath, in large letters: "Cobblers to the Caliph".*

*Cut to: the prison.*
*(RC is in a cage-like cell, bars on three sides. A large guard, stripped to the waist, stands in the cell with him. In the next cell, a pretty, dark-eyed girl sits on the floor, bound and gagged.)*

**RC:**
*(to guard)* Three days I've been sitting here, you know. I wasn't even allowed one call. I know they haven't invented phones yet, but you'd think they'd let me shout out the window. *(To girl)* What are you in here for, darlin'? Hope they're not going to chop your head off. What a waste. Pity they don't have mixed cells, ain't it? Eh? I say, I wish he was where you are and you was in here.

*(A whoosh of blue smoke and the guard, in the girl's clothes, is tied up in the other cell. The girl, stripped to the waist (and back to the camera) is in RC's cell. He reacts, and quickly covers her with his coat.)*

**RC:**
Here, put this on. Mustn't let those loose. They should be kept on a leash – they'll cause a riot. That's better. Gawd, all this blue smoke! I thought at first it was the Kebabs coming in for dinner. *(He goes and sits cross-legged on the table.)* They cook 'em at the table here, you know. And if you complain, they cook you at the table. Gawd, I wish I was a thousand miles from here!

*(Whoosh! Blue smoke – RC is gone, leaving the girl wide-eyed as RC's coat vanishes, leaving her clutching her modesty)*

*(RC flies through the air, this time on the prison table. He opens the drawer in the table, takes out air-sickness pills.)*

*A desert island.*

*(RC appears, lands with a bump, which rolls him off the table. As he picks himself up, he hears a voice calling faintly: "Let me out, oh master" he looks round, in the table drawer, etc. finally realises that the voice is coming from the old bottle, which is hanging on a piece of string around his neck. He forces the cork out of the bottle. A whoosh – he drops it. A close-up on the bottle as it lies on the sand. Smoke streams from it and forms a cloud, which clears to reveal RB as a twenty-foot high genie.)*

**RC:**
Crikey! It's the incredible hulk!

**RB:**
What is your wish, oh master?

**RC:**
My wish?

**RB:**
You have one more wish. The first one brought you to Baghdad on a carpet.

**RC:**
And the second one brought me here on a table. Next wish I make I'll be careful where I'm sitting. I'd hate to arrive anywhere on a flying toilet.

**RB:**
It would indeed be an inconvenience.

**RC:**
Yes. So it's the old three wishes, is it?

**RB:**
Four.

**RC:**
Four wishes? Why four?

**RB:**
Special offer. This week only.

**RC:**
Oh, that's fortunate. So I got two more.

**RB:**
No, one. You wished the girl into your cell.

**RC:**
Oh well, my last wish has got to be – take me home, to London, wasn't it?

**RB:**
I regret, Master, I am allowed only ONE voyage through TIME. If I took you to London now, you would find it a vast area of evil-smelling rubble.

**RC:**
Oh – like the last dustman's strike. Well, I'd like to have a think about it for a while. Matter of fact, I ain't in any particular hurry to leave here at the moment.

*(We fade on the idyllic desert island landscape.)*

**VOICE OVER:**
Time passes – and Archie, knowing he can't escape, settles into a life of peace and plenty on his Robinson Crusoe Island. Companions were supplied, at no extra charge, by the accommodating Genie ...

*(Fade up on palm tree, with monkey in it. Tilt down to where RC, dressed now as Robinson Crusoe, sits with six beautiful black girls around him. RC is lounging back, contentedly sipping out of a coconut shell.)*

**RC:**
*(to girl)* Where's Friday?

**GIRL:**
It's her day off.

**RC:**
I thought Thursday was her day off.

**GIRL:**
No, Thursday is Tuesday's day off.

**RC:**
Oh, is that right, Tuesday? *(Another girl nods, giggling.)* Let's see, who are you then?

**GIRL:**
I'm Monday.

**RC:**
It's Monday today, isn't it?

**GIRL:**
Yes.

**RC:**
Oh, good!

*(A strange noise is heard. RC and the girls react. The noise is that of Dr Who's Tardis, which materialises, in its familiar fashion, on the sand. RB emerges, dressed not as Dr Who, but as Wurzel Gummidge.)*

**RC:**
It's the Tardis!

**WURZEL:**
Oh ay, me dears? What be you all doing a-sitting about here by the seaside, eh? A sunnin' of yourselves. Nice here, ain't it?

**RC:**
Gawd – it's all a bit mixed up, this. Who do you think you are, mate?

**WURZEL:**
I be Dr Who, that's who I be. Who be you be?

**RC:**
No, no, you used to be Dr Who, but now you're Wurzel Gummidge.

**WURZEL:**
Oh dear! I must have got the wrong head on. Oh ay! It's all coming back to me now, as the sailor said when he spat into the wind. It's that there Jon Pertwittee, he be Dr Whosit, baint he?

**RC:**
No, you're Jon Pertwee.

**WURZEL:**
Who, me? No, I be Dr Gummidge. Oh, I be all confused now. I be going off to find Dorothy.

**RC:**
Don't you mean Aunt Sally?

**WURZEL:**
No, Dorothy up the Yellow Brick Road. Ta-ta, me dears.

*(Goes off, singing "If I only had a Brain".)*

**RC:**
He's a nutter.

*(The black girls look bemused. RC, however, is quick to realise that the Tardis stands there, its door open.)*

**RC:**
Listen, girls – I'm off. *(Hurries to the door of the Tardis.)* It's been nice knowing you. All the best. And don't worry – if this doesn't work, I'll be back on Friday by Tuesday.

*(He disappears inside and shuts the door.)*

*Inside Tardis.*
*(A close-up of a bank of dials. RC's hand turns dial to "London" and another to "20th century". Outside, we see the Tardis de-materialise. The girls look bemused again)*

*(The Tardis materialises against a brick wall. RC emerges. He is now dressed normally in his modern clothes, as in first scene. He looks across at his old house. From behind the Tardis, RB as genie appears. RC reacts.)*

**RC:**
How did you get here? I thought you couldn't travel through time.

**RB:**
There is a nail sticking out of the Tardis at the back. You can travel through anything when your loin cloth gets caught on a nail.

**RC:**
You got a point there.

**RB:**
I nearly had, several times. Hair-raising.

**RC:**
Well, listen, you can't walk about like that. Hide behind there till we can get you some clothes. Can you get any smaller?

**RB:**
I'll try, oh master.

*(RC crosses to his house, rings bell. Old man answers.)*

**OLD MAN:**
Yes?

**RC:**
Oh – er – Mrs Barber in?

**OLD MAN:**
Never heard of her.

**RC:**
Oh. She lives here.

**OLD MAN:**
No she don't. I live here.

**RC:**
Oh … I gotta find her. Mrs Barber.

**OLD MAN:**
Ring up the police. There's a box over the road.

*(He indicates the Tardis)*

**RC:**
Oh yes – how long has that been there?

**OLD MAN:**
Ever since I've lived here. Thirty years.

**RC:**
Thirty years?

**OLD MAN:**
I come here in 1985. Thirty years ago.

**RC:**
Oh. Right, ta.

**OLD MAN:**
Righto, mate.

*(Shuts the door.)*

*(RC nods to himself, realising. He hurries back into the Tardis. Inside, his hand is seen moving dials back to 1982. He immediately re-emerges, crosses the road and rings the bell again. His wife, Doris, answers the door.)*

**DORIS:**
Where you been?

**RC:**
Sorry to have been so long, Doris.

**DORIS:**
I thought you'd just gone down to get a paper. You've been gone three hours!

**RC:**
Three hours?

**DORIS:**
Your supper's ruined.

**RC:**
That's nothing new, is it?

**DORIS:**
You're drunk. Come on, get inside.

*(RC goes in. From behind the Tardis, the huge head of the genie peers out, nonplussed.)*

*Fade out – fade in.*

**VOICE OVER:**
And so Archie once more picked up the threads of his life … except that now he had a new found friend.

*(A close-up of RC as he walks along the street. Widen to see RB as genie. He now wears ordinary flat cap and raincoat, but is about eight feet high.)*

**RC:**
I feel stupid walking along with you as big as that. I get laughed at in the pub. Have you tried to get smaller?

**RB:**
Indeed, oh Master, I have used all my powers, but alas, to no avail. May Allah forgive your unworthy pig of a servant ...

**RC:**
And for Gawd's sake talk proper – not all that Eastern rubbish.

**RB:**
Righto, Squire.

*(They walk away down the road and the scene ripples and dissolves, as in a flashback, to a close-up of RC in the pub. It is quite crowded and animated. RC, in close-up, is talking.)*

**RC.**
So that's my story, darlin' – me wife has left me, and all I've got now is that great load of lard over there.

*(We see RB sitting on the floor in the corner, still eight foot tall. The pretty blonde girl RC is talking to nods sympathetically.)*

**BLONDE:**
What a shame.

**RC:**
Yeah. 'Nother drink?

**BLONDE:**
Yeah, ta.

**RC:**
*(calls to barman)* George! Another Bacardi and Coke, and two beers. Pint for me, gallon for him.

**GEORGE:**
Right, Archie.

**BLONDE:**
Here – why can't you wish more wishes?

**RC:**
I lost me bottle. Anyway, I had one final wish left. And that was granted. I got what I wanted.

**BLONDE:**
What was that?

**RC:**
Come back to my place and I'll show you.

*(The blonde reacts in puzzled amusement. RC laughs.)*

*The suburban street.*
*Night – a moon. RC and girl are walking away from the camera. They are laughing.*

**BLONDE:**
You what? You mean I'm coming all the way home just to have a look at your extension?

**RC:**
That's about the size of it.

**BLONDE:**
*(giggling)* What is?

**RC:**
*(giggling)* Eleven foot by nine foot six.

*(They collapse with laughter and, arm-in-arm, go away down the moonlit suburban street.)*

# PHONEY

*Man in phone box, dialling. Female voice answers.*

**FEMALE VOICE:**
Number please?

**MAN:**
Is that Interpol?

**FEMALE:**
This is the exchange, sir. What number

did you require?

**MAN:**
Interpol. I want to speak to Interpol.

**FEMALE:**
Hold the line, sir.

*(A pause. Buzzing and clicking.)*

**POLICE VOICE:**
Wandsworth police station. Can I help you, sir?

**MAN:**
I want Interpol, please.

**PC:**
I'll connect you with Scotland Yard, sir. Hold on.

*(More clicking.)*

**SCOTLAND YARD VOICE:**
Scotland Yard here. Who do you wish to speak to, sir?

**MAN:**
Interpol.

**SCOTLAND YARD:**
Is it priority, sir?

**MAN:**
Er – yes, please.

**SCOTLAND YARD:**
Hold the line please.

*(more clicking)*

**INTERPOL VOICE:**
Hello. Interpol here.

**MAN:**
Oh, Interpol? I want to send some flowers by wire to my mother.

# MILEAWAY

*A pretty country road. A high shot, as a little open sports car comes over the hill. In it sits RC. A mild-mannered civil servant, and his wife, a tall, forbidding blonde. The car draws to a halt by a signpost. Muriel (the wife) consults a road map on her knees.*

**RC:**
*(looking at sign)* Podmores End. Never heard of it. Are you familiar with Podmores End, dear?

**MURIEL:**
*(icily)* Not at all.

**RC:**
Lucky Podmore.

**MURIEL:**
Don't make pathetic jokes, Brian. You haven't the faintest idea where we are, have you?

**RC:**
I know exactly where we are, Muriel. We are lost. That's where we are. *(Looking at sign)* What's that other name? I can't see from here.

**MURIEL:**
Well, get out then.

*(RC gets out of car to inspect sign. A close-up of sign. It says "Mileaway – ½ mile".)*

**RC:**
It's a place called Mile-away, half a mile away. But it's only a footpath.

**MURIEL:**
Well, at least there will be someone who can tell us where we are.

**RC:**
Righto. Are you staying here?

**MURIEL:**
No, it's too hot. I'm being bitten all over by gnats as it is.

**RC:**
I think they're attracted by your aftershave.

**MURIEL:**
Brian!

**RC:**
Perfume. Sorry – Freudian slip. And talking of Freudian slips, mind where you put your feet round here.

*(She descends from the car.)*

**MURIEL:**
Do you think there will be anywhere we can spend the night?

**RC:**
Bound to be some sort of pub or inn. Might be nice.

**MURIEL:**
Mm. A single bed, mind.

**RC:**
What, for the two of us?

**MURIEL:**
Don't be facetious, Brian. You know how set I am on a single bed. I won't be moved on that.

**RC:**
I wouldn't dream of trying to move you on any kind of bed, dear. Come along.

*(They set off down the path. Cut to them emerging from a cart-track, or similar, into a village street. A close-up as they stop and stare. Music over. We cut to their point of view. The village street we see is a street of Elizabethan times. Peasants with carts, ragged children, horses and sheep in the street. The locals give them strange stares as they go about their business. One middle-aged peasant approaches them.)*

**PEASANT:**
Good day, Master, Mistress. I do see by your apparel, in shape and form most foreign to mine eye, that you be strangers

to this valley and these lands. I give you welcome, Master.

**RC:**
Thanks awfully. Er – sorry to disturb you on your carnival day. We were wondering if there was an inn where we could spend the night. Single beds, of course.

**PEASANT:**
There be the inn, good master – yonder, there.

*Cut to: inn – close-up sign "The Boar's Head".*

**PEASANT:**
But I must warn you straight -the landlord here
True to his title, "land-lord" doth possess
And is in sooth the Lord, of all these lands.
He is our Thane, our Duke, our governing Peer
And he doth rule, and over all hold sway.

**RC:**
Ah yes, I know the type. *(To Muriel)* Bit of a big-head.

**PEASANT:**
Shall I convey thee to my good Lord's door?

**RC:**
Yes, certainly. I'll soon sort him out. He's not even in the *Good Food Guide*.

*(Suddenly, shouts off. Cut to: the door of the inn. Bolts are drawn, the door is flung open – chickens hurtle out. A nearby child looks terrified. A servant girl is propelled out, held by the scruff of the neck by RB, as the landlord – a Henry VIII type figure, of Falstaffian proportions.)*

**RB:**
Thou poxy wench! If I do but catch thee once more with thy greasy hand in my money-bags, I'll wrap thy legs round thy neck and hang thee up by thy garters for the crows to peck at! Now, be gone!

*(He kicks her into the street. As he does so, he spies RC and Muriel. He struts over to them.)*

**RB:**
What have we here? Upon my troth, look now,
'Tis bold Sir Thomas Thumb, I do declare!
Thrice welcome, good Sir Tom, and to thy spouse.
*(aside)* If that is what she be – such frozen looks dispute she is Mistress of his bed.

**MURIEL:**
Single beds, Brian.

**RC:**
Yes, good evening. Do you think you could accommodate us? In single beds? Both of us, that is. Separately.

**MURIEL:**
In the same room.

**RC:**
But facing different ways. What I mean is, can you put us up?

**RB:**
What, put you up? I, marry, that I shall!
My microcosmic Lord, thou shalt be up
As tall as any subject in the realm.
Thou shalt take dinner seated on a cask
Of good red claret, earmarked for the feast.
Astride this mount, it's tap between thy legs
Thou shalt replenish all the serving maids.

*(Muriel looks disdainful.)*

**RB:**
Put up indeed, the highest in the land
Thou shalt sit here, with me, on my right hand.
Thy frosty spouse, however, by my crown
Should not be up, nay, she should be laid down.

**MURIEL:**
That reminds me, Brian. Hot water bottles.

**RC:**
Ah yes – are the beds warm?

**RB:**
There is a wench, who for an honest groat
Will warm thy bed with warming pans of coals
Or whatsoever method you devise
'Twixt she and you – the girl knows all the ways. *(Looking at Muriel)* As to this glacier – this Siberian stone.
Give me its latch-key, I will warm it straight. *(He slaps her roundly on the roundel of her rear.)* Come, enter, and prepare ye for the feast.

*(Music as he sweeps inside, scattering children and chickens. Muriel is standing aghast.)*

**RC:**
Come on then, dear. *(They start to follow him)* I hope he takes Barclaycard.

*(They enter the inn. Mix to: inside the inn.)*

*(A tracking close-up of goblets being filled from a jug by a serving wench. Lots of raucous noise. The faces of the diners, laughing, eating. The serving wenches, queuing up to fill their jugs from the cask, on which sits RC, legs astride it. RB on his left – pan to the frosty-faced Muriel.)*

*(Shots of the crowd stuffing their faces – a jester wanders round, hitting people on the head with a sheep's bladder balloon. RB, eating and tearing at a chicken. He burps, then throws one leg of chicken over his shoulder.)*

*(It hits a footman standing behind him. RB throws the other leg. It lands in the cleavage of a enormously-busted middle-aged woman, who stares down at it. The footman laughs, RB throws his tankard over his shoulder. It hits the footman, who stops laughing. Large-busted woman laughing. A drunk passes, holding chicken bone. Sees woman's cleavage, removes her bone, replaces it with his one, goes off eating hers.)*

*(The musicians – maybe four or five -start up*

*a dance with drum and tabor. People get up to dance. RC is grabbed by the big-bosomed woman and led onto the floor. The dancers, as part of the dance, suddenly draw each other closer and part again. RC's face splats into the large lady's bosom, recoils, and is dragged in again. Muriel sits on her own, frostily. The crowds laugh and applaud, the dogs eat scraps from the rush-covered floor. Muriel is suddenly surprised by something under the table. It is RC, who emerges.)*

**RC:**
It's alright, it's only me, dear.

*(He is dishevelled.)*

**MURIEL:**
You promised you would never touch me there, Brian.

**RC:**
I'm sorry, Muriel – I didn't mean to grab your bad knee. I'm hiding from that woman. I had to suddenly drop down. Luckily, she's got such a big bosom, she can't see the floor.

**MURIEL:**
I think I would like to go to our room now, Brian. I want to listen to *Book at Bedtime* on Radio 3.

**RC:**
Yes. Bit hectic, isn't it? They're always the same, these Henry VIII Suppers. I don't even know which room we're in.

**MURIEL:**
Well, ask him.

*(Indicating RB, who is involved with a serving wench.)*

**RC:**
*(crossing round to RB)* Excuse me, mine host, but we'd like to retire.

**RB:**
So shall you, good Sir Tom – sweet dreams. *(They start to go.)* But stay! Afore ye go, there's reckoning to be made

Thou must, for this night's work due recompense
In full account of cost be now discharged. This is the custom in these whereabouts–
No man shall sleep until he pay his dues.

**RC:**
*(to Muriel)* Oh, obviously a Union man. Barclaycard? Or perhaps used fivers?

*(He produces both.)*

**RB:**
*(staring at the money)* What? Papers, bills and promissory notes? Nay, this is not a London counting house! Were not the vittals real? The meat not warm? Was not the wine wet, did the cheese not bite? How then can we accept some airy pledge. The promise of some future settlement? *(Grabs him, threateningly)* One shilling in the silver or the realm. The honest coin that bears our good Queen's head.

**MURIEL:**
A shilling?

**RC:**
Oh, well, why didn't you say so? *(To Muriel)* Must be National Trust, or the Arts Council. Lord Montague's probably behind it. *(Hands over coin)* There you are, my man. There's 5p. Come along, Muriel.

*(They start to leave.)*

**RB:**
Stop! This coin is counterfeit! Restrain them!

*(RC and Muriel are grabbed.)*

**RB:**
Bear witness all – that some strange alien face doth masquerade hereon for Good Queen Bess "Elizabeth the Second" the legend bears. We know, God knows, that there be only one!

**RC:**
But look ...

**RB:**
But me no buts, thou scurvy knave
This counterfeiting is a heinous crime
The punishment is clear, and widely
known.
The forfeiture of all your goods and
wealth
And for your further humblement and
shame
To spend the night imprisoned in the
stocks
Away with him.

*(He is taken out.)*

**RB:**
Yet hold his wife close by.
She, being but a chattel of his house
Is likewise forfeit to our royal claim
Go, woman, and prepare her for the night
With perfumes, unctions – dress her all in
white
The ice is white that floats in Arctic sea –
But ice must melt – and melt then so shall
she!

*(A cheer as she is taken out.)*

*Cut to: RC in stocks – or rather, a pillory –
hands and head. (He stands there, deserted.*
*Camera pulls back, he is on a box. The stocks
are under a large tree.)*

**RC:**
This would never have happened if we'd
stuck to Trust House Forte. *(He looks round
at the twilight)* It's going to be damn cold
standing here all night. At least they could
have given me something on my head.

*(Above him, in the tree, a boy drops a hen's
egg. It lands and bursts on RC's head.)*

**RC:**
Sorry I spoke.

*Cut to: a bed-chamber, a large four-poster.*
*(RB carries in Muriel, in revealing night attire.*
*He throws her onto the bed. As she bounces,*
*she shows a lot of leg and promise. A close-up*
*of her, bosom heaving, as we hear sounds of*
*RB tearing off his clothes.)*

*Mix to: next morning. Sunny.*
*(Muriel is hurrying along, looking only*
*slightly the worse for wear. She emerges from*
*the footpath, to find RC sitting in the*
*passenger seat, his arms and hands in the air,*
*as if still in the stocks.)*

**RC:**
Ah – there you are, dear – are you alright?

**MURIEL:**
I'm not sure – I think I'm possibly quite
well. Why are you doing that, Brian? You
look silly.

**RC:**
The stocks, dear. I've just sort of set like it.
You'll have to drive. Have you had much
sleep?

**MURIEL:**
Not a lot.

*(She half-smiles to herself.)*

**RC:**
I've just noticed. That sign isn't there any
more. The one that said "Mileaway". *(We
see that it isn't.)* Muriel, do you think we
dreamt it? God, what a nightmare.

**MURIEL:**
Oh, I don't know ... *(she smiles warmly at
him)* All set, Brian, dear?

**RC:**
Fine. You're very relaxed this morning.

**MURIEL:**
I'm just looking forward to the drive,
that's all.

**RC:**
Well, don't drive too fast. In this position,
I might fly away.

**MURIEL:**
*(laughing)* Let's have a little music, shall
we? *(She turns on the radio.)*

*Cut to: a radio. (It is standing by the four-
poster, in which RB sits, dressed in night cap*

*and Elizabethan frilly night shirt. He is smoking a cigarette and counting fivers. He comes across RC's Barclaycard – opens a small box on the bedside table, and throws it in with the rest. The Irish DJ's voice comes from the radio.)*

**DJ:**
Well, now, with such beautiful weather you should all be out in the country, not sitting indoors listening to this rubbish – why, there's places out there that you've never even heard of. Believe me, it's worth it. Go and find yourself an adventure. It may change your life.

*Cut to: RC and Muriel. (She smiles at him as they drive along. He turns to her and manages to flap one hand at her as they zoom off over the horizon.)*

# THE AMATEUR PLAY

*A false proscenium – looking like a village hall stage. Tatty velvet curtains, closed. On each side, enormous posters saying: "Meadowfield players present* Weekend in Mayfair *by Gerald Barrington".*

*These are written in an amateur signwriting hand, in red and blue (about six foot high, four foot wide).*

*Through the curtains comes the vicar. He blinks at the lights.*

**VICAR:**
Thank you – just a quick word before we start off. Due to circumstances beyond his control, the lad who was playing the part of Rodney had to get married on Saturday, and is at the moment having a wonderful time up a Swiss Alp. George Biggins, however, has agreed to read the part at an hour's notice, and has shut the butchers shop early especially. My wife is still playing one of the lovers, so we hope for a

bit of fun there. By the by, if there are any men who wish to join the Dramatic Society, please come forward. My wife, who also produces the shows, has been desperately short of men for years. In fact, when I tell you that Arnold Corbett is playing three parts in the show, you'll realise just how short the men are round here. Anyway, please see her after the performance backstage. If you can get round – no room to swing a cat back there! Young Trevor will have to find another hobby. Incidentally, we painted all the scenery ourselves. Right, on we go, let's get on with it! Thank you.

*(He disappears through the curtains.)*

*The set is made up of flats painted by amateurs. The pictures are real, but they shake when the door opens. The door opens up and out, but can only open about ten inches as it hits the side wall (no wing space): people have to squeeze in.*

*Window in back wall, with painted Mayfair houses backing, also about ten inches away. Shadows of window on backing.*

*Furniture – a very low settee (smallish) 1950s G plan. Table and two kitchen chairs (tatty). Cocktail cabinet (awful). A painted-on fireplace. A hat stand, also painted on the wall, which has a nail for hanging a real hat on.*

*Another door, where the milkman appears, is on the back wall.*

*"Weekend in Mayfair"*
*The play*

*The curtains part, to see the back of the vicar disappearing out of the door. The door only opens about ten inches, so it is not easy. A large maid is on stage, with a feather duster, dusting. A loud sound effects record is heard to be put on; it is of a car arriving. It stops.*

**MAID:**
Good gracious. The master. And me with me dumplings on the table.

*(She squeezes off. Immediately, RC and the woman enter. RC in boiled shirt and 1928 dinner jacket – high collar, etc. woman in short twenties evening dress, full skirt. RC has "greyed-up" hair at the sides only, badly done with white make-up. His suit is rather crumpled, his complexion ruddy. The woman is, of course, the vicar's wife, but made up far too heavily as a raving beauty.)*

**WOMAN:**
So this is the elegant Mayfair flat I've heard so much about. It's beautiful. Tell me, what's it like being a successful novelist, Charles?

**RC:**
*(with a rural accent)* Unutterably divine, darling. And yet at the same time, devastatingly boring. Money isn't everything, you know.

*(He hangs his hat on the fake peg and looks out of the window. His shadow is seen on the houses opposite.)*

**WOMAN:**
Money? Money doesn't bring happiness, but it enables you to be miserable in comfort.

**RC:**
What has money brought me?

**WOMAN:**
You've got your yacht, in Cannes *(pronounced cans)*. You're so lucky – you can simply lie on deck and sunbathe all summer. Heaven.

**RC:**
I get tired of lying in Cannes. One feels so like a sardine. Cocktail?

*(He crosses behind sofa and trips over something behind it – we cannot see what.)*

**WOMAN:**
Divine.

*(the cocktail cabinet is freestanding and RC disappears completely behind it.)*

**WOMAN:**
*(drifting up level with it)* What are you looking at me like that for?

**RC'S VOICE:**
*(behind cabinet)* Because I love you, you little fool

**WOMAN:**
I know – isn't it heaven? What have you got there?

**RC'S VOICE:**
It's my new cocktail-shaker. Isn't it divine?

**WOMAN:**
Heaven.

**RC'S VOICE.**
Olive?

**WOMAN.**
Yes Charles?

**RC'S VOICE:**
Olive?

**WOMAN:**
Yes, Charles?

**RC'S VOICE:**
Stuffed?

**WOMAN:**
No, just a plain olive, thanks Charles.

**RC'S VOICE:**
Very well, Cynthia.

*(He emerges, hands cocktail to her – she moves down left of sofa – he crosses behind it.)*

**RC:**
Cheers.

*(He trips over thing behind sofa.)*

**WOMAN:**
*(as they sit on sofa)* When will we be married, Charles?

**RC:**
Just as soon as my dreadfully boring divorce comes through. After all, I have a grown-up son, remember. Still, let's not think of him. He's miles away, at Oxford.

*(The maid squeezes on.)*

**2ND MAID:**
Master Rodney, sir.

**RC:**
What?
*(amazed)*

**2ND MAID:**
Master Rodney, sir.
*(same tone of voice)*

**RC:**
*(thinking she has gone back)* What?

**2ND MAID:**
Master Rodney, sir.
*(same tone of voice)*

*(RC helps to squeeze maid through door, then turns to woman and says)*

**RC:**
What?

**WOMAN:**
Rodney?

**RC:**
My son.

*(RB squeezes on, in dinner jacket, much too small, carrying French's acting edition. He wears glasses and is made up much too young. He wears a black toupee, also hobnail boots.)*

**RB:**
Hello, Pops.

**RC:**
Rodney! Why aren't you up at Oxford?

**RB:**
*(reading)* They sent me down, Pops.

Dashed rotten luck, wasn't it?

*(He stands in front of RC.)*

**RC:**
I must phone the governors immediately. How dare they treat someone as sensitive as you are in this beastly manner. Turning you away as if you were some country bumpkin. Cynthia will mix you a cocktail.

*(He squeezes out.)*

**WOMAN:**
*(going to him)* You!

**RB:**
What are you doing here, Snithia? I thought I'd never see you again.

**WOMAN:**
Charles – your father – doesn't know about us, does he?

*(She goes up towards the cocktail cabinet.)*

**RB:**
I've told him.

*(Woman looks surprised, indicates with a nod towards the book. RB looks again.)*

**RB:**
I've told him nothing.

*(He trips over thing behind sofa.)*

**WOMAN:**
That's a relief. Cocktail?

*(She disappears behind cabinet.)*

**RB:**
Well, as long as it's a little one. I'm not really old enough.

*(Woman reappears with two cocktails. RB puts down his book to receive one from her.)*

**WOMAN:**
Oh, Rodney! Do you remember what I

said to you that night at Oxford in the shrubbery?

**RB:**
*(quickly picking up his book and reading)*
Well, as long as it's a little one. I'm not really old enough. Er – no. What?

**WOMAN:**
I said I know we both know what we're doing. We both know that. We both know what we were doing to each other, but I knew I was doing something to you that you didn't know about.

*(RB scratches his head, and displaces the toupee. He quickly goes behind the cocktail cabinet, and re-emerges wearing it back to front.)*

**WOMAN:**
There was something that you couldn't know about that I was doing to you. A young, innocent boy – how could you know I was corrupting you.

*(A pause. RB looks off left.)*

**RB:**
Door – door!

*(He knocks on the cocktail cabinet.)*

**WOMAN:**
Oh, God! Is there no privacy anywhere?

**RB:**
If you want people to leave you alone, you should have your doorbells disconnected.

**WOMAN:**
*(sotto voce)* Knockers.

**RB:**
Eh? Oh. If you want people to leave you alone, you should have your knockers disconnected.

*(He opens door in back wall. This opens fully, to reveal a cardboard cut-out of a milkman.)*

**RB:**
Not today, thank you.

*(He closes door again.)*

**WOMAN:**
Oh, Rodney. *(Lies back on sofa)* Come here, my own sweet boy!

**RB:**
*(tripping on thing behind sofa)* How radiant you look, Snithia. I could sing your praises forever. I don't know where to start. Turn over. *(Woman turns and lies on her stomach. RB turns the page.)* What a curious expression, Snithia. What are you thinking?

**WOMAN:**
It mustn't happen, Rodney, it can't happen; not this way. Oh, but it must – it must – I don't care about the world! Kiss me!

*(RB now studies his book for quite a while – turns page, etc., then suddenly drops it and starts to grapple with Cynthia on the couch. His hobnail boots are much in evidence and so are her directoire knickers. RC enters, dressed as the grandfather. Same dinner jacket, but badly made up – white moustache, old white wig, walking stick, bent double, etc.)*

**RC:**
What's this? Rodney, is that you? Who have you got under there? I recognise that face. What's going on? And, what is more important, *(trips over thing behind sofa)* what is that bloody thing?

**RB:**
Grandfather! Pops has just popped out. Fancy a cocktail?

**RC:**
No, thank you. You keep your filth to yourself. I'm going to look for my son and tell him that his Cynthia is flat out on the sofa, on top of which there's his son behaving under-handed behind his back, under his very nose.

*(He opens door at back. Milkman cut-out is still there. RC jumps in alarm.)*

**RC:**
Oh! Excuse me!

*(He pushes past it. It falls over.)*

**RC:**
He's fainted.

*(An ad-lib. He hurries off.)*

**WOMAN:**
It's no good. I can't go on like this. Things seem to be getting on top of me lately.

**RB:**
In that case, I'll get off. *(He does so, then realises)* In that case, I'll get off back to Oxford.

**WOMAN:**
No – not yet. One last fling, my dearest boy. I need your tenderness, your innocence, your warmth. My arms await you!

**RB:**
I'm coming back on. *(He gets back on to her – she pushes him off.)* Oh. Tuesday. I'm coming back on Tuesday.

**WOMAN:**
Too late, dear Rodney. I shall have returned to the South of France. What is the time?

*(A whirring, and the painted clock (which says twenty to five) strikes two.)*

**RB:**
One o'clock.

**WOMAN:**
I shall leave at once. So, Rodney – this is the end.

*(The curtains start to close. RB waves them back. They re-open again. RC enters, dressed in top hat and black beard, and a cloak over his dinner jacket.)*

**RC:**
Just a minuit!

**RB:**
Who are you?

*(The maid squeezes on, and announces)*

**MAID:**
Monsieur Gerard.

*(She tries to squeeze off, but gets stuck in the door. A small scruffy dog enters, obviously the vicar's wife's. It runs all over the set. They all ignore it.)*

**WOMAN:**
Gaston!

**RC:**
Parbleu! So I was right! You are here!

**RB:**
Snithia – who is this old girl?

**RC:**
I am her husband! Gaston Gerard at your service!

*(He raises his hat – his beard is attached to it. He replaces hat and beard as if nothing had happened.)*

**RC:**
I come from France – didn't you get my letter?

**RB:**
Husband?

**WOMAN:**
It's true! I've deceived everyone. You, Rodney, your father, your grandfather – I didn't want any of you – all I wanted was adventure!

*(She sits on the dog.)*

**RB:**
Well, if that's how things are, then I'm off.

*(He goes to door, where maid is still stuck.)*

**RB:**
I'm going back to somewhere where I know I'm always welcome.

*(He crawls underneath the maid's skirts to get off. She gives a squeal as he disappears.)*

**WOMAN:**
Come, Gaston, come and sit here!

*(She pats the sofa – the little dog leaps onto it. RC goes behind sofa, trips on thing, proceeds round and joins her on sofa.)*

**WOMAN:**
You'll have to forgive me, you know.

**RC:**
Oui, oui, cherie. As long as you promise me never to let any man touch you again, ever.

**WOMAN:**
I promise you this, darling – no man will kiss me on the lips again. From now on, it's all over.

*(The curtain is pulled. Opened again quickly. RC without beard, woman, RB, maid and cardboard milkman take bow. Curtains close.)*

# THE FOREIGN FILM

*A cinema interior: distorted music and throaty french dialogue in background. Very few in audience, mostly men, silent, intent. Enter Mr and Mrs Titheradge. They are about sixty, very suburban and un-with-it. They are also very wet. She removes her plastic rain hat and he shakes water from his cap, which he then replaces.*

**SHE:**
*(as they settle)* Ooh! Dear! What a downpour! We were lucky to find this, Jack. I didn't know there were any cinemas in Soho. I thought it was all restaurants. Hey, that was a lot of money,

15 shillings each. Why didn't we go in the cheap seats?

**HE:**
That is the cheap seats.

**SHE:**
Oh! I'm splashed right up me stockings. Whenever I put on new stockings it's the same – it pours with rain and I get splashed right up 'em. *(Looking at screen)* What's it called, Jack?

**HE:**
I dunno.

**SHE:**
It's foreign, isn't it?

**HE:**
I dunno.

**SHE:**
I think it's foreign. Well, it's not English, anyhow. Yes, it's one of them foreign films. *(They watch and we hear passionate dialogue.)* Mrs Cook across the road has got some bedroom curtains like that – only they're more of a blue. Here, I like that eiderdown, don't you, Jack? *(We see Jack beginning to get interested.)* I think I'll try and get one of those with my Green Stamps ... I've got nearly eight books now. Here, isn't she like Muriel?

**HE:**
Who?

**SHE:**
Elsie's girl.

**HE:**
No. Nothing like her.

**SHE:**
Oh, I think so. A bit bigger perhaps ... although Muriel takes a forty now, you know. We had an awful job getting a bridesmaid's dress to fit her. Great big lump, she is. *(Jack is staring pop-eyed at the screen.)* Now that's just Muriel, that is. Just takes her clothes off and drops them

281

anywhere, all round the bedroom. No sense of tidiness, girls these days. If she'd got up ten minutes earlier, she wouldn't have to rush about like that. *(Jack is transfixed. we hear a bath being filled.)* Now those are the soap-racks I was telling you about, Jack – they got them in Harris's. They're continental special design. There, you see the way she's leaning over it to turn the taps off, well you can't scratch yourself on them. They're all curved over, with no sharp edges. Lovely shape, aren't they?

*(Jack is sitting there, shaking. We hear the man's voice (off-screen) and a lot of splashing. He sounds passionate.)*

**SHE:**
There's a lovely loofah he's got there. I wonder if you can get those on the Green Stamps.

**HE:**
*(gulping)* I doubt it.

**SHE:**
That's what I need. There's a bit of my back I can never get at. Oh look, she's having the same trouble, see? Oh, he's giving her a hand now ... *(cut to Jack: his cap is steaming.)* Now, what's he doing? Oh, they must be trying to save water. Still, you'd think he'd let her get out of the bath first, before he got in, wouldn't you? *(The music swells up off screen.)* Ooer. What does *Fin* mean? Oh, it's the end. We must have missed the best part. *(Another bit of music starts up.)* Oh, "Look At Life No. 94 ... Do It Yourself". There you are, Jack – this'll be more interesting for you.

*(Fade on Jack, sweating and steaming.)*

# STAR TREK

*Original opening captions if possible, with RC's voice over, as Captain Kirk. If not available, we copy as near as possible.*

After captions, cut to: Scene 1: the control room. As near as possible to the original. essential are sliding-doors at entrance, which appear to be automatic, a computer-type piece of equipment, with hole for things to come out of and an overlay "viewer" on which we see stars and a planet (zoom in on caption boards for this). Also a seat for Captain Kirk, Lieutenant O'Hara and Mr Scott. The above three principals, plus a couple of extra men, are in position at the start of this scene.*

**SCOTT:**
Approaching unidentified planet now, sir. Warp three.

**RC:**
*(As Kirk – seated at controls)* Distance?

**SCOTT:**
3,800 miles, captain.

**RC:**
Velocity?

**O'HARA:**
*(a white girl)* 7,500 miles per hour, captain.

**RC:**
Chronometric scale?

**O'HARA:**
Similar to our own, sir. 21st century AD.

**RC:**
Precise time at present moment?

**SCOTT:**
Three minutes past eleven.

**RC:**
You don't say – where the hell's the coffee? And come to think of it, where's Mr Spock? I want him to run checks on this planet before we land.

**SCOTT:**
He just slipped out for a moment, captain.

**RC:**
What for?

**SCOTT:**
He's only human, sir.

**RC:**
That's just it, he's not. He's a Vulcan. He told me they never had to go at all. Keep a steady course, Scotty, I'm going to find Spock. *(He rises)* Hey! *(Looks down at himself)* I'm much smaller than I used to be! What's happened? Scotty! Look at me!

**SCOTT:**
Sir?

**RC:**
I've got smaller. Come over here.

**SCOTT:**
*(approaching)* Good gracious, so you have, sir. How could that have happened?

*(The automatic doors open – RB enters, with pointed ears, as Mr Spock.)*

**RB:**
Pray excuse me, captain, I was delayed. *(He stares)* Captain Kirk, I don't know if you are yet aware of it, but certain physical changes have taken place in your body, resulting in a somewhat abbreviated version of your erstwhile good self.

**RC:**
Never mind my body, Mr Spock – what about yours?

**RB:**
I regret that I, too, have become affected, but in a different direction – that is, outwards, as opposed to downwards. I am approximately twice as heavy as I was. I suggest we take steps to investigate the phenomena immediately – especially in your case, captain.

**RC:**
Why me more than you?

**RB:**
With respect, captain, if a thing swells it can only get bigger, but if it shrinks, it could disappear altogether.

**RC:**
What?

**RB:**
You are very small, captain.

**RC:**
And you're like the side of a house!

**RB:**
Verbal fisticuffs will get us nowhere, captain. Let us consider – has anyone else on board been affected?

**RC:**
Lieutenant O'Hara certainly looks the same size and shape to me – still as attractive as ever.

*(A shot of her, at her controls.)*

**RB:**
*(eyeing her)* Hmm. One detail may have escaped your notice. Yesterday she was a negro.

**RC:**
You're right, Mr Spock! *(calling)* Lieutenant O'Hara! How do you feel?

**O'HARA:**
Oh, I'se just fine and dandy, Captain Kirk. Don't you worry yo' head 'bout lil ole me!

**RB:**
It's still working on her.

**SCOTT:**
*(who has been looking into viewer on "computer" device)* Captain Kirk, sir!

**RC:**
What is it, Scotty?

**SCOTT:**
There seems to be something wrong with the computer banks, sir. I'm getting no information on the planet at all.

*(RC and RB move to computer.)*

**RC:**
Spock?

**RB:**
(peering into "viewfinder") There appears to be a malfunction in the electronic brain-cells themselves, captain. Some force is being exerted which has the effect of twisting the cell-patterns, producing a kind of insanity within the machine.

**RC:**
Insanity? That's crazy!

**RB:**
That is another way of putting it, certainly.

**RC:**
Here – let me feed it a question. (Switches on and speaks into small microphone.) Co-ordinates, please, of the planet in our immediate flight-path.

(He presses button once.)

(The computer chugs and tings and bangs away for a few seconds – then a final twang – and a card comes out of the output hole. RC picks it up.)

**RC:**
(reading it) "Your weight is 8 stone two, and you will meet a short dark stranger." That's ridiculous. (Into mic. again) Precise details, please. Type of planet. Land Mass. Atmosphere. Life Forms.

(He presses button four times. The "viewer" flashes four times, then same noises as above. After final "twang" – RC takes out strip of paper from the hole and holds it up.)

**RC:**
Four passport photos.

**RB:**
Allow me, captain. (He speaks into mic.) Full report please, on computer brain itself. Self-analysis and diagnosis on "over-ride sanity" circuit. (to Kirk) That should do it, if anything will, Captain.

(Same noises as before. Then we cut to the actual opening in the computer, through which the messages come. A paper cup, being filled up with black coffee. Spock's hand comes in and takes it out.)

**RB:**
I think we may safely deduce that the computer is completely out of its tiny mind.

**RC:**
That does it. Scotty – prepare to beam us down to the planet's surface. This force must be coming from down there, Spock.

**RB:**
I'm quite certain you're right, captain. We must investigate at once.

**RC:**
Let's go. As soon as we enter the transporter-room, beam us down, Scotty – and then circle the planet and stand by.

(They exit.)

**SCOTT:**
Aye, aye, sir. (He crosses to computer and tastes the cup of coffee) Well, I'll say one thing – you make a lovely cup of coffee.

(The computer burps.)

Scene 2: the transporter room.

RB and RC are already standing in position.

**RC:**
Okay, Scotty – beam us down. Go!

**SCOTTY'S VOICE:**
(over intercom) Aye, aye, captain. Beaming now.

(RB and RC start to fade, but don't disappear completely.)

**RB:**
Increase power, Mr Scott. We haven't gone yet. (RB disappears completely, RC still half there.) Spock has gone, Scotty. I seem

to be stuck.

*(RC disappears – RB fades back a bit.)*

**RB:**
Something's wrong with the machine –
I'm back.

*(RC flicks back suddenly.)*

**RC:**
Me too. Over-ride, Scotty! I'm beginning
to feel like a yo-yo.

*(They both fade away and disappear. a
pause.)*

**RC'S VOICE:**
We're still here. For Pete's sake, Scotty!

**RB'S VOICE:**
Try the booster, Mr Scott.

*(They begin to fade back – but only the
bottom half of RB shows.)*

**RB'S VOICE:**
This is ridiculous. *(The legs walk round RC.)*
I'll try and fix it – I'll join you later.

*(The legs walk away, out of shot. RC fades in
and fades out as we cut to: camera zooms
slowly in on planet, surrounded by stars.)*

**RC** *(voice over):*
Captain's log, star-date 2150. Mr Spock
and I finally managed to land on the
planet XJ 340, after trouble with the ship's
computer. We set out to search for the
source of the strange evil force which had
changed our shape.

*Scene Three: a room in the palace of Kanhuth,
on the planet*

*RC and RB enter, ray-guns in hand.*

**RC:**
Seems deserted.

**RB:**
It would appear so, captain. However, Mr

Scott beamed us down as near to the
force-field as possible. We must be within
a few feet of it. We should proceed with
caution.

**RC:**
Search the room.

*(They begin to do so. In the centre of the room,
a sort of plinth, on top of which is a black
metal box, with a knob on the top. RC is
searching in a corner. RB approaches the black
box, touches the knob. Then he lifts the black
box up by the knob. Underneath, like a large
cheese on a dish, is a head – green, with wires
coming from its temples. It looks to be
completely detached, resting on a chromium
square block. It is obviously alive. It looks at
him evilly. RB puts back the cover before he
realises what it is. He has moved away, and
suddenly stops.)*

**RB:**
Captain!

*(He beckons RC over and then lifts the cover
off again.)*

**RC:**
Good grief.

**HEAD:**
Greetings, earthman.

**RC:**
Greetings. Are you in charge here?

**HEAD:**
There are many kinds of life-form who
serve me.

**RC:**
So you're the head?

**HEAD:**
I am the Master.

**RB:**
Tell me, Headmaster, is it you who have
been disrupting our starship and
changing our physical shapes?

**HEAD:**
The ray emanates from the machine behind me. I control it by thought waves.

**RC:**
But why? Why?

**HEAD:**
Revenge! Revenge!

**RC:**
I see! I see! Go on – go on.

**RB:**
Captain, if we're going to say everything twice we're never going to get out of here. I suggest once is enough.

**RC:**
I'm sorry, I'm sorry. I mean, I'm just sorry. Once.

**RB.**
Revenge, I believe you said.

**HEAD:**
Yes – I loaned my body to the scientists for experiments – *(furious)* and they never returned it. They left me here with this machine – using my brain as a sort of clockwork machine! Me! Who used to love life! Wine, women and song! I lived for them!

**RB:**
Well, at least you can still sing.

**RC:**
Does no one bring you food?

**HEAD:**
What good is food? I have no stomach.

**RC:**
Tough.

**RB:**
And women?

**HEAD:**
The same thing applies.

*(RB looks at RC.)*

**RC:**
*(explaining)* He has no inclination.

**HEAD:**
I'm becoming a vegetable.

**RB:**
*(takes RC aside)* What is your opinion, captain?

**RC:**
*(to RB, quietly)* I think he's off his head.

**RB:**
True. An evil force that must be dealt with.

**HEAD:**
I'd be better off dead.

**RB:**
I think that could be arranged.

*(He suddenly slams the cover over the head and then runs to the machine which is emitting the ray. He turns it onto the black box, then moves forward to the black box and is about to pick it up.)*

**RC:**
Spock! Keep back – you could get contaminated!

**RB:**
Leave me, captain – beam aboard and wait for me on the starship.

**RC:**
I'll have the medical unit stand by.

*(He exits. Spock removes the black cover. underneath is a cabbage. RB stares at it. Then a strange thudding noise is heard. RB looks apprehensive and backs away from the door. We fade.)*

*Scene Four: Captain Kirk's cabin on the starship.*
*A small affair, one door; the main essential is an overlay blue window in the back wall – three foot tall by four foot wide. (Note: the impression to create here is that RC is now six feet tall so everything to scale.)*

*RC is standing next to a couch-type bed. O'Hara, who is now a negress, and must be about eight inches shorter than RC, is offering him a drink from a tray.*

**RC:**
*(taking it)* Thanks, Lieutenant O'Hara. Glad to see you've got your colour back. I'm back to my normal six feet again. Spock must have overcome the creature and nullified the ray. The question is, is he OK? *(Enter Scotty)* Scotty – is Spock back yet?

**SCOTTY:**
*(on monitor)* No, captain. And I don't like it, being down here on the planet's surface. Permission to blast off again, sir?

**RC:**
Certainly not, Mr Scott. Not without Spock.

*(He looks out of the "window" where we see the planet's surface – typical backcloth à la science fiction magazine.)*

**RC:**
Somewhere out there, there are many life-forms – who knows – one of them may have got Spock!

*(The thudding noise is heard again. They freeze. Then in through the window peers the vast head of RB (on overlay). The head fills the window.)*

**RB:**
Good day, captain. I've come to say goodbye.

**RC:**
Goodbye? Spock, what's happened?

**RB:**
I became contaminated – and just grew and grew. I intend to stay here until I become normal size again. Farewell!

**RC:**
But that's terrible. Terrible!

**RB:**
Don't worry, captain. You were right about the other life forms – one of them did get me. Say goodbye, Angelique.

*(An enormous under-dressed girl peers in, displaying a bosom about four feet across. She smiles and waves, then stands up and turns round, displaying a bottom about four feet across. It walks away from us and we see Spock eventually, walking with her. An amazed look from RC, and we bring up the music, as per original.)*

# UPSTAIRS, DOWNSTAIRS

*Credits:*
*We copy the steel engraving-type captions of the series, finishing with an engraving of the outside of the Bellamy house. We go in on this, mix through to studios.*

*Scene 1: the drawing room – a May morning, 1907.*

*Mr Bellamy (RC) suave, elegant, an MP sits reading a letter. His wife, beautiful and witty, is toying with some embroidery.*

**MARJORIE:**
Well?

**RC:**
What?

**MARJORIE:**
What does it say?

*(She is eager.)*

287

**RC:**
I haven't quite finished reading it. Be patient, my dear.

**MARJORIE:**
Patient? A letter is delivered by hand from no less an address than Buckingham Palace itself, and my husband asks me to be patient. Richard, really!

**RC:**
I'm sorry, my dear, to be a trifle slow. Reading wasn't my best subject at Eton. That's why I had to give up any ideas of following a profession and become an MP.

**MARJORIE:**
Well, how far have you got?

**RC:**
Well, I'll tell you this much, it's addressed to both of us.

**MARJORIE:**
Here, let me read it. *(He gives it to her.)* To Sir Richard and Lady Bellamy …

**RC:**
There you are, I'm right so far.

**MARJORIE:**
I have the honour to inform you that his Majesty – oh! – would deem it a privilege to dine with you on May the 21st at eight o'clock, at your residence in Belgrave Square. His Majesty will, of course, be incognito. I have the honour to remain, etc. Arthur Wormington, private secretary to his Majesty – Oh, Richard – I think I'm going to faint.

*(She collapses into his arms.)*

**RC:**
Here, lie on the sofa, and I'll undo something for you.

**MARJORIE:**
No, no, there's no time for that. I'm too excited. Oh, Richard! The King, dining here! It must be because of that chance meeting at the garden party. You

remember – you weren't there.

**RC:**
How can I remember if I wasn't there?

**MARJORIE:**
I mean, I told you about it. I met him – and now he wants to dine here! And all because I offered him a pressed tongue sandwich.

**RC:**
Are you sure that's all you offered him?

**MARJORIE:**
Don't be silly, Richard. Now we must prepare. It must be kept a secret from the neighbours. Remember, he will be incognito the whole time.

**RC:**
From what I hear, he always is these days. Can't do his liver any good. I'll ring for Hudson.

*(He goes to bell-rope. As he is about to pull the rope, Hudson (RB) enters. RC doesn't hear him and pulls the bell.)*

**RB:**
*(immediately)* You rang, sir?

**RC:**
*(turning round quickly)* Ah, Hudson. That was quick.

**RB:**
I came in just before you rang, sir.

**RC:**
That's what I mean. Your mistress wants a word with you.

**RB:**
*(alarmed)* What, you mean she's here, now? In the house? Oh, my goodness!

**RC:**
*(explains)* Lady Bellamy. *(Indicating his wife.)*

**RB:**
*(relieved)* Oh, I see, sir. Sorry. Milady?

**MARJORIE:**
We are expecting a very distinguished visitor for dinner on Friday, Hudson.

**RB:**
*(to RC)* Would it be a fellow MP, sir?

**RC:**
No, no – someone of far greater stature than me.

**RB:**
Oh, really? I wonder whoever that could be?

**MARJORIE:**
His Majesty, Kind Edward.

**RB:**
The Seventh?

**MARJORIE:**
Naturally. Edward the Sixth died in 1553.

**RC:**
Did he, by jove? That's something else they didn't teach us at Eton. Just a minute, that can't be right. That would make this one over three hundred years old.

**MARJORIE:**
No, silly – there have been others in between.

**RB:**
Excuse me, milady – perhaps while you're sorting that out, I could go and inform the staff. *(He starts to go, then remembers)* Oh, milady, the reason I came in, in the first place, was to ask whether I could use the morning room this afternoon for my evening classes.

**RC:**
What?

**RB:**
Only we're all working this evening, and

so I thought I'd have them this afternoon, and the morning room is ideal.

**RC:**
Hang on a minute, I'm confused. You're not asking for the whole day off, are you?

**RB:**
Oh no, sir. I'm working this morning and this evening. It's just this afternoon I want off, for the evening classes.

**RC:**
In the morning room.

**RB:**
Yes, sir.

**RC:**
Alright then, Hudson – just try to put in an appearance from time to time.

**RB:**
Certainly, sir, milady. Will that be all?

**RC:**
Yes, thank you, Hudson. Nice to have passed the time of day with you. *(RB exits. To Marjorie)* What are these evening classes, anyway?

**MARJORIE:**
He gives the maids lessons in deportment and physical fitness. He likes to show them a few wrinkles.

**RC:**
I'm sure he does. Still, the King's visit should give the maids something to occupy them. I bet he can't wait to tell them the news.

*Cut to: close-up of a maid, scrubbing a floor. She suddenly reacts violently to an attack from behind.*

**KITCHEN MAID:**
Ooh!

*(We pull back a little as RB bends down and says in her ear)*

**RB:**
The King's coming to dinner!

**MAID:**
Ooh!

*Cut to: another maid.*
*Back view on her on a pair of steps, dusting the picture rail with a short feather duster. Close-up of her face. Suddenly she reacts in the same way.*

**PARLOUR MAID:**
Ooh!

*(We pull back a little. RB is there. He too has a small feather duster, as the maid found out. He steps up and whispers in her ear)*

**RB:**
The King's coming to dinner!

**PARLOUR MAID:**
Ooh!

*Cut to: door with "servants bathroom no. 1" painted on it in gold lettering. Pull back to reveal RB, peering through keyhole. Sounds of water running and maid's voice, singing. RB enters quickly, clouds of steam emerge, sound of a slap.*

**HOUSEMAID:**
*(off)* Ow! Coo, that didn't half hurt, that did.

**RB:**
*(off)* The King's coming to dinner!

**HOUSEMAID:**
*(off)* Ooh!

*(RB appears again, wiping his soapy hands on his apron. He goes to next door, which says "servants bathroom no. 2" on it. He opens it, clouds of steam emerge. Sound of a loud slap, as before. Then a loud splash. RB reappears with a bucket over his head. He removes it. He is drenched. We cut inside. In the bath is a surly-looking gardener, gnarled, with a filthy old hat on, smoking a filthy old pipe and scrubbing his back at the same time.*

*We fade out.)*

*(Fade in – close-up of desk calendar – "Friday May 21st". The great day. RC is in a brocade dressing gown and is speaking, or rather shouting, into the telephone.)*

**RC:**
Hullo! Hullo in there! Is anybody in there? Hullo, mother. MOTHER! *(Marjorie enters)* Mother, if you're in there, answer me. *(Putting it down in disgust)* Dashed new-fangled things. Spend a fortune having the thing installed and then it doesn't work. Just can't make mother hear at all.

**MARJORIE:**
Mother's not on the telephone.

**RC:**
That's no excuse. *(Then realising)* What?

**MARJORIE:**
Listen, I've something much more important to talk about. I've just been having a word with Rose, the head housemaid. She's very distressed, Richard.

**RC:**
I absolutely deny it. Her whole story is a tissue of lies. I was at an all-night sitting. What did she say?

**MARJORIE:**
She merely told me that Hudson, the butler, is missing.

**RC:**
Oh, that's different.

**MARJORIE:**
Have you got a guilty conscience, Richard?

**RC:**
Certainly not. You can't afford one if you're an MP. Did you say Hudson is missing?

**MARJORIE:**
He hasn't been seen since this morning.

Apparently a man in a bowler hat called at the front door and, after a hurried consultation, left again – followed, five minutes afterwards, by Hudson. One of the maids saw him later this morning with a large bag in Burlington Arcade.

**RC:**
Did the maid recognise her?

**MARJORIE:**
Recognise who?

**RC:**
The large bag he was with. It wasn't Gerty from the Gaiety, was it? I know he's been hanging round the stage door after her, ever since he saw her as Dick in the Panto.

**MARJORIE:**
I don't know what you're talking about. All I know is that the King is coming to dinner tonight, and we are without a butler!

**RC:**
Good grief! What are we going to do?

**MARJORIE:**
You will have to be the butler, Richard.

**RC:**
Me? I couldn't. I've never buttled in my life. I wouldn't know how to begin.

**MARJORIE:**
Look, his Majesty doesn't know you – and I'm not having a strange butler in the house tonight. We've got six hours to prepare.

**RC:**
No, it's impossible – my tailcoat is at the cleaners.

**MARJORIE:**
Then you'll have to wear Hudson's. Richard – I'm determined.

*(Close-up of RC's resigned face.)*

*(Mix to: the house in Belgrave Square. A*

*policeman saunters past. A nursemaid goes in the opposite direction, pushing a pram. The policeman stops and turns. We hear the faintest sound of a carriage and pair approaching. A close-up of the policeman as we hear the carriage stop. Footsteps approach. A look of recognition and a salute from the policeman. Then a close-up of the front door. The shadow of the King's top hat and cloak falls on the door. A walking stick comes into shot, presses the doorbell (they did have electric bells in those days!) after a moment, RC comes to the door, wearing gold-rimmed spectacles like Hudson's. He bows slightly)*

**RC:**
Good evening your, er, Lord, sir, Mr Windsor.

*(The King's top hat is handed over to RC. He goes to take it – we see a very large, long black coat-sleeve with no hand in sight. Eventually the hand arrives out of the sleeve and takes the hat.)*

*Cut to: the dinner in progress.*
*(The table is set very elaborately – for two. The King (RB) sits on the right of Lady Marjorie. RC is at the sideboard. Three maids hover about, assisting. As we cut, the King is roaring with laughter. He is obviously getting on very well with Lady Bellamy.)*

**RC:**
Soup, milady?

**MARJORIE:**
Thank you, Hudson.

*(RC places plates before them, then prepares to ladle out soup from a tureen held by a maid. To do so, he has to roll up his sleeves like a magician. He glares at his wife.)*

**KING:**
He's going to do a conjuring trick! Can you pull a rabbit out of the soup?

**RC:**
Why not? That's what went into it. That and a few other things.

**KING:**
Such as what?

**RC:**
Such as this sleeve, for instance. Feel that, it's soaked. Would milady mind very much if I removed my coat to serve the soup?

**MARJORIE:**
You will do no such thing, Hudson. Where's your decorum?

**RC:**
Could be anywhere under this lot.

**MARJORIE:**
Kindly serve the soup, Hudson, and don't be impertinent.

**RC:**
Very well, milady.

*(He ladles one dollop into each plate, ungraciously.)*

**MARJORIE:**
*(her hand on his)* More wine, Teddy?

**KING:**
Thank you – delightful. Where do you get it?

**MARJORIE:**
My husband gets it specially. *(Looking into his eyes.)*

**KING:**
Where from?

**MARJORIE:**
Downstairs.

**RC:**
*(to himself)* You'll get it specially upstairs if you carry on like this, my girl.

**MAID:**
*(surprised, but interested)* Were you talking to me, sir?

**RC:**
Shut up. *(Coming back to them, loudly)* More soup?

*(He ladles some into Marjorie's plate.)*

**MARJORIE:**
No, thank you, Hudson.

**RC:**
Oh. *(He picks up her plate and pours it straight back into the ladle, then pours the ladleful into the King's plate and puts the plate back in front of the King.)*

**KING:**
Please – no more.

**MARJORIE:**
Oh, but I insist – it's oyster soup. *(With a wink)* A little more, Hudson.

*(She picks up the King's plate, holds it out.)*

**KING:**
*(knowingly)* Oh, I see. You think I will be needing it later.

*(He leans over to whisper in her ear. She reacts, giggling, and moves the plate out of range just as RC pours a ladleful out, his eyes on her the whole time. The consequence is that the hot soup lands not in the bowl, but in the King's lap.)*

**RB:**
*(leaping up in pain)* Ow! Och hoots, Sir Richard, you've scalded me – Ooh – oh, I'll never be able to wear a sporran again!

*(RC and Marjorie stare at him)*

**RC:**
Just a minute. Good grief – Hudson!

**MARJORIE:**
What on earth does this mean?

**RB:**
I'm sorry, milady, to deceive you. It was with the best intentions.

*(Taking off his false beard.)*

**MARJORIE:**
But why?

**RB:**
The King's secretary called this morning and cancelled the visit – and I just hadn't the heart to tell you.

**RC:**
Good gracious – you did it all – out of loyalty?

**RB:**
Yes, sir. Oh milady, will you ever forgive me?

**MARJORIE:**
Of course, Hudson – come upstairs and I'll see how badly you're hurt.

**RB:**
Oh, it's nothing, milady.

**MARJORIE:**
Nonetheless, it might need a poultice.

**RC:**
Now, just a minute … you're not taking him upstairs – not after the way you've been carrying on.

**MARJORIE:**
Then he must remove his trousers here. Come along, Hudson.

*(She starts to get his trousers off. Hudson resists feebly.)*

**RC:**
Now look here …

*(He starts to take his coat off. The maid enters, stares at Hudson's long johns)*

**PARLOUR MAID:**
*(flustered)* Milady – quick – can I have a word with you?

**MARJORIE:**
What is it, Rose?

*(Before she can answer, King Edward VII walks in)*

**MARJORIE:**
Your Majesty!

*(Everyone bows and/or curtsies low.)*

# THE ONEDIN LINE

*Stock opening of boat etc. as per original TV programme. After opening captions cut to close-up of RC as James Onedin. He sits at a ship's table, with charts, sextants, etc. He is working on his charts. The wind howls – a storm is obviously imminent. It is night. storm music over.*

*(There is a knocking at the door – a hammering.)*

**RC:**
Come in!

*(RB enters as Mister Baines, the first mate. He wears oilskins of the period and sou'-wester. As he enters, the wind blows all the papers off Onedin's desk, etc.)*

**RB:**
Beg pardon, cap'n!

**RC:**
What is it, Mister Baines?

**RB:**
*(shouting over the wind)* There's a terrible Nor-nor-easter blowing up, sir – could reach gale force in a matter of minutes. A lot of fork lightning over to the west. The rain's falling in bucketfuls, cap'n and if that wind goes on increasing at its present rate, it could snap the mast off any ship in the line, sir!

**RC:**
Good God! Well, all I can say is, thank heaven we're not at sea.

**RB:**
Yes sir, that would be dreadful.

**RC:**
Shut that blasted door, man, there's a terrible draught – is the back door open?

**RB:**
Yes cap'n – it's your maid. She's in the garden, getting in washing.

*(He shuts the door – wind subsides a little.)*

**RC:**
That's better. Well, Mister Baines, what brings you to my house? It must be something important to drag you out of the Dirty Duck on a night like this.

**RB:**
Oh, 'tis true, cap'n, I do like my pint of ale, but there are some things in this world that, when they happen, do stop a man from drinking. And closing-time is one of 'em.

**RC:**
Ah, so you were thrown out, eh?

**RB:**
No, cap'n – I just came to tell you that the latest addition to your fleet is all ready in port, refitted and ready to sail.

**RC:**
My new cargo ship? It's arrived?

**RB:**
Last night, sir. I thought perhaps you and me might go and look at her first thing in the morning, if you've a mind.

**RC:**
Of course I've a mind. I'm not daft. You need brains to build up a fleet of cargo ships as I've done, Baines. Brains, Baines, brains!

**RB:**
Yes sir, yes sir, yes sir.

**RC:**
And I've done it from nothing – all on my own. My father was no help. Sometimes I used to think his head was full of cotton-wool.

**RB:**
Why, sir?

**RC:**
I saw a bit of it sticking out of his ear once. And now, the latest addition to the line. *(Pours out two glasses of port from a decanter.)* Let's drink to it, Baines – I'm sorry I have to offer you this rather inferior port wine, but the weather's been so bad I couldn't get to the off-licence. Anyway, you're so drunk you won't know the difference.

**RB:**
That's alright, cap'n – any port in a storm. To the newest addition to the line, sir – here's health.

*(They clink glasses.)*

**RC:**
May she always prosper – here's to her the – do you know, Mister, I don't know her name.

*Cut to: the quayside. It is now dry and the following morning. RB now wears cap and reefer jacket. RC is dressed authentically as James Onedin.*

**RB**
"Saucy Sue", cap'n. Ain't she a beauty?

**RC:**
Excellent, Mister Baines, excellent. Trim and proud. Fast, I should imagine, too – and yet that air of strength and reliability characteristic of the class. What's she like to handle, have you heard?

**RB:**
Jones, the pilot, says she responds quickly, manoeuvres well – I've been all over her already – she's as solid as a rock and a lot more comfortable than the older ones of

the same size.

**RC:**
"Saucy Sue", eh?

**RB:**
That be her name, cap'n. I can't wait *(calling)* I say, Sue!

*Cut to: big, beautiful, blonde wench, lounging on a pile of rope. She has bare feet and a chest to match. (She gets up bouncily and moves out of frame. She enters frame and joins RB and RC)*

**SUE:**
Hello, sailor!

**RC:**
Look, why don't you slink over to the tavern and wait for me – I'll be with you in time to buy your second pint. I've just got to look at a ship. What's it called, Baines?

**RB:**
*(as Sue moves off)* "The Dependable", cap'n.

**RC:**
How very unexciting.

*(Watches Sue go.)*

**RB:**
I reckon her bottom will need a lot of attention.

**RC:**
Quite. Still, first things first. Come on.

*(They head off in the opposite direction.)*

*Mix to: stock shots of ships at sea. Mix from this to the captain's cabin – not very large, but with an alcove for the bunk which is curtained to give complete privacy. (RC is looking out through the porthole, through a large telescope on a stand.)*

**RC:**
*(suddenly shouting)* Land Ho! *(He leaves the telescope and goes towards the cabin door.)* Mister Baines!

*(RB enters.)*

**RB:**
Aye, cap'n?

**RC:**
Land ho, Mister Baines.

**RB:**
Land, sir? There ain't no land for miles, cap'n.

**RC:**
Really? Look, man – through the telescope. What's that small blob on the horizon?

**RB:**
That's not on the horizon, cap'n, that's on the end of the telescope. Ar. A seagull did it, cap'n.

**RC:**
Oh, I see. Any other messages?

**RB:**
Eh? Oh yes, cap'n, I was just coming to report a stowaway on board. Found him in one of the lifeboats ...

**RC:**
What? The blackguard. Bring him in at once.

**RB:**
Bring in the prisoner, Martin!

*(Two sailors bring in the stowaway, who is dressed in oilskins and sou'-wester. They throw him roughly to the ground)*

**RC:**
*(angry)* So. Try to stowaway on my ship, would you? Try and swindle an honest seaman out of the money for a passage? You're a parasite on the back of society. Well, my fine fellow, a ship's captain has the power to deal with the likes of you. By the time I've finished with you, you'll wish you'd never been born. Take him out, tie him to the yard-arm, strip him and give him a taste of the rope's end.

**RB:**
*(shouting)* Get up! And take that hat off in the presence of the cap'n!

*(RB grabs the stowaway, helps him up and snatches off his sou'-wester. The stowaway's hair cascades down over her shoulders – we get a close-up of a beautiful girl, for the first time.)*

**RC:**
Good God! A woman! You see that, Baines?

**RB:**
Yes, sir. Is she still to be stripped and given a taste of the rope's end, cap'n?

**RC:**
Now don't get hasty. You're always a bit inclined to be hasty. Let's compromise a little, shall we? Let's just take off your oilskins for a start, shall we, my dear?

*(He assists her – she reveals the expected charms – dressed in a boy's torn shirt and skin-tight trousers. This is all duly noted by RC)*

**RC:**
Oh, yes. Well! Perhaps not the taste of the rope's end. You probably don't like rope's end, do you – perhaps you'd prefer something else a bit tastier? *(Calling)* Bring this lady a cheese sandwich! Now, you sit down here and get your breath back. We're both breathing rather heavy. *(Catches Baines' scornful eye)* What are you looking at, Baines?

**RB:**
I take it we can leave the girl's plight in your hands, sir.

**RC:**
Exactly, Baines. I shall set her to work for me. She shall be my cabin boy. Don't worry, I shall see that she works her passage, as any stowaway would. What is your name, girl?

**GIRL:**
Ophelia O'Hanaflanagan, sir.

**RC:**
O – what?

**RB:**
Phelia, cap'n. Permission to go aloft, sir?

**RC:**
Aye, buzz off, Baines. I have to instruct my new cabin boy in her duties. *(Baines plus the two sailors exit.)* But first, my dear, tell me why you stowed away aboard my ship?

**OPHELIA:**
I wanted to travel and make a name for myself.

**RC:**
Well, you've come to the right place. If you play your cards right, you can do both at once. Now, it will be your duty to do the dusting, bring me my early morning tea and polish my sextant. Look, come through here and I'll show you where I keep the hammocks ...

*(They exit, as we fade to night: a storm at sea. stock film. Long shots of the ship having a tough time staying afloat. Quite a bit of this, then cut to close-up of RB in sou'-wester, etc. on the bridge – but too close to see exactly where.)*

**RB:**
*(shouting)* Hoist your missen! Reef the Topsail! Batten down all hatches! *(About six bucketfuls of water hit him. He gasps and recovers.)* Hold her, Mister Granville. Bear over the Bowspit!

*(Another six bucketfuls hit him. He groans and leaves frame.)*

*(More stock film, then RB, outside RC's cabin door.)*

**RB:**
Cap'n! Are you coming up on to the bridge? The storm's at its height.

**RC:**
(off) I'm afraid I've got much too much to do in here at the moment.

(Cut to: RC, in his bunk. An arm comes into shot and caresses his cheek.)

**RB:**
But we need your experience up there, cap'n.

**RC:**
I'm sorry, but I'm using most of it down here.

(The arms pull him out of shot.)

(Stock shots of storm, lightning, etc.)

**RB:**
(in close-up on bridge again) Heave to, Mr Granville! Keep her into the wind. (The water hits him again.) Hoist your Mainsail!

(The water again – he collapses.)

(Cut to: RB approaching door again, hammering on it.)

**RB:**
Cap'n! I can't keep her upright. She's rolling a lot!

**RC:**
(half smothered by Ophelia) How d'you think I feel?

(More lightning – RB on bridge again.)

**RB:**
Top your rigging! (Water hits him again.) Oh, Gawd!

(Close-up hand banging on door again.)

**RB:**
Cap'n – you gotta come up. It's a filthy night up here!

**RC:**
(beating off an attack by Ophelia) It's pretty heavy weather down here as well.

**RB:**
I tell 'ee, cap'n. It's touch an' go. I doubt if I can hold her on my own.

**RC:**
Don't give up, Baines! I'm not.

(RB in despair, groans and staggers off. A streak of lightning in the sky – then mix to calm, daytime, film of ship.)

Cut to: captain's cabin. RC, still in shirt and trousers, is seated at breakfast, which consists of rum and ship's biscuits. Ophelia, now only in her shirt, is serving him.

**OPHELIA:**
More rum, cap'n?

**RC:**
No, thanks, my dear, not at breakfast. It's a bit early for me. God, what a night.

**OPHELIA:**
I do love you, cap'n.

**RC:**
And I love you, too. And that's the first time I've ever said that to a cabin boy.

(She sits beside him on bench. Suddenly a sound of shouts, cries and a naval gun. Then a banging on the door.)

**RC:**
What's going on?

**RB:**
Cap'n – we're about to be boarded.

**RC:**
Boarded? By whom?

**RB:**
(off) Pirates!

(RC rushes to porthole – looks out. Sounds of muskets, shouts – music over. RC slams porthole- cover over.)

**RC:**
He's right, you know. He's not wrong.

**OPHELIA:**
Oh dear.

**RC:**
Don't worry, my love – you're safe in here with me.

**OPHELIA:**
Aren't you going out to fight?

**RC:**
No – I shall stay here to protect you.

**OPHELIA:**
I'll go out and fight, too.

**RC:**
What, and leave me here on me own? Don't be so daft.

**RB:**
*(off)* Are you coming out, or aren't you, cap'n?

**RC:**
No, you carry on – I have every confidence in you.

**RB:**
*(off)* Aye, aye, sir. *(Then shouting)* Stand by to repel all boarders!

**RC:**
*(to girl)* Sounds like a landlady I had once. Come, sit down. *(They sit. The dreadful cries and clashes of steel and shots continue.)* Well, how pleasant this is. How different my life has suddenly become.

**OPHELIA:**
Are you sure Mister Baines can manage on his own?

**RC:**
Why not? He saw us through last night without a scratch, didn't he? Which is more than can be said for you, my dear.

**OPHELIA:**
Oh, Captain.

*(She snuggles up to him.)*

**RC:**
I shall never forget the first moment I saw you yesterday, when you took off your hat and your hair all fell out over your shoulders.

**OPHELIA:**
Were you surprised?

**RC:**
Well, it was a bit of a shock – it usually means an attack of scurvy.

**OPHELIA:**
They sound as if they're getting closer.

**RC:**
Don't worry – they'll never get past that door. Baines won't let them. He's not only tough, but he uses his head.

**OPHELIA:**
What's it made of?

**RC:**
Solid oak – not a knothole in sight.

**OPHELIA:**
No, I meant the door.

**RC:**
Oh, the door – no, I don't know what that's made of–

**OPHELIA:**
Listen!

**RC:**
What?

**OPHELIA:**
It's gone quiet.

**RC:**
So it has. Perhaps they're fighting on carpet.

**RB:**
*(off – knocking on door)* It's all over, cap'n.

**RC:**
Ah! Well done, Baines – I knew you'd beat 'em.

**RB:**
They beat us, sir. I'm a prisoner. Are you coming out?

**RC:**
What? No fear. Ophelia and I have got enough rations in here for months. Plenty of rum and ship's biscuits. *(She joins him near the door -he puts his arm round her.)* Tough bunch, are they?

**RB:**
They are, sir. *(Cut to close-up: RB with cutlass at his throat.)* Been at sea for months, without setting eyes on a member of the opposite, as you might say, sir. Makes a body a bit edgy, that do. However, they've promised not to kill me if I do as they say.

*Cut to: RC and Ophelia.*

**RC:**
Then I advise you to agree, Baines. I'm staying in here. The fewer men out there with that lot, the better.

**RB:**
*(close-up)* Ar. You may be right at that, cap'n.

*(Pull back to reveal RB is held by four girl pirates, dark and gypsyish. They gaze at him hungrily. One picks her teeth.)*

**RB:**
I'd just like to say if I don't see you again, cap'n, it will have been wonderful.

*(He is dragged off by the piratesses. Music up.)*

# COLDITZ

*Caption – as in the original series, with theme music.*

*Scene one: the yard of a castle.*

*As many extras as we can spare (or stock library film of yard from the original) two men are throwing a ball to each other, others are crowded in a circle, talking. Close-up of a man looking up as the sound of a lorry is heard. The lorry arriving. It stops – four guards get out of the back escorting RC as the RAF air gunner (as played by David McCallum in the series) with pencil moustache and ruffled hair.*

**RC:**
So this is Colditz. They'll never keep me in here!

*(Close-up as he looks up at the castle. He is roughly pushed in the back by one of the guards. They march him away – overlaid is the sound of heavy marching feet in echo. They pass the group seated in a circle and march round a corner, out of sight.)*

*(Cut to: round the corner, the guards come into view. RC, however, isn't with them. They realise this and Captain Helmut cries "halt". They run back round the corner. The group is seated there, still chatting. The Germans look suspiciously at them, then a guard points out of shot. We cut to RC walking away in the middle distance. He has his trousers rolled up, his jacket tied round his waist like a skirt, his scarf tied round his head and he carries a bucket and broom. He looks from the back like an old charwoman, but we know it's him. The guards run after him and grab him.)*

**RC:**
Just testing you.

*(As he starts to remove his scarf, we cut to: studio.)*

*Scene 2: the prisoners' dormitory or rather, a corner of it, next to the latrines (as per original set for Colditz).*
*Two-tier wooden bunks, etc. On one of these lies Chapman, a prisoner, tall, thin. Perhaps two others, non-speaking, also two chaps throwing a ball to each other.*

*(RC is brought in by a guard. Chapman gets up to greet him.)*

**CHAPMAN:**
Hello, there.

**RC:**
My name's Carter. George Carter. *(Shaking hands)* How are you.

**CHAP:**
I'm Dicky.

**RC:**
I don't feel so good myself. How long have you been here?

**CHAP:**
Four years.

**RC:**
Four years, cooped up here? No wonder you're feeling dicky. Haven't you tried to escape?

**CHAP:**
My name's Dicky.

**RC:**
Oh, I see.

**CHAP:**
And don't think you're going to escape from here. The place is impregnable.

**RC:**
Don't you believe it, chum. That's what they said about Doreen Phipps. How wrong they were.

**CHAP:**
Were they?

**RC:**
Well, I'm paying her thirty bob a week. Judge for yourself. *(He moves around, sizing the place up.)* No, we'll soon be out of here.

**CHAP:**
You'd better have a word with Captain Whitmore.

**RC:**
Where is he?

**CHAP:**
I'm not sure, I …

*(There is a banging from inside one of the latrines.)*

**RB:**
*(inside the loo)* Anybody there? I'm stuck. The door's jammed. Hello *(etc. as he bangs on the door.)*

**CHAP:**
That's him. *(Calling)* Coming.

*(They eventually succeed in prising open the latrine door. RB comes out, dressed as an army captain.)*

**RB:**
How do you do – Whitmore. I'm the escape officer.

**RC:**
Carter, sir.

*(RC salutes. RB salutes back – he has an oil can stuck on his little finger.)*

**RB:**
Sorry about the oil can. Can't get my finger out. Got it stuck, trying to oil my bed springs.

**RC:**
Really, sir? Is this a mixed dormitory then?

**RB:**
Oh yes, rather. Officers and men.

**RC:**
Oh, I see. You had me going there for a minute. I thought perhaps I wouldn't bother to escape, after all.

**RB:**
Ah. Well, I'm sorry to disappoint you, but the only woman on the camp is the Matron.

**RC:**
What's she like?

**CHAP:**
Blonde. And big with it.

**RC:**
I like big women.

**RB:**
Luckily for you, she's a vegetarian.

**RC:**
Why?

**RB:**
She'd have you for breakfast.

**RC:**
Oh. I see. Right, that does it. I'm getting out of here.

**RB:**
Now listen, Carter. Sit down. It's not as easy as all that. We have a code of conduct here. Of course you want to escape. Everybody does. But it has to be organised. You need papers. Money. Clothing. A cover story. And that means none of this "go it alone" stuff. We've built up a specialist team to deal with every aspect, and each escape has to be planned. Planned down to the very last detail, do you understand?

*(The door is opened by a guard. RB tries to make a dash for it.)*

**HELMUT:**
*(entering)* Get back! *(RB is dragged back by guards and flung onto one of the bunks.)* Flight Lieutenant Carter!

**RC:**
Yes?

**HELMUT:**
Hauptmann Ulrich wishes to speak with you. He is second in command. Quickly, please! You will come now.

**RC:**
Alright, keep your hair on, Fritzy.

**HELMUT:**
*(removes hat – he is bald.)* I have no hair. And I have no time to waste.

*(Hits RC with hat.)*

**RC:**
*(going)* Touchy lot, aren't they?

*Scene Three: Hauptmann Ulrich's office.*

*RB as Hauptmann Ulrich, seated at desk. We hear feet approaching, a knock on the door.*

**RB:**
Kommen zie herein!

*(RC enters with helmut and guards.)*

**RB:**
Ah Carter, sit down please.

**RC:**
*(looks around)* There's no chair.

**RB:**
*(quietly)* Well, stand then. We don't run this place for your comfort, Carter. *(RB takes file from drawer of desk.)* I just wish to make a few things clear to you before you begin your stay here at Colditz. This is a top security prison and there is no escape. You are now in the hands of experienced prison officers. If you try to escape, here is a list of the men you have to deal with. *(Reads)* Hauptmann Leitz, Sturmbann-fuhrer Schmelling, Standartenfuhrer Hessler, Unterwebel Blateau and Uppengruppenferanstarter ge-grossler Pintwinkler. Do you understand all this?

**RC:**
Yes – luckily my father kept a delicatessen.

**RB:**
Really?

**RC:**
Yes – that was before he went into show business.

**RB:**
Show business? What did he do?

**RC:**
He was an escapologist.

**RB:**
So! It runs in the family, eh? *(Looking at file)* I see that he was in the first war.

**RC:**
Yes.

**RB:**
Did he stay in the army after the war?

**RC:**
No, he couldn't get out quick enough.

**RB:**
"He then continued with his act – being dropped into the Thames in a padlocked trunk."

**RC:**
Yes, it killed him.

**RB:**
Why?

**RC:**
He couldn't get out quick enough.

**RB:**
I see. Well, my dear Flight-lieutenant *(getting up and moving across the room)* I hope you won't entertain any thoughts of following in your father's footsteps. *(Close-up)* Because I can assure you, escape is impossible. *(Looks around)* Carter? *(Cut to: long shot – RC is out of sight. RB looks under desk.)* Come out, Carter!

*(RC crawls out.)*

**RB:**
I promise you, you will never manage it. Now *(goes to other side of desk, takes out papers)* here is your prison number and the address to which letters should be sent … *(he again looks up. No one is in sight again, he walks over to large cupboard)* …

and they will then be forwarded to your family via the Red Cross. *(He opens the cupboard. RC is standing in it.)* Understand?

**RC:**
Yes, perfectly. *(Stepping out of cupboard)* You realise, of course, that it is every officer's duty to try to escape?

**RB:**
Of course I realise it, Flight-lieutenant *(goes to desk, picks up the file)* it's just that I thought I might save you a lot of wasted time and energy. *(Long shot – no one there again)* I mean, after all *(goes to filing cabinet)* there are many more profitable ways of passing the time, don't you agree?

*(He opens the top drawer of the steel filing cabinet. RC's head appears to come out with it.)*

**RC:**
I suppose you're right.

*Scene four – the dormitory.*

*RB as Whitmore, with Chapman, sit on bottom bunk. Two other prisoners are throwing a ball to each other.*

**CHAP:**
Sshh! I think he's coming back.

**RB:**
Is that you, Carter? How's it going?

**RC:**
*(emerging from under bed)* Pretty good. Another couple of feet.

*(He hands RB two socks full of earth.)*

**RB:**
Oh, thanks. How much further to go?

**RC:**
I've just told you, two more feet.

**RB:**
Oh, I see – I thought you meant *(indicating socks.)* Here you are, Chapman.

*(Gives socks to Chapman, who empties the earth into the drawer of his locker.)*

**CHAP:**
Isn't it someone else's turn to provide the socks? *(As he puts sock on his foot)* What about you, Whitmore?

**RB:**
I've got a potato in mine.

**CHAP:**
I shall be able to grow them in mine if this goes on.

*(Approaching footsteps, marching. They halt. The door opens and in comes the matron. A large, curvy blonde, all knickers and knockers, as they say, but a wonderful actress.)*

**RB:**
Morning, matron.

**MATRON:**
Good morning, Vitmore, Chepman. I am happy to inform you that the RAF have dropped a load of Red Cross parcels for you.

**RB:**
Marvellous!

**MATRON:**
Unfortunately, when they hit the ground they were flattened completely. Only one survived.

**RB:**
How?

**MATRON:**
I was sunbathing on the roof and it landed right on top of me. It bounced.

**RB:**
It would.

**MATRON:**
Bring it in, please.

*(A guard brings in the box.)*

**RB:**
*(opening it)* Oh well, that explains it. It's a load of balls.

*(He takes out a rubber ball. The matron eyes him, and exits briskly.)*

**RC:**
Right, lads, this is it. I'm going to make my final bid for freedom. If I'm not back in three hours, come through the tunnel and investigate.

**CHAP:**
Good luck, Carter. Drop us a postcard!

**RC:**
I'll do better than that. As soon as I get to France, I'll send you a letter. Bye, skipper.

*(RB and RC shake hands. RC goes under the bed.)*

**RB:**
Well, now all we have to do is wait.

*Cut to: clock on locker. Cross-fade to three hours later. Caption over: "3 hours later".*

**RB:**
Well, it's three hours later. I'm going through to investigate.

*(He crawls under the bed. A close-up of Chapman, listening to marching feet as they pass the door.)*

*Scene five – a close-up of a cupboard. One door opens, RB crawls out, dusty. He stands up and stares.*

**RB:**
Good lord!

*Cut to: RC and matron on top of bed, suspenders in evidence. We are in matron's bedroom.*

**RB:**
What are you doing?

**RC:**
You've got to take it where you can get it.

**RB:**
You never told me the tunnel came out in matron's room.

**RC:**
Pure coincidence. Bit of luck though, wasn't it?

*Scene six: the dormitory – night.*

*RB and RC in same clothes, but blackened faces, à la commandos. Chapman is with them.*

**RC:**
This time it's got to work.

**RB:**
Don't see why it shouldn't. We've got papers, money. Once we get over that wall, we stand a damn good chance.

**CHAP:**
Got the sheets tied together?

**RC:**
Only two. Most of the chaps have been damn mean about parting with their sheets. Selfish baskets. You were the only one who volunteered.

**CHAP:**
That's alright.

**RB:**
Just two sheets, eh? How high's the wall?

**CHAP:**
Eighty feet.

**RB:**
Hmm. Just have to drop the last bit. Right, come on then. *(To Chapman)* Bye, Chapman, old sport. See you after the war. *(Opens door.)* All clear.

**RC:**
Cheerio, Dicky. And thanks again for the sheets.

*(He goes.)*

**CHAPMAN:**
Bye. *(Closes the door and goes to the bunk bed.)* Who needs sheets? *(Calling under bed)* Coming, matron!

*(He begins to climb under the bed.)*

*Scene seven – the escape*

*This should be a montage – night shots of the castle, close-ups of RC and RB with blackened faces, scurrying here and there, climbing, listening, etc. Lots of mood music and sound effects – marching feet, etc. Finally, a shot of dummies of RB and RC landing at the foot of a high wall. Then a closer shot of them.*

**RC:**
Well, we're over. You alright?

**RB:**
Fine. I suggest we stay put under the shadow of the wall until morning.

**RC:**
Good idea. *(He puts a blanket round their knees as they huddle together for warmth.)* Goodnight, Whitmore.

**RB:**
Night, old boy.

*(They close their eyes.)*

*Cut to: early morning. Sunlight.*

*(They are still asleep against the wall. Shouting can be heard in the distance. A shadow looms over them suddenly. It wears a peaked cap.)*

**VOICE**
*(off)*: Good morning, gentlemen. So you got over the wall, did you? *(They start to stir and open their eyes.)* You will be sorry, I can assure you.

*(They stare up in dismay. Cut to: big close-up of man with big cap on.)*

**MAN:**
Velcome to Butlitz.

*(Now, at last, a shot of the scene. It is Butlins holiday camp at Bognor Regis. The man wears a striped blazer, white trousers and a coloured peak cap. Holiday-makers stroll about. We zoom in dramatically to the barbed wire on the top of the fence. We freeze-frame and superimpose the word: "Butlitz" in the same lettering as the opening titles. Music crashes in – slow fade.*

# OPEN WINDOW

*Signature tune and caption: "Open Window," followed by a second caption: "A programme in which minority groups tell the world about their problem. This programme has been made entirely by amateur talent from within the groups, and the BBC takes no responsibility for it (and neither does ITV). This programme was originally made in black and white, but will be shown in colour."*

*(All the above over a picture of an open window – camera zooms slowly in on it.)*

*Cut to: another picture. Flat countryside. Caption over – "this week – flat is horrible".*

*(RB in garden, talking to camera.)*

**RB:**
I find digging in my garden is a bit of therapy and helps me to gain strength to carry on expressing my beliefs to a thoroughly sceptical and pig-headed world. *(Caption over – "flat earth society".)* Because being in a minority can be very depressing, when people just won't believe you or take any notice of you. *(Shouts at barking dog)* GET DOWN, SALLY! Even when you have irrefutable evidence that the world is flat when your wife has actually fallen off it. My wife actually fell off it. I very nearly did myself, I only just managed to stop myself – GET

DOWN, SALLY, DAMN YOU! When you have actually experienced it, then it's no good saying the earth is round, because it isn't, any more than a ten pence piece is round. It's not, it's flat. So I ...

*(Dog leaps on him, he falls out of frame.)*

*Interior – house.*
*Cut to: RC, at piano, in the middle of a song. He is singing flat – "Drink to me only with Thine Eyes". He has long, straight hair over his ears. As he finishes the song, the caption appears over: "the flat singer's society".*

**RC:**
*(speaking to camera)* I have sung flat all my life. I love music and wished to make it my profession, but my father is a piano tuner and has turned me out of the house, with the advice "Get it up or give it up". But music is my life; I've got all of Rod McKinar's records, which proves that it's not that I don't appreciate good music, because I don't. It's just my flat voice. I just can't get it up as high as the others. That is why I try to look like a musician, and wear my hair long, to try to hide the fact that I have no ear.

*Exterior – garden: a girl with flat chest.*

**GIRL:**
You may think, to look at me that I haven't a thing to worry about, but I have. Well, two things, like, really. *(caption: "flat chest society")* My bosoms. I've tried everything. I've tried that bust-developing cream, but it tastes horrible. I've tried stuffing a couple of lemons up inside my sweater, but boys only squeeze them and I get covered in juice without really enjoying it. Everything's been getting on top of me lately. It's horrible being flat. A man likes something comfortable to lie his head on. He doesn't want a walnut in his ear. The only benefit I've ever derived from being flat was that I made a black bikini out of two eye patches I got on the National Health. But people on the beach called me the Lone Ranger.

*Exterior – street.*

*(RB walks along in shopping area, flat-footed, with passers-by behaving as they would normally, looking at camera, etc.)*

**RB'S VOICE OVER:**
People laugh at me in the street when I go to work and I say to them, it's all *(Caption: "flat feet society")* very well for you to laugh but it's not much fun when your feet are flaming flat. Doctors say they can't do nothing about it. The medical term for it is "flat feet" and that's it, ain't it? *(Cut to close-up – RB on park bench)* That's what I'm up against. My instep's level with me sole. One is supposed to be lower than the other, but it isn't. It's level. Which means that there's more to get dragged through the mud. What I feel is that I have missed out. There's lots of things I can't do, like, ballet dancing – *(pause)* things like that. The ballet *(pause)*, and I think the Government oughter do something about it.

*Exterior – street.*

*(RC at window of large car, in bowler hat, etc.)*

**RC:**
My society is growing all the time. A lot of people have joined over the past year. *(Caption "Flat Broke Society")* Everything's gone, as far as I'm concerned. This isn't my car. The chauffeur bought it off me last year when things got difficult. He very kindly gives me a lift to work every day. Sweet of him, isn't it? *(Cut to chauffeur, smiling)* No, I can't afford a big car like this. I've got a very small one. I just take it out on Saturday mornings, just to give it an airing. *(He gets out of car)* This is not my suit – I got it at a jumble sale. Thirty-eight pounds. My wife found it, didn't you, dear? *(Cut to close-up – wife's face, nodding and smiling.)* The trousers are very good *(cut to trousers and shoes)* but the sleeves are too long. *(Cut to RC showing sleeves).* However, my wife likes it, and it will do for now – until the time we can both

afford to have one.

*(Widen to reveal the trousers are on the wife – with a bra. RC has long suit jacket only, with suspenders and socks. They turn and walk away.)*

*Cut to: a front-room, in fairly awful taste.*

*RC as husband in seedy, straight-haired wig, moustache and sideburns. RB as his wife.*

**RC:**
*(voice over)*: Of course it's a problem. It's a big problem. Well, you can see for yourself. It's obvious what a big problem I've got. *(By now we can see RB as wife.)* It's very difficult living in a tiny flat, with a woman as big as this. *(Caption: "flat-dwellers society")* It was different when we first met. I was living in two rooms overlooking the Cromwell Road.

**RB:**
I had a flat behind.

**RC:**
'Course, now it's all changed. And it's a very difficult thing to come to grips with. The kitchen is tiny with a sliding door. If she bends over the sink, she's liable to sit on the gas stove; and the whole flat smells of fried bacon. It's a big problem.

**RB:**
I have to put tin foil in my knickers.

**RC:**
The bedroom is very pokey. *(RB agrees, muttering)* Just room for the bed. If she's in bed first I have to climb over her, and that's no fun, is it, when you're tired. I rang up the Council to see if they could help; they suggested spiked boots. Silly. *(Cuckoo noise.)* I think everybody in flats has got a problem. I've got a big one; let's hope Mrs Thatcher gets in. I'll present her with it. And that's that. *(Sound fades. RC goes on talking.)*

**RB:**
*(commentator voice over)*: All the people

you have just seen are members of flat societies of one sort or another. I think you'll agree that, as they put it, "Flat is Horrible". We hope this programme has brought to light their private problems. Everyone has got one – but each one is different.

*Cut to: a series of actual clips from the previous interviews.*

**FLAT SINGER:**
*(RC)* I just can't get it up as high as the others ...

**FLAT EARTH:**
*(RB)* My wife actually fell off it ...

**FLAT CHEST:**
*(girl)* Everything has been getting on top of me lately ...

**FLAT BROKE:**
*(RC)* I've got a very small one – I just take it out on Saturday mornings – just to give it an airing.

**FLAT FEET:**
*(RB)* One is supposed to be lower than the other, but it isn't – it's level. Which means that there is more to get dragged through the mud.

**FLAT DWELLERS:**
*(RC, RB)* I've certainly got a big one – let's hope Mrs Thatcher gets in. I'll present her with it.

**FLAT DWELLERS:**
*(RB)* ... a flat behind.

**FLAT FEET:**
*(RB)* ... that's what I'm up against.
**FLAT CHEST:**
*(girl)* ... It's horrible.

**FLAT EARTH:**
*(RB)* ... It's flat.

**FLAT DWELLERS:**
*(RC)* ... And that's that.

*(Freeze frame on this, Caption over: "flat is horrible. The end".)*

# I MARRIED A POLTERGEIST

*An Edwardian "semi" in the provinces. outside, on the front door, hangs a funeral wreath. Noise of a party is heard.*

*Cut to: inside the room, sandwiches disappearing off a plate, as hands grab them. Loud party chatter. Two ladies in black, with lots of make-up, gossip in a corner.*

**AGNES:**
Certainly a good do, isn't it?

**MAVIS:**
Lovely. Who did the food? Did his sister do it?

**AGNES:**
He hasn't got a sister.

**MAVIS:**
Who's that over there then?

**AGNES:**
That was her sister.

**MAVIS:**
Oh, poor thing. *(looks round)* He seems to be enjoying it, anyway.

*(Points discreetly to RB as Jim, stuffing his face.)*

**AGNES:**
If you were asked to pick out the bereaved husband, you'd hardly pick him, would you?

**MAVIS:**
He's not sorry. He was glad to see the back of her.

**AGNES:**
Well, he was certainly never too pleased with the front of her.

*Cut to: RB eating. Cut to: RC, as Harold, approaching RB through the chattering guests. He reaches RB.*

**RB:**
Hello, Harold. Sandwich?

**RC:**
Hello, Jim. No thanks. Just wanted to express my condolences.

**RB:**
*(quietly)* Needn't bother, Harold. I'm not going to miss her. I couldn't have stood much more of her.

**RC:**
I know that. Everybody guessed it, of course. But I know it.

**RB:**
What?

**RC:**
Being psychic, as you know.

**RB:**
Oh, yes?

**RC:**
Someone has dropped a vol-au-vent on the floor.

**RB:**
Gosh, do you know that because you're psychic?

**RC:**
No, because I'm standing in it.
**RB:**
Oh dear. Oh well, it's alright, it's not the front room carpet. She was terrible about that, Jennifer. Her mother bought it for her. Great big, ugly, blotchy-purple thing.

**RC:**
Her mother?

**RB:**
No, the carpet. I had to take off my shoes before I was allowed on it. And her mother used to sit there, with that smug expression on her face. I used to long to jump all over it with big muddy boots on.

**RC:**
Her mother's face?

**RB:**
Absolutely. And the carpet. And Jennifer. It was her mother who instituted the kitchen blackboard. Jennifer used to write the day's orders on it in chalk. Jobs for me to do, messages if she wasn't speaking to me, that sort of stuff. Big black thing hanging there, spoiled the look of the kitchen.

**RC:**
I'm still getting these mental pictures of her mother.

**RB:**
Quite. She literally led me a dog's life, Jennifer. She used to take me for walks, I had to fetch her slippers, she even made me sit up and beg for my food. So then, when I heard she was having an affair with the postman, I did what anyone in my position would have done. I bit him in the leg.

**RC:**
Well, you're free of her now, Jim. Do what you like, go where you please. You didn't kill her, by any chance, did you?

**RB:**
'Course not. Being psychic, you should know that.

**RC:**
Oh, we don't know everything. Otherwise, for instance, I wouldn't have to ask you where your lavatory was when I needed it, which I do now.

**RB:**
Oh, sorry – through there, just on the left.

**RC:**
Ta.

*(He goes.)*

*(A large, bosomy, middle-aged woman approaches RB, with a smile.)*

**WOMAN:**
Hello, Jim. Do you think I look good in black?

**RB:**
You'd look better out of it.

**WOMAN:**
Jim, really! That's not like you!

**RB:**
No. Well, I'm not like me. Never have been, really.

*(She reacts, and goes.)*

*Cut to: the front door. (The guests are leaving, RB seeing them off. RC among them. RB closes the door and leans against it.)*

**RB:**
*(sighs)* Alone at last!

*(Suddenly, a vase smashes against the wall beside his head. He looks around, shocked. Then he quickly looks into the room where the party was. No one. Looks into the front room – silent and empty – the purple carpet presiding over the heavy old furniture. He looks into the kitchen. No one. Zoom in on the blackboard. written on it is the single word: "Jennifer")*

*(RB rubs it out with the yellow duster which hangs there for this purpose. He leaves the kitchen, starts to go upstairs. A crash in the kitchen. He rushes back. On the floor is a broken dish. Tilt up to reveal the blackboard. On it, the words: "Leave this blackboard alone")*

**RB:**
*(recoils, then angrily)* Shan't! Shan't! *(grabs the duster and rubs out letters)*. I've had

enough of you, Jennifer. You're not ruling me any more. I've finished with you.

*(The board in close-up. Writing appears – the words: "Oh no")*

*Cut to: RB, watching, then back to the board. It now says: "Oh no, you haven't".*

**RB:**
Oh yes I have, Jennifer – you and your rotten mother.

*(He leaves the kitchen, goes into the hallway, to the phone and dials.)*

**RB:**
Harold? Jim. Listen, can I see you in the pub? It's urgent. Yes, I know you've just got back, but you'll have to come out again. Something's happened. Couldn't tell you at the funeral, 'cos it hadn't happened at the funeral. Five minutes? Right. Bye.

*(He returns to the kitchen. A cup smashes near his head. The blackboard says: "Go to bed. You're drunk")*

**RB:**
No, I'm not, but I will be shortly. I'm going to the pub!

*(He turns to go and a saucepan hits him on the back of the head.)*

*The pub. Two drinks put down on a table. widen to reveal RC, still in black tie and armband.*

**RC:**
Thanks. Where are the nuts?

**RB:**
Did you ask for nuts?

**RC:**
No – I just had a feeling that you would bring some.

**RB:**
A psychic feeling?

**RC:**
No, just a greedy feeling.

**RB:**
Well, what am I going to do, Harold?

*(He reseats himself, moving away the glasses from their previous rounds)*

**RC:**
You've heard of the astral body?

**RB:**
What's that, like the Psychical Research Society?

**RC:**
Your astral body is what some people believe rises from your own body when you're asleep, and floats about. Haven't you ever felt, in dreams, that you seem to be floating above yourself, looking down at yourself? And your real self is below, looking up at yourself looking down at yourself. Have you felt that ever?

**RB:**
Yes, I have.

**RC:**
Well, that's your astral body. Either that, or the drink.

**RB:**
So you mean …

**RC:**
Yes. Jennifer's astral body is rising from the grave and floating about your kitchen, throwing things at you. She has become a poltergeist.

**RB:**
But what can I do?

**RC:**
Stay out of the kitchen. She will eventually run out of crockery.

**RB:**
Then what?

**RC:**
She'll start on the bedroom.

**RB:**
Good grief.

**RC:**
You'll just have to hope that she gets tired of it.

**RB:**
Not Jennifer. She's relentless.

**RC:**
Well, unless you can stop her astral body rising from the grave, you're lumbered. Just buy yourself a tin helmet and don't bend down in the bath. *(Picks up new glass)* Cheers!

*(RB's face, brooding on this)*

**RB:**
Cheers.

*The kitchen: day.*

*(All quiet. RB returning from the pub, opens door, looks in. We see a jug rise from a shelf and hurtle out of frame. It crashes near RB. The blackboard says: "Where have you been?" RB hurriedly shuts the door and, as the crashes continue within, looks into the front room, at the big old pieces of furniture. He nods to himself.)*

*Outside the house: night.*

*(RB is loading the front room furniture onto an open truck ("acme rent-a-van"). He is almost finished. He staggers out with half a table and throws it onto the truck. He gets into the cab and starts the engine.*

*(Now a montage – RB arriving at the cemetery, taking things off the truck, staggering under the load of a corner-cupboard across the graveyard, and the ever-increasing pile of furniture on the grave. An owl watches this macabre spectacle. Eventually, a close-up as RB throws the last object onto the pile!)*

**RB:**
Now, get out of that, you old bat. And I don't give a hoot!

*(The owl looks disapproving, and does give a hoot.)*

**RB:**
*(looking up)* Well, you can please yourself.

*Cut to: inside the house, the same night.*

*(RB enters front door. He looks into now-empty front room. Only the carpet is there, in all its patterned monstrosity. He looks into the kitchen. All quiet. The blackboard is empty. He closes door and stands in the hall. He nods in satisfaction and goes quietly upstairs.)*

*Exterior house: day.*

*(RB in raincoat, leaves for the office. Day turns to night in the same shot. RB returns from work with newspaper. He enters the front door.)*

*The kitchen: night.*

*(RB sitting with tea, scones and jam, contentedly munching. Suddenly, a whoosh and a loud bang. RB reacts. Another whoosh and several bangs, coming from outside. RB grabs newspaper. Zoom in on the date – November 5th. RB looks up in consternation.)*

*A bonfire – it is the pile of furniture. (Skinheads and other hooligans dance around it, laughing and drinking from cans. Others let off firecrackers.)*

*(RB's little car approaches the camera and he gets out. The flickering firelight is reflected in his glasses. His expression is gloomy.)*

*The kitchen.*

*(RB enters. All quiet. The blackboard says: "Try to cremate me, would you?" and all hell breaks loose. RB tries to dodge the flying crockery. We see many objects lifted up as if by invisible hands, crashing round RB's head. he tries to leave the kitchen, but a narrow*

*broom cupboard falls across the door, so that it cannot be opened.)*

*(He moves around the kitchen. Overhead cupboards open. A whole pile of spice bottles bounce on his head, one by one. An enormous jar of brown rice tips, spilling the contents on him, as further pieces of crockery burst round him.)*

*(A bag of flour falls and bursts on his head. He grabs a big saucepan and puts it over his head. A broom flies out of the cupboard and hits the saucepan with a clang. He comes out, looking dazed, and collapses on the floor. Above, on the work surface, a bottle of milk tips over. A close-up as the milk pours over RB's head. Chaos around him as we mix to: the pub)*

*A caption: "Six weeks later".*

*(RC and RB are sitting at their usual table. RC drinks. we see that RB has a few cuts and bruises still showing)*

**RB:**
Well, when I finally got out of there, I thought what a good idea! So I had the body exhumed and cremated!

**RC:**
Has it worked?

**RB:**
Like a charm. And guess what I did with the ashes?

**RC:**
You sprinkled them all over the front room carpet!

**RB:**
How did you know?

**RC:**
I'm psychic – remember?

*(Their laughter takes on an echo-like quality as we mix to: the front room. There, on the carpet, lies an upturned urn. Trailing from it, the spilled ash. We pan along a thin line of*

*ash – and we find it forms itself into the words: "I will be back". The laughter distorts into an unintelligible shriek.)*

# QUIET WEDDING

*A church. The bridegroom waits. Organ music playing. The vicar (RB) approaches the groom (RC) and speaks in a whisper.*

**RB:**
Good morning.

**RC:**
Good morning, Reverend.

**RB:**
Nervous?

**RC:**
Yes, I am rather. *(sheepishly)* I've had hiccups all morning.

**RB:**
Oh dear – well, there's no need to be – although it's a rather solemn service, it is nevertheless a happy one, and a joyful occasion.

**RC:**
Oh yes.

**RB:**
You must forgive me if I sound a bit nasal.

**RC:**
Oh – we've all got colds as well, haven't we, dad? Mum's chest is bad – must be something going round.

**RB:**
No, mine's actually hay fever – always get it at Harvest Festival time – it's all the flowers.

**RC:**
Oh yes – Leticia gets that.

**RB:**
Leticia?

**RC:**
Leticia, my – my intended.

**RB:**
Oh, the bride.

**RC:**
Yes – I was going to say wife, but that's not till tonight. That's not till after the service, I mean.

**RB:**
Quite. Ha ha. Not straight after the service, I hope? *(Smiling)*

**RC:**
No, no. Anyway, she's had it for a week.

**RB:**
What?

**RC:**
Hay fever.

**RB:**
Oh, quite.

*(The organist starts to play "Here comes the Bride")*

**RB:**
Ah. Here she comes. Takes your places, please.

*(The bride approaches, and stops. The organ finishes playing. Silence.)*

*(Girl, looking at RC, sneezes.)*

*(RC, looking at girl, hiccups.)*

**RB:**
Dearly beloved, we are gathered here in the face of the congregation, to join together this man and this woman in holy matrimony. Which is an honourable estate, and therefore not to be taken in hand inadvisedly, lightly or wantonly, but reverently, discreetly, advisedly and

soberly, duly considering the causes for
which matrimony was ordained.
Aaahchoo!

**RC:**
Hic!

**RB:**
Therefore if any man ...

**BRIDE:**
Zsst!

**RB:**
... if any man can show any Aaaahchoo!
any just cause why they m-m-m-mmahay
not lawfully be joined together let him
speak now or foo-forever hold his peace.
Aaaahchoo!

**BRIDE:**
Zsst!

**RC:**
Hic!

*(A silence, broken only by mum's chest
wheezing heavily.)*

**RB:**
Hah-hah-Harold Frederick, wilt thou take
this woman to be thy lawful wedded
wife?

**RC:**
Hic!

**RB:**
Wilt thou love her, comfort her, honour
and keep her, in sickness and in her-
heahealth, as long as ye both shall live?

**RC:**
Hic! I will. Hic!
**RB:**
Aaaahchoo!

**RC:**
Hic.

**BRIDE:**
Zsst!

**DAD:**
*(into hankie)* Honk!

**RB:**
Leticshoo! Leticshoo! Leticia Muriel–

**BRIDE:**
Zsst!

**RB:**
Wilt thou have this man to thy wedded
husband.

**RC:**
Hic!

**DAD:**
Honk!

**RB:**
Aaaahchoo! Wilt thou love, honour and
keep him, in sickness and in Haychow!
And forsaking all others keep ye only
unto him as long as ye both shall lachoo!

**BRIDE:**
I whizzt!

**RC:**
Hic!

**RB:**
Who giveth this woman to be married to
this man?

**DAD:**
Honk!

*(steps forward)*

**RB:**
Aaaahchoo!

*(The sneeze blows off dad's toupee. He ignores
it.)*

**RB:**
*(putting on the ring)* I, Harold Frederick ...

**RC:**
I, Hic Harold Frederick hic...

313

**RB:**
Take thee, Leticshashoo!

**RC:**
Take thee, Lettic-isha.

**RB:**
To my wedded wife.

**RC:**
To my wedded hic wife hic!

**RB:**
*(desperately)* To have and to hold from this day forward, for better for worse, for richer for poorer as long as we both shall live, Aaaahchoo!

**RC:**
I diccoo.

**RB:**
For as much as Harold Frederick and Aaahchoo Muriel have consented together, by the giving and receiving of a ring, I pronounce that they be man and wahey! together. You may kiss the bride.

**RC:**
But we didn't finish the Hic!

**RB:**
Kiss the bride – please!

**BRIDE:**
Come on, Harold.

*(They kiss – RC hics and the bride sneezes during the kiss.)*

**DAD:**
Honk!

**RB:**
I'm sorry I had to cut it short, but the hayayaay …

**RC:**
But – Hic! – if we haven't had the full service, we're not properly married.

**RB:**
Well, you'll just have to come next month and we'll fi-fi – finish it off.

**RC:**
But what about the Hic! honeymoon?

**RB:**
I should go ahead – at least it will cure your hiccups. Aaaahchoow!

*(A pile of apples collapses behind him as the wedding party hurries out.)*

# CHEERS

*A cocktail bar with glass doors leading to a terrace behind it. A crowd of well-dressed people, all chattering loudly in a tight group. RB emerges from the middle.*

**RB:**
Righto everyone – I think I've got the order – you all go and wait on the terrace, I'll get the waiter to bring the drinks out.

*(He approaches the bar.)*

**BARMAN:**
Good evening, sir, what would you like?

**RB:**
A large gin and tonic to start with. Very large.

**BARMAN:**
Sir. *(He goes into action)* Ice and lemon?

**RB:**
If there's room in the glass, yes.

**BARMAN:**
And what else, sir?

**RB:**
Well now, I've only just met these people, don't know them at all. Friends of the wife, you know. So now, let's see. The lady in the sack dress wants an enormous

brandy. The young man with the flat head wants a rum and Coke. Andy, the tall chap – he's Scottish; he wants a pink gin with lemon. The girl with the boobs wants a White Lady. My wife will have a Scotch on the rocks. The woman with bare arms behind her wants half a bottle of the house wine. And the old man with the shifty eyes wants a rough cider. *(RB drinks his gin.)* But before that, I'll have another large gin.

**BARMAN:**
Very good, sir.

**RB:**
Right, so that's an enormous brandy and a rum and Coke, a pink gin, a White Scotch, a wine and a cider and lemon on the rocks.

**BARMAN:**
Pardon, sir?

**RB:**
The lady in the sack dress, brandy. The flat head, rum and Coke. The Scotsman behind, a white gin. The lady with the pink boobs, a cider and … just a minute.

*(He dashes out to the group, who can all be seen chattering at him for a few seconds. He returns to the bar.)*

**RB:**
*(indicating glass)* Is that mine?

**BARMAN:**
Yes, sir.

**RB:**
Good. *(Drinks it.)* Same again, please.

**BARMAN:**
Yes, sir.

**RB:**
Now, I've got it. One brandy, one rum and lemon, a pink thing, a white lady with double boobs, rough rocks, wine on the house and a big bottle.

**BARMAN:**
Pardon, sir?

**RB:**
Don't worry, it's all under control. The lady in the sack wants a tall Scotch. The bare lady with the behind wants a rum and Coke. My wife will have an old man on the rocks, and the girl with the shifty boobs wants a big bottle of brandy on the house. The young man with the flat wife wants an enormous wine … the white lady with the pink … just a minute. *(He goes to the group and returns, as above.)* Is this mine?

**BARMAN:**
Yes, sir.

**RB:**
Good. *(He downs it in one.)* Same again, please. Now then. Are you listening? Simple. I'll have a gin and tonic.

**BARMAN:**
*(placing it down in front of him)* There it is, sir.

**RB:**
Either one?

**BARMAN:**
Yes, sir.

*(RB manages to pick it up.)*

**RB:**
Have a beer.

**BARMAN:**
No, thank you, sir.

**RB:**
Right. *(Thumping counter)* Now, I do exactly what I'm knowing. Here goes. The randy girl with the big bottle wants a rough Scotsman. The tall lemon wants a double Coke on the rocks. The bare woman with the boobs like the side of a house wants a pink old man; the enormous man with the flat gin wants my wife with a beer behind. And the

white lady wants a sack of Coke. Simple enough. What are you having?

**BARMAN:**
Look, sir–

**RB:**
Look. Ready? This is it. Cancel all previous orders. Just give me a sack of Coke, two large rocks, two pink boobs, an enormous lemon and a large bare lady of the house.

**BARMAN:**
Right, sir. I'm glad we finally got it sorted out.

*(He deposits on the bar, a small sack of coke, two rocks, a pair of pink model boobs and an enormous lemon. A large (almost) bare showgirl comes from behind the bar where she has been hiding and she and RB walk off towards the group, carrying the props.)*

# BAR ROOM SKETCH

*A corner of a reasonably trendy bar.*

*(RB sits on a stool, finishing a drink. the girl behind the bar, very attractive, slightly barmaid-ish, lots of eyelashes. RB hands her his empty glass. He is a middle-aged lounge lizard and is about to try and "pull" the barmaid.)*

**RB:**
Same again, my dear.

**GIRL:**
Large gin and tonic?

*(She starts to pour it.)*

**RB:**
You're new here, aren't you?

**GIRL:**
No. I've been here two years.

**RB:**
Oh. Must be me then. That's why I've never seen you here before – I've never been here before.

*(He laughs like the twit he is.)*

**GIRL:**
*(smiling)* That would account for it.

*(RC enters and sits on stool next to RB.)*

**RB:**
Two years, eh? You must like it. The work, I mean.

**GIRL:**
You meet a lot of people.

**RB:**
Yes, of course you do. You must be a pretty good judge of a person, aren't you?

**RC:**
Tomato juice, please.

**GIRL:**
Small one, sir?

**RC:**
Er – yes, why not.

**RB:**
Yes – you're a pretty good judge alright. Pay well here, do they?

**GIRL:**
Alright.

**RB:**
I should think a pretty girl like you must be worth her weight in gold to a place like this.

**GIRL:**
Flattery will get you nowhere.

**RB:**
No, I mean it – you're a very pretty girl.

**RC:**
Very.

*(RB looks at him. RC eats a crisp from the bowl. RB looks back at the girl.)*

**RB:**
Very attractive. You must have been told that before.

**GIRL:**
*(flirting)* Once or twice, yes.

**RB:**
Do you think you're attractive?

**GIRL:**
I'm too tall.

**RB:**
I like tall girls.

**RC:**
So do I.

**RB:**
*(turning to RC)* Did you say something?

**RC:**
Who me? No.

**RB:**
The taller the better.

**RC:**
Quite.

**RB:**
What?

**RC:**
Pardon?

*(RB glares at RC. The girl tries to smooth things over.)*

**GIRL:**
You – er – you local?

**RB:**
Me – good heavens, no. Just travelling through. Staying at the Plough. Ever been there?

**GIRL:**
Mm. Nice bedrooms.

**RB:**
*(surprised at this move)* Oh? Really? You know the bedrooms at the Plough, do you? You interest me enormously.

**RC:**
And me not quite so enormously.

**RB:**
Look, old chap, I'm trying to have a private conversation with this young lady. Now drink up and puddle off, will you?

**RC:**
*(to girl)* Tomato juice, please.

*(The girl glares at him, takes his glass, starts to pour another.)*

**RB:**
Ignore him, perhaps he'll go away. Listen, my dear, what time do you finish here tonight?

**GIRL:**
Half-past ten. Why?

**RB:**
I was just thinking. Would you like a drink?

**GIRL:**
No, I don't think so.

**RC:**
Go on, have one.

*(RB ignores him.)*

**RB:**
Why not? Don't you drink?

**GIRL:**
Oh, yes, I like a vodka – trouble is, two of them and I'm anybody's.

**RB:**
Well, just have one.

**RC:**
A double.

*(RB controls himself with difficulty.)*

**RB:**
Look, please don't think I'm trying to get you drunk. I didn't mean that at all.

**GIRL:**
You sure?

**RB:**
No, really, honestly, I didn't.

**RC:**
I did.

**RB:**
*(desperate)* It's just that I find you very attractive indeed. Beautiful.

**RC:**
Fantastic.

**RB:**
And I'd love to take you out for a meal.

**RC:**
Me too.

**RB:**
Because you're friendly, and charming, and you've got such terrific …

**RC:**
Knockers.

*(RB grabs RC and frogmarches him out. A crash off. RB marches back, dusting his jacket. RC marches back behind him. RB goes to bar, not seeing RC. They both sit.)*

**RB:**
*(to girl)* I'm sorry about all that – if you feel like a meal afterwards, ring me at the Plough. Here's my card.

*(He turns and leaves, without seeing RC.)*

**RC:**
And if you do go out for a meal, don't be late home, Lillian, 'cos we've got to get up early tomorrow. Your mother's coming over.

*(He sips his tomato juice.)*

# A CLINIC IN LIMERICK

*A notice reads: "Limerick clinic. Consultant: R. Kelly, MD, assistant J. Long PhD. Please hang up your coat for ear, nose and throat. For a blister, see sister".*

*(A dizzy nurse sits at table. Patient enters, bent double)*

**NURSE:**
Good day, sir. Have you an appointment?

**PATIENT:**
I was just bending down and this joint went at the back of my thigh. I was just passing by …

**NURSE:**
Step through here and I'll rub on some ointment.

**PATIENT:**
No, I'll just wait and see Doctor Smithers.

**NURSE:**
I'm afraid he is no longer with us.

**PATIENT:**
Oh, a new one, eh? Nice?

**NURSE:**
Well, his hands are like ice. And while you're undressing, he dithers.

**PATIENT:**
I've begun to feel weak at the knees.

**DOCTOR:**
*(over the intercom)* Will you send in the next patient, please?

**NURSE:**
In you go. Be a man! *(As the patient goes to the door)* I'll just switch off that fan – when you're stripped, there's a terrible breeze.

*(They both pass through into the consulting-room)*

**DOCTOR:**
Lord save us – he hops like a rabbit. *(He gets up, goes to the patient and holds his own arm outstretched.)* Grab my arm. *(The patient attempts to.)* Come on, man! I said, grab it.

*(The patient tries – the doctor pushes him in the back, trying to straighten him out.)*

**DOCTOR:**
Well. We'd best oil the springs. Come on, take off your things.

*(The nurse removes her uniform in one zipping movement.)*

**DOCTOR:**
Not you, nurse!

**NURSE:**
I'm sorry – just habit.

*(She picks up her uniform and goes out.)*

**DOCTOR:**
My name's Doctor Kelly – sit down. Oh, you can't – never mind, Mr ...

**PATIENT:**
Crown.

**DOCTOR:**
Just go round by the screen.

*(They go behind a screen – patient cannot be seen because he is bent over, but doctor can.)*

**DOCTOR:**
Now then, what's to be seen? Had your holidays yet? Aren't you brown! Oh, my gosh – hold your breath – grit your teeth! Your braces are caught underneath. Well, you are in a state – we were almost too

late. If they'd snapped, you'd have needed a wreath. Now, there's one way to make you unbend–

*(He brandishes a large pair of scissors, then disappears behind screen. A loud "twang" and the patient straightens up in agony.)*

**PATIENT:**
Ow, my ... *(twang!)*

**DOCTOR:**
There, you're cured, my friend -I'm a Limerick man; I make sure, if I can, that you get the joke right in the end!

# THE REGIMENT

*The living room of the colonel's residence – a stone's-throw from the barracks at Rawlpore, india. Time: 1894.*

*The room is overdressed, oppressive, above all, a feeling of heat. Sunblinds, etc. insect noises. The distant cries of a sergeant-major, and men drilling, marching feet.*

*(On the chaise longue, dressed from head to toe in white, lies the colonel's lady. She reclines, fanning herself languidly. She is beautiful, thirty and very hot. Next to her, in a wider chair, sits the colonel (RB). He is whiskered, dressed in full uniform, sixty and sweating profusely. After a moment or two he speaks.)*

**COLONEL:**
*(mopping his forehead)* Gad! The heat!

**EDITH:**
It's the hot season.

**COL:**
Yes – that's what does it. Phew! I hope it's not curry again tonight.

**EDITH:**
It always is.

**COL:**
The only thing they can make in this God-forsaken country. *(Pause.)* Would you like whisky?

**EDITH:**
Fire water.

**COL:**
Yes, quite. Tea?

**EDITH:**
It takes two hours to get cool enough to drink.

**COL:**
Fancy a game of cards?

**EDITH:**
No – it's too hot for that.

**COL:**
There must be some little thing I can tempt you with.

**EDITH:**
It's too hot for that as well.

**COL:**
True. Yes, thinking about it, I think you're right. Still, it's nice thinking about it. I think I'll have a gin. *(Rings handbell on table.)* Gad, the heat! Look at all this mess *(indicating drinking glasses on table)*. Damn filthy swine of a house boy. Mahmud! Where the devil are you?

*(Enter an Indian house boy dressed in as little as possible within the conventions of the period.)*

**COL:**
Now look here, you damned beggar, Colonel-massa want all-same great big gin-tinkle, all-same full up top big big overflowing very little tonic water. You all-same lazybones, no sit about on big fat verandah, clear up all-same glasses in all-same living-hut or big Colonel-massa will all-same give you sack and big bag to put it in, understand? You all-same out on your big, fat, all-same ear! Savvy?

**HOUSE BOY:**
*(shrugging)* It's all the same to me, dear.

*(He minces out.)*

**COL:**
We must be nearer the border than I thought! Damned cheeky swine! Thank God, Corporal Bligh is starting work here this afternoon. He should be here by now.

**EDITH:**
Corporal Bligh?

**COL:**
My batman. You remember him.

**EDITH:**
Of course I do, George. I'm hardly likely to forget him. He undresses you every night in the bedroom.

**COL:**
Oh, of course. Damned good batman, Bligh. Dashed keen.

*(Door opens and Corporal Bligh (RC) enters. Efficient, respectful and breezy. The perfect gentleman's gentleman. He carries the glass of gin for the colonel.)*

**BLIGH:**
Good afternoon, sir – madam. Your gin, Colonel.

**COL:**
Bligh! Good lad – you've arrived already. Splendid.

**BLIGH:**
Yessir. Thought I'd pop over a bit early. Bit warmish today, sir.

**COL:**
Warmish! I don't think I can stand it much longer. Gad! What must it be like for the lads on parade.

**BLIGH:**
They'll stick it, sir. It's the honour of the regiment, sir.

**COL:**
The regiment. Yes. I must get out there, inspect them. Least I can do. *(Drinks gin.)* Where's my helmet? *(Picks up pith helmet.)* Gad, this thing weighs a ton – and it's too small *(which it is)*. Can't something be done about it?

**BLIGH:**
We could try taking the pith out of it, sir.

**COL:**
*(after reacting slowly to this)* Most of the chaps do that already.

*(He exits.)*

*(Bligh goes behind the chaise longue.)*

**BLIGH:**
Everything to your satisfaction, madam?

*(Edith immediately grabs him and pulls him over the back of the chaise lounge. He rolls on top of her. They finish up on the chaise, sitting, in an embrace.)*

**EDITH:**
You know everything is NOT to my satisfaction, Corporal. Ever since that first accidental brush in the bedroom. It's all your fault, you wonderful creature.

**BLIGH:**
That first accidental brush in the bedroom, as you put it, was not my fault, madam. I happened to be using the brush, but it was you who turned round quickly. There was little I could do.

**EDITH:**
And you did it beautifully.

**BLIGH:**
Well, that's as may be.

**EDITH:**
There was no maybe about it. Kiss me.

**BLIGH:**
But supposing the colonel comes back and catches us?

**EDITH:**
Let him.

**BLIGH:**
But the honour of the regiment!

**EDITH:**
Damn the honour of the regiment! What about my honour?

**BLIGH:**
Ah, well, if you're going to start living in the past.

**EDITH:**
*(she reacts)* It's the future I'm concerned with. The immediate future. Tonight?

**BLIGH:**
Tonight? Where?

**EDITH:**
In the clearing where we met that evening. I'll never forget that first moment when you came up behind me and grabbed me by the azaleas. Look at me! I'm trembling in your arms – my lips are burning, I've got pins and needles all up my back.

**BLIGH:**
That's not passion, it's prickly heat. You ought to be lying down.

**EDITH:**
That's what I keep telling you!

**BLIGH:**
Look, madam, if you think I'm making love to you in broad daylight, you're mistaken.

**EDITH:**
Let's go down into the cellar *(She goes to the cellar door, opens it and looks down.)* It's not broad daylight down there.

**BLIGH:**
I'm sorry, but I'm not sinking to those sort of depths.

321

**EDITH:**
It's quite a shallow cellar.

**BLIGH:**
Nevertheless, I'm afraid it's beneath me. Gad, if only you weren't so beautiful, if only it weren't so hot.

*Cut to: a parade ground, backed by low, wooden army huts. A thin, red line of soldiers standing to attention, the colonel inspecting them. He stands at one end of the line with sergeant major. He starts to walk along the line, slowly looking them up and down. A shot of the men's sweating faces as we pan them. Back to colonel – he stops, looks down. We track along the men's feet, stop at one who is standing in a pool of liquid.*

**COL:**
*(staring at man)* Do you want to go somewhere?

**SOLDIER:**
Yes, sir. Anywhere.

**COL:**
What? *(To sergeant)* Is he all right?

**SERGEANT:**
He sweats rather a lot, sir.

**COL:**
Oh, I see. Alright, men. In view of the extreme heat, you may all undo the top button of your tunic!

*(The men begin to do this, carefully. Close-up of one man. As he undoes the button, steam pours out from his tunic. We see others steaming, then cut to a long shot – we see steam rising all around the little group. The colonel and the sergeant exchange a look and mop their brows.)*

*Cut to: the living room.*
*(Edith, now without her dress, in white corset, bloomers above the knee, black stockings, bare shoulders, is smouldering on the sofa. Bligh stands by the door.)*

**BLIGH:**
Look, I've got to go. I've got to starch the colonel's front for tonight.

**EDITH:**
Oh, very well. Go. But don't expect me to be any different when we next meet. I shall still want you, desperately …

*(During the following dialogue the colonel enters. The door hides Bligh from his sight, opening onto him. He takes off his hat, is about to hang it on the peg near the door, but stops to listen to Edith's speech. Bligh creeps round the door, takes the hat from the colonel, who still doesn't realise he's there and goes out, quietly shutting the door.)*

**EDITH:**
I shall always want you. You did something to me that no one else has ever done. Not so violently, at any rate. You awakened something in me – something that had been lying dormant since I was a young, frightened girl at her first hunt ball. There's been a lot of hunt balls since then, but never any quite like the first. And so it was with you – I've never known anything that has moved me so much – or so often.

**COL:**
*(now on his own by the door)* What the devil are you on about, old thing?

*(Edith turns and reacts – how much has he heard and where is Bligh?)*

**EDITH:**
Oh – I didn't hear you come in.

**COL:**
Never moved you so much or so often? Sounds like an advert for Pickfords.

*(He realises as he goes to hang his hat that it's already on the peg.)*

**EDITH:**
I'm sorry, I was rambling. I think I'm out of my mind.

**COL:**
Nonsense. Talking of being out of things, what happened to your dress?

**EDITH:**
I took it off. It's this accursed heat.

**COL:**
I know. That's what drives a man mad. The heat. Like that chap who disappeared last month – Captain Wilcox. The Professor, they called him. Mad as a hatter, through the heat.

**EDITH:**
What happened to him?

**COL:**
Just vanished overnight. Took two hundred feet of water pipes with him. Pinched them from stores. Mind you, he was always inventing things. He invented a thing called the smelephone.

**EDITH:**
The what?

**COL:**
The smelephone. It was like a telephone, only when it rang you could smell it. He said it was for the benefit of the deaf. Just shows how mad he was. When they answered the phone they couldn't hear what the person was saying anyway.

**EDITH:**
I know how he felt. George – we must leave here at once.

**COL:**
What?

**EDITH:**
We must leave the camp. I can't stay here a moment longer. Now. We must go now!

**COL:**
But we can't, old thing – we're halfway through the bridge tournament. I haven't paid my mess bill, or anything. And there's another reason as well.

**EDITH:**
What?

**COL:**
I'm the Commanding Officer.

**EDITH:**
You won't be for long if I speak my mind.

**COL:**
What the devil do you mean?

**EDITH:**
I'm having an affair with Corporal Bligh.

**COL:**
(shouting) Corporal BLIGH?

(Bligh enters.)

**BLIGH:**
You called, sir?

**COL:**
I want a word with you, sir!

**BLIGH:**
Is it about your stiff front, Colonel?

**COL:**
No, it's not about my stiff front, Corporal Bligh. Is it true, about you and Edith here?

**BLIGH:**
Well, perhaps. I suppose you could think that. Is what true, sir?

**COL:**
That you had an affair with her. Is it all true? That you've caressed her, touched her, fondled her, kissed her?

**BLIGH:**
Well – only bits, sir.

**COL:**
Which bits? Point them out!

**EDITH:**
I can't stay here a moment longer – I must get out of this stifling atmosphere.

323

*(She picks up a small parasol and makes for the door.)*

**COL:**
Come back, woman – you've got nothing on!

**EDITH:**
I don't care!

*(She exits.)*

**COL:**
I'm going to fight you, sir. *(he starts to take off his coat)* For the honour of the regiment. I may be twice as old as you, but what I give away in age, I make up for in weight.

**BLIGH:**
At least.

**COL:**
Come on, put 'em up.

*(He adopts fighting attitude)*

**BLIGH:**
*(takes off coat)* Very well, Colonel – but only for the regiment.

*Cut to: the parade ground, as before. (The line of men see Edith approaching in corset and bloomers with parasol. The men all start to steam again. Then one faints. They all faint as she approaches, except one big, grizzled, tough lump of British beef, who stands to attention. The sergeant is next to him. Edith passes them, then–)*

**SERGEANT:**
Why didn't you faint, Higgins?

**HIGGINS:**
*(gruffly)* I'm not interested in women, Sarge.

*(He spits on the ground.)*

**SERGEANT:**
Oh? And what are you interested in?

**HIGGINS:**
Give us a kiss and I'll tell yer.

*(He smiles winsomely at the sergeant.)*

*Cut to: the living room.*
*(The colonel and Bligh, still with their jackets off, are enjoying a whisky and soda together.)*

**COL:**
Much more sensible, deciding not to fight. Too damn hot for anything like that. No damn woman is worth it.

**BLIGH:**
I'm glad I managed to make you see reason, Colonel.

**COL:**
Quite, quite. So, you were fly-weight boxing champ of the Army, were you?

**BLIGH:**
A few years ago now, sir. Lot of water flowed under the bridge since then.

**COL:**
I wish some of it would flow through here. Gad, it's stifling. Just the sort of weather for a native uprising, this.

**BLIGH:**
I doubt it, sir – too lazy, I …

*(A distant banging is heard. A sort of booming thud. The men look at each other.)*

**COL:**
What did I tell you? It's started. Gunfire.

**BLIGH:**
That's not guns, colonel. That sounds as if it's coming from the cellar.

**COL:**
*(listening at cellar door)* You're right! *(Picks up large Indian club as weapon.)* Stay here – I'll take a look.

*(He goes.)*

*(Edith bursts in, sees Bligh.)*

**EDITH:**
Are you alone?

**BLIGH:**
The colonel's in the cellar.

**EDITH:**
The drunkard. Harry, forgive me. I'm sorry, but it would never have worked. Our positions are so very different.

**BLIGH:**
Well, there's not much I can say to that, is there?

**EDITH:**
It was just the heat. *(despairingly)* This infernal, eternal heat! Will it never end?

*(The cellar door opens – the colonel emerges with a mad-eyed, bearded, straggly-haired man in filthy, tattered captain's uniform. He is on the verge of collapse. He carries a piece of iron piping.)*

**COL:**
You remember the Professor, who disappeared with the water pipes?

**WILCOX:**
I knew I could do it! It was all in my head.

**BLIGH:**
Captain Wilcox!

**COL:**
He's been down there for a month. No wonder we've been so damned hot. Damn fool's gone and invented central heating!

*(Edith faints, as the professor dances about, half collapsing, and colonel and Bligh restrain him as the music swells up.)*

# DRESS SHOP QUICKIE

**RB:**
Er – cocktail dresses, please.

**GIRL:**
Certainly, sir – what size is your wife?

**RB:**
No – it's not for my wife – it's for me.

**GIRL:**
For you?

**RB:**
Yes – I'm about an 18, I think. Anything but blue – blue doesn't suit me.

**GIRL:**
Yes – well, I'll just get the manager, sir – he'll deal with you.

**RB:**
No, no – I don't need the manager – I'll just browse around for a while if I may.

**GIRL:**
I'm sorry, sir – I've been forbidden to serve gentlemen with ladies dresses. It's a rule of the management.

**RB:**
But it's only for fancy dress!

**GIRL:**
Yes that's what they all say. A lot of your sort come in here. *(calls off)* Mr Buller!

**RB:**
What do you mean, my sort?

**GIRL:**
I've got my orders – the manager deals with this sort of thing. *(calls)* Mr Buller?

**RC:**
*(off)* Yes?

**GIRL:**
There's another of those fellahs wanting a cocktail dress.

**RC:**
(*off*) Oh – I'll deal with him, Miss Jones.

(*RC enters – he wears a cocktail dress, covered in sequins.*)

**RC:**
Now sir, anything in particular? Something off-the-shoulder? Perhaps in pink – now here's a super little dress ...

# THAT'S WHAT I SAID

(*RC and girl sitting up at L-shaped bar. RB enters. Large-bosomed barmaid approaches him. She wears a very low-cut sweater.*)

**RB:**
(*to barmaid*) Good evening. Tickle your botty with a feather tonight.

**BARMAID:**
I beg your pardon?

**RB:**
Particularly grotty weather tonight.

**BARMAID:**
Oh. Yes, isn't it.

**RB:**
That sweater looks a little risky.

**BARMAID:**
Pardon?

**RB:**
I said, I'd better have a little whisky.

**BARMAID:**
Oh. I thought you said something about my sweater.

**RB:**
No, no – that's very nice.

**BARMAID:**
Thank you.

**RB:**
Mustn't get the hiccups or they'll fall out.

**BARMAID:**
What did you say?

**RB:**
I said, I've just heard the cricket score, they're all out.

(*RB moves over to RC and girl, who had her arm round RC's neck.*)

**RB:**
Who's this silly ass with the ugly daughter?

**RC:**
I beg your pardon?

**RB:**
I said, I wonder if you'd pass the jug of water.

**RC:**
Oh.

(*He does so.*)

**RB:**
Thanks awfully, you dozy fish-face.

**RC:**
Pardon?

**RB:**
I said, thanks – awfully cosy, this place.

**RC:**
You know, if you don't mind my saying so, you seem to sound as if you're saying things other than what you say you are saying, if you understand me.

**RB:**
(*indicating his large moustache*) Oh dear – I'm afraid it's this moustache, it sort of muffles the sound. My wife likes it so, otherwise I'd shave it off, and drown

it in the sink.

**GIRL:**
Otherwise you'd what?

**RB:**
Shave it off – I'm sounding indistinct.

**GIRL:**
Oh, quite.

**RB:**
You're a nice girl – do you drop 'em, for a friend?

**GIRL:**
What?!

**RB:**
I said, have you dropped in on your friend?

**GIRL:**
Oh, no, he's my boss. He's an accountant.

**RB:**
Oh, I see. My name's Gollinson, by the way. I sell long hooters to alligators.

**RC:**
You what?

**RB:**
I sell computers and calculators. So this is your secretary, eh?

**RC:**
Yes – we're working late at the office.

**RB:**
Ah! Going back for a tease and a cuddle.

**RC:**
Yes, we're going back because the VAT's in a muddle. Miss Jones is new – I had to sack my last girl.

**RB:**
Why, did she ignore your advances?

**RC:**
That's it, yes. She was a big bore at dances.

**RB:**
I bet this one's a right little goer.

**RC:**
Yes, she does write a little slower, but I don't mind.

**RB:**
I know the type – she's one of the "mad with desire" brigade.

**RC:**
How funny you should know that!

**RB:**
What?

**RC:**
Her dad's in the fire brigade. Well, we must go. I want to look up your skirt and down your dress.

**GIRL:**
Eh?

**RC:**
I want to look up Lord Burton's town address.

**GIRL:**
I think it's somewhere in my drawers.

**RB:**
That sounds like an invitation.
If I were you, I'd lurch through those doors and get her back to the office.

**RC:**
I will. I'll search through her drawers and get her a bag of toffees.

*(The girl exits with RC.)*

**BARMAID:**
Funny sort of chap.

**RB:**
Yes. But let's talk about you. You'll never drown, with those water wings.

**BARMAID:**
I beg your pardon?

**RB:**
You should wear brown with those sort of things.

**BARMAID:**
It's not really your moustache – you're actually saying those things on purpose, aren't you?

**RB:**
Only trying to drum up a little trade, that's all.

**BARMAID:**
What sort of trade?

**RB:**
I sell deaf-aids.

# BAITED BREATH

*(A party. RB and hostess talking.)*

**RB:**
Well, Harriet, a scintillating crowd here this evening, as usual. How do you do it? You seem to be able to breathe life into any old dull collection of people …

**HARRIET:**
Yes, talking of breathing life, Roger, have you been on the garlic?

**RB:**
Good lord, you mean my breath? No, not me.

*(He breathes on her.)*

**HARRIET:**
No – well, there's someone polluting the atmosphere round here – I wonder who it can be?

*(RC approaches and greets them.)*

**RC:**
Hello, Harriet!

*(His "aitches" are very strong, and so is his breath. Harriet reels.)*

**RC:**
*(to RB)* Hello, Hartley! *(RB blanches, but recovers.)* Harry Hartley.

**RB:**
*(trying is best to face RC)* How do you do, Mr Hartley.

**RC:**
*(He tends to stand rather too close to people.)* How do you do. Actually, it's Huntington-Hartley, but who cares about a hyphen?

**RB:**
Quite. *(He takes out his handkerchief, and pretends to mop his brow, hiding behind it.)*

**HARRIET:**
*(staggering slightly)* Must look after the guests. See you later!

**RC:**
Bye, Harriet. Hasta la vista. *(To RB)* Helluva good hostess, Harriet. Hundred per cent. You alright, old chap?

**RB:**
*(turned away)* Yes – something in my eye, I think …

**RC:**
Let's have a look.

*(Peers into RB's eye.)*

**RB:**
No – it's alright – just watering a bit. Probably hay fever. *(Realises.)* No, not hay fever, I didn't mean hay fever …

**RC:**
Horrible thing, hay fever. I had it at Harrogate on holiday. Horrid. Had to hibernate in the hotel the entire holiday.

**RB:**
*(collapses on to settee)* Sorry – must sit down. Bit faint.

**RC:**
I can give you the name of a good hay-fever man. Cured mine.

*(He sits next to RB on settee.)*

**RB:**
Oh – expensive?

**BOTH:**
Harley Street.

**RB:**
Yes, I was afraid so.

*(Stands up – RC does the same.)*

**RC:**
Well, no good waiting for the National Health – hopeless.

**RB:**
*(despairs)* No, actually I use the old wives' remedy. You twist your neck round and hold your breath for as long as possible.

*(He turns his head the other way, takes a deep breath.)*

**RC:**
Oh – I didn't know about that one. There are some strange old wives' tales about though, aren't there? *(RB grunts.)* Some fairly strange young wives' tales about, too, especially round these parts. Things they get up to. You married? *(RB nods and grunts.)* Children? *(RB nods.)* How many? *(RB grunts.)* Oh, no, can't answer, holding breath, of course. I've got three. All at boarding school. Gosh, you can hold your breath a long time, can't you? *(RB nods in agony.)* Yes, all at school now. Helen's at St Hilda's, Harold's at King Henry's in Hertfordshire and Hector is at Harrow-on-the-Hill. *(RB's eyes popping out – he finally exhales.)* Ah! You're back! Hip hip hooray!

**RB:**
Oh!

*(Collapses on sofa again, flat out.)*

**RC:**
Oh dear! You've overdone it. Lack of oxygen to the brain.

**HARRIET:**
*(rushing in)* What's happened?

**RC:**
Stand back, everybody–

**HARRIET:**
What are you going to do?

**RC:**
I'm going to give him the kiss of life.

*(RB, with a yell, leaps up and runs out.)*

**RC:**
*(to Harriet)* Good gracious! What the hell is up with him, Harriet?

**HARRIET:**
*(reeling)* I'm sorry, Harry – halitosis!

**RC:**
Had he? I didn't notice. *(He takes her arm and walks off with her.)* Well, I wouldn't perhaps because I did have a teensy bit of garlic, I think, in the dressing at lunchtime. You know how it is.

*(People reel back as they pass on their way out of the room.)*

# THE BOGLE OF BOG FELL

*Night. The interior of a dark, cobwebby, Scottish castle. A huge fireplace, with a log fire smouldering fitfully. Chickens strut about and nearby a goat is eating the curtains. Next to the fire sits RB, as an old Scot, covered in red hair and plaid.*

**RB:**
Welcome to Cockahoopie Castle. I have a story to tell, so strange that it will make

your blood run **cold,** freeze your gizzard and perish the **rubber** in your inner tubes. But whisht! Before **I** begin, let me stoke the fire. *(He calls)* McWeenie! Put another piece of peat on **the fire!**

*(RC appears, as a replica of RB, same hair and clothes. He carries a wickerwork log basket.)*

**RC:**
We're running out o' peat. There's not much of him left now – only his right leg.

**RB:**
Never mind which part – will it burn?

**RC:**
It should do, it's his wooden one.

*(He produces a wooden leg from his basket. RB takes it, puts it on the fire.)*

**RB:**
Poor old Pete! Home cremation is a tradition in these parts. And so much cheaper.

*(He picks up large bellows.)*

**RC:**
By the by, Andrew, the MacDonalds are here – they've been waiting twenty minutes. Poor wee things are getting awful cold out there.

**RB:**
Well, bring them in, man.

**RC:**
I will, I will. *(He starts to go, then turns back.)* Do you want mustard on yours or ketchup?

**RB:**
Mustard. Now get out and stop interrupting. Go on, away with ye!

*(He puffs at him with the bellows and RC flys away backwards and out of sight.)*

**RB:**
Now, where was I? Oh, just here. The

story I'm about to tell concerns the Bogle of Bog Fell. Don't worry, it's not all going to be in rhyme, that was by accident. Angus Bogle was a mild-mannered wee man, who came to a tragic end. Finding that his wife was unfaithful to him, he cut her off without a shilling. Whereupon she cut him off with a bread knife, and he died intestate, leaving no money to anyone. And from that day onwards, his ghost haunted the area around his native village of Cockahoopie. The village itself was steeped in history ever since it had been pillaged by McNenemy and his Barbican Hordes, who drank all the whisky and left it alcohol-free.

*Cut to: film of mountains and village, etc.*

**RB:**
*(voice over)* Soon after he died, the Bogle's ghost began to appear to various of the villagers; always at full moon, just after closing time.

*(A man walks along a country road – goes behind bush to relieve himself. He stands behind bush. RC, completely white, as the Bogle, rises up from behind bush with a wide-eyed grin on his face. Man reacts in fear – starts to run off, comes back to do up his zip, then runs off. RC disappears. The man runs towards us, and stops near a tree in the foreground. RC appears from behind the tree. man rushes off again.)*

**RB:**
*(voice over)* It was a truly terrifying sight. One young man, out with his dog, was so petrified that everything stood on end.

*(Young Scot in kilt sees RC scuttling up the road. His hair stands on end (trick wig). Cut to: his dog – the dog's hair is also on end. Cut to: the man's sporran – it stands on end.)*

**RB:**
*(voice over)* He was a very popular young laddie after that, as he relayed to the lassies the gist of his experiences.
*(Young man, surrounded by girls in the heather.)*

**GIRL:**
Tell us about when everything stood on end, Jimmy.

**RB:**
*(voice over)* Mrs MacMuck, the widow of poor old Mick MacMuck, the sewage worker, had been a bag of nerves ever since her husband died. Before that she'd just been a bag. She would go to enormous lengths to protect herself from the Bogle.

*(Widow Macmuck in her bedroom – long (floor-length) nightie. She locks door. Three bolts. Chain. Puts chair under door knob. Small chest pushes up against chair. Looks under bed, sees chamber pot. Gets into bed, throws back the covers to find RC is there, grinning. She is terrified and frightens him as she screams. She dives through window, lands on a man walking past. Meanwhile, halfway up a highland road, RC appears, running away.)*

**RB:**
*(voice over)* The Bogle himself was very timid and always hid himself away in his favourite hiding place – the toilet of his wee cottage. In life, ever since he was a bairn, he had always hid there when he was really frightened ...

*(Cut to: RC as Angus Boyle, but when alive. He is at the side of his cottage, gardening. A knock is heard. He cautiously goes to the corner of the house and peers round at the front door. There stands a woman with a tray. A large notice on the tray reads "flag day". terror on RC's face. He runs into the loo and shuts the door. A puff of smoke from his pipe comes through the little circular holes cut in the door. The chain is pulled.)*

**RB:**
*(voice over)* And so, even now, as a ghost, when frightened by the widow, he sought retreat and safety in the toilet ...

*(RC, as ghost, rushes into toilet as before. This time, a large woman in a nightie emerges, terrified.)*

**RB:**
*(voice over)* ... which wasn't much fun for the new owners. *(The chain is pulled.)* A so a plan was hatched to catch the Bogle of Bog Fell. Residing in the village was Professor Monty MacDougal, *(a shot of a detached house, day)* the inventor of the now world-famous MacDougal's self-raising trousers, for people who can't get up in the morning. His brilliant, drink-riddled brain was brought to bear upon the problem ...

*(Cut to: RB as professor, white hair and moustache, standing next to a blackboard, on which is his design.)*

**PROF:**
*(to camera)* The idea is this. When the Bogle dashes into the lavatory and pulls the chain, this knocks the large boulder down this specially-built ramp and it falls to the ground, rolling to the other end of the toilet. This will cause the whole structure ... *(he points to his plan on the blackboard)* ... to overbalance, thus trapping the Bogle inside. Any questions?

**VOICE**
*(off)* Yes, what time do they open?

**PROF:**
Any minute. Come on, let's have one.

*(A stampede is heard, as he rushes out of frame. A door slams.)*

**RB:**
*(voice over)* And so the plan was put into action. Strangely enough, it was the Professor himself, returning home even drunker than usual one night, that was to be the cause of the Bogle's downfall.

*Night. RB as professor, staggering along the road – houses, etc. in evidence. He leans against a wall, singing. We see a sign on the wall –"flour mill". He staggers along the wall and leans against a barn door. It gives way, he falls inside. Crashes, etc. He staggers out, now white from head to foot. Staggers out of shot. A pair of lovers, hand in hand, walk along the*

331

*village street. They approach a corner. RC appears from one side, grinning. The couple take flight. Then RB, all white, appears at the other side. RC, terrified, rushes away. RB looks vaguely surprised. RC running up the road, away from us.*

**RB:**
*(voice over)* And so the Bogle sought to take refuge in his usual place. *(The toilet door – RC runs into frame, looks around and goes inside)* What he didn't realise was that the crafty Professor had moved it …

*(We now see that the toilet is balanced on the edge of a cliff. The chain is pulled. A rumble is heard. The toilet starts to topple and, in very slow motion, falls onto the rocks of the glen below, shattering to pieces. The dust settles, we mix to: RB in the castle, by the fire.)*

**RB:**
And from that day to this, the village has been known as Bog Fell – because that's where the bog fell, you see. One last thing I'll say to ye – the tale I've told you may seem strange, and almost impossible to believe – but if it's not true, may I be blown to smithereens, and the various parts of my body be distributed and scattered throughout the length and breadth of Scotland, including the Trossachs. Good night.

*(The camera widens a little and settles as RB takes a drink. He explodes – his clothes fall to the ground.)*

# PATIENTS, PATIENTS

*A doctor's waiting room. Twelve patients sit round the walls. RB and RC sitting next to each other.*

**RC:**
Slow, isn't he?

**RB:**
Who?

**RC:**
The doctor. Slow.

**RB:**
Difficult job.

**RC:**
I know. But he's still damned slow. You've got to admit it. That last woman has been in there so long, I've forgotten who's next.

*(A man emerges from the surgery door. A bell rings. All the patients get up and converge on the door. A man goes in eventually. The others sit down, grumbling.)*

**RC:**
That's why she was in there so long – she went in for a sex change. *(Bell rings.)* There you are, you see. Utter confusion. Nobody knows where they are. It's enough to make you sick.

**RB:**
These people are sick.

**RC:**
Listen, whose side are you on?

**RB:**
Difficult job.

**RC:**
Never mind "difficult job". It's a difficult job sitting here in confusion with a broken arm.

**RB:**
Broken arm? Is that why your leg's in plaster?

**RC:**
There you are, you see. Show you how confused I am. It's not that I've come about. Good God, no good coming to him with this leg. I'd have been here for months. Set that myself. The wife plastered it. She does all the decorating in our house. She's very keen. She wanted to

give it a coat of green emulsion, but I wouldn't let her.

**RB:**
I like it in white. Why are you here?

**RC:**
Been getting pains in my back. Just there.

*(He indicates, just above the waist.)*

**RB:**
Lumbar.

**RC:**
It is – a dead lumbar. Interferes with all sort of activities.

**RB:**
The lumbar region. Just there.

*(Touches RC's back.)*

**RC:**
Ow! That's it. How come you know so much about it?

**RB:**
I'm a doctor.

**RC:**
You are? What are you doing here then?

**RB:**
I'm not very well.

**RC:**
Oh dear, I'm sorry to hear that. What's the trouble?

**RB:**
Headaches, run down sort of thing. How long have you had this back trouble?

**RC:**
Couple of months.

**RB:**
*(gets out stethoscope from bag)* Look, lie down across these seats – excuse me, madam.

*(Moves woman. RC lies down, RB examines him.)*

**WOMAN:**
*(to girl)* What are they doing?

**GIRL:**
*(who has overheard)* He's a doctor.

**WOMAN:**
Is he? Perhaps he'll sound my chest. *(she goes to RB, taking off her jumper)* It's me chest, doctor – could you have a listen?

**RB:**
Hang on a minute …

*(The other patients all crowd round him, trying to ask for an examination – shouting and pushing.)*

**RC:**
Don't push!

**RB:**
Get back, everyone.

**RC:**
I was here first.

*(They still clamour.)*

**RB:**
*(above the noise)* Listen, quiet everyone! Just take off your clothes and form an orderly queue – I'll see you as soon as I can.

*(They all take off their clothes and stand around in their underwear, still chattering.)*

**RB**
*(to girl who hasn't removed her clothes)* Hey you, come along – get those clothes off.

**GIRL:**
Oh, me as well?

**RB:**
Of course you as well.

*(She does so.)*

**RB:**
Now, who's next? *(They all clamour.)*
Quiet! Look, we're never going to get
through this lot – I need some help.

**VET:**
I'm a vet, can I help?

**RB:**
Marvellous! *(To crowd)* Anyone with pains
in their legs, over there with that
gentleman.

*(Indicates vet, some people go to him.)*

**VET:**
*(to middle-aged man)* What's your trouble?

**MAN ONE:**
Hardpad.

**VET:**
Oh, right.

*(Takes pills from bag.)*

*(The girl is now with RB.)*

**RB:**
Now, why are you here?

**GIRL:**
I'm waiting for my husband. He's in there.

*(Indicates surgery.)*

**RB:**
Oh, sorry. You can put your clothes on
again then.

**GIRL:**
Oh, do I have to?

**RB:**
Of course you don't, my dear young lady.
*(He takes her to a chair and engages her in
conversation.)* Next! *(they all clamour again).*
Quiet!

**VET:**
*(shouting)* Could I have a second opinion
over here?

**RB:**
*(shouting back)* What's the trouble?

**VET:**
This man's got a broken leg – do you
think he ought to be shot?

**RB:**
Certainly not.

**VET:**
His wife's given the OK.

**RB:**
Look, quiet everybody. Listen! Will you
please form yourselves into couples and
try to diagnose each other.

*(They all start to examine each other and talk
about their complaints. Some lie on the floor,
the chairs, etc.)*

**RC:**
*(lying on his stomach, talking to girl, who is
examining his back)*
No, it's lower than that …

*(Suddenly three policemen burst in.)*

**SERGEANT:**
Alright, this is a raid. You're all under arrest!
Get your clothes on as fast as you can.

*(Everybody does so. It is, of course, chaos.)*

**SERGEANT:**
Alright – quiet! *(They settle down.)* Now
then. It's not really a raid, but we were in
the caff next door, and we couldn't hear
the juke box for the terrible row in here.
Just keep quiet and behave yourselves –
otherwise I'll nick the lot of you!

*(The policemen exit. All is quiet. The nurse
enters from the surgery, showing out
the girl's husband.)*

**NURSE:**
*(in a whisper)* Next, please.

*(RC gets up and starts to go in. The nurse then
turns and whispers to the others.)*

**NURSE:**
Thank you for being so patient.

*(RC turns, reacts to RB as he goes into surgery.)*

# THE SWEAR BOX

*(Please note – whenever the word "farmer" is used – a cuckoo noise is heard. Likewise a "buzz" for the word "plonk", and a "boing" for the word "clown".)*

*A country pub. RB enters, is greeted by barmaid.*

**BARMAID:**
Evening, Mr Parsons.

**RB:**
Evening, Dolly. How's the (farmers) beer? Flat as (farmers) usual?

**BARMAID:**
Now watch it, Mr Parsons – you'll have to mind your language in here from now on – look here.

*(She points to a box on the counter. It says "swear box" on it.)*

**RB:**
Oh – a swear box. That's a (farmers) good idea. Is it for charity?

**BARMAID:**
The church fund, five pence a time.

**RB:**
Oh – you'll make a (farmers) fortune out of me.

**BARMAID:**
You're right – you owe it fifteen pence already.

**RB:**
Fifteen (farmers) pence?

**BARMAID:**
Twenty now.

**RB:**
Oh, right. Have you got change for a (farmers) quid?

**BARMAID:**
You won't need much change of you go on like this.

**RB:**
That's true. Too (farmers) right I won't.

*(RC enters. Greets RB.)*

**RC:**
Evening, Joe.

**RB:**
Hallo, Gilbert.

**RC:**
Coo, it's a bit (farmers) nippy out there tonight. Shouldn't be surprised if we're not in for a (farmers) great fall of (farmers) snow tomorrow. That's all we (farmers) need.

**BARMAID:**
And I need twenty pence, Mr Robbins.

**RB:**
*(pointing at box)* Got a (farmers) swear box in here. Go on, have this on me.

*(Puts a few coins in the box.)*

**RC:**
Hey, that's a (farmers) good idea.

**RB:**
For the church, five pence a time.

**RC:**
Quite right too. About time this lot in here did something for the (farmers) church.

*(Puts coin in box.)*

**RB:**
Too right. Dozy lot of (plonks).

**BARMAID:**
Whoops – that one costs you ten pence.

**RB:**
You what? You never (farmers) told me that!

**BARMAID:**
You didn't (farmers) ask me. It's five pence for a (farmers) and ten pence for a (plonk).

**RC:**
Look, never mind all that (farmers) rubbish. I'm standing here like a (plonk) without a drink. Pint of best, Dolly. And what will you have, Joe?

**RB:**
Five pounds worth of silver, then we'll take this box over there, *(picks up swear box)* sit down and have a civilised (farmers) conversation. *(They sit, the box between them on the table.)* So, how's your love life, Gilbert?

**RC:**
(farmers) non-existent, mate. How's yours?

**RB:**
Not all that (farmers) grand. Got in a (farmers) argument with the (farmers) wife about going to the (farmers) dogs on (farmers) Friday night – I (farmers) told her I was (farmers) going anyway and she (farmers) hit me round the (farmers) head with a (farmers) saucepan.

*(The barmaid, bringing RC's beer, also carries a bag of silver. She pours all of it into the box and gives RB the empty bag.)*

**RC:**
What did you do?

**RB:**
I hit her back – silly old (clown).

**BARMAID:**
*(returning)* Mr Parsons!

That will cost you a pound!

**RB:**
A (farmers) pound? This is getting a bit (farmers) expensive.

**RC:**
I think she's making a (plonk) out of you, charging you a (farmers) pound for a (clown).

*(Enter a vicar.)*

**VICAR:**
Good evening, Dolly – good evening, gentlemen. A double lemonade and water, please. I say – this swear box seems mighty full.

*(He lifts it up.)*

**RC:**
Yes – and Dolly tells us all that money is going to the (farmers) church!

**RB:**
That's a nice surprise for you, eh Vicar?

**VICAR:**
Surprise? I'm the (plonk) who (farmers) thought of it.

# HOW TO CARE FOR THE SICK

*(N.B: dialogue and actions to run concurrently.)*

**VOICE OVER:**
The care of the sick is a very worthwhile subject for study – and a knowledge of first aid is a must for everybody today –

*(We see a man, dressed in white coat, standing with first aid box. Tighten slowly onto box.)*

**VOICE OVER:**
And the most important thing to

remember in first aid, is to keep the patient calm–

*(We see shot of woman with saucepan stuck on her head, rushing around the room wildly. The man grabs her and shakes her vigorously.)*

**VOICE OVER:**
Don't try to remedy the situation yourself–

*(Man trying to knock saucepan off with hammer.)*

**VOICE OVER:**
Simply lie the patient down, cover with a blanket and get them to drink plenty of hot, sweet tea–

*(Man lies woman on floor, covers with a blanket and tries to pour a cup of tea under the saucepan. Eventually pours tea from teapot down handle of saucepan.)*

**VOICE OVER:**
Calmness is the keynote always when dealing with a patient–

*(Man in white coat wheels trolley into room where girl patient is in bed.)*

**VOICE OVER:**
A blanket bath, for instance, can be an unnerving experience if a person is unused to it–

*(Man turns way at trolley, girl slips off nightie underneath the blanket and puts it on side table. Man turns, and lifts corner of blanket with one hand. Reacts – the soap in his other hand shoots up into the air. He shakes.)*

**VOICE OVER:**
When bandaging an injured limb, do not do so in such a way that the limb is difficult to cope with–

*(Man finishes bandaging male patient with one arm down to his side and the other straight up in the air. Patient departs, having to bend at right angles to open the door.)*

*(Pan over to reveal another man, his arms bandaged at right angles in front of him. He is holding a cup of tea. He can't get near enough to drink it.)*

*(Cut to: man in wheelchair, arms stretching straight out, banging on the railings.)*

**VOICE OVER:**
If an arm is bandaged correctly, it can often still be gainfully employed–

*(Patient with arm at right angle to his body, lying in bed. Nurse approaches and bends to get something out of cupboard. She suddenly leaps up, outraged. Patient looks innocent.)*

**VOICE OVER:**
Cheerfulness is a great asset, but remember that one must never treat a patient's disability too lightly–

*(Patient on bed, lying with both legs bandaged straight up in the air, so that he is an "L" shape. Man in white coat comes with the trolley, pours out medicine into spoon and suddenly pushes down on patient's legs, causing him to sit up – the spoon goes into his mouth and the man pushes him back down again, then up, then down, like a seesaw.)*

**VOICE OVER:**
Make sure you know how to handle equipment properly, and that it is in a safe condition–

*(Two men in white coats carry in male patient on stretcher. They approach the bed feet first. The man at the feet puts down his end, and the man at the head doesn't, so the patient slides straight under the bed. Another angle – he is hauled out and put on the bed. The two men walk out. The bed immediately folds in half and the patient is doubled up like a jack-knife.)*

**VOICE OVER:**
Finally, be attentive at all times to the needs of the patient, and never be caught off-guard for a moment. Remember, he's in your hands–

*(Man in white coat with "L"-shaped man sitting in wheelchair. The man stops to light a cigarette, letting go of the chair. A long shot – the wheelchair runs down a hill, hits a low wall and the patient pitches straight out of it and disappears from view.)*

# DOCTOR SPOONER REVISITED

**RB:**
*(as presenter)* Some time ago, we visited the abode of Dr William Spooner, the Oxford Don who, a hundred years ago, was confusing all and sundry with his unique habit of transposing the first letters of two adjacent words – hereafter known as "Spoonerisms". It was he who had proposed a toast to the queer old dean instead of the dear old queen. It was also he who shocked the wife of the new bursar of the college. What he meant to say was that, coming into contact with so many high-spirited young geniuses, she would be soon be as mad as a hatter, of course. Instead of this he said, she would soon be had as a matter of course. And so, in a special reconstruction, we return once again to the peaceful confines of Dr Spooner's house in Oxford …

*(Mix to: a Victorian vicarage – the garden room, with French windows to the garden. Mrs Spooner sits in a wicker chair, sewing. Enter RB as Dr Spooner with basket with flowers in it.)*

**MRS S:**
Good morning, William.

**RB:**
Ah, good ray, Dosey. I mean, good day, Rosie.

**MRS S:**
You were up early, dear. Where have you been?

**RB:**
I've been rolling the strose bushes – strolling in the rose bushes. They love so smelly this morning.

**MRS S:**
You do adore your garden, don't you?

**RB:**
Indoo I deed – I mean indood I dee. Nothing makes me gappier than a spot of hardening. But I fear I have neglected it of late – and there is so much to do at this time of year. It's the rutting season for tea-cosies, you know.

**MRS S:**
The rutting season? For tea-cosies?

**RB:**
No, no, my dear – the cutting season for tea-roses. I declare, you're getting as mad as me!

**MRS S:**
Is that what you intend to do today, my love?

**RB:**
No, the roses must wait. The first thing I have to do is to spray my flies against greenbeans. And while I'm at it, I think I'll black my dooberries as well.

**MRS S:**
Oh, that reminds me, I need some vegetables for dinner. Would you mind me a farrow?

**RB:**
Mia Farrow? What has she got to do with it?

**MRS S:**
I'm sorry, dear, I mean, could you find me a marrow?

**RB:**
Oh, I see – a mere tip of the slung. Alas, my dear, I cannot. The garden gate must have been left unlocked. Someone has nip-toed in and tipped my barrow in the mud.

**MRS S:**
You mean tip-toed in and nipped your marrow in the bud?

**RB:**
I couldn't have bet it putter myself; I'll wager it was that villainous landlord of the Wig and Pistle.

**MRS S:**
What, little Billy Humphries?

**RB:**
Exactly. Little Hilly Bumphries. He's jealous of my prowess in the Shower Flow.

**MRS S:**
My name is Rose, dear.

**RB:**
No, the shower flow. The annual shower flow.

**MRS S:**
Oh, I see.

**RB:**
Don't you remember? Last year he sabotaged my peas. He covered them with creosote, and left the sore little pods to die.

**MRS S:**
The sore little pods? Oh, the poor little–

**RB:**
Exactly.

**MRS S:**
William, are you sure it's him? Perhaps it was the bees.

**RB:**
Bees can't open a garden gate.

**MRS S:**
But how do you know the gate was open?

**RB:**
I saw next door's dog loo-ing things on the dawn.

**MRS S:**
Their pet poodle?

**RB:**
Yes, their pod pettle.

**MRS S:**
Pretty Polly?

**RB:**
Yes, prilly potty. That villain! He'll pay for this. I've a good mind to creep over there and put dertiliser on his failures.

**MRS S:**
William, dearest, don't get so upset. I will help you with the garden when I get time. At the moment we both have other duties – our students, remember?

**RB:**
Good heavens. Took at the line! I mean like at the tomb! I've hissed a mystery lecture.

**MRS S:**
And I have a Divinity class waiting. Let us hurry, dear William, and not keep them waiting any longer. *(She takes his arm.)* Dearest! You are my William – the sweetest sweet William that ever grew.

**RB:**
And you are my Rose – the ricest nose I ever picked.

**MRS S:**
But you know – you're much too gashionate to be a pardener.

**RB:**
And you're much too titty to be a preacher!

*(They exit.)*

# THE TWO RONNIES:

# THE SERIALS

One of the most popular elements of *The Two Ronnies* were the weekly cliff-hanger serials. Throughout the show's 12-season run, these serials were penned by Gerald Wiley (with one exception, the fondly recalled *Phantom Raspberry Blower of Old London Town*, which was co-credited to Spike Milligan. This was, in fact, adapted and expanded on by Ronnie from an original half hour by Milligan that had made up one of the *Six Dates With Barker* series back in 1971). As Ronnie mentions in his foreword to these books, for various unfathomable reasons, the scripts for these serials have been lost. However, three still remain – *Done To Death* and *Death Can Be Fatal* (both featuring the Barker/Corbett alter-egos of Piggy Malone and Charley Farley) and one of the most popular of all the serials, the futuristic gender-bending *The Worm That Turned*, which of course featured the late Diana Dors as the Commander.

# THE WORM THAT TURNED

## EPISODE ONE

**VOICE OVER:**
The dateline is 2012, England is in the grip of a new regime of terror, traditionally a land of brave heroes and great statesmen – Nelson, Wellington, Disraeli, Churchill. Britain now laboured under the yoke of a power guaranteed to strike terror into the hearts of all men: the country is being run by women.

It all started with Margaret Thatcher. Housewives all over England delighted at her rise to power, voted more and more women in, and more and more men out. A few years later the Germaine Greer knicker uprising made 1984 a far more terrifying year than even George Orwell predicted. Men's clubs were abolished, gentlemen's toilets closed, creating widespread distress among thinking and drinking men everywhere. Ailing livers naturally were the first to go to the wall. The advance of feminism was by now making itself felt in public and traditional spheres, names of buildings were changed. The Houses of Parliament were still the Houses of Parliament, but immediately the all-woman government took over, Big Ben was renamed Big Brenda.

By 1998 the newly-formed state police had established their headquarters in the old Tower of London. This historic fortress with its grisly associations of torture and executions had been given the name of a former folk heroine, as was now known to all and sundry as Barbara Castle. The state police marched around the country in squads. They were omnipotent and carried all before them – quite a lot behind them as well. It had become, in short, an England completely dominated by the female sex, even the Union Jack had now become the Union Jill, a sad travesty of its former self. Women were the breadwinners; they gave the orders, they made the decisions; they were the union leaders, the captains of industry and the men? Well, let's start with this one.

*(We see RC dressed as a woman – "Janet".)*

Cartwright, JW is employed as a tea boy at the secret police headquarters in Barbara Castle. He has a pass with his photograph on it, pinned to his overall. He lives in a two-roomed flat in Perivale and he is the worm that is about to turn. His main adversary, everybody's main adversary, was the commander of the state police, a woman with an iron will and underwear to match.

**COMMANDER:**
Now, ladies, it has been suggested by certain opposition factions that men should once again be allowed to revert to wearing trousers and I can see that to you as well as to me this whole concept is unthinkable. They must be kept in frocks if we are to retain the control which we have fought so hard to achieve. Trousers have always been the symbol of the male overlord. Here in England, trousers were traditionally always worn by the head of the family. In those olden days all women had an image of their perfect man.

**JANET:**
Nice strong black one for you, wasn't it?

**COMMANDER:**
And yet deep down there was always a

resentment, a spirit of rebellion which was ready at any time to burst to the surface. When our mothers and grandmothers burnt their bras way back in the 70's, what did this reveal?

**JANET:**
Nothing at all for you, as far as I remember.

**COMMANDER:**
It revealed that at last women, the creators of life, the protectors of the young, the guardians of the future, were ready to assume the mantle of leadership. The master stroke, however, was to insist on the changeover in traditional dress. Once the men had to wear the frocks, they were subjugated. As soon as we took their trousers away, they were putty in our hands. After all, what did they have left?

**JANET:**
Two lumps and a sponge finger.

**VOICE OVER:**
While on the other side of London, another downtrodden male *(RB in dress – "Betty")* goes about his everyday chores, only half conscious of the seeds of rebellion which are growing inside him.

**BETTY:**
*(answers phone)*
Alright, I'm coming, I'm coming. Hello? Oh it's you, Janet. Yes, how are you? No, no, no, not at all. No, no, just doing a bit of housework. I don't know why I bother either. Yes, I work and slave to keep it all clean and tidy. She just comes home, slumps down in an armchair, falls asleep in front of the television set. Just broken two of my blasted fingernails as well. Look, are you coming round as usual this afternoon? Well, yes, I made a cake. No, nothing fancy, no – just a plain one. Well, got to watch the old figure. I can't get into that blue dress she bought me for my birthday, daren't tell her. Right, OK. See you later, bye. *(He spots a ladder in his tights.)* Oh damn, new pair on his morning

*Later:*

**BETTY:**
Ah, hello Janet, do come in.

**JANET:**
Thanks.

**BETTY:**
Let me take your coat.

**JANET:**
Oh, well how are you, Betty old chap?

**BETTY:**
Oh fine, fine, mustn't grumble, sit down. Now, a nice cup of tea.

**JANET:**
Oh, you've changed the curtains, haven't you?

**BETTY:**
Yes, yes, yes. Oh, before I forget, the Drama Club have been on and they said would I be in this year's production again. I said I would if you would – I presume you would, wouldn't you?

**JANET:**
Oh, rather. Yes, wouldn't miss that for worlds. What is it?

**BETTY:**
Well, of course you know they've made them change the titles of all the plays that have sexual connotations.

**JANET:**
Oh, they're not doing … *Juno and the Pea Hen*?

**BETTY:**
No.

**JANET:**
Moby Dillys?

**BETTY:**
No, you remember the one that used to be called *Little Women*, now it's called *Little Men*. You'd be good for the lead in that, I

should think.

**JANET:**
Which part is that?

**BETTY:**
Arthur, the eldest daughter.

**JANET:**
Oh, it gets so complicated. Betty, old chap, I'm in trouble.

**BETTY:**
In trouble? Don't tell me John's pregnant?

**JANET:**
No, no, no. She's fine. No. It's just that I'm being spied on at work.

**BETTY:**
At the Castle?

**JANET:**
I think the secret police have heard about my collection of chauvinistic films. I'm sure the house is going to be searched any moment.

**BETTY:**
Well, you'll have to get rid of them.

**JANET:**
I can't, you see, not before Thursday. You know I'm having the private show in the auction rooms. It'll be the last because it's just getting too risky. Do you know that you can get three months' hard labour for showing a Humphrey Bogart?

**BETTY:**
So you want me to spread the word to the rest of the lads, eh?

**JANET:**
Yes, if you would, in the secret code. Tell them sewing circle meets on Thursday as usual, same place.

**BETTY:**
Does he mind you using his auction rooms?

**JANET:**
Who? Greta? No, he's a great chap, Greta. He'd give you the dress off his back if you asked.

**BETTY:**
Right, so as it happens, I shall be seeing some of the lads in the morning.

**JANET:**
Oh, really? Why? Are you going to keep fit?

**BETTY:**
No, having my roots done.

*At hairdresser: a row of men sitting under dryers.*

**BETTY:**
Cheryl, Cheryl. Susan, give Cheryl a knock, will you. Damned old fool, as deaf as a post, give him a knock.

**CHERYL:**
Come in.

**BETTY:**
Cheryl, sewing evening Thursday, all right?

**CHERYL:**
Oh, good, good. Oh, Thursday. Ah, me wife goes out with her boozing pals.

**BETTY:**
Pass it on, will you?

**CHERYL:**
Yes. Gracie, Gracie, don't know how to turn these damned things off.

*(A worried-looking Janet enters.)*

**BETTY:**
Janet, what the devil are you doing here, old boy?

**JANET:**
Shhh, police.

**VOICE OVER**
Who are the police looking for? Will Janet be discovered? Will the policewoman see him, or will the vanishing cream do the trick? Is Betty a man to be trusted? Find out next week in another exciting episode of THE WORM THAT TURNED.

# EPISODE TWO

**VOICE OVER:**
The year is 2012. England, traditionally a land of heroes and great statesmen, is in the grip of a new regime: the country is being run by women. They are the breadwinners, the rulers and their state police strike terror into the hearts of the subjugated male. In short, the roles have been completely reversed. It is the man, not the woman who now wears the frock. Even their names are feminine. But one poor downtrodden worm is about to turn. This man is Janet Cartwright. Employed as a tea boy at police headquarters, Janet has one friend he can trust: Betty Chalmers. Our story starts one afternoon over a cup of tea.

**JANET:**
I think the secret police have heard about my collection of chauvinistic films. I'm sure the house is going to be searched any moment.

**BETTY:**
Well, you'll have to get rid of them.

**JANET:**
I can't, you see, not before Thursday. You know I'm having the private show in the auction rooms. It'll be the last because it's just getting too risky. Do you know that you can get three months' hard labour just for showing a Humphrey Bogart?

**VOICE OVER:**
Next day in the hairdressers, Janet and Betty are surprised by a raid from the secret police.

**POLICEWOMAN:**
Do you have a customer by the name of Ursula Debenham? Tall, balding with a beard?

**OWNER:**
Eh, no. I don't think so.

**POLICEWOMAN:**
He's wanted for petty crimes against the state. Stand up. Name?

**PHYLLIS:**
Phyllis Willis.

**POLICEWOMAN:**
Is that a joke?

**PHYLLIS:**
My father thought so. Just 'cos he had a silly name, he gave me one.

**POLICEWOMAN:**
Your father?

**PHYLLIS:**
Dillys Willis.

**POLICEWOMAN:**
Papers. Have you recently shaved a beard off this man?

**OWNER:**
No, ma'am.

**POLICEWOMAN:**
Carry on. Any of you see or hear, it's your duty to report him.

**BETTY:**
What was his crime?

**POLICEWOMAN:**
Playing illicit rugby and pipe smoking.

*(Cut to: Janet on the phone.)*

**JANET:**
Hello, Shirley, old boy. How are you? It's me. I'm just ringing up to say, sewing circle evening Thursday, all right, you know what I mean? Yes, it is. Good drying

weather though. Mine was on the line ten o'clock this morning. Oh, have you? No, I haven't got a rich wife to buy me a dryer. No, I don't mean it. Yes. All right then, see you Thursday. Yes, bye.

*(Cut to: Betty on the phone.)*

**BETTY:**
Yes, yes, Thursday. Usual place, auctioneers, yeah fine. How's George? Is she? Amazing woman. Is she still playing left half for Brentford? Give her a good kiss on the goal mouth for me, will you. Bye.

*(Auction rooms – several men, all in dresses, occupy seats in rows before a large screen.)*

**JANET:**
Evening chaps, evening. Just a word before we start. I'm afraid this is going to be the last film shown for a while. I know, I know, I know, but we can't help it. I'm afraid I've got to go under cover, there's been a little dicky bird has told me there's been a bit of a leak and I might get raided. And so here we are, however, and tonight. So make the most of it, that's what I'm really trying to say, sit back and enjoy yourself, because tonight we're going to have a John Wayne film.

*(All the men cheer. The lights go down. The film starts. A man stares at Betty – he stares back, suspiciously. Is it really a man? Is that moustache real? After a few moments, the man gets up and leaves. Betty follows him into the toilet.)*

**BETTY:**
*(stopping her)* Here, you're a woman!

**WOMAN:**
*(producing revolver)* Be quiet!

**BETTY:**
Who are you?

**WOMAN:**
State police.

**BETTY:**
You taking me in?

**WOMAN:**
Yes.

**BETTY:**
Where, to the Castle?

**WOMAN:**
Yes.

**BETTY:**
It's rather a long journey. Do you think I might go to the toilet?

**WOMAN:**
All right.

**BETTY:**
Well, can I take my hands down?

**WOMAN:**
If you must.

**BETTY:**
Well, it's essential, very difficult otherwise. Look, could you please turn round and face the other way?

**WOMAN:**
No.

**BETTY:**
Oh! In that case I will. *(While pretending to use the urinal, Betty drops a piece of soap, taken from the wash basin, onto the floor.)* I'm ready.

**WOMAN:**
Then move.

*(She slips on the soap and Betty grabs the revolver, but drops it. They fight, during which Betty manages to get the gun again and shoots the woman in the behind.)*

**WOMAN:**
*(calling after Betty)* You shot me in the behind.

*(She collapses head-first into toilet bowl.)*

*(We cut back to the end of film, as Betty enters. She whispers in Janet's ear.)*

**JANET:**
What? You what? Shot her in the what? In the where? Good grief. Well, I should think she would faint. I'll go and have a look.

*(Janet looks in the toilet, and returns.)*

**JANET:**
Did you say fainted, old chap? She's dead.

**BETTY:**
Dead? But she was only shot in the backside. You can't die of a shot in the backside.

**JANET:**
She didn't die of a shot in the backside. She died of her head down the toilet.

**BETTY:**
She was drowned.

**JANET:**
She was drowned, yes. They're after both of us, Betty old chap.

**BETTY:**
They certainly are, Janet old boy. The thing is: what are we going to do with the body?

**VOICE OVER:**
What will happen now? Are Janet and Betty doomed? Can the toilet keep its grisly secret, or will the police flush it out? Don't miss next week's enthralling episode of THE WORM THAT TURNED.

# EPISODE THREE

**VOICE OVER:**
The dateline is 2012. England is in the grip of a new and terrifying regime: the country is being run by women. Their secret police are everywhere. Men, downtrodden and subjugated, are forced to wear dresses and to have only feminine lives. Janet's illegal showing of male chauvinist films to the men's sewing circle has been discovered by a secret police spy and, in a scuffle, Betty accidentally shoots her and our heroes are left with the grisly task of concealing the body. When Betty arrived home that night, his wife Brian was already in bed.

**BRIAN:**
How was the sewing circle tonight, darling?

**BETTY:**
What? Oh fine, fine. Usual sort of thing you know, everybody sewing things.

**BRIAN:**
How's yours coming along?

**BETTY:**
What?

**BRIAN:**
The thing you're sewing?

**BETTY**
Oh, oh, oh fine. I've nearly finished it actually. It's– I've just got to embroider, embroider around the neck, you know.

**BRIAN:**
I thought you were making a pair of French knickers?

**BETTY:**
Er yes, yes I am, yes, but they're reversible. You see, you can put your arms through the leg holes and wear them as a bolero.

**BRIAN:**
Or upside down as French knickers?

**BETTY:**
Er, yes.

**BRIAN:**
Bit draughty.

**BETTY:**
Oh, I'll shut the window.

**BRIAN:**
No, French knickers.

**BETTY:**
Oh, draughty. Yes, round the, round the neck, yes–

**BRIAN:**
Very sexy though.

**BETTY:**
Yes; don't do that, Brian, not tonight. I've got a bit of a headache actually.

*Next day:*

**BETTY:**
*(on phone)* Hello, oh hello, Janet. Yes, no, no, no. Brian's gone. I got into a big row this morning – I forgot to do her packed lunch. Where are you phoning from?

*(We see Janet at Barbara Castle.)*

**JANET:**
*(on phone)* I'm in the Commander's office, so I'm risking my neck, old chap. Listen, it's about the films: we must bury them in the garden. Well, your garden. I've only got a window box and that's full of my radishes. Hardly worth demolishing them to make room for *Gone with the Wind*. I know it's apt, but that's not the point. There are 37 films to get rid of before I'm caught red-handed – and some unfinished business in the Auction Rooms.

*Auction rooms:*

**AUCTIONEER:**
Gone, Mr Thompson. Next Lot 324, Victorian oak wardrobe with fitted drawer.

**PORTER:**
This one, ma'am.

*(He opens the door. the body of the woman falls forward towards camera.)*

*(Cut back to Commander's office)*

**JANET:**
*(on phone)* Well, look, I'll bring the films round in the car this afternoon. I'm on early shift. What about 2.30? Oh, and there's one other thing, oh–

*(The Commander enters. Janet pretends to dust the phone; then replaces it.)*

**COMMANDER:**
What the hell do you think you're doing?

**JANET:**
I'm dusting the desk.

**COMMANDER:**
Sitting down?

**JANET:**
Dusting the chair. It's a new directive from the efficiency department. Very good for the figure as well.

*(He wriggles about in the chair.)*

**COMMANDER:**
That will do. I can use that method to dust my own chair just as efficiently.

**JANET:**
More so, you've got better equipment. Well, I'll be off then, ma'am.

**COMMANDER:**
Just a minute. Name?

**JANET:**
Julie.

**COMMANDER:**
Where is your identity badge?

**JANET:**
In the wash by mistake on my other pinny.

**COMMANDER:**
Don't you know it's a punishable offence

not to wear it? Name?

**JANET:**
Julie, Julie Andrews.

**COMMANDER:**
Sounds familiar.

**JANET:**
Well, it probably is. My great grandmother was very, very famous in showbusiness.

**COMMANDER**
Really?

**JANET:**
Yes. Eamonn Andrews.

**COMMANDER:**
Julie Andrews, you will report to this office at nine o'clock when you will be disciplined.

**JANET:**
Yes, ma'am.

**COMMANDER:**
It won't take long, but I can assure you that you will not use that particular method of dusting again for quite a long time. Jump to it.

*(Cut to garden – Janet and Betty digging, burying the spools of film.)*

**JANET:**
You all right then?

**BETTY:**
No, I've just split my knickers.

**JANET:**
Pass me some more cans of film then. Ah, what one's this then?

**BETTY:**
*Robin Hood.*

**JANET:**
Errol Flynn, he's a real man's man.

**BETTY:**
Yeah, bit of a lady's man too, I understand.

**JANET:**
Come on then, otherwise your wife will be home.

**BETTY:**
All right.

*(Daphne, a nosy neighbour, peers over the fence. Janet and Betty try to conceal their actions from her.)*

**DAPHNE:**
That's a big hole.

**BETTY:**
Oh, I see, I thought you meant the split in my knickers.

**DAPHNE:**
Are you digging that for the wife?

**BETTY:**
No, I'm planting rhubarb.

**DAPHNE:**
Rhubarb? That far down?

**BETTY:**
Oh yes, yes. It's marvellous. You see, by the time it's grown you've got sticks six feet long. I saw it on television – Penelope Thrower.

**DAPHNE:**
Listen, the butcher's got some lovely fillet in. Thought you could surprise the wife tonight.

**BETTY:**
Oh, yes. Thanks very much Daphne, old chap, but I don't really feel in the mood for fun and games at the moment.

**DAPHNE:**
OK, just thought I'd mention it. Cheerio.

*(He leaves.)*

**BETTY:**
Cheerio, old sport.

**JANET:**
Has he gone then?

**BETTY:**
Yes, let's get cracking.

*(They are interrupted by the arrival of the milkwoman.)*

**MILKWOMAN:**
Hello, cheeky. I thought I knew that face.

**BETTY:**
Don't be so rude, you saucy monkey. Give me two pints and a flavoured yoghurt. You're very late?

**MILKWOMAN:**
It's Friday. I'm collecting the money. Anyway, I left you till last today. I thought I'd get a cup of tea and my legs up.

**BETTY:**
You'll get a slap round the face if you don't behave yourself. Now, be off with you. I'll pay you Monday. Go on.

**MILKWOMAN:**
Oh well, no harm trying. Ta ta sunshine.

*(Leaves.)*

**BETTY:**
Dear.

**JANET:**
I thought you said you enjoyed complete privacy in this garden? If I'd known, I'd have laid on some tea and cakes.

**BETTY:**
I know, it's incredible, isn't it? Who'll be next, I wonder?

*(On cue, Brian arrives home – reaction from RB and RC.)*

*Cut to: later, inside the house ...*

**BRIAN:**
Of course you realise I'm going to have to report you, don't you, Betty?

**BETTY:**
To the state police, you can't!

**BRIAN:**
I must. It's my duty as a woman. I shall go on Monday.

**BETTY:**
But Brian, I'm your husband, Betty. Thirteen years we've been married, doesn't that mean anything to you? I mean, look at us on the wall there, thirteen years.

**BRIAN:**
Unlucky for some.

**BETTY:**
That's a great help, isn't it? I suppose you realise what they'll do to me?

**BRIAN:**
I know what I'd like to do to you. You disgust me – those disgraceful films – you deserve all you get.

**BETTY:**
Well, in that case, why wait till Monday? Why not pick up the phone now?

**BRIAN:**
Simply because I need to have the use of you one more time.

**BETTY:**
The use of me?

**BRIAN:**
I need a partner tomorrow night.

**BETTY:**
Oh, of course. I'd forgotten. The Annual Staff Dance.

*(Cut to the dance: Betty sits in* Come Dancing *type frilly dress, with sequins. Janet arrives in almost identical flowery dress. She sits next to Betty.)*

**JANET:**
Evening Betty, old boy.

**BETTY:**
Sit down.

**JANET:**
Why? What's up?

**BETTY:**
My wife is going to report us to the secret police.

**JANET:**
What?

**BETTY:**
We've got to get out, go into hiding, but before we do, we must get hold of our identity files so they won't know who they're looking for,. All photographs will have to be destroyed. Look out.

**CYRIL:**
Hello, Betty. May I have this dance?

**BETTY:**
Not at the moment, thanks, Cyril. My girdle's killing me. It's really a big nuisance.

**CYRIL:**
How about you, Janet?

**JANET:**
No, I'm afraid mine's being a small nuisance.

**CYRIL:**
Come round to my place and I'll fix it for you.

*(She winks lecherously, and leaves.)*

**BETTY:**
Silly old crumpet.

**JANET:**
When's your wife going to report us?

**BETTY:**
I'll tell you later. There's no time now, but the point is those identity papers. Now you work at the place, you've got a pass, you'll have to smuggle me in – you game?

**JANET:**
Is there another way?

**BETTY:**
No, no, no. I know it sounds crazy, trying to break into the Tower of London–

**JANET:**
For God's sake, don't let anybody hear you call it by its old name. That's treason.

**BETTY:**
Whatever you call it, it's going to be blasted difficult to get in there.

**JANET:**
It's just not very safe, that's all.

**BETTY:**
All right, all right, have it your own way old boy. All right then, we're going to break into Barbara Castle.

**VOICE OVER:**
Will Janet and Betty succeed in their desperate plan, or will the Commander thwart it? Will she herself be thwarted? To find out who thwarts what and to whom, tune in next week to another eccentric episode of THE WORM THAT TURNED.

# EPISODE FOUR

**VOICE OVER:**
The year is 2012 in an England which has now been entirely taken over by women, where women are the breadwinners and the decision-makers and where men are completely subjugated, forced to wear dresses and given feminine names. Our story concerns two men, Janet and Betty. These two downtrodden specimens are on the run, wanted for crimes against the state by the dreaded secret police.

*Outside the Barbara Castle.*

**JANET:**
Now as soon as I get inside I'll go to the lavatory.

**BETTY:**
Pardon?

**JANET:**
The lavatory – the window looks out onto the street. That's it up there.

**BETTY:**
Oh yes, yes.

**JANET:**
I'll stick my pass out of the window–

**BETTY:**
You'll do what?

**JANET:**
My pass, I'll stick it out of the window and you grab it.

**BETTY:**
No, I'm sorry, I can't hear a damn thing with this cottonwool. I'm going to have to take it out.

*(Removes cottonwool from ear.)*

**JANET:**
Well, what's it there for?

**BETTY:**
Well, it's those cannons on the parapet, they go off every hour on the hour. I thought I'd take a bit of precaution, that's all.

**JANET:**
Well, that's part of the plan. You'll have to get used to the cannons. Now, you take my pass, change the photo and get in with the pass. I'll be waiting outside with the bucket.

**BETTY:**
Right. Good luck, Janet old chap.

*(Janet enters the Castle, Betty waits against the wall. Soon she is approached by a woman.)*

**WOMAN:**
How much, dearie?

**BETTY:**
I beg your pardon?

**WOMAN:**
You're rattling your keys. How much?

**BETTY:**
How dare you, madam. I'm not a common streetwalker.

**WOMAN:**
Well, what you rattling your keys for then?

**BETTY:**
I happen to have the palsy.

**WOMAN:**
Oh, beg pardon, I'm sure.

*Cut to inside Castle.*

**GUARD:**
Why have you got two buckets?

**JANET:**
Double time, Sundays.

**GUARD:**
Well, get on with it.

*Cut back to outside.*
*(The pass drops from the window, Betty drops her handbag when picking it up.)*

**BETTY:**
Oh, damn.

**WOMAN:**
Oh dear, allow me.

**BETTY:**
Oh, thank you very much. *(He bumps into woman and knocks her over.)* I'm sorry, it's these darned shoes. I'm awfully sorry. I'm

so clumsy, I'm awfully sorry ... you're fine, you're absolutely fine. Oh, do excuse me, don't worry about it. I'll, I'll be out of your way in no time at all. There, that's all right, I'll leave the rest, it's only money, isn't it? I've got piles. Which reminds me, I wouldn't sit there too long on that cold pavement ...

*Cut to inside castle. (Betty has got in with the pass. She sidles up to Janet.)*

**BETTY:**
There's too many people about for my liking.

**JANET:**
The sooner we get into that Record Office the better. We've got to find a cleaning trolley from somewhere. Now, come on.

*(They find trolley and start to move off. A big, hairy man in a cross-over pinny appears and scowls at Janet.)*

**JANET:**
This'll do.

**DEIDRE:**
Where the hell do you think you're going with my trolley, Cartwright?

**JANET:**
Now– Oh, Betty this is Deirdre, Deirdre Collinwood, this is Betty Chalmers who's new here.

**DEIDRE:**
Well, he don't look very new to me. What's your game, you rat?

**JANET:**
Now don't start bullying, Deirdre.

**DEIDRE:**
Who's going to stop me? Your friend Betty? You going to save your little friend, eh?

**BETTY:**
As a matter of fact, he was seeing if you've got something.

**DEIDRE:**
Got what?

**JANET:**
Boot oil.

**DEIDRE:**
What boot oil?

**JANET:**
Boot, it's a new directive, you see. I mean, if an officer comes to you and she's got squeaky shoes and you haven't got it, you're for it.

**DEIDRE:**
Boot oil?

**JANET:**
What do you mean? Haven't you got any then?

**DEIDRE:**
But I don't know nothing about it.

**JANET:**
You better get up the supply and get yourself some then.

**DEIDRE:**
Boot oil, right I will.

**JANET:**
And don't forget to get both sorts.

**DEIDRE:**
Eh?

**JANET:**
Black and brown. *(Deirdre leaves)* We'll be black and blue if we're still here when he gets back. Come on.

*Cut to outside office.*

**JANET:**
Right, it's four minutes to ten. At ten o'clock the gun fires three times at fifteen-second intervals. Now you have got to use these three bangs to cover any noise you might make.

**BETTY:**
What I need is a machine gun to cover the noise of my knees knocking.

*Inside the office. (Betty looks for files while Janet chats to guard. She rattles buckets when the cannons go off.)*

**GUARD:**
Did you have to make all that noise? The guns go off every day.

**JANET:**
I know, I know, I'm sorry. It's my nerves, you know I can't bear noise of any sort. I once joined the silent order of a monastery, had to leave.

**GUARD:**
Why?

**JANET:**
They were such noisy eaters.

*(Cannon noise.)*

**JANET:**
Oh dear, oh dear. Oh, I'm sorry, was that the last one?

**GUARD:**
Yes, only three.

**JANET:**
Oh, thank heaven for that.

*(She dusts near the desk, then smiles at the guard.)*

**JANET:**
I'm going to ask you to stand up, I'm afraid. I want to just dust your chair.

**GUARD:**
What?

**JANET:**
It's a new directive, all chairs have to be dusted. (*As the guard stands, Janet spreads glue on the seat while Betty nips out of the office.*) I'll be off then. All finished behind there, Betty? All nice and tidy. Off we go,

don't get up. Bye.

**BETTY:**
Bye.

*Cut to outside Castle.*

**BETTY:**
As soon as she sees that mess, they'll be after us.

**JANET:**
No, she won't I stuck her trousers on the chair.

*(We see their papers burning in their cleaning buckets.)*

*The Castle corridor – we see two girls dressed as Beefeaters pass by. Betty and Janet leap out and overpower them, dragging them behind a pillar. They re-emerge wearing the beefeaters' clothes.*

**JANET:**
It's forbidden to impersonate women now, you know. Danny La Rue's still locked up in here somewhere.

*(They see Deirdre coming towards them.)*

**JANET:**
(*as beefeater*) You, face the wall. You deserted your post and lost your trolley.

**DEIRDRE:**
How do you know that?

**JANET:**
We know everything.

**BETTY:**
It's because we eat so much beef, you see.

**JANET:**
You are a stupid nitwit.

**BETTY:**
You certainly are, bend over.

*(He kicks Deirdre's backside, and they move on.)*

*Cut to commander's office.*

**COMMANDER:**
We must find them. They must not be allowed to escape.

**OFFICER:**
But they burnt their identity papers. We have no photographs to go on.

**COMMANDER:**
Silence, one is short, the other is fat. They won't get far. They must be got rid of, liquidised.

**OFFICER:**
Don't you mean liquidated?

**COMMANDER:**
No, we have a new method.

**VOICE OVER:**
What will happen to our heroes, Janet and Betty? Have they burnt their boats, as well as their papers? Have they jumped out of the frying pan into the liquidiser? Find out next week in another excruciating episode of THE WORM THAT TURNED.

# EPISODE FIVE

**VOICE OVER:**
The dateline is 2012. Dear old England, land of heroes, is being ruled with a rod of iron by a new regime. The country is now being run entirely by women. They govern, they are the breadwinners, they wear the trousers. Men, completely subjugated, are now the housewives forced to wear dresses and given feminine names. But some of the worms are about to turn, among them these two men, Janet and Betty. Knowing that they are wanted by the dreaded secret police for crimes against the state, our heroes break into headquarters to steal their own identity papers, hoping to cover their tracks. But as they meet the next day

during their routine daily shopping trip, they know that never again will their lives be quite the same.

**JANET:**
Here's the sugar. How are you getting on?

**BETTY:**
Fine, all I need now is coffee and powdered milk.

**JANET:**
Powdered milk, for the country?

**BETTY:**
Well, we can't just leave a note outside for the milkgirl, can we? I mean, no one must know we're there. How long will it take to get there?

**JANET:**
Oh, about a couple of hours.

**BETTY:**
Oh, fine. Well, I'll put all this lot in the car. I'll shave off the moustache–

*(They are interrupted by the arrival of Cynthia.)*

**JANET:**
Hello, Cynthia. How's Arthur? She had the baby yet?

**CYNTHIA:**
Yes, a boy.

**JANET:**
Oh, good. What are you going to call him?

**CYNTHIA:**
Marigold.

*(She leaves.)*

**BETTY:**
I'll pick you up in an hour and before we can say Jill Robinson, we'll be tucked away in your little country hideout, just the two of us.

**JANET:**
No. Three of us.

**BETTY:**
Who?

**JANET:**
Herbert, my pet mouse.

**BETTY:**
What?

**JANET:**
Oh, yes, I take him everywhere with me.
I've got him with me now.

**BETTY:**
Where?

**JANET:**
Yes, he's in my bag, he's in a little tobacco
tin. Look, here he is.

**BETTY:**
Oh well, if you must, you must. But you
have to realise, Janet old chap, we're going
to be very tight on food.

**JANET:**
Oh, he doesn't eat a lot of food, just a little
bit of cheese. Edam, he likes this. This'll
do.

**BETTY:**
Oh, how long does that last?

**JANET:**
Oh, about a year.

**BETTY:**
Won't it be all mouldy?

**JANET:**
He likes it mouldy, oh yes.

*Exterior country lane. (Police seen around the
area. Janet and Betty wait behind the fence.
Janet appears very tall. Betty is dressed as a
yokel. A policewoman guard approaches.)*

**GUARD:**
That your car down there?

**BETTY:**
Oh, what car is that, my dear?

**GUARD:**
The one in the lane.

**BETTY:**
Oh, what lane is that, my dear?

**GUARD:**
The lane at the back of the house.

**BETTY:**
Oh, what house is that, my dear?

**GUARD:**
This house.

**BETTY:**
Oh, this house, oh that lane. Oh what,
what car is that, my dear?

**GUARD:**
Have you got a car?

**BETTY:**
No, no, never had car. No, we've never
had a car in our lives, no! Well, we had
one once, it was a little mini, but we had
to get rid of it, 'cos he couldn't get in it,
he's so tall, you see. He's so very, very tall.

**GUARD:**
He doesn't say much.

**BETTY:**
No, he's deaf and dumb, aren't you?

**JANET:**
Yes.

**BETTY:**
Well, he's deaf anyhow.

**GUARD:**
He heard you.

**BETTY:**
Oh yes, he lip reads, you see, lip reads.

**JANET:**
Pardon?

**BETTY:**
You lip read.

**GUARD:**
I'm looking for a short man.

**BETTY:**
Yes, I'd prefer one myself.

**GUARD:**
Keep your eyes and ears open, both of you, do you understand?

**JANET:**
It's about a quarter past five.

*(The policewoman stalks off. Janet, behind the fence, steps off her orange box.)*

*Cut to interior house.*

*(They are removing the costumes.)*

**BETTY:**
Where did you get all this stuff?

**JANET:**
The pantomime costumes from the Drama Club. They asked me to look after them a couple of years ago, still here.

**BETTY:**
Lucky for us they are. I mean, what were the ones we're wearing?

**JANET:**
The two yokels, Sarah and Henry, what were in *Jill and the Beanstalk*? They were two extra characters we put in to sing the song, "You can drive a horse to water, but a pencil must be lead". Not as bad as the principal boy singing "I did it her way".

**BETTY:**
Still, these things definitely got us out of trouble.

**JANET:**
They'll be back.

**BETTY:**
You think so?

**JANET:**
Oh, I'm sure of it and I can't be standing on a box all the time.

**BETTY:**
No, that's true. Has this place got an outside toilet?

**JANET:**
Yes.

**BETTY:**
I mean, if they find you in there without your box.

**JANET:**
Exactly, I'll be caught short.

*(Auction rooms – several men, all in dresses, occupy seats in rows before a large screen.)*

**JANET:**
... hope they're not going to be long, I've got cramp.

**BETTY:**
Where?

**JANET:**
In my hindquarters.

**BETTY:**
Don't be silly. I'm your hindquarters.

*(The police girls in their skimpy uniforms are peering underneath carts, their own hindquarters very much in evidence.)*

**JANET:**
Wish I had my catapult.

**BETTY:**
Why?

**JANET:**
Some bulls eyes to be scored over there.

**BETTY:**
Don't talk about bulls at the moment, old chap. I'm in a tricky position back here. If there's a bull in this field, he might charge us.

**JANET:**
Well, I hope not. I haven't got any money with me.

*(The police chief decides to abandon the search and marches the others off. A group of real cows gather curiously around the fake one.)*

*Cut to interior house.*

**BETTY:**
That milkmaid turning up was a nasty moment.

**JANET:**
She must have been pretty shortsighted to be taken in by this lot.

**BETTY:**
I'd love to have seen her face when she groped round my udders and I handed her a bottle of milk through a flap in the back.

**JANET:**
She didn't half yell.

**BETTY:**
That's what attracted the bull.

**JANET:**
That's when I decided we ought to make a run for it. I mean I would have been all right. I could have just stood there eating the grass – you would have born the brunt of it.

**BETTY:**
Yes. Well now, they're off the scent for a while, but they're still in the village. We've somehow got to get right away from the area.

**JANET:**
We need a vehicle with four wheels, rather than four legs.

**BETTY:**
Yes. Not only that we need a vehicle with a couple of good safe places to hide in …

*Cut to: a cart, approaching down a lane. On the back, two dustbins marked "pig swill".*

**VOICE OVER:**
Is this the end for our two heroes, Betty and Janet? Is it possible the police pigs will see through the pig swill? Or is it a load of hog wash? Don't miss next week's enchanting episode of THE WORM THAT TURNED.

# EPISODE SIX

**VOICE OVER:**
The year is 2012. England now languishes under a new reign of terror, a regime guaranteed to strike fear into the hearts of all men. The country has fallen into the hands of man's primeval enemy, woman. Women now govern, they are the breadwinners, men are completely subjugated, they are forced to do the housework, to wear frocks, they even have feminine names. And the dreaded secret police see that these new stringent measures are enforced. Our heroes in this tragic tale are two simple, honest, straightforward Englishmen, Janet and Betty. Wanted by the secret police for crimes against the state, they were hiding out in an old cottage. When the area is surrounded, they have to find another method of breaking through the road block.

*(The chief policewoman searches the pig swill and finds nothing. She dismisses the cart. Janet and Betty's feet protrude from beneath a tarpaulin as the cart moves off, safe for the moment.)*

*Cut to: a field beside a lane – Janet and Betty eating a picnic.*

**JANET:**
Good thing I brought this knife.

**BETTY:**
Yes, I was just looking at that. How many

blades has it got?

**JANET:**
Twenty-seven. I've had it since I was a Brownie.

**BETTY:**
Is that what you opened these tins with?

**JANET:**
Yes, the only thing that's broken is the thing that takes the stones out of horses' hooves. Well, it's not broken actually, it's bent. Melanie Harper did that at school.

**BETTY:**
Oh, how?

**JANET:**
Sat on it … Melanie.

**BETTY:**
Yes, yes. Thick skinned. Wonder what he's doing?

**JANET:**
He's an actress. Oh yes, just played the lead in *Hairy Queen of Scots* at the National.

**BETTY:**
Now then, anything else you'd like to eat, old boy?

**JANET:**
Well, what is there?

**BETTY:**
Well, there's some chocolate here or there's a Pa's bar.

**JANET:**
Oh I'll have that. I'll have a Pa's Bar, yes.

**BETTY:**
Now we really must get organised if we're going to contact my brother-in-law.

**JANET:**
Don't you think it's a mite dangerous, old boy? I mean we're less than thirty miles from my cottage. The police are bound to

be spreading out.

**BETTY:**
If we're going to go to ground, it's our only hope.

**JANET:**
Yes, you're sure this is the pub he works at?

**BETTY:**
What, the Green Woman? Yes, yes, absolutely positive, yeah. It's a good pub. Brian and I used to come down and visit him sometimes at weekends, not that she ever liked him really.

**JANET:**
Oh, he's not her brother then?

**BETTY:**
No, no, he's my sister's husband.

**JANET:**
Oh, which sister is that?

**BETTY:**
My younger sister, Harold.

**JANET:**
Well, what's your brother-in-law's name?

**BETTY:**
Diana.

**JANET:**
Oh, and he's bound to cycle down this road on his way to work?

**BETTY:**
Yes, it's the only road. You see the pub's about a quarter of a mile down there. Right, now then, I've got some drawing pins, I've got some tin tacks and I've got a few large fish hooks for good measure. Come on, we'd better get sprinkling.

*Exterior lane (they have sprinkled pins and tacks all over the road).*

**JANET:**
How's that?

**BETTY:**
Yes, that should do it.

**JANET:**
Bit drastic, don't you think? Wouldn't it be better to jump out of the bushes and wave at him?

**BETTY:**
No, no, he wouldn't stop. He was once stopped on his way back from getting some groceries by what he thought was a man, turned out to be a woman in a dress.

**JANET:**
Good lord.

**BETTY:**
It was terrible. She assaulted him. He came back with his frock all torn. Fortunately, she never laid a finger on his groceries.

**JANET:**
Just as well. Look out, who's this?

*(A car approaches, stops, and a man gets out. It is Betty's brother-in-law, he stares at them.)*

**BETTY:**
Good grief, Diana!

**DIANA:**
Betty! Good gracious, what are you doing here?

**BETTY:**
What are you doing here, in a car? What happened to the bike?

**DIANA:**
I've been fiddling the housekeeping. What are you doing here?

**BETTY:**
No time to tell you now. Get in quick, Janet. Look, turn the car round and I'll tell you as we go.

**DIANA:**
But I'm supposed to be–

**BETTY:**
Never mind all that, just hurry. Come on.

**VOICE OVER:**
Betty and Janet lose no time as they travel to tell Diana the whole story. He in turn informs our two heroes that the pub now belongs to him and like the true blue old-fashioned chauvinist he is, offers them a job. And so the very next night, in this sleepy little village far from the madding crowd …

*Cut to: pub. (Janet is working as a barmaid, collecting glasses.)*

**WOMAN:**
Here, you're a nice little thing. What're you doing in a dump like this then?

**JANET:**
Just pin money. My wife's away in the Navy.

**WOMAN:**
Here, come and sit in my lap.

**JANET:**
Oh, I don't think there's room for both of us.

*(Cut to Betty, with lady pianist.)*

**BETTY:**
Do you know "My little grey home in the West"?

**PIANIST:**
No, how about my little brown flat down the road? It's nearer.

**BETTY:**
What about "After the Ball"?

**PIANIST:**
No, I meant, after you finish here.

**BETTY:**
Oh, shut up. Excuse me.

**WOMAN:**
And what's your name, my dear?

**BETTY:**
Beryl, madam.

**WOMAN:**
Married?

**BETTY:**
No, no, no.

**WOMAN:**
Thought not. I can read men like a book.

**BETTY:**
Oh really, what system do you use?

**WOMAN:**
Braille.

**BETTY:**
Oh, really.

**DIANA:**
Oh, Janet, can you take an order in the other bar. Man in a green dress.

**JANET:**
It's all go round here, isn't it?

*(A woman is studying Betty, gives him a wink.)*

*Cut to: next morning.*
*(Betty is hoovering the empty bar.)*

**JACK:**
Good morning, Betty.

**BETTY:**
No, no, my name is Beryl. Beryl Cambridge, ma'am.

**JACK:**
No it's not, it's Betty Chalmers. We were at school together. You were Captain of the netball team. I was watching you last night.

**BETTY:**
Shhh, not so loud.

**JACK:**
I used to see you when I was on my way

back from cricket, in your frilly netball skirt. I used to think you were the most wonderful creature on earth. But I was only thirteen and you were seventeen.

**BETTY:**
 I'm sorry, I can't place you.

**JACK:**
Oh well, a lot of water has flown under the bridge since then.

**BETTY:**
Yes, quite a few gin and tonics as well. I doubt if I'll get into that netball skirt now.

**JACK:**
Still got that twinkle in your eye, though.

**BETTY:**
Look.

**JACK:**
Betty, you do know there's a big reward offered for your capture, don't you? It's in all the papers. Don't worry, I'm not going to give you away.

**BETTY:**
What, then?

**JACK:**
I want to keep you for myself.

**BETTY:**
What?

**JACK:**
I want to hide you. I've got a nice little house a couple of miles from here. We could renew old acquaintances and no one to disturb us.

**BETTY:**
But I never knew you.

**JACK:**
Well, I knew you, in my dreams.

**BETTY:**
Grief!

**JACK:**
Well, what do you say?

**BETTY:**
Well, I don't mind if you don't.

**JACK:**
Can't wait.

*Cut to: Jack's house.*

**JACK:**
Pour me a gin and tonic, would you?

**BETTY:**
Yes, yes, of course. How do you like it?

**JACK:**
Seven parts gin, one part tonic.

**BETTY:**
Slice of lemon?

**JACK:**
When I want a lemonade I'll ask for one.

**BETTY:**
I say, you're wearing pyjamas.

**JACK:**
Mmm, won't you join me?

**BETTY:**
What, in your pyjamas?

**JACK:**
Well, maybe you could start off in this?

**BETTY:**
What's that? Oh, I say, that's a pretty nightie, isn't it?

**JACK:**
Why don't you try it on? Take a shower, hurry back.

**BETTY:**
Yes, all right. I'll take a shower and then try it on and hurry back.

**JACK:**
Even better.

**BETTY:**
I say, it's jolly nice of you to hide me like this. Do you think you'll be able to hide my friend, Janet, as well, you know, later on?

**JACK:**
Later on. Let's have a day or two to ourselves first, shall we? He'll understand. I mean, you did put that in your note, didn't you?

**BETTY:**
A day or two, yes.

**JACK:**
Well, go on, you're wasting time. *(RB leaves. On phone)* Hello, state police? I wish to speak to somebody about one of the missing men, Betty Chalmers.

**VOICE OVER:**
So Jack is up to no good after all. What will happen to Betty? Will the police send their special squad to get him? As he steps from the shower, will he be grabbed by the heavies? Find out next week, in another extraordinary episode of THE WORM THAT TURNED.

# EPISODE SEVEN

**VOICE OVER:**
The dateline is 2012. England labours under the yoke of a reign of terror. Every Englishman is now at the mercy of his age-old enemy, woman. Women now rule, women govern, women earn the daily bread and the dreaded state police strike fear into the hearts of all and sundry. The poor downtrodden male, forced to wear a frock and even given a feminine name, is a sad caricature of his former self. Two such caricatures are our two heroes, two fine, upstanding specimens of English manhood, Janet and Betty. Wanted by the secret police for crimes against the state, our heroes are forced to go to ground in a remote village

in Herefordshire and find work in a pub owned by Betty's brother-in-law, Diana. It isn't long, however, before Betty is recognised by a former school chum who still seems to have a crush on him.

**JACK:**
You, you do know there's a reward out for your capture, do you? It's all in the papers. No, don't worry. I'm not going to give you away.

**BETTY:**
What then?

**JACK:**
I want to keep you for myself.

**VOICE OVER:**
But having lured our hero to her house, she shows herself in her true colours.

**JACK:**
Hello, state police? I wish to speak to somebody about one of the missing men, Betty Chalmers.

*Cut to interior house.*
*(Betty and Jack are eating lunch.)*

**BETTY:**
I feel so silly sitting here in my nightie at two o'clock in the afternoon!

**JACK:**
It belonged to my late husband.

**BETTY:**
There you are you see, sitting here in a dead man's nightie.

**JACK:**
He's not dead.

**BETTY:**
You just said "my late husband".

**JACK:**
He was always late, so I divorced him.

**BETTY:**
Oh, I see. Well, I still feel silly sitting

here in it.

**JACK:**
Perhaps you'd rather be lying down in it?

**BETTY:**
No, no, no, it's not the sitting, it's just the nightie, you know.

**JACK:**
Would you feel better sitting up without the nightie? If so, take it off.

**BETTY:**
No, no, no, no. What I mean to say is, a nightie's for going to bed in.

**JACK:**
Well, that's just what you'll be doing, when you've finished filling your face. Ready?

*Cut to later in the meal. (Betty is now on the cheese, while Jack watches, puffing on her cigarette.)*

**JACK:**
Now, my darling, I'm going to take a shower and a bath.

**BETTY:**
Shower and a bath, why? Did you miss out yesterday or what?

**JACK:**
No, I shower off the dirt first and then when I'm nice and clean I have a bath.

**BETTY:**
Isn't that rather like carrying coals to Newcastle, though of course if you had been carrying coals to Newcastle, you'd need a bath, wouldn't you? Though of course if you lived in Newcastle you couldn't have a bath, because you do keep the coal in the bath in Newcastle–

**JACK:**
You are rambling again, my darling.

**BETTY:**
Yes.

**JACK:**
I do believe you're nervous. What are you, man or mouse?

**BETTY:**
I'm not sure. Tell you what, this cheese tastes very good though.

**JACK:**
Now in ten minutes I shall be in the bath. I want you to rush in and scrub my back with a loofah.

**BETTY:**
Rush in?

**JACK:**
Absolutely hurtle.

**BETTY:**
Is it a rough loofah?

**JACK:**
Very rough.

**BETTY:**
Be careful you're not facing the wrong way.

*A telephone box nearby. (Janet speaks with a phoney foreign accent.)*

**JANET:**
Hello, could I please speak with Betty Chalmers.

**BETTY:**
Oh it's you, Janet old boy.

**JANET:**
How did you know it was me?

**BETTY**
Oh well, you're using that voice that you use when you played the Frenchman in *See How They Run* at the drama club, you know the one that was in …

**JANET:**
He was a German.

**BETTY:**
Oh, was he? Better disguise than I thought.

**JANET:**
Look, never mind about that. I've got your note. All it's got on it is this woman's address and "Something's come up". What are you doing there? What are you up to?

**BETTY:**
Well, I'm sipping champagne and preparing to dash in with a loofah.

**JANET:**
Listen, I wouldn't advise you to do that, old boy. Are you in the room on your own?

**BETTY:**
Listen, how did you get hold of her phone number?

**JANET:**
Well, everybody's got her phone number. She's well known for it.

**BETTY:**
What?

**JANET:**
She's been picked up so often she's starting to grow handles.

**BETTY:**
Oh goodness, really?

**JANET:**
What's more she's betrayed you.

**BETTY:**
She's what?

**JANET:**
The police are all round the house.

**BETTY:**
Where? Well, just a minute. *(He looks out of window.)* You're right, you know. Listen, I'm trapped in here, old chap.

**JANET:**
Where is she now?

**BETTY:**
What? Oh, she's in the bath, blast her.

**JANET:**
Right, I'll get your brother-in-law. I've got a plan to get you out of there, but you have to deal with the woman.

**BETTY:**
How?

**JANET:**
Just keep her quiet somehow. Keep a lookout for us, right?

**BETTY:**
How can I keep her quiet?

**JANET:**
Well, I don't know. You know, try champagne or something. Right, bye.

*Cut to: outside bathroom.*

**JACK:**
*(from within)* Who's that knocking at my door? Betty, said the fair young maiden.

**BETTY:**
It's only me from over the sea, said Barnacle Betty, the sailor.

*(He enters.)*

**JACK:**
Well, darling what do you think. Haven't lost my figure, have I?

**BETTY:**
No, but I think you're about to lose your balance.

*(A thud and a splash is heard. Betty rushes out, brandishing the champagne bottle. Cut inside to see Jack, unconscious in her bath.)*

*Cut to: outside the house. A van arrives. Janet, in false beard, gets out, with Diana.*

**DIANA:**
Good afternoon, madam. We've brought your order, a barrel of brown ale, and want to collect the empty one. Can we come in? Thank you.

*(They roll in a large barrel. Outside, the police watch suspiciously. After a while, the barrel re-appears. Diana is now accompanied by Betty in the false beard. Guess where Janet is? Of course, she's in the barrel.)*

*Cut to: inside the van. (Janet is climbing out of the barrel as they travel along the bumpy road.)*

**BETTY:**
You all right?

**JANET:**
Yeah, pretty dizzy. Otherwise no damage done.

**BETTY:**
Oh good.

**JANET:**
Oh good lord!

**BETTY:**
What's the matter? What's the matter?

**JANET:**
Oh, Herbert, he's still in the handbag. Wonder how he managed to survive the journey? Mice get dizzy like we do, you know.

**BETTY:**
Yes, I suppose they do.

**JANET:**
Oh yes, he's all right.

**BETTY:**
Well, congratulations old boy, you certainly got me out of a very ticklish situation there.

**JANET:**
Really?

**BETTY:**
Yes, pretty frightening-looking loofah in there. Well, you know things are getting pretty desperate, old chap. I mean the police are everywhere. They're bound to catch up with us sooner or later.

**JANET:**
Don't despair, things are not as desperate as that. I've had a word with Diana who's got a few friends in the know and there's still a ray of hope.

**BETTY:**
What? Where?

**JANET:**
I've got an address of an organisation, an underground organisation.

**BETTY:**
To hide us?

**JANET:**
We shall need fake papers, a change of clothing and a lot of nerve.

**BETTY:**
Where're they going to hide us?

**JANET:**
No, they're not going to hide us, even better than that, they're going to give us a chance to start a completely new life, free, completely free.

**BETTY:**
How?

**JANET:**
They plan to smuggle us over the border.

**BETTY:**
You mean–?

**JANET:**
Yes.

**BETTY:**
Into Wales!

**VOICE OVER:**
Will Janet and Betty succeed in their daring plan? How long before the police realise our heroes have them over a barrel? Find out next week in the final exhausting episode of THE WORM THAT TURNED.

# EPISODE 8

**VOICE OVER**
The year is 2012. England, once a land of heroes, has now become a land of downtrodden men. And who has trodden down on them? Women. Women now rule the land with an iron rolling pin. Aided by the commander of the dreaded state police they have completely subjugated men, forced them to wear the frocks, even called them feminine names. No more heroes, there remain only martyrs hounded at every turn by the dreaded secret police. However, our story concerns two miserable specimens who refuse to relinquish their claims to manhood, Janet and Betty. Wanted by the secret police for crimes against the state, they have been forced to hide out in the country. The police, however, track them down after a callous betrayal by a former school chum, a girl called Jack. However, they made a daring escape inside a barrel and as the brewery van drives them to safety, Janet tells Betty of a glimmer of hope on the horizon.

**JANET:**
I've got an address of an organisation, an underground organisation.

**BETTY:**
To hide us?

**JANET:**
We shall need fake papers, a change of clothing and a lot of nerve.

**BETTY:**
Where're they going to hide us?

**JANET:**
No, they're not going to hide us. Even better than that, they're going to give us a chance to start a completely new life, free completely free.

**BETTY:**
How?

**JANET:**
They plan to smuggle us over the border.

**BETTY:**
You mean–?

**JANET:**
Yes.

**BETTY:**
Into Wales!

**VOICE OVER:**
And so accompanied by Betty's brother-in-law, Diana, our heroes visit a certain dress shop in a nearby market town which specialises in the latest dresses for men.

**SALESMAN:**
May I help you, sir?

**JANET:**
Yes, my friend and I, we'd both like something in blue.

**SALESMAN:**
Blue, sir? What kind of blue?

**JANET:**
True blue?

**SALESMAN:**
I think we might have something to suit you in the stockroom. It's upstairs. Follow me, would, you sir.

*Cut to: stock room. (This is like a large operations room, seen so often in British war films. Lots of activity – men scurrying about, etc.)*

**BETTY:**
Good lord.

**SALESMAN:**
Julius! Two new visitors!

**JULIUS:**
Coming.

*(A Kenneth Moore type appears, obviously in charge of operations.)*

**JULIUS:**
How do you do, Julius Armstrong, though we prefer surnames only here.

**BETTY:**
Chalmers, B.

**JULIUS:**
Yes, I heard you were coming.

**JANET:**
Cartwright, J P.

**BETTY:**
Oh, what's the "P" for?

**JANET:**
Petula.

**BETTY:**
Oh, is it? That's funny, I had an uncle Petula.

**JULIUS:**
As I say, it will be Chalmers and Cartwright except of course, we'll have to change the names on the false papers. Now, come round here and pull up a couple of chairs. Let's see, a couple of good Welsh names. How about Ianto Evans and Di Owen? They're a couple I got out of the Welsh copy of the Yellow Pages, smuggled over the border last month. Bagg, bring some coffee, would you. That's Bagg, good man, unfortunate name, made even worse by his father christening him Edna.

**JANET:**
Edna Bagg?

**JULIUS:**

It might be some obscure reference to his mother. Right, photos. Come round here, would you. Right, sit there, would you. Right. Right. Ah, here's coffee. Thanks Bagg. Oh, Bagg, take these off will you. Ready Thursday?

**BAGG:**

Sir.

**JULIUS:**

Splendid. Good man, Bagg. Local chemist, you know. Got a man in the developing department. Good chap, bit gay, known as the original poof in boots. He's one of us, but he's also one of them, if you know what I mean. Now who's going to do the talking?

**BETTY:**

What, apart from you, you mean?

**JULIUS:**

At the border – best if only one of you talks.

**JANET:**

Oh, you'd better do that, Betty old chap. You do the Welsh accent much better than me. He played the lead in *Under Milk Wood* at the dramatic club and mine always comes out sort of, you know, Pakistani.

**JULIUS:**

Fine. Now as a cover story, you're a couple of Welshmen going across the border to visit relatives, maybe a wedding. Wear a corsage of carnations.

**BETTY:**

Oh, is that the usual thing for weddings in Wales, carnations?

**JULIUS:**

Oh, yes. Yes, men always wear them. Women tend to go for a leek at weddings.

**BETTY:**

Well, it's the excitement.

**JULIUS:**

Yes, well carnations then. Melanie, two corsages of carnations for Thursday.

**JANET:**

Pink for me, Melanie.

**JULIUS:**

One pink, one white. White all right for you, Chalmers?

**BETTY:**

Yes, fine.

**JULIUS:**

White goes with everything.

**BETTY:**

Fine.

**JULIUS:**

All right.

**BETTY:**

Fine.

**JULIUS:**

Right. Now keep it bright and breezy and above all keep going when you're across the border. You'll be met the other side by two of our agents, Bob Newton and Ivor Jones.

**JANET:**

Women.

**JULIUS:**

No, no, no. Men, men, no female domination over there. Welsh men have men's names, that's why you're travelling as Ianto and Di and not Megan and Myfanwy. Any questions?

**JANET:**

Yes, I've got a question. Would you mind very much if I brought Herbert with me? He's my pet mouse, I've got him here.

**JULIUS:**

I don't see why not, no quarantine restrictions. But I shouldn't show him unless you have to, they might decide to get awkward. He doesn't squeak or anything, does he?

**JANET:**
No, of course, he doesn't. He's as quiet as a mouse. Isn't he, Betty?

**BETTY:**
Quieter if anything.

**JULIUS:**
Oh, that'll be fine. Right, fine. All right?

**BETTY:**
Fine.

**JANET:**
Fine.

**JULIUS:**
Right. Come over to this map, would you? Now then, we'll take you by road up here in the car, to this point here. Ahead of you you'll see the border post and the barrier across the road. Simply get out of the car, turn round and wave goodbye to us as if we've given you a lift and then carry on towards the guards. Have your papers ready then they don't have so long to stare at you. And we all wish you the utmost luck.

*Cut to later – at the border. (Janet and Betty approach the uniformed women on guard.)*

**BORDER GUARD:**
Papers. Where are you going?

**BETTY:**
Well, we're going to a wedding, isn't it? My next door neighbour's niece, Blodwyn. Beautiful girl she is, yes, outstanding you might say in every direction, lovely. Has to be squeezed to be believed it does, and only seventeen too.

**BORDER GUARD:**
Ah, a minor.

**BETTY:**
No, she's marrying a miner. He's a nice bloke.

**BORDER GUARD:**
What about you?

**BETTY:**
Oh he's with me.

**BORDER GUARD:**
I spoke to him.

**BETTY:**
I know, but he's a bit shy, you see.

**BORDER GUARD:**
Shut up. You answer me.

**JANET:**
Oh yes, I mean, definitely with my friend here, look you indeed to goodness. I'm on my way, we're on our way to a yacky dar, with my hoppo here, you know. At the wedding really–

**BORDER GUARD:**
You're not Welsh.

**BETTY:**
No. No, he's not, he's not. He's Indian.

**BORDER GUARD:**
Indian?

**BETTY:**
Yes, his grandpa came over here you see. Oh in the seventies I think it was, and opened up a take-away in Merioneth, since when the family have never looked back.

**BORDER GUARD:**
He doesn't look Indian.

**BETTY:**
No, no, well they've never looked black either. Never look back or black. Well, there's all colours of Indians, isn't there? There's Red Indians, there's White Indians, lot of inter-breeding goes on out by there, see. Well, it's the weather you know. Oh yes, there's nothing else to do in the rainy season.

Ronnie Barker in the 1960s, just as his writing career was taking shape

(L-R) Ronnie Corbett, Ronnie Barker and John Cleese in "Three Classes" pose – the sketches were a regular highlight of the *Frost On Sunday* series

Ronnie always admired physically funny men, but got many of his laughs from the clever manipulation of words

Ronnie as General Futtock with Michael Hordern as Hawk the Butler, in the 1969 (almost) silent film, *Futtock's End*

(L-R) Ronnie as Lord Rustless with Mary Baxter and Jo Tewson in 1970's *Hark At Barker* episode, "Rustless On Cooking"

(L-R) David Jason as Dithers, Frank Gatliff as Badger, Jo Tewson as Miss Bates and Ronnie as Lord Rustless in *His Lordship Entertains*, 1972

Ronnie Barker as Piggy Malone and Ronnie Corbett as Charley Farley – heroes of *Done To Death* and *Death Can Be Fatal*

Ronnie Barker and Ronnie Corbett ending an episode of *The Two Ronnies* in familiar style with a song

Ronnie Barker and Ronnie Corbett were always inventive in *The Two Ronnies*; just part of why their humour endured so well, for so long, here as *Marionettes*

Ronnie in familiar 'spokesman' role from *The Two Ronnies*

Ronnie Barker in the title role of *Clarence;* the last television sitcom he wrote and starred in, with co-star Jo Tewson

**BORDER GUARD:**
All right, all right, don't keep on. Go on you're cleared.

*(Suddenly, through the border-post gate steps the Commander, the head of the government they last encountered at Barbara Castle. She wears a pale blue uniform and looks not unlike Field Marshall Goering, the Nazi.)*

**COMMANDER:**
Just a minute. Well, well, well, if it isn't the two worms that turned. Come inside, please.

**JANET:**
Oh, God, that's the finish.

**BETTY:**
What are you doing here? How did you know?

**COMMANDER:**
A little bird told me, a little bird you left tied up in her bathroom. She said you'd head for the border and she was right. Guards, this calls for a little celebration.

**GUARD:**
Yes, Commander.

**COMMANDER:**
Go into the village and get me some champagne.

**GUARD:**
Champagne, Commander?

**COMMANDER:**
A magnum, a couple of magnums. I wish to celebrate with my two old friends here.

**GUARD:**
We have no transport.

**COMMANDER:**
Well, take my car and hurry and make sure the champagne is cold.

**GUARD:**
Will you be all right here alone, Commander?

**COMMANDER:**
Of course, these are my friends. They won't harm me. Hurry. Here, the keys.

**GUARD:**
Come on.

**BETTY:**
Why did you do that?

**COMMANDER:**
Why? Because, my dear Betty, the regulations state that I'm not allowed to shoot you in cold blood. That wouldn't be justice.

**JANET:**
Since when has that bothered you?

**COMMANDER:**
But if you try to escape I can shoot you in the back and that's what you're going to do. That's why I've sent away the witnesses, my little friend.

**JANET:**
You can't do that.

**COMMANDER:**
Why can't I?

**JANET:**
I might refuse to turn round.

**COMMANDER:**
Then I shall shoot you in the front and then the back. You have two minutes to live, both of you. Is there anything either of you want to say?

**BETTY:**
Yes, there's something I'd like to say. Something which I know men all over England would like to say to you, whoever they are, wherever they may be. The rich man in his mansion, the poor man in his lowly cottage, I know I speak for all of them when I say, brrrrrrrr.

*(A juicy raspberry.)*

369

**COMMANDER:**
Very amusing. You know where you're going to get the first bullet as you walk away. Well, and have you got an insult for me, something that will make sure you get shot in the raspberry too?

**JANET:**
No, mine's in the nature of a last request.

**COMMANDER:**
How romantic. What is it?

**JANET:**
I want to smoke a pipeful of tobacco before I die.

**COMMANDER:**
You know that pipe smoking by men is a crime.

**JANET:**
Well, you can always send me to prison after you've shot me in the back.

**COMMANDER:**
You're right, it doesn't really apply in your case, does it? Certainly, go ahead, smoke your pipe. Tobacco, the age-old masculine weakness that brought the arrogant male eventually to his knees and allowed women to assume their rightful place in society as rulers – rulers through strength, strength. The might of womanhood will prevail for the very reason that we are invested with many strengths. Strength of character, strength of will, strength of purpose, greater strength than mere men could ever achieve. We are invincible, we have no weaknesses.

*(The Commander screams as she sees the mouse in the tobacco tin.)*

**JANET:**
You have one, this one. Mice, the one female weakness. Commander, get the gun, Betty.

**COMMANDER:**
Take it away.

*(The mouse is now on the floor. She backs into a corner, screaming.)*

**JANET:**
I'm afraid not. It's going to stand guard over you till we're well on our way. Goodbye, old friend, I'm going to miss you. There used to be a play once called *Of Mice and Men* – very famous. Who knows, one day, Herbert, you may be even more famous as the mouse who saved a man, two men, perhaps the whole of mankind. Guard her well, Herbert, and if she moves a muscle, straight up her trouser leg.

*(Betty and Janet walk away, over the border.)*

**VOICE OVER:**
And so ends the tale of the worm that turned, or does it? Was it just a story, or will it happen? That is in the future. For the present, our heroes are safe in a new land. Safe in a land where men are men and women are glad of it. A land where women constantly keep a welcome in the hillside and something warm in the oven.

*Song: we see the miners at the pit-head singing "Land of my Fathers". Then a panoramic view of the whole valley. In front of the miner's choir stand Betty and Janet, restored to men's clothing, with miners' lamps and helmets, their coal-besmirched faces grinning as they finish the song.*

# DONE TO DEATH

## EPISODE ONE

**VOICE OVER:**
Our story starts on the morning of the 1st of April – an apt date, you may think, for the strange charade that was about to unfold itself. Then again, perhaps you may not think that. It's up to you. What you think is your own affair. The fact remains that Piggy Malone, private eye and secret eater, was on his way to his office situated in the heart of unfashionable Neasden, over a greengrocers shop in the Harrow Road.

*(Over this, shots of large calendar with date – April 1st – people and traffic in Harrow Road. Then RB walking through crowds, eating a ham sandwich.)*

**VOICE OVER:**
He entered the door at the side of the shop, pausing only to acknowledge the cheery smile of the proprietor. *(Terrible ugly scowl from greengrocer. As RB passes, he throws fruit at him)* And mounted the stairs, two at a time. He was in no particular hurry, but it saved wear and tear on the carpet. *(Close-up on RB's feet)* He opened the first door on the right and strode in – a mistake he often made. *(Still close-up on feet. We see man's legs with trousers round his ankles.)*

**MAN'S VOICE:**
*(gruff)* Oi! I'm in here!

**MALONE'S VOICE:**
Sorry.

*(Door closes, feet continue along corridor to another door.)*

**VOICE OVER:**
Waiting for him on that spring morning, as usual, was Malone's trusty assistant,

Charley Farley, a failed undergraduate who occasionally rode to hounds, and invariably walked to work.

*(RC as Charley, with newspaper. Enter RB.)*

**VOICE OVER:**
Without a word, Charley handed Malone the morning paper.

**CHARLEY:**
Here you are.

**VOICE OVER:**
Silently, Malone took it.

**MALONE:**
Thanks very much.

*(He looks at headline – his eyes widen.)*

**VOICE OVER:**
There, in the paper, was the first in what was to be a long list of surprises ...

*(Dramatic musical sting – then: close-up of newspaper – the headline says "Woman found on Heath". Next to it is (quite by chance) a picture of Mr Heath. Widen a little to show that Mr Heath's photo has another headline underneath "Prime Minister at London Airport".)*

**MALONE:**
*(sits and reads)* A woman's body was found this morning on Hampstead Heath, strangled with her own garter. The body is estimated to be about 31 – the legs about 28 1/2, and the bust about 44. The police were able to identify the body by a coat of arms tattooed on the lady's back – a unicorn rampant, and the family motto "Ready when you are". She was the wealthy Lady Brimstone, of Brimstone Grange, Surrey – widow of Lord Arthur Brimstone, the Treacle millionaire. Well?

**CHARLEY:**
Sounds like a case for us, Chief.

**MALONE:**
You reckon?

**CHARLEY:**
Certainly. I've looked up the family in "Burke Peerage" – there's a swarm of relatives, all penniless. Any one of them could have a motive. And if she's put all her money into treacle, it's not going to be easy to get hold of.

*(Miss Whizzer, a small, bouncy, scatterbrained secretary, enters. She brings coffee in paper cups.)*

**MALONE:**
Quite. And they'll all be up there, ready to contest the will.

*(As Miss Whizzer bends over desk to give RC his coffee, RB notices her back view – she is facing towards the camera.)*

**MALONE:**
You've forgotten again, Miss Whizzer.

**MISS WHIZZER:**
*(putting her hand behind her)* Oh, sorry, Mr Malone. I got up in such a hurry this morning.

**MALONE:**
That's all right. Bring me a buttered bun, would you?

**MISS WHIZZ:**
Righto.

*(She bounces out.)*

**MALONE:**
Brimstone Grange, eh? Sounds inviting. A trip to the country.

**CHARLEY:**
Yes – you've looked a bit peeky lately – a change of beer will do you the world of good.

**MALONE:**
Anything we ought to finish off here first?

**CHARLEY:**
Nothing that can't wait. Business hasn't exactly been brisk. *(Looking at file marked "outstanding")* Couple of lost pension books; oh, and the Mrs Thompson poisoning case.

**MALONE:**
What, the window-box affair?

**CHARLEY:**
Yes – while she was leaning out of the window talking to a neighbour at the front, someone crept round the back and sprayed her prize begonia.

**MALONE:**
And it went yellow?

**CHARLEY:**
That's it.

**MALONE:**
We can't waste time on trivialities. Drop her a card and tell her to put the whole thing into the hands of a solicitor. We've got a murder to solve. Strangled with her own garter, eh?

**CHARLEY:**
We're taking the case then?

**MALONE:**
Yes.

**CHARLEY:**
I'll go and get the tandem round the front then.

**MALONE:**
It's not much to go on, Charley.

**CHARLEY:**
No. P'raps we'd better go by train, eh?

**MALONE:**
Go and pack – ride the tandem down to Brimstone Grange – I'll phone and say we're coming, then follow by train. We

should be just in time to catch the funeral!

*Cut to: Brimstone Grange.*
*(RB and RC ride up on tandem. They dismount, hear laughter, rather raucous, from about twenty people, obviously a party going on.)*

**CHARLEY:**
Sounds as if the funeral's in full swing.

**MALONE:**
Better take a look.

*(They enter the house through the front door. We see a large table, with about fifteen or twenty people sitting at it, all eating, drinking and making merry. We see shots of various guests and relatives – mostly played by RC or RB.)*

**VOICE OVER:**
And so it was that Piggy Malone and his intrepid assistant, Charley Farley, came face to face with the Brimstone family, surely the most bizarre funeral feast the fat detective had ever clapped eyes on. At this moment in time they were just faces – but faces he would grow to know and hate before many days had passed.

*(Shot of RC as bearded old professor, with two white mice in a cage, feeding them with a pipette.)*

**VOICE OVER:**
There was Professor Amos Brimstone, the rightful heir – 72 years old, eminent gynaecologist and tug-of-war champion of the thirties, who at the moment was trying to get his pet mice drunk. *(Camera pans to RB as the Dowager Lady Brimstone.)* Next to him, the Dowager Lady Agatha Brimstone – ex Gaiety Girl, reputed to have been kissed on the lips at Balmoral by Edward VII, and in many other places as well.

*(Reaction shot of the detectives. Then shot of RC as the young rip, with his bride – a sweet and innocent type.)*

**VOICE OVER:**
Further along the table, young Billy Brimstone, with his brand new blushing bride, Brenda, was busily trying to brief her about the birds and the bees before bedtime.

*(RB as northern tycoon joins RC and bride, raises his glass to them. Shot of RB and RC as detectives.)*

**CHARLEY:**
Is this a funeral – or a wedding?

**MALONE:**
Bit of both, by the look of it.

**VOICE OVER:**
As indeed it was. Uncle Jo Brimstone, the bankrupt tycoon, who, at this moment, toasted the bride and groom, had decided to combine the two occasions in order to save time and money. It was he himself who had designed the unusual cake.

*(A shot of bride and groom cutting the cake – it is black and white – half and half.)*

**VOICE OVER:**
Two other pairs of eyes watched the proceedings with mixed feelings. *(cut to RB as German, RC as frail old lady.)* Nellie Trembler, the Dowager's lady companion and Otto Van Danzer – a permanent guest in the house ever since he had been flown over from Frankfurt in 1954 by the late Lord Brimstone, to act as military adviser in the grouse-shooting season. It was no secret that Otto was madly in love with Brenda, Billy's bride.

*(Shot of RC kissing Brenda. Shot of Otto crushing a meringue with his bare hands.)*

**VOICE OVER:**
There remained but three people in the room worthy of a more than cursory glance before the drama is allowed to unfold itself – and they were gathered at the far end of the table, drinking heavily.

*(Shot of RC as doctor, Blanche, a voluptuous*

femme fatale, dressed in low-cut black dress and a tough-looking evil butler.)

**VOICE OVER:**
Pike, the sinister butler, Doctor Grist, the family physician, an eccentric, who had often been found in bed with his patients, and wore his stethoscope always – even in the bath, and last, but by no means least, the well-endowed Blanche Brimstone, sister of the deceased, who they said was like Mount Everest, she had been conquered few times, and then only by men willing to suffer great personal hardship, working in groups of three or four.

(Reaction shot of detectives, ogling Blanche.)

**VOICE OVER:**
Meanwhile, in another part of the grounds, the gardeners went about their duties. No one knew their names, but they worked with a relentless enthusiasm. At present, they were in the vegetable garden, engaged in moving a hole from one end to the other.

(RC is taking the last spadeful of earth out of a hole and putting it onto a small pile. RB is just finishing taking earth off the same pile, and putting it into a hole which is now almost filled in. They mutter to each other all the time in a rustic way. As soon as they are satisfied that RB's hole is full up, RC starts to dig a third hole in order to get earth to fill up the second hole.)

**VOICE OVER:**
They worked on, little knowing that disaster was about to descend once more upon the Brimstone household.

(Shots of them working – suddenly a prolonged distant scream – they look up, startled. We cut to a close-up of a knife in the old professor's back, and the scream, which continued through the cut, is now twenty times louder. Dramatic music as scream ends.)

(Shot of detectives – RB leaves shot, going towards where professor is lying face downwards on the table. RB lifts professor's head from out of the cream gateau into which he had fallen – cream and cherries all over his face – he is unrecognisable.)

**MALONE:**
It's the Professor!

(He lowers his face into the gateau again.)

**BLANCHE:**
(slinking into shot, breathing heavily) Is it murder?

**CHARLEY:**
(approaching the group) Well, it's not arson, is it, dear?

**MALONE:**
(loudly) I don't want anybody to leave this room! Oh. (Shot of the room – they have all gone.) Especially you, madam.

**BLANCHE:**
I knew this would happen. Inspector – you are from Scotland Yard, aren't you?

**MALONE:**
No, Neasden High Road, P G Malone.

**BLANCHE:**
There's something I must show you. Come to my bedroom while we've got the chance.

**MALONE:**
Oh, right.

**BLANCHE:**
When you've seen it, you'll realise what I've been going through.

**MALONE:**
I understand, madam. Charley, stay here and look after the body. (Then quietly, in his ear) If I'm not down in an hour, bring up a couple of pork pies, will you?

**CHARLEY:**
I'll do better than that, Chief – I'll send the Army in!

*(RB gives RC an old-fashioned look, and starts to move off with Blanche.)*

**VOICE OVER:**
Questions tumbled over each other in Malone's seething brain. What did Blanche know of the murder? What was she going to show him in the bedroom? Had he got clean underwear on? Had he cancelled the milk? One thing was certain – there would be very little sleep for Malone that night.

*(Shot of Blanche, smouldering – shot of RB, gulping. Shot of RC, tutting – body with knife in foreground. Move in on it.)*

*Caption: next week – Episode Two "Viewing The Body".*

# EPISODE TWO

*Titles, scenes from previous episode.*

**VOICE OVER:**
The place Brimstone Grange, the date April 2nd, the day Wednesday. Piggy Malone, unsuccessful private eye and Cornish pasty expert, and his undaunted assistant, Charley Farley, a man who said little and knew less, found themselves in the middle of one of the most extraordinary murder mysteries since *The Mousetrap*, now in its 82nd year.... Mr Brimstone lay murdered, a knife in his back and his face in a trifle. The beautifully upholstered Blanche Brimstone had urged Malone to go to her bedroom, saying she had something vital to reveal to him and Malone didn't need much urging – in fact he'd had the urge before she even asked him. Charley Farley was left alone with the body.

**CHARLEY:**
Stone the crows.

*(The door opens and the formidable Lady Brimstone lumbers in.)*

**LADY BRIMSTONE:**
That sounds like a very nasty habit, young man. Still, I don't suppose you mean it literally. Just an expression.

**CHARLEY:**
Tell me, madam, what do you know of this murder?

**LADY B:**
Only what you told me, Mr Farley.

**CHARLEY:**
I've told you nothing.

**LADY B:**
Then that's exactly how much I know about it, nothing.

**CHARLEY:**
I see. Would you be prepared to answer a few questions?

**LADY B:**
Certainly.

**CHARLEY:**
Right. I'll try and think of some. Question one. Why did you return to the scene of the crime so suddenly?

**LADY B:**
I didn't return to the scene of the crime as you put it, I simply came back to get me handbag. And I resent that word, suddenly. With my legs, you don't do anything suddenly.

**CHARLEY:**
I'll bear that in mind. Question three.

**LADY B:**
What happened to question two?

**CHARLEY:**
I'm coming to that. Question four, what have you got in your handbag that you don't wish me to see?

**LADY B:**
Oh well, let me see now. There's a photo of me in bathing drawers.

**CHARLEY:**
Anything else?

**LADY B:**
I think was wearing a picture hat and plimsolls at the time, I can't quite remember.

**CHARLEY:**
I don't mean that. I mean, anything else in the handbag?

**LADY B:**
No, no, absolutely nothing.

**CHARLEY:**
Very well Lady Brimstone, if that's the way you wish to play it.

**LADY B:**
How do you want me to play it, with a limp?

**CHARLEY:**
Look madam, I refuse to stand here and bandy legs with you. Now, one final question. Is there a bathroom on this floor?

**LADY B:**
Just outside. Why?

**CHARLEY:**
Don't be personal.

*(He leaves room. Lady Brimstone takes out poison. Woman enters – she is Lady Brimstone's constant companion. A smaller-scale version, but equally ga-ga. Her name is Nelly Trembler.)*

**WOMAN:**
Has he gone, Jemima dear?

**LADY B:**
Yes, yes. All's clear, he suspects nothing. Mind you, there was one nasty moment.

He tried to get his hands on my Dorothy bag!

**WOMAN:**
Ooh, disgusting, I don't know what the younger generation is coming to. Well, I've cut the cheese into little pieces and put it on little pieces of bread.

**LADY B:**
Oh good. Then all we have to do is to put a little drop of arsenic on each one and that will be that.

**WOMAN:**
Oh, I do hope we're doing right, dear.

**LADY B:**
Of course we are. It serves them right for trying to kill other little creatures. One should live and let live.

**WOMAN:**
Exactly, so let's put plenty of poison on to make absolutely sure.

**LADY B:**
Yes, come along then, let's hurry, because there's a programme I want to see on television when we've finished.

**WOMAN:**
Oh?

**LADY B:**
It's all about two clergymen, who don't wear any underclothes.

**WOMAN:**
What's it called?

**LADY B:**
The Nickerless Parsons Show.

*(They Exit.)*

**VOICE OVER:**
And so they went, leaving the room empty and the television critic of *The Sunday Times* wondering whether to quote that last remark as the worst joke of the year. Meanwhile, in a large,

comfortable bedroom, with a view of the rolling hills, a woman answering to roughly the same description was deeply engrossed with a fat detective, who couldn't keep his eyes off her bedroom biscuit tin. It was Blanche and she was about to give him a piece her mind, which was the last thing he wanted at that moment.

**BLANCHE:**
Would you mind going behind the screen? I want to change my clothes.

**PIGGY:**
Seems a funny arrangement. Why don't you go behind the screen?

**BLANCHE:**
I'm too tall. I'll show over the top.

**PIGGY:**
I'm as tall as you are.

**BLANCHE:**
I know, but it doesn't matter if you show over the top. You're not changing your clothes.

**PIGGY:**
Yes, that makes sense, yes. Quite.

*(He goes behind screen and can see quite clearly over the top.)*

**PIGGY:**
Right, carry on.

**BLANCHE:**
I'd rather you sat down.

**PIGGY:**
Oh yes. *(he falls)* Is there a chair?

**BLANCHE:**
Over there. (*He sits over there. He is now in full view*)

**PIGGY:**
Oh yes, thank you. No, that's not right, is it? Oh, just a minute, excuse me (*He moves chair to behind the screen*). Ha, that's better.

Now do you mind if I ask you a few questions?

**BLANCHE:**
*(cannot hear him behind the screen)* What did you say?

**PIGGY:**
Pardon?

**BLANCHE:**
I didn't hear what you said.

**PIGGY:**
I said, do you mind if I ask you a few questions?

**BLANCHE:**
Sit down!

**PIGGY:**
Oh yes, very well. But I get the feeling you're trying to hide something.

**BLANCHE:**
Yes, and I'm finding it extremely difficult with you bobbing up and down like a jack-in-a-box.

**PIGGY:**
Talking of boxes, who's the local undertaker?

**BLANCHE:**
A man called Grout. He and his wife run the business. They've got a daughter called Debbie.

**PIGGY:**
Oh, thanks. Pretty?

**BLANCHE:**
Very. Why do you ask?

**PIGGY:**
Oh, I don't know. It's just nice to know where you …

*(Two hands appear from a panel in the wall behind and Piggy is strangled. Dramatic music. Piggy eventually breaks free.)*

**BLANCHE:**
(*oblivious*) What's that?

**PIGGY:**
That was an attempt on my life, that's what that was, madam. Two hands grabbed me through a secret panel, wearing gardening gloves.

**BLANCHE:**
Who would want to murder you? No, Mr Malone, that was meant for me.

**PIGGY:**
Possibly. But if you'd been standing behind the screen here changing, you'd have been standing up, wouldn't you?

**BLANCHE:**
So?

**PIGGY:**
Do you mind coming here a minute? Ah ha. So if you had been standing here, you couldn't have been strangled. But you could have been – hmmm. Are any of the gardeners desperately in love with you?

**BLANCHE:**
I've no idea, there are so many of them

*Cut to: the ground outside. Gardeners go about their work.*

**VOICE OVER:**
There were indeed many gardeners employed at Brimstone Grange and even the smallest of them was no bigger than the rest. And underneath his smock beat a heart just as strong, just as lustful as any man in the district and he loved the Lady Blanche. He would mutter her name to himself as he wheeled his wheelbarrow.

**SMALL GARDENER:**
My Blanche, my Blanche.

**VOICE OVER:**
Sometimes, because he was an idiot, he would say–

**SMALL GARDENER:**
Blancmange, blancmange.

*Cut to: corridor in house.*

**VOICE OVER:**
Only one other man in the household equalled his lust – Pike, the butler. He was a lustful and a stealthy man, in fact everything he ever did was either stealthy or lustful. At the moment he was being both as he approached the bedroom door, behind which Blanche and the overweight Malone were in conference. Blanche suddenly tired and not quite knowing what to do next, lay on the bed and smoked. Malone, suddenly not tired and knowing exactly what to do next, stood by the door and steamed.

*(Cut to: Pike outside the door. Charley creeps up on him.)*

**CHARLEY:**
(*catching him*) Looking for something? You're a bit of a snooper, aren't you, eh?

**PIKE:**
Yes, sir. I do snoop a bit.

**CHARLEY:**
Why, why do you snoop?

**PIKE:**
Why, sir?

**CHARLEY:**
Why do you do it, why do you snoop about?

**PIKE:**
Well …

**CHARLEY:**
Go on, admit it. You like it, don't you, snooping about?

**PIKE:**
Well …

**CHARLEY:**
Come on.

**VOICE OVER:**
It was indeed, the Dowager Lady Brimstone and Nellie Trembler, her aged companion, who never went anywhere alone unless they were together. They had somehow managed to become imprisoned inside the same outside WC or, as Shakespeare once put it–

**CHARLEY:**
It's the two old ladies locked in the lavatory. Don't go in there. I think it's a trap.

**PIKE:**
No, sir, it's a lavatory. Mind you, it did give me a bit of a nip once. I was–

**CHARLEY:**
Don't pull the chain.

*(Lavatory explodes. The toilet seat ends up round RC's neck.)*

**VOICE OVER:**
Once more the unknown killer had struck, this time killing two birds with one stone, and old birds at that. Where would he strike next? Was he a madman or simply a lunatic? Would Charley get to the murderer before the murderer got to Blanche? Would Malone get to Blanche before Blanche got her clothes back on? One thing was certain, there would be very little sleep for anyone that night.

# EPISODE THREE

*Titles, various shots from previous episodes.*

**VOICE OVER:**
Malone, the fat detective, and his tireless assistant, Charley Farley, were in a tight corner. Murders were coming at them thick and fast. First the lady on Hampstead Heath, then the professor. Now, two old ladies blown up in the lavatory. Who was next for the chop? Was it Malone himself?

*(Shots of professor in trifle, explosion of loo, etc. From previous episode.)*

**PIGGY:**
*(looking up)* No, I'm the steak and kidney pie – he's the chop.

*(Wider – we see that he and Charley are being served by the butler. They tuck into their food.)*

**CHARLEY:**
What news from the doctor? Have they found him?

**PIGGY:**
Not yet. He was seen leaving the house about an hour ago. Probably on a call. What did you find out about the professor's death?

**CHARLEY:**
Well, whoever stuck that knife in his back was a much-travelled man.

**PIGGY:**
Why?

**CHARLEY:**
It said British Railways on the handle.

**PIGGY:**
But surely the doctor wouldn't use a British Railways knife? He'd use a scalpel.

**CHARLEY:**
Yes – by God you need them with that railway food – I had a meal going up to Birmingham the other day …

**PIGGY:**
To kill the professor with.

**CHARLEY:**
What?

**PIGGY:**
The scalpel.

**CHARLEY:**
Oh, quite – he could have given the old ladies arsenic.

**PIGGY:**
With the scalpel, you mean?

**CHARLEY:**
In the bottle.

**PIGGY:**
Nasty. *(They both start talking with their mouths full.)* So the doccah glut my flings round the cormarer in spike of habben at a grump plog.

**CHARLEY:**
Yg. Wib urrw glower in grundeming from ve viggle.

**VOICE OVER:**
*(as they continue to converse unintelligibly)* The doctor obviously had a lot to answer for. And while the two detectives stuffed their faces, the doctor himself was going about his normal duties in the village.

*Cut to: bedroom – double bed. (Two people, completely hidden under blankets. Doctor's black bag in foreground. A bit of movement under the blankets.)*

**DOC:**
*(under blankets)* Say ah!

**GIRL'S VOICE:**
*(deep breath, then)* Ahhh!

**DOC:**
Again.

**GIRL:**
*(sighing)* Again.

**DOC:**
I see.

*(They emerge. He is dressed, she is not. Their heads appear over the blanket.)*

**DOC:**
Well, my dear, there's nothing I can do for you. What you need is a good chiropodist.

**GIRL:**
Thank you, doctor.

**DOC:**
Not at all. Yo can get up. Keep off fatty foods, cakes and sofas. I'll see you in a week. Or I may pop round tonight. *(Phone rings.)* Answer that, it might be the phone.

*(He goes to get his bag.)*

**GIRL:**
*(answering phone)* Brimstone ninety-nine.

**DOC:**
*(putting stethoscope to her bosom.)* Again.

**GIRL:**
Brimstone ninety-nine. Yes, he's here. *(Handing doctor the phone.)* It's for you.

**DOC:**
*(putting the phone into his bag)* Thanks. I'll answer it later. I must get back to the Grange. *(He cuts through telephone cord with scissors.)* I've a feeling that all is not well back there. Goodbye.

*(As he goes, we hear a voice from the phone in the bag saying "Hello? hello?")*

**VOICE OVER:**
Did the doctor have some strange premonition that Malone wished to question him? If so, he was wrong. Malone and Charley weren't even within a mile of the Grange. They were on the golf course. *(Cut to: various pretty shots of golf course.)* Sherlock Holmes, when he wanted to think – or to relax – played the violin. The large, economy-sized Malone had tried this, but had been advised to give it up by a leading heart specialist, who lived next door to him. So he had taken up golf and now, whenever he had a tough assignment, he and Charley *(shot of Charley, lighting pipe, with a caddie next to him)* would play a few holes and talk their way through the case. In the strange half-world of murder and suspense which Malone inhabited, golf was the one thing that kept him from going mad.

*(Shot of Malone in sand bunker going mad. Then relaxed, peaceful shot of Charley and caddie watching.)*

**VOICE OVER:**
Charley, too, enjoyed the game and although not in the same class as Malone, still contrived to give his overweight boss a run for his money.

*(Charley addresses the ball on the fairway, swings. A perfect stroke. The ball goes straight towards the green. Reaction of RB – he swipes at ball in bunker, it flies out and lands in golf bag on caddie's back. The caddie does not realise. Malone says nothing as they all walk towards the green.)*

**VOICE OVER:**
But the evil presence of the Grange was nevertheless still at hand. The gardeners, ever watchful, lurked behind very bush – silent, primitive and, by all accounts, for the most part, completely insane.

*(Shots – sinister, not too comic – of gardeners, melting into the scenery, peering through bushes, etc.)*

*(Charley, about to play, looks behind him. Sees six or seven gardeners behind the trees. Charlie swings. As the ball is about to land, a gardener suddenly appears and holds out a shovel. The ball bounces off the shovel and the gardener disappears. Cut to another gardener with shovel. He again deflects the ball so that it now returns towards Charley. It lands at his feet. Close-up of RB, smiling. He takes another ball out of his pocket, drops it down his trouser-leg, onto ground. No one sees. He steps back and slices it into the woods. The screech of a crow being hit by a golf ball. Reaction RB.)*

*Cut to: a wide romantic shot of Blanche in a negligée, riding a magnificent horse in slow motion.*

**VOICE OVER:**
But even as another crow fell victim to Malone's deadly inaccuracy, the beautifully busty bulk of Blanche

Brimstone was approaching the two second-rate detectives with all the grace and erotic charm of a petrol advertisement.

*Cut to: the green. (The caddie puts down the bag and RB's original ball rolls out of it, rolls to within six inches of the hole. RC putts. Ball goes to within three inches of the hole and stops. Intercut with Blanche riding in slow motion – close-up of the two golf balls, then Blanche's boobs. RB looks at the golf balls, then kneels down and, using his golf club as a billiard cue, knocks his ball off RC's and into the hole. Blanche rides up. Dismounts.)*

**BLANCHE:**
*(bosom heaving)* Oh, I'm out of breath!

**PIGGY:**
*(staring at bosom)* Yes, I know.

*(Close-up of Piggy, he starts to breathe heavily. Intercut shots of Blanche, Piggy and bosom, all breathing heavily. Then the caddies. Then a group shot, all breathing heavily. Malone sits down, so does Charley. They are all now out of breath.)*

**PIGGY:**
If you've come to see the game, I'm afraid you've missed it.

**CHARLEY:**
Pity. We could lay another game.

**PIGGY:**
What, for instance?

**CHARLEY:**
I mean another game of golf.

**BLANCHE:**
No, no. I'd love to, but I can't. It's the doctor at the Grange. Dr Grist. He's ill. Pike, the butler, found him half an hour ago.

**PIGGY:**
Where?

**BLANCHE:**
Just outside the garage. He was in a coma.

**CHARLEY:**
I hate those rotten Italian cars.

**PIGGY:**
He's fainted, you fool. Come on, we'd better get back. Where is he now?

**BLANCHE:**
Pike said not to move him, but the ground seemed so damp. So I put him in my bedroom. I thought he'd be more comfortable in familiar surroundings. *(she leaves them and mounts her horse)* You'll probably be here before me – this horse is so damned slow.

*(She rides off in slow motion again.)*

**PIGGY:**
Come on!

*(They leave.)*

*Cut to: a shot of their motorcycle combination. It is covered in gardeners. Like monkeys, they are climbing all over it, curiously peering in at it. There are about eight of them now. Suddenly one of them looks up says "sshh!" then listens, then makes a dash for it. They all scatter rapidly. When RB and RC arrive, they have disappeared. RB and RC leap onto the bike and sidecar, and roar away.*
*We intercut between the slow-motion Blanche and the speeded-up shot of the motorbike. Then cut to the house.*

**VOICE OVER:**
But, in fact, it was the superbly streamlined Blanche who reached the house first. *(she rides up, now speeded up, rapidly dismounts and goes inside)* Closely followed by an exhausted, overweight detective and a tired-out, tireless assistant.

*(The motorbike – now in slow motion – arrives. They get off and float towards the door. Malone falls over, gets up again and enters the house.)*

*Cut to: the bedroom.*
*(The doctor is lying in bed, a wide grin on his face. Malone, Charley and Blanche are looking down at him.)*

**PIGGY:**
I don't like the look of him.

**CHARLEY:**
No. Ugly, isn't he?

**PIGGY:**
Charley – wait outside the door. Keep guard.

**CHARLEY:**
Right.

*(He leaves.)*

**PIGGY:**
Why is he smiling?

**BLANCHE:**
I don't know – he was like that when I found him.

**PIGGY:**
*(lifts bedclothes and looks inside)* Hello, what's that?

*(Puts his hand under bedclothes.)*

**BLANCHE:**
What's what?

**PIGGY:**
A note – pinned to his pyjama trousers. *(reads)* "Don't weep for me – I died of love".

**BLANCHE:**
So he's dead!

**PIGGY:**
Certainly. *(Indicating the note)* He admits it. Was he a lonely man?

**BLANCHE:**
Oh, no. He had loads of friends – mostly women.

**PIGGY:**
So when he says h died of love, he doesn't mean not enough love.

**BLANCHE:**
On the contrary. He probably means too much of it.

**PIGGY:**
Lucky swine – no wonder he's smiling. *(Stares – then lifts bedclothes again.)* Just a minute. He's wearing my pyjamas!

**BLANCHE:**
Yes.

**PIGGY:**
Aha! Then how did that note get there? You must have pinned it there yourself.

**BLANCHE:**
I …

**PIGGY:**
What really happened between you and the doctor? Did he really die of love, Mrs Brimstone?

**BLANCHE:**
You really want to know? Very well – I'll show you!

*Cut to outside the door (RC listens)*

**PIGGY:**
*(voice off)* Keep away from me!

*(Then crashes, and yells, and groans and grunts – sounding like a cross between a fight and an orgy. RC reacts. He opens the door to look in – Blanche's negligée flies out and wraps itself round his head. The door is slammed shut again. He removes the negligée and we see that he has a bra on his head.)*

*Cut to: a shot of the house – twilight. The crashings and bashings can be heard over. (A group of gardeners, muttering and chattering, are digging a hole. We zoom in as they move away – it is a grave.)*

**VOICE OVER:**
Was Blanche the killer? Had Malone bitten off more than he could chew? What was worse – had he brought another pair of pyjamas? Or would Blanche creep into his bedroom and do for him what she had done for the doctor? One thing was certain – there would be very little sleep for Malone that night.

*(A long shot of the house – the gardeners wander towards it. The crashings continue.)*

*Caption: next week – Episode Four "Blood will Out."*

# EPISODE FOUR

*Titles, shots from previous episodes.*

**VOICE OVER:**
Once again, our podgy and intrepid hero, Piggy Malone, and his slightly more tepid assistant, Charley Farley, had managed to be in the right place at the wrong time, and another murder had been committed behind their backs.

*(Dissolve to dining room – RC and RB are having breakfast.)*

**VOICE OVER:**
The latest victim, Dr Grist, had apparently died of an overdose of love, according to a note pinned to his pyjama trousers. Malone and Charley checked through the facts carefully next morning, while tucking into bacon and sausages, trying desperately to digest them.

**PIGGY:**
Fact one, four people have been murdered since we got here four days ago.

**CHARLEY:**
Right, chief.

*(Writes on pad.)*

**PIGGY:**
Fact two. We haven't found any clues at all yet.

**CHARLEY:**
Right.

*(Writes on pad.)*

**PIGGY:**
Fact three. There are still five more people left.

**CHARLEY:**
Right.

*(Writes.)*

**PIGGY:**
Therefore – Question: Was I silly to get a weekly return? Would I have been better off with a monthly?

**CHARLEY:**
That seems to me a pessimistic attitude, chief – sooner or later, we'll get him.

*(Pike, the butler, enters with dishes.)*

**PIGGY:**
Or her.

**CHARLEY:**
*(looks at pike)* Her? *(puzzled)*

**PIGGY:**
*(quietly)* It could be a her.

**CHARLEY:**
You mean he could be a woman in disguise?

*(A shot of Pike, looking like Jerold Wells.)*

**PIGGY:**
Not him – the murderer. Could be a her. *(calling)* Pike!

**PIKE:**
*(jumps and drops something)* Yessir?

**PIGGY:**
I'd like a word with you, my good man.

**PIKE:**
*(approaches)* Yessir?

**PIGGY:**
As you know, four people have been murdered in this vicinity recently.

**PIKE:**
I had heard, sir.

**PIGGY:**
Doesn't that strike you as odd?

**PIKE:**
No, sir.

**PIGGY:**
Oh it doesn't, eh?

**PIKE:**
No, sir.

**PIGGY:**
Come on, Pike, what are you trying to hide?

**PIKE:**
It's a bit of bacon, sir *(produces it from behind his back)* I didn't get no breakfast.

**PIGGY:**
Listen Pike. You were jealous of the Doctor. Admit it – wouldn't you have liked to get your hands on him?

**PIKE:**
No, sir!

**CHARLEY:**
What about Blanche? Miss Brimstone?

**PIKE:**
Yes, I'd like to get my hands on her, sir.

**PIGGY:**
No – he means she wanted to get her hands on him.

**CHARLEY:**
And your hands would be on her as soon as her hands were on the money?

**PIGGY:**
Isn't that right?

**PIKE:**
I'm confused, sir. I don't know whose hands are on what, now sir.

**PIGGY:**
Alright – you can go.

*(Pike goes to the door.)*

**CHARLEY:**
Oh – one more thing, Pike.

**PIKE:**
*(returning)* Yessir?

**CHARLEY:**
Would it be possible to have another sausage?

**PIKE:**
Oh, certainly, sir. *(He gets the dish from the side table.)* I'll say one thing, sir. *(He looks around furtively, then whispers)* Old Jack knows.

**PIGGY:**
What's that?

**PIKE:**
It's a sausage, sir.

**PIGGY:**
No, what did you say?

**CHARLEY:**
He said "Old Jack knows". Who's old Jack?

**PIGGY:**
Come on, Pike. Tell us.

**PIKE:**
*(at the door)* That's more than my job's worth.

**PIGGY:**
*(a thought strikes him)* What is your job worth?

**PIKE:**
£2500 a year, sir.

*(He goes.)*

**PIGGY:**
Hey, that's not bad. *(He hurries to the door.)* Is that all found?

*(At the door he bumps into Blanche in her negligée.)*

**BLANCHE:**
Good morning.

**PIGGY:**
Oh, good morning, Miss Brimstone.

*(He is affected, as usual, by her beauty.)*

**BLANCHE:**
I'm starving. How do the grapefruits look this morning?

**PIGGY:**
*(eyeing her bosom)* Very nice indeed.

*(She passes him and goes to side table.)*

**CHARLEY:**
Miss Brimstone – "Old Jack" mean anything to you?

**BLANCHE:**
Old Jack? Yes, he lives all alone in the old fisherman's cottage on the cliffs.

**CHARLEY:**
Really? Alone, eh? Odd.

**BLANCHE:**
What's odd about it?

**CHARLEY:**
Why would he want to live in an old fisherman's cottage?

**BLANCHE:**
He's an old fisherman. I'll take you to see him if you like – I quite fancy a day on the beach.

**VOICE OVER:**
This chance remark from the beautifully proportioned Blanche, which seems insignificant at the time, was to mean even less in the ensuing pattern of events.

*Cut to: a cliff path. A signpost saying "Old Jack's cottage" pointing one way; another sign saying "to the beach" pointing down another path. (RB, RC and Blanche enter and look at the sign.)*

**VOICE OVER:**
Piggy Malone, unable to resist the idea of Blanche in a bikini, had decided to give Charlie the important task of questioning Old Jack, while he himself remained on the beach to keep an eye on, as he put it "our principle witness".

*(RC says farewell and leaves in the direction of Old Jack's cottage. RB and Blanche run off towards the beach. We pan down signpost. At the bottom is a pot of paint and a brush. A hand wearing a gardener's glove comes in and takes the pot out of shot.)*

*Cut to: them dashing down to the beach (speeded up), disappearing behind two adjacent rocks and hurling their clothes up into the air. Then cut to Blanche in bikini (slow motion again) as she floats in all her glory towards the sea. Cut to: RB comes out from behind his rock (speeded up), runs towards the sea, takes a flying leap. Cut to: him landing on his stomach in one inch of water. A pained expression.*

**VOICE OVER:**
Meanwhile, Charley Farley, a man who had once played wing three-quarters for the England team, found himself in the unlikely situation of introducing himself to a man he had never met.

*Cut to RC and Old Jack (RB), a man who is all hair, except for his eyes, dressed as a*

*fisherman. He sits in an old armchair. RC is on a stool, a cassette tape recorder and microphone at the ready.*

**CHARLEY:**
Now then, Jack, I want you to tell me, in your own words, what you know of the murders.

**JACK:**
Er–

**CHARLEY:**
Hang on, just a minute. I'll just check if we're recording. *(Into mic)* Hello testing 1 2 3 4 5 4 3 2 1 Hello, hello, 2 4 6 8 Mary at the cottage gate 1 2 3 4 Mary at the cottage door. If he hollers let him go, England! Bom bom bom England! Bom Bom Bom. Right, we'll just see if that's recorded all right.

*(Presses button, listens, nothing.)*

*Cut to: the beach.*
*Shot of Blanche with saucy yachting cap on, about to look through a telescope. Shot of Malone looking at a lifebuoy on a hook. He removes it and throws it into the sea. It sinks immediately. He looks puzzled. Blanche looks through telescope – her point of view, panning round countryside. Suddenly, we pan onto a group of gardeners, all creeping about as usual in a sinister fashion. Suddenly an enormous monster crawls into the picture. It looks like a horror film animated model of an insect. Blanche is horrified. Malone grabs the telescope – sees that there is a fly on the lens. Flicks it off. They laugh and run into the water.*

*Cut back to Old Jack's cottage. RC now has the back of the tape recorder off.*

**CHARLEY:**
It's brand new, this is. It should work – it fell off the back of a lorry. Now, let's be logical. Tape recorder. Battery or mains? Not plugged into mains. Therefore should work off batteries. Not working. Why not? Answer. No batteries in it. *(Looks inside.)* Correct. Sorry Jack, shan't be a

minute. I'll have to plug it into the mains. That wall light will do. *(Cut to shot of unlit gas light.)* Oh, you've got gas lighting. Ah. Well, that won't work. You probably need a special adapter for that.

*Cut to the beach.*
*(RB and Blanche splashing water at each other. Intercut between the two – three playful splashes, then close-up on RB as about four gallons of water hit him, knocking him backwards. Cut to Blanche, giggling. Cut to RB getting up, running after Blanche. They disappear into a solitary beach hut. RB shuts the door – the hut completely collapses.)*

*Cut to the top of a telegraph pole (RC attaching a wire to one of the terminals).*

**CHARLEY:**
That should do it.

*(He climbs down out of frame.)*

*Cut to the beach. (RB is now buried up to his neck in sand. Blanche is draping seaweed around his head. Close-up of RB – he suddenly looks alarmed. Cut to wide shot just in time to see the waves break over his head as the tide comes in. Blanche giggles as she runs away up the cliff path. Final long shot – the tide coming in.)*

*Cut to Old Jack's cottage (RC with tape recorder.)*

**CHARLEY:**
Right, Jack. It's finally working. Now tell me all you know.

**JACK:**
Er – ar oi in er oh ha ha wor oi ee oh ugger amar er oi oh ar an all eh her ag roit of…

*Close-up RC. (He looks at camera – raises his eyes to heaven in despair.)*

*Cut to the house.*
*(Blanche, still in bikini, carrying her dress, strolls up to the door. As she approaches, Pike rushes round the corner.)*

**PIKE:**
Miss Blanche! Quick! Come round to the vegetable garden.

**BLANCHE:**
I've told you, Pike, it's all over between us.

**PIKE:**
No, no, not that Miss Blanche – the gardeners! Oh, it's terrible! Terrible!

*(RC arrives on the scene and joins them. He carries a stuffed fish in a glass case.)*

**BLANCHE:**
What's that?

**CHARLEY:**
Old Jack gave it to me. What's happened?

**PIKE:**
Oh, it's terrible!

**BLANCHE:**
Come on!

*(They all run round the corner to the vegetable garden. We see a pair of gardener's legs sticking out of the soil. They react in horror. We cut to their point of view – wider. There are about eight or nine pairs of legs sticking out of the ground in rows, like plants.)*

**CHARLEY:**
All murdered. Buried alive.

*(A close-up of Blanche, looking guilty.)*

**VOICE OVER:**
Only Blanche knew the answer to that question.

*(Cut to Malone's head, half submerged in waves. A seagull perches on his head.)*

**VOICE OVER:**
Had she deliberately left him there to die? What was the significance of the seagull? Would Malone get the message? The fish that Old Jack had given to Charley – was it a red herring? *(A close-up of the fish held by RC. It winks.)* Only one thing was

certain – there would be very little sleep for anyone that night.

*A long shot of the gardeners' feet.*

*Caption: next week – "Dead Men's Shoes"*

# EPISODE FIVE

*Titles.*

**VOICE OVER:**
The latest disaster to hit Brimstone Grange, scene of many a gory murder in the past week, was the mass murder of the gardeners – buried in their own vegetable patch. Neither Piggy Malone, our fat hero, or the undaunted Charley Farley, his assistant, had been at the scene of the crime.

*Cut to Blanche. (Surveying the scene of horror, she faints gracefully.)*

**VOICE OVER:**
It was too much for the hot-blooded but highly strung Blanche. She collapsed on the ground in a dead faint.

*(Malone, now completely dressed, rushes in, takes in the scene, talks rapidly with RC.)*

**VOICE OVER:**
Malone and Charley knew there was only one thing to do – get back to the house as quickly as possible.

*(Malone tries to pick up Blanche. RC eventually helps him. Malone carries her off on his own. He staggers, falls and they both lie there on the ground. RC rushes up. He tries to pick up Blanche, half gets her up then falls backwards, her on top. She recovers, looks resigned, then she picks up Malone and gives him a fireman's lift. Wide shot to show she is also dragging RC by his coat. She strides out towards the house like a true amazon.)*

*Cut to Blanche's bedroom.*

*(All three are lying on their backs on Blanche's bed. Blanche has now changed into a tight-fitting cat-suit.)*

**VOICE OVER:**
Three hours later, they were still no nearer to solving the mystery. Malone had suggested that they all relax and make their minds a blank – a method he had used with some success ever since his early school days – and in this, they had found the beautifully-built Blanche more than co-operative.

*Close-up of Blanche.*

**BLANCHE:**
Whose turn is it?

**CHARLEY:**
I think it's Malone's – but he's asleep.

**BLANCHE:**
*(turns to Malone, he sleeps.)* Then it's your turn again. If you like.

**CHARLEY:**
Would you like?

**BLANCHE:**
I don't mind – if you think it helps.

**CHARLEY:**
*(thoughtfully)* I think it does.

**BLANCHE:**
*(looking at him)* Fine. OK?

**CHARLEY:**
OK. I spy with my little eye, something beginning with "T".

**BLANCHE:**
*(suddenly getting up)* Otto!

**CHARLEY:**
No. That begins with "O". These begin with "T".

**BLANCHE:**
It must be Otto! The murderer!

**CHARLEY:**
What makes you say that?

**BLANCHE:**
Look, Charley, there's only him left. And Pike the butler.

**CHARLEY:**
How about young Billy Brimstone and his brand-new blushing bride, Brenda? They're still alive and kicking.

**BLANCHE:**
How do you know?

**CHARLEY:**
They're in the room next to mine.

*(He waves his arm across her, indicating his room. He accidentally brushes against her.)*

**BLANCHE:**
That's my point.

**CHARLEY:**
Oh, sorry.

**BLANCHE:**
No, I mean that's exactly what I mean. Otto is insanely jealous of Billy. He's always been in love with Brenda – everybody knows that.

**CHARLEY:**
I didn't.

**BLANCHE:**
No, I mean everybody who is anybody. I think we should keep a very close eye on Herr Otto Van Danzer! Remember – he's a crack shot!

*Cut to: a row of eight bottles on a wall. (They shatter, one by one, until only one is left.)*

*Cut to: Otto with a peashooter. (He shoots another pea. The last bottle falls. He looks satisfied. He sees something and suddenly looks insanely jealous)*

*Cut to: RC as Billy and his bride Brenda are walking towards the woods. (They carry a*

*picnic basket and travelling rug. Otto ducks down from sight as he follows the happy pair. He carries a shot gun – close-up – dramatic music.)*

**VOICE OVER:**
And so it was, that on that gloomy (or bright) afternoon, a strange game of chess was to play itself out – and the overweight detective and his fearful assistant, Charley, were to find themselves mere pawns in a deadly battle for survival.

*Cut to RB and RC : standing by a cottage watching Otto following Billy and Brenda. (They creep after him. A milkman sees the detectives creeping about. He looks puzzled. Otto creeps through the undergrowth.)*

*(RB and RC creep through the bushes. They creep into frame, stop by a tree and creep out again. The milkman creeps into frame then and follows them out.)*

*(Billy and Brenda are walking along. They see another couple coming towards them. They smile. As the other couple pass, Billy and Brenda turn to look at them, turn, look surprised, giggle. We see retreating couple – she has her dress tucked in her knickers and he has his shirt tails hanging out.)*

*(We see Otto approaching a low wire fence with a notice near it. It says "cattle, control-electrified fence". Otto starts to put one leg over it. Close-up of his riding boots. As the leg comes down the other side, the wheels of his spurs go whizzing round with a loud electrical buzzing, and a yell of pain comes from Otto. He leaps off quickly.)*

*(Billy and Brenda are setting up their picnic. Billy is blowing up two large plastic chairs. Brenda kisses him. As she does so, we hear a strange squeaking noise as the air escapes from the blow-up armchair. He then has to start blowing it up all over again.)*

*(Otto watches from behind a tree. Piggy and Charley watch from the long grass nearby.)*

*(The milkman watches from inside a bush. A*

*rather bedraggled housewife comes into his shot.)*

**HOUSEWIFE:**
*(whispering)* You didn't give me my change!

**MILKMAN:**
Oh, sorry madam. *(Gives her change. She crawls out of shot.)*

*(The picnic – Billy and Brenda, with cups of tea and plenty of dainty sandwiches, are about to sit on their blow-up armchairs. They do so. Two loud pops. The chairs deflate rapidly.)*

*Cut to: Otto, gleeful, pea shooter in hand.*

*Close-up of Billy eating. (A gypsy violin is heard. Widen to include Brenda. They look at each other lovingly. We cut wider still and see Otto dressed as a gypsy violinist, approaching. He walks round them, serenading them in the usual manner. They take very little interest in him, then Billy notices his spurs and leaps up.)*

**BILLY:**
Stop! You're an impostor! You're Otto Van Danzer – I recognised your spurs.

**OTTO:**
So! You have discovered my secret. *(Makes a grab for Brenda.)* I'm taking your pretty young wife with me. I warn you, if you try to follow me, she will die.

**BILLY:**
You – you German pig!

*(Sits on ground.)*

**OTTO:**
*(dropping Brenda immediately)* You dare to call me names? I demand satisfaction.

*(He throws down his glove. It lands in a large gateau. RC picks it up, slaps RB's face with it, leaving a lot of jam on the face.)*

*(We see the detectives watching, as is the milkman. Billy and Otto go off for the duel.)*

**VOICE OVER:**
So Otto Van Danzer, a recognised crack-shot, was to fight a duel with young Billy Brimstone, a man whose inaccuracy was well known. Even at his London club he had never once got his umbrella into the stand at the first attempt.

*(We see Brenda clearing up the picnic, tearful. She throws sandwiches into the bushes. We see Malone rummaging around, finding a sandwich and eating it. Over this, two pistol shots. He stops munching. He and Charley run off in the direction of the shots.)*

*(Another clearing: Malone, Charley, the milkman and Brenda all appear from the bushes. They look horrified. Billy lies dead on the ground. Otto appears to be standing to attention, gun in hand. Blanche also now appears from the bushes with a bunch of primroses. She gasps, runs forward to Otto and touches him. He falls forward revealing a noticeboard against which he was propped up. It reads "please do not throw stones at this notice".)*

**VOICE OVER:**
What did it mean? Had they really killed each other? Or was that strange noticeboard merely part of the killer's fiendish sense of humour? And what was Blanche doing in the woods? Had she gone there simply to pick her nosegay? *(Shot of Malone and Charley approaching Blanche.)* Malone intended to find out. One thing was certain – there would be very little sleep for Malone that night.

*Caption: next week – Episode Six "No Flowers by Request".*

# EPISODE SIX

*Titles, shots from previous episodes.*

**VOICE OVER:**
The latest victims, done to death in the
continuing gory story of Brimstone
Grange, were none other than young Billy
Brimstone, who had been married for
only a fortnight – what the Sunday papers
would describe as a two-week bridegroom
– and Otto Van Danzer, oily German
crack-shot, and hitherto chief suspect in
this bizarre affair. Piggy Malone, second-
rate private eye and inveterate glutton,
and his more fastidious but equally
pathetic assistant, Charley Farley, had
witnessed the whole affair and spent a
long time at police headquarters, helping
the police with their enquiries.

*(Mix to police car arriving at Brimstone
Grange. Piggy and Charley get out, with sacks
over their heads. They bid a muffled "cheerio"
to the police driver.)*

**POLICEMAN:**
Oh! Er – could we have our sacks back,
please. They're my mum's ones she keeps
for the onions.

**PIGGY:**
Oh yes, certainly.

**CHARLEY:**
Sorry.

*(They hand back the sacks. A third person has
got out of the car with a sack on. The
policeman spots this.)*

**POLICEMAN:**
No, you don't get out here Mrs Parsons –
we're not at your house yet.

**MRS P:**
Oh.

*(She is helped back into the car. It drives off.
Piggy and Charley wave it off.)*

**PIGGY:**
Come on – let's go in.

**CHARLEY:**
Wait, chief – you realise there's only Miss
Blanche left? And Pike, the butler?

**PIGGY:**
*(dramatic)* You mean …

**CHARLEY:**
*(dramatic)* Exactly!

**PIGGY:**
What?

**CHARLEY:**
What?

**PIGGY:**
What do you mean?

**CHARLEY:**
How do you mean?

**PIGGY:**
You said "Exactly".

**CHARLEY:**
I meant "exactly what you were going to
say".

**PIGGY:**
I wasn't going to say anything.

**CHARLEY:**
Oh. Well, what I was going to say was, the
murderer must be Pike, the butler.

**PIGGY:**
Or Blanche.

**CHARLEY:**
Exactly.

**PIGGY:**
I suggest we approach them both with
caution.

**CHARLEY:**
Right.

*(They stealthily open the door.)*

*Cut to: inside house.*

*(Dramatic suspense music, played mostly on violins, sawing away as the two detectives creep round the house. We cut to a shot of them spotting something. Their eyes widen. Cut to what they see–)*

*(A curtained alcove. We see the toes of three pairs of feet protruding from beneath the curtain. One moves slightly. Charley grabs a heavy brass ornament to use as a club, as Malone cautiously approaches. His point of view as we move in – a sort of "Psycho" feeling – the violins screeching away. Malone's hand comes into shot, grabs the curtain. He pulls it aside. The camera does a fast pan down to three violinists, scraping away like mad. They are sitting on chairs. They stop, raggedly, as they are discovered.)*

**PIGGY:**
What the devil are you doing here?

**1ST VIOLIN:**
Oh, er – we're rehearsing. For the musical evening tonight.

**CHARLEY:**
Musical evening? What musical evening?

**1ST VIOLIN:**
Miss Blanche always has a musical evening on the first Thursday of the month. She loves anything musical.

**CHARLEY:**
Does she, indeed. I must show her my cigarette box.

*(Blanche enters, in a ravishing evening gown.)*

**BLANCHE:**
Ah, gentlemen – you're back.

**PIGGY:**
Is it true, madam, that you are holding a concert here tonight?

**BLANCHE:**
Yes – but never mind that now. Come to my bedroom. I've got something to show you that will make you go hot and cold.

*(She goes.)*

*(The two men look at each other. Then both make a rush for it through the door.)*

Cut to: close-up of letter. *(Piggy is reading it. They are all in Blanche's bedroom.)*

**PIGGY:**
*(reading aloud)* "I am out to get you. I will kill you like I killed all the others. You will die a horrible death, I promise you. Very best wishes, Anonymous" … Do you know this man?

**BLANCHE:**
It can only be from Pike. He's the only one left.

**PIGGY:**
And yourself, of course, madam.

**BLANCHE:**
But I wouldn't threaten my own life!

**CHARLEY:**
No, chief, stands to reason. Otherwise, if she continued to ignore the note, she'd be forced to kill herself.

**PIGGY:**
Exactly! She could commit suicide and make it look like murder! That would incriminate Pike and she would get away scot-free!

**BLANCHE:**
Except I'd be dead.

**PIGGY:**
True. I see. Right – anybody else got any ideas?

**CHARLEY:**
Where is Pike?

**BLANCHE:**
I haven't seen him all day. You don't think he's hiding somewhere, do you?

**CHARLEY:**
Wherever he is, whatever he's doing, Miss

Blanche, one thing is certain. From now on, neither of us must leave your side for a moment. Ever.

*Cut immediately to a shower curtain, with water spraying onto it. We pull back as we hear all three of them singing "Raindrops Keep Falling on my Head" and giggling and splashing about, all very happy. We can vaguely see three shapes.*

**BLANCHE'S VOICE:**
Well, what shall we all do today? Any ideas?

**PIGGY'S VOICE:**
Could all go to the pictures.

**BLANCHE'S VOICE:**
Oh yes – what's on at the local, anyone know?

**CHARLEY'S VOICE:**
The Hitchcock picture – you know – *Psycho.*

*(Suddenly, the camera, which has been slowly moving round the room, picks up someone's head coming into view. Shock stuff. It is in silhouette – rather heavy. Cut to reverse angle – it is a stuffed gorilla, on which are draped the three bathers' clothes. It looks very unfrightening, from the front.)*

**VOICE OVER:**
The two detectives worked tirelessly to safeguard the life of the splendidly-proportioned Blanche. And it was here that Charley Farley, failed undergraduate, was to shine – bringing his keen mind to bear on the problem of a foolproof warning system. Malone was content merely to look in occasionally, and receive a progress report.

*(We see Charley working at a table with drawings, ruler, etc. Blanche joins him, looking over his shoulder. Then a shot of Malone approaching Blanche's bedroom.)*

*Cut inside. (He opens the door. A bag of flour bursts over his head.) Cut to Charley, pleased.*

**CHARLEY:**
Well, that works alright.

**PIGGY:**
Yes, it's very good.

**CHARLEY:**
Ah!

**PIGGY:**
Exactly. Where's the string?

*(Charley hands him the string, then various shots of them both winding string round table legs, under chairs, etc. Music. General documentary feel.)*

**PIGGY:**
That's more like it.

*(He is surrounded by string.)*

**CHARLEY:**
Yes. Now, how are you going to get out?

**PIGGY:**
Er. Don't worry, I'll go through this door and come round.

*(He goes out of the door.)*

*Cut to Charley, waiting. (He looks thoughtful. The door opens, Piggy enters and is hit by the flour again.)*

**PIGGY:**
Hm.

*(Mix to: even more strings everywhere. Piggy by the door, Charley by the other door.)*

**CHARLEY:**
Right. That's definitely got everything wired up. OK. Go out and try it, chief.

**PIGGY:**
No, no, no, you go out and try it. Go on.

**CHARLEY:**
Oh. Alright.

*(He exits. Shot of Piggy by the main door,*

*waiting. Shot of Charley entering other door. Shot of Piggy, being hit by the flour again.)*

**PIGGY:**
Hm.

*(Fade out – fade in. All the strings are gone, the room is free of flour. RB and RC sit either side of the door, with a poker.)*

**CHARLEY:**
I suppose this is simpler.

**PIGGY:**
Definitely. Mind you, it means we've got to sit up all night.

**CHARLEY:**
I'm ready to do anything to protect Miss Blanche. Where is she, by the way?

**PIGGY:**
She's er – *(looking concerned)* The last time I …

*(They both look at each other in alarm, then rush out of the door.)*

*(The corridor outside Blanche's bedroom – Piggy and Charley rush out and bump into Pike, who is outside the door.)*

**PIGGY:**
Ah – where is Miss Blanche, my good man?

**PIKE:**
I'm not sure, sir.

**PIGGY:**
Then search for her, man! Her life has been threatened.

**PIKE:**
Yes, sir.

*(He hurries off, round a corner. The two detectives walk down the corridor. A couple of paces, then RC stops RB.)*

**CHARLEY:**
Hang on, chief.

**PIGGY:**
What?

**CHARLEY:**
That was Pike!

**PIGGY:**
Good God! After him!

*(They rush back, look round the corner. Cut to their point of view: an empty corridor.)*

**CHARLEY:**
Disappeared. I suggest we search for Miss Blanche, chief. We must get to her before he does!

*(Cut to the grounds. RC and RB walking, looking.)*

**VOICE OVER:**
It was three hours later when they finally found her.

*Cut to a lawn and some bushes. We see a pair of female legs, naked, lying behind a bush. Reaction of RC and RB. They rush forward. Cut to reverse angle Blanche, in brief shorts, lying on tummy behind the bush, on the lawn, reading.*

**BLANCHE:**
Hello, boys.

**CHARLEY:**
Oh, Miss Blanche! I'm so glad we've found you. I've been so worried – when I saw your legs lying on the grass, I didn't know where to put myself!

**BLANCHE:**
Naughty boy!

**PIGGY:**
I don't want to alarm you, madam, but Pike is back.

**BLANCHE:**
I know. I've seen him. I think he's quite harmless.

**PIGGY:**
You may do, but I'd still like to have a word with him.

**BLANCHE:**
*(getting up)* Well, let's all go and look for him.

**PIGGY:**
Any idea where we should look?

**BLANCHE:**
Well, where would you expect a butler to be? I should think he's probably hanging around the kitchen.

*Cut immediately to Pike, a rope round his neck, hanging in the kitchen. A stool overturned, Pike's legs hanging down in foreground of shot.*

*Cut to dining room. (Blanche, RB and RC enter.)*

**PIGGY:**
I suggest you get him in here at once.

**BLANCHE:**
Very well – I'll ring for him.

*(She pulls bell rope.)*

*Cut to kitchen – the legs dangling as before. They rise up, out of frame. Cut back to Blanche – she lets go of rope. Cut back to kitchen – the legs drop back into frame.*

**VOICE OVER:**
So the butler didn't do it, after all. And if he didn't, then who was the mysterious killer who lurked unseen in the dim corridors of Brimstone Grange?

*Cut back to dining room. They wait. Then close-ups of Blanche, Charley and Piggy.*

**VOICE OVER:**
Piggy Malone and Charley Farley had already agreed to sleep in Blanche's bedroom to protect her. Or was it to protect each other?
One thing was certain – there would be very little sleep for anyone that night.

*Caption: next week – "Two Flies in Her Parlour"*

# EPISODE SEVEN

*Titles, shots from previous episodes.*

**VOICE OVER:**
The trail of death and destruction that had dogged the footsteps of our overweight hero, Piggy Malone, and his much maligned assistant, Charley Farley, continued relentlessly. The beautiful Blanche Brimstone, who was admired throughout the country and whose puppies had won prizes at Crufts, was now the only surviving member of the household. The latest victim of the killer was Pike, the butler … *(cut to Pike's legs hanging in the kitchen)* … who had been discovered in the kitchen, hanging from the bell rope. *(Cut to dining room. They ring for him. Cut to kitchen. His legs go up on the rope.)* Piggy Malone eventually located the body and returned to the dining room, where Blanche and Charley waited anxiously.

*Cut to the dining room. Blanche and Charley in a passionate clinch on the sofa as Piggy enters. Cut to after Piggy has broken the news.*

**BLANCHE:**
He was obviously preparing dinner when it happened. The rest of the staff left days ago. It's terrible. Terrible! What are we going to do?

**CHARLEY:**
Well, we could eat out.

**PIGGY:**
Yes, that's true.

**BLANCHE:**
No, no – don't worry – I'll prepare dinner. You stay here and rest.

You must be worn out, poor things.

*(She exits.)*

**CHARLEY:**
Do you think we should let her go on her own, chief?

**PIGGY:**
We'll have to risk it, Charley. I'm starving. Anyway, I want to talk to you. Why would anyone want to kill Pike? Surely he wouldn't inherit the money?

**CHARLEY:**
Could be another motive entirely, chief? *(Picks up briefcase.)* I've taken the liberty of making out one of my charts. *(He removes a large piece of paper from the briefcase. It is folded many times.)* This shows all the suspects, with cross-references to all their motives, and opportunities to commit all the various crimes.

*(He unfolds it – it gets bigger and bigger – RB helps him. Eventually they fix it to the wall. It is 12 feet by 6' 9".)*

**CHARLEY:**
You'll notice I've used code words so nobody can understand it, chief, should it fall into the wrong hands.

**PIGGY:**
Good work. I presume you can understand it, can you?

**CHARLEY:**
Oh, yes. It's all in my head. Now with this column, we have the various methods of death that could be used: Balloons, Trouble and Strife, Glug glug glug, Gardens of Babylon, etc; then on this column …

**PIGGY:**
Hang on. What do all those mean?

**CHARLEY:**
Oh, sorry – Balloons, that means blown up. I mean, a balloon is blown up, isn't it? Then Trouble and Strike – that's knife.

Glug glug glug – that's drowning. And Gardens of Babylon – hanging. Hanging Gardens of Babylon, see? It's all quite simple.

**PIGGY:**
What's this – "potatoes"?

**CHARLEY:**
Eh? Oh, that means nothing.

**PIGGY:**
Nothing?

**CHARLEY:**
That's just a space. If I've got any empty spaces, I just fill them up with potatoes.

**PIGGY:**
Oh, I see. And you reckon this chart is going to show us who's been doing the murders?

**CHARLEY:**
I think you'll find if we study it for long enough, yes. Sooner or later, the killer will emerge.

*(A close-up of Charley as he says this. A tearing sound. We cut to a wider shot of chart – Blanche has opened the door behind the chart and walked in, giving the effect of stepping through the chart. Dramatic music.)*

**BLANCHE:**
Dinner will be ready in fifteen minutes. I'm sorry – did I interrupt something?

**PIGGY:**
No, madam – your entrance was very timely. Very timely indeed.

**BLANCHE:**
Oh, good. Perhaps you'd like to open a bottle of wine.

*(She goes again.)*

**PIGGY:**
Good God! Why didn't we think of that before? Blanche Brimstone! Of course!

**CHARLEY:**
You mean – she committed these horrible crimes?

**PIGGY:**
Why not?

**CHARLEY:**
But what makes you think it's her?

**PIGGY:**
Motive, opportunity – they're all there. But there's one reason that outweighs all the others, Charley.

**CHARLEY:**
What's that?

**PIGGY:**
She's the only one that's not dead.

**CHARLEY:**
That's true. So. We've been fooled all the way along. Nothing but a big front.

**PIGGY:**
Just a series of boobs.

**CHARLEY:**
It sticks out a mile when you think about it.

**PIGGY:**
I don't know how she keeps it up. Look, Charley, there's a couple of points I'd like to discuss.

**CHARLEY:**
I thought we were discussing them.

**PIGGY:**
No – what I mean is, dinner. You realise, of course, that it is in fifteen minutes?

**CHARLEY:**
Good grief! And she's preparing it, with her own fair hands!

**PIGGY:**
Ever heard of poison?

**CHARLEY:**
Oh, my God! And we've got to eat it – otherwise she'll suspect something.

**PIGGY:**
Exactly! I wonder what devilish concoction her warped mind is going to produce?

*Cut to a plate of baked beans. (Blanche hands the plate to Piggy.)*

**BLANCHE:**
There we are, Mr Malone. Eat them all up, make you a big boy!

**PIGGY:**
*(reluctantly)* No – that's far too many – you have those, I'll have yours.

*(He gives her his beans. They are sitting in a line, on one side of the table. They all have a plate of beans in front of them.)*

**BLANCHE:**
Nonsense! I wouldn't hear of it.

*(She returns Piggy's plate to him. While she is doing so, Charley steals hers and puts his plate in front of her.)*

**PIGGY:**
Please! I insist – they give me indigestion.

*(he puts his plate in front of her, taking her plate, which was Charley's)*

**BLANCHE:**
Oh, very well. *(Then, to Charley)* You like beans, do you, Charley?

**CHARLEY:**
*(thinking he's got the unpoisoned plate)* Oh yes.

**BLANCHE:**
Then you have this large helping.

*(Swaps plates with Charley.)*

**CHARLEY:**
I say, chief.

**PIGGY:**
Yes?

**CHARLEY:**
I think you've got the plate that I started with.

**PIGGY:**
Oh, really? Sorry.

*(They swap quickly. They both look satisfied and laugh, uneasily – each thinking they've got Blanche's plate.)*

**BLANCHE:**
Well, let's eat – they'll be getting cold. *(They all tuck in, heartily.)* You know, isn't it silly? I've got my own plate back. I remember the little crack on the side.

*(Reaction – mouths full, alarmed.)*

**BLANCHE:**
Come on, eat up. There's plenty more.

**VOICE OVER:**
And so our two pathetic heroes ate a frightening three-course meal of beans, beans, and more beans … *(mix to the three of them with coffee cups)* … they all retired to bed, with indigestion, whilst outside, fog began to build up in the channel.

*(Shot of door marked "WC" – liner's fog horn sound over.*
*Cut to the bedroom. The two men, with their suitcases on Blanche's bed, unpacking.)*

**PIGGY:**
Well, I'm not sleeping with her.

**CHARLEY:**
Well, I'm not. I'm having the camp bed.

**PIGGY:**
Oh no, that's my camp bed. I'm having that. You'll have to go in with her.

**CHARLEY:**
Look, it was me who took the trouble to lug the camp bed all the way up here. "Why take a camp bed to a large country

mansion?", you said. "It's like taking coals to Newcastle", you said. Well, now your coal has come home to roost, so you can put that in your pipe and smoke it. You've burned your boats and I'm going to lie in it. So there.

*(Blanche has entered, in a very feminine fluffy negligée.)*

**BLANCHE:**
What's going on, boys?

**PIGGY:**
Oh, we were just arguing about who's going to sleep with you.

**BLANCHE:**
Oh. Why not both of you? It's a very big bed – there's plenty of room for all of us. You did say you'd protect me!

**CHARLEY:**
Oh, oh dear. I'm sorry, but I can't. I haven't brought any pyjamas. Look.

*(Indicates his suitcase.)*

**PIGGY:**
What?

**CHARLEY:**
You've got yours, I see, chief. It'll have to be you.

**PIGGY:**
Now hang on–

**BLANCHE:**
Don't worry – I know what we can do. Come with me, both of you.

*(She ushers them into the bathroom. Piggy, with his pyjamas in hand, glares at Charley as they go through the door.)*

**BLANCHE'S VOICE:**
*(off)* Now, give me that. You take that, you have that – and I'll have this – there. There we are.

*(Rustle of clothing throughout the speech,*

*then Blanche emerges, dressed in Piggy's pyjama top only. It is big enough to cover what is necessary.)*

**BLANCHE:**
*(over her shoulder)* I like wearing men's pyjama tops. Don't you find it attractive, Charley?

**CHARLEY:**
*(off)* It would be all the same if I did, wouldn't it? *(Cut to Charley, who enters, wearing Piggy's pyjama bottoms. They come all the way up to his neck. The drawstring is, in fact, tied round his neck. His arms are inside the legs.)* I couldn't do much about it in this lot.

**BLANCHE:**
I think they look adorable, don't you, Mr Malone?

*Cut to Malone, who is wearing Blanche's negligée.*

**PIGGY:**
Don't ask me. Look, I feel ridiculous in this.

**BLANCHE:**
It's all in a good cause. Come on, into bed.

**CHARLEY:**
Could someone give me a hand?

*(They lift Charley into bed. Malone gets in, but Blanche hesitates.)*

**BLANCHE:**
I'll just clean my teeth. Shan't be a moment.

*(She exits to adjoining bathroom.)*

**PIGGY:**
*(when she has gone)* Why have you got your hands inside the trousers? If she attacks you, you're defenceless.

**CHARLEY:**
Oh no, I'm not. I'm holding a blunt instrument inside here.

**PIGGY:**
What is it?

**CHARLEY:**
A brass candlestick. Have you got the automatic?

**PIGGY:**
Yes, it's tucked in my matching briefs. What do you reckon she's doing in there?

*Cut to bathroom. A close-up – striped toothpaste going onto a toothbrush. Shot of Blanche, brushing her teeth. Cut back to bedroom.*

**PIGGY:**
We'd better put her in the middle, Charley.

**CHARLEY:**
Right, chief – then we shall know where she is. Anyway, I'm not sleeping next to you. Not in that nightie.

**PIGGY:**
Don't be so daft – I wouldn't …

*(There is a crash from the bathroom as if some jars or bottles have fallen into the washbasin.)*

**PIGGY:**
What's that?

*(They both rush out of bed, RC still with his arms inside trousers. They exit into bathroom. We cut inside. They stare in horror at Blanche lying there, dead in the empty bath, her legs over the side. She clutches the tube of toothpaste. Dramatic music.)*

*Mix to the dining room.*
*(Both men are dressed again. RC sits in a high-backed chair, RB at dining table. They are both facing away from the door.)*

**PIGGY:**
Poisoned. No doubt about it. But how?

**CHARLEY:**
Exactly.

**PIGGY:**
We all ate the beans, then we all drank the coffee – and after that, no one ate or drank anything.

*Cut to the door.*
*(The handle turns slowly. The door opens about two inches. Cut back to Malone, unaware of this.)*

**PIGGY:**
We all came to bed, then she went to clean her teeth and – my God! The toothpaste!

*(A close-up of Malone as he realises. Then a voice, out of vision, says –)*

**PROFESSOR:**
Precisely. The poison was in the stripes.

*Cut to the Professor, who died in the first episode. (He looks very much alive now and holds a pistol in his hand.)*

**PIGGY:**
*(staring)* Professor! But – but you're dead!

*(Charley is hidden by the high-backed chair.)*

**PROFESSOR:**
It would appear not.

*(Reaction on Charley – he cowers in his chair.)*

**VOICE OVER:**
So the Professor had not died after all. Piggy Malone was stunned. Charley Farley's brain began to race – had the Professor seen him? Where had he left his blunt instrument? Why hadn't he followed his mother's advice and become a window dresser?

*(A shot of the professor sitting down opposite Malone at the dining table. The gun is still pointing at Malone.)*

**VOICE OVER:**
One thing was certain – there would be very little sleep for anyone that night.

*Caption: next week – "The Final Act"*

# EPISODE EIGHT

*Titles, shots from previous episodes.*

**VOICE OVER:**
The final act in the terrifying saga of Brimstone Grange was about to unfold itself. Piggy Malone, a pitifully boring, over-fed private eye, and his equally pathetic, underweight assistant, Charley Farley, had at last come face to face with the homicidal maniac who had murdered ten people in six days – a new British all-comers record. The fiendish Professor Amos Brimstone held them at gunpoint while he indulged in an orgy of self-confession, a popular pastime among murderers the world over. There seems to be no escape … One slim chance lay open to Charley … *(Cut to wide shot wherein we see that Charley is hidden from view by the wing-back chair.)* … it was just possible that the Professor hadn't seen him. It was a risk he had to take.

*(Charley starts to slide out of his chair without being seen.)*

*Cut to the Professor and Piggy at the dining table.*

**PROFESSOR:**
Yes, I did it. I killed them all – partly for the money – but mainly, simply because I enjoyed it. I've always wanted to know what it felt like to kill someone. Now I know. It's a nice feeling, Malone.

**PIGGY:**
You're off your bloody head. That gun's not loaded.

**PROFESSOR:**
You think not?

*(The pistol comes up into shot and fires past Piggy's ear. Cut to the other side of the wing*

chair – a bullet hole through the back of the chair. Piggy gets up, terrified that Charley has been shot. Charley isn't in the chair. Cut to Charley waving from under the table. Piggy sees him and pretends to be examining the bullet hole as he takes a visiting card out of his pocket and writes three words on it. As he returns to the table, he drops it near Charley, who picks it up and reads the words "Tie shoelaces together".

**PIGGY:**
That's a pretty nasty hole you've made in that armchair, Professor. If anyone had been sitting there, it could have been nasty.

**PROFESSOR:**
But there wasn't, was there? Which reminds me – where's that obnoxious assistant of your's – Mr Farley? I thought he never left your side.

**PIGGY:**
Well, he, er, he has to sometimes, doesn't he? He's only human. He'll be back in a minute. It never takes him very long.

(Cut to Charley tying the Professor's laces together, then cut back to Professor.)

**PROFESSOR:**
Well, you may rest assured I will be ready for him, Mr Malone.

**PIGGY:**
But the door's behind you, my dear Professor.

(Cut to Charley – he has finished the shoe laces. He pokes his head out from under the cloth and tugs at Piggy's trousers. Piggy looks down.)

**CHARLEY:**
(whispering) OK.

**PROFESSOR:**
(alarmed) What was that?

(He looks round at door.)

(Piggy, catching the Professor off guard, knocks the gun out of his hand. It slithers down the dining table and crashes off the end.)

**PIGGY:**
(triumphant) Now, Professor – it's you against me. We'll just see who can run the fastest!

(Both men leap up. The Professor runs off out of door. Piggy minces after him with his shoe laces tied together.)

**PIGGY:**
(furious) Not my shoelaces, you damn fool!

(Charley emerges from under table. They argue pathetically.)

Cut to a car driving away from the Grange at speed.

**VOICE OVER:**
And so the wily Professor escapes for the moment, the clutches of the law. But Piggy and Charley were not beaten yet …

(Mix to Piggy's London office. The two of them are on the phone. Miss Whizzer is pouring tea. Piggy is eating sandwiches.)

Back in London, they discovered that the mad Professor was on the board of a well-known chemical company. They accordingly made plans to waylay him when he attended the next board meeting, at the firm's head office in Southall the following Friday. (Mix to very tall office block. Cut to sign – "Brimstone Chemicals ltd, 14th floor".) They rendezvoused at the head office the day before, and finalised their scheme.

Cut to Piggy and Charley entering building, walking past sign, into lift and out. The number 14 is on a notice by the lift door.

**PIGGY:**
Now, this is my scheme. We change all the numbers of the floors so that when he

arrives and takes the lift to the 14th floor, he will get out and see it marked 15th. Now, he will simply walk down the stairs to the floor below, which is unoccupied. And we'll be waiting for him.

**CHARLEY:**
But why change all the numbers on all the floors?

**PIGGY:**
So that he's confused and will naturally get back into the lift and start again. That way we'll make sure he eventually gets out at the right floor. The right floor for us, that is.

**CHARLEY:**
Exactly. It's a marvellous scheme, chief. However did you think it up?

**PIGGY:**
It was in a film on telly last night. Right – we'd better get started.

*(They each get out a screwdriver and start to remove the floor number board from the wall.)*

**VOICE OVER:**
And so the trap was laid. Next morning, at precisely 10.57am, the mad Professor, brutal killer of almost a dozen people, walked sedately to a board meeting of the Brimstone Chemical Company – completely unaware of the net that was closing inexorably around him.

*Cut to the Professor walking in through the doors. He carries an umbrella. Cut to Charley, hiding behind something, watching.*

**VOICE OVER:**
With split-second timing, Malone was about to take his place on the floor below. *(Shot of Malone, inside lift.)* Fate, however, was about to take a hand, in the shape of Dulcie Latimer – typist.

*Cut to Piggy's point of view. Dulcie is bending down, lifting tray of coffees from floor, knickers in evidence. Malone stares.*

**DULCIE:**
Could you hold the lift, please. *(She straightens up and enters lift with tray.)* 17th, please.

*(Malone looks annoyed, but presses button. Dulcie smiles at him, warmly.)*

*Cut to 17th floor – it says "15th". The lift door opens. Dulcie comes out, stares at notice.*

**DULCIE:**
This says 15th floor.

**PIGGY:**
Ah – that's wrong. This is the top floor, 17th.

**DULCIE:**
Oh. Could you open this door for me?

*(Indicating office door.)*

**PIGGY:**
Er – all right. *(He leaps from the lift, opens the door, the lift doors close. He just fails to get back in.)* Damn.

**DULCIE:**
Thanks.

*(She goes.)*

*(Close-up of Piggy's annoyance. Shot of professor getting in lift.)*

*(Back to Piggy waiting by lift. Door open. He steps in as Professor steps out. They both do a take … but the doors close before either of them can do anything about it. Close-up of Malone. He waits for doors to open. They do. He peers out. Umbrella comes into shot and hits him on the head. The Professor leaps upon him. They struggle as lift doors close on them.)*

*(Inside lift – they fight. The Professor swings at Piggy with the umbrella. Close-up of the umbrella hitting the floor indicator sign. It smashes. Another swipe at Piggy.)*

*Cut to a door opposite the lift. Sign on door*

*says "Magnifique Model Agency Ltd". (Five girls in bikinis and heavy eye make-up come out and wait for the lift. It arrives. Doors open. Piggy and the Professor seem to be behaving quite normally as the girls get in.)*

*(Inside lift – the doors close. They are unable to fight. The lift stops.)*

*(Outside lift – the girls get out.)*

*(Inside lift – the doors close. RB and RC leap on each other once again.)*

*(Outside lift – floor number 6. A little old lady waits. Lift arrives. Doors open. RB and RC on floor of lift, fighting. Reaction of old lady.)*

*(Inside the lift – the old lady watches the doors close, unable to get in. RB and RC continue to roll around the floor. The doors open and close very quickly as a man bends down to pick up a large cardboard box. We just glimpse him before the doors shut. The men fight. Door opens. The little old lady belts the staggering professor with her umbrella. Knocks him back into the lift again. The doors shut before she can get in. They fight.)*

*(Outside the lift – the man with the cardboard box is just putting it down. The lift doors open. He quickly picks it up and tries to get into the lift. The doors squeeze the box and lots of tins of peas fall out of the bottom of it.)*

*(Inside the lift – the doors close and the man has to remove the box. The men fight.)*

*(Outside the lift – close-up of the old lady, waiting. As the doors open, she leaps in on top of the fighting men.)*

*(Inside the lift – the doors close. The Professor lunges at Piggy with his umbrella like a sword. Piggy side-steps, umbrella point goes into wall panel, smashing it. Sparks everywhere, terrible whining lift noise. The men, and the old lady, all lurch and fall over.)*

*(Outside lift – floor number 3 – lift doors partly open and close once again, very quickly. This happens over several other floors – 15,*

*then 2, then 11, then 1. When they reach number 17, this time the doors open fully and the two men and the old lady stagger out. The old lady staggers back in again and the doors close. Piggy recovers, grabs the umbrella and gets to his feet just as the Professor sits up.)*

**PIGGY:**
Have you had enough?

**PROFESSOR:**
It was the lift that beat me – not you, my friend. I never could stand very high speeds. That's the trouble with the world today – speed, speed, speed. Well, thank heaven I shall soon be out of it.

**PIGGY:**
What do you mean?

**PROFESSOR:**
You don't think I'm going to let you take me alive, do you?

*(He backs away towards a large window of frosted glass.)*

**PIGGY:**
What can you do? You have no weapon.

**PROFESSOR:**
Haven't I? Haven't I? You notice that number near the lift?

**PIGGY:**
What – 17?

**PROFESSOR:**
Exactly. The 17th floor! Don't try and stop me, Malone. *(shouting)* Goodbye, frail world!

*(He takes a run towards the frosted window, screaming as he goes.)*

*Cut to the outside of the building, wide shot. A crash of glass as the professor flies out of the ground floor window. He lands in a flower bed.*

*Cut to Charley, now with two policemen.*

**CHARLEY:**
That's him. Come on lads – let's move in. *(They start to move towards the flower bed – leaving the shot.)*

*Cut back to Piggy near lift. (The lift doors are open. He is sitting mopping his brow. Two girls from the typing pool approach him. They look at him.)*

**PIGGY:**
*(heroically)* Yes, I'm alright. Now.

**1ST GIRL:**
Oh, right.

*(The girls get in the lift.)*

**PIGGY:**
*(suddenly realising)* Don't go up in the lift! It's too fast!

*(But too late, the doors are almost closed. Whip pan up and whoosh sound effect.)*

*Cut to outside the lift – sign says "top floor". (the doors open. The two girls look dizzy. They go to step out – pan down to their feet. Their knickers are around their ankles.)*

*Mix to Malone's London office. Close-up of large, jovial, loud, well-spoken gent who is talking to RB and RC.*

**GENT:**
But what I still don't understand is how the Professor managed to appear to be killed right at the beginning of the case and then to conceal himself in the house without being spotted by the servants.

**PIGGY:**
Simple. He simply grew a beard, which made him look exactly like his elder brother. Then he invited him down for the weekend and killed him. Pushing his face into the trifle helped.

**CHARLEY:**
And of course the fellow was deaf and dumb anyway, which made it a lot easier.

**GENT:**
Well, I'm damned glad you've managed to clear it all up – it's been a messy business. A messy business. Well, I'd better get back to the yard. Lot to do this morning. *(Starts to take his coat off – revealing bib and brace overalls.)* All those apple boxes to shift. Can I leave my coat here, dear?

**PIGGY:**
Yes, all right. *(Gent starts to go.)* Oh Daisy, just a minute.

**GENT:**
What, love?

**PIGGY:**
Would you put a couple of bunches of bananas aside?

**GENT:**
Righto, dear. Well, off we go. Woman's work is never done.

*(He camps off.)*

**VOICE OVER:**
And so the sage of Brimstone Grange drew to a close. Piggy Malone and Charley Farley were once more about to sink back into obscurity. *(Miss Whizzer enters with visiting card – she hands it to Piggy.)* Once more it was to be the unending dreary day-to-day tasks of an unsuccessful private eye.

*(Close-up of Piggy and Charley, looking at card. Cut to shot of two large-busted girls entering. One big, one small. The men get to their feet.)*

**VOICE OVER:**
Or was it?

**1ST GIRL:**
We work at the nudist camp, and we need protection …

**VOICE OVER:**
One thing was certain – there would be very little sleep for anyone that night.

# DEATH CAN BE FATAL

## EPISODE ONE

*Titles:*
*Roulette wheel spinning. Dramatic music.*
*Wheel slows down. Stops. Suddenly (jump*
*cut) we zoom in fast on ball but instead of the*
*number, there is a skull. The skull almost fills*
*the screen, black on a blood-red background.*
*Superimpose the word "Death", then "can be*
*fatal".*

*Silhouette stills of Piggy Malone eating a*
*sandwich – superimpose below "starring Piggy*
*Malone". Similar stills of Charley, writing in*
*notebook, scratching head with pencil.*
*Superimpose words "and Charley Farley".*
*Finally, open-ended shot of roulette wheel*
*spinning, over which we can superimpose the*
*title of each episode.*

*End titles.*

*Shots of Marseilles – the docks area, quayside,*
*the hotel de ville and the grand cours, the road*
*joining the new town to the old.*

**VOICE OVER:**
Marseilles – city of intrigue. Smuggling
centre for the drug traffic of the western
world. Crime lurks behind every corner –
filth and degradation in every gutter. And
worst of all, the town (like most places
abroad) is crawling with foreigners.

*Shots now of Venice.*

**VOICE OVER:**
Venice – memorial to the lost glories of
the Renaissance – and the only town in
Europe to have found a way of keeping
prostitution off the streets.

*Shot of the Grand Canal.*

**VOICE OVER:**
But our story begins many, many miles
from teeming, steaming Marseilles – not
on the banks of the Grand Canal in
Venice, but on the banks of the Grand
Union Canal in Watford.

*Cut to long shot, canal at Watford. (Piggy*
*Malone and Charley Farley preparing to fish.)*

**VOICE OVER:**
Piggy Malone, overweight private
detective, and his undernourished
assistant, Charley Farley – failed
undergraduate and former hit man for the
Brownies – were having a day off. And
Charley was about to teach his boss the
gentle art of fishing.

*(Charley is showing Piggy how to fish. Piggy*
*wears his usual raincoat and hat, but Charley*
*has removed his sports jacket and he has with*
*him an impressive array of fishing gear,*
*including six or seven fishing rods and lots of*
*accessories.)*

**RC:**
Now then, chief, *(holds up float)* this is
called a float. Guess why?

*(He throws it in the water. It goes under.)*

**RB:**
Because it sinks.

*(RC peers into the water, nonplussed.)*

**RC:**
Funny, must be a dud. I'll have to take
that back. It's supposed to float. No point
in calling it a float if it sinks.

**RB:**
No, quite. Floats sinking – contradiction
in terms, isn't it? I mean, sinks don't float,
do they?

*Cut to the water – a wash basin, with taps,*
*floats by on the current.*

405

**RB:**
*(staring at it)* Apart from that one. Terrible what people dump into canals these days, isn't it? That float hasn't come up again. You've lost that.

**RC:**
Oh well, never mind. I've got plenty more. We're out to enjoy ourselves. I'll be over there adjusting my tackle.

**RB:**
Pardon?

**RC:**
I like to spread it all out on the grass.

*(He goes out of shot before RB can question this. RB opens a polythene box – takes out slice of bread and starts to eat.)*

**RB:**
*(calls to RC )* This bread's a bit stale, isn't it? Any meat with it?

**RC:**
That's the bait, chief. *(Concerned)* Are the worms alright?

**RB:**
*(Looking into box, alarmed.)* I hope so.

**RC:**
Now, here's your rod, chief.

*(Hands him complicated-looking rod and reel.)*

**RB:**
Perhaps I'd better watch you do it first. I've never watched people fishing.

**RC:**
Look, chief, there's a lot of nonsense talked about fishing. There's nothing complicated about it. There are three golden rules. Three things you have to do, that's all. My old grandad told me this, when I was about that high.

*(Indicates his own height.)*

**RB:**
When was that, last week?

**RC:**
No, no, be fair – he said three things. Never mind all the clap-trap. Do three things and you can't go wrong. Put some bait on the hook, see that the line is attached to the rod and throw it in the water. That's all *(hands him rod.)* Go.

**RB:**
Right then. Bait on the hook.

*(Does so.)*

**RC:**
Bait on the hook, yes.

**RB:**
See that the line's attached to the rod.

**RC:**
Correct – and the last thing?

**RB:**
Throw it in the water.

**RC:**
Got it! Go on, then.

**RB:**
Right.

*(He throws the rod into the water. It sinks and disappears.)*

**RC:**
Ah. *(Patient, but anguished)* No. Not the rod in the water, just the ... Er – let's have our lunch while I rethink it through.

*Cut to duck or swan, then back to Piggy and Charley. (Charley is just finishing fixing up cleft sticks in which to prop the fishing rods. Piggy is eating sandwiches.)*

**RC:**
There we are, now we just rest the rods in these *(does so)* and we don't even have to hold them. They're as safe as houses. Just lie back and enjoy the solitude.

*(They lie back. After a beat, three boys ride by on bicycles, snapping the fishing rods. They ride out of frame. RC and RB look after them as they disappear into the distance.)*

*Another time-passing shot of the canal. Now a shot of RC holding yet another rod in the water. RB is reading a Tarzan comic.*

**RC:**
Well, at least it's a day out. At least we can forget the worries of all those criminal cases. Well, both those criminal cases.

*(Close-up of the float, dipping in the water. It goes under.)*

**RC:**
Hello, I've got a bite!

*(He pulls and winds in his reel. Close-up as he reels in, then looks amazed. Cut to the water – a man in frogman's gear comes up, holding the line. He removes his snorkel, etc. And speaks with a French accent.)*

**FROGMAN:**
You are ze famous Bridish detecteefs, on 'oliday?

**RB:**
What were you doing down there, my good man?

**RC:**
He's a frogman, chief.

**RB:**
I know that. I can tell by his accent. I still want to know what he was doing down there.

**FROGMAN:**
Top secret. Read ziss.

*(Hands Piggy a note, in a plastic bag.)*

**RB:**
Who are you?

**FROGMAN:**
Undercover man.

**RC:**
More like an underwater man.

**FROGMAN:**
No stupid jokes, if you pleez!

**RC:**
I'm sorry.

*(Piggy glares at him, then returns to note.)*

*Cut to: Stratford Johns and Frank Windsor on a small launch moored against the bank of the canal, some hundred yards or so away from RB and RC.*

**SJ:**
Peculiar. Frogman up there, talking to two idiots on the bank. Up to no good, I shouldn't wonder.

**FW:**
Now, now, sir – don't get involved. We're on holiday, remember. Frogmen probably feel the need for conversation same as anybody else.

**SJ:**
Mmm. *(Shakes head.)* Fishy.

**FW:**
Ooh, dear. *(Winces at the pun.)* I don't think this holiday is doing you much good at all.

*Cut back to RB reading note to RC.*

**RB:**
"... I can tell you no more now, except that it is a case of international importance. It is imperative that you meet the head of MI6 at once. The fate of nations is at stake. Hoping this finds you as it leaves me, in the pink. Yours ever, British Intelligence."

*(RC looks amazed.)*

**RB:**
Well? What do you reckon, Charley? Do we accept the case?

**RC:**
International importance!

**RB:**
We can hardly refuse, can we?

**RC:**
Well, I don't know. I've got that roast chicken in the oven.

**RB:**
You can't think about a roast chicken at a time like this – when the fate of nations is at stake!

**RC:**
I've done roast potatoes all round it.

**RB:**
*(torn)* Oh Gawd, have you? *(To frogman)* Can we report a bit later on?

**FROGMAN:**
It must be at once!

*(RB and RC look at each other – they nod to each other.)*

**RC:**
You're on. Where do we go?

**FROGMAN:**
Follow me!

*(He dives.)*

*(RB and RC look at each other, a resigned sigh and they leap into the water.)*

*Cut to Stratford Johns and Frank Windsor.*

**SJ:**
I've heard of throwing the little ones back – I didn't think they threw the fat ones back as well.

*Cut to a close-up of Piggy's hat floating on the water. (Piggy's hand comes up from under the water and pulls it under.)*

**VOICE OVER:**
What is the murky secret of the canal? Is

MI6 running Watford? What will happen to Charley's roast chicken? Don't miss next week: "Passage to Marseilles".

*(Music swells.)*

# EPISODE TWO

*After titles, various shots from previous episode.*

**VOICE OVER:**
Piggy Malone, the fat, little-known detective, and Charley Farley, his little, little-known assistant, once again found themselves involved in a strange world of intrigue and secrecy. While quietly fishing in the canal at Watford, they are approached by a foreign frogman and told to report immediately to MI6. And like the courageous, patriotic, foolhardy idiots that they are, they agree.

*(Shots of Piggy and Charley jumping into canal; Piggy's hand surfacing to reclaim hat.)*

*Cut to the office of MI6.*
*Old-fashioned, a lot of polished wood doors and furniture. (A man, suave, greying at the temples, is reading the newspaper. A secretary is searching through a filing cabinet on the other side of the room.)*

**MAN:**
Have you found that file yet, Miss Willow?

**MISS W:**
No, I haven't. When you've got a minute, I wouldn't mind you going through these drawers.

*(We see the drawers she is referring to. Also, as she is bending over the cabinet, we see hers. The man raises his eyebrows slightly, then looks back to his paper.)*

**MISS W:**
I don't know where to look.

**MAN:**
Neither do I. *(But he carries on looking at his paper.)* It says here in my stars that I'm going to meet a short dark stranger and a fat, grey stranger. Bit specific, isn't it?

**MISS W:**
That sounds like the men we located at Watford, sir.

**MAN:**
Does it indeed. I think you'd better have our chaps investigate this star-gazer bloke. He's getting a bit too accurate. I don't want my private doings splashed across the newspapers. Especially before I've done them.

*(Phone buzzes. Miss Willow answers.)*

**MISS W:**
Oh, hello Elsie. Yes. Oh, are they? Righto, Elsie, send them in. Yes. Bye Elsie. *(puts down phone)* That was Major Cartwright, sir.

**MAN:**
What does he want?

**MISS W:**
Mr Malone and Mr Farley have got out of their wet clothes and are ready to see you, sir.

**MAN:**
Oh fine. Er – they have got into some other clothes, haven't they?

**MISS W:**
Oh yes. We lent them some uniforms. They're quite decent.

**MAN:**
Oh good, I'm glad. We don't want someone coming and corrupting you on your first week here, do we?

**MISS W:**
*(giggling)* No.

**MAN:**
Not till I've had a go, anyway.

*(The door opens – Piggy and Charley enter, both in very ill-fitting traffic warden uniforms, with peaked caps.)*

**MAN:**
*(angrily)* Oh, now what! Look, the car is parked perfectly. Nine inches from the kerb, no yellow lines, not across anyone's entrance – you jumped-up little Hitlers come barging in here ...

**MISS W:**
This is Mr Malone and Mr Farley, sir.

**MAN:**
What? Oh – oh, I see. So sorry. Of course, the clothes. How do you do. *(They shake hands.)* Do park yourselves somewhere, won't you?

**RB:**
Thank you. Would you mind telling us what this is all about?

**MAN:**
Certainly. But first, what can I get you to drink?

**RC:**
Er – Martini, please.

**MISS W:**
Shaken or stirred?

**RC:**
Er – both, please.

**RB:**
Ginger beer shandy.

**MAN:**
Half pint?

**RC:**
*(as if he has been addressed)* Yes?

**MAN:**
No, sorry- *(To RB)* Did you want a half pint?

**RB:**
No, pint will do, thanks.

**MAN:**
Oh, right. See to that, will you, Miss Willow? I'll just have some tea.

**MISS W:**
Pint?

**MAN:**
No, just a half, thanks. *(She Exits.)* Now then, gentlemen. Straight to the point – drugs – drugs and world domination. Now I'm not talking about your ordinary dope-pushers; this is a special drug which has been developed, we think, in Marseilles. At least we know the headquarters of the smuggling ring is centred in that area.

**RC:**
Excuse me, are you "M"?

**MAN:**
What?

**RC:**
"M". You know, the head of MI6. "M".

**MAN:**
Oh, no. "M" is retired. No, it's "N" now. But he's on holiday. And "O", the second-in-command, he's got compassionate leave, His mother's got a bit of back trouble.

**RB:**
Who are you then?

**MAN:**
I'm "P".

**RB:**
Oh, I see. You were saying about this special drug – what's it for?

**MAN:**
Ah, now this is the whole crux, if you'll forgive the word, of the matter. I'll say it slowly – a certain organisation is seeking to undermine authority all over the world by administering to important people a certain drug which has the effect of making them clumsy.

**RC:**
Clumsy? Did you say clumsy?

**MAN:**
Clumsy.

**RB:**
I see. You mean, these people are made to look foolish, and so lose respect in the eyes of the public.

**MAN:**
Exactly. And you can see it happening. You only have to watch British television.

*(He crosses to map on wall which is on a roller blind. He releases the blind. It goes up revealing an underlay screen.)*

**MAN:**
I first noticed it some time ago with Tommy Cooper. Now Tommy Cooper used to be a wonderfully smooth performer, but lately he's been getting decidedly clumsy.

**RC:**
Yes, I've noticed that. Gets it all wrong, doesn't he? I've noticed that.

**RB:**
*(defending him)* He was the first man to knock down Muhammed Ali.

**MAN:**
That was Henry Cooper. Anyway, the point is, this clumsiness is spreading. Take a look at this film compiled by our research department.

*(We now cut to a tape sequence. Occasional reaction shots from the to detectives.)*

*(Mr Wilson speaking at a meeting. Close-up as he knocks over water and mops it up with his handkerchief. A newsreader who drops his papers or squirts ink onto his shirt as he puts his pen away. Procession of state – in close-up, the man with the mace clouts one of the judges as he swings round. Well-known minister going into the houses of parliament. In close-up he trips over milk bottles. Miss*

*world steps on her robes and falls flat on her face.)*

**RB:**
I see what you mean. Stupid, isn't it?

**MAN:**
We've got to stop it.

**RC:**
Not half. I mean, once it reaches *Coronation Street*, where are you? If Ena Sharples loses her dignity, what hope would there be for any of us?

**MAN:**
What worries me is if it gets to the Royal family.

**RB:**
The Queen's speech at Christmas would be a fiasco, wouldn't it? One long laugh from start to finish.

**MAN:**
So, gentlemen. Our aim: to locate the vice ring in Marseilles and render them inoperative.

**RC:**
Wipe them out, you mean? Because we don't go in for a lot of violent work, not Mr Malone and myself. We're more your civil cases, divorce and breach of promise.

**RB:**
Yes, a lot of ladder work – peering through windows, that sort of thing. We're more sneaks, really.

**MAN:**
And that's precisely why you've been chosen. We've got a heavy mob that'll come and clear up after you. All we want you to do is to get the formula for the drug.

**RC:**
The formula?

**MAN:**
So that our chemists can research

antidotes. That's what matters. You've got to get that formula. What do you say, lads?

**RB:**
What if we say no?

**RC:**
Yes, what if we refuse?

**MAN:**
I'll have you shot.

**RC:**
*(immediately)* Well, I'm game. Are you, chief?

**RB:**
Oh yes, fine. Now, when do we start ...

*(Their voices fade down as the voice over comes in and we slowly mix to film.)*

**VOICE OVER:**
And so our two heroes take the first step on the road to murder and mayhem. But already they are marked men. In some ill-lit corner of a café in Marseilles, two of the underworld's arch villains are, even now, completing the first stage of their plan to conquer the world, and the evil tentacles of their organisation are already reaching out to Whitehall.

*(During this voice over, we see various shots of Marseilles, first a wide quay side shot, then a narrow alley, a doorway, then moving towards a heavy bead curtain. It is swished aside by the camera to reveal RB in panama hat and dark glasses, and white double-breasted suit. RC, Japanese, with thick pebble glasses and pinstripe suit, à la "Oddjob" in the Bond films.)*

*(When we first see them, RB is being handed a note by an anonymous waiter. He reads it quickly.)*

**RB:**
Ah. All is proceeding according to plan. Well done, Oddknob.

**RC:**
*(who cannot sound the letter "l")* Prease, Mr Greensreeves, how many times must I tell you my name not Odd-knob. I am called Bob-Job. This nickname given to me by rate ramented master before he rost his rife in a Rundon night-crub. I must be called Bob-Job. Nothing but Bob-Job!. And if you don't rike it, you must bruddy well rump it.

**RB:**
Waiter! Bring some Turkish coffee. *(Looks at watch.)* Do you realise, Bob-Job, that in London now, it's just about time for afternoon tea?

*(He chortles insanely, joined by Bob-Job.)*

*Cut to the MI6 office. Close-up of cup of tea, shandy and Martini on tray. Pull out. (It is carried by Miss Willow. She puts it down on the desk. The tray also contains a plate of sandwiches.)*

**MAN:**
Ah – help yourselves, chaps. Thank you, Miss Willow, you've saved our lives. I was just thinking, if I don't get that cup of tea soon, I shall die.

*(He drinks tea, smacks his lips appreciatively and then starts writhing and groaning in agony. during a pause in the groaning, Miss Willow speaks, in close-up.)*

**MISS W:**
Oh, didn't I put any sugar in?

*(The man's only reply to this is to die, horribly. RB and RC rush to him.)*

**RC:**
He's dead. Poisoned.

**MISS W:**
Oh my Gawd. I – I'd better get the next in line.

*(She rushes out.)*

**RC:**
How terrible. That's a terrible thing to happen to anybody, isn't it?

**RB:**
You're sure he's dead, are you?

**RC:**
He's dead alright.

**RB:**
Oh. Will it be alright if I have this other sandwich then?

**RC:**
Yes, I don't want it. Did she say she was going to get the next in line?

**RB:**
Yes, that must be ...

**RC:**
Yes. "Q".

*(The door opens and a suave, elderly, well-groomed gent appears, accompanied by Miss Willow.)*

**RB:**
Are you "Q"?

**Q:**
Yes. Are you?

*(Over RB's reaction, the voice over comes in.)*

**VOICE OVER:**
And so, as Charley comforts a weeping Miss Willow, questions seethed around in Piggy Malone's thick skull. Who holds the secret of the Clumsy drug? Is this man really "Q", or is he just playing at it? Who'd got to the tea and poisoned "P"? Don't miss next week: "Into The Web".

*(Music swells. Fades.)*

# EPISODE THREE

*Titles.*

*After titles, shots from previous episodes accompany voice over.*

**VOICE OVER:**
Piggy Malone, one of Britain's best-known losers, and Charley Farley, a man who would have had what it takes if someone hadn't taken it first, were in a tight spot. They had orders from MI6 to locate the formula for the deadly "Clumsy drug", which was undermining the authority of famous and important people all over the world. No sooner had they accepted the case, however, than their superior was brutally poisoned. This, then, is the story so far – except for viewers in Scotland, where the story is as follows.

*(We now see similar shots in the office but everyone is dressed in tartan, with kilts and tam o'shanters. "P" dies after drinking the tea, as usual.)*

**VOICE OVER:**
Piggy McMillan and Chairleigh Fairleigh, those two braw bricht cocks o' the North, are called into the headquarters of Scottish Intelligence in Sauchiehall Street, after hearing of a terrible drug which quietens down Scottish football fans. It renders a haggis harmless, and can be a contributing factor in rotting the kilt. So when the chief is slipped a wee dram in his tea, there is nothing for it but to send for Dr Finlay.

*End of Scottish sequence.*

*Now a shot of the office. ("P" is lying dead. RB and RC – "Q" absent.)*

**VOICE OVER:**
Meanwhile, back in civilisation, the hunt is on.

*Mix from office to shots of London airport.*

**VOICE OVER:**
Piggy and Charley arrive at London Airport, the first hesitant step on a downward path that could lead to destruction ... *(Shot of RB getting out of taxi.)* And if you're wondering why Charley doesn't seem to be around, remember that the air fares have all gone up again.

*(Pass over to large, black trunk, strapped to taxi's luggage compartment. This obviously contains Charley. The taxi driver, RB and a burly porter eventually get the trunk, still upright, onto a trolley. RB pays taxi driver, who leaves.)*

**PORTER:**
Blimey! Whatever have you got in there?

**RB:**
Nobody.

*(Reaction of curiosity from porter. They enter the terminal. Close-up of Piggy's hand removing sandwich from vending machine. Wider – we see Piggy and trunk.)*

**CHARLEY'S VOICE:**
*(from within)* Why have we stopped, chief?

**RB:**
I'm just having a snack.

**RC:**
I'm fed up with this.

**RB:**
Look, it's all money, isn't it? Money saved.

**RC:**
But why is it always me?

**RB:**
Don't be daft – where would we get a trunk my size?

*(A middle-aged lady has entered and now approaches, having heard Piggy's last remark.)*

**LADY:**
Were you addressing me?

**RB:**
No, I was talking to myself.

**LADY:**
Why?

**RB:**
I'm insane.

**LADY:**
Oh!

*(She is nonplussed and walks out of shot.)*

**RC:**
Here, chief.

**RB:**
What?

**RC:**
Can I have a drink now?

**RB:**
Are you sure you want one?

**RC:**
Yes, I fitted up all the rubber tubes specially. The funnel is in the carrier-bag with the orange juice.

*(RB takes out of the carrier bag a medium-sized funnel and a half-gallon orange juice container. He then places the carrier bag on top of the trunk to shield his next operation, which is to insert the funnel in a hole in the top of the trunk.)*

**RB:**
Ready?

**RC:**
Yes, go on.

*(RB starts to pour. After a second he stops.)*

**RB:**
Alright?

**RC:**
I'm not getting any.

**RB:**
Well, I'm pouring it in.

**RC:**
Well, there's nothing coming through, chief.

**RB:**
You must have got the tubes mixed up.

*(He pours some more in, then we widen to see that halfway down one side of the trunk, at just the right height, a stream of liquid is pouring out in an arc.)*

**RB:**
Yes, I thought so. It's all coming out the side. I'll try the other hole.

*(He does so. This hole is about halfway down the side. He once more pours in the juice. Now we can see a separate shot of the lady standing near the vending machine, staring at Piggy and the trunk in horror. She sees Piggy standing up against the trunk and the liquid still pouring out. She obviously suspects the worst.)*

*Cut to: exterior of the Hotel Metropole, Marseilles.*
*Then a shot of a corridor in the hotel. The outside of room no. 13. (A porter, streaking with sweat and almost collapsing, is just leaving the room. Piggy's face appears.)*

**RB:**
Merci, mon brave.

*(The porter groans and staggers out of shot. Piggy closes the door.)*

*Cut to inside the room.*
*(Piggy goes to the trunk, which is now on its side. He turns the key and opens the lid towards us, masking the inside. RC gets out in a cramped, bent position, then manages to straighten up. He then speaks into the trunk.)*

**RC:**
Come on then.

*(Cut to RB's face. He stares in astonishment.*

*Then cut back to trunk as a small, attractive girl clambers out, her hair awry, her dress creased and crumpled.)*

**GIRL:**
Thanks for the lift. Bye.

*(We follow her to the door.)*

**RB:**
What's all this? What's she doing in there?

**RC:**
Couldn't refuse her, really. She's working her way across the Continent. I got friendly with her this morning.

**RB:**
Not as friendly as you got with her this afternoon, I bet. You've been squashed together in there all through the flight. She must have been the excess baggage they charged me for.

**RC:**
Well, I couldn't eat or drink. I had to do something. Mind you, the loading and unloading was pretty dodgy. At one stage, when they tipped us completely upside down, I thought I'd bitten off more than I could chew.

*(He reaches into the trunk, takes out a battered carrier bag – removes striped pyjamas from it and lays them on one of the two single beds.)*

**RC:**
Right, that's me unpacked. I wonder if it's the sort of hotel where you put your shoes out to be cleaned?

*Cut to a small room somewhere within the labyrinth of the hotel. (Two swarthy Middle-Eastern servants in filthy white waiters' coats, shapeless and baggy, with trousers to match, are cleaning shoes. They are RB and RC as Marmaduke Lepjohn and Mustapha Djiun respectively, and they each wear a fez.)*

**MUSTAPHA (RC):**
*(slyly)* I have certain information to impart to Your Highness.

**MARMADUKE (RB):**
Very well then, impart it. I am all ears.

**RC:**
I know.

**RB:**
What?

**RC:**
I will tell you now. I am told ...

*(He looks around.)*

**RB:**
Yes?

**RC:**
I am told – I will not tell you who told me – but I am told ...

**RB:**
What are you told?

**RC:**
I'm telling you.

**RB:**
You are not telling me. You keep telling me you are told, but you are not telling me what you are told. Kindly tell me at once without further "to-do"ment, or I'll punch you in the mouth with my big fist, you little scoundrel.

**RC:**
Listen, if you don't play your beads right, I won't tell you at all.

**RB:**
Very well, but don't get camp.

**RC:**
I am not.

**RC:**
Ah, I am told *(conspiratorially)* that the two English fools have arrived in the hotel.

415

**RB:**
The detectives?

**RC:**
Those are the very them of which I speak.

**RB:**
Aha! Then we are to spy on them as arranged by the almighty Mr Greensleeves?

**RC:**
And the oriental snake in the ointment, Mr Bob-Job.

**RB:**
Aha.

**RC:**
We must start at once. There is no time like the future! Ha, ha, it will be great sport.

*(He begins to polish shoes vigorously.)*

**RB:**
Now, now, don't get excited.

**RC:**
*(polishing away)* I am not getting excited.

**RB:**
You are.

**RC:**
I'm not.

**RB:**
You are. Those are suede shoes you are polishing. You see? Now then ...

*(As RB calms him down, we mix to Piggy and Charley in their hotel room. Piggy is washing his face with his hat on; Charley is trimming his shirt cuffs with scissors.)*

**VOICE OVER:**
And even as our two shabby heroes prepare to hit the town in search of the Clumsy Drug, there approaches one more player in this grim drama of love and death. As yet, she has never taken part in

the latter, but what a performer in the former.

*(Over this last time we see lift doors open – very close shot of girl's legs. We track back as they walk down the corridor, still in close-up.)*

**VOICE OVER:**
She is the fabulous Madame Cocotte – beautiful, sultry manageress of the Hotel Metropole – a goddess who is destined to win the heart of at least one of the English detectives, apart of course, from being one in the eye for both of them. *(Cut to her low-cut bosom as she walks.)* Having heard of the Britishers' arrival, she was on the move. *(Back to tracking shot of legs.)* And when she was on the move, nobody else could keep still for long either.

*Cut to: close-up on girl's hips from behind as they swing almost out of shot as she slinks down the corridor.*

*Cut to: close-up of stuffed animal on wall. Its ears or horns suddenly stand up straight.*

*Cut to: girl's legs above knee, her split skirt revealing her beautiful nether limbs.*

*Cut to: waiter and man with whisky glass. They stand, both staring out of shot at girl. Waiter sprays soda siphon into man's glass continuously. Neither of them notice.*

*Cut to: her hips again.*

*Cut to: a fruit machine. She passes it. As soon as she has cleared frame, it pays out. A Jack pot.*

*Cut to: her hips and legs, this time from the side in profile.*

*Cut to: close-up – snooker ball going into pocket.*

*Cut to: close-up – old man standing up, chalking billiard cue. His eyes pop out as he sees girl out of frame.*

*Cut to: her back, which is bare to the waist.*

*Cut to: (reverse film) lots of billiard balls shooting back up out of the pocket.*

*Cut to: close-up of door – no. 13. A hand knocks on it. RC 's voice cries "Come in."*

*Cut to: other side of door, close-up. The door is opened and we see, for the first time, the lovely face of Madame Cocotte.*

*(A reaction from both RC and RB, separately.)*

**MADAME C:**
Good evening. My name is Madame Cocotte.

**RC:**
*(stunned)* Is it really?

**RB:**
Pleased to meet you.

**MADAME C:**
I am the manager of the hotel.

**RC:**
Oh, good. I say, that's a responsible job for a young lady like you. What's it like, being the manager here?

**MADAME C:**
I manage.

**RC:**
Yes, I bet you do.

**MADAME C:**
I came to welcome you and wondered if you might both like to join me after dinner for a little drink in my private quarters.

**RC:**
Oh, I'm sure we would. You wouldn't object to drinking in her private quarters, would you, chief?

**RB:**
No, that would be very nice indeed, Madame ...

**MADAME C:**
Eloise. Eloise Cocotte.

**RB:**
Oh, yes. Very nice.

**MADAME C:**
Shall we say about eight?

**RC:**
*(to RB)* Shall we?

**RB AND RC:**
About eight.

**MADAME C:**
I shall look forward.

*(She turns to go and, in doing so, knocks over a vase on a tall stand near the door. It crashes to the ground.)*

**MADAME C:**
Oh, mon dieu! I am sorry to be so clumsy.

*(Reactions from RB and RC. They look at each other. Then a reaction from Madame Cocotte, her hand to her mouth, realising what she has said. Without another word, she turns and leaves the room.)*

**VOICE OVER:**
Is this the first evidence of the Clumsy Drug, here in this very hotel? Will Charley Farley go drinking in Madame's private quarters? Has Piggy Malone been drinking them in already? These, and very few other questions, will be answered, in another thrilling episode next week: "A Drug On The Market".

# EPISODE FOUR

*After usual titles, cut to shot of previous episodes.*

**VOICE OVER:**
Piggy Malone and Charley Farley, our pair of private eyes, who were renowned for

making a spectacle of themselves, were on the trail of the sinister drug which was causing embarrassment to leading public figures all over the world – the Clumsy Drug. Having traced the gang to Marseilles, our podgy hero and his underweight assistant had come up against a brick wall, in the shape of Madame de Cocotte, the manager of the Hotel Metropole. And if you've ever come up against a brick wall shaped like Madame Cocotte, you'll know what I mean.

But suddenly Madame Cocotte herself had become clumsy. What strange spell was she under? Was she herself a victim of the dreaded drug? As soon as she had left the room, Charley Farley was on the scent.

*(Charley is crouching by the pieces of broken vase.)*

**RC:**
Chief! Look! Here's a note. Either she dropped it, or it was inside the vase.

**RB:**
*(Crosses into frame and crouches with him.)* What's it say?

**RC:**
*(reading)* "I must be careful what I write. But the following message may be of interest to you in locating the whereabouts of what you seek".

**RB:**
That must mean where the formula's hidden. Go on then, read the message.

**RC:**
*(reading)* "A sketch map you have to find. Enough time you must give yourself; room thoroughly to search every ladies' bed, under which you will find it printed on".

**RC:**
Every ladies' bed. It's printed under a bed, this map then.

**RC:**
*(shaking his head)* There's more to this note than meets the eye, chief. It's a puzzle.

**RB:**
*(rising)* Well, don't puzzle it out down there, you'll get cramp.

*(RB crosses to bed, lies down, flicks through magazine.)*

**RC:**
*(after a pause)* Chief, I think I'm getting it!

**RB:**
I told you. Point your toe. Walk about a bit.

**RC:**
The message. I think I'm getting it. Where's some paper?

*(He picks up a piece of card from the desk and starts to copy out the note.)*

**RB:**
Oh, good. *(Picks up phone.)* Er – I think I'll order something to eat, shall I? What do you want?

**RC:**
I'm not interested in food, chief. I can't do two things at once.

**RB:**
Oh, I can. *(Speaks into phone)* Oh, room service? I fancy a nibble of something. Could you send me up a waitress? Thank you.

**RC:**
*(finishing his writing)* Come here, chief, and look at this.

*(RB crosses to RC at desk. Close-up of message, written out like this :*
    *a sketch map you have to find*
    *enough time you must give yourself*
    *room thoroughly to search every ladies'*
    *bed*
    *under where you will find it printed on.)*

**RB:**
So what? You've just written it out again.

**RC:**
But watch!

*(He takes scissors, cuts the card down the middle, swaps it round so the second piece is in front of the first. Sticks the two halves together with Sellotape.)*

**RC:**
Now read it, chief.

**RB:**
*(reads)* "You have to find a sketch map. You must give yourself enough time to search every bedroom thoroughly. You will find it printed on under where." You will find in printed on, under where? *(The meaning suddenly becomes clear to him.)* Oh – you will find it printed on underwear! That's brilliant, Charley.

**RC:**
Thank you, chief. So we've got to search the hotel bedrooms to find some ladies' underwear with a map drawn on it.

**RB:**
Top or bottom?

**VOICE OVER:**
And so the search was on. But the odds were heavily against them – and so were most of the women whose rooms they entered.

*Cut to: a long hotel corridor. At the far end the corridor turns a corner. A scream is heard. Then a woman's voice – "How dare you. What are you doing in my room?" During this line another scream is heard, and another woman's voice – "Leave my room at once. Whatever next!" etc.*

*(Two doors open, one on either side, at the far end of the corridor. RB emerges from one, RC from the other. They shake their heads and enter the next two rooms. More screams and shouts of "Get out", "I am in the bath", "please, my husband and I wish to be alone", etc.)*

*(They again emerge and meet. They look desperate. Then they spy a chambermaid in mob cap and black dress, knocking on a door in the foreground. "Come in," says a female voice. She enters the room. RB and RC exchange a nod.)*

*(Optical wipe to the corridor once again. Two strange chambermaids in mob caps come round the corner. It is RB and RC. They each knock on a door. "come in" is heard. They enter the rooms.)*

*(M. Phillipe, the middle-aged under-manager, comes round the corner. He is a pompous fool with a little moustache. A porter approaches him. They stop, exchange a word – porter gives him a note and leaves. M. Phillipe stands looking at note, when RC comes out of the door. RC sees M. Phillipe and starts to dust the door and a nearby picture frame furiously with his feather duster. He dusts down the door frame. When he is quite low down, he suddenly jumps up. M. Phillipe has goosed him.)*

**M. PHILLIPE:**
Are you new?

**RC:**
No. Very old.

**MP:**
Very droll, mon petit.

*(He walks away. The camera pans with him and he collides violently with RB, who is waiting just out of shot.*

**MP:**
*(recovering, angrily)* Get on with your work, both of you!

*(He goes round the corner.)*

*(Another optical wipe – and we see RB still as chambermaid, coming out of yet another bedroom – when round the corner comes the porter, pulling a large wicker laundry basket on wheels. He ignores RB.)*

*Cut to: the basket. (The lid is raised and RC*

*peers out, covered in laundry. He throws a rolled-up garment out of shot. RB catches it. He unrolls the garment which proves to be a large pair of silk bloomers. Printed on them in large letters: "the dreadnought bloomer co". RB reverses them and we see the words: "they shall not pass".*

*Cut to: round the corner. The under manager speaks to the porter.*

**MP:**
Has the hotel flag come back from the laundry yet, Alphonse?

**PORTER:**
The flag, Monsieur?

**MP:**
It has its own special box.

*Cut to: laundry basket. (A flat cardboard box, about 2ft by 1ft by 4 inches, begins to emerge from under the lid.)*

**PORTER:**
Oh, yes.

*(He throws back the lid. There is the box on top of a pile of clean laundry. He hands it to M. Phillipe.)*

**MP:**
Merci. Our glorious tri-colour must not be absent from our flag pole for a moment longer than necessary. Three cheers for the blue, white and red. N'est-ce pas?

*(He departs. Cut to a close-up of the laundry basket as it is pulled along once more. RC emerges, draped in the French flag.)*

**VOICE OVER:**
But still the search went on!

*Cut to: the reception area of the hotel. Potted palms and gilt, turn of the century decor. A reception counter in one corner, also an ornate phone on a table, 2ft 6 inches high. (Miss Grimsberg, a girl with an American accent, is speaking on the phone, leaning with her elbows on the table.)*

**MISS G:**
Sure, baby. I work here. Here in the hotel. Oh, about three months. Well, it certainly makes a change from college ...

*(During this RB enters in close-up. Reacts to girl. Cut to RB's point of view – girl's short, full skirt from the back. He approaches and lifts up her skirt without the girl noticing. Close-up of his face. His jaw drops. We do not see what he sees, but we guess. He releases the skirt and backs away.)*

**MISS G:**
*(continuing her speech into phone)* ... sure ... I just play it cool. Right.

*(RB reacts again at this, in light of what he has just seen. RC enters.)*

**RC:**
What about her?

*(Indicating girl.)*

**RB:**
I've just checked.

**RC:**
Well? What news?

**RB:**
None whatsoever.

**RC:**
Oh, just ordinary, were they?

**RB:**
No.

**RC:**
What then?

**RB:**
I've just told you, none whatsoever.

**RC:**
Oh! You mean ...

**RB AND RC:**
*(together)* None whatsoever ...

**RB:**
Yeah.

**RC:**
Oh, I see. No luck there then.

**RB:**
Depends which way you look at it, doesn't it.

*(MP rushes in to speak to Miss Grimsberg.)*

**MP:**
Miss Grimsberg! Where is Madame la Manageress? Madame Cocotte? Where is she?

**MISS G:**
I really don't have any idea, sir.

**MP:**
The flag, it has disappeared. There has been a terrible mix-up. Look out of the window.

*(He rushes her to the window.)*

*Cut to: a flagpole against the sky and fluttering gaily from it, a pair of frilly knickers. Cut back to M. Phillipe and Miss Grimsberg.*

**MISS G:**
Oh, oh dear. Oh, my sainted aunts.

**MP:**
Oh, you recognise them?

**MISS G:**
No it's just an expression, Monsieur Phillipe ...

**MP:**
*(leaving)* Something must be done quickly. This situation cannot be allowed to go on!

*(An old lady has come in and approaches him.)*

**OLD LADY:**
Monsieur ...

**MP:**
Not now, I beg you, Madame! I have things to do. *(To Miss G)* I must get to the bottom of this. Miss Grimsberg, get those knickers down at once!

*(He exits and the old lady reacts in surprise. Cut to RB and RC.)*

**RB:**
Hm. I'm afraid it's a case of locking the stable door after the horse has bolted.

*Cut to: the flagpole. The knickers, in close-up, descending. A hint of "lights out" bugle-call is the background music. The camera follows it down to discover the two Middle-Eastern porters, Mustapha and Marmaduke (RC and RB).*

**RC:**
There we are, down they come, down they come.

**RB:**
Most satisfying, Mustapha. Remove them from the rope so that we may search for a label inside them, which may indicate whose loins they formerly girded.

**RC:**
*(finding a label)* Ah. Here is one label. And a name – it is Saint something.

**RB:**
Saint somebody?

**RC:**
Obviously a religious personage of some description. A nun perhaps.

*(Still peering at label.)*

**RB:**
No, no, too frilly. Wait. Is it Saint Mickel?

**RC:**
Saint Mickel?

**RB:**
A celebrated British saint, who is often to be found inside people's underwear. Is

that what it says, "Mickel"?

**RC:**
No. I can see it now. It says "Saint Christopher, Hong Kong".

**RB:**
Ah. It is a filthy foreign imitation. Saint Christopher is the saint who watches over people when they are travelling.

**RC:**
But not, I hope, when they are travelling up a flagpole in their underwear?

**RB:**
No, no. That would be stretching things a bit far.

**RC:**
Talking of going too far, strange things and wondrous events are happening in the hotel. The head porter is telling me that on the third floor, several ladies have had their panties removed.

**RB:**
*(after thinking about this for a second)* Must be the hot weather.

**RC:**
Yes, that's what it is.

**RB:**
Yes ...

**RC:**
Either that, or that naughty window cleaner. You know, the one with ...

**RB:**
Oh yes, him.

*(As they gabble on, we mix to the exterior of the hotel.*
*The villains arrive in a limousine – Mr Greensleeves and Bob-Job. They get out of the car and enter the hotel.)*

*Cut to: the reception area. (They pass through.)*

*Cut to: the corridor. (Piggy and Charley are just emerging from Madame C's room. Round the corner come the villains. They pass each other, look back, suspicious.)*

*Cut to: inside Madame's room. (Start with a close-up of her bursting with laughter. Cut wider. They are all laughing)*

**MADAME C:**
Yes, they have taken my briefs alright. The ones with the map carefully drawn on them.

**MR GREENSLEEVES:**
*(RB)* A map which they think will take them to the Clumsy Drug formula.

**BOB-JOB:**
*(RC)* But which will merely lead them to our villa and to their death. A lingering, loathsome death. A death they will remember for the rest of their lives.

**RB:**
But which we three will regard as merely the removal of a couple of stupid obstacles in our path. The path that leads to world domination.

**MADAME C:**
Oh, Mr Greensleeves, you put everything so beautifully!

*(They look at each other and laugh again. RC, smiling and pouring drinks for all of them.)*

**VOICE OVER:**
Once again, our two dull-witted heroes have been tricked. Will they discover they have been incorrectly briefed? Will Piggy embark on another wild goose chase? Or will Charley persuade him to keep his hands to himself? Find out in next week's episode: "Fork Right For Disaster".

# EPISODE FIVE

*After usual titles, various shots from previous episodes.*

**VOICE OVER:**
Events in the Clumsy Drug case have taken a turn for the worse. Our two dauntless detectives, hopelessly duped by international villains in Marseilles, were now studying a piece of false evidence planted on them by the beautiful Madame Cocotte – a map, drawn on a pair of her own briefs. And Piggy and Charley were even now desperately trying to grasp what was behind them.

**RC:**
*(indicating map)* ... through the mountains, curve round to the right, and from then on it's a straight run to the village.

*(A close-up of his finger tracing the route.)*

**RB:**
Yes. Looks simple enough. But I'm not sure. I get this odd feeling.

**RC:**
Well, you're bound to get an odd feeling looking at a map on a pair of knickers. It's a funny thing to do, isn't it?

**RB:**
No – I'm just not sure.

**RC:**
What aren't you sure of?

**RB:**
I don't know.

**RC:**
Oh well, if you don't know what you're not sure of, you can't be sure that you're not actually sure of it, can you?

**RB:**
What?

**RC:**
Are you certain you don't know what

you're not sure of?

**RB:**
Positive.

**RC:**
Oh well, that proves it.

**RB:**
Look, never mind all that. You've got to go and talk to her.

*(A change of location – exterior. They walk or stand.)*

**RC:**
Who, me?

**RB:**
Yes – get to know her. Worm your way into her affections. Get her to slip into something more comfortable. Find out if she's straight, underneath it all.

**RC:**
Straight? What, you mean all that could be a false front?

**RB:**
Why not?

**RC:**
It looked pretty real to me. I'm not sure, chief ...

**RB:**
Listen, we've got to know. After all, she was with those two shady-looking characters, the little one and the fat one.

**RC:**
All right then, chief. I'll try. It's all in the course of duty.

**RB:**
'Course it is. I mean, in this game, you're either on the job or you're not.

**RC:**
Quite. Er, chief–

**RB:**
What?

**RC:**
What will you be doing?

**RB:**
Don't worry – I've got other fish to fry.

*Cut to: the terrace of the hotel.*
*Close-up of frying pan, with steak sizzling – it is being served to a hungry-looking Piggy. The table is laden with fruits, bread rolls, salads, etc. Very mouthwatering.*

*Cut to: Madame Cocotte's bedroom.*
*(She is seated on the sofa. She wears a semi-transparent housecoat. A knock on the door.)*

**MADAME C:**
Enter.

*(Charley enters.)*

**RC:**
Good evening.

**MADAME C:**
Ah, Monsieur, come in. Is there any way I can be of service?

**RC:**
Yes. I'd like you to have a look at my plumbing.

**MADAME C:**
Ooh la la – you are having trouble?

**RC:**
Yes – every time the man in the next room pulls the plug, my toilet flushes. It can be very unnerving when you're not expecting it.

**MADAME C:**
I'm sure it can. I'm afraid nothing can be done until the morning now – but perhaps I can offer you a little champagne by way of consolation?

*(She is very friendly.)*

**RC:**
Oh, don't open it specially for me.

*(He sits on the sofa.)*

**MADAME C:**
No, no – in this hot weather I keep it on the ice all day, ready for the evening. Ready for a nice gentleman like you.

*(Pours champagne.)*

**RC:**
Oh, who's that?

**MADAME:**
Who?

**RC:**
The gentleman who's like me?

**MADAME C:**
I mean you, cheri. I must say I think you are very cute. Why don't you take off your coat?

**RC:**
*(Still sitting, he does so.)* I hope I'm not disturbing you.

**MADAME C:**
Well – only a little. *(She sits close to him.)* Perhaps a little more now you have taken off your coat.

*(She leans over him.)*

**RC:**
*(struggling a little)* I'll just hang it up.

**MADAME C:**
Let me.

**RC:**
No, no, the walk will do me good.

*(He gets up and hangs the coat over a chair. He turns, and sees that Madame Cocotte is sitting, rolling down her stockings and showing a lot of leg as she does so.)*

**MADAME C:**
I hope you don't mind me removing my stockings – they are too hot around my legs.

**RC:**
Oh yes. Like footballers.

**MADAME C:**
Pardon?

**RC:**
They roll their stockings down. Not usually this early in the game though.

**MADAME C:**
You say such strange things, cheri. Come here.

**RC:**
Look, why don't you slip into something more comfortable?

**MADAME C:**
*(with a smile)* The only thing that is more comfortable than this is nothing. Kiss me.

*(They kiss, passionately.)*

**RC:**
*(close to her)* There's something I'd like you to accept from me, Madame. Will you?

**MADAME C:**
Of course I will, darling. *(They are clasped together in each other's arms.)* Now?

**RC:**
All right. Here we are then. *(Takes bag from pocket.)* Have a jelly bean.

*Cut to: the terrace.*
*(Piggy is just finishing his meal. A discreet burp behind his hand. RC staggers up to the table.)*

**RB:**
That was quick. What happened?

**RC:**
Well, I got carried away.

**RB:**
And?

**RC:**
She got carried away.

**RB:**
Well?

**RC:**
We both got under way.

**RB:**
And?

**RC:**
Then she got called away.

**RB:**
What's that supposed to be? The first verse of Ta ra ra boomdeay? You mean to say you didn't find anything out at all?

**RC:**
Well, I'll tell you one thing. She's hot stuff. My jelly beans melted.

**RB:**
Well, it doesn't matter anyhow. I've got another idea. While you've been off enjoying yourself, I've been sitting here thinking.

**RC:**
Oh yes? You think too much, you know. You're overweight as it is.

**RB:**
All right, all right. Listen, where's that Polaroid you took of those two villains?

**RC:**
Here.

*(He produces it from his pocket.)*

**RB:**
Ta. Evil-looking pair, aren't they? *(We cut to the photo of Mr Greensleaves and Bob-Job.)* Right, now tomorrow is the Hotel Fancy Dress Dance, right?

**RC:**
Tomorrow, yes.

**RB:**
It's the perfect opportunity. If we disguise ourselves as these two, we can talk to Madame Cocotte as they would. Her defences will be completely down.

**RC:**
They won't you know – she's going as Boadicea.

**RB:**
Don't worry. Whatever defences she puts up, we'll penetrate them. We'll just go in and fight dirty, like Lee Marvin. We can't be any dirtier than that great fat sinister slob in the dark glasses, and that evil little Oriental runt.

**RC:**
Absolutely, chief. So it's disguises, eh?

**RB:**
Yeah.

**RC:**
Which one do you want me to be?

*(Piggy gives him a jaded look.)*

*Cut to: the ballroom of the hotel.*
*(A quartet of fake gypsy musicians play tango and rumba numbers, and about eight couples are in evidence, six of whom are in fancy dress.)*

*(RB anc RC enter as Piggy and Charley, disguised as Greensleeves and Bob-Job. RB has an ordinary pair of glasses, which he has smoked over. RC has ordinary glasses with Sellotape all round to make them look like pebble glasses. He also has a distinctly yellow look, much more than necessary. RB has a bad straw-like wig. Their clothes, however, are perfect replicas of the real thing. They both give fairly rotten impersonations, voice-wise. They stand in the half-shadow of a potted palm.)*

**RB:**
*(in Piggy's voice)* I can't see a bloody thing in these glasses.

**RC:**
Me neither. What is it, cocoa?

**RB:**
No, I smoked 'em over a candle.

**RC:**
Mine's sticky tape, cut into strips.

**RB:**
That's clever.

**RC:**
Trouble is, there's bits sticking up. I'm frightened to blink in case I can't open my eye again.

**M. PHILLIPE:**
*(coming forward to greet them)* Ah, bonsoir Monsieur Greensleeves – we are honoured.

**RB:**
*(bowing graciously)* Where is Madame Cocotte, Phillipe? We expected to find her waiting to greet us.

**MP:**
I regret she has not yet made an appearance, Monsieur.

**RC:**
*(who mistakenly gets his "r"'s wrong instead of his "l"'s)* She is plobably in her loom, lighting a few letters. She will alive, never flear. She loves a bit of levelling.
*(Addressing a nearby guest)* I have known her make the lafters ling, and louse up the whole village.

**RB:**
*(out of the corner of his mouth)* Don't overdo it. Ah! Madame Cocotte. Ravishing, ravishing!

*Cut to: Madame C dressed rakishly as Boadicea. (She joins them, giving them rather an odd look.)*

**MADAME C:**
Good evening, gentlemen. No fancy dress?

**RB:**
No, my dear. At my time of life one becomes too set in one's ways to try to be someone else. I'd rather save my energy for other things.

*(A chuckle.)*

**MADAME C:**
In that case, why not join Miss Grimsberg over there – she is dressed completely in balloons.

**RB:**
Really?

**MADAME C:**
Yes – she's feeling a bit lonely – no one can get near her.

*Cut to: Miss Grimsberg, arms, legs and head visible amid a big bunch of coloured balloons.*

**RB:**
Oh. Well, I'm willing to try. *(As he goes)* Anyone got a pin?

*(He laughs a sinister laugh as he goes.)*

**RC:**
*(to Madame C)* Well, how are you, my little lay of sunshine?

**MADAME C:**
*(amused)* Your little what?

**RC:**
It's an English explosion.

**MADAME C:**
Oh – you have lived in England?

**RC:**
Yes.

**MADAME C:**
Where?

**RC:**
Near the liver at Loehampton.

*Cut to: the doorway. (Standing there are the real villains – RB and RC as Greensleeves and Bob-Job. Zoom in fast, dramatic music.)*

**RB:**
*(looking round)* What the devil's going on, Bob-Job.? Look over there.

*(Bob-Job looks – cut to his point of view – see Charley talking to Madame C, and then Piggy talking to Miss Grimsberg.)*

**RB:**
Those two British idiots, what are they up to?

**RC:**
I'm not sure, Mr Greensleeves, but I don't rike the rook of it.

**RB:**
Neither do I. It may be a trap. Keep close together and head for the French windows.

*(They start to move when suddenly a fusillade of shots rings out. They both drop down behind a sofa as a scream is heard. The other guests look in the direction of the shots.)*

*Cut to: Piggy and Miss Grimsberg. She is now wearing only six balloons, strategically placed. (Piggy pops another one with his pin, leaving five. Piggy does his imitation of Greensleeves' laugh.)*

**RB:**
There goes another!

**MISS G:**
*(annoyed)* Please!

*(Piggy looks round and notices the hush.)*

*Cut to: Greensleeves and Bob-Job looking over the top of the sofa, angrily. (Piggy reacts in embarrassment at their presence. He takes off his glasses – two black rings of soot are around his eyes.)*

427

**VOICE OVER:**
And even as the villains are confronted by our heroes' pathetic attempts at impersonation, two waiters of unknown origin prepare to serve the speciality of the house – a double dose of the already Clumsy Drug.

*(During the above we see a long shot of the kitchen with RB and RC as the two Middle-Eastern gents, complete with fez and dirty white coats. We shoot at first, however, from behind them so we cannot see who they are or what they are doing. Then a close-up of a large iced cake. Into it is plunged a rather over-sized hypodermic – deadly-looking nonetheless.)*

**RB:**
One double dose injected directly into the centre of this noble example of the confectioner's art, and the drug will permeate into all parts.

**RC:**
Paralysing any person permitted to partake of a portion.

**RB:**
Precisely.

**RC:**
One piece, and poof!

**RB:**
Pardon?

**RC:**
Poof!

**RB:**
Oh yes.

**RC:**
They become as clumsy as a bull in a knocking shop.

**RB:**
China shop.

**RC:**
What?

**RB:**
China!

**RC:**
Yes, any part of the world whatsoever. Now ...

*(They continue to chatter together as we fade up the final voice over, cutting back to the ballroom, for various shots.)*

**VOICE OVER:**
So once more a sinister net is cast that may land our heroes in trouble. Will Piggy refuse a piece of cake? Has he ever refused a piece of cake? And what of Madame Cocotte? Will she offer Charley a bit? And what will happen to Miss Grimsberg when the balloon goes up?

*(Over the last line – a close-up of Piggy, then Madame C and Charley, then Miss Grimsberg and her balloons. Two more bangs make her jump and look round at Piggy.)*

**VOICE OVER:**
Don't miss next week's enthralling episode: "The Bitter Bit".

# EPISODE SIX

*After usual titles, voice over and shots from previous episodes.*

**VOICE OVER:**
The Clumsy Drug affair. Piggy and Charley, having tracked the gang to Marseilles, had managed to secure a map of the villains' hideout, drawn on a pair of ladies' panties. But even as they studied the contours, the beautiful owner of the aforementioned unmentionables was planning to give our two heroes a dose of the dreaded Clumsy Drug itself, planted inside the speciality of the house. At the fancy dress dance, Piggy and Charley, disguised as the two villains, were confronted by the real villains themselves and the balloon went up. Piggy alone ate

the cake and the awful effects began to show themselves as the loyal Charley helped him back to their hotel bedroom.

*Cut to: bedroom.*
*(RC opens the door.)*

**RC:**
Come on in, chief, and shut the door.

*(RB enters, bangs his head on the door, staggers back and knocks over vase on pedestal by door.)*

**RC:**
Here, you'd better sit down. The drug is obviously quite powerful.

**RB:**
Yes.

*(He sits on very delicate, thin upright chair, which collapses underneath him. He gets up, sits on the settee, his arm flops out onto an occasional table next to it, knocks lamp over.)*

**RC:**
*(trying to ignore the damage)* Does it hurt at all?

**RB:**
No – it doesn't hurt. Just can't quite control your movements, that's all.

*(He removes his panama hat clumsily. It falls to the floor.)*

**RC:**
*(making light of it)* According to London, it only lasts a short while.

**RB:**
Yes, as a matter of fact, I think it's wearing off already.

*(Crosses his legs and falls straight off the sofa.)*

**RC:**
Anyway, I've ordered you a drink. I must go and clean that stuff off my face, won't be long. Then I'll help you get to bed.

*(Exits to bathroom.)*

*(RB sits back on settee. A knock. A waiter enters with whisky and soda siphon and glasses on a tray.)*

**RB:**
Ah, thank you.

*(Gets up.)*

*(The waiter puts tray down, waits for tip. RB tries to get his hand into his trouser pocket. He eventually manages it, gropes about, pulls out a handful of coins and throws them up in the air.)*

**RB:**
Put it on the bill, would you?

*(The waiter looks daggers and goes. RB picks up tumbler upside down and pours whisky over it. Puts it back on the tray, right way up. Tries to pour whisky into it and misses. He gradually steers the bottle over it, then presses soda on the wrong side. Turns siphon round, again presses wrong side. Picks up siphon and glass, but soda water misses and goes all over the front of his trousers. He puts down siphon and glass, sighs.)*

*(RC enters – same clothes, wiping his face with a towel.)*

**RC:**
Here, let me do that, chief. You ought to rest. They say this drug's got some nasty side effects.

**RB:**
*(looking at his trousers)* Pretty horrible front effects an' all.

*(RC pours new drinks.)*

**RC:**
Well, don't worry, we'll soon have you in bed. That's the ...

*(He stops and stares in the direction of the door.)*

*Cut to: close-up. A note is being pushed under the door. (RC picks up the note, opens it.)*

**RC:**
It's from Madame Cocotte. *(Reads)* "I am in deadly danger. Meet me at midnight in the El Fatale Club, 17 Rue de Remarques ...

**RB:**
17, where?

**RC:**
Rue de Remarques. It's in the old town, chief.

**RB:**
Oh yes, go on.

**RC:**
*(reading)* "Wait for me there. Please, please. Then, in a private room, I will reveal everything to you."

**RB:**
Hm. Put like that, we can hardly refuse, can we?

**RC:**
Do you think you're fit enough, chief? You're still a bit clumsy.

**RB:**
It's another two hours yet – it'll have worn off by then.

**RC:**
All right, chief. *(Hands RB his drink, takes his own.)* For the sake of that poor, unprotected, magnificently built woman, we'll go! To th El Fatale Club!

*(He offers up his drink as a toast. RB raises his glass, hits RC in the nose with it, then throws the contents into his own face.)*

*Cut to: sign saying "Rue de Remarques".*

*Cut to: sign: "El Fatale club".*

*Cut to: interior of the club.*

*A smoke-filled, low-lit dive. A very "Turkish*

delight" feeling about the place, but filthy with it. At one end of the room, a small alcove, through which the villains can peer unnoticed. Weird Turkish music. (Piggy and Charley are being seated by a greasy waiter at a table in the foreground.)*

**RC:**
That's fine, thank you.

*(The waiter produces a menu that appears to be two foot high by one foot wide, and hands it to Piggy. It is, however, a concertina-type folded card, with four folds, so it is really two foot high by four feet wide. Piggy holds this in front of them both for a few seconds, completely hiding both of them. Then he folds it again and hands it to the waiter.)*

**RB:**
Two light ales, please.

**WAITER:**
You eat something?

**RC:**
Er ... *(waiter takes knife from belt menacingly)* One of those please.

*(Stabs finger at menu. The waiter glares and exits.)*

**RB:**
Bit of a dump, this, isn't it?

**RC:**
A real den of iniquity!

*(The drinks arrive. They drink. Charley spills his.)*

**PIGGY:**
Oh, my God! They must have drugged the drinks. You feel all right?

**RC:**
No, the drink's OK.

*(Tries to mop it up with his hankie.)*

**RB:**
But you were acting clumsy.

**RC:**
That's not the drug. I just am clumsy sometimes. Just naturally clumsy, you know.

*Cut to: a belly dancer. The camera tracks past her to the alcove where, in the half light, we see the villains (RB and RC as Greensleeves and Bob-Job).*

**RB:**
They've arrived. Those British fools have walked right into our trap.

*Cut back to Piggy. (The belly dancer is now next to him. He looks at her. Close-up of her belly dancing. Close-up of Piggy's face. Close-up belly, close-up plate of jelly on plate Piggy is holding. It wobbles in the same rhythm. Dance ends, applause from onlookers. Close-up as jelly slows down and stops as Piggy puts it on table. A few couples get up and start dancing.)*

**RC:**
Well? Are you going to try some, chief?

**RB:**
No, thanks I've gone off it. Where's this woman got to?

**RC:**
*(looking round the room)* She's probably pouring herself into one of those low-cut dresses she wears.

**RB:**
Like that girl over there, you mean. *(Cut to girl with enormous boobs in low-cut dress.)* You don't get many of those to the pound. *(Drinks, then looks at watch.)* I wonder what's holding her up.

**RC:**
What, that girl, do you mean?

*(Still looking at her.)*

**RB:**
No – Madame Cocotte.

**RC:**
Oh, nothing. It's all there –

I've seen her in a negligée.

**RB:**
*(sighing)* I mean, why is she late?

**RC:**
Oh. Here, chief, do you think we look a bit spare sitting here? A bit suspicious, like?

**RB:**
Yes – you may be right. Perhaps we'd better dance.

**RC:**
I think that might make us look even more suspicious. You get arrested for that round here, you know.

**RB:**
I didn't mean together.

**RC:**
Oh!

**RB:**
I meant pick out a couple of birds.

**RC:**
*(looking out of frame)* Frankly, I don't advise it, chief.

**RB:**
Why?

**RC:**
The only two birds who aren't dancing are sitting over there.

*Cut to: two rather masculine-looking old ladies in blue-rinse wigs, dressed like us tourists – big handbags, etc. They look very surly.*

**RB:**
Oh dear. Here – they're men, ain't they?

**RC:**
I don't know. But I wouldn't like to try and find out. It would be a terrible disappointment either way.

431

**RB:**
I'm sure they're fellahs. Look out, they're moving.

*(We see the two women get up and go through an alcove. They enter a door marked "dames".)*

**RB:**
Oh well – shows you how wrong you can be.

**RC:**
I still don't fancy tripping the light fantastic round the dance floor with them, though.

*(Once again the floor has cleared and once again the belly dancer emerges and begins to gyrate.)*

**RB:**
Look, she's obviously not coming.

**RC:**
Something's happened to her.

*(The belly dancer is once more at Piggy's elbow.)*

**RB:**
Come on, let's go. I've had a bellyful of this place.

*(They rise and start to leave.)*

*Cut to: Greensleeves and Bob-Job. (Greensleeves gives a nod to the waiter, who exits. They continue to watch, smiling.)*

*Cut to: a dark alley containing the entrance to the club. A Turkish doorman stands outside. (Piggy and Charley come out and walk towards camera. We suddenly hear a gruff voice with a French accent out of vision.)*

**GRUFF VOICE:**
'Ave you a light, Monsieur?

*(RB and RC turn, startled. It is the two "ladies" they saw in the club. Now it is obvious they are men, and "heavies" at that.*

*They grab Piggy and Charley, hands over mouths and half-nelsons on their arms, and push them out of shot.)*

*Close-up of the inscrutable doorman, over which we hear car doors slamming and a car roaring away.*

*Cut to: car roaring away.*

**VOICE OVER:**
Is this the end for our two heroes? What of Madame Cocotte? Is she in some bedroom somewhere, lying in wait with a silencer? Or lying in silence with a waiter? Find out next week in another exciting episode: "Villa Of Villainy".

# EPISODE SEVEN

*Titles as usual, with scenes from previous episodes.*

**VOICE OVER:**
Piggy and Charlie on the trail of the dreaded Clumsy Drug, which was being used to make fools out of public figures, had tracked the gang to Marseilles, but had been lured into a trap at the notorious El Fatale club, situated at number 17, Rue de Remarques. As they left, they were attacked by two thugs disguised as lady tourists and taken by car to a lonely villa a few miles out of town. There, waiting for them, stood the fascinating Madame Cocotte, widely acclaimed for her beauty, and publicly known for unveiling things for charity, while, at the same time, she was secretly concerned with drugs, shifting quantities of amazing proportions. At this moment, however, as she shifted her own amazingly proportioned quantities towards the car, there was but one thought in her head: murder.

**MADAME C:**
Welcome gentlemen to the Villa D'Aston, my little country bottom.

**RC:**
Seat, country seat.

**MADAME C:**
Oh yes, seat. Is pretty, no?

**RB:**
Yes, very nice, yes.

**MADAME C:**
Shall we go in and sit down? We can be more comfortable.

*Cut to: inside house.*

**MADAME C:**
*(to "ladies")* Now go, get back to town and take off that terrible make-up and the clothes. You disgust me. You think I am foolish, a poor, frail, unarmed girl to cope with two men. But I am not unarmed. My arms are on my legs. You see, I only have to lift my legs, then you are dead. *(She reveals pistols strapped to her thighs.)*

**RC:**
What a terrible way to go.

**MADAME:**
Don't worry, cheri, I do not intend to kill you – yet. M. Greensleeves will be my first victim.

**RB:**
Greensleeves, but he's the head of your gang?

**MADAME C:**
Not for much longer. Bob-Job and I are going to take over the business.

**RB:**
That little Japanese crook?

**MADAME C:**
I like him.

**RB:**
I wouldn't trust him further than I can throw him, which is not as far as I'd like to.

**MADAME C:**
I didn't say I trusted him. I like him. I like all men who are shorter than I am. That's why I have asked those two villains not to arrive until tomorrow. I have a little unfinished business with you, cheri.

**RC:**
I've run out of jelly beans, if that's what you're after.

**MADAME C:**
You are so sweet. Oh, it may interest you to know that while you were searching the hotel for a pair of panties, on which was printed a map of this hideout, you were completely wasting your time.

**RB:**
Why, we found a pair with a map on them. Yours, they were.

**MADAME C:**
Of course, but they were a pair of big red herrings.

**RB:**
Not the pair I saw weren't. They would have hardly covered a tiddler.

**MADAME C:**
You are so foolish. All the time you looked for a map, the formula itself was written on another pair.

**RC:**
Another pair? Whose?

**MADAME C:**
The ones I am wearing at this moment. Come, let's go to my room, we can be alone much more comfortably. Goodnight, M Piggy.

**RB:**
Here! Aren't you going to untie me?

**MADAME C:**
Perhaps tomorrow

**RC:**
See you later, chief. Hope you get

a good night.

**RB:**
Yeah, not as good as you're going to get, I bet.

**RC:**
What can I do, chief? My hands are tied.

**MADAME C:**
We'll think of something. Goodnight.

*(They exit.)*

*(Piggy finds he is tied up next to a spear, which is digging into his rear. He manoeuvres himself so that he can get the spear to cut the ropes that bind his wrists.)*

**VOICE OVER:**
And so as Charley Farley lay upstairs with his conscience pricking him, Piggy Malone suffered a similar sensation, though not in the same place. At last he was free. Now, with the door bolted and barred from the outside, there was nothing he could do but wait.

*(Next day. Madame C enters.)*

**MADAME C:**
Good morning. Did you manage to get some sleep?

**RB:**
Yes, what did you manage?

**MADAME C:**
Oh, I managed.

**RB:**
Yeah, I bet you did. Where's Charlie?

**MADAME C:**
I have locked him in the bedroom. He is a little exhausted.

**RB:**
He's a little exhausted rat, upstairs with you pandering to his foibles, me down here, sitting on me own ...

*(We hear a car pulling up outside.)*

**MADAME C:**
It is them – Greensleeves and Bob-Job. Don't make a sound.

*(Greensleeves and Bob-Job enter.)*

**RB:**
Good morning, my dear. I trust we're not too early for our appointment?

**MADAME C:**
*(producing a gun)* Not at all, especially as today your appointment is with your maker.

**RC:**
An excellent device, my dear. Double-barrelled, I see. Do you need any help re-roading?

**MADAME C:**
No, no. I have three bullets – one here, another two in this one. Listen, there's no time to lose. I'll go upstairs and get my passport and then come back and finish off this fool. Stay and guard him. I lock the door behind me.

*(She leaves the room. Piggy lunges at Bob-Job. There follows a fight, in which Piggy manages to knock out the villainous Japanese. He finds Charley and they are just in time to see her running towards her car.)*

**RB:**
Come on, she's getting away.

**RC:**
She's still wearing those pants with the formula on.

**RB:**
Oh, you've seen it?

**RC:**
Not half.

**RB:**
Did you learn it?

RC:
No, there was too much to remember.

RB:
Oh, really?

RC:
Mmm. I shall never forget it.

*(Madame C drives off in car. They follow down a winding road that leads to the coast.)*

VOICE OVER:
Our two intrepid detectives were on the horns of a dilemma as they chased the bold, bad, beautiful Madame Cocotte. At any moment she may throw caution to the wind and her knickers out of the window. Or did she intend to sit tight on the information? Don't miss next week, the final gripping instalment: "Double Exposure"!

# EPISODE EIGHT

*Titles, scenes from previous episodes, as before.*

VOICE OVER:
The sordid affair of the Clumsy Drug, which had led our two ill-fated detectives to Marseilles, was drawing to a close. The villains, one dead and one half-dead, were no longer a problem. All that remained now was to get hold of the formula. A difficult, dangerous, but not unpleasant task, bearing in mind that it was written on a pair of panties worn by the woman in the car ahead of them. And Piggy was already baring it in mind as they gave chase.

*(RC and RB in car, giving chase.)*

RC:
She's heading for the coast road.

RB:
We mustn't lose sight of her. If she

manages to dodge us long enough to destroy the formula, we've had it.

RC:
At least she can't take 'em off while she's driving, can she?

RB:
It has been known.

*(We are now in the docks area, near some warehouses. Madame's car comes speeding round corner, stops. She jumps out and runs towards a warehouse. RB and RC's car arrives. They stop and run after her. Madame runs around a corner and dives into a doorway. RB and RC run round corner and do the same. We see the sign on the door – "International feather bed co".)*

*Cut to: inside the warehouse.*
*(Piggy and Charley stand, listening. All is still and silent. Madame's long and shapely leg slowly appears round a corner, followed by her gun. A shot. RB and RC duck. Echoing footsteps are heard running. Then a door slams; then silence. RB and RC indicate that they will split up. Dramatic music as they move through the warehouse.)*

*Cut to: the door.*
*(RC puts his ear against it, reacts as if he hears something. He suddenly throws the door open and drops to the ground.)*

*Cut to: inside the little room looking towards the door.*
*(RC is on the ground and in the foreground of the shot is a pair of female legs. RC grabs the desk lamp and hurls it past camera. A crash, and all the light is extinguished as he dives towards the legs. Screams, yells and scuffles in the black-out.)*

*Cut to: inside another room. A pile of mattresses in plastic covers, also about a dozen pillows in a heap.*
*(RB enters stealthily, peering round the door first. He comes in, closes the door. Suddenly Madame C grabs him round the neck, one hand over his mouth. RB twists round, throws her on a pile of mattresses. She lands, her*

*hand goes to her pistol. Click! it is out of ammunition. Piggy, in close-up, looks relieved. Madame C grabs a pillow and takes a swing at him. Hits him on the head.)*

*(The pillow bursts; feathers everywhere. RB grabs pillow. He hits her. His pillow bursts. Then he tackles her and they fight as the feathers float around them like a snow storm.)*

*Cut to: outside the room Charley was in. (He comes out very quickly and locks door. He is extremely dishevelled and out of breath. He leans against the wall, gasping, then sits on the floor, trying to get his breath back.)*

*Cut to: RB approaching. (He too is exhausted and covered in feathers. RC looks up.)*

**RC:**
I got her, chief! She's in there.

**RB:**
What do you mean, you got her. I got her. Look! *(From his pocket he produces a pair of orange briefs with some figures written on the back.)* Here they are. Here's the formula.

**RC:**
*(puzzled)* Then who ...

*(He quickly unlocks the door. A very dishevelled girl appears, her hair all over the place, her glasses bent. She looks puzzled and blinks at them both.)*

**RC:**
I'm terribly sorry, Miss.

*(The girl smiles dazedly.)*

**GIRL:**
That's alright, cheri!

**RC:**
You see, I was trying to find the formula.

**GIRL:**
I 'aven't fought like zat since ze office party. Excusez-moi – I must tidy up.

*(She shuts the door again.)*

**RC:**
So – you got them, chief.

**RB:**
After a struggle, yes. I nearly got me face kicked in.

**RC:**
Where is she now? Locked in?

**RB:**
No need. Poor kid – she never stood a chance.

**RC:**
Why? What happened?

**RB:**
She hit me with a pillow and it burst. The whole room was filled with feathers, floating about everywhere.

**RC:**
You mean ...

**RB:**
Yeah. She was tickled to death.

# SONGS

## A PINT OF OLD AND FILTHY

In 1964 Ronnie Barker was filming the Galton and Simpson scripted movie, *The Bargee*, alongside Harry H Corbett. As a way of passing the time between set-ups, he started writing parody lyrics of Edwardian music hall songs. He showed these lyrics to Galton and Simpson, who were impressed and amused. By the time he was a regular on *Frost On Sunday*, Ronnie had penned several more songs and showed them to musical director Laurie Holloway, who suggested setting them to music and making an album out of them. The result was released in 1969 as *A Pint of Old and Filthy*. "The title indicates that some of them are old and some of them are filthy. Or both," explains Ronnie. "And I don't know how successful they were, but they were published and I enjoyed it very much."

# NOT TOO TALL AND NOT TOO SHORT

**VERSE ONE:**
I haven't been out with a girl for years –
Now maybe you think I'm slow
No, that's not the reason: I'll tell you why–
I'm particular, you know.
Some girls are two a penny,
And others a halfpenny each.
I don't want them – the girl I seek
Must be a perfect peach.

**CHORUS:**
Not too tall and not too short,
Not too thick or thin;
She must come out where she should come out,
And go in where she should go in;
She mustn't have much too much behind,
Or much too little in front;
If ever I have a girl again,
That's the girl I want.

**VERSE TWO:**
I heard about a girl called May,
She sounded quite a catch.
"She's only five foot five" they said,
"With golden hair to match."
But when I met her in the woods
I knew I'd been sold a pup;
'Cos she was taller lying down
Than when she was standing up.

**REPEAT CHORUS:**
Not too tall ... etc.

**VERSE THREE:**
Then I met Rachel Rosenbloom,
An Irish girl from Wales.
She had a face like a summer's morn,
And a shape like a bag of nails.
"Could I only see your face," I said
"I never more would roam.
So bring your dear sweet face to me,
And leave your body at home."

**REPEAT CHORUS:**
Not too tall ... etc.

**VERSE FOUR:**
At last I met my heart's desire,
A girl called Annie More.
She walked in beauty as the night,
With legs right down to the floor.
I pressed my suit, she creased her frock,
We had a splendid spree–
She was the girl I'd been looking for,
Now her husband is looking for me.

**REPEAT CHORUS:**
Not too tall ... etc.

# I BELIEVE IN DOING THINGS IN MODERATION

**VERSE:**
I'd like to introduce myself to all you lovely men,
My name is Miss Golightly, and I'm on the loose again;
My engagement to the Duke of Diss was broken off in May,
And he sent me to the South of France for nine months holiday.
Now I'm back in circulation, I've rejoined the social whirl–
I'm really awfully popular, and have been since a girl,
But I do have certain standards, and I never let them drop–
I'm very good at most things, but I do know when to stop.

**CHORUS ONE:**
If I'm drinking at a party, then I stop when I'm half-tight–
I believe in doing things in moderation.
If I'm dining with a man, I only stop out half the night,
I believe in doing things in moderation.
I went out with a footballer – he really was sublime,
I said "Are you a half-back?" as I sipped his gin and lime,

He said "No, I'm centre-forward" so I
stopped him at half-time,
I believe in doing things in moderation.

**PATTER:**

Oh, I've met some men in my time. I met
one last week.
He was gorgeous. I said "Marry me!" He
said "I can't, I'm not working at the
moment." I said "Never mind, I can
always have you repaired!"

**CHORUS TWO:**

When cuddling with a motorist, I don't
mind if he swerves,
I believe in doing things in moderation.
I tell him "Take your time and please go
easy round the curves,"
I believe in doing things in moderation.
The meanest man in London, once lured
me to his lair,
He asked for my hand in marriage, so I
told him then and there–
I just held up two fingers and said "That's
all I can spare,"
'Cos I believe in doing things in
moderation.

**PATTER:**

I was a nurse in the Boer War, you know –
oh, those soldiers – they were always
trying to get me into trouble. One night I
was in the ward and this soldier
whispered "Give us a kiss, nurse"
And I said "Certainly not!" and he said
"Oh come on, one little kiss," and I said
"No! It's against the rules. Nurses must not
kiss the patients – matron's orders. And if I
hear another word out of you I shall get
out of this bed and report you." I mean,
you've got to draw the line somewhere,
haven't you?

**CHORUS THREE:**

I met a charming golfer – oh, he's really
awfully bright,
I believe in doing things in moderation.
He's teaching me the game – I played a
round with him last night.
I believe in doing things in moderation.
"Now this one is a two-stroke hole," he
said, which sounded fun.

"So just give me a chance and I will show
you how it's done."
I finally gave him half-a-chance, and he
got it in in one!
Oh I believe in doing things in
moderation!

# I GO OOMPAH

**VERSE ONE (SPOKEN):**

My father was in the Swiss navy,
Und he yodelled all day, on the deck.
Till one day he slipped, and fell off the
ship
Und broke both his voice, und his neck.
In his will he had left me his "oompah",
A euphonium that I learned to play.
And now when folk ask what I do all day
long,
I just show my euphonium and say:

**CHORUS ONE:**

Oompah ... Oompah,
I just sit alone and go oompah.
I find it enchanting, so good for the mind
It helps me to leave all my worries behind.
I go Oomph ... Oompah
It fills me with constant delight.
And when day is done, I find it such fun
To go oompah-pah all through the night.

**VERSE TWO:**

When I first tried to find rooms in
London,
The landladies were a disgrace.
They just took one look at my oompah
And closed the door right in my face!
But one lady I called on was different,
She had not seen an oompah before.
She invited me into her parlour
And as soon as she'd closed the front
door–

**CHORUS TWO:**

Oompah ... Oompah,
I gave her a bit of the oompah.
She found it enchanting, so good for the
brain,

And each time I stopped she said "Do it again!"
I went Oompah ... Oompah,
And now we've become man and wife
And as long as I keep going oompah,
She'll be happy the rest of her life!

# THEY TELL ME THERE'S A LOT OF IT ABOUT

**VERSE ONE:**
When I got home last Wednesday I was feeling rather queer,
A little out of sorts, you'll understand:
I found a little drinking-house, conveniently near,
And went in with my threepence in my hand.
The barmaid she was six foot two, and every inch a gent–
With a figure like a well-made double bed;
"What can I do for you?" she said, and on the counter leant–
And I stared into her feather-boa and said–

**CHORUS:**
They tell me there's a lot of it about,
They tell me there's a lot of it about–
Some get it here,
Some get it there,
Others seem to pick it up any old where;
It's definitely on the increase,
Of that there is no doubt;
It's not a thing that you can put your finger on,
But there's certainly a lot of it about.

**VERSE TWO:**
On looking round my property, imagine my dismay,
To find the fence all broken, by the door;
So I popped round to the carpenters to tell him, right away,
My perimeters had fallen to the floor.
He brought some wood, all full of holes –
"They're knot-holes," he explained –

"If they're not holes, what are they then?" I cried.
"Of course they're holes – they're knot-holes," he replied in accents strained
"The hole's there, but the knot is not inside."

**REPEAT CHORUS**
Well! ... They tell me there's ... etc.

**VERSE THREE:**
In the old Egyptian desert, there's a frightful lot of sand,
And in crossing it, one's mouth gets awfully dry.
My camel got the hump one day, it got quite out of hand–
Just lolloped off, and left me there to die.
I strolled about for days and days, as thirsty as could be,
Till round the corner came an Arab bold.
I cried "Water, water, water" as I clutched him round the knee,
And his answer made my fevered blood run cold;

**REPEAT CHORUS:**
Well! ... They tell me there's ... etc.

**VERSE FOUR:**
Two honeymooners, rather tired, preparing to retire,
Began to kiss and cuddle on the bed,
His love it was so ardent that the bedclothes caught on fire–
"Quick, dearest! Through the window – jump" he said.
Her nightie caught upon a nail, she nearly fell right through it,
She hung there, with her arms flung open wide:
The lady in the flat beneath said "Kindly pass the cruet"
And the firemen down below as one man cried–

**REPEAT CHORUS:**
Well! ... They tell me there's ... etc.

# I CAN'T STAND BY AND WATCH OTHERS SUFFER

**VERSE ONE:**

I mingle a lot with society,
I'm well known by the gentry, you see–
I often go round to Quaglino's;
And he sometimes comes round to me.
I sat next to a beautiful lady
When I last went around there to sup;
She was wearing a frightfully low-cut gown–
You could see she was well brought up:
She began to converse rather freely,
Her one pleasure, she said, was to cook–
She described what she did with her dumplings
Till I didn't know which way to look.
Just then, an itinerant waiter
Dropped a large ice-cream right on her chest;
As it slid out of sight she cried "Help me!"
"It's freezing! Oh quick! Do your best!"

**CHORUS ONE:**

Well, I can't stand by and just watch others suffer,
No, I have to go and try to make amends–
So I held her down by force,
And applied hot chocolate sauce,
And ever since we've both been bosom friends!

**VERSE TWO:**

One night at the club I'd been drinking
And was staggering home, about three–
Well, I'd missed all the cabs, and decided
It was their turn to try missing me.
As I zigzagged along the embankment
(As I said, I'd had several halves)
On the bridge stood the butcher's young daughter,
I could tell it was her by her calves.
She spoke in a disjointed fashion
"All the lights have gone out of my life–
I know it's not meet, but there's so much at stake,
I shall chop out my heart with a knife!"
I murmured "That's tripe – you're a chump, dear"
(T'was the language she best understood)
She replied "If I had but the guts, sir,

I'd throw myself into the flood!"
(She was Northern)

**CHORUS TWO:**

Well, I can't stand by and just watch others suffer–
And other people's fear just makes me brave.
So like the dear kind soul I am
I threw her underneath a tram,
And saved her from a very watery grave.

**VERSE THREE:**

As I wandered through a cornfield last September
A couple sat beneath the harvest moon
And I saw the lady cuddling the fellow,
Persuading him to have a little spoon;
First he wouldn't, then he would, and then he didn't–
Then he tried to, and he couldn't, just the same.
Then he wondered if he should or if he shouldn't,
As he didn't even know the lady's name.
No, finally he decided that he oughtn't–
As he'd always wished he hadn't, once he had;
Then he asked her "Is it really that important?"
And she said it was, which petrified the lad.
Well, she lay there on one elbow, so romantic,
And he stood there, undecided, on one leg;
In her eyes I saw a longing that was frantic
Like a cocker-spaniel, sitting up to beg.

**CHORUS THREE:**

Well, I can't stand by and just watch others suffer–
It makes me suffer so myself, you see:
So I pushed, and he fell over;
They were married in October,
And they've called the baby Cyril, after me!

# OUR MARY ANN, IS WITH A HAIRY MAN

**VERSE ONE:**
There's a girl down our street
Pretty as can be.
Mary Ann's her name and
She never smiles at me.
She likes men with whiskers,
And when she's about
With her latest fellow, why
The kids all shout–

**CHORUS:**
Our Mary Ann, is with a hairy man,
Our Mary Ann, is with a hairy man,
Fetch dad quick,
And stop it if you can
'Cos a hairy man is dallying
With our Mary Ann.

**VERSE TWO:**
Once she went a-gathering
Watercress for tea,
Down by the brook she saw
A man behind a tree
She knew he was a Scotsman
Because his knees were bare.
But when she saw his sporran, why
She went quite spare!

**REPEAT CHORUS**

**VERSE THREE:**
One day her uncle
Took her to the zoo.
She saw the lions and tigers
And the baby kangaroo
But then the big gorilla
Snarled at her with rage,
She gave a little giggle and
She jumped inside the cage!

**REPEAT CHORUS**

# BLACK PUDDING MARCH

**VERSE ONE:**
A soldier lad was far from home, a-
fighting at the wars
To win the day for dear old England's
name
They'd sent him off to Africa to battle
with the Boers
To do his best, though he was not to
blame.
He thought of his old mother, a sitting all
alone
At supper and a lump came to his throat.
He took up pen and paper to send a letter
home
And his eyes were filled with tears as he
wrote:

**CHORUS ONE:**
Send me a lump of your old black
pudding
That's the stuff that I love most
Send me a lump of your old black
pudding
And a slab of dripping toast
We're fighting to make this old world
good enough
For folk who really care
So send me a lump of your old black
pudding
And I'll know that you're still there.

**VERSE TWO:**
A Scottish lad was over there and he was
fighting too
And thinking of his homeland far away.
He thought of all the things his darling
Maggie used to do
As they wandered through the heather on
the brae
And then a dreadful longing seemed to fill
his Scottish heart
As he pictured Maggie sitting by the fire
And he wrote these simple words to her
"Although we're far apart
There's really only one thing I desire–

**CHORUS TWO:**
Send me a lump of your dear old haggis
That is what I'm craving for the noo

If I could just get my hands on your dear
old haggis
I would know that you're still true
I've never seen a haggis like my dear old
Maggie's
And although I'm far from home
Just send me a lump of your dear old
haggis
And I'll know you feel the same.

**VERSE THREE:**
An Irish boy lay wounded in the camp
that very night
But the suffering and pain he bravely bore
And he watched the others writing
And he wished that he could write
To his Colleen back on dear old Erin's
shore
But his wound would not permit it
So he just lay back and thought
Of the little patch of green that he called
home
Of the humble little cottage and the girl
for whom he thought
And his loving thoughts went winging
o'er the foam

**CHORUS THREE:**
Send me a parcel of Irish stew, dear
Wrap it up and send it piping hot
If I could just dip bread in your Irish stew,
dear
Then I'd know you've not forgot
There's nobody nearly as good as you,
dear
With yer taters and yer meat
So send me a parcel of Irish stew, dear
And my life will be complete.

**VERSE FOUR:**
They're fighting to make this old world
Good enough to live in, side by side
So with yer stew and yer haggis and yer
old black pudding
You can keep them satisfied.

# NOT ROUND HERE

**VERSE ONE:**
This village is a friendly place – I live with
Mrs Meek,
And so do seven other men as well;
She keeps a little lodging house – I moved
in Wednesday week –
And I'm very well looked after – you can
tell.
There's nothing that I lack, except one
thing; that is to say,
An object usually found beside the bed.
So to the nearest household stores I
trotted, straight away,
But when I told them what it was, they
said–

**CHORUS ONE:**
Oh, you won't get those round here!
No, you won't get those round here;
Well, there isn't any call for them – round
here.
Why not just forget about them?
You're much better off without them!
No, you won't get no alarm-clocks, not
round here!

**VERSE TWO:**
One sunny morning, Daisy Jones leapt
gaily out of bed,
And went to spend a weekend on a yacht;
The sea-breeze blew her skirts about, and
Daisy, blushing red,
Became aware of something she'd forgot–
A part of her apparel that she couldn't be
without,
And still appear a lady, so to speak;
So to the nearest draper's shop she went,
and blurted out
Her shy request, and heard the draper
shriek–

**CHORUS TWO:**
Oh, you won't get those round here!
No, you won't get those round here;
Well, there isn't any call for them – round
here.
Why not just forget about them?
You're much better off without them!
Not handkerchiefs with lace on, not
round here!

**VERSE THREE:**
Young Archibald was getting wed to lovely Betty Blue,
The poor chap was so scared he could have died!
He trembled when he thought of all the things he'd have to do,
On the day that Betty Blue became his bride.
Our hero's tum felt absolutely full of butterflies
As at the local chemist's shop he called:
He asked for what he wanted, with a glazed look in his eyes,
And the girl behind the counter loudly bawled–

**CHORUS THREE:**
Oh, you won't get those round here!
No, you won't get those round here;
Well, there isn't any call for them – round here.
Why not just forget about them?
You're much better off without them!
No! Not stone hot-water bottles! Not round here!

# I PUT IT IN THE HANDS OF MY SOLICITOR

**VERSE ONE:**
I've always been a careful man – I don't go out in fog;
I don't believe in saying "Boo" to geese;
I don't converse with Irishmen, I never stroke a dog,
And I always raise my hat to the police.
And so when trouble comes my way, I do not fuss or shout,
I simply carry out this little plan;
I just put on my ta-ta, I go forth, and I seek out
The opinion of a proper legal man;

**CHORUS ONE:**
And I put it in the hands of my solicitor–
Yes, I put it in the hands of my solicitor.
So if trouble troubles you

You will know just what to do,
Simply put it in the hands of your solicitor.

**VERSE TWO:**
I ventured out one Friday morn when no one was about,
To buy a pound of apples, for a tart;
I was edging down the High Street, when I heard the butcher shout,
As round the corner rushed his horse and cart.
It hit a stone, the cart collapsed, the horse dropped to the ground,
And something nasty hit me in the eye;
It proved to be a piece of tripe, marked "one and eight a pound";
It was sticky; it was horrid; it was high.

**CHORUS TWO:**
So I put it in the hands of my solicitor
Yes, I put it in the hands of my solicitor–
And the butcher went to "Clink"
For creating such a stink,
When I put it in the hands of my solicitor.

**VERSE THREE:**
One day Miss Flo, a shapely lass, whilst on the river bank,
Removed her clothes and dived in, pleasure bent–
A passing navvy spied her skirt, and took it, for a prank.
And wrapped his dinner up in it, and went.
This thoughtless crime was soon revealed, poor Flo came to a stop
While still half-dressed – imagine her despair!
She had her blouse and feather-boa to cover up her top,
But she'd nothing left to cover her – elsewhere.

**CHORUS THREE:**
So she put it in the hands of her solicitor
*(spoken)* Yes, the whole thing.
She put it in the hands of her solicitor;
Having carefully weighed her case,
He then sued for loss of face!
When she put it in the hands of her solicitor.

# ALL SORTS

**VERSE ONE:**
Off for a week at the seaside,
Oh, what a jolly affair!
Off for a pint, and a paddle–
All sorts of folk will be there.
Last year I stayed at Miss Knocker's;
Really, the food was a crime–
Sausages; all shapes and sizes,
That's what she served all the time:

**CHORUS ONE:**
There were small ones, tall ones, rolled up
in a ball ones,
Long ones, strong ones, horrible and
high,
Pale ones, frail ones, thereby hangs a tale
ones,
Red ones, dead ones, and ones that
wouldn't die.
Edible, treadable, some that were
incredible,
Bashed ones, mashed ones, not a pretty
sight;
Tangled, mangled, very nearly strangled,
Washed ones, squashed ones, you got 'em
every night.

**VERSE TWO:**
Out for a blow in the evening,
Stroll down the prom after dark;
Down past the pier and the lighthouse,
Then take a turn round the park;
They say all the world loves a lover,
In the park that is certainly true–
They are so busy loving each other,
That you've hardly got room to get
through!

**CHORUS TWO:**
There are slim ones, grim ones, pretty
little prim ones,
Shy ones, sly ones, fancy ones and plain
Rough ones, tough ones, cannot get
enough ones,
Some who hadn't been before, and
wouldn't come again.
Squat ones, hot ones, give me all you've
got ones,
Game ones, tame ones, putting up a
fight–

Vast ones, fast ones, try to make it last
ones,
Everybody spooning on a moonlit night.

**VERSE THREE:**
Dow for a dip in the Briny!
Laughing and splashing about.
Watching the girls in the water,
Waiting for them to come out.
Stroll past the back of a beach hut,
Glimpsing the ladies behind;
All in their best bathing-dresses,
Each one a different kind:

**CHORUS THREE:**
There are green ones, lean ones, stringy
runner-bean ones,
Black ones, slack ones, barrels and
balloons–
Fat ones, flat ones, welcome-on-the-mat
ones,
Tiny little orange ones, and big full
moons;
Square ones, bare ones, toss-'em-in-the-air
ones,
Bright ones, tight ones, lollipops and
lumps;
Town ones, brown ones, wobbling up and
down ones,
Dainty little spotted ones, and great big
bumps.

**CODA:**
It takes all sorts to make a world
Or so they always say–
And down by the sea all sorts you'll see,
On a seaside holiday!

# BILLY PRATT'S
# BANANAS

**VERSE ONE:**
Little Billy Pratt, what a funny fellah
Sold bananas on the street, they were so
big and yellah
They soon became quite famous and
wherever people meet
They vowed they were the ripest and the

best they'd ever ate
And now throughout the land you'll find them near at hand
You'll see them in the Café Royale if you go there to sup
Whenever men and women meet, they're always popping up
You don't win silver cups no more at races and gym-kha-nas
The prize is now a handful of young Billy Pratt's bananas.

### VERSE TWO:

You'll find them in the nicest homes, at court they're "just the stuff"
They do say that his Majesty just can't get enough
I know a wealthy widow in the better part of Ealing
And every time I visit her I get a lovely feeling
I drink her fine old brandy and I smoke her fine Havanas
And all I give her in return are Billy Pratt's bananas.

### VERSE THREE:

I took Mary Jane to church, it was a lovely wedding,
We'd been betrothed for fourteen years to save up for the bedding,
The folks all started throwing rice, which very nearly struck me
One chap threw milk and sugar, and an Indian threw some chutney.
They wrote "Just Married" on my back, they played all sorts of tricks,
They nailed my topper to the floor, they filled our bags with bricks.
But still the worst was yet to come, I gave my bride a kiss
Then climbed the hill to Bedfordshire to start our wedded bliss.
"Oh Jack," she said as she undressed, "what's in your pyjamas?"
And I found out that it was one of little Billy Pratt's bananas.

# BANG, CRASH, OOH, AH ...

### VERSE ONE:

I live
Down in Peckham Rye
17 Canal Street
It's a proper "pals" street
We're all
Friendly as can be
One big happy family.
But the
People next to us
Had a little daughter
Proper little snorter.
She would
Fight with all the boys
My! You should have heard the noise
Every day you'd hear her in her old back yard
Knock the living daylights out of some young card ...

### CHORUS:

Bash, Crash,
Ooh, Ah,
Whizz, bang, ding, dong. There they go again.
Grunts, groans, cries, moans.
Leave him alone, girl, do!

### VERSE TWO:

That was
Twenty years ago
Now she's quite a big girl
Doesn't care a fig girl.
She got
Married last July
To a fellah six foot high.
But she
Hasn't changed a bit
When they have row, why
You should see the fur fly
Poor chap
Doesn't stand a chance
She's leading him a right old dance.
Every night she starts as soon as he comes in
Giving him a licking with the rolling-pin.

### REPEAT CHORUS

**VERSE THREE:**

Mind you
I'll say this for her,
Though her temper's strong, it
Doesn't last for long, it
Soon e–
vaporates away,
Long before the break of day.
When they
Wander up to bed
She's apologising
He's philosophising.
Then they
Start to bill and coo,
Just like married couples do.
But oh dear me, this doesn't mean we get
a peaceful night–
The noise when they are making up is
worse than when they fight!

**REPEAT CHORUS.**

# NELL OF THE YUKON

My tale is a weird one – 'twas found, long
ago, In a book on my Grandpappy's shelf;
So hush while I tell it, and don't make a
sound,
'Cos I'd want to hear it myself.

It was writ in the days when the Yukon
was rich,
And the miners got drunk every night.
It was writ all in red, by my old Uncle Jed,
'Cos he was the one as could write.

Now the story begins with a quarrel, one
night,
Between Jed and his pretty wife, Nell;
She'd lost all his dough at the gambling
saloon,
And one of her garters as well.

Now Nell was a gal with a wonderful
shape;
She could hit a spitoon at ten paces;
When she went on the town, she wore a
tight gown,

And was seen in all the right places.

Well, she'd come home that night, just a
little bit tight,
And she threw off her clothes in disgust.
"What's the matter?" said Jed, and she
drunkenly said
As she undid her corset "You're bust!"

Now Jed knew what she meant, all his
gold she had spent,
And he sat there awhile, making faces;
Then as she bent over to unlace her boots,
He gave her a belt, with his braces.

Nell gave a great jump, with her hand to
her rump,
And a yell all Alaska could hear,
Then she made a quick run, and she
snatched up Jed's gun,
And she poked it inside of Jed's ear.

"That's the finish," said Nell, "I've had all I
can take,
Do you hear me? – Get out of my sight!"
Well, old Jed could hear – and the gun in
his ear
Made him hear even better that night.

So he quitted the shack, and he never
looked back,
And he set out to search for more gold:
But his luck it was out, and he wandered
about,
Till at last he was dying of cold.

So he dragged himself into a nearby
saloon,
Which was known as the "Barrel of Glue"
It was one of those joints where the men
are all men,
And most of the women are, too.

The place was a gambling hell, it was
clear;
Every man jack was betting and boozing–
Three miners were winning a strip poker
game,
And a girl with no clothes on was losing.

Jed sat down at a table and bought
himself in

By producing his very last dollar;
And he started to deal with hope in his
heart,
And three aces under his collar.

And he won thick and fast; when the
evening was past,
He owned all the gold on the table–
As well as six mines, and a three-quarter
share
In a Mexican showgirl called Mabel.

Then in walked Black Lou, with a sackful
of gold,
And he challenged poor Jed, with a leer–
"One cut and one call, and the winner
takes all,
And the loser must buy all the beer."

What could Jed do? He hated Black Lou,
As everyone did in those parts;
So Jed shuffled the cards, and both players
cut,
And both players cut – Ace of Hearts!

Then up jumped Black Lou, and his face
went bright blue,
(Which astonished a passing physician)
And he used a foul word that no one had
heard
Since the time of the Great Exhibition.

"You cheated, you swine!" said Lou with a
whine,
As he grabbed Uncle Jed round the neck;
And he started to squeeze, till Jed dropped
to his knees,
And with one final wheeze, hit the deck.

The whole saloon froze as Black Lou drew
his gun
"Alright, stranger!" said he "Have it your
way."
When in rushed a woman – and as Lou
turned round,
She spat straight in his eye, from the
doorway.

It was Nell! There she stood, and she really
looked good
As she grabbed Jed, and rushed him
outside–

And they didn't stop running for seven
long miles,
Till they found themselves some place to
hide.

'Twas a room booked by Nell in a sleazy
hotel,
A dollar-a-night double-roomer.
It was built out of driftwood, and named
"The Savoy"
By some guy with a quick sense of
humour.

Well, they flopped on the bed – "Thank
the Lord," said old Jed,
"My gambling days are behind me,
But I'm puzzled, dear Nell, and I want to
hear tell,
How in hell's name you managed to find
me?"

"I've been wandering too, all around, just
like you,"
Said Nell, "and the thought makes me
wince;
And the reason, my dear, was that whack
on the rear –
I just ain't sat down, ever since."

And they lay there awhile, then Jed, with
a smile
Said "I'll never more leave this old town–
We'll find peace, you and I" – but he got
no reply,
For young Nell was a-sleeping – face
down.

# JEHOSAPHAT AND JONES

Of all the various musical characters the two Ronnies presented in their show, one of the most popular and enduring was the post-Woodstock, long-haired country and western duo, Jehosaphat and Jones. They first appeared in the early days of the show and stayed with the duo through to their final series, recorded exclusively for Australia's Channel 9. In 1973, the stool-bound duo even cut an album.

Presented here – beginning with an introductory sketch from the show – is The Jehosaphat and Jones Songbook (peddle steel guitar to be imagined).

## JEHOSAPHAT, JONES AND GUESTS

*RB and RC discovered on stools. Intro into the first number – "The Muck about Song", which they both sing.*

**VERSE ONE:**
Luella Sue O'Hara is the girl who lives next door,
I've known her since-times I was six
And she was only four
And now that we have both grown up
It's very plain to see
No matter how hard she tries to grow
She's still two years younger than me.

**VERSE TWO:**
When we was little scruffy kids
I'd play in my back yard
We didn't have no TV set
'Cos times was awful hard
But when she tried to ask me round
To her back yard instead
So we could play together
This is what I always said.

**CHORUS ONE:**
Don't come around here asking me out
I ain't coming out, just to muck about
You have to muck about on your own, my dear,
'Cos I'm gonna muck about here.

**(CODA)**

Trundling a truck about, wadding a duck about,
I'm gonna muck about here.

**VERSE THREE:**
Then ten or twelve years later on
She grew up overnight
Her legs got long and slender and
Her blouse got awful tight
But when I asked her if she'd like
To visit me next door
She only answered "You're too late,
'Cos now I know what for".

**CHORUS TWO:**
Don't come around here asking me out
I ain't going out just to muck about
You'll have to muck about on your own, my dear,
'Cos I'm gonna muck about here.

**(CODA)**

I'm not struck about
Can't run amok about
Don't give a buck about
Folks here roundabout
Let them cluck about
I'm just tuckered out
– I'm gonna muck about here.

*(Applause at end. Mix to pre-VT.)*

449

*(Caption "The Surprises" over long shot of RB and RC , blacked up, with straightened, bouffant hair-do's, identical floor-length dresses. Heavily made up, orange lipstick, etc. RB has his teeth in.)*

*(They sing the proper words of black magic, miming two girls voices. They move identically as they sing.*

**BOTH:**
That old black magic has me in its spell.
That old black magic that you weave so well.

**RC:**
Those icy fingers up and down my spine.

**RB:**
That same old witchcraft when your eyes meet mine.

**BOTH:**
That same ole tingle that I feel inside
And then that elevator starts to glide.

**RC:**
And down and down I go.

**RB:**
Round and round I go,

**BOTH:**
Like a leaf that's caught in the tide.

**RC:**
I should stay away, but what can I do?

**RB:**
(What can she do?)

**RC:**
I hear your name.

**RB:**
(She hears my name)

**RC:**
And I'm aflame.

**RB:**
(And I'm fair game) Aflame, with such a burning desire
That only your kiss

*(RC kissing noises.)*

**RB:**
Can put out the fire.

**RC:**
(Water, water)

**BOTH:**
Oh, you're the lover I've been waiting for,
The note that fate had me created for
And every time your lips meet mine
Darling down and down I go
Round and round I go,
In a spin, loving the spin I'm in,
Under that old black magic called love.

*(The orchestra then repeats, from the beginning, while RC and RB move without singing, for the first two lines.)*

**RC:**
*(Third line) (Turns his back and puts his arms round himself, and runs "icy fingers" up and down his spine.)*

**RB:**
*(Fourth line) (Three bumps with his hip on eyes meet mine.)*

**RC:**
*(Fifth line.) (Rattles his bracelets three times, and we hear bells. Squeezes his left boob once, we hear motor horn.)*

**RB:**
*(Sixth line) (Takes off his earrings and drops them down his bosom – swanee, whistle and splash.)*

**RC:**
(sings) And down and down I go.

**RB:**
(speaks) Round and round I go.

**BOTH:**
In a spin, loving the spin I'm in, under
that old black magic called Love!
*(Applause at end. Mix to pre-VT.)*

*(Caption – Gary Schmutter over long shot of
RB as Gary Glitter, with spangle suit, wig and
very high platform shoes.)*

**RB:**
(waves arms about and sings) You oughta
be in my shoes,
My shoes, my shoes
People try and buy shoes
Just like mine
If you pay the price youse
Should get high shoes
When you've got your high shoes
You'll feel fine.

You put your left leg out
You put your left leg in
You put your left leg out
And you shake it all about
You give it all you've got, the whole night
through,
And you sometimes put your back out,
too.
Ooh!

*(He hobbles off.)*

**BACKING VOICES:**
*(off)* Get off-get-off, get off-get-off, etc.
*(Fading away.)*

*Mix to pre-VT.*

*(Caption: "Elton Bog" over long shot of RC
seated at piano as Elton John, with enormous
glasses.)*

*(Intro to song.)*

**RC:**
*(sings)* Oh, I have got a woman
I give her this and that
But she's got a taste for all the things
that make her fat.

**CHORUS:**
Oh baby

Every night she's choc-a-bloc
We do the roll-mop rock cake cheese roll
peppermint rock.

**VERSE TWO:**
I rock her to the left,
I rock her to the right
She said "I like a man who like a rock all
night".
I took her to the sweetshop
I said it's all for you,
She said I only like my rock when it's
lettered right through.

**REPEAT CHORUS**

*(Musical break: half-verse and chorus, during
which RC changes glasses.)*

**RC:**
I took her to the cafe
For a fancy casserole
The only thing she fancied
Was the luncheon meat roll
I took her for a picnic
I took her for a stroll
We sat among the rocks but she wouldn't
have a roll.

**REPEAT CHORUS**

*(Applause to end. Mix to studio (live).)*

*(RB and RC as Jehosaphat and Jones.)*

**VERSE ONE**
**RC:**
A man said to a bar-maid, now mix me a
drink,
A cocktail made up of whatever you think,

**RB:**
She mixed it, he drank it, and went quite
cross-eyed,
And three hours later he came to, and
cried.

**CHORUS:**
I'd like to try another like the one
I had before.
I so enjoyed the last one that I'm coming
back for more.

The effect is not immediate, but it's worth waiting for.
So oblige me with another, like the one I had before.

**RC:**
(spoken) ... Only bigger!

### VERSE TWO:
**RB:**
A man sat in a drug-store, and he called for the boss.
He said you sold me a pep pill to give to my boss.
I put it on the shelf on the wall near my bed
It fell into the coffee pot and I swallowed it instead.

### BOTH:
### (CHORUS AS BEFORE)
I'd like to try another like the one I had before.
I so enjoyed the last one that I'm coming back for more.
The effect is not immediate, but it's worth waiting for.
So oblige me with another, like the one I had before.

**RB:**
(spoken) ... Only stronger ...

*(Fade.)*

## UP CAT POLE CAT

**BOTH:**
(chorus) Up cat pole cat juniper tree
Lying in the yard with a bellyful of water melon
Don't pick cotton and I don't plant grass
Out in the open, sitting on my corn patch.

**RC:**
Down in Louisiana where the corn is high
Keep a jumping up to see the gals pass by

Down by the river where the bulrush grows
Watch the gals a-swimming there without no hesitation.

**REPEAT CHORUS**

**RB:**
Met Mary Ellen by the old barn door
I know just what she's a-waiting for
Up in the loft where the oil lamp flickers
I lost my heart and she lost her parasol.

**REPEAT CHORUS**

**RC:**
Annie was kissed by the preacher's son
She said "Now, what you been and gone and done?"
He said "I've been at the end of my wits
Even since the night I grabbed you by the currant bushes.

**REPEAT CHORUS**

Town folk come here, try to settle down
Pretty soon it's gonna be a great big town
They build their roads and houses and then
They all have to move to the country again.

**REPEAT CHORUS**

## STUTTERING BUM

**RB:**
Oh, Mary Lou, I'm a-calling you
Up on the telephone
To say thanks for coming to the dance with me
And letting me take you home;
I'm sorry I seemed so nervous
And started to stammer and sweat
But it s-started as s-soon as I saw you
And I ain't got over it yer-yet

I stared at your great big Ber-B-B-Ber-Ber
Beautiful blue-green eyes
I wondered if you Fer-F-F-Fer-Fer
Flirted with all the guys;
When you smiled I nearly Sher-Sh-Sh-
Sher-Sher
Shot right out the door
'Cos I'd never seen such pretty little Ter-T-
T-Ter-Ter Teeth before

I ain't yer-usually a bashful boy
I've took out other gals
I've kissed them on their ber-b-b-ber back-
door step
And per per per per promised to be pals
but
Since I first caught sight of you
On the Brownsville Buggy ride
Why, I've become a ser-ser-stuttering bum
And my tongue's perpetually ter-tied

My Cer-C-C-Cer Cer Cer C-C-Cer Cer
Collar gets awful tight,
When I Fer-F-F-Fer-Fer feel you close
As I Der-D-D-did last night;
I get a funny feeling in my Ber-B-B-Ber Ber
Ber B-B-B-B-B brain
And I can't Wer-Wer Wer till I per-p-p-per
I Jer-just gotta see you again

(instrumental break)

She said she'd see me Saturday
And I put down the phone
My tongue is back to normal now
Now I'm once more alone.
But next time that I meet her
On Saturday night around ten,
You can ber-bet your ber-bottom dollar I'll
be
A ser-stuttering bum again

I'll grab her by the Ber-b-b-ber-ber barn
And per-p-p-push her inside
I'll take my cer-courage, in both hands,
And ask her to be my ber-bride.
And if she holds my cer-cer-clammy hand
And tells me that she would,
I'll Fer-fer-fer-fer-fer fetch a preacher right
away
And that'll cure my stutter for good

That's good! That's Ger ger, ger-ger-ger, g-
g-ger-ger
Ger-ger, ger-g-ger ger good!

# RAILROAD MAN

**BOTH:**
They told me when I left the jailhouse
"Now try to go straight if you can"
Now I'm doing fine, 'cos I'm on a straight
line
A-working for the railroad man, oh Lord,
A-working for the railroad man.

**RB:**
They said "Lay tracks for the railroad
'Cos steam means speed and power
So I'm doing by best and I'm travelling
west
About 15 feet an hour, oh lord,
About fifteen feet an hour.

**RC:**
Oh I crouched all night laying track down
And the wind on my back made me choke
And I felt that the bottom had fell out o'
my life
Till I found that my braces had broke, oh
Lord,
I found that my braces had broke.

**RB:**
Someone had stole my hammer,
But I still got to earn my bread
And life ain't so grand, when you're
standing on your hands,
And driving in the rivets with your head,
oh Lord,
And driving in the rivets with your head.

**BOTH::**
There's a curve in the track up yonder
I think it's the beginning of the end;
I've tried going straight, but sad to relate
I think I'm a'going round the bend, oh
Lord,
I think I'm a'going round the bend.

# BLOWS MY MIND:

**BOTH:**
The river's flowing, up the hill
It keeps moving I keep still
Some folks say that thinking makes you blind
And when the wind is blowing from behind
It blows my mind.

Questions filter through my brain
Who makes water? What makes rain?
Is bakin' powder made from bakin' rind
And when the wind is blowing from behind
It blows my mind.

Painted girls and neon light
Lord, you made the darkness bright
The hole in my blue jeans is hard to find
But when the wind is blowing from behind
It blows my mind.

I'll go home and change my clothes
Brush my hair and blow my nose
A barrel-organ's life is one long grind
And when the wind is blowing from behind
It blows my mind.

# WE KNEW WHAT SHE MEANT

**RC:**
My cousin Pauline was a Tennessee Queen
As pretty a critter as you've ever seen
But she was so dumb that no matter how she tried,
When she opened her mouth she'd put her foot right inside.

**BOTH:**
(chorus) We knew what she meant
We knew what she meant
We heard what she said
But we knew what she meant

**RC:**
She invited the preacher to her house, they say
She said "It's a party, I'm 19 today
Ma's bought me a dress and a bonnet so cute,
So come up and see me in my birthday suit."

**REPEAT CHORUS**

**RC:**
She went to a dance hall one night on her own
And she smiled at a young man who stood all alone
He remarked that he'd not had the pleasure before
And she answered "Come on then, let's get on the floor".

**REPEAT CHORUS**

**RC:**
One day she went into a department store
And she said to the guy who was stood by the door
"I need some material to make a new belt
Perhaps you can tell me where I can get felt?"

**REPEAT CHORUS**

**RC:**
She said "I once met a guy with dark wavy hair
So we rushed off to Alaska for a quick love affair
But I came back disappointed with a cold and a cough
We were both frozen stiff and I just broke it off."

**BOTH:**
We knew what she meant
We knew what she meant
We heard what she said
But we knew what she meant.

# SHE AGREES

**VERSE ONE:**
I got myself a gorgeous gal
She lives just out of town
She's always most agreeable
Whenever I'm around
We never ever quarrel and
She sees my point of view
She just agrees with everything
(Well, that's not strictly true).

**CHORUS ONE:**
('Cos) She agrees we're like the bees
And the birds up the trees
She agrees that love is
Wonderful and right–
She agrees in every way
With everything I say
But she won't agree to do
What I asked her to last night.

**VERSE TWO:**
She's such a healthy sort of gal
She plays all kinds of sports
She's a wonderful all-rounder when
She's wearing tennis shorts
She's great upon the golf-course, she's
An expert rifle shot;
And when she plays a game she gives
It everything she's got.

**CHORUS TWO:**
(Oh) She plays baseball she plays pool
She plays hockey for the school
She can ski, and swim, and fence
And fly a kite–
Throw a dart or bounce a ball
She'll play any game at all
But she wouldn't play the game
I asked her to last night.

**CODA:**

**RC:**
She agrees that I'm sincere,
And she thinks that I'm a dear.

**BOTH:**
But she won't agree to do
What I asked her to last night.

**(REPEAT CODA)**

**RB:**
She agrees that I've got class,
And she thinks that I'm a gas.

**BOTH:**
But she won't agree to do
What I asked her to last night.
No, she won't agree to do
What I asked her to last night!

# GAL FROM ARKENSAW

**VERSE ONE:**
She was a big, fat, welcome on the mat,
True blue Southern gal,
Met her down in Arkensaw, never saw the
Gal before, but she seemed a real cool pal
She could rustle cattle and her sister
From Seattle, she used to do it as well
She was a big, fat, what d'you think of
that?
Uptight downtown belle.

**VERSE TWO:**
She was a huge, tall, really on the ball
Great big loving dame
Travelled with the rodeo, working in the
Stripper show, no two shows the same
Country show or cattle fair, she would
drop
Her underwear, everyone enjoyed it, you
could tell
She was huge, tall, no complaints at all,
Uptight downtown belle

**VERSE THREE:**
She was a great, proud, say it out loud
Bubbling ball of fire
To the guys who came to see, she would
always guarantee
Temperatures would shoot up higher
Didn't have to prove it 'cos when she
began to move it,

Boy, how the crowd would swell.
She was a great, proud, wonderfully
endowed, uptight downtown belle.

**VERSE FOUR:**
She was a large, fine, try one of mine,
Rattling big success
Seemed to be the one for me, seemed a lot
of fun to me,
But she made my life a mess
Took my gold, left me in the cold, didn't
even
Leave me my heart
She was a large, fine, lay it on the line,
Regular downtown tart.

# IN THE SUMMERTIME

**VERSE ONE:**
**BOTH** *(throughout):*
What I mean
There's a dream
Of a queen
Who I've seen
In New Orleans
In the Summertime

**VERSE TWO:**
She's so lean
So serene
And she's clean
I've never seen
Such a Queen
Of seventeen
In the Summertime

**MIDDLE EIGHT:**
In the Summertime
There will come a time
At the moment I'm
Working overtime
For a pal o' mine
So I'll have a dime
To git to New Orleans.

**VERSE THREE:**
Her eyes are green
Just like a bean
Her legs are lean

And just between
Ourselves, I mean
To love that queen
In the Summertime.

**VERSE FOUR:**
Her name is Jean
It's Jean Christine
Her boyfriend Dean
Is really mean
He's a Marine
And so obscene
Nearly all the time.

**VERSE FIVE:**
I mean
To steal the scene
I'll win his Jean–
The old routine
Will melt that queen
Like margarine
In the Summertime.

**VERSE THREE** *(repeated):*
Her eyes are green
Just like a bean
Her legs are lean
And just between
Ourselves, I mean
To love that queen
In the Summertime.

# IT DON'T MEAN THAT I
# DON'T LOVE YOU

**VERSE ONE:**
Now just you listen to me, darling
What I say to you is true
If you really want to leave me
That's entirely up to you
But believe me when I tell you
I am really not to blame
All your silly fears are groundless
I still love you just the same.

**CHORUS:**
It don't mean that I don't love you
Just because I never speak
And I never give you presents–
Take you swimming in the creek;
Just because I hate your cooking
Oh, please don't get in a stew–
Just because I'm not your grandma,
Doesn't mean I don't love you.

**VERSE TWO:**
It don't mean that I don't love you
When I punch you in the nose
And go out with other women
Never buy you any clothes.
How can we remain together
With so many ifs and buts?
It don't mean that I don't love you–
But my wife – she hates your guts.

# NEIGHBOURS

**RC AND RB:**
(chorus) Heat up the coffee
Serve up the stoo,
Pull up a chair
'Cos we're neighbours, me and you.
You take the golf-clubs
I'll take the car
What's yours is mine
'Cos that's what neighbours are.

**VERSE ONE** (*spoken*):
**RB:**
John and Joe were neighbours
They lived side by side
Joe, he was a bachelor
John, he had a bride
They borrowed from each other
Just like neighbours do
Said Joe, "Why keep two lawn-mowers
When only one would do?"

**REPEAT CHORUS**

**VERSE TWO** (*spoken*):
**RC:**
Young John drove home, to Joe's house

And returned his neighbour's car
Then popped in through Joe's back-door
To borrow a good cigar;
On the couch lay his own wife, Molly
With her cheeks so blushing red
She said "Poor Joe's
TV don't go,
So he switched me on instead".

**REPEAT CHORUS**

**VERSE THREE** (*double verse, spoken*):
**RB:**
"I wish we had a baby,"
Said John to his wife one day
" 'Cos neighbour Joe's got a baby-carriage
He wants to give away"
So they both looked under the gooseberry bush
And telephoned the stork
But it never came, and it seemed a shame
To take an empty pram for a walk.

**RC:**
John went away on a business trip
And he spent a year at sea
When he came back he found his wife
With a baby on her knee
She said "Joe brought it over
One night as I lay asleep
The stork left twins at Joe's house
So he gave me one to keep".

**REPEAT CHORUS**

# DIMPLES

Oh, the dimples in her cheeks
And the ribbons in her hair
And the rosebuds on her lips
And that lacy underwear
(spoken) Oh, the dimples in her cheeks!

There's a gal who lives near me
Pretty as a pin
Whenever I go by her place
She always lets me in
She's a gal without no brains

457

She's simple, so they say
But when I take her in the woods
She always knows the way.

Oh, the dimples in her cheeks
And the sunburn on her knees
And the music in her voice
And she tries so hard to please
(spoken) Oh, the sunburn on her knees!

When first we met she was wearing pants
And pushing an old iron plough
At first I thought she was a boy–
But I don't think so now.
Sometimes we go for buggy rides
And other times we walk
I'd like to ask the gal her name
But we don't get time to talk.

Oh, the dimples in her cheeks
And the freckles on her back
And the starlight in her eyes
And she loves my brother Jack
(spoken) What a shame she married Jack.

## THE GIRL WHO'S GONNA MARRY ME

She can sow, she can hoe
She can read, she can write
She can cook a man a breakfast in the
middle of the night
She can cut up a chicken
She can cut down a tree
Wow! That's the gal who's gonna marry
me.

She can dig, she can jig,
She can juggle, she can jump,
She can drive a fella crazy with a wiggle of
her rump
She can stand in the saddle
She can sit on your knee
Wow! That's the girl who's gonna marry
me

She can joke, she can smoke
She can drink a dozen beers,
She can move a grand pianner, she can
move a man to tears
She can pour out her heart or
She can pour out your tea
Yep! That's the gal who's gonna marry me.

She can roast, she can toast
She can boil, she can bake
She can cut a fella dead and she can  cut a
slice of cake
She can cook a fella's goose and
She can fry a fricassee
Yep! That's the gal who's gonna marry me

She can sweep, she can weep
She can giggle, she can grin
She can play a little poker, she can play a
little gin
She's as spicy as a pickle
And sweeter than a pea
Hup! She's the gal who's gonna marry me.

# MORE SONGS

The following songs, many of which are musical medleys, were penned by Ronnie for *The Two Ronnies*, except where noted.

## ELIZABETH AH HA!

**PRESENTER:**
Owing to the great success of *Elizabeth R*, the BBC historical series, an American company has commissioned a further series for the autumn. In order to make it more acceptable to Transatlantic audiences it has been met to music, but the essential flavour has been retained by using only traditional English airs. Here then, is a preview of the BBC's latest venture, entitled *Elizabeth, AH HA:*

*Cut to throne room. Courtiers in attendance. Fanfare of trumpets. Enter RB as Queen Elizabeth.*

**RB:**
My Lord Chancellor! Where is the keep of the privy chamber?

**COURTIER A:**
I am here, your Majesty.

**RB:**
The lock needs repairing. I just met three old ladies coming out. They said they'd been there since Saturday. However. Are we all here?

**COURTIER B:**
We are your Majesty.

**RB:**
Good, then we can start.

*Musical intro into "The Vicar of Bray".*

**RB:** *(sings)*
In good King Charles's golden days
When morals were appalling
His majesty was always in
When Nell Gwynn came a-callin';
She plied him with her oranges
(Twas known through the land, boys)
So full was he of vitamin C
That he could hardly stand, boys

But now those bad old days are gone
And I am on the throne, sirs.
A virgin queen I shall remain
I mean to held my own, sirs.
I have a big four-poster bed
No man has dared to leap in,
And woe betide the twit who tries
To creep in while I'm sleepin'.

*Coda – to "Rule Britannia".*

**RB:**
Rule Britannia, marmalade and Jam
I wouldn't give you 2d for your chances chaps
Elizabeth the First I am.

**RB:**
Well, gentlemen, what did you think of that?

*A wood (as used in the game of bowls) rolls onto the set, closely followed by another.*

**RB:**
Is someone trying to tell me something?

**COURTIER B:**
Sir Francis Drake wishes to see you your Majesty.

**RB:**
Oh, of course – I thought I recognised them.

**COURTIER B:**
He is without, ma'am.

**RB:**
Yes, he would be. Bid him enter at once.

*(Fast version of "Blow the Man Down" as play on. Enter RC as Francis Drake.)*

**RC:**
Good evening, folks. My goodness, what a time I've had getting here. Terrible traffic round the Isle of Wight. Bowsprit to bowsprit all the way. Finally some silly seaman backs into me and knocks me figurehead off. I'd have been better off coming by boat. Your majesty. *(Kisses her hand.)*

**RB:**
Why, Sir Francis Drake – the knights are getting short.

**RC:**
I was just telling the folks why I'm late.

**RB:**
I heard. Couldn't you have persuaded your crew to go the other way?

**RC:**
They wouldn't need much persuading, dear, not that lot. It's a treat to get back to normality.

**RB:**
Where are your sailors now?

**RC:**
They're camping on Plymouth Hoe.

**RB:**
What Hoe?

**RC:**
Oh yes, there'll be plenty of that, don't you worry. Buy I didn't come here to talk about the crew. I came here because I want to woo.

**RC:**
To woo? To woo who?

**RC:**
To woo you!

**RB:**
You do? Ooh!

**RC:**
So if you'd stop playing trains for a minute, I'll tell the people all about it.

**RB:**
Oh, spare my blushes, do.

*(Music intro to "Lass of Richmond Hill".)*

**RC:**
*(sings)* At Hampton Court there lives a lass
As broad as she is high
Those ample charms I'll take into my arms
Or know the reason why.
This lass so sweet has great big feet
And shoulders like an elephant
The fact that I'm skint, and she's worth a mint
Is really quite irrelevant.

You're well and truly caught,
Sir Francis Drake's in port.
With any luck you'll be Mrs Duck
Sweet lass of Hampton Court.

**RB:**
That's all very well, Francis, but while you've been away, The Earl of Essex has been
seeing quite a lot of me.

**RC:**
Well that's not difficult. The Earl of Essex, eh – you don't mean that you've let him....

**RB:**
Certainly not. You know very well I don't believe in Essex before marriage.

**RC:**
I knew I shouldn't have been away so
long!

**RB:**
I know. A whole year – tell me about your
travels, dear Francis.

*Intro into "Billy Boy".*

**RB:**
*(sings)* Where have you been all the year,
Francis dear, Francis dear
On the seas, or merely on the beer?

**RC:**
To the Spanish fleet went I
And I made the Spanish fly.

**RB:**
Oh, you sank it?

**RC:**
No, I drank it, oh my darling Lizzie dear.

**RB:**
Did you sail the seven seas, Francis dear,
tell me please
Did you see the sights a sailor sees?

**RC:**
To the Orient I've bin dear,
And I've heard the voice of India.

**RB:**
In Darjeeling?

**RC:**
No, in Ealing, oh my darling Lizzie dear.

**RB:**
Are your travels over yet, Francis dear,
Francis pet,
Aren't you getting tired of getting wet?

**RC:**
Yes my travels new are done
And I'm home to have some fun,
Let Sir Francis lead you some dances
Oh my darling Lizzie dear.

*They dance with the courtiers. At the end of*

*the number RC grabs RB.*

**RC:**
Marry me Lizzie. *(He pulls her onto a couch,
she lands on top of him.)*

**RB:**
Let me get up, you clown. This Virgin en
the ridiculous. *(He gets up.)*

**RC:**
Oh Lizzie, I pray you, spurn me not.
You're than I could ever want in a
woman. About six stone more.

**RB:**
But I am another's.

**RC:**
Well, there's plenty for everybody! I know,
it's that varlet Essex. When he spoke with
you earlier, I didn't like the way he made
certain remarks touching your chastity.

**RB:**
Really? I never noticed. It's difficult to tell
in these farthingales.

*Courtier A rushes on.*

**COURTIER A:**
Your majesty! The Spaniards are at the
door!

**RB:**
Oh, not again. I bought two strings of
onions last week.

**COURTIER A:**
No – 'tis the Armada! The Spanish ships
are approaching England!

**RC:**
Then I must depart. I must set sail from
Plymouth at once. But never fear, when
England once more is safe, when the grim
shadow of war is banished once again
from these shores, I shall return.

**RB:**
I'll leave your supper in the oven.

**RC:**
Goodbye dearest Elizabeth until we meet again.

*Intro to "The girl I left Behind".*

**RC:**
So it's off I go to fight the foe
With the fleet that you assigned me

**RB:**
And I'll stay at home, and sit upon the throne
So you always know where to find me.

**RC:**
Though my life they take, they cannot break
The chains of love that bind me.
As I sink in the drink, I shall always think
Of that hefty girl behind me.

**BOTH:**
*(to "Rule Britannia")* Rule Britannia, tis time for our goodbyes,
Next week, Henry the Fourth Part One, on ice.

*Music to finish.*

# THE PIPE BAND

*An empty stage.*
*Off stage the pipers strike up. They march on, with RB and RC .*
*They stand and sing.*

*Tune: "Amazing Grace".*

**BOTH:**
Amazing Grace, how sweet the sound
She played upon a whistle -

**RB:**
To show you how, she charged a pound

**BOTH:**
Behind the "Dog and Thistle".

**BOTH:**
Amazing Grace is truly grand
Gigantic Greta's grander

**RC:**
But if you want a lingering death

**BOTH:**
Try Merciless Miranda.

**BOTH:**
Most Scottish girls are tickled pink
By a sporran and a feather

**RB:**
But men in kilts should steer well clear

**BOTH:**
Of a girl called Prickly Heather.

**BOTH:**
Amazing Grace is truly great
Fantastic Freda's faster.

**RC:**
But Earthquake Ethel's quite unique -
She's an absolute disaster.

*Tune: "The Bonnie Bonnie Banks of Loch Lomond".*

**RB:**
In the last highland games
They called out our names
And they made us take part in the races:
Oh I tossed the caber,

**RC:**
An I put the shot

**RB:**
And you put it in some damn funny places.

**RB:**
They thought they would risk us
With throwing the discuss –
We stood by the walls of the castle
But they'd wrapped up the thing
And we couldn't break the string
So we all had to play "Pass the Parcel".

**RC:**
The bloke next to me
He was sixteen stone three
And we stood side by side 'neath the
ramparts -
He said with a grin
If I didn't let him win
He would break every bone in my band-
parts.

**RC:**
So I took the High Jump
And he took the Long Jump –
For all I know he's still travellin' –
The crease in his trousers will never meet
again
'Cos he got in the way of the javelin.

*Tune: "Blue Bells of Scotland".*

**RB:**
Oh where, tell me where,
Has my Sunday sporran gone?
I hung it out to dry
On the line, and now it's gone.
I think someone enticed it
With a biscuit or a bone
And I hope, in my heart,
It has found a decent home.

It never barked at stranger.
Or chased the next door's cat
It just used to lie
Curled up upon the mat
I hope it's not run over
And it comes back safe, again
Oh so sad beats my heart
Cos a new one's three pound ten.

*Tune: "Over the Sea to Skye".*

**RC:**
Speed bonny boat, like a bird on the wing,
Rowed by a sturdy crew,
Though this wee boat is a beautiful thing
It doesn't contain a loo.

*Tune: "The Ball of Kirriemuir".*

**BOTH:**
The Chief of Clan McPhillistine
Laird Loganberry of Perth

Once gave a ball at Kirriemuir
To celebrate his birth
With enough supplies of whisky
For to fill the forth of Firth
Which naturally caused jollity
Hilarity and mirth.

**RC:**
And some folk drank till they were drunk
And others did the same
And some folk didn't bother –
They were drunk before they came.

**RB:**
The only man who didn't drink
Was flat upon the floor
And he'd been there since last year
Sleeping off the year before.

**CHORUS BOTH:**
They were drinking in the pantry
They were drinking in the hall
They were hanging out the windows
They were hanging on the wall
And the bonny pipes were playing
But nobody danced at all
They were all too busy drinking
At Laird Loganberry's ball.

**RB:**
There were twenty kinds of whisky there
To everyone's delight
When someone asked for water, why
It nearly caused a fight

**RC:**
Some girls were drinking rum and pep
And others gin and lime
But most girls didn't drink at all,
They never had the time.

**RB:**
Oh the Duchess, who was twenty stone
Could hardly keep awake
She threw off all her garments and
She jumped into the lake.
She terrified the fishes
Who scattered pretty quick
And she floated in the moonlight
Like a Scottish Moby Dick.

**RC:**
Oh she frightened Jack the Ripper
She was such an awful sight
Then along came Jock the Kipper
Who was hoping for a bite.
He plunged into the water, with
His harpoon dripping wet
And he scored a hit amidships
Then he gaffed her with his net.

**CHORUS BOTH:**
They were drinking in the pantry....etc.

**RB:**
A piper had too much to drink
How much he couldn't tell
He'd ruled himself with whisky, then
He'd filled his boots as well

**RC:**
He'd filled up all his pockets with
As much as he could steal –
And then he burst his bag pipes and
He sprayed an eightsome reel.

**RB:**
A very drunk American
In kilt and tartan socks
Sat by the lake at midnight
Drinking whisky on the rocks

**RC:**
He climbed up on the castle walls
For everyone to see
And danced a jig and shouted
"All the highballs are, on me."

**REPEAT CHORUS**

*Tune: "A Scottish Soldier".*

**VERSE 1:**
He was a soldier, a Yiddish soldier
Who wandered far away
From Golders Green one day
He went quite barmy
And joined the Army –
The Queens own Highland four by twos.

**CHORUS:**
And he worked in the cook house there

With his knees all bare, cooking Kosher fare
And serving latke soups to the hungry troops
Far from Golders Green, his home.
And how he proudly gave his kilt a swish
When the band piped in the gefilterfish
And he'd prepare each stylish Yiddish dish
Just like Momma made back home.

**VERSE 2:**
But now our soldier, our Yiddish soldier
A man so bold and brave
Lies in a hero's grave
In some far corner
Of somewhere foreign
At last his sporran's come to rest.

**CHORUS 2:**
He sailed away, for, to fight the foe
At some highland show, up in Scapa Flow
A flying haggis in a cookhouse brawl
Caused our poor young lad to fall.
But now he's up there, and he's grown some wings
And he's probably, lost some other things
That's why an angel stands around and sings
Cos there's nothing else to do.

**VERSE 3:**
But like I told yer, that Yiddish soldier
Will never be forgot
Wherever soup is hot
His name will linger
On every finger
When pickled herrings, are passed around.

**CHORUS 3:**
But never more will he serve a lobster-ball
He has answered now that final bagel call
There's just a brown mark on the cookhouse wall
Where the haggis did its worst.
But now he's up there, and he can't go wrong
Serving Kosher meals to the angel throng
And there we leave him, as we end our song,
Far from Golders Green his home.

# THE IRISH FOLK GROUP

*Three Irishmen – RB as violinist, RC as guitarist and clog dancer. A N Other on drums. They all have short, jet black hair and red necks, costumes are navvy like, flat caps etc.*

*Caption: Peter Cutter and the Boggers.*

**PETER: (RB)**
Good evening, Ladies and Gentlemen from Pete Cutter and the Boggers. Now as this is our very first visit to this country, I'd like to say that it's wonderful to be with you once again.

**SEAN: (RC)**
We've got some brand new songs for you – they're so new we haven't even heard 'em ourselves yet, and we sincerely hope that we are going to enjoy them; so here we go – *(counting them in)* – 4, 5 -

*Tune: "I'll Have A Drink".*

**RB:**
Twas on a Monday morning in the middle of the night
I dreamt that I had woken up, it gave me such a fright.
I thought I'd got insomnia, it nearly made me weep.
But luckily, when I woke up, I found I was asleep.

**BOTH:**
Singing, I'll have a drink with youse,
I'll have a beer,
But if I catch you with the wife,
I'll thump you round the ear.

**RB:**
Twas on a Tuesday morning, and the woman I was wid
She said that she was thirsty, and she asked me for a quid
"Oh I could drink the river dry,"
Says she "I do declare"
Says I "The river's got a bank, so borrow a quid from there"

**BOTH:**
Singing, I'll have a drink with youse,
I'll have a gin,
But if I catch you mucking about
I'll bash your teeth right in.

**RB:**
Twas on a Friday morning and it really was a trial
The wife she craved affection, but I couldn't raise a smile,
My get-up-and-go has got up and went but I don't care no more –
When I think of the places my get-up-and-go
Has got-up-and-been before.

**BOTH:**
Singing, I'll have a drink with youse,
I'll have a stout,
But if I catch you wid the wife
I'll bash your brains right out.

*A musical figure to finish with.*

*After song No.1.*

**RB:**
Now, before we carry on, I'd like to introduce both of the trio to you – first of all, my name is Pete Cutter, and I'm a Peat cutter, and these two here is called the Boggers, on account of they both work in the bog, cutting peat. Now this here is Sean, and he is the champion bogger of the South West – ah, he's a marvellous little bogger. And he has learned to clog dance in the bog. Haven't you, Sean?

**RC:**
Oh, I have indeed, yes, learned to clog dance, yes, in the bog, yes.

**RB:**
And that's not easy cos you get your feet very very wet in the bog, when you're dancing in it.

**RC:**
Especially if somebody pulls the chain.

**RB:**

Now I usually play the bones during this
number, but I've got a terrible headache,
so I'm going to play two sticks of rhubarb
instead. Here we go now – the song is
called "Thump, thump".

*Tune: "Thump Thump".*

**RC:**

I love the girls, I take 'em behind the shed
I don't know what to say to 'em,
cos I'm simple in the head –
But I've got a little trick, that pleases 'em
I've found,
I just lift up me left leg, and thump it on
the ground
*(thump thump with foot)*
So if you're with a lady and you don't
know what to do
Just remember this advice what I am
giving you
If she's eighteen or eighty, you'll please
her I'll be bound
If you just lift up your left leg and thump
it on the ground.
I met a girl in Liverpool,
I thought that I would try,
To give her a quick *(thump thump)*
me lads, as she was passing by,
I *(thump)* her once,
I *(thump)* her twice,
She stopped and gave a smile,
We're married now, and so I can
*(thump thump)* her all the while!

*RC now does his Irish dance, while RB plays
the rhubarb.*
*During the dance, RC gets a couple of
shillelaghs and, as he dances, lays them down
like crossed swords. He then dances on the
opposite side of the stage – then picks them up
again, and holds them up to the audience as
the number finishes.*

**RB:**

And now, finally, here is a sad song with a
moral – it's title is, "It pays to listen." And
that's what it's called an' all.

*Tune: "It Pays To Listen".*

**RB:** *(spoken, with piano, colla voce)*
There's a corner of old Ireland
That is all the world to me
And I visit it as often as I can
And all I have to do is catch
A bus from North West Three,
To Camden Town, to see me Uncle Dan.

He's an ugly man is Uncle
With a face like a carbuncle -
"I'll tell you why" says he
T'will break your hearts
The fact is, I must mention,
That I didn't pay attention
When the Angels were a-handin' round
the parts

*Now song goes into tempo.*

**BOTH SING:**

When the angels gave out brains,
I thought that they said "trains"
And I missed mine as I usually do –
When they handed out the eyes
I thought that they said "ties"
And I asked for one of brown
and one of blue.

**RB:**

When they passed out the chins
I thought that they said "gins"
And I ordered a double one for me

**RC:**

When they gave out the noses,
I thought they said "roses"
And I chose a great big red one,
as you see.

**CHORUS:**
**BOTH:**

Oh what a mess I'm in
Oh what a mess I'm in
If only I had listened
To those angels when they spoke
I'd not be in the mess that I am in.

**RB:**

When the angels gave out hair
I thought they said fresh air

And so I asked for plenty up me nose
When they gave out bellies
I thought that they said jellies
So a great big pink and wobbly one I
chose.

**RC:**
When they gave out the ears
I thought that they said Beers
So I ordered mine with handles on,
instead
When they gave out the necks
I thought that they said sex
And now I'm old I can't hold up my head

**CHORUS:**
**BOTH:**
Oh what a mess I'm in,
Oh what a mess I'm in,
If only I'd listened
To those angels when they spoke
I'd not be in the mess that I am in.

*Repeat last three lines, as a build-up to finish
with.*

# GILBERT AND
# SULLIVAN

*Tune: "Here's a How-de-do".*

**BOTH:**
Hello how diyou do
We are bringing you
Songs by Sullivan and Gilbert
Hope they're going to fill the bill, but
Let us not waste time
Let us start the rhyme.

*Tune: "Yum Yum".*

**RB:**
We, won't,
Sing anything that is glum (Yum yum)

**RC:**
For this is the season
That gives us a reason

For drinking and filling our tum (Yum
yum)

**RB:**
I must say it's alright for some:

**RC:**
I eat what I like and don't put on a pound,

**RB:**
I like what I eat that is why I'm so round,

**RC:**
Just keep off the starches

**RB:**
I've got fallen arches,
With carrying this lot around.

*Tune: "The Flowers that Bloom in the Spring
Tra la".*

**RC:**
The flowers that bloom in the spring tra la,
Are blooming all over the place

**RB:**
The girls in the chorus that sing, tra la,
Each one is a beautiful thing, tra la,

**BOTH:**
A flower of feminine grace,

**(CHOIR:**
A flower of feminine grace.)

**BOTH:**
There's Lily and Iris, and Daisy, and Rose,
There's also Sweet William, but he's one of
those,
But our favourite flower
She blooms by the hour
At twenty-six Bloomsbury Place.

*Tune: "Take a Pair of Sparkling Eyes".*

**RB:**
And now a little song dedicated to my
dear wife.

*RB sings, unaware that he is being watched
by his wife.*

**RB:**
Take a pair of bloodshot eyes
And a nose that's round and red
And a set of loose false teeth
Picture two gigantic thighs
And a pair of knobbly knees
With enormous boots beneath

Some men have pretty women
To go ridin' with, or swimmin',
Or parading round the park
Not for me those smiles and dimples
It's just bandy legs and pimples
So, if I fancy a saunter, I go after dark

Take a pair of rubber lips
And a pair of bumpy hips
And a voice just like a knife
Like a knife,
A complexion as green as grass, it's a farce,
yes alas!
That's what I see every day
*(he sees wife glaring)*
In my looking glass!

*Tune: "Three Little Maids".*

**RC:**
Three little maids one night I met
Each one a perfect little pet
Popped to the pub for something wet
Three little maids came too

Three lemonades I ordered first
That didn't satisfy their thirst
Then I realised the worst
Three lemonades won't do

They said "Let us try champagne"
Then they tried it once again
"Now we'll try the beer" they said
"Then we must be off to bed"

Well…
Fourteen pints and six gins later
Went upstairs for a baked "potato"
I woke up with the hotel waiter –
The three little chicks had strayed
Three little maids – unmade!

*Tune: "He is an Englishman".*

**BOTH:**
But now pray let us sing
Of that patriotic thing
That we call an Englishman
A -a true blue Englishman
Though best by Income Taxes
They clutch their Union Jackses
And they wave them when they can
From the Khyber to the Congo
You will find a Pete or Pongo
That Intrepid Englishman
That ill-fated
Celebrated
Under-rated
Dear Old Englishman

*Tune: "Buttercup".*
*(sung to fat girl on seat)*

**RB:**
Dear little buttercup9
Sweet little buttercup
Nonsense of course you're not fat
But dear little Buttercup
Lift your left buttock up
You've squashed my opera hat flat:
*(He retrieves it.)*

*Tune: "When I Was a Lad".*

**RC:**
When I was a lad of seventeen
I took my girls upon the village green
When I was a lad of twenty-one
I took 'em in the hayloft which was much
more fun,

**CHORUS:**
He took 'em in the hayloft which was
much more fun,

**RC:**
But now I'm middle-aged you know
I take 'em anywhere they want to go
And when I'm old, why you can bet
I'll have to take what I can get.

*Tune: "The Sunny Spanish Shore".*

**RC:**
Now its Christmas once again
*(Drum, Drum, Drum, Drum)*

Peace on earth goodwill to men
*(Drum, Drum, Drum, Drum)*
And of course to ladies too
*(Drum, Drum, Drum, Drum)*
They're the ones that see us through
*(Drum, Drum, Drum, Drum)*
When the relatives all come
*(Drum, Drum, Drum, Drum)*
Aunts and Uncles, Dad and Mum
*(Drum, Drum, Drum, Drum)*
And the air begins to hum
*(Drum, Drum, Drum, Drum)*

**BOTH:**
Very merry Christmas and the same to
you
What a very pretty bonnet, why it looks
brand new
Are you comfortable? Very.
Will you take a glass of sherry?
It's so nice to see you merry,
Oh, sit down please do.

**CHOIR:**
So nice to see you merry, oh sit down
please do.

**RB:**
When a trumpet blasts your ear
*(Drum, Drum, Drum, Drum)*
You awake at 5 o'clock
*(Drum, Drum, Drum, Drum)*
Then the children all appear
*(Drum, Drum, Drum, Drum)*
With an orange in a sock
*(Drum, Drum, Drum, Drum)*
And you wish that you were dead
*(Drum, Drum, Drum, Drum)*
And they thump you on the head
*(Drum, Drum, Drum, Drum)*
Till they get you out of bed
*(Drum, Drum, Drum, Drum)*
And it's

**BOTH:**
Look what Father Christmas brought
along for me
Can I have another sweetie from the
Christmas tree
And you try to mend a dolly
While pretending to be jolly
Them you sit upon some holly

And you spill your tea

**CHOIR:**
You sit upon same holly and its agony.

**RC:**
Quite apart from noise and fuss
What does Christmas mean to us?

**RB:**
It's a thing that we can share
It's a family affair

**RC:**
When we're once more far away
We will think about today

**RB:**
And then perhaps we'll say

**BOTH:**
Oh, they -
Really did it nicely as it should be done
There were such a lot of presents. and we
all got one
Such pretty snowy weather
It was nice to be together
Such a very merry Christmas, oh we did
have fun!

**CHOIR:**
Such a very merry Christmas, oh we did
have fun!

# THE SHORT AND FAT MINSTRELS

*Opening: Robert E Lee.*
*Taken slowly, then building to speed. Sung as girls enter.*

**FAT MEN:**
See them shuffling along,
Hear them singing this song
Just bring a big pal
A fat gal,
If she's fat and heavy
Get down on the levee.

**SMALL MEN:**
*(Will you)* let those little gals through
And if they're very small, we'll take two

**ALL:**
We're short and fat, but,
That don't stop us singing,
All these songs we're bringing to you.

*Tune: "Swanee River".*

**RB:**
Way down upon the swanee river
I met Kate Maguire
Two onions and a pound of liver
That's how she won my desire

She knew just how to cool my dinner
Oh! shut my mouth -
No chance of ever getting thinner
Down in the deep-fried South

All the steaks were rich and fatty
All the beans were tinned
That's why my heart is burning ever
That's why I'm gone with the wind.

*Tune: "Swing Low Sweet Chariot".*

**RC:**
I looked cross the water, and what did I see,
Standing on the sea-front at Frome
A gal with a bust that measured fifty-three
Looked like St. Peter's in Rome.

Her name, was Harriet –
A stripper at the Hipperdrome
Swing low, sweet Harriet
Took four men to carry her home.

*Tune: "Blue-tail Fly (Jimmy Cracked Corn)".*

**RB:**
A gal whose date had let her down
She got so tired of waiting round
She said if I ain't in bed by ten *(pause)*
I'm a-going back home again.

**CHORUS:** *(all)*
Gimme that corn, and I don't care,
Gimme that corn and I don't care

It ain't no worse than you hear elsewhere
That's about all you can say.

**RC:**
A man in a bank saw a lady stop
And tuck some cash in her stocking-top
He said my, my what a large amount
*(pause)*
I'd like to open a joint account.

**CHORUS:** *(all)*
Gimme that corn, and I don't care,
Gimme that corn and I don't care
It ain't no worse than you hear elsewhere
That's about all you can say.

*Tune: "Smilin' Through".*

**RB:**
There's a little brown road winding over
the hill
To a little white car factory
There's a little green gate,
Where the red pickets wait
To stop blacklegs who
Keep sliding through
Like Me.

*Tune: "Beautiful Dreamer".*

Beautiful Dreamer, starting to snore,
Lying curled up on the factory floor,
Work day is over, sleepy young head,
Kiss the shop-steward and go home to
bed.

*Tune: "Raquel (Camptown Races)".*

Oh Raquel Welch, I love your left
Doo-Dah, Doo-Dah
I sit and think of Raquel's left
Doo-Dah all the day
Is it bigger than the right?
It's very hard to say
But that's the one that'll get my vote
On national Doo-Dah day.

*Tune: "Swanee".*

**RB:**
Ronnie, how I envy, how I envy
dear little Ronnie

I'd give the world to be
Just like young R.C.
Six stone four and five foot three
But Mammy's
Waiting for me
Cooking for me
Spuds and spaghetti
You'll find the jokes ain't
Funny no more
When you're stuck in the pantry door

**RC:**
Ronnie, how I envy, how I envy,
dear big fat Ronnie
If only I had grown
I'd be so full-blown
Eighteen stone of skin and bone
And fat that
Keeps you cosy
Warm and rosy
When nights are chilly
I'd be a great big
Crowd on my own
If only I was eighteen stone.

**ALL:** *(with Choir)*
Swanee, how I love yah, how I love yah
My dear old Swanee.

**RC & RB:** *(with Choir)*
The folks at home will be
So glad to know, we're
Working at the BBC-ing you, next
Week, if they'll allow us to come back
On the telly –
So once gain, we'll
Say cheerio,

**ALL:**
The short and fat Minstrel Show?

# NANA MOUSSAKA AND CHARLES AZENOUGH

*The production area. RB in silhouette as Nana. Greek music plays. Lights up as RB walks down to mic. Applause.*

**NANA:**
Good evening everybody, it is wonderful to be back on television again – I have only been away for a few months, but I am so glad to find you still sitting there. You are very patient, thank you. My friends in the band are glad to be back also – they are a very friendly group of boys. I am friendly with all of them. One at a time, of course.

*Music starts to play, quietly, behind next speech.*

**NANA:**
The first song I would like to sing for you tonight, is a story all about a young boy who works in a fairground, who is very sad, because no one will visit his stall. All the gay young men walk past with their friends, and patronise the swings and the roundabouts and the hoopla stalls, but none of them seem to want to throw thing at his coconuts. And he cried out to them "Why do you not want my coconuts? They are big and hairy, and rounded, like a young Greek warriors arms. Some of them are as big as my head – and others aren't. Look at them, as they stand there, all in a row. Aren't they lovely? All they need is a flick of the wrist, and they will be yours:

*The music is now fast, and has built up, like Zorba, into a Greek version of lovely bunch of coconuts. Suddenly it cuts out.*

**NANA:**
The song is called "Stormy Weather". But before I sing it to you, let me introduce my special guest this evening, a Frenchman who has delighted so many ladies all over the world by his

471

performance, and I'm sure he will be doing the same tonight, but before that, he has agreed to come on this programme and sing to us. Ladies and gentlemen - Charles Azenough.

*Play on music as RC comes on as Azenough.*

**RC:**
Good evening, ladies and gentlemen my dear Nana, it is wonderful to be here – where are we?

**NANA:**
At the BBC in London, Charles.

**RC:**
Ah beautiful. I am on this lightning world tour – I don't know if I'm on my head or on my heels.

**NANA:**
I thought you were on your knees.

**RC:**
Oh now now Nana. It's quality that counts, not quantity. And this world tour is proof. It shows that a little can go a long way.

**NANA:**
Yes, I have been warned about you.

**RC:**
Oh come now – you think I would make love to you behind your back?

**NANA:**
If you do ad I get to hear about it, there will be trouble. *(To audience)* We are only joking ladies and gentleman. Charles, what are you going to sing tonight?

**RC:**
It is called "Love Goes Over My Head." *(sings)* As I travel through life
in my search for a wife
I am on the look-out for a small one –
but of all the sweet girls
that I meet in this world
why do I always fall for the tall one?
it is not that I'm shy

I can always get by
when I'm telling a girl how my heart is –
but I soon lose my cool
'cos you feel such a fool
when you take a step-ladder to parties.

Yes it has to be said
though I long to be wed
love goes over my head.

In a small crowded bar
I met Fifi Lamarre
and her eyes held the promise of heaven
but when she left her seat
and she rose to her feet –
I found she was six foot eleven.
We would walk through the town
with the rain pouring down
it was really a soggy affaire-a
though each time that we met
I never got wet,
'cos I sheltered beneath her brassiere-a.

Yes it has to be said
it was just like a shed
it went over my head.

You may say it's my fate
that I exaggerate,
when I say love's above and beyond me
in society's whirl
I meet all kinds of girl
I have glamour and love thrust upon me
maybe after a show
there are girls that will go
somewhat further, perhaps, than they ought to –
it's no good, I have tried
when we lie side by side
I find I've got no-one to talk to.

Even when I'm in bed
yes, it has to be said
love goes over my head.

**NANA:** Thank you Charles, that was delightful. And now I'd like to sing for you a medley of well-known English songs, translated into Greek for me by my agent, Takis Tenpercentomi. But for those of you who don't understand Greek, they have been translated back into English by my good friend George Copalodathis.

*Into medley – during which the sub tiles come up, on a roller, across the screen, like autocue. Nana sings in cod Greek, to the tune of –*

*Tune: "Daisy Daisy".*

**NANA:**
Little flower, Little flower, kindly reply to my question.
I am on the borders or insanity, due to my passion.
Our wedding will be unfashionable,
Because I am unable to pay for part of a railway train.
But you'll look lovely over the back of a tandem.

*Tune: "Home on the Range".*

**NANA:**
A house, a house on the kitchen stove
Where the expensive and other animals enjoy themselves.
Not very often do we overhear a !! @ ?? @ ?? !! *(sound effect)* and the weather forecast is not wet and windy.

*Tune: "Pop Goes the Weasel".*

**NANA:**
225 grams of rice at 4p a kilo,
225 grams of molasses.
In this way our cash is used up.
The small furry animal explodes.
Up and down the main highway,
In and out of the well-known public convenient house.
In this way our cash is used up –
Another furry animal explodes.

*Tune: "Bye Bye Blackbird".*

**NANA:**
Please put my annoyance in a suitcase –
I am about to leave, singing in a bass voice
Goodbye, negro lady.
Where someone is waiting – sugar is very agreeable to the palate, and so is she
Goodbye, negro lady.

No one here can follow my reasoning
Stories of ill fortune by the handful
Manufacture something for me to sleep on
Switch on the bedside lamp, I may be detained at the office.
Negro lady – that's your lot.
*(Then in English, as a finish)* Black bird –
Bye bye!

**NANA:**
Thank you so much – and now it is time to leave you – Charles – let us sing together before we go – have you enjoyed it?

**RC:**
It has been wonderful...

*Tune: "Intro into Last Bit of Offenbach's Orpheus Can-can".*

**RC:**
It's so nice to come along
From the land where we belong
And if you sing a foreign song
Then no one knows when you go wrong

**RB:**
Dance with me in Zorba's dance

**RC:**
You might fall and ruin your chance

**RB:**
If I do I'd fall on you
My little shock absorber!

**RC:**
Nana! Nana!
You're so very Greek to me

**RB:**
La La La La
You look very weak to me.

**RC:**
How I love Greece
Axle grease and candle grease

**RB:**
Your so dainty

473

Want you for my mantelpiece.

*Intro music to main theme.*

**RB:**
You, gorgeous little Frenchman
Will you be my Henchman

**RC:**
Well it all de-
pends what you want henching darling

**RB:**
I love your Gaelic manners
Wish that you were Nana's
I would take you home and have you
stuffed.

*Repeat main theme.*

**RC:**
No, that is not for me
Cheri, I can't agree
Cheri, I'd find that things would get on
top of me
But I'm glad to be invited.

**RB:**
I am quite delighted
To have you on the show
And now I really think it's time for us to
go.

**RC:**
Let us embrace each other now we have
to part

**RB:**
And let me clasp you to my heart

*They embrace – RC 's face in RB's cleavage.*

**RB:** *(spoken)*
Oh, I felt a proper Charlie.

**RC:**
And I felt a right Nana!

**BOTH:**
Goodnight.

*Music finishes last chords of can can.*

# THE WELSH MINERS

*Darkened stage – we can just see the lights on the helmets of the miners glowing in the dark. Music starts as lights go up, revealing chorus of twenty men (eighteen plus RB and RC ) the tune is Bread of Heaven. The choir hum the first verse, then RC and RB sing, from their place in the back row.*

**BOTH:**
Here you see two amateur performers

**RC:**
I am Evan, he is Dai.

**RB:**
Though he's small, and I'm enormous
He can get much lower than I
Me and Evan,
Me and Evan,
All we want to do is sing

**RC:**
Like Anything –

**BOTH:**
All we want to do is sing.

*They both move out of the back row and come to the front.*

**CHOIR:**
Dai and Evan
Dai and Evan,
All they want to do is sing (Like anything)
All they want to do is sing.

*Tune: "Sospan Fach".*

**ALL:**
We earn our living at the coal face
We labour to make an honest crust

**RB & RC:**
We might have a young face or an old
face
You can't tell behind this ruddy dust
Rough and tough, and black as the ace of
spades

**ALL.**
Rough and tough and black as the ace of spades

**RB & RC:**
There's no colour problem, down the pit

**ALL:**
They say, that if we used our brains boys
We'd leave the mines and start life anew

**RB:**
But coal dust gets into your veins, boys,

**RC:**
And a lot of other funny places too.

**RB:**
Pit head baths, they don't remove the black

**RB & RC:**
In the nude, we stand there back to back,
Like a ton, and a half, of nutty slack.

**ALL:**
Rough and tough, and black as the ace of
Spades

**RB & RC:**
Though we strike, for differential grades
We'll still all be black legs -

**ALL:**
Johnny-bach!

*Tune: "All Through the Night".*

**RB:**
Took the train and went to Swansea
Last Friday night
Took a girl to have some fun, see

**CHOIR:**
Last Friday night

**RB:**
Wouldn't let me kiss or hug her
She'd just come to watch the rugger
Sent her home, the stupid Blodwen
Last Friday night.

**RC:**
My wife is a real fanatic

**CHOIR:**
All through the night

**RC:**
She's fixed goal posts to the bedposts
All painted white
In her dreams, she roars like thunder
Rips the bedclothes all asunder
Giving me an "up and under"
All through the night.

*Tune: "The Ash Grove".*

**RB:**
I met a girl called Megan
Oh she'd got a wooden leg, an'
A wouldn't it be nice sort of
Look on her face.
Now Megan was a cockney
And her one knee it was a knock knee
And the other one had woodworm
All over the place
Megan's flat wasn't far from us
And she made me a solemn promise
To show me her Dylan Thomas
On a bookshelf in the loo –
But my sides started shakin'
When she said her name was Megan
Bacon
You can guess what I had for breakfast
And very nice too.

**RC:**
I met a girl called Sally
Who worked in the Rhondda valley
Giving lessons in ballet
And she charged half a quid.
I danced with Myfanwy
And Myfanwy said "can we?"
I fell flat on Myfanwy,
An' we damn nearly did.
Then I met another girl called Shirley
Who was big beefy broad and burly
Her hair it was short and curly
She played scrum half for Rhyl;
But the nicest was Amanda
When I kissed her on her veranda
She asked me to stop and
I'm stopping here still.

*Tune: "Men of Harlech".*

**ALL:**
Once a year, they valleys ringing
With the sound of Welshmen singing
At the Fancy Dress Eisteddford
Down in Gogogoff.

**RB:**
It was such a grand Eisteddford
Opened by the Duke of Bedford

**RC:**
I went dressed as Robert Redford
On his half day off.

**RB:**
Everyone competing

**RC:**
Drinking, smoking, eating.

**RB:**
Songs were sung
And leeks were sprung
And things were seen that wouldn't bear
repeating –

**RC:**
Our conductor, Albert Stratton
Trouserless, but with his hat on
A ribbon tied around his baton
Had won second prize.

**ALL:**
Through the valleys of the Rhondda
Singing songs from way back yonder

**RC & RB:**
But our minds were bound to wander
When we've had a jar

**RB:**
Blodwen's bosoms cause a rumpus
Specially when she's wearing jumpers
Less like knockers, more like bumpers
On an old Ford car.

**RC:**
Megan's on the brandy
Grannies smashed on shandy
Auntie Glad's gone raving mad

With a randy handy man from
Tonypandy.

**RC & RB:**
Men of Harlech, alcoholic
Reeked of garlic, fun and frolic

**RB:**
What a load of –

**RC:**
Most symbolic

**RC & RB:**
So say all of us

**ALL:**
And so say all of us,
And so say all of us
Oh don't go down the mine, dad
Oh don't go down the mine dad
Oh don't go down the mine dad –

**RC & RB:**
There's plenty of coal in the bath

**RB:**
And now, before we go like, please
welcome some of the opposite, if you'll
pardon the expression, sex. We were to
have had the ten wise virgins on the
show, but during rehearsal we found out
that three of them weren't wise; and the
other seven – well....

**RC:**
Yes. The other seven wanted too much
money. So here instead, are five beautiful
girls from Rhyl.

*Girls enter. They are dressed in floor length,
clinging white dresses. Orchestra start to play
"Land of my Fathers" in slow waltz time. The
girls waltz with RB & RC and three other
miners from the choir.*

**RC & RB:**
We're just like our fathers, we love all the
girls
The tall ones, the short ones, with straight
hair or curls.

There always seems to be, lots of fish in the sea
Don't care if they're winkles or whales.

**CHORUS:**
Whales, snails, monkeys with big bushy tails
We love them every one, and when all's said and done,
We're glad we're all females and males.

*Repeat chorus – five couples dance behind the choir, come out again for last notes. The girls' dresses and faces are now black, covered in hand marks.*

**ALL:**
We're glad we're all females and males!

# THE WOMEN'S GUILD CHOIR

*Two banks of flowers. Hydrangeas, etc. Perhaps a couple of pillars. Eighteen ladies, all dressed alike, standing in three rows, on raised differing levels. In the front RB. And RC as two of the ladies. Dresses with corsages. They all hold music books.*

*Tune: "Now is the Month of Maying".*

**ALL:**
Now is the month of Maying
When merry lads are playing
With a fa la la la la la la
With a far la la la la
*(We cut to another woman singing.)*
Each lying on the grass
*(Cut to RB and RC watching her.)*

**RB:**
She's such a silly ass:

**ALL:**
With a fa la la,
La la la la la la la,
La, la , la la la.

**RB:**
Just like a donkey braying

**RC:**
I don't think she'll be staying

**ALL:**
With a fa la la la la la la
With a fa la la la la.

**RC:**
Her firm is moving South
She works for Rent-a-Mouth

**ALL:**
With a fa la la -
La la la la la la la la la la la.

**RB:**
She looks a bit like Flo
That's a horse I used to know.

**ALL:**
With a fa la la,
La la la la la la la, la, la la la la.

*Tune: "Nick Nack Paddywack".*

**ALL:**
This old man he played one
He played nick-nack on my drum,
Nick Nack Paddywack, give a dog a bone,
This old man came rolling home.

**RC:**
Her old man, next to you,
Needs a damn good talking to,
Nick nack paddy whack, now she's in the club,
He's off boozing down the pub.

**RB:**
My old man he plays hell
After all the girls as well
Nick nack paddy whack give him half a chance
He'd lead me a right old dance.

**RC:**
My old man's just as bad
Thinks himself a proper lad -
Nick-nack paddywack, lock him in the loo

That soon cools his how-de-do.

**RB:**
Her old man, he's the same
He's in love with what's-her-name.
Big jaws, droopy drawers, standing at the end
Known to all as man's best friend.

**ALL:**
This old man he played nine,
He's as bad as yours or mine,
Dick, Jack, Harry, Mac, Trevor, Doug or Mike
All old men are all alike.

*Tune: "Nymphs and Shepherds".*

**RB:**
Cynthia Shepherd has gone away,
Gone away,

**RC:**
Where's she gone?

**RB:**
Her mother won't say
Saturday she packed and went away

**RC:**
Denis Grove,
Denis Grove across the way
He went away, on Saturday
Now wait, I know what you're going to say,
'Praps he went on holiday

**RB:**
Yes and Cynthia met him half-way

**RC:**
That's not like Cynthia at all,
She's not the sort of girl to muck about

**RB:**
You're joking!
I've often seen her stop and take a bloke in

**RC:**
Oh Elsie
He'd really have to urge her, cos her father is a verger

And her mother is a vegetarian.

**RB:**
The daft young cow

**RC:**
Now now now, now now now, now now now,
It'll turn out right you'll see

**RB:**
Oh very well
But time will tell

**RC:**
You are just as bad as me,
You are always putting
Two and two together and making three

**RB:**
Just remember what I say
Come what may
She'll be in the family way
One fine day
That's why she's gone away

*Tune: "Cockles and Mussels".*

**RB:**
We've got a new milkman
His skin is like silk, man:
His van's full of goodies
He brings round to sell
He's full of surprises
He's got eggs of both sizes
He's got half-cream, and full-cream,
And whipped cream as well.

But he's leaving next Sunday
And he starts work on Monday
At the New Fish and Chip shop
Just down by the Green –
But I'll still drool with hunger
At my fancy fish-monger
He's got cockles and mussels
Like you've never seen.

**ALL:**
Alive alive O -
Alive, alive O -

**RB:**
Oh, no doubt about it, they're

**ALL:**
Alive, Alive O.

**ALL:**
Oh dear what can the matter be

**RC:**
I went to the hairdressers Saturday
There we sat like hens in a battery
While the young man did our hair
The first one to do me his name it was
Michael
He wanted to give me a ride on his cycle
And much as I'd like a good cycle with
Michael
I don't trust his cross-bar so there.
The second one he was a Welsh boy called
Billy
He wanted to show me the hills of
Caerphilly
I wouldn't trust Billy beyond Piccadilly
There's no mountain climbing up there.
The Manager thought that he'd just keep
his hand in
He promised to show me his flat on the
landing
But when we got there it was nothing
outstanding
In fact quite a pokey affair.
Oh dear, I learnt on Saturday
No good, responding to flattery
That won't recharge your battery
I'll do my own bloody hair.

*Tune: "The Pipes of Pan".*

**RC:**
Have you heard about young Mandy
At the annual dinner dance

**RB:**
(Hurry up and tell me what, what, what)

**RC:**
Someone laced the punch with Brandy
And she never stood a chance

**RB:**
(Drunk she got, silly clot)

**RC:**
That's not all she lost that night
A policeman so they say
Found her knickers a mile away
In Harrow,
On someone's barrow
Wrapped round a marrow
Marked half-a-crown.

**ALL:**
Oh-h-h…

**RB:**
Hurry, hurry, hurry, I've got to go and
cook a flan
My husband Keith has lost his teeth
He flushed them down the pan,
In the can –

**RC:**
I'll speak to Anne, her husband Dan's
The sanitary man
You never know where they may turn up

**BOTH:**
 In-

**ALL:**
The merry merry pipes of Pan!

*Music to finish.*

# HELLO SAILOR

*(A cyclorama with a mast, flags and two prop
cannons, arranged at the back – as for a
theatrical tableau. Orchestra strikes up – "All
the Nice Girls Like a Sailor" – and on march a
lot of naval ratings – as many as we can get.
They countermarch across the stage, and then
RB and RC come on as two members of the
W.R.N.S. They are dressed as ordinary ratings
– white blouse, hat, skirt etc. They sing the
following songs, with a bit of marching and
hornpiping, as considered necessary.)*

*(Tune: "A Life on the Ocean Wave".)*

479

**BOTH:**
A life on the ocean wave
Is better than walking the street
If a sailor's life you crave
Then up and follow the fleet.

**RB:**
Oh the skipper's awfully sweet
When he comes for his Sunday treat

**RC:**
Well – when you're abroad
You're bound to get bored

**BOTH:**
And it's nice to get off your feet –
When you're out with a sailor boy
The answer's always "Yes"

**RC:**
I'm the captain's pride and joy

**RB:**
And I'm the officer's mess

*(They march away during the next intro, and return together in time to sing tune: "Hearts of Oak".)*

**BOTH:**
So cheer up my lads
If you need us, we're here
We've already had
Quite a varied career

**RB:**
Oh we've both been around

**RC:**
Though we're not very old

**RB:**
We've been kissed in the crows nest

**RC:**
And held in the hold.

**BOTH:**
Hearts of oak, we have got

**RB:**
Cos me bra's made of wood *(knock).*

**RC:**
We always are ready

**RB:**
Steady girl. Steady

**RC:**
Oh she's as bad as me
But we're both pretty good

**BOTH:**
We love playing games
On the deck, or below
With a bottle of rum
And a quick Yo ho ho

**RC:**
Though our fish nets get torn
In a game of sardines

**RB:**
And we sink pretty low
When we play submarines

**BOTH:**
For a joke or a jar
With a bloke who's a tar
We always are ready
Steady girls, steady
We travel round the world
But we don't go too far.

*(Tune: "Drunken Sailor".)*

**RB:**
I had a date with a drunken sailor
Thursday night with a drunken sailor
Had a fight with a drunken sailor
Early Friday morning.

**RC:**
Heigh ho, and up she rises
She's got knees of different sizes
One's very small, but the other wins prizes
Early in the morning.

**RB:**
Out in a row boat with this sailor
All tarted up like Elizabeth Taylor
Shouting at each other through a small
loud hailer
Early in the morning.

The fog got thicker and so did the sailor
The night got darker and he got paler
Then we were hit by a bloody great whaler
Not a word of warning.

**RC:**
They were hit by a bloody great whaler
Early in the morning.

**RB:**
Lost the oars and the small loud hailer
Hung up me blouse and tried to sail her
Used my brassier as a baler,
Early in the morning.

**RC:**
Heigh ho, up she rises
She got big by exercises
Measure her bust in school cap sizes
Six and seven eighths.

**RB:**
I saved that sozzled saturated sailor
Took him back to my caravan and trailer
Gave him a sniff of my Vick inhaler
Early in the morning.
He took off his suit and prepared to retire
Dried his bell bottoms by the fire
They weren't his own, he'd got 'em on hire
From the local Moss Bros.

**RC:**
Heigh ho, up she rises
They have suits of different sizes
The pockets are full of little surprises
Early in the morning.

**RB:**
Cold and wet and much much frailer
Three sizes smaller, two shades paler
I finished up with a shrunken sailor
Early in the morning.

**BOTH:**
Early in the morning.

*Tune: "Bobby Shafto."*

**RC:**
Bobby Shafto's gone to sea

He'll be back in time for tea
He's in charge of the W.C.
On the channel ferry.

Every morning he departs
With his telescope and charts
Off for a glimpse of foreign parts
On the channel ferry.

Bobby Shafto's tall and strong
His legs are thin and his hair is long
He looks like a lavatory brush gone wrong
On the channel ferry.

But I have a little plan
To marry Bobby if I can
Cos I love a W.C.-going man
On the channel ferry.

*Tune: "Rule Britannia."*

**BOTH:**
And so we now salute
That gallant crew

**RB:**
The captains, the commanders
And the cabin boys
Who sail the ocean blue

*(They dance, showing the flag.)*

I love each one

**RC:**
And I've had fun
With quite a few,

**BOTH:**
We wear the colours
The flag of great renown –
And we'll never let them
Be pulled down.
June and Tania, the darlings of the waves
Just try blowing your hornpipe
We're your slaves.

*(Coda)* Rule Britannia
The old red, white and blue
We shall never leave you
We love you.

*(The cannons fire and the Union Jack knickers fall to the ground.)*

# THE BRASS BAND

*(Genuine brass band march on, playing. They countermarch immaculately. Among them are discovered RB with bass drum, RC with cymbals. They come together and sing – "The Stein Song."*

**RB:**
Evening Jack and how are you? *(Drum.)*

**RC:**
Fine, how's yourself.

**RB:**
Don't ask *(drum)* me *(cymbal)*.

*(They part, next 16 steps they countermarch, then come together again.)*

**RB:**
Mavis put me on a diet
She says if me tum gets big *(drum)* ger *(cymbal)* I'll be too fat to reach the Drum *(drum)* Jack *(cymbal)* and lots of other things as well.

*(During the next twiddly middle-eight, they march. Then they meet for the chorus again.)*

**RB:**
Tell me, how's your love life Jack.

**RC:**
Full of the joys of spring mate.

*(They mark time on the spot.)*

**RB:**
Is it still that six foot brunette?
The one with the enormous *(drum cymbal drum cymbal)*.

**RC:**
Yes, her name is Mary Jane
Works at the mattress factory

She says that life, like a bed is what you make it
As long as you take it lying down. *(Drum cymbal.)*

*(Introduction into "Where Did You Get That Hat?" during which they march away and return in time for the verse.)*

**RC:**
Where did you get that hat?

**RB:**
I got it from the stores –
Isn't it a little one
I think it must be yours.

**RC:**
I have got a big one

**RB:**
I'm quite sure of that

**RC:**
I didn't mean my flaming head

**RC:**
And I didn't mean your hat!

*Tune: "Anchors Aweigh".*

**RC:** *(indicating tuba player)*
Old Herbert's drunk again
He's well away *(drum, cymbal, drum)*
He's got a bottle with a
Rubber tube poked down his trousers
He sips then plays away

**RB:**
With any luck *(drum, cymbal, drum)*
We'll all get showered with Scotch
If he decides to blow instead of suck.

*(Segue to soldier's chorus (Faust) and marching. A short intro, then – )*

**RC:**
I don't half fancy a drink myself

**RB:**
They should put beer on the national health

**RC:**
You'd hear a different show tonight
The brand would get hissed
And Mozart and Lizst –

**RB:**
You're probabaly right.

*(They march to repeat chorus, a short intro, then – )*

**RB:**
As soon as we both finish here *(drum, drum)* Why don't we, have a meal, round the Chinese
Or else, I shall go off me nut,
Cos me stomach thinks me throat's been cut *(drum, drum)*.

**RC:**
I'd much rather go round the pub
To re-float me kidney that is sinking
I don't want to fill up with grub
That little space that I've reserved to pour some drink in.

*Tune: "Ain't it a Pity".*
*(RC marches off, separating from RB.)*

**RC:**
Ain't it a pity, the pubs in the city
All close at half past ten
If I had the power, they'd close for an hour
Then open up again *(cymbal)*
I could get chronic on vodka and tonic
Till any time I like
Then while the policeman watched my car
I'd nip home on his bike.

**RB:** *(singing the counterpoint, on his own, as he marches)*
Oh how I'd love
To eat anything I want-ed
Bangers and beans
And enormous lumps of fried bread
Fed chop and chips
And steak and kidney pies
By a girl who likes cooking
Who's big and good looking
Whose dumplings are double the size,
Oh –

*(They both come together and repeat their own versions, together, as a counterpoint, then carry on with the tune together –)*

**BOTH:**
And then we'll all have a damn good time

**RB:**
All peaches and cream *(cymbal, drum)*

**RC:**
And vodka and lime *(cymbal, drum)*

**BOTH:**
To eat and drink ain't a blinkin' crime
Enough is enough, let's go and get stuffed, together.

*(During intro to "Entry of the Gladiators" – )*

**RB:** *(spoken)*
Here it comes then – last number, "Entry of the Gladiators".

**RC:** *(spoken)*
Yeah – see you at the stage door straight after, alright?

**RB:** *(spoken)*
Right – don't be long, the Chinese shuts at eleven, I can't wait…
*(sings)* Prawn chop suey and a chicken fritter

**RC:**
Large Drambuie and a pint of bitter
Corkscrews and waiters

**RB:**
Rice and potatoes
Hurry up and finish with these bleedin' gladiators

**RC:**
Three pink gins and a Napoleon brandy
Two dry sherries and a half of shandy

**RB:**
I'll run amok! Two crispy duck!

**RC:**
Wishing you the best of luck

**RB:**
Herbert's drunk so much he can hardy stand

**RC:**
I have got a somewhat similar occasion planned

**BOTH:**
So before it all gets out of hand
It's goodnight from the boys in the band.

*(Band does big eight bar finish, RB and RC march round, meet and march off together, with the band.)*

# BALL AND SOCKET

*(A grand piano and potted palms. RC sits at the piano, RB stands beside it. They are dressed as "Hinge and Bracket". Play on music and applause. They both begin to babble away as the applause dies down.)*

**RB:**
Good evening ladies and gentlemen, it's wonderful to be with you again, isn't it dear?

*(RC nods and trills up the piano in glee.)*

**RB:**
Yes, she's been terribly excited all day - don't overdo it dear, because I want you to tell the ladies and gentlemen what we are going to do for them this evening – off you go.

**RC:**
Well, what we'd like to do tonight, Dame Evadne and I, bearing in mind that.....

**RB:**
Don't forget to tell them about Jubilee year, dear –

**RC:**
Yes, bearing in mind that it is Jubilee year

**RB:**
Yes, they know that now dear, I've just told them that.

**RC:**
We thought we would take a peep back into the past at other important, royal years.

**RB:**
Ah yes, thank you, Hilda. First of all, the Coronation of Edward the Seventh. 1902.

**RC:**
My goodness – as long ago as that. It seems like only last year.

**RB:**
No no, you're thinking of the repeats on ITV dear.

**RC:**
Oh, yes – wonderful, wasn't it? Probably cost more than the real thing, dear.

**RB:**
I wouldn't be surprised. I actually met King Edward, you know. Oh yes. Well, when I say met, he came to the house – I was a tiny, tiny baby gel, lying on my tummy on a bearskin rug. And apparently I turned my head, like that, and gave him a big wide smile. It was apparently very big, even in those days, wasn't it dear.

**RC:**
Oh, enormous. I've seen the photograph.

**RB:**
Yes, alright, yes, that's enough about that – carry on.

**RC:**
Well of course, 1902 was the hey day of the music hall. Gertie Gitana, Marie Lloyd, Vesta Tilley.

**RB:**
And of course my favourite, George Tickle. Do you remember him? The famous female impersonator.

**RC:**
Oh yes. Bent as a fork.

**RB:**
Pardon dear?

**RC:**
Camp as a row of silver sausages dear.
Queer as a tin of sardines.

**RB:**
Yes, never mind dear. Well ladies and
gentlemen, I would very much like to sing
one of George Tickle's famous drag songs.
You'll have to bear with me, because
remember, I'm a woman playing a man
who is playing a woman – aren't I dear?

**RC:**
Oh, at least.

**RB:**
Yes. The song is called "Moderation"
Thank you.

*RB sings "I Believe in Doing Things in
Moderation".*

*(Editor's note: See "A Pint Of Old and Filthy".)*

**RC:**
Now the year is nineteen hundred and
eleven – Coronation year of George the
fifth and our Beloved Queen Mary.

**RB:**
The dear thing. Oh yes – she loved Gilbert
and Sullivan, and of course, so did
everybody else.

**RC:**
Oh dear me yes. I loved Gilbert, you
know.

**RB:**
Not personally did you dear?

**RC:**
Oh no, but I knew him intimately. He
wrote this version of "I have a song to
sing, O" specially for me. He came to my
house in Primrose Hill one wintry
afternoon, and I offered him something
warm in the conservatory, and he wrote
me this. I do hope you'll like it.

**RB:**
Of course. they will. I adore this one
because I'm allowed to play my
tambourine in between. Off you go, dear.

**RC:**
I have a song to sing- O

**RB:**
Sing me your song-O

**RC:**
I sing of a man who is six foot tall
Who's legs are strong and hairy
Whose muscles bulge right through his
clothes
With some of these and lots of those
Who I saw last night as he danced on his
toes
In the dance of the Sugar Plum Fairy.

**CHORUS BOTH:**
Hey, de, Hey de, misery me, lackaday-dee

**RC:**
He plainly shows he's one of those
Trust me to pick a fairy.

**RC:**
I have a song to sing-O

**RB:**
Sing me your song-O

**RC:**
I sing of a man who's a sporting man
Whose skin is bronzed and shiny
Whose face is lean, whose eyes are bright
Who hits each ball right out of sight –
I played a round with him last night
And his handicap is tiny.

**BOTH:**
Hey, dee, Hey dee, misery me, lack a day
dee,

**RC:**
If you'd been on the green you'd have

seen what I mean,
His handicap is tiny.

**RC:**
I have a song to sing-O

**RB:**
Sing me your song-O

**RC:**
I sing of a man who is bald as a coot,
Who's fat, and who's old, and who's tame,
dears,
Cos after all, it must be said
No matter whom we ladies wed
After twenty years of board and bed
They end up exactly the same, dears
Hey-dee, hey dee, misery me, lack a day,
dee,
Though the flame has gone, they
smoulder on,
And they end up exactly the same, dears.

*(After song, applause.)*

**RB:**
1910 was the year when I sung my first
little song in public – I was nine years old.

**RC:**
Good gracious – let's see – that makes you
76.

**RB:**
Yes, never mind that dear, I was hoping
you wouldn't – anyway, it was so sweet –
It went like this –
I had a little puppy once,
When I was just turned four
My mother bought it for me
From a gypsy at the door;
Oh how I loved that puppy dog
The sweetest little thing
I used to take it for a walk
Upon a piece of string,
But soon my pup began to grow
It's face got quite distorted;
And when the postman knocked the
door,
It didn't bark, it snorted.
It grew a little curly tail
And got so fat, that one day

We realised it was a pig –
So we had it for lunch on Sunday!

*Song No.4: "The Ash Grove"*

**BOTH:**
With Mabel and Molly
We thought that it might by jolly
To spend our summer holi-
-days down on a farm
We wanted no dramas
With gentlemen farmers
So we wore very thick pyjamas
So we'd come to no harm.
But we found what made us tick
Was certainly nothing rustic
And we can't wait to get our bus tic-
-ket back to Vauxhall –
Young girls from the city
When down to the nitty gritty
Find cows and chas-titty
Just don't mix at all.

*(Tune: "The Minstrel Boy")*

**RC:**
The farmers boy, his name is John
And he works hard for his wages
The baggy trousers he has on
Have been in the family for ages
Old and patched, but they still work hard
So used to him they've grown, now
If he's out courting and he loses them
They trot home on their own, now.

*(Tune: "Early One Morning".)*

**RB:**
Early one morning, just as the sun was
rising
I heard someone saying in the valley
below,
"Mind where you're putting it,
You've got your foot in it"
But who it was and what it was and why
I'll never know.

*(Tune: "Where the Bee Sucks".)*

**BOTH:**
Where the bee sucks

**RB:**
Where the bee sucks

**RC:**
Where the bee sucks

**BOTH:**
There suck I:-
Where the pig-sties, there sty I
Where the pig-sties, there sty I
Not a sight to please the eye
They look no wide, they smell so high
If it gets worse, I shall die-ie-ie-ie-ie
After summer merrily, merrily,
After summer, merrily.
Merrily, merrily, wondering why,
They built the farmhouse, right next to
the sty
Merrily, merrily, Wondering why
They built the farmhouse, right next to
the sty,
They built the farmhouse, right next to
the sty.

Where the cow-pats, there pat I
Where the cow-slips so do I,
In the meadow grass I lie
Tis there I lie and swat the fly
On a cow-pat I do lie-ie-ie-ie-ie….
After summer merrily, merrily,
After summer, merrily.
Merrily merrily, shall I live now
There with the cow-pat, that comes from
the cow.
Merrily, merrily, shall I live now.
There with the cow-pat, that comes from
the cow.
Right in the cow-pat, that comes from the
cow.

**BOTH:**
Goodnight.

*(Orchestral play off.)*

# THE CHELSEA PENSIONER

*(The setting – a park – a realistic backcloth. In front of this a tall hedge and a row of ornamental iron railings. A green park bench in front of the railings. The time is 1976 but the park as looked the same since 1910. The orchestra plays "The Boys of the Old Brigade."*
*RB enters pushing RC in an old fashioned wheelchair. They are old Chelsea pensioners. RC has a white beard. RB stops the chair centre stage.*

**RB:** *(puffing)*
Ooh – I'll have to stop a minute. Whew!
*(he struggles to get out a large handkerchief, mops his brow)* Cor – fair puffs you out, don't it?

**RC:**
What, climbing up that hill?

**RB:**
No, getting your hanky out. Still, the fresh air does us good.

**RC:**
Yes. I like a bit of a walk.

**RB:** *(after giving him a look)*
It's the Queen's birthday today you know.

**RC:**
How old is she now.

**RB:**
I was trying to work it out. She was born in 1820, so that makes her about a hundred and fifty six.

**RC:**
What?

**RB:**
Fancy being that age. I should think she's very glad she's not alive.

**RC:**
Yes. Mind you, she was always older than us.

**RB:**
I should thinks he was! Some of them girls as we used to know would be getting on a bit now.

**RC:**
Yes, my little sister's seventy eight now you know.

**RB:**
Doesn't seem a minute ago, does it Albert?

**RC:**
No. You and me used to get round a lot of girls in them days, didn't we eh?

**RB:**
Yes, well I did. You used to say you did.

**RC:**
Watcher talking about? I loved 'em all. Beautiful girls they were.

*(Orchestra starts to quietly play "Mademoiselle from Armantieres".)*

**RC:**
D'yer remember the French girls? What was their names?

**RB:**
Madeleine and Millicent.

**RC:**
That's it, yes.

*Tune: "Mademoiselle from Armantieres".*

**RB:** *(sings)*
Madeleine came from Armantieres
Parlez-vous
Madeleine loved the navy and the army too
She surrendered every night
But she never went down without a fight
Inky pinky parlez-vous.
Millicent came from Clapham Road, Waterloo

**RC:**
She was a girl who did what she
Oughter do –

To officers she was always prone
But the private they were left alone
Inky winky Waterloo.

**RB:** *(speaks)*
Do you remember Daisy?

**RC:**
I remember them all.

*(Tune: "Daisy, Daisy".)*

**RB:** *(sings)*
Daisy, Daisy how can we ever wed
You're so lazy, you never get out of bed
I think it would be much quicker
If I brought along the vicar
For the honeymoon
This afternoon
And just let him say grace instead.

**RC:**
Mary, Mary lived with her aunt at Crewe
Strong and hairy, stood about six foot two
When I told her I'd never marry
She changed her name to Harry
Her great big feet
Now pound the beat
Cos she's one of our boys in blue.

*(Tune: "K-K-K-Katie".)*

**RB:**
K-K-K-Katie, was terribly matey
She'd k-kiss me on the mat behind the d-door;
But he f-father
Got into a lather
And he kicked me on the c-c-c-cobbled floor.

*(Tune: "Just Like the Ivy".)*

**RC:**
I first met Ivy
When I was quite small
She was the other side
Of an eighteen foot wall
She tired to entice me
With a sweet night of sin
So I took a run At it
And pole-vaulted in.

*(Tune: "Mary from the Dairy".)*

**RB:**

I fell in love with Mary from the dairy
And little Mary fell in love with me,
She was such a pretty sight
In the cowshed every night
The pull of every udder
Made me shudder with delight.
She was the very cream of all the dairy
But I turned out to be the biggest clot –
I married little Mary from the dairy –
Now she's milking me for everything I've
got.

**RC:** *(spoken)* Oh dear, so many of 'em.
Where are they all now.

**RB:**

You remember Phyllis Hooter?

**RC:**

Who?

**RB:**

The Honourable Phyllis Hooter. Don't
you remember? The posh girl we met at
the railway station.

**RC:**

Oh yes – we had our dress uniforms on, so
she didn't know we were ordinary people
– she asked us to that big dance at her
house.

**RB:**

That's it. We had a good old time there.

**RC:**

Yes. Blimey, there was a lot of girls there,
wasn't there? You remember?

**RB:**

Not half. I can remember all their names.
Every one.

*(Tune: "Phil the Fluter's Ball".)*

**RB:** *(sings)*

There was Jean there was June
There was Janet there was Jennifer
And Jane and Joyce and Jaqueline

And Juliet and Joan.
There was Lilly who was silly
There was Bessie who was messy
There was Annie with her granny
And Fanny on her own.
And they all stood around looking rather
ineffectual
Their feet close together and their
bottoms tot he wall
And some were thick, and other
intellectual
And some were fairly sexual, and other
weren't at all.

There was Clare there was Chris
There was Connie and Clarissa
And Cecilia and Charity and Caroline and
Kate.
There was shrinking little Violet
Who doesn't want to marry yet
And bulging little Harriet
Who can't afford to wait.
Clarissa you could kiss her
You could meddle with Melissa and
Vanessa you could press her and
Caress against the wall.
You could have fun with Nicola
But if you tried to tickle her
You'd end up with Virginia
Who wouldn't do at all.

There was Cora, Dora, Nora, Thora,
Flora and Felicity
Their sweetness and simplicity
Enchanted one and all
Though we fancied every one of 'em
We finished up with none of 'em
We both went home together
From Phyllis Hooter's ball
*(repeat)*
We both went home together
From Phyllis Hooter's ball.

**RC:**

Still – lovely to look back on, isn't it?

**RB:**

Yes. I think we'd better get off back. You're
getting too excited, I can feel the chair
vibrating.

**RC:**
Not me, old son. Not any more – all I'm interested in tonight is me dinner.

**RB:**
Yes – I'm afraid it's goodbye to all that.

**RC:**
Yes – goodbye, little girls, goodbye.

*(Tune: "Goodbye Dolly Gray".)*

**BOTH:** *(sings)*
Goodbye girlies we must leave you
Though it breaks our hearts to go –
We're no longer in the running
Cos we're past it now you know
We just think about the old times
Each dog has its day – We'll remember
with affection –

**RB:** *(spoken)*
'Ere Albert, come on – it's my turn in the pram.

*(They change places, RC wheels RB off.)*

*(Both (sing) "Goodbye Dolly Gray.")*

The following two songs were written by Ronnie for the 1976 Chichester Festival, artistic director Keith Michell

# I CHANGED THE WORLD (WALTZ)

*(Nothing to do with Hitler.)*

*During the introduction to the waltz, a man dressed as a Viennese gentleman of the 1870s enters. He sings: (in a thick German accent).*

**VERSE ONE.**
All through the ages
Of History's pages
The men that make war
Have made love that we're sure
Of, and love that is made is

Most often with ladies
And ladies have babies
Who grow up to fight.

**VERSE TWO**
As I've already told yer
That grown up young soldier
Or sailor will fancy
Some Nell or some Nancy.
Those soldiers and sailors
Succumb to blackmailers
Divulging their secrets
In boudoir, by night.

**CHORUS**
Changes,
in men's destiny
The course of,
world history
Can all be,
put down to me,
Because of my little invent-shon...
Schon....Schon...

**VERSE THREE**
I am ze invendor
Of ze ladies suzpendor
That small piece of fabric
Works better than abric
Cadabra when dealing
With gentlemen feeling
The need for some comfort
A chum for tonight

**VERSE FOUR**
That ring of bright metal
Is bound to unsettle
Those fingers unlocking
That black shocking stocking,
And he's dead as mutton
If that rubber button
In any way fails to
Arouse and excite

*(Enter the chorus girls – all legs and suspenders. They have eight or sixteen bars of dancing, as the waltz tempo increase. They continue to dance as the Inventor resumes the song:)*

**CHORUS**
So, because of these things,

I've, been, the downfall of kings
My, anarchic heart sings
To think how I've crippled convent-shon,
Schon....Schon....

*(He dances with the girls.)*

**VERSE FIVE**
I am the invendor
Of ze ladies suspender.
Brave generals quiver
They shake and they shiver
They all live to rue it
The ones who undo it
And lay themselves open
To scandal and snide.

**VERSE SIX**
Thus tough girls and frail girl.
And dark girls and pale girls
These white-thigh-and-tail girls
Have wheedled and won.
They've tumbled great nations
They've caused resignations
Their victims suspended,
Up-ended, undone.

**CHORUS**
Each new country that's born
Each new map that is drawn
Each new flag that's unfurled
I did it – I changed the world –

**CODA REPEAT**
I did it – I changed the world!

*(They dance round to a whirling finish, as the waltz builds. To a crescendo.)*

## QUEEN BESS SINGS

*(To the tune of "Greensleeves".)*

When Daddy dallied, and strutted and
strayed
With some ladies' maid in a woodland
glade
And penned this tune for the hit parade
Hew as monarch of all he surveyed....

The ladies' maid was as good as laid
For the King commanded and she obeyed
And she joined the throng who had made
the grade
For they all would succumb to my father.

While conqu'ring Kings their titles take
I remain a virgin for Daddy's sake
I sleep with no one, I stay awake –
For to tell you the truth, I would rather.
I go through the motions with some
young rake
I dally with Raleigh, play ducks with
Drake
But the whole damn thing's such a
dreadful fake
Because I am the son of my father.

**PATTER:**
*(spoken)* It is true England. My father
Henry, Got rot his socks, brought me up
as a maid instead of a man. He feared the
sexual competition that a younger man, a
prince of the blood, might provide at
court. It was therefore kept a closely
guarded secret. The whole thing was
carefully tucked away out of sight. By the
royal nanny usually.

So ever since I was sweet sixteen
A principal boy in reverse I've been;
Because the old man wouldn't let it be
seen
That a son was as good as his father.
But it's taken it's toll, if you know what I
mean
Now I'm middle aged, balding and faintly
obscene.
I have finished up dears, just a silly old
queen
A virginal son of my father.

# THE JAMBOREE SHOW

*The Chorus enter in usual fashion – finally RB and RC. When everyone is on stage, the lyrics begin.*

**ALL**: *(Refrain)*
We're sailing along with
The wind in our hair
And our knees are all bare
And we haven't a care
But
We will be there if
There's work to be done
'Cos with us it's not work
It's just fun!

*(Repeat)*

Just wear a grin
And take life on the chin
Keep away from the gin
Then your ship will come in

**RB & RC:**
So stick close together
And when troubles come
You can always fall back
On your chum

**ALL:** *(middle section)*
Boredom is our *(stamp)* enemy
We don't allow it around;
If you've got the *(clap)* energy
Why not come round to our camping-
ground.

*(Change key)* Oh, Oh,
Oh Oh Oh We're

**RB & RC:** *(Refrain)*
Drifting through life with
A song in our hearts
And we all know our parts
So that when trouble starts
We will be there, boys, and
We will be keen
'Cos, we're doing it all
For the Queen!

**ALL:** *(Coda)*
We're not easy riders
We're just a load of country-siders

Sailing along with the wind in our hair
And the world's all right!

**RC:**
Hello, everybody. Hello gang!

**CHOIR:**
Hello, skipper!

**RC:**
Here we are again, this is your old pal skipper Chuck Ferris, welcoming you to another Jamboree Show, and I hope you're all ready to go, 'cos I know we're all going to have a lot of fun. With me tonight, as usual, is your old friend, Buster Gunnersbury...

**RB:**
Hi there, listeners!

**RC:**
And we're going to commence by starting off straight away with one of your old favourites – the "UM PAH DAY" song.

*Tune: Scout Song "Um Pah Day".*

**RC & RB:**
Um pah dee, Um pah day
Here's a silly game to play
When you sing an old-time song
Change the words as you go along:
Um pah doe, Um pah dee
It's so simple, you'll agree
But in this life, if you know where to go
You'll have a lot of fun with your um pah
doe

**CHOIR:** *(Chorus)*
Um pah ding, Um pan dong
Sing these words and you can't go wrong
Um pah Um pah Um pah doo
And an Um pah doo to you.

**RC:** *(behind cut-out)*
Little Jack Horner sat in the corner
Eating his Christmas Pie
He put in his thumb, and pulled out a
plum
As big as his Um pah die

**RB:** *(behind cut-out)*
Twinkle Twinkle little star
How I wonder what you are
Up above the sky so high
You remind me of my UM PAH DIE

**CHOIR:***(Chorus)*
Um pah ding, Um pah dong
Sing these words and you can't go wrong
Um pah Um pah Um pah doo
And an Um pah doo to you

**RC:** *(behind another cut-out)*
Mary Mary, quite contrary
How does your garden grow
With silver bells and cockle shells
And plenty of UM PAH DOE

**RB:** *(behind another cut-out)*
Jack and Jill went up the hill
To fetch a pail of water
Jack fell down and broke his crown
And Jill let her UN PAH DAYS fall down

**CHOIR:***(Chorus)*
Um pah ding, Um pah dong
Sing these words and you can't go wrong
Um pah Um pah Um pah doo
And an Um pan doo to you.

**RC:**
Thank you, thank you – that one always
goes with a swing, and it's all good clean
fun.
And now, in more serious mood, Buster
Gunnersbury is joined by young Roger
Hopkins, in a dramatic monologue
entitled "Be a chap with a purpose."

*(Cut to RB and young lad, in limbo.)*

**RB:**
All right, lad – do you want to tell me why
you stole that chocolate biscuit? Were you
– hungry?

**ROGER:**
No skipper. It was – just something to do.

**RB:**
Something – to do? You're just wasting
your life, Roger. You'd better pull yourself

together, son, and take this good advice
from me: -
Be a chap with a purpose
Be a fellow with an aim
Though life's a moving target
Try and hit it, just the same

Take up the bow of honesty
Screw up your strength, and pull:
And in the field of cleanliness
You're bound to hit a bull

Be a man who is merry
Be a guy who is gay
And if life seems topsy-turvy
Try it up the other way

If you're in a narrow tunnel
And it's black, and you are blue;
If you've a friend at the other end
He's bound to pull you through

Be a gent who is gentle
Be a pal who isn't proud
Don't try to be a big knob
Or stand out in a crowd

But if a chum falls on hard-times
Just offer him your hand
And let him grasp it firmly
It will make you both feel grand

So remember as you go through life
And travel, near or far
It isn't what you say, or think
Or what you do, or are-
It's what you think, it's what you say,
It's what you are, and do!
Just live by that – and then, you'll stay
Alive your whole life through

**RC:**
Well, that's it, folks; once again the old
clock's beaten us and it's time to say
goodnight -come on Buster. *(RC hurries
back to join RB.)*

**RB:**
Cheerio, everybody: from all us gangsters
here it's good luck till we meet again, and
don't forget -Stay Bright
Do Right

**RC:**
Don't get tight
Or high as a kite

**RB:**
Try not to fight
Stay home at night

**RC:**
Keep out of sight
And you'll be all right!

**BOTH:**
Goodnight:

*(Into last chorus of "Sailing Along".)*

**ALL:** *(Refrain)*
We're marching along and
We're all side by side
And our legs are astride
And we do it with pride
Step forward bravely
And then you will find
You can rely on your comrades behind

*(Coda)* We're not easy riders
We're just a load of country-siders
Sailing along with the wind in our hair
And the world's all right!

*(Big finish and all wave.)*

# PEARLY KINGS

*Eight dancers 4 male, 4 female – 10 extras, but not all as pearly kings etc.*

*To tune of: "Knees up Mother Brown."*

**BOTH:**
Pearly kings are we,
We've brought the family

**RC:**
Curly kids and burly males

**RB:**
Dogs with pearly curly tails

**RC:**
Pearly whirly girlies
With pearly twirly frocks.

**RB:**
Pearly surly mothers-in-law
With bleedin' ugly clocks.

*Tune: "Segue: What a Rotten Song".*

**ALL.**
Oh my! Everyone's a swell
Every coster jacket cost a packet
Can't you tell?
Do try, to join us for a spell
When you're in the Old Kent Road.

*Into Cockney rhyming song.*

**RC:**
If you're cockney, same as me
It's amazing, you'll agree,
How we've conjured up a language all our
own.

**RB:**
'Cos we're talking all in rhyme
And we talk it all the time
It's the most peculiar lingo ever known.
(Too right!)

**RC:**
Now your plates they are your feet,
'Cos they rhyme with plates of meat.
And your Hampstead Heath are teeth,
that's fairly clear.

**RB:**
And your teeth are in your mouth,
which is called your North and South,
And a pint of Pig's Ear means your pint of
beer.
So you can

**BOTH:**
Put up your plates,
Take out your Hampsteads
And pour a pint of Pigs
Down your North and South.
Put up your feet
Take out your teeth, pour a pint of beer
Down your mouth. (See?)

**RC:**
Now your trouble and your strife,
That is what you call the wife,
'Cos she's been one since the day that you
were wed.

**RB:**
If you've got a load of kids,
Then they're called your saucepan lids,
And your bed upstairs, that's called your
Uncle Ned.

**RC:**
But you never call them stairs,
They're your Apples and your Pears,
That you climbs up when the currant bun
has set

**RB:**
When you smoke an oily rag,
It really means your fag,
Your dog-end, dimp, or snout, or
cigarette.
So you can

**BOTH:**
Tuck in the Saucepans,
Put out your Oily,
Chase the Trouble, up the Apples,
To the Uncle Ned -
Tuck in the Kids,
Put out your fag,
And chase the wife upstairs
And go to bed.

*(spoken)*
**RC:**
Now the roads not called the road,

**RB:**
It is called the frog and toad

**RC:**
And the Pub's the Rubber-dub, we all
know that.

**RB:**
And a tumble down the sink

**RC:**
Is the cockney name for drink

**RB:**
And your titfer is your hat – your titfer-tat.
So you can

**BOTH:**
So you can put on your titfer
Go down the frog
To have a little tumble
In the Rubber -
Put on your Hat
Go down the road
To have a little drinky
In the Pub.

*After Cockney rhyming song, RB seated with
large girl – RC approaches.*

**RC:**
Who were you with last night?

**RB:**
The big beauty on my right -
That's Shirley, from Purley, my sweet little
gnome.

**RC:**
What's her nickname when she's at
home?

**RB:**
They call her Boiled Suet Pudden
She eats like a good 'un.
Make sure she gets enough to scoff
Or else she'll have your whiskers off
And when she does a knees-up
She is anything but wooden
Cos every ounce begins to bounce
Yes every pound just flies around
Yes every stones got a life of it's own
Yes every hundred weights a plate of
Boiled Suet Pudden.

**RB:** *(to girl)*
How yer doing dearie? Feel a little weary?

**RC:**
Got a little query -

**RB:**
What's that?

*Segue to tune of "Where Did You Get That Hat?"*

**RC:**
How did she get that fat?
Look how it all sticks out.

**RB:**
Eating this and noshing that
And swiggin' lots of stout.

**RC:**
I should like to have one
Just the same as that
If I stood underneath them two
I wouldn't need a hat.

**RC:**
Where d'you find her, old pal?

*Tune: "My Old Dutch".*

**RB:**
I went wife-swapping with me china Gert
And we both had a gin too much –
And I ain't a-kidding – that's the piece of skirt
That I swapped for me dear old Dutch
Now if I go home again, without a doubt
I'll come out on a bloomin' crutch.

*Segue to "Knocked 'em in the Old Kent Road*

**RC:**
Your old girl will do her nut
Knock you off your feet, Bill.

**RB:**
Half the bleeding street will –
Ain't you got a little dear.

**RC:**
Got a little nice one here. *(Indicates girl.)*

*Segue to -"Any Old Iron".*

**RC:**
Fanny O'Brien
Fanny O'Brien
Funny little Fanny O'Brien
With a pearly king
It's the same old song

I'm a little bit short,
But I won't be long.

I'll take you off to church one day
With spats and a collar and tie on -
Then I'll always know
I've got sweet F.O.
Fanny O'Brien.

*Segue to "Carolina in the Morning".*

**RB:**
Nothing could be finer
Than to seize and squeeze your china
Without warning.
Smoochin' with my Shirley
My Sweet pearly girly early
In the morning.

**RC:** *(indicating Fanny O'Brien)*
Mines petite and tiny, she's
The belle of the ball,

**RB:**
She wears buttons bright and shiny
On her undies an' all!
That's why this old Apachy
Wakes up bruised and rather scratchy
In the morning!

*The dancers do a soft shoe shuffle to same tune, first eight lines, then pick up the tempo, to a whirling knees-up.*

*Segue to "Knees up Mother Brown".*

**ALL:**
Dear old London Town
Dear old London Town -
It's the only place we know
On and on and on you go

**RB & RC:**
Pearly lads and lasses
Kings without a Crown.

**RC:**
Dukes and Earls with button pearls

**RB:**
And Queens without tiaras – ra-ra

**ALL:**
Boom-de-ay
Ta-ra-ra Boom-de-ay.

**RC:**
We've had some fun today

**RB:**
Now there'll be hell to pay.

**ALL:**
Ta-ra-ra Boom-de-ay
Ta-ra-ra Boom-de-ay
We'll dance the night away
In London Town,
Oh!

**RC:**
We will paint the Town.

**RB:**
We'll paint it Watneys Brown,
I'm gonna drink like a bloomin' toff.

**RC:**
I'm gonna dance till me buttons drop off

**BOTH:**
Oh lor' love yer London
We'll never let you down
Wind or wevver, here forever

**ALL:**
Dear Old London Town.
Diddle-iddle a-dah
Diddle-iddle a-dah

**RC:**
Rule Britannia.
And other pubs as well -

**ALL:**
Diddle-iddle a-dah
Diddle-iddle a-dah

**RB:**
There'll always be an England
While there's a Rose & Crown

**BOTH:**
Wind or wevver, here forever.

**ALL:**
Dear old London Town.

# THE BARBERS SHOP

*A large Victorian sign, black on white – "Four chairs, No waiting." Pull back to reveal the four chairs, of the swivel type, but old fashioned. There is a door to the street, hat stand, basins etc. A customer is seated in one of the chairs – a barber is cutting his hair.*

**1st BARBER:**
Beautiful morning sir.

**1st CUSTOMER:**
Mm.

**1st BARB:** *(sings)*
Oh what a beautiful morning -

*(Another customer enters.)*

**1st BARB:**
Morning, sir. *(calls out)* Customer, Mr Green.

*(2nd Customer sits in 2nd chair, 2nd Barber enters.)*

**2nd BARB:**
Morning sir. Just a trim?

**2nd CUST:**
Please.

**2nd BARB:**
Rain seems to have stopped

**2nd CUST:**
Yes.

**2nd BARB:** *(sings)*
It ain't gonna rain no more no more

*(3rd Customer enters.)*

**BOTH BARBERS:**
Morning, sir – customer, Mr Brown.
*(3rd Customer sits in chair.)*

**RB:** *(Enters as barber.)*
Morning, sir. Short back and sides?

**3rd CUSTOMER:**
Please.

**RB:**
Thought so. I could see that the minute you walked in the door. *(Sings)* The minute you walked in the door, Boom-boom…

*(4th Customer enters.)*

**ALL BARBERS:**
Morning, sir. *(Calls)* Customer, Mr White.

*(Customer sits in 4th chair)*

**RC:** *(Enters as barber.)*
Morning, sir. Anything on it?

**4th CUST:**
Er-could you cut it first?

**RC:**
Very good, sir. Then I'll put a drop of this on it. *(Takes bottle from pocket.)* It's called "Moonlight". Very nice. *(Sings)* Moonlight becomes you, it goes with your hair .....

**4th CUST:**
Could you get on with it please?

**RC:** Certainly sir.
*(They are all snipping away.)*

**RC:**
Nice, that Moonlight though. *(Sings)* Oh by the light, of the silvery moon etc.

*They all join in, one by one, and sing the song, twice, with the correct words. During it, they get hot towels, all moving in unison, and singing in close harmony – miming to their own track. At the end of the number they remove the hot towels. All the men are completely bald. The barbers go into their*

*next number – "Whiffenpoof Song".*

**ALL:**
They are four little chaps who have lost their hair -Baa – Baa – Baa
They are bald as a coot in the barbers chair Baa – Baa – Baa
Gentlemen, now you've got room to think,
Smooth as a baby's, round and pink,
Used by flies as a skating rink, Baa – Baa – Baa.

*RB strikes his customer on head with a tuning fork, and they go into next number.*

"Dixie" *(I think).*

**RB:**
Now don't upset yourselves
and don't feel rotten
Your hair is gone but not forgotten.

**QUARTET:**
Hip Hooray, Hip Hooray,
For today's your lucky day.

**RB:**
There's some wigs in the cupboard and I don't know where I got 'em
But they're made of Nylon mixed with cotton.

**1st BARB:**
Get away *(hold note).*

**2nd BARB:**
Get away *(hold note).*

**RC:**
Get away.

**RB:**
It's a fact.

*Quartet, as they all move round, get wigs out of cupboard.*

**CHORUS:**
Do-do-do-do-do-do-do-do,
Doo-way, Doo-wah,
Do do ba-ba-ba-ba-ba doo-ay

De dap bap bap bap bap, ah -
Doo-way. Doo-way, Doo-way
bap bap ba bap ah

*(RB appears with large pot marked "glue" and large paint brush.)*

**REPEAT CHORUS**

**RB:**
Now they could be rather tricky
To keep, in place –
What we need is something sticky and
We'll splash it on all over.
*(He pastes their heads across the top.)*

**QUARTET:** *(as they place wigs on three of the men, and RB returns the glue to the cupboard)*
By gum, they're stuck,
A strong man couldn't lift 'em;
The best of luck
You'll never ever shift 'em.
*(they repeat the last line slowly, with a wandering harmony*
*finish)* You'll never ever shift 'em.'

*(On this last line, RB takes wig off barber's head, and puts it on the remaining customer, leaving the barber now completely bald. The barbers go into their next number: "Down by the Riverside".)*

**RC:** *(feeling customer's chin)*
Now how's the chin this morning, sir?
It's on the hairy side.

**ALL:**
It's on the hairy side

**RC:**
The Grizzly-beary-side
So kindly take this warning, sir –
Be on the wary side

**ALL:**
In case you scratch the
gal that you adore.

*(RC has fetched bowl of soap and shaving brush.)*

**RC:**
A shave is what's intended, sir.

**ALL:**
Makes you feel good inside.*(They get soap.)*
Makes you look good outside
Hold up your head in pride.

**RC:**
This soap is recommended sir,
Contains insecticide.

**ALL:**
Gives each little spot what for.

*(They are all lathering their customers faces. We now segue into next number: "The Old Rustic Bridge".)*

**1st BARB:**
I'm thinking tonight of my love far away,
Adrift on the deep, splashing foam.

**ALL:**
Splashing foam. *(They do so.)*

**1st BARB:**
Since he sailed away; each
night I softly pray.

**ALL:**
The tide will bring my loved one
safely home.

**1st BARB:**
He said, as we parted
"Don't cry, Maggie dear,
I've left you my old telescope

**ALL:**
My telescope.

**1st BARB:**
May your passion still burn
as you watch for my return,
For while there is life, there is hope.

**ALL:**
There is soap.

*(They now scrape away with cut throat razors.)*

**1st BARB:**
So at night, by the light
of the pale misty moon
And at noon, when the sun's rays are
sharp.

**ALL:**
Razor sharp.

**1st BARB:**
I watch from the shore, till the day when,
once more

**ALL:**
The tide brings my loved one back to me.

*(They all get buckets of water.)*

**1st BARB:**
And in dreams every night,
by the old fire light,
His boat on the shore I see

**ALL:** (I see!)

**1st BARB:** *(slower)*
After many close shaves

**ALL:** Close shaves!

**1st BARB:**
The billowing waves
Have washed my dear loved
one back to me!

**ALL:** *(repeat)*
Have washed my dear loved
one back to me!

*(On the last note, they hurl water into the faces of the customers. This, we hope, knocks off the wigs, so they are once again bald.)*

*Tune: "Good Night Ladies".*

**ALL:**
Good night, baldies
Good night, baldies
Good night, baldies -It's time to leave you
now.

*(They all go and get the mens bowler hats*

*from the hat stand, and fill them with shaving soap as they sing.)*

**RB:**
Now that you have lost your hair

**RC:**
You're all bare,

**ALL:**
We don't care,

**RB:**
Stick your hats on fair and square

**BOTH:**
Then no one will know

**ALL:**
Goodbye, baldies,
Goodbye, baldies, Goodbye, baldies –
It's – time – to – leave -you NOW!

*(On the last word, jam the hats on the customers heads -the soap shoots up through a hole in the hat in the old pantomime fashion, reaching a height of about eight feet, we hope, as the last note is held.)*

# THE RUSSIAN CHOIR

*Fade up on choir in silhouette (35) in uniform.*

**VOICE:** *(off)*
Ladies and Gentlemen, from Russia, the
St. Petersburg Male Voice Choir.

*Fade up lights*
*The choir sing an authentic Russian folk song – short. We pan along them. Various shots to establish authenticity. Then pan past RC and RB, singing with the others, as the song finishes. At end of song, RB steps forward.*

**RB:**
Good evening, and thank you.
*(Caption: Vasilievitch Kharkoff).*

And may I say how wonderful it is to be in your terrible country. My name is Kharkoff – and for a start-off, I would like to ring up the iron curtain by introducing to you my gentleman friend, Vladymir Pestov.

*(Super caption over RC – "Vladymir Pestov." RC steps forward.)*

**RB:**
You are Pestoff?

**RC:**
No, I like it here.

**RB:**
Da, it's good. My friend is a little defective. He has defected to the West, and has asked
to go in the political asylum.

**RC:**
The House of Commons.

**RB:**
Da, dats it. We now are singing for you our first song, which, as always, is our vulgar boating song. Thank you please.

*Volga Boat Song.*

**ALL:**
Yo Heave Ho
Pull once More
We must reach that far, sandy shore.

**RB & RC:**
Sandy Shaw
Sandy Shaw
Let's all try and pull
Sandy Shaw

**RB:**
We must reach those far off shores

**RC:**
All we need is a couple of oars
Ivan and Boris

**RB:**
Elsie and Doris
Waters splashing

**RC & RB:**
Yo heave ho

**RC:**
Pull once more
Pull like stink

**RB:**
But don't pull the plug, or
The boat will sink
We don't carry lifebuoys and we're glad we haven't got 'em

**RC:**
A sailors not a sailor till he's been on the bottom

**RB:**
I'm getting heavier
Eating too much caviar

**CHOIR:**
Like an Irish navvy our
Boris will get

**RC:**
My name is Vladymir
And when I was a kid
I came from Vladyvostock and
I'm Vlady glad I did

**RB:**
The waves they are calling
Rising and falling
Up and down and to and fro
Rising and falling,
I feel appalling
I think I'm
About to Heave – Ho! *(Looks decidedly ill.)*

**CHOIR:** *(fading)*
Yo heave ho
Yo heave ho, etc.

*Fade to silhouette.*
*Lights up, applause.*

**RB:**
Thank you, thank you. It is a great privilege to be here with you dis evening and a delight to see all you English gentlemen wid your laddies. It is nice to

501

see all your beautiful laddies. In Russia it's illegal. Women only. Now, if we may, we give you a muddly of English songs, which all have RED in them. We took all of the ones we are liking, and meddled them up into a muddly. Thank you please.

*RB & RC pick up balalaikas and appear to play them throughout next number.*

**RB & RC:**
Give me some

**CHOIR:**
RED

**RB & RC:**
Roses for a blue lady – la la la la la la la la

*(They play a few bars, then at a suitable point, RB interrupts.)*

**RB:**
Little Bo Peep, she lost her sheep
And didn't know where they grazed
When Mary had a little lamb
The doctors were amazed

*(Continue with "Red Roses" – then RC interrupts.)*

**RC:**
Georgie Porgie Pudding and Pie
Kissed the girls and made them cry
When the boys came out to play
He kissed them too, and now he's gay

*(Segue into "Red Sails in the Sunset")*

**CHOIR:**
Red sails in the sun set

**RB & RC:**
…huit neuf dix

**CHOIR:**
Way over the sea

**RC & RB:**
D. E. F. G.

**CHOIR:**
Oh carry my

**RC & RB:**
2. 3. 4.

**CHOIR:**
Home safely to me

**RC & RB:**
fah so lah te

*(Segue into "Red Red Robin" – 4 bars intro.)*

**RB & RC:**
When the RED RED

**ALL:**
Robin goes bob bob bobbing along, along

*(Continue with orchestra to a suitable point, then RB interrupts.)*

**RB:**
Little Ted Heath has lost his teeth
And doesn't know where to find them
There's been so much back biting on the back bench
They'll probably find them behind them.

**CHOIR:**
When the red red robin goes etc.

*Three girls, as Russian dancers, in peasant skirts, dance on. Very traditional folk dancing. RC interrupts*

**RC:**
Roses are red
Violets are too
But Mabel's a traitor
Cos hers are blue
*(Girls show knickers to prove it)*

**ALL:**
When the red red robin goes bob bob bobbing along

*(End of number.)*

**RB:**
Thank you, thank you. And now, as a

final, we would like to finish you off with
one of your own folk tunes, "Green Grow
the Rushes-O", which we have adapted
for ourselves. And here is my gentleman
friend to say "goodnight".

**RC:**
Hello. And thank you for letting me wish
you a good night.

**RB:**
Thank you for letting us put up with you.
Thank you please!

*(Intro – "Green grow the Rushes-O")*

**RB:**
I'll sing you one, O.

**ALL:**
Red grow the Russians, O

**RC:**
What is your one, O?

**RB:**
One is one and all alone and that is Greta
Garbo

**RC:**
I'll sing you two, O

**CHOIR:**
Red grow the Russians, O

**RB:**
What is your two, O?

**RC:**
Two, two, for women's lib,
Now they've burnt their bras, O

**RB:**
And they'll turn white
In the middle of the night
If you cover them with Blanco
I'll sing you three, O

**CHOIR:**
Red grow the Russians, O

**RC:**
What is your three, O?

**RB:**
Three p, for another cup of tea
Two two for women's lib
Now they've burnt their bras, O

**RC:**
And they'll go brown
When the sun goes down
If you hang them out the window
I'll sing you four O

**CHOIR:**
Five, six and seven O

**RB:**
What is your Seven, O?

**RC:**
Seven for the Seven Deadly Sins
And six for the Common Market

**RB:**
Five pence a mile to drive your car
And four pounds ten to park it

**CHOIR:**
Three p, for another cup of tea.
Two, two, for women's lib
Now they've burnt their bras, O

**RC:**
My wife Yvonne
Should keep hers on
She's built like a commando

**RB:**
At darts she's a flop
With her double top
But she's got a full house for Bingo

**ALL:**
One is one and all alone, and ever more
shall be so.

*Orchestra up to finish.*
*Play off.*

# THE LAUGHING TAXMAN

*(From "Lines From My Grandfather's Forehead")*

I am a tax inspector
A jolly chap that's me
I deal with your assessments
And drink a lot of tea
You'll always find me laughing,
You'll never see me cry,
I find out what you're earning,
And then I bleed you dry.

**LAUGHING CHORUS**

I check the bills you send me
I find out what you've bought
I look through your expenses,
Then cut them down to nought.
I squeeze out every penny
You all pay up like mice
And if I catch you cheating
I make you pay it twice!

I send you forms and pamphlets
It's fun without a doubt
To ask a lot of questions,
And try to catch you out
There's only one man's tax forms
I leave there on the shelf –
Oh yes, I make quite certain,
I don't pay tax myself.

**LAUGHING CHORUS.**

*Revolver shot. Ronnie groans, body falling.*

**MAN:**
Got you, you swine.

# WHAT AM I GOING TO DO ABOUT YOU?

*(From "Lines From My Grandfather's Forehead")*

Since I first met you

I can't forget you
I want you for my own, but
You won't be hurried
You've got me worried
You always want to be alone, but
I must arrange dear
For you to change dear
And see my point of view
For you suggest dear
All that is best dear
The things that I like are like you *(crunch)*

You remind me of a slice of raspberry tart
I'd love to take a bite right out of you
You're as pretty as a costermongers cart
Succulent as Irish Stew (with dumplings)
You remind me of a golf umbrella
Just before the rain soaks through
And what is so ironic
You want it kept platonic
What am I going to do about you?

You remind me of a Picture-house in Stoke
You're friendly you're warm and you're dark
When you wear that dress with flowers round the yoke
You remind me of St. James Park (Last Thursday)
You're as sparkling as the Crystal Palace
As Jazzy as a co-respondent shoe
My brain is in a whirl
If only you weren't a girl
What am I going to do about you?

You're an absolute fizz on the dance floor
With that low-fronted dress that you wear
And when we do the Big applie
They remark, what a beautiful pair
(they're lovely)

You remind me of the Lord Mayor's Show
Cos I think you're the biggest thing in town
You're, just like a book by Edgar Allan Poe
When I pick you up I cannot put you down (till bedtime)

You remind me of a knife and fork and spoon
And I'd love to eat breakfast with you

Yet you never say goodnight
Without putting up a fight
What am I going to do about you?

You say that you must be home early
That staying out late isn't fun
Yet when you went racing with Curly
You came home at twenty-to-one (hot
favourite)

You remind me of a pair of Oxford Bags
I don't feel quite at home without you
now
You're like Everest with all its icy crags
I don't think I'll get over you somehow
I'm beside myself I'm jumping up and
down
Behaving like the monkeys in the Zoo
I wonder just supposing
I were to try proposing
What about trying that with you?
That's what I'm going to do about you.

## THE PALLADIUM
## CAN-CAN

Here at the Moulin Rouge
My repertoire is huge
I offer wine and laughter -
Forget the morning after.
The girls are here to tease
To tickle and to squeeze
And I am here to please you
Here at the Moulin Rouge.

My food is all superb
Each vegetable and herb
Each entree and hors d'oeuvre
I know that you will loevre!
My home-made garlic soup
Will make you loop the loop
You'll find out who your friends are
Here at the Moulin Rouge.

But these girls –
To me they are adoring
They're the toast
Of all the married men
late at night

When all their wives are snoring
They creep out for
A crepe suzette
And creep back home again

These nights in gay paree
They take their toll of me
My head aches and my heart aches
And every other part aches.
I serve the best champagne
And drink it like a drain
My gherkin's always pickled
Here at the Moulin Rouge
I keep a private room
Where couples can consume
A tasty cold collation
With mutual admiration;
A quiet tête-à-tête,
With plenty on their plate -
No extra charge for service
Here at the Moulin Rouge.

My meat balls
Are served up on elastic
My frog's legs
Are such a pretty sight:
I've been told
My coq-au-vin's fantastic
They like it so
Because I make
It different every night.

## BUNDLES OF FUN

*Two old clowns, in full make-up and wigs, sit
at a bare trestletable in front of pieces of
cracked mirror propped up on tin make-up
boxes. A tented "dressing-room", in an obscure
corner of the bigtop. Straw on the floor.*

*They sing:*

**VERSE ONE**

**RB:**
People don't want clowns no more –
We seem to be out of fashion now
We seem to have lost our dash, somehow
We seem to have lost our "clout" -

505

**RC:**
People don't think we're funny no more
Comedy seems to have passed us by
It's just moved on, don't ask us why,

**BOTH:** And left us down and out.

**CHORUS ONE**

**RB:**
But . .
I remember the day, when,
Everyone loved the clown,
I remember the day whenever
The circus came to town
All the kids in the neighbourhood
Ran after you down the street,
Everyone's next door neighbour would
Knock on the wall as hard as they could
They're here, they're here!
Come out and give 'em a cheer!

**RC:**
And the elephants holding each others
tails
Came lumbering through the crowd
Pulling the cages which held the lions
And the liberty horses trotting proud.
And the men on stilts, and the acrobats
Came tumbling through the town,
And behind them all to tremendous
cheers
The hero of the day appears
The Clown – the Clown!
Everyone loved the Clown!

*RB hits RC on the head with enormous
hammer.*

**VERSE TWO:**

**RC:**
People don't want clowns no more –
The things we do don't make 'em laugh.
The comical car that falls in half
No longer stops the show

**RB:**
People don't go for our gags no more
The slippery planks and buckets of paste
It's sheer hard graft just gone to waste

**BOTH:**
And nobody wants to know.

**CHORUS TWO**

**RC:**
I remember the day when
The clowns were the only thing
I remember the day when -
Ever we entered the circus rig
That joyful sound, that magical roar
Would surge up from the crowd,
And as each prat-fall shook the floor,
And little Joey came back for more,
The laughs were loud!
The laughs were long and loud!

**RB:**
And the flour-bags bursting all over the
place
And the custard pies that flew
And the soda siphon full in the face
And the baggy trousers filled with glue
Joe on his square-wheeled bicycle,
And Jacko's gigantic ears
And the final chase round the edge of the
ring
And you feel no pain, and the only thing
Are the cheers! The cheers! You never
forget the cheers!

*RC throws bucket of water into RB's face.*

*RB begins to take off his wig.*

**LAST VERSE:** *(spoken)*

**RB:**
People don't want clowns no more
I tend to blame the telly meself.

**RC:**
That's what put us on the shelf
That's what did us in...
*(he begins to take off his wig)*
It's all too sophisticated now
There's entertainment round the clock.

**RB:**
From breakfast TV to late-night rock
It's one long bleedin' din.

**RC:**
There's too many of us at it now.
The Goodies started the rot.
Now everyone's jumped on the gravy train
The competitions too hot.
There's Little & Large, and Morecambe & Wise,
And Canon & Ball an' all,
The fat one, and the little one,
Whose names I can't recall

**RB:**
Still, come on, Jacko, we can't sit here
There's too more shows tomorrow night,
Two more chances to get it right
Providing family fun.
Let's get moving, there's a dear...
It's half-past twelve and I'm soaking wet,
There's the elephant cage to clean out yet.
Come on, or we'll never get done.

*They shamble off.*

# BOLD SIR JOHN

*This is sung by RC and RB. And other dancers, with a solo by a high tenor: someone like Fred Tomlinson.*

**VERSE ONE:**

**ALL:**
Bold Sir John was young and fair
And bold Sir John was gay;

**SOLOIST:**
He said "I'll tread the morning dew
To take the air, and listen to
The twittering of the birds all day
The Bumblebees at play"

**RC:**
The twit

**RB:**
The twit

**ALL:**
The twit
The twit
The twittering of the birds all day.

**RC:**
The bum

**RB:**
The bum

**ALL:**
The bum
The bum
The bumblebees at play.

**VERSE TWO:**

**ALL:**
Bold Sir John he went his way
Observing natives farce

**SOLOIST:**
"Dear Mother Earth, oh tell me pray
Why elephants live so long they say?
Your flies live but a day, then they
Drop dead upon the grass".

**RB:**
Your flies
Your flies *(stares at RC 's trousers)*

**ALL:**
Your flies
Your flies
Your flies live but a day, then they

**RC:**
Drop dead
Drop dead *(glares at RB)*

**ALL:**
Drop dead
Drop dead
Drop dead upon the grass.

**VERSE THREE:**

**ALL:**
Now bold Sir John he met a maid
As on her back she lay

**SOLOIST:**
"Please show respect, and come not near
For I've seen many a maiden here
Get lost among the new-mown hay
So doff your hat I pray."

**RC:**
Get lost

**RB:**
Get lost.

**ALL:**
Get lost
Get lost
Get lost among the new-mown hay.

**RB:**
Sodoff

**RC:**
So doff

**ALL**:
So doff
So doff
So doff your hat I pray.

**VERSE FOUR:**

**ALL:**
When bold Sir John returned home
They gave him gin to try;

**SOLOIST:**
"Nay fill me not with liquor up,
Nor give me grain or grape to sup,
Pour cowslips dew into my cup
A puritan am I".

**RC:**
Pour cow --

**RB:**
Pour cow -

**ALL:**
Pour cow -Pour cow -Pour cowslips dew
into my cup

**RB:**
A pu

**RC:**
A pu

**ALL:**
Up you
Up you
Up you-ritan am I.

*Four-bar flourishing finish.*

# COUNTRY HEAVEN

*RB as rather swarthy, scruffy singer with
guitar and mouth organ.*
*Caption: Lightweight Louie Danvers*

An old country singer lay dying
At the end of a long, weary life
And he lay with his loved ones around
him
Three dogs, seven horse, and a wife
Oh Mary, the voices are calling
They're calling and telling me to go
But before I set out on my journey
There's one thing that I gotta know

Do they play country music in Heaven?
Are there still four square beats to a bar?
Can I find a backing group amongst the
angels?
Can I swap my plucking harp for a guitar?
Cos I can't, I just can't leave my music
It's the thing that has served me so well
So if I can't play my music in Heaven
I'll go play my music in Hell.

And with that, he lay back on his pillow
With a sad dreamy look in his eye
And his soul saddled up and departed
For that pearly stockade in the sky.
And there stood Saint Peter a-waiting
And he opened that big rhinestone gates
"But before I go in" said the Singer
"St. Peter, I must know my fate" -

Do they play country music in Heaven?
Are there still four square beats to a bar?
Can I find a backing group amongst the
angels?

Can I swap my plucking harp for a guitar?
Cos I can't, I just can't leave my music
It's the thing that has served me so well
So if I can't play my music in Heaven
I'll go play my music in Hell.

"Come inside now," said Peter, and rest
you –
Change out of them dirty old things
Try these breeches of snowy white
buckskin
And a waistcoat with slits for your wings,
Yes you can play your music in heaven -
And your gee-tar is safe in your hands
There is no room in hell for a singer
Cos it's too full of Rock and Roll bands.

So he played Country music in Heaven
And there were four-square beats to the
bar,
And he found a backing-group among the
angels,
And he swapped his plucking harp for a
guitar.

## MAE WEST

*RB, dressed as Mae West, standing by a grand
piano, with pianist seated.*

**MAE:**
Hi there folks. Glad you could come up
and see me. Come a little closer why don't
you? Ohh! That's enough. *(To pianist)*
Hows about giving me a tickle in A flat,
honey?
*(Pianist plays "intro" to song, which is spoken
to the music.)*
My first name's Mae – and my second
name is West,
I'm the kind of shady lady who'll put
hairs upon your chest;
Now some folks say I'm overweight, but
take a tip from me –
Life begins at 47 – 37 – 43.
Know what I mean?

I've got a little penthouse, where I'm
nearly always pent,

Well, it's really just a bedroom, but at least
it pays the rent;
I'm working on my latest book – I write
from six till ten,
So pop in if you've an inkling, and I'll fill
your fountain-pen.

My past is all behind me – I'm reformed,
as you can see;
My motto once was "love for sale" but
now I give it free.
Come up to my apartment, and I'll drive
away your cares;
But you'd better be in training – it's up
fourteen flights of stairs.

*(Spoken, over end of song) –*
That's why nobody comes up and sees me
no more! Ohh!

## FATS WALLER SONG

People say
That love is here to stay
Forever, and a day
But that just ain't the way
Love is a flower.
Pluck it, and its sure to die
(Bye and Bye – yes)

I have heard,
That love is just a word
A little wingless bird
But I think that's absurd
Love is a boot
That kicks you in the stomach when
you're down (oh yes)

Love ain't worth the candle –
It ain't no door to fairyland
Cos as soon as you grab that door-handle
It comes right off in your hand
(Believe me -)

Me and you,
Our loving days are through
'Cos you found someone new
And if that's really true –
Love is a ticket, on a

One way trip right outta my heart
(Ba-da-di-da, da-di-do)

No more strife
I've had my slice of life
I'll put away the knife
And go back to the wife –
Love was a fire.
But now you're just another old flame
('Can't even remember your name – oh
yes.)

# LADIES' NIGHT

*A small classical orchestra, all male, in
evening dress, on the usual tiered rostrum.
About twelve feet of rostrum depth in front of
the orchestra. The conductor enters, and starts
to play the Ballet Egyptian, as per cassette,
edited version. They play the first 15 seconds,
and just as they come to the end of the main
theme, RC and RB enter as char ladies. They
stand and listen. The main theme is repeated
– they enjoy the music, walk to the centre, get
out their scrubbing brushes, and scrub in time
to the music. Then, at a given point, they take
their sweeping brooms, and brush in time to
the music. At the end of the whole section,
they begin to sing:*

**RB:**
Me and Mrs Higginbottom come here
Every morning to look after the band
Scrub the stage and empty out the
kettledrums
And polish the conductors stand.

**RC:**
Rain or shine we're always at the ready
And we're never lackadaisical or hateful
Where else could you meet so many
fellers
We are just a pair of scrubbers who are
grateful.

**RB:**
Look at them, they look so charming

**RC:**
Some of them are quite alarming
When they play their obligato

**RB:**
Half of them are pizzicato,
Trombones, like gravel, have always quite
excited me.

**RC.**
I love to travel, I'm more of a French Horn
girl, you see
Sunkissed nights on the Mediterranean

**RB:**
Pillow fights with a randy Romanian

**BOTH:**
We dream of love when the music plays.
*(They dance with their brooms to the slow
waltz section, they then sing again:-)*

**RB.**
Me and Mrs Higginbottom love it when
We get put on those orchestra jobs
My first husband used to play the organ
So I've always quite liked twiddling knobs.

**RC:**
I can claim no musical connections
Though I used to have an Uncle in the
woodwind
But he would eat radishes for supper
And was consequently not a very good
wind.

**RB:**
Every week, we work till Sunday

**RC:**
Have it off, then back on Monday
Tuesday Wednesday Thursday Friday

**RB:**
Keeping the performance tidy.
Sometimes, there are times when
I would like a go myself.

**RC:**
I could make music, with anyone off the
bottom shelf,
So when they go for their tea-break,

Here's the kind of sound that we make,
Let the work go hang while we both have
a bang.

*Visual f/x.*

*The saucepans and buckets etc. On the trolley
must include 8 items which, when hit produce
the following musical notes:*

*F (the third note above Middle C)*

*G (the note above that)*

*A (the note above that)*

*B (the note above that)*

*C (the note above that, which is an octave
above Middle C)*

*D (the note above that)*

*E (the note above that)*

*G (two notes above that)*

*also wooden spoons and/or dishmops to hit
them with.*

*During this last line, trolley is uncovered. It
contains large array of saucepans, teapots,
buckets, tins of liquid soap etc., which can be
played and are pitched to a definite note.
The orchestra plays a bright version of
"Chinatown". After a suitable "intro" RC and
RB play the melody with handmops, wooden
spoons etc. On the saucepans. A washboard is
also in evidence, and scrubbing brushes of
course. At the end of the first section or
chorus, they sing and accompany themselves,
backed by the orchestra.*

**RB:**
*(sings)* Camden Town, my Camden Town,
High rise flats so gay

**RC:**
That's where I met Harry Brown
In a flat in Camden Town

**RB:**
Now they're going to pull them down
Oh what a disgrace

**RC:**
That's what Harry tried to do
But I slapped his face.

*They play another chorus, then sing final one.*

**BOTH:**
Camden Town, dear Camden Town
All my childhood dreams
We could live on half a crown
No one seemed to wear a frown.
Now you're sad and tumble-down,
But you'll always be
Camden Town, my Camden Town,
You are home, to me.

*Big musical finish.*

## McCLEARY'S GOLD

I woke one morning when the sun was
high
It was a big red melon in a big blue sky
But a wind from the East warn blowing
up, kinda cold.
I looked at my watch, it was still on it's
chain
I could see by the time, it was gonna rain
I thought it's just the day to search for
McCleary's gold.

Now McCleary was a guy, so I've heard tell
He could ride a horse, and could ride it
well.
But he couldn't shoot a gun, to save his
doggone life
He took a pot-shot, at the sheriff, and
missed
By all accounts he was a little bit drunk
So they strung him up, made a widow
outta his wife.

Now he'd had his gold, in a little old
shack
Beyond the creek, near the railroad track

And his widow, Betty Jane, she lived there
still
I knocked on the door, and she let me in
We sat in the parlour, and we drank pink
gin
And we drank till the sun went down
behind the hill.

Now Betty Jane was a woman and a half
And she liked to love and she liked to
laugh
And she giggled and groped around like a
love-sick kid;
She dragged me off to her boudoir-room.
And I thought of McCleary in his tomb
And a shiver shot through my shirt-tail,
so it did.

Now I ainta gonna say what went on that
night,
But I quit the shack in the early light
And I staggered out like a wrestler leaving
the ring.
Now I can handle myself in a fight,
But she floored me fifteen times that
night
But I was so damn drunk I didn't feel a
thing.

And I realised, as I sat in the cold
I'd found romance, but I'd found no gold
And I'd come out just as poor as I'd gone
in.
It was just as well, 'cos behind a tree
A beady eye was glued on we
A no-good gambling-man called Mickey
Finn.

Now Mickey had been chasing Betty Jane
And our little romance had caused him
pain
You could tell by the way he ground his
teeth and spat
And the way he stiffened, and went all
tense
And banged his head on a nearby fence,
And crossed his eyes and danced on his
Stetson hat.

Now Mick was mean, and Mick warn slick
And nobody wanted to meddle with Mick
In spite of the fact that he's only five foot
three.

When he draws his gun, you take my tip,
You run! Cos when he fires he fires from
the hip
Which means he always hits you in the
knee.

I staggered to my feet and back indoors
Where Betty Jane lay in her vest and
drawers
While Mickey let loose with everything
he'd got.
He was shouting crazy and throwing
rocks
I jumped for cover like a blue-tailed fox
And from then on things began getting
kinda hot.

Now I ain't a guy to stick out my neck
They can call me a coward but what the
heck
If you don't surrender, you end up dead
and brave
I decided, if the gold was there,
Then Mickey Finn, he could have my
share.
So I started looking round for something
white to wave.

I rushed tot he other side of the room
And I stuck the drawers up on a broom
And I waved them out of the window for
Mick to see
But his jaw went loose and his face went
puce.
He thought they were a trophy, not a
truce
To show him Betty Jane had given in to
me!

He began to let loose with everything he'd
got
And Betty Jane's drawers got riddled with
shot
When suddenly, my eyes fell outta my
face -
Out through a hole in that wonderful pair
A stream of coins fell through the air
McCleary's gold – I'd found its hiding-
place.

I hurriedly wrote a note to Mick
Saying "Stop the shooting and get here
quick

We'll call it quits and share McCleary 's
gold."
I wrapped it round a rock he'd thrown,
But my aim ain't quite as good as his own
He caught it with his head, and it laid him
flat out cold.

Well that's the story of McCleary's gold,
Remember men, you've all been told
These widow-women might be middle-
aged and plain
But don't let that stop you, take a tip from
me
Just try your luck, it could very well be
She's sitting on a fortune, like Betty Jane.

# KID COAL-HOLE AND
# THE MONKEYNUTS

*A sandy, rocky, tropical studio set. (See LP
Cover "Doppelganger")*
*RB as Kid Creole, in white etc., and three girls
dressed as LP.*
*The arrangement similar to "There's
something Wrong in Paradise". The girls work
and move in unison, as backing.*

**VERSE ONE:**
I was sitting on the beach
Playing marbles with me coconuts
When I heard a sort of screech
And I must admit it froze my guts
I walked back along the shore
Where the smell of sea-weed fills the
breeze
There I found my cockatoo
Lying there among the Banyon trees

**CHORUS ONE:**
There's something wrong
Me Parrot's died
He's lying there
Upon his side
I'm sorry but I can't decide
Whether to have him boiled or fried.

**GIRLS:**
O-oh! O-oh! O-oh! O-oh!

*Shots of girls, large toy parrot, etc. Etc.*

**VERSE TWO:**
Now I'm sitting drinking rum -
Ain't nobody left worth talking to;
'Cos I've lost my little chum
Everybody loved my cockatoo
He would whistle at the girls
Blow a raspberry at the policeman's wife -
Taught the missionary to swear,
Now all he's good for is the carving-knife

**CHORUS TWO:**
Now hear my song, me parrot's died
He's lying there, upon his side
I guess the only thing to do
Is fricassee of cockatoo.

**GIRLS:**
O-oh! O-oh! O-oh! O-oh!

*The girls pour sacks of monkey-nuts still in
their shells, over RB, they dance ankle-deep in
monkey-nuts etc. as cutaways.*

# THE ROAD SWEEPERS

**VERSE ONE:**
Out in the street
You'll find us morning noon and tea-time
on our beat
A-sweeping up the bits of litter round
your feet
To keep the highways and the byways
nice and neat
Let me repeat
Out in the street
You'll find us out there in the cold or in
the heat
It is our duty to perform and to complete
The sort of work that can be hardly called
a treat
Not very sweet.

**MIDDLE SECTION:** *(one)*
Just a couple of working blokes
Doing our jobs like other folks
Putting up with all the jokes
From the passers-by.

513

**CHORUS ONE:**
Somebody has to do it
Somebody has to do it
No-body wants a mucky job
But somebody must go through it.
Somebody's got to lift it
Shovel it up and shift it
Sweep it and scrape it
Squash it and shape it
Kick it around, and try to get rid of it
Keeping it nice and tidy
So long as we're paid on Friday
What's the point in making a lot of fuss -
Though we may all pooh-pooh it
Somebody has to do it
And somebody's decided that it's us!

**VERSE TWO:**
It ain't much fun –
It is the sort of work a lot of people shun
But then it can't be said that we' re the
only one
There are a lot of other jobs that must be
done
That ain't much fun.
Now take the Queen
Although the work she has to do is nice
and clean,
It must be tiring being on the public scene
And looking fresh as paint no matter
where she's been
And still serene.

**MIDDLE SECTION** *(two)*
It may look like just a game
All that glamour, all that fame
maybe so, but just the same
Rather her than me.

**CHORUS TWO**
Somebody has to do it
Somebody has to do it
Nobody wants to be the Queen
But somebody must go through it.
Opening public functions,
Banquets and balls and luncheons
Ruling the land and
Waving her hand and
Changing the guards and trooping the
colour and
Training a Derby winner, getting the Duke
his dinner,

Baby-sitting for the Prince of Wales -
Smiling and looking regal
Acting like Anna Neagle
To do the job she must be hard as nails.

# MARIONETTES

*A graphic border, or vignette, representing a
small proscenium arch. RC and RB as
marionettes -real heads pushed through a
black cloth, with their own arms used as feet,
attached to small bodies and dangling false
arms. Introduction music over this, and into
the first song. The music has a "twenties" feel
throughout.*

**VERSE 1.**
**BOTH:**
Summer Holidays are here,
Kids are gathering on the pier
Come to see if we're still here
The dancing Marionettes.

**VERSE 2.**
**RB.**
Watch our tiny tootsies fly

**RC.**
Step so neat and jump so high

**BOTH.**
Kick each other in the eye
The dancing Marionettes.

**MIDDLE EIGHT:**
Legs forever tangling
Jokes we can't resist
Little arms a-dangling
Fleet of foot and limp of wrist.

**VERSE 3.**
**RC.**
Now you know just why we're keen

**RB.**
Keen to show you what we mean

**BOTH.**
Take you through the tap routine

Of the dancing Marionettes.

*Then, the following sequences in order.*

*1. RB and RC "dance" with their false legs, to the same melody.*
*2. We pull back to reveal a total of ten girl marionettes – we use a black vignette to cover top and bottom of screen, so that we can get ten in a row. The false bodies have tiny frilled skirts, and tap-shoes with bows. They do a short routine.*

*3. RC and RB sing the following short number, with the camera cutting to the girls as and when required.*

**RC & RB.**
Can't beat a tap dance
It makes a chap dance
A simple sap dance
Like me –
Tickle and slap dance
Hop, step and clap dance
Can't beat a tap dance
No siree!

**MIDDLE EIGHT.**
You can beat carpets, you can beat eggs,
You can beat a hasty retreat
You can beat time, but you can't beat legs
Twinkling toes and flashing feet.

**VERSE 4**
So my dear chappie
Just make it snappy
Keep tapping happy
And free!

*4. Now the girls come from behind the marionettes bodies, to reveal that they are dressed exactly as the dolls are. They do a tap routine to the same melody.*

*5. Now we go into a "black theatre" situation (i.e. Overlay) and we see only the eyes and legs of the girls. They dance, and are joined after a few bars by RC and RB – but we see only the heads and the trousers and shoes of the Ronnies (boy dancers in the trousers!) They do a few bars.*

*6. Repeat a final chorus, with RC and RB as marionettes again, but girls for real, tapping to a big finish.*

# COY GEORGE

*RC as Boy George – plus two girls dressed as firemen with hoses – non-practical, of course. Musical arrangement similar to "Do you really want to Hurt Me".*

**VERSE:**
Oh my heart it is on Fi-yar *(Fire)*
And it's burning just for you
'Cos you fill me with desi-yar
And you warm me through and through

Yet you won't fulfil my yearning
You just dampen down my dreams
Putting out the fire that's burning
Throw cold water on my schemes

**MIDDLE SECTION:**
Every night
I'm all alight
When you're around
So tell me why
You always try
To cool me down.

**CHORUS:**
Do you really want to squirt me?
Do you really want to make me wet -
Do you really want to squirt me?
Do you really want to make me wet…

*Instrumental section – cutaways of RC at instruments, and noncontinuity bits with girls and odd props, cups of tea – extra long pigtails with lavatory pulls on the end, etc.*

**SECOND CHORUS:**
Do you really want to squirt me?
Do you really want to hose me down -
That would ruin all my make-up
Mess my hair and spoil my nice new gown

*The girls now turn towards camera with practical hoses, but there is a sheet of glass over the camera – RC then appears behind glass, water running off it – etc. etc.*

*Fade out.*

# CHLOE LOON & DANNY JONKWORTH

*RB as Chloe, RC as Danny, on typical set.*

*RC's own voice is used, but impersonator needed for RB's Cleo voice. After a longish intro, to establish characters, RB sings the song.*
*The tune is a jazz version of "Three Blind Mice".*

**RB:**
Three blind mice,
(I said) Three blind mice
See how they run
My, My! how they run.
They all ran after the farmer's wife
She cut off their tails with a carving-knife
Never saw such a thing in my life
Those three blind mice.

*Instrumental – solo sax (RC) for the duration of one chorus, as above. Then RB sings the following very fast, à la Cleo Laine.*

**RB:**
Listen everybody while I tell you all the story of
THREE BLIND MICE
Living on a farm in Arizona where the owner was a
Real mean
String Bean
Married to a farming man.
Well -

Late one Friday evening they were leaving Harry's bar and they were
ALL BLIND DRUNK
Staggering and slipping over
Tottering and tripping over -
Each others tails

Now the farmer's wife was a-waiting
Out on the veranda cutting vegetables for dinner
And without no hesitating
With a speed that makes you shudder
She cut off each mouses rudder
Oh Lord! you should have
HEARD THEIR WAILS.

*Instrumental – solo sax (RC) This time RC has enormous saxophone. Cut to: RB. Think bubble supered on to RB's head – "He's Sax Mad". The saxophone notes travel up to a very high passage. Cut back to: RC. He has tiny saxophone.*

**RB:**
Now you've heard the story of the gory situation of the
THREE BLIND MICE
Living on a farm in Arizona where the owner was a
Real mean
String bean
Married to a farming man,
So when you're sitting boozing
And your vision you are losing don't for-
GET THOSE MICE!
Keep away from other farmers'
Wives because the little charmers
Might cut off your tail! Whoa!

**RC:**
Three blind mice,

**RB:**
Three myopic mice

**RC:**
See how they run

**RB:**
Golly! How they run

**BOTH:**
They all ran after the farmer's wife

**RB:**
She cut off theirs with a carving knife

**BOTH:**
Which certainly ruins the old love-life

**RC:**
Those three…*(held note)*

**RB:**
Ba ba da be-be-be ba,

**RC:**
Blind…*(held note)*

**RB:**
Ba doo da de de de do

**BOTH:**
Mice!

# CHAS AND DAVE
## – PUB SONG

*A London pub decorated for Christmas.
Musical introduction as the camera reveals RB
and RC as Chas and Dave, they are
surrounded by boys and girls (dancers) in their
christmas finery, who possibly join in the
chorus, along with some Fred Tomlinsons, etc.
RB is at the upright piano, RC plays a banjo.*

**RB:**
Christmas comes but once a year

**RC:**
It's just as well

**RB:**
A time for all to have good cheer

**RC:**
It's that as well

**BOTH:**
Christmas comes but once a year
A pipe full o' baccy and a belly full o' beer
Relatives come from far and near

**RB:** *(spoken)*
WELL! You can't have everything can
you?

**RC:**
Mum brings in the turkey roast

Oh, ain't it nice?

**RB:**
Round the fire, warm as toast

**RC:**
Toilet's just like ice

**BOTH:**
Too much noise and too much grub
Pity they have to, shut the pub
Roll on Boxing Day:

**CHORUS:**
**BOTH:**
Oh but we
Wouldn't be without it
Wouldn't be without it
Ain't no doubt about it
Wouldn't be without it
Wouldn't be without our Christmas cheer
Specialeeeeeey….
Around this time of year.

**RC:**
Father talking politics with his paper hat
on
Mum is going bonkers 'cos the Christmas
cakes been sat on,

**RB:**
Uncle's gone to pieces since he got that
jigsaw puzzle
Auntie Nora bought it him – he bought
her a muzzle.

**RB:**
Christmas comes but once a year

**RC:**
It's just as well

**RB:**
A time for all to have good cheer

**RC:**
It's that as well

**BOTH:**
Christmas comes but once a year
A pipe full o' baccy and a belly full o' beer
Relatives comes from far and near

517

**RB:** *(spoken)*
Well. You can't have everything can you?

**RB:**
Newly weds Lorraine and Dan

**RC:**
Gawd! They can't half scoff

**RB:**
She wants to have the telly on

**RC:**
He wants to have it off.

**BOTH:**
Chocolate papers, cigarette butts
I think I'm going crackers and nuts
Roll on Boxing Day.

**CHORUS:**
**BOTH:**
Oh but we
Wouldn't be without it
Wouldn't be without it
Ain't no doubt about it
Wouldn't be without it
Wouldn't be without our Christmas cheer
'Specialeeeeeey….
Around this time of year.

**RB:**
Gather round for the Christmas speech

**RC:**
Gawd save the Queen

**RB:**
Someone's mucked the picture up

**RC:**
Her face is green

**RB:**
Can't go out, because it's pouring

**RC:**
Grandma's jawing Grandad's snoring

**RB:**
Cat's been sick on the parquet flooring

**RB:** *(spoken)*
STILL! You can' t have everything can
you?

**RC:**
Presents round the Christmas tree .
Just take your pick

**RB:**
Pine needles fall into your tea

**RC:**
Gives it a kick

**RB:**
I'll never eat again the rest o' me life

**RC:**
Milk's gone sour and so's the wife

**BOTH:**
Rabbit, Rabbit, Rabbit, Rabbit,
Yap Yap Yap Yap, Rabbit Rabbit

**CHORUS:**
**BOTH:**
Oh but we
Wouldn't be without it
Wouldn't be without it
Ain't no doubt about it
Wouldn't be without it
Wouldn't be without our Christmas cheer
'Specialeeeeeey….
Around this time of year.

●◆

# DEVIL'S BREW

I'll tell you a tale
I learnt along the trail
As I rode to Wyoming long ago
It's a sad sorry story
(The details they are gory)
Of a man and a gal named Mary Jo.

**CHORUS:**
Mary Jo – Mary Jo
Oh you went the way you didn't have to
go
You could of been my wife

And lived a peaceful life
But you left me on my own and hurt me
so.

Now Mary was a farmer
A reg'lar rustic charmer
And she drove her daddy's tractor to and
fro.
Her little sister Liza
Was forking fertiliser
So Mary was the one I got to know.

We were married in the spring
I was happy as a king
As we kissed and crooned and cuddled
All day long
Oh her cooking was just fine
And she brewed her home-made wine
And that was where it started to go wrong.

**REPEAT CHORUS:**
Mary Jo, Mary Jo
Oh you went etc

Of the wine we drank our fill
Then she built herself a still
To make a little moonshine whiskey too;
I shall always curse the day
When that moonshine came my way
And I first fell victim to the devils brew.

Now the sheriff rode from town
And he tracked that whiskey down
And they grabbed my wife and wouldn't
let her free
And they didn't heed her tears
And they gave her seven years.
On a prison diet with nought to drink but
tea

**REPEAT CHORUS**

Now that prison diet was fine
Cos she didn't drink no wine
It was me that had got hooked upon the
stuff.
I was drinking now for two
And before each day was through
I had had about eleven times enough.

When her prison time had done
Mary Jo became a nun

It was me that died of drink and went to
hell
Now with a ghostly wail,
I tell this grisly tale
To riders down the trail, they know so
well.

**LAST CHORUS:**
Now you know
'Bout Mary Jo –
Try not to be a stupid so and so
If you want a peaceful life
Just drink tea and love your wife
Or you'll go the way you do not have
to go!!

# YUKON SONG – SOME DAYS THESE DAYS

Some day these days will be known as the
Good old Days
Some day these ways will be known as the
Good old Ways
Folks of the future won't recall our names
Just faded photographs in old-fashioned
frames.
They'll sit and talk of the days, when Men
were men
And women were all stocking tops and
stays.
Then through their memories they'll live
again
The passion of those good old-fashioned
days
(You bet your bottom dollar).

Some day these days will be known as the
Good old Days
Some day these ways will be known as the
Good old Ways.
So make the most of whatever you've got
right now,
Each day that passes won't come back
anyhow!

The Here and Now very soon becomes
"way back when"
And life itself is just a passing phase.
We'll never ever see the like again

Of those good old-fashioned,
(when passion wasn't rationed)
Those Good old-fashioned Days.

## GIRLS I'VE MET

I knew a girl called Jeannie
She was nothing but skin and bones
I knew a girl called Janie Scott
She had bumps where Jean had not
I knew a girl called Susie Strong
Her feet were large and her legs were long
Her feet were so large that it is said
She had to take her pants off over her
head.

I'm talking about
Girls – Girls I met
Ice is cold and waters wet
Up is up and feathers is down
That's what makes the world go round.

I knew a girl called Droopy Drawers
Her ears stuck out like taxi doors
Tall as a pole and thin as a candle
Hard to please but easy to handle
Took her out in the wind and rain
She blew round like a weather vane
By the fire, warm and snug
Melted her upon the rug.

I'm talking about
Girls – Girls I've known
Oats I've scattered, seeds I've sown
Up is in and down is out
(You all know what I'm talking about).

I knew a girl called Jennifer Goafer
She had hips like a well-stuffed sofa
If she sat on you she'd squash you flat
(Boy! I sure kept out of THAT)
She was buxom, big and round
Gave good value, pound for pound
Like a mountaineer, upon a climb
I conquered her a bit at a time.

I'm talking about
Girls, Girls I've seen
Faces I've known and places I've been

Tales I've told and songs I've
That's what makes the world go bang.

I knew a girl called Big-time Bella
'Til I found out she was a fellah
We parted friends and everything
But he never sent back the engagement
ring
I knew a girl called Topsy Turvey
She was cute and she was curvy
She was sweet and she was sunny
Now I'm paying her alimony.

I'm talking about
Girls, girls I've known
Birds that nested, and have flown
Black or white or pink or brown
That's what makes the world go round!

## ONE GOOD TURN

*RB as Barry Norman.*
*caption – "One good turn – with Barry*
*Normal."*

**RB:** *(very fast)*
Good evening to you, and welcome to
what promised to be, but doesn't seem to
have turned out that way, an interesting
series of old film clips and when I say old,
do I mean old! I suppose I do, really,
otherwise I wouldn't have said it.
Discovered recently behind a stack of
toilet rolls in the private loo of the head of
drama BBC 1, old, faded and cracked, but
then who isn't, nevertheless we thought it
worthy of an airing. It features Arthur
Halliday, the Vagabond Lover, who toured
the music halls with one of the first one
man shows ever, so called because that
was usually the size of the audience. A
great favourite with the ladies, he was a
very upright, forthright, and downright
disgusting character, who lived to a ripe
old age, getting riper as he got older, until
he finally died of drink, women, and
horses at the age of 63. He was to have
been buried in a pauper's grave, but the
pauper objected, so he had to have one of

his own. Here he is, in his prime, in 1932, singing his most popular ballad, "Life's Highway." See how it grabs you and what's more important, where…

*(Mix to – black and white, fuzzy, scratched film.*
*Theatrical set with proscenium arch. A very cardboard version of a rocky cliff top. Sky (slightly wrinkled) rocks and tufts of grass. A two-dimensional cut out of rocks in foreground, large enough to contain a "trampette" for bouncing and jumping off. Arthur Halliday (RB) enters, in cloak and hat, black tights etc. He sings the following song with various acrobatic tricks interspersed.*

**RB:**
I
Travel along life's highway
With never
A worry or care at all
I wander through every byway
Hoping that I may
Not fall;
You
Never will hear me grumble
No!
Everything's fun for me
You
Never will see me stumble
A hop and a skip and I'm free!

*(He turns a complete somersault, in very long shot 0 double needed.)*

When
Worldly cares beset you
Wracked
With pain and misery
Don't
Let old man trouble get you….
*(He does a few steps of eccentric dancing in long shot.)*
Take a hop and a skip, like me.

*(A musical break, during which he marches round the rocks, does a standing somersault and a trampoline jump over some rocks.)*

I
Never have any money –

Money
Only brings grief and sin
Just
So long as the day is sunny
I'll simply face it
And grin –

*(He marches out of shot and immediately flies on stage on a kirby wire – double used.)*

I
Never know where I'm going
I
Haven't the least idea

*(Exits on wire – marches on in close up.)*

Just
So long as the grass is growing
There's no point in knowing –
No fear!
Don't
Let trouble come and find you –
Stay
Fit and fancy free –
Leave
Your worries far behind you
Take a hop and a skip and a jump…

*(He jumps over cliff – large water splash – he reappears to sing last two words.)*

Like me!

# THE SIT COMS:

# HIS LORDSHIP
# ENTERTAINS

"Fawlty Towers Mark One" is how Ronnie describes this, his first stab at writing situation comedy (under the pen name of Jonathan Cobbold). And the comparison is an interesting one, given that His Lordship appeared a full three years before John Cleese's similarly hotel-bound classic. One of his most popular characters, Lord Rustless had first appeared as the linking character on *Hark At Barker* in 1969, although Ronnie claims he first found the character whilst playing Lord Slingsby-Craddock in Alan Ayckbourn's *Mr Whatnot*, several years before. (Ayckbourn wrote Rustless's scenes in *Hark At Barker*.)

The series continued two of Ronnie's long running associations with other actors – Josephine Tewson played Bates (they had first worked together back on the Frost shows and on stage in Tom Stoppard's *The Real Inspector Hound*) and David Jason who played Dithers.

Rustless's show debuted on BBC2 on 5 June 1972 and ran for seven weeks. Sadly, it is believed that the BBC wiped the tapes of those show, leaving these scripts all that remains of *His Lordship Entertains*.

# EPISODE ONE

*The hall of the hotel. Rustless is on the phone behind the obviously new reception desk. He wears an alpaca jacket.*

**RUSTLESS:**
Yes madam. I see. You'd like a double room with bath on the third. Preferably on the first floor. Double room, yes. Does the bath have to be double? No, single bath, overlooking the Downs. I see. That's the room. Not the bath. No. Quite. Yes, it would. Well, I have a double room overlooking the Downs but no bath. Or I have a single room with bath. Your husband? No. Not unless he slept in the bath. Overlooking the Downs, yes. Mind you that's the second floor. Yes, I should think your best bet is to overlook the bath, and have a first floor double room overlooking the car park.

*(Miss Bates enters, and places letters in pigeon holes.)*

**RUSTLESS:**
So that's on the third. *(writes in book)* No the rooms on the first but you're coming on the third. What name is it? Mr & Mrs Kingstanley-Hartington-Browne-O'Sullivan? I see – are you sure you can manage in a double room? Oh well I look forward to seeing you all – both. Thank you madam, *(puts down phone.)* Morning, Bates.

**BATES:**
Good morning milord. Nice bright morning,

**RUSTLESS:**
Is it? I haven't really surfaced yet, I was up till three in the billiard room drinking brandy with that idiot in room seven. Good grief, what a bore he is.

**BATES:**
Why didn't you go to bed?

**RUSTLESS:**
Damn fool had lost the cork out of the brandy bottle. Obviously the only thing

to do was to stay up till we'd finished it;

**BATES:**
Why?

**RUSTLESS:**
Well, you know that stuff evaporates. By the way, that was another booking, I've put 'em into room eleven.

**BATES:**
Oh super. Aren't you pleased?

**RUSTLESS:**
Not really. That's my room.

**BATES:**
Oh dear.

**RUSTLESS:**
It's alright I'm getting used to it. I keep a little weekend case ready packed now, so I can change rooms at a moment's notice. I'm beginning to enjoy the life, wandering hither and thither, never knowing where I'm going to lay my head next. Sort of indoor tramp.

**BATES:**
Well, things will soon sort themselves out. We've only been open as an hotel for ten days. Still, I think it's going to work. People seem to like the idea of staying in a real stately home.

**RUSTLESS:**
Let's hope so. It's either that, or hand the whole place over to the National Trust. And I'm damned if I'm going to do that. People tramping all over the golf course.

**BATES:**
Oh no.

**RUSTLESS:**
It's one of my few remaining pleasures, to be able to play golf in private. I mean, if a chap hits a bad ball, then he wants to feel free to voice his opinion of that ball – its size, shape, possible ancestry and so on, both in the singular, and if necessary, the plural. And the last thing you want is to

have a crowd of tourists hanging around while you're digging up the rough or having a slash in the bushes.

**BATES:**
*(not sure of that last remark)* Er – quite. Well, I'd better go and see if Mr Badger has managed to wheedle the lunch menu out of cook.

**RUSTLESS:**
How are you managing Bates? Keeping your chin up? Head above water? Holding your own?

**BATES:**
Oh I think so, milord – I'm rather enjoying it.

**RUSTLESS:**
Bit of a change from copying out my memoirs, and doing my income tax, what?

**BATES:**
Oh, but it's worth it. I love this place, I've always loved it, ever since that first day I came to work here. Do you know that's twenty-seven years ago in August, milord, I was a young girl then.

**RUSTLESS:**
A fresh-bloomed rose, what?

**BATES:**
I'm afraid my petals are beginning to fade a little now.

**RUSTLESS:**
Nonsense old chap. You don't look a day over fifty.

**BATES:**
I'm forty six milord. I was just nineteen when I first came to work here.

**RUSTLESS:**
My god, that's right, During the war, wasn't it? That stray incendiary bomb fell on the potato shed, and the whole lot went up. We were eating roast potatoes for a week I remember.

**BATES:**
I used to tremble and go bright red every time I came into the room

**RUSTLESS:**
Really? They never affected me like that – just gave me heartburn.

*(A man approaches from outside – he is tall, well spoken and unpleasant. He approaches the desk.)*

**RUSTLESS:**
Good morning.

**BATES:**
I'll cut along. Excuse me.

**RUSTLESS:**
Righto, Bates. Now sir, can I help you?

**MAN:**
I wonder if you can.

**RUSTLESS:**
Well, I'm willing to have a stab. Did you want a room?

**MAN:**
I'm not really sure.

**RUSTLESS:**
Oh. Well perhaps you'd like to sit down and have a bit of a think about it I mean I don't want to sway you one way or the other.

**MAN:**
What I'd really like to do is to look at the register.

**RUSTLESS:**
Well, I don't think you'd get much of an idea from that. I mean all the rooms look alike in the register – sort of oblong blank spaces. Totally devoid of charm.

**MAN:**
I want to know if you've had my wife here.

**RUSTLESS:**
I beg your pardon?

**MAN:**
She's been hob-nobbing with another man, and I'm trying to locate them.

**RUSTLESS:**
I see; and you have reason to believe that they may be hob-nobbing here.

**MAN:**
Why not?

**RUSTLESS:**
Why not indeed? This is as good a place to hob-nob as any. *(Produces register.)* Here we are.

**MAN:**
You don't object?

**RUSTLESS:**
Certainly not. The British Hotel Register is an open book.

**MAN:**
*(finds two pages stuck together)* Then why are these pages glued together?

**RUSTLESS:**
*(peering at it, then managing to open them)* Sorry about that – it's not glue, it's marmalade. The boy who does the boots has a habit of having his breakfast on it in the mornings. Very messy eater. Now then …

**MAN:**
Who's that, for instance? *(pointing to name.)*

**RUSTLESS:**
*(reading)* Muriel Lovat. Number four. I see she describes herself as a splinter. *(Looks again.)* Oh no, that's a piece of orange rind. Damned marmalade. Spinster. Oh yes – very old Wears a trilby hat, and likes to go to bed with a digestive biscuit. That wouldn't be her.

**MAN:**
No.

**RUSTLESS:**
She's about the only single woman staying here at present. All the others are married couples.

**MAN:**
Ah, but not necessarily married to each other.

**RUSTLESS:**
How dare you. Are you suggesting that I am keeping a disorderly house?

**MAN:**
I'm suggesting that my wife and her gentleman friend may be misbehaving here without your knowledge. Who's this? Mr and Mrs Cohen.

**RUSTLESS:**
Ah, now I've got a feeling that that's an assumed name.

**MAN:**
Aha! What makes you think that?

**RUSTLESS:**
They're Chinese. Sweet couple.

**MAN:**
Why ever should they call themselves Cohen?

**RUSTLESS:**
I don't know – it's probably the Chinese equivalent of Smith.

**MAN:**
*(suspiciously)* I get the feeling you're trying to hide something.

**RUSTLESS:**
My dear chap, I …

**MAN:**
I'd like a room. *(He begins to sign the register.)*

**RUSTLESS:**
Oh, alright. Early morning tea?

**MAN:**
Breakfast at six o'clock. Cold orange juice,

cornflakes, cold toast, cut very thin, and a glass of cold milk. And I want it sharp at six.

**RUSTLESS:**
I see. Tell you what, as it's all cold, I'll give it you now – you can take it up with you – save disturbing you in the morning;

**MAN:**
I want it to be fresh, at six!

**RUSTLESS:**
It'll be fresh alright, over in that East Wing. I'm afraid it's a basement room, but quite dry. I'll get the page-boy to deal with your luggage.

*(Rings a bell on the desk. An aged man dressed as a page-boy with pill-box hat emerges from a blanket chest on the set.)*

**RUSTLESS:**
Good god, Dithers, what the devil are you doing in there?

**DITHERS:**
I got moved out of my room last night, for that American couple.

**RUSTLESS:**
Yes, but my dear old chap, you should be up and about before this time in the morning. It's a quarter to ten. Now, this gentleman is going into number thirteen, and he wants his bags taken down.

**DITHERS:**
Eh? Oh, ah. Come on then sir. Putting you in the dungeons are they?

**MAN:**
The dungeons?

**RUSTLESS:**
Don't worry, they're all scrubbed out and white-washed. Like new. Only thing wrong is the towel-rings – rather high up on the wall. Still, you can easily reach them if you stand on that big block of wood with chop marks on it. Pleasant dreams.

**MAN:**
I'm not going to bed yet.

**RUSTLESS:**
Oh no quite. Might see you at lunch.

*(Dithers and the man go. An old man with a deaf aid walks slowly and stonily through the hall.)*

**RUSTLESS:**
Good morning, Mr Blunt.

*(The man takes no notice, stares stonily ahead.)*

**RUSTLESS:**
Morning Mr Blunt. *(No response.)* How are you this morning? I'm very well, and you? Yes, I'm fine. Good, glad to hear it, Thanks. Not at all. What do you fancy for the two-thirty?

**DEAF MAN:**
Laughing Boy's got a chance.

*(He goes out. Rustless looks nonplussed.)*

*(A little old lady, who entered the room a few lines earlier, now approaches the desk.)*

**OLD LADY:**
Did I hear you mention lunch, milord?

**RUSTLESS:**
That's right, Mrs Ringer, Why do you ask?

**OLD LADY:**
I was just wondering whether it will be cold today.

**RUSTLESS:**
Well, of course it depends what time you want it. If you have it at twelve-thirty it'll be hot, but by about a quarter to three it's usually getting pretty tepid.

**OLD LADY:**
I'd like to see the menu.

**RUSTLESS:**
Yes, by jove, so would I. Where's that

damn cook?

*(Badger, the butler, enters.)*

**RUSTLESS:**
Ah, there you are, Badger. Has cook decided what's for lunch yet? Mrs Ringer's taste buds are on the move.

**BADGER:**
I'm afraid a decision hasn't been reached yet milord. Er – could I have a word with you in private?

**RUSTLESS:**
Certainly; Mrs, Ringer, shove off, would you, there's a dear – get Dithers to give you a game of rounders.

**OLD LADY:**
I'll write some letters in the morning room.

**BADGER:**
Ah. I'm afraid the morning room won't be open till this afternoon.

**OLD LADY:**
Oh.

**RUSTLESS:**
Yes, someone's holding some evening classes in there.

**OLD LADY:**
Would it be alright if I just sat in my bedroom?

**RUSTLESS:**
I don't see why not, as long as you keep your boots off the bedspread. Oh, by the way, you're not hiding from your husband, are you?

**OLD LADY:**
My husband? Oh no. He was called, many years ago.

**RUSTLESS:**
Called? Called up you mean?

**OLD LADY:**
I hope so. And do you know, although he is under the ground, I see him every day.

**RUSTLESS:**
Oh, I see. Coal-miner is he?

**OLD LADY:**
He is one of the chosen.

**RUSTLESS:**
Oh, a Jewish coal-miner. Not many of those about.

**BADGER:**
I think Mrs Ringer means he's passed on, milord.

**RUSTLESS:**
Oh dead? Oh dear, I'm sorry to hear that. Recently, was this?

**OLD LADY:**
Over forty years ago.

**RUSTLESS:**
Beginning to got over it are you?

**OLD LADY:**
I shall never get over it.

**RUSTLESS:**
Oh, don't say that. Give it time, give it time.

*(The old lady goes out.)*

**BADGER:**
I'm afraid there's a crisis in the kitchen, milord.

**RUSTLESS:**
Oh good grief – it's not the tea leaves blocking the sink again is it?

**BADGER:**
No – it's Cook.

**RUSTLESS:**
Cook? Blocking the sink? What's she doing, got her leg down it?

527

*(Bates enters.)*

**BADGER:**
No it's not the sink – Cook refuses to cook.

**BATES:**
I beg your pardon, Mr Badger.

**BADGER:**
Cook won't cook, Miss Bates.

**BATES:**
Oh lawks!

**RUSTLESS:**
But that's unheard of. Cooks always cook. It's like saying a banker won't bank, or a jockey refuses to jock. What's the matter with the damn woman?

**BADGER:**
It's the menu being in French – she says she's not a French cook, she's an English cook.

**RUSTLESS:**
But dammit she doesn't have to cook in French. We're not expecting her to turn up with frogs' legs – just churn out the usual rubbish and leave you to interpret.

**BADGER:**
I told her that, but she seems to think her best work loses something in the translation.

**RUSTLESS:**
Most of it defies translation. I'd better go and sort her out.

**BADGER:**
I'll tell her you're on your way, milord. *(He exits.)*

**BATES:**
I think perhaps you ought to read this before you go milord, it may have a bearing on the conversation. *(Hands him a letter.)*

**RUSTLESS:**
What's this?

**BATES:**
From the Hotel Association. Something about a food inspector coming to see us.

**RUSTLESS:**
Damned cheek – don't they think we're clean, or something?

**BATES:**
Apparently, it's a common practice.

**RUSTLESS:**
It is. Dashed common. When's he coming?

**BATES:**
It's all there in the letter, milord. He will arrive without notice.

*(Enter Dithers – he starts to make his bed, inside the linen chest.)*

**RUSTLESS:**
I knew that man was up to something. Fellah's a blackguard.

**BATES:**
Who, milord?

.

**RUSTLESS:**
Damn chap's here! Dithers just put him in the dungeon.

**BATES:**
I don't follow you.

**RUSTLESS:**
Comes in here with some cock and bull story about being unable to get hold of his wife's whereabouts.

**DITHERS:**
Eh?

**RUSTLESS:**
So that's what's he's up to, eh? Right. It's all hands to the pump. We'll play him at his own game. We mustn't let him know that we know who he is.

**BATES:**
Why not?

**RUSTLESS:**
Well, if he knows we know, he'll know we're doing what we do because we knew who he is. If he thinks we don't know, he'll know we're doing it because we always do what we're doing whether we know who he is or not, because we've no way of knowing who he is. Is that clear?

**DITHERS:**
No. I don't even know who ho is.

**RUSTLESS:**
Who?

**DITHERS:**
The man who's not supposed to know who he is.

**RUSTLESS:**
No, no, no. He knows who he is – it's us who don't know who he is.

**DITHERS:**
Well why ask me?

**RUSTLESS:**
I didn't ask you, you asked me, you damn fool.

**DITHERS:**
Well it's no good asking me – I don't know who he is.

**RUSTLESS:**
No, but I do

**DITHERS:**
Well, what's his name then?

**RUSTLESS:**
I've no idea. Let's have a look. *(Gets the register.)* Piddler.

**DITHERS:**
Eh?

**RUSTLESS:**
*(indicates book)* Piddler. Says here.

**BATES:** *(looking at book)*
I think it's Pedder. There's no L in it.

**RUSTLESS:**
*(looking closely, then removing something from book)* Marmalade again. Would you kindly tell the boot boy to stick to cornflakes in the mornings, Bates – he's throwing the office work into complete confusion. Pedder eh? And what does he call himself in the letter?

**BATES:**
Arkwright. G L Arkwright.

**RUSTLESS:**
There you are you see? Nothing like it. Right. Now it's obvious that we've got to get organised. Don't want to lose the licence after only ten days. Bates, hold the fort here, I'm going down to sort Cook out – stop her using that old set of false teeth for putting the edge round the steak and kidney pies, that sort of thing. Dithers!

**DITHERS:**
Ar?

**RUSTLESS:**
Tidy up here. And for god's sake smarten yourself up, man. Look at you. Comb your hair, and do try and straighten up. Stand up, come on, chest out, stomach in, shoulders back!

**DITHERS:**
I can't stand up any straighter.

**RUSTLESS:**
Well, 'course you can't – you know why? You've get your waistcoat done up to one of your fly buttons.

**DITHERS:**
Au-er. *(Dithers does the button up properly.)*

*(Badger enters.)*

**BADGER:**
Cook says will you be long, milord? Only she's preparing "oeufs en cocotte" and she wants to knew what cocotte means.

**RUSTLESS:**
Cocotte? Well it's obvious. Roast chicken. I'll go and see to her. Now remember, I want this whole place to have an air of efficiency – let's all try and look as if we know what were doing. Is that understood?

*(He comes out from behind the desk – we see that he is wearing pyjama trousers. He exits.)*

**BATES:**
Oh dear I do hope it's all going to be alright. Look you'd better hoover in here, Dithers – I must write up some of these bills.

**DITHERS:**
Righto. *(He goes.)*

**BATES:**
Hope no one sees his Lordship on the way to the kitchens. Did you notice, Mr Badger? He had his jimmy-jams on.

**BADGER:**
His what Miss Bates?

**BATES:**
His pyjamas. I'm not awfully sure he's going to be able to cope with running this place as an hotel – I mean, it's his own home – he was brought up here.

**BADGER:**
I've no doubt he'll muddle through as usual, Miss Bates. After all, he was a major-general.

**BATES:**
I know, but a hotel's somewhat different from the army, isn't it.

**BADGER:**
Not really, Miss Bates – there are just as many rules and regulations. The only difference is the food's slightly better in the army.

**BATES:**
Were you in the army, Mr Badger?

**BADGER:**
No I'm afraid not. Of course – when the war started I was a mere lad.

**BATES:**
Yes, yes, so was I. But didn't you do National Service, after the war?

**BADGER:**
I did try to get into the RAF but I was turned down.

**BATES:**
How funny – so was I, for the WRENS. Why wouldn't they have you in the RAF?

**BADGER:**
Flat feet.

**BATES:**
Oh with me it was my chest. *(Badger looks puzzled)* I mean I have a weak chest. Not a flat one. *(she blushes)* Well, it's not all that … I mean … it's not enormous, but it's … er – would you excuse me, Mr Badger *(backing out)* There's a couple of points I want to check up on in the office. *(she goes, flustered)*

*Cut to: the kitchen.*

*(Effie, the maid, is working at a table. Rustless enters.)*

**RUSTLESS:**
Ah, there you are, Effie old thing. What are you doing down here? I thought you usually performed in the bedrooms.

**EFFIE:**
*(Mouths, silently as usual.)*

**RUSTLESS:**
Oh really? Yes, I suppose you do. Must get very tiring – all that bending about. Yes. Well, I must say I like the look of your dumplings.

**EFFIE:**
*(Mouths.)*

**RUSTLESS:**
Oh, are they? It's been so long, I've forgotten. How do you keep them so fresh looking?

**EFFIE:**
(Mouths)

**RUSTLESS:**
Silver paper? What, wrap them up overnight you mean?

**EFFIE:**
(Mouths.)

**RUSTLESS:**
Oh I see. Stops them going lumpy. Yes. Brush them with milk, and sprinkle sugar on the top. Well, I must say, they're positively mouth watering. Can't wait to sink my teeth into one. Oh, and talking of sinking teeth, where's Cook? I've get some news for her that'll frighten her to death, with any luck.

**COOK:**
(entering) Oi!

**RUSTLESS:**
Ah, Cook.

**COOK:**
Nobody's allowed in here, I'm creating the lunch.

**RUSTLESS:**
Cremating would be nearer the mark.

**COOK:**
Have you been poking your nose into Effie's secrets?

**RUSTLESS:**
Certainly not. She's been telling me about her apple turnovers

**COOK:**
And you've been looking over her shoulder.

**RUSTLESS:**
Of course not. It would be impossible.

Now listen to me, Cook. We've got a food inspector prowling around the place and, by a unanimous decision, it has been decided that you should step down in favour of a younger man.

**COOK:**
Who?

**RUSTLESS:**
Bates.

**COOK:**
She couldn't cook her way out of a paper bag.

**RUSTLESS:**
No, but she's very good at getting rid of paper bags full of the muck that you've cooked. The point is, this inspector chap's coming into the kitchen, and –

**COOK:**
He's not you know.

**RUSTLESS:**
What?

**COOK:**
It's me bottling day. No civil servant's coming snooping around here when I've got me soft fruit on the table.

**RUSTLESS:**
Now look here –

**COOK:**
And that goes for everybody. Miss Bates and all. So you can put that in your pipe and smoke it.

**RUSTLESS:**
I don't smoke a pipe.

**COOK:**
Exactly.

**RUSTLESS:**
I see. Is that your last word?

**COOK:**
No.

**RUSTLESS:**
Oh. What is your last word?

**COOK:**
Good riddance.

*(She slaps some dough into a pile of flour on the table causing a great cloud of flour to arise. Rustless retreats hastily.)*

*Cut to: the hall again.*

*(Badger is being approached by the old lady – who is now accompanied by her friend who is also about 72.)*

**OLD LADY:**
Do you think my friend and I might have some coffee?

**BADGER:**
Certainly madam – I'll get the maid to bring you some right away. *(He exits.)*

*(The old lady returns to her friend.)*

**FRIEND:**
So as I was saying – this boy was really struck on me – really struck. Of course, at that time I was only seventeen, of course, I was thinner. *(She is enormous.)* And I had this cotton dress, with this broderie anglaise all gathered at the neck and you know the back of Fanshaws?

**OLD LADY:**
Pardon?

**FRIEND:**
The back of Fanshaws Breweries?

**OLD LADY:**
Oh yes.

**FRIEND:**
Well of course that was all fields then, and this boy took me into this field and I caught this dress on some wire and it all tore, right up to the waist. And of course the poor boy didn't know where to look? Well he could see my drawers you see and what's the name of that thing that looks

like a water tower at the top of the hill?

**OLD LADY:**
Pardon?

**FRIEND:**
That thing with the fence round it with spikes on?

**OLD LADY:**
Oh – er …

**FRIEND:**
Anyway, we went in there so I could sew up the dress. Of course being torn at the back I had to take it off, do you see and –

*(Dithers enters, Hoovering – drowning the voice of the old lady and her friend, who nevertheless keeps talking.)*

*(Dithers Hoovers near them, then lifts up the old lady's legs to Hoover underneath, much to her surprise. He does the same thing to her friend who doesn't stop talking.)*

*(Effie, the maid, enters. Dithers is obviously a devotee of hers, and stares at her as she approaches with the coffee. The Hoover motor dies down, i.e. is switched off, but as she bends down to place the tray onto the low table, Dithers's eyes light up as he sees her knickers, and at the same time the Hoover leaps into life again. He stares. Effie goes – and he Hoovers on.)*

*(Mrs Pedder and her lover enter. She is a large attractive woman of about 37 or 38 – a "full blown rose", rather heavily made up. Her lover is perhaps a little younger, a smoothie. He "pings" the desk bell four times. Dithers alters the grandfather clock to four o'clock. Miss Bates enters, and goes to desk.)*

**LOVER BOY:**
Good morning.

**MISS BATES:**
Oh. Good morning sir, madam.

**LOVER BOY:**
We'd like a double room.

**BATES:**
Well, we're rather full at the moment, sir – for how long would it be?

**MRS PEDDER:**
Just tonight.

**LOVER BOY:**
Er – yes, really, only tonight. Really.

**BATES:**
Yes, well I think we could manage the one night. If you wouldn't mind over looking the car park.

**LOVER BOY:**
Oh, I think we're willing to over look that, aren't we Rosie?

**MRS PEDDER:**
Well, I am if you are.

**LOVER BOY:**
Yes, we've decided to over look it. Just this once.

**BATES:**
Oh splendid. Would you sign the register please? Number eleven.

*(They both sign the book. Miss Bates takes it back.)*

**BATES:**
Oh, Smith. I see. Oh, and you've put Mrs Smith.

**MRS PEDDER:**
Naturally.

**BATES:**
Yes, oh, well that's lovely then. Yes.

**LOVER BOY:**
My name really is Smith – I can show you my birth certificate.

**BATES:**
No no – it's just that it looks funny in the book, that's all. Our first Smith!

**LOVER BOY:**
I don't doubt there'll be plenty more, eh?

**BATES:**
Quite. *(To Dithers, who has reappeared)* Dithers, show Mr Smith and this – Mrs Smith to number eleven, would you?

**DITHERS:**
Righto. Overlooks the car park you know.

**LOVER BOY:**
Yes, we've been all over that already.

**DITHERS:**
*(interested)* Oh? Bumpy, ain't it? *(They exit.)*

**OLD LADY:**
Did they say Smith, dear?

**BATES:**
That's right, yes.

**FRIEND:**
I knew a Smith once.

**OLD LADY:**
Yes. I believe I did.

**FRIEND:**
Really? You don't happen to know his name do you?

**OLD LADY:**
It was Smith, as far as I can remember

**FRIEND:**
Oh. Mine was Robinson.

**OLD LADY:**
A Smith called Robinson?

**FRIEND:**
Yes. Worked at the Smithy. Blacksmith. Extraordinary muscles.

**OLD LADY:**
Yes, their arms do get very strong.

**FRIEND:**
No, these were in his head.

**OLD LADY:**
Oh.

*(Rustless enters.)*

**RUSTLESS:**
No go, Bates – Cook's not having any.

**BATES:**
What?

**RUSTLESS:**
She refuses to budge out of the kitchen. She's quite adamant. So there's only one thing left to do.

**BATES:**
What's that?

**RUSTLESS:**
Nobble her. Kidnap her, put her behind locked doors, till old Pedder's left the premises. Now, it's not going to be easy.

*(Pedder enters and approaches the desk. Bates sees him first.)*

**BATES:**
*(loudly)* Hello, Mr Pedder!

**RUSTLESS:**
*(without taking breath)* Because with the state of the common-market, we're going to be buying baked beans singly, so much each. Ah, Mr Pedder – everything satisfactory?

**PEDDER:**
The tap drips, and my wife is still being unfaithful to me.

**RUSTLESS:**
Perhaps the washer's loose. On the tap, I mean.

**PEDDER:**
I won't be in to lunch. *(He goes.)*

**RUSTLESS:**
Did I hear aright? By jove, that's given us a bit of breathing space. It's nearly eight hours till dinner. Now then, we must decide the best plan of attack. We've got to lock Cook up somewhere. We've got to pick somewhere where she's bound to go sooner or later –

*Cut to: film.*

*(Close up – WC. On door – pull out to reveal Dithers just finishing fixing a bolt on the outside of the door.)*

*Cut to: Rustless, stationed at the end of the corridor.*
*(Rustless gives a signal, and Dithers darts away.)*

*(Long shot – Cook approaching.)*

*(Close up – of her, to establish her face. She enters the loo. Dithers comes into frame, shoots the bolt across.*
*Close up of Rustless listening. He hears the loo flush.*
*Rustless approaches door. He and Dithers stand, waiting.)*

*(Close up – the vacant/engaged sign on the door, it clicks over from engaged to vacant.)*

*(There is a tug at the door. It is rattled vigorously.*
*Reaction shot of the men smiling. Then, over this shot, a curious creak and a thud. Rustless silently slides back the bolt, and gingerly opens the loo door. The little window is open, and through it we can see Cook walking away from us, across the lawns. Reaction of the two men.)*

*(Long shot – part of the back of the house. Cook, carrying a plastic pail of kitchen garbage, approaches the dustbins. Medium shot as she opens one of then, and empties her rubbish. From behind her, suddenly, from nowhere, appear Dithers and Rustless. One covers her mouth they lift her into the dustbin.)*

*(A low angle close up of the lid going down on her head. Medium shot of Rustless holding the lid down, while Dithers threads rope through the handles and secures it.)*

*(Close up of Dithers – to speed this tying business up.)*

*(The men retreat to a safe distance.)*

*(Close up of bin, shaking.)*

*(Reaction of Rustless, watching. Over this, a sudden crunch and clang.)*

*(Men stare.)*

*(Long shot – the dustbin's bottom has been kicked out, and it now proceeds to run off, leaving a little pile of rubbish. It crashes into the wall with a tremendous clang, rebounds off, and hurries off towards the house.)*

*(Reaction of men – foiled again.)*

*(The front of the house.)*

*(Dithers in goggles sits on an old motorcycle and sidecar. Cook, dressed now for outdoors, comes from the house and gets into sidecar.)*

*(Close up of Dithers – he looks up towards bedroom window.)*

*(Close up of Rustless giving thumbs up sign in the window.)*

*(Long shot – they drive off.)*

*(A country lane. A long, straight, open road. The motor-cycle approaches and passes camera. Just past the camera it splutters and stops.)*

*(Close up of Cook, looking surprised.)*

*(Medium shot as Dithers gets off, gets spanner from his pocket and starts banging about on the motorcycle.)*

*(Close up of Cook being shaken about.)*

*(Medium shot – Dithers remounts and kicks the engine into life again.)*

*(Long shot – the motorcycle roars off, but the sidecar stays where it is.)*

*(Close up reaction of Cook.)*

*(Close up of Dithers as we see over his shoulder, the gesticulating figure of Cook as she recedes rapidly into the distance. Success at last.)*

Cut to: the dining room.

*(A sad pianist and an eager lady cellist are giving a rough approximation of "velia" from the Merry Widow.)*

*(We pull out to see that the old lady and her friend are eating – the deaf old man, and about seven other guests also. They are being served by a very young, slow waiter, and the buxom Effie. Badger and Miss Bates are in attendance.)*

*(Miss Bates is now dressed as a waitress. Mr Pedder is seated at his table. Rustless enters, dressed as a chef, pushing a trolley on which is a large covered dish, and smaller dishes, all covered.)*

*(He arrives at Pedder's table.)*

**RUSTLESS:**
Good evening, Mr Pedder. You ordered the beef, I believe.

**PEDDER:**
Yes, that's right.

**RUSTLESS:**
Thank you.

*(He opens a dish. It contains surgical gloves. Miss Bates helps him on with them. He then lifts up the surgical mask which is round his neck and covers his nose and mouth with it. He now looks completely like a surgeon.)*

*(Miss Bates puts on rubber gloves, opens the dish, revealing a joint of beef and then hands*

535

*Rustless carving knife and fork. He carves one large slice.)*

*(Miss Bates, meanwhile, picks up a dinner plate, using surgical pincers, and places it in front of Mr Pedder. Pedder is looking amazed at this behaviour. Just as Rustless is about to place the meat on the plate Badger picks up the plate and polishes it with a napkin. Rustless places the meat deftly on to the table cloth.)*

**PEDDER:**
*(leaping up)* Oh my God!

*(His action knocks the vegetables, which miss Bates was about to dish out, all over the floor.)*

**RUSTLESS:**
Oops! I'm damned sorry about that Mr Pedder.

**BADGER:**
If you'll hand me the forceps, Miss Bates, I will return the meat to the plate.

**RUSTLESS:**
You will do no such thing, Badger. It would be most unhygienic! You don't know who's been drumming his fingers on that tablecloth! No, no, don't touch a thing. Allow me, Mr. Pedder.

*(Rustless picks up the tablecloth by its four corners and heaves it off the table. With a great clatter of crockery and cutlery.)*

**RUSTLESS:**
Now. Let us start again.

*Cut to: the corridor outside the bedroom of Mrs Pedder and lover boy. (the door opens and lover boy comes out.)*

**LOVER BOY:**
*(to Mrs Pedder inside the room. )* I'll tell him to put two bottles on the ice, just in case.

**MRS PEDDER:**
*(voice off)* Don't be long, darling.

**LOVER BOY:**
Just a couple of ticks, Rosie my love.

**MRS PEDDER:**
*(appearing at the door)* I'll be waiting. (*Gives him a plonker on the lips.*)

**LOVER BOY:**
I'll try and make it one tick.

*(He goes, she closes the door and we cut back to the dining-room.)*

*(Pedder is now seated at another table. Rustless prepares to carve again. As before, they go through the same routine for a few seconds, then suddenly, pedder leaps up and stares; the food goes flying again.)*

*Cut to: Lover boy, speaking to the young waiter, asking for champagne to be put on ice.*

**PEDDER**
That's him! That's the blackguard who's hob-nobbing with my Rosie!

**RUSTLESS:**
Look, I do wish you'd sit still Mr Pedder – you're never going to taste the food at this rate.

**PEDDER:**
I don't want to taste the damn food.

**RUSTLESS:**
But that's what you're here for.

**PEDDER:**
I'm here to find my wife. Is she staying here?

**RUSTLESS:**
But aren't you the Food Inspector?

**PEDDER:**
Am I hell. I breed pigs.

**RUSTLESS:**
Really? Congratulations. Oh, what a relief.

*(A shot of lover boy going out.)*

**PEDDER:**
Look, are you going to tell me if that man is a resident?

**RUSTLESS:**
What? Certainly. Anything, anything, my dear old chap. Yes he's a resident alright. Number eleven. Calls himself Smith.

**PEDDER:**
I bet he does. Has he got a woman with him?

**RUSTLESS:**
Not half. Big filly. Looks as if she rides.

**PEDDER:**
Which room are they in, did you say?

**RUSTLESS:**
Number eleven – come on, I'll show you.

*(They hurry out.)*

**BATES:**
Oh gosh, what a relief. I say, do you think there's going to be a fight up there?

**BADGER:**
I hope so! Come on.

*(They start to follow, as we cut to)*

*(The corridor outside the bedroom. Pedder flings open the door, and rushes in.)*

**LOVER BOY:**
*(voice off)* No, look here!

**PEDDER:**
*(off)* You swine!

*(A heavy punch is heard and a groan from lover boy, followed by furniture crashing. Rustless, outside the door, winces and moves away a little.)*

**MRS PEDDER:**
*(voice off)* Now William don't get excited …

**PEDDER:**
*(voice off)* As for you –

**MRS PEDDER:**
*(voice off)*: No – William, stop it – put me down — don't you dare –

*(A scuffle is heard followed by the noise of Mrs Pedder being spanked by Mr Pedder.)*

**PEDDER:**
*(over this)* I'll teach you to go gallivanting off with some sneaky little gigolo –

*(Over this, Mrs Pedder yells. Rustless sidles up and peers through the door.)*

**RUSTLESS:**
So that's why they call her Rosie.

*(Miss Bates and Badger arrive, in time to see Pedder emerge dragging Mrs Pedder by the arm. She clutches her behind.)*

**PEDDER:**
I'd like my bill, please.

**RUSTLESS:**
Certainly, sir – both rooms? Yes, well naturally. See to that Bates, would you. Badger, I think Mr Pedder will need some help with his baggage.

*(A close up reaction on Mrs Pedder – she is livid. As they go, lover boy emerges from the bedroom with a black eye, dishevelled.)*

**RUSTLESS:**
Ah, Mr Smith, I presume you're off as well, what?

**LOVER BOY:**
The name's Arkwright. I'm supposed to be here as Food Inspector but I think all things considered, I'll be off. I'll send word to the department that all is in order. Sorry about the mess.

**RUSTLESS:**
You're the food inspector? Oh , I see. I thought you and Mrs Er – his, er – her were just here for a, er – week-end

**LOVER BOY:**
Yes – I foolishly thought I could combine

the two, but I was wrong.

**RUSTLESS:**
Quite. Never mix business with pleasure, old fruit.

*(They move off down the corridor.)*

*Cut to: the hall.*

*(Rustless and lover boy walking towards the door.)*

**RUSTLESS:**
Pity you didn't have a chance to sample the food – excellent cook – very hygienic.

*(Cook enters – bedraggled, covered in mud, looking furious.)*

**COOK:**
What happened about dinner?

**RUSTLESS:**
Ah – er this is my aunt Matilda. Wonderful person – wrestles in mud. Curious hobby, but she seems to enjoy it.

*(He chunters on as the credits roll.)*

# EPISODE TWO

*"There's Safari at the Bottom of My Garden"*

*Scene: the reception hall of the hotel. Rustless is on the phone.*

**RUSTLESS:**
Yes, certainly sir. Yes, I can give you a nice double room on the second floor: Well, when I said "give" of course – er, I mean you'll have to pay for it. Yes, naturally. Oh yes, very pleasant outlook, over the golf course. Beautiful room. Charles the Second is supposed to have slept in it: but, as Lady Catherine de Neauville was with him at the time, I doubt if he got a wink all night. What? Amenities? What, you mean constant hot housemaids and water, all that sort of thing? Oh I see. Things to do. Well, there's the golf course. Seventeen holes. Seventeen. Yes. Well it was eighteen holes, but some damn fool got his foot stuck in the hole at the fourteenth. His caddie managed to prise it free with a five-iron, but the fellah's plimsoll remains. Can't shift it. Squirrels have stuffed it full of nuts. Yes. What? Well, what else, well, there's the Billiard-room. Snooker? No, I'm afraid not. Not enough balls. Only got three, you see – two white ones and a red one. Yes. Unless you like to bring your own. Oh, you don't possess any. No.

*(The old lady guest has entered. She totters over to an armchair and sits.)*

**RUSTLESS:**
Well, what about museums? We've got a geological museum at Passmore Green. Full of amazing old fossils. Went to school with two of them. No. No, not in your line. Something more exciting. Well, Wednesday is our Ludo evening. Play a lot of Ludo – Hello? Hello? Damn fella's rung off. Morning Mrs Ringer.

**OLD LADY:**
Good morning milord.

**RUSTLESS:**
You haven't got any snooker balls in your room, have you?

**OLD LADY:**
No, I don't think so. What are they like?

**RUSTLESS:**
They're like billiard-balls, only more numerous.

*(Bates enters. She carries a ledger.)*

**BATES:**
Morning, milord, sorry I'm late. I took this ledger to bed with me.

**RUSTLESS:**
Really? What happened to Teddy?

**BATES:**
Oh. Oh no, he's fine, milord. How – how did you know about him?

**RUSTLESS:**
I noticed him the other day when I was in your room, checking your drawers for woodworm.

**BATES:**
Oh yes, of course, yes.

**OLD LADY:**
I think I've got woodworm.

**RUSTLESS:**
Really? It's possible. Paraffin's the answer. Put plenty of paraffin into the holes. That'll kill it.

**OLD LADY:**
Oh, I must try that.

**RUSTLESS:**
Yes, and the sooner the better. We don't want it spreading to the furniture.

**BATES:**
Any more bookings, milord?

**RUSTLESS:**
No. Chap's just been on the phone asking about the amenities. Told him about the golf and the Ludo, but he didn't seem awfully impressed. Rung off. You know, when you think about it, there's damn-all to do around here Bates, unless you're a drunk, or you suffer from sleeping sickness.

**BATES:**
Perhaps we should introduce Ludo twice a week, milord.

**RUSTLESS:**
No, no, Bates: I'm afraid Ludo is a minority sport. I can't see it drawing the crowds. I've got this AA form to fill up here, look. So far I've put down – "Excellent cuisine; licensed bar; golf-course; bedrooms sixteen; bathrooms four;" now if I add to that "Ludo-boards

one, snooker balls none" I mean it's going to turn them away in droves, old thing. We've got to find something a bit more exciting for the customers. Any ideas?

**BATES:**
When I was a girl in India we used to get up to all sorts of exciting things. One of the native house-boys, Mahmud his name was, used to take me on excursions into the jungle. He was wonderful.

**RUSTLESS:**
Really.

**BATES:**
Yes – We used to take a picnic lunch and sit in the undergrowth and he would teach me all about nature.

**RUSTLESS:**
I say, steady on old chap, ladies present.

**BATES:**
Of course, Mummy would have had a fit if she'd known – because in those days it wasn't considered the thing to do.

**RUSTLESS:**
Yes – even today it's still frowned upon in parts of Surrey. But weren't you frightened? I mean, sitting in the jungle, eating cucumber sandwiches, with the likelihood of being jumped on at any second by a great hairy beast?

**BATES:**
Oh no milord – Mahmud would never dream of anything like that. He was a gentleman.

**OLD LADY:**
I think I'll go to my room. *(She starts to go.)*

**RUSTLESS:**
Yes, I think I should. Conversation's taken on a damn tricky turn. If it gets any hotter I may be forced to join you.

*(Old lady exits.)*

**BATES:**
Anything the matter, milord?

**RUSTLESS:**
I think we've got our wires crossed, Bates old fruit – I meant, in the jungle – when you – I say! Just a minute!

*(A thought strikes him.)*

**BATES:**
Milord?

**RUSTLESS:**
Lions! That's what we want! We must bring in lions!

**BATES:**
Lions, milord?

**RUSTLESS:**
Not that there are any in India, of course. You don't remember having seen lions in India, do you Bates?

**BATES:**
Well they did open a Corner House in Calcutta once.

**RUSTLESS:**
Not Lyons, man – lions. King of the jungle, big-game, that sort of lion. That's what we need. Turn the place into a safari park! That'll bring 'em in. By jove, Bates, that's it!

**BATES:**
Oh dear.

**RUSTLESS:**
The old Duke of Thing does it – so does old Lord Whatsit. Can't fail. Let 'em drive round in their cars, trying to catch a glimpse of the wild life. They'll love it. Listen – get the staff in here at once, we've got to get things moving.

**BATES:**
Very good, milord *(She goes.)*

**RUSTLESS:**
Rustless old chap, you're on to a winner!

*(A girl enters, and goes to the letter-rack near Lord R.)*

**RUSTLESS:**
*(roaring like a lion)* Aaahhhrrr!!!

*(Girl jumps a foot in the air.)*

**RUSTLESS:**
Exciting, isn't it?

*(Fade down.)*

*(Fade up.)*

*(The reception hall is now transformed. Strange potted plants, bamboo screens, and a large totem pole in the centre of the room. The doors all have signs over them written on birch-bark, saying "cannibal hot-pot" with "dining room" in brackets, "fire-water hut" (bar), "devils magic box" (TV Room), "lagoon" (bathroom).*

*(Or there could perhaps be signs with arrows stuck onto the totem pole pointing in different directions.)*

*(Badger, the butler, is talking to Bates.)*

**BADGER:**
I think we've covered everything, Miss Bates.

**BATES:**
Oh, yes, Mr Badger, it looks lovely. Very atmospheric. Wherever did you get that beautiful totem-pole?

**BADGER:**
My brother-in-law – you may recall he's under-manager at the Co-op.

**BATES:**
Oh – I thought they were mainly groceries.

**BADGER:**
No, no, Miss Bates – he is a member of the Light Opera group in Passmore, and they've just finished doing *Annie Get Your Gun*, and so I was lucky enough to secure

it at very moderate cost. In fact, I rather think they were pleased to be rid of it. They were having great difficulty in incorporating it in their next production.

**BATES:**
Oh, what's that?

**BADGER:**
*The Sound of Music.*

**BATES:**
Oh, yes. It's enormous. Is it Polynesian?

**BADGER:**
Polystyrene, actually. *(He taps it.)*

**BATES:**
No, what I meant was ...

*(Rustless enters, dressed in full big game hunter's outfit, with solar topee, etc.)*

**RUSTLESS:**
Ah, there you are, chaps. Found this upstairs in me trunk. Haven't worn it for years. What d'you think, Bates? Catches the flavour, what?

**BATES:**
Oh, very much so, milord.

**RUSTLESS:**
Don't smell of mothballs too much, do I?

**BATES:**
*(sniffing)* Well – I'm sure it will wear off, milord.

**RUSTLESS:**
Quite. Where's Dithers.

**BADGER:**
He's awaiting delivery of the lion, milord. He's going to supervise its unloading at the stables.

**RUSTLESS:**
Ah, first class. I hope it's alright. Damned expensive things to hire, you know.

**BATES:**
Do you think one lion is enough, milord?

**RUSTLESS:**
It'll have to be for the time being – we'll have to keep moving it about in its cage – people will think it's a different one.

*(Dithers enters, dressed in his page-boy suit.)*

**RUSTLESS:**
Ah, Dithers! Has it arrived?

**DITHERS:**
Ar. I put it in the paddock, like you said. It's a big-un.

**BATES:**
Is – is it fairly docile, Mr Dithers?

**DITHERS:**
Eh?

**BATES:**
It didn't snarl at you, did it?

**DITHERS:**
Oh no, seemed contented enough. Where do you want the cage put?

**RUSTLESS:**
What? I thought you said you'd put it in the paddock.

**DITHERS:**
Oh no – put the lion in the paddock. Cage is still on the back of the lorry.

**BADGER:**
You mean to say you've released the lion?

**DITHERS:**
Ar. Can't have a Safari Park if the lions are locked up. Got to run about wild.

**RUSTLESS:**
Good God man – it's a bit sudden, isn't it? Have you warned the postman?

**DITHERS:**
That's alright, he's got his bike.

**RUSTLESS:**
I know, but damnit, he can't go very fast on that.

**DITHERS:**
He will when the old lion gets behind him! *(chuckling)* Anyhow, we shall get our letters delivered a lot quicker! *(He starts to go then sniffs)* Terrible smell of mothballs in here.

*(He exits.)*

**RUSTLESS:**
The man's a lunatic. Look Bates, we can't let the postman sail in here without warning – if he sees that lion it'll be a terrible shock. He won't know his parcel from his elbow. Look, ring him up and tell him if he's got any letters for us, not to deliver them by hand; just – er – post them on to us. *(thinks)* No, wait a minute – that doesn't work, does it?

**BATES:**
Not really, milord.

**RUSTLESS:**
Hm. If we're not careful, things could get very ugly.

*(Enter Cook.)*

**COOK:**
Oi!

**RUSTLESS:**
What did I tell you. Hello, Cook – what are you doing in here? I thought I told you to remain below stairs.

**COOK:**
There ain't no man who could keep me below stairs.

**RUSTLESS:**
Oh, I don't know. I dare say a good carpenter could manage it. What d'you want anyway?

**COOK:**
It's this menu she's given me to get ready.

**RUSTLESS:**
*(taking it)* What's the matter with it? *(reads)* Kangaroo Soup – Parrot Pie – Fricassee of Elephant. Did you think of this, Bates? Sounds damn good.

**COOK:**
Sounds damn daft to me. How d'you expect me to turn out that sort of trash?

**RUSTLESS:**
Simple. You just turn out your usual trash, and we call it by different names.

**COOK:**
What, Kangaroo Tail Soup?

**RUSTLESS:**
Give 'em oxtail. One tail tastes very like another, I should imagine.

**COOK:**
It's Australian, anyhow.

**RUSTLESS:**
Well, serve it upside down. What about this Parrot Pie Bates? What did you have in mind for that?

**BATES:**
I think chicken pie would suffice, milord.

**RUSTLESS:**
Exactly. Stick a few coloured feathers in it.

**COOK:**
Eh?

**RUSTLESS:**
Those ones out of your Sunday Hat would do a treat. I'd be glad to see the back of those.

**COOK:**
My aunt Doris left me that hat in her will.

**RUSTLESS:**
Really? What did she die of, fowl-pest?

**COOK:**
Look, I haven't got time to stand here mincing words with you. I've got the

butcher dangling on the other end of the 'phone, waiting to know my intentions.

**RUSTLESS:**
Really? I should marry the man, put him out of his misery.

**COOK:**
I'll get him to serve me one of his best legs, and I'll see what I can do with it.

*(She goes to the door.)*

**RUSTLESS:**
Yes – that'll do very nicely for the Fricassee of Elephant.

**COOK:**
*(at the door)* You're off your chump! *(She exits.)*

**BATES:**
D'you think perhaps I ought to go after her, milord? Perhaps I could explain in a little more detail.

**RUSTLESS:**
Good idea, Badger.

**BATES:**
Perhaps we could lay up a few sandwiches for this evening at the same time, Mr Badger? – Just for the three of us? In case Cook still doesn't get the message?

**BATES:**
An excellent idea, Miss Bates – I'll attend to that at the same time. I think I know where I can lay my hands on some pâté.

*(He goes.)*

**BATES:**
Just in case, milord.

**RUSTLESS:**
Quite. I say, talking of laying your hands on some pâté, where is Effie? I haven't seen her all day.

**BATES:**
*(looking at watch)* She should be in the

morning-room about now, milord, dusting her bric-à-brac.

**RUSTLESS:**
Good Lord, mustn't miss that. I – er – I'll just go and see that she's safely indoors. Can't be too careful with that lion about.

*(Mr Quick enters, with suitcase.)*

**RUSTLESS:**
Ah, guest arriving. *(to Mr Quick)* Good day sir – Welcome to the Jungle.

**QUICK:**
Good afternoon.

**RUSTLESS:**
If you'd care to sign the register, I'll summon a bearer. *(Goes behind counter and starts to beat a large tom-tom with his hands saying, as he beats.)* Pleasant weather for the time of year, isn't it? Looks like the monsoon's given us a miss. Ah, Dithers.

*(Dithers enters, picks up the suitcase, and balances it on his head.)*

**RUSTLESS:**
Take this great white hunter to number nine hut.

**QUICK:**
Er – just a minute. Before I sign in, I'd like to know a bit more about the Safari Park.

**RUSTLESS:**
Ah. Well perhaps you'd show the gentleman round Bates. Dithers, clear off for a minute. *(Dithers goes out again.)* Oh, excuse me won't you – I've got to have a word with the bric-à-brac.

*(He exits.)*

**BATES:**
Yes *(a beaming smile)*. Well, erm – what can I tell you?

**QUICK:**
Livestock.

**BATES:**
Pardon?

**QUICK:**
How many head?

**BATES:**
Er – well, ... one.

**QUICK:**
One head?

**BATES:**
Yes.

**QUICK:**
One head of livestock.

**BATES:**
Just the one, yes. A lion. But he's extremely fierce.

*(The old lady has entered.)*

**QUICK:**
I'm sure.

**BATES:**
That's just at present – we hope to have lots more very soon when the – er – breeding season starts.

**QUICK:**
He can't breed on his own.

**BATES:**
No that's true, he'll need a friend – er, naturally. But ... Can I help you Mrs Ringer?

**OLD LADY:**
*(quietly to Bates)* I can't seem to find the Ladies.

**BATES:**
Oh, sorry – it's confusing, isn't it? I couldn't find it myself! It's all changed, now we've got all this foliage. If you just go behind the totem-pole, Mrs Ringer.

**OLD LADY:**
Pardon?

**BATES:**
The door to the Ladies. Behind the totem-pole.

**OLD LADY:**
Oh, I see.

*(She goes.)*

**BATES:**
Sorry about that sir – anything else I can tell you?

**QUICK:**
No thanks. I thought this was a genuine wild-life preserve. Obviously it's a complete sham. If I were you, I would remove that advertisement in *The Times* at once. Otherwise I shall consider writing them a stiff letter, advising them that they are liable to a court action for misrepresentation.

**BATES:**
Oh yes. Er – perhaps I could write to you when we've got lots more animals?

**QUICK:**
If you like – send it care of Lincoln's Inn. Sir Geoffrey Quick, Q.C. K.C.B.

*(He exits)*

**BATES:**
Good gracious – a judge!

*(The old lady reappears through the foliage.)*

**BATES:**
*(flustered)* Ah – Mrs Ringer, did you find it? Well, that's a relief, anyway.

*(The old lady raises her eyebrows, and departs.)*

**BATES:**
*(more flustered)* Oh dear!

*Cut to: the morning room – a small room, with French windows, which are slightly ajar. (Rustless enters, and finds Effie, the maid, dusting a number of pieces of ornamental china on shelves.)*

**RUSTLESS:**
Ah, there you are Effie old thing. I was worried about you. Have you been indoors all day?

**EFFIE:**
*(Speaks, noiselessly, as always.)*

**RUSTLESS:**
Oh you have? In the garden just now? Oh, you saw him? *(Effie keeps on mouthing.)* Big staring eyes, snarling. Yes, that's the one. Did he attack? Oh, I see. Just kept staring at your vegetables. Then what happened?

**EFFIE:**
*(Mouths some more.)*

**RUSTLESS:**
Suddenly turned on his heel and stalked off into the undergrowth. Yes – oh, no doubt about it. Yes. *(She nods.)* Well, you had a lucky escape my dear. No, what I came to tell you was that the lion we ordered has been rather prematurely released by that damned idiot Dithers, and is prowling about the grounds. Now you've no need to panic, because ...

*(The lion – prefilmed, on overlay, appears to be outside the French windows. Effie sees it, and goes wild-eyed.)*

**RUSTLESS:**
What's the matter? *(She clutches at him.)* Now look, it's perfectly alright, all the doors and windows are shut ... *(Effie notices that the French windows, are, in fact open and promptly faints in Rustless's arms.)* Oh Good God, now she's passed out on me, I ... *(He turns and sees the lion.)* Ah. Oh, Er ... *(He hoists Effie over his shoulder in a fireman's lift.)* Er – good dog! Now. Back away, slowly. Effie – stare him straight in the eye. *(Effie is staring at him with her knickers.)* That's the idea. Don't turn your face away for a moment ... *(He backs out of the door.)*

*(The hall. Bates is on the phone.)*

**BATES:**
No. No madam – well, it's just that we've not been operating for very long as a Safari Park, and we're sort of working up to it gradually. Your husband lived in Africa – yes ... Well no ... *(Rustless enters, still rather out of breath – he has deposited Effie somewhere en route.)* One lion isn't much, I agree. No. No, very well madam – perhaps when we get some monkeys your husband would feel more at home. Yes. Goodbye Madam.

**RUSTLESS:**
Who was that, Bates?

**BATES:**
Another cancellation, milord.

**RUSTLESS:**
Another?

**BATES:**
The gentleman who was here earlier also left when I told him we only had the one lion. In fact, he as good as threatened a court case for misrepresentation, milord.

**RUSTLESS:**
Good grief – who the devil was he?

**BATES:**
Sir Geoffrey Quick – *(meaningfully)* – Q.C. K.C.B.!

**RUSTLESS:**
That's not how you spell Quick.

**BATES:**
No, no milord – he's a judge.

**RUSTLESS:**
Oh I see. Damned tricky. Well, what are we going to do, Bates old fellow? What?

**BATES:**
We'll have to get some more animals, milord. People aren't going to be satisfied with one.

**RUSTLESS:**
Dammit all, Bates, we can't afford to fork out hundreds of pounds a week on animals – that'll be all the profit gone. We've spent a fortune as it is, doing the place up.

**BATES:**
Well, people will expect to see something for their money, milord – even if it's at a distance.

**RUSTLESS:**
*(idea)* By jove Bates, that's it. Why didn't I think of that before. Let's see – yes – Badger, Dithers – he could be a gorilla —

**BATES:**
Whatever do you mean, milord?

**RUSTLESS:**
Costumes, Bates old chap. Costumes! They're a damn sight cheaper to hire than animals – get 'em sent down from London by train.

**BATES:**
But won't people know?

**RUSTLESS:**
At a distance, Bates! You said it yourself. Put old Dithers in a skin, he'd look exactly like a gorilla a hundred years away. Come to think of it, he does now. Without a skin. Close to. Badger can be a lion – and you can be – er – well – you'll think of something.

**BATES:**
Yes milord, but ...

**RUSTLESS:**
And tell you what – we'll get all the stags' heads and big-game trophies out of the gun-room and dot them about in the grounds – people won't go too near them – stands to reason. *(Badger enters)* Ah, there you are, Badger – you're going to be a lion, old thing.

**BADGER:**
A lion milord?

**RUSTLESS:**
Yes – we're all dressing up as animals – got to get this Safari idea off the ground. Give the customers what they want.

**BADGER:**
But what about dinner, milord? I'm supposed to officiate as head waiter.

**RUSTLESS:**
Well, you'll just have to pop in and out – do the best you can. I know it's not exactly going to be a picnic, but it's all hands to the pump when duty calls.

**BADGER:**
Very good milord.

**RUSTLESS:**
Oh, and Badger – try and record some animal noises off the radio – we'll stick the tape recorder in the grounds to add atmosphere. Better still – I've got some Percy Edwards records upstairs – tape those – save a lot of trouble.

**BATES:**
Don't forget there's Effie 'n Cook, milord.

**RUSTLESS:**
Bates, please! Kindly watch your language.

**BATES:**
No, Effie and Cook, milord.

**RUSTLESS:**
Oh, sorry, thought it wasn't like you Bates. Well, now Effie – don't know. Giraffes about the nearest. Those legs. Amazing. They go right up one side and down the other.

**RUSTLESS:**
I should imagine a giraffe costume would be rather difficult to cope with milord – especially whilst making beds.

**RUSTLESS:**
True, true.

**BATES:**
How about an ostrich, milord?

They've got long legs.

**RUSTLESS:**
Good idea, Bates. She'd look damn good with her head stuck in the sand. And cook, milord?

**RUSTLESS:**
Yes. On reflection, I don't think we'd better put Cook into an animal skin. In her present mood, she's liable to bite somebody, and then we'd have to have her shot. I say, that's a damn good idea!

**BATES:**
Milord!

**RUSTLESS:**
Only joking, Bates old chap. I'm not that desperate. No, she'll have her hands full turning out the parrot pie and the moose.

**BATES:**
Oh, goody – I love mousse. Is it orange or chocolate milord?

**RUSTLESS:**
Neither. It's brown, with big furry antlers. Now come on, you two – don't stand about! Get weaving. Bates, on the phone to the costumiers ... I want those things here by the early train tomorrow. Badger – help Dithers with the stags heads and the stuffed birds. By this time tomorrow, this place is going to make London Zoo look like a pet-shop!

*(Fade out.)*

*(Fade in.)*

*(The hall, as before, next morning. Rustless is standing beside a bowl of goldfish.)*

**RUSTLESS:**
Hup! *(He holds a pencil over the bowl.)* Hup! Jump! Come on, damn you, over the pencil. *(He blows a whistle)* hup! *(Dithers enters, dressed in the full gorilla costume, mask and all – but with his pill-box hat on.)*

**RUSTLESS:**
*(noticing him)* Ah, Dithers. Morning. Have those costumes arrived yet?

**DITHERS:**
Eh?

**RUSTLESS:**
Oh, yes, I see they have. Sorry – it was the hat that fooled me. Are the others dressed up yet?

**DITHERS:**
Ar – just coming.

**RUSTLESS:**
Ah, splendid. Know anything about training goldfish, Dithers?

**DITHERS:**
Ar.

**RUSTLESS:**
Oh, you do?

**DITHERS:**
Ar. Can't be done.

**RUSTLESS:**
Nonsense, man. They do it with dolphins. Here, have a go with this pencil, there's a good chap. Get 'em to jump over it. It's only a question of patience.

*(Badger enters, dressed as lion – a very realistic head.)*

**RUSTLESS:**
I say, Badger, that's magnificent! It is Badger, isn't it? *(Badger nods.)*

**RUSTLESS:**
Splendid. Now – *(he hears someone approaching)* Look out – someone coming. Hide!

*(Dithers grabs a newspaper and sits in an armchair – we can still see his hairy legs and hands. Badger stands behind a piece of furniture – possibly a cupboard of some sort – so that only the lion's head is showing. The old lady enters.)*

**RUSTLESS:**
Ah – morning Mrs Ringer.

**OLD LADY:**
Good morning. I'd like some coffee, please.

**RUSTLESS:**
Certainly. *(Picks up internal phone)* Coffee for Mrs Ringer, please.

*(The old lady notices Badger's head.)*

**OLD LADY:**
Is that a new head you've got there, milord?

**RUSTLESS:**
Er – no, no, same old one. I'm afraid I haven't shaved this morning.

**OLD LADY:**
The lion's head, there.

**RUSTLESS:**
*(Looking round, and jumping slightly as he sees where Badger is hiding.)* Oh, oh, that, yes, bit of extra colour. *(He pretends to be writing in a ledger.)*

**OLD LADY:**
*(seeing Dithers)* Who – who is that?

**RUSTLESS:**
Er – *(confidentially)* New guest.

**OLD LADY:**
*(staring at Dither's legs – he is wearing plimsolls)* Is he Italian?

**RUSTLESS:**
Yes, he is.

**OLD LADY:**
They're very hairy, the Italians, aren't they?

**RUSTLESS:**
Quite. Matter of fact, he's over here for the British Hairy Legs contest. He's European Champion. I wonder if you'd mind having your coffee in your room – it – er –

gives him hayfever.

**OLD LADY:**
Really?

**RUSTLESS:**
Yes. Never touches the stuff. Drinks nothing but hair-restorer. He's got an enormous villa in Italy, crammed with the stuff.

**OLD LADY:**
Oh? *(going)* I should imagine he's a count.

**RUSTLESS:**
Oh, I'm sure of it. *(She has gone.)* Good grief, that was a narrow squeak. Now, come on, out of here as quick as you like.

*(Bates and Effie enter. Bates is in a fancy dress white rabbit skin with her face showing through, and Effie in a showgirl's costume, covered in pink ostrich feathers, very low-cut.)*

**BATES:**
Here we are, milord.

**RUSTLESS:**
Great balls of fire, Bates, what in Hell's name are you doing in that lot?

**BATES:**
I thought I'd be a bunny, milord.

**RUSTLESS:**
Yes, but my dear old chap, that's not going to fool anybody, is it?

**BATES:**
I thought I could stand a very long way away milord.

**RUSTLESS:**
What, Aberdeen, somewhere like that? No, no, won't do at all. Best thing you can do is keep backing out of the bushes – people might think you're a polar bear. *(Looking at Effie)* And what have you come as, my dear?

**BATES:**
Oh, yes, I'm afraid the costumiers have

made an enormous boob with Effie's rig out.

**RUSTLESS:**
So I see.

**BATES:**
I did ask for an ostrich costume with lots of feathers, and that's what they sent.

**RUSTLESS:**
Yes. Never mind – you can wear it tonight in the dining room – should liven up dinner a little. Right, now buzz off the lot of you, before anybody sees you. Badger, you take the car, drop Dithers and Bates off in the spinney, and then get back here and prowl around the lower lawn. See you at dinner – and good luck!

*(They go out, chattering. Rustless goes to goldfish bowl again, on the desk.)*

**RUSTLESS:**
Hup! Hup! *(He waves his pencil. The old lady returns.)*

**OLD LADY:**
Were you addressing me?

**RUSTLESS:**
*(covering up)* No, I was addressing this envelope. *(He writes on envelope.)*

*(A middle-aged couple enter, with their daughter – a daft-looking plain girl of about twenty.)*

**RUSTLESS:**
Ah! Welcome! Welcome to the New and Improved Safari Park. You couldn't have come at a better time. I promise you – you've never seen animals like we've got here! *(He pushes over the register, happily.)*

Cut to: film.

*(Rustless and the three guests outside the hotel – Rustless points – they get in car and drive off. Rustless, in closeup, waves them off.)*

*(Rolls Royce stops on road near spinney –*

*Bates and Dithers get out, and go off into the bushes. Badger, still in lion's head, etc. Drives on.)*

*(The guests, driving along. A shot, inside the car, pointing at something they see.)*

*(Car's point of view – various stags' heads, in a row, peering round trees. The last one is a skeleton only – no fur. Reaction on the mother and daughter, in the back seat.)*

*(Close up father, driving. He looks to his right. His eyes widen in surprise.)*

*(Point of view (his), Badger (looking like a lion) slowly overtakes in the Rolls Royce.)*

*(Close up. Reaction again from father – he swerves.)*

*(Long shot – from behind cars. Guests' car goes completely off the road, into the bushes, hitting a tree.)*

*(Close up. A large stuffed vulture on the branch of the tree. The bird swings round and hangs upside down.)*

*(Close up. Father getting out of car, dazed.)*

*(Bird drops onto father from above. Mum and daughter get out of car, shaken.)*

*(Medium long shot. Bushes by roadside. Bates, in her white rabbit skin, backs out of bushes, a close up of this. She waits a few seconds, then goes back in again. Then her head peeps out, looks round – sighs – goes back in. Her rear end reappears.)*

*(A small wooden shed, with "gents" and "ladies" notices on. Dithers, in close up, looking round. He goes into "gents". A man comes along, goes into "gents". He immediately rushes out again, in long shot, and runs over near the bushes, close up looking round – no? one about . He goes into bushes, in long shot. We hear elephant's roar (tape recorder) very loud – the man rushes out again, and into the "ladies". In the same shot, three women rush out of the "ladies", and*

*round the corner behind the shed. The gorilla comes out of the "gents" and walks past the "ladies" and round the corner. Immediately we hear screams, and the three women appear on the opposite side, and rush into the "gents". The tape recorder says – "and now for another of my favourites – the sheep". The man appears sheepishly from the "ladies", and the women appear sheepishly from the "gents". As Percy Edwards imitates a flock of sheep, they cross each other, and return to their respective loos.)*

*(An old car – a young couple sitting near the rear wheel, on the grass, eating sandwiches. Bates, rear appears from the bushes, the young couple don't notice it.)*

*(The family – dad, mum and daughter – walking along in the grounds – they see a sign saying "cafeteria". The front of the cafeteria – a huge rhino's head on the door. Two of the women from the "loo" sequence are approaching it. Shot of the family approaching the side of cafeteria. At the front, the woman opens the door. At the side, the family see what appears to be a rhino looking round the corner. They stop, petrified. The rhino backs off, as the women go into the cafe and shut the door. The family approach, cautiously. The front door again – the third woman opens the door. The side – the rhino suddenly appears again, somewhat faster than the last time. The family drop everything and run.)*

*(Bates's rear end again. Pull out, to reveal young couple getting up, and getting into the car. C/u of exhaust pipe, as car revs up. Black smoke and soot shoot out. The car roars off. C/u Bates rear end – a large black circle of soot on it.)*

*Cut to: a small corner of the dining room.*

*(The old lady is being served by Badger, now in waiter's uniform)*

**OLD LADY:**
*(with menu)* "Fillet of Mountain Lion"? What's that like?

**BADGER:**
Rather like steak, Madam.

**OLD LADY:**
Oh good, well I'll have that.

**BADGER:**
Certainly, Madam. You'll enjoy it. I eat an awful lot of it myself.

**OLD LADY:**
Oh?

*(Badger turns, and walks out of shot. His lion's tail is sticking out from underneath his coat. The old lady reacts.)*

*Cut to: the lounge hall.*

*(Rustless is talking to a man in a raincoat and bowler hat.)*

**MAN:**
I'm sorry, your Lordship – but that's the law, when these sort of outbreaks arise.

**RUSTLESS:**
Yes, but I mean to say – six weeks quarantine! I'm trying to run an hotel here. I can't afford to lock the doors for six weeks.

**MAN:**
I know how you feel sir, but there's nothing I can do about it. Hard-pad is hard-pad.

**RUSTLESS:**
It may be Hard-pad to you, but it's bloody hard luck for me, isn't it?

**MAN:**
Well, I'll send you the necessary forms to fill up. Oh, I take it you've got licences for all these animals – gorilla, lions, bear, ostrich, et cetera?

**RUSTLESS:**
*(lying)* Er – naturally – about the place somewhere.

**MAN:**
Good. Otherwise we have to shoot them. Well, I'll be off. Happy Hunting! *(He goes.)*

**RUSTLESS:**
And the same to you! *(to himself)* Damned Hard-pad. *(Goes to door leading to rest of hotel.)* All right, you can come out!

*(Bates, Dithers, Badger and Effie come out.)*

**BATES:**
Has he gone, milord?

**RUSTLESS:**
Yes – and we're all in quarantine for the next six weeks.

**BATES:**
Quarantine?

**RUSTLESS:**
Quarantine, Bates. Confined to Barracks. Jankers – spell in the Glass House. There's an outbreak of Hard-pad. Think yourself lucky you weren't all shot. Get those skins packed off to the costumiers, Bates, we'll forget the whole idea. We'll have to think up some other gimmick. Let's face it, we've got six weeks. *(Feels in his coat pocket, brings out handful of mothballs.)* Good grief, no wonder I reek of mothballs! I remember now – I won these off Sergeant Major Pickett in a game of marbles in 1937. They've been in there ever since. Mind you, they were a lot bigger then. Seem to have shrunk. Bally moths have been at 'em I suppose. Anyone care for a game, wile away a bit of time?

*(General murmurs of "no thank you" from the rest.)*

Well, in that case I'll wish you goodnight.

**BATES:**
Where are you going, milord?

**RUSTLESS:**
This morning Miss Ringer invited me to a couple of hands of Old Maid in her bedroom. I don't know the game myself, but it sounds a damned sight more interesting than marbles! Goodnight! *(He goes.)*

# EPISODE THREE:

*"Brightly Dawns our Wedding Day"*

*Scene: the hall. Rustless is on the phone.*

**RUSTLESS:**
What? Yes, it is marvellous to hear your voice again – must be weeks since I've spoken to you, old dear. Twelve years, is it? My goodness, doesn't time fly. Yes, of course I remember you. You're my sister. Harriet, isn't it? Yes. Oh, of course, yes, you went to Australia, that's right. I must say, I can hear you perfectly – you might be in the next village. Oh, you are in the next village. Well, good grief, you must come on over. You still married? Oh, sorry to hear that. Nine years ago. Poor old Jack. Jim. Yes. I meant Jim. What did he die of? Nothing serious, I hope, Cold eggs? Oh, old age. Yes. Well, there's a lot of it about. Yes. What? ... Oh, I see ... Yes, yes, sort of hotel, now – saves giving the place to the National Trust ... What? Your daughter? Yes, damn good idea. Who's she marrying? Some man. Mm. Yes, I'd be delighted. We can fit you all in somewhere. Have to have a word with Miss Bates, of course – a lot of extra work. Haven't had a wedding in the house since 1948. Poor old Freddie married that old Countess for her money, you remember? Terrible tragedy. Old Freddie's still terribly cut up about it, you know, Why? Damn woman's still alive, that's why. Can't seem to shake her off. *(Bates enters.)* *(Seeing Bates)* Well, must ring off – see you Friday sometime, then. Wonderful. 'Bye. Yes, leave it to me. Look forward to it. 'Bye bye. *(Replaces phone.)*

**BATES:**
You haven't seen Mr Dithers anywhere,

have you, milord? He promised to have a look at Mrs Ringer's overflow pipe.

**RUSTLESS:**
Really?

**BATES:**
She thinks the birds must have been nesting in it.

**RUSTLESS:**
Yes. Could be nasty. Last time I saw him was very early on, hoovering the bowling green. Takes a great pride in that bowling green, old Dithers.

**BATES:**
Yes – I'll go and see if he's still there.

**RUSTLESS:**
No No, Bates. I've got something more important to talk about. Sit down a minute, old thing.

**BATES:**
Oh. Very good, milord. *(she does so)*

**RUSTLESS:**
Now. What would you say if I were to say "Wedding" to you?

**BATES:**
*(taken aback slightly)* Wedding, milord?

**RUSTLESS:**
Wedding, Bates. The marriage of twin souls. Two hearts intertwined, that beat as one. Cake, confetti, telegrams, and old boots. How does that strike you?

**BATES:**
Oh, milord! Well – I never expected – I mean, it's so unexpected.

**RUSTLESS:**
Yes. I expect it is. It's only what one would expect. Never mind – think about it.

**BATES:**
You mean you want me to ...

**RUSTLESS:**
Have a brood, Bates, have a brood.

**BATES:**
You mean – babies, milord?

**RUSTLESS:**
Babies? Who said anything about babies? No, no, that would be jumping the gun a bit, old fruit. No, the point is, do you think you could cope with a wedding, and reception, and all that? Or would you rather delay it? I mean, I don't mind whether we have the wedding or not, if it's going to be too tiring for you. I mean, you're the one that's going to have to bear the brunt.

**BATES:**
*(quickly)* Oh, no, no milord. I think one should get married. Otherwise it wouldn't be – well, I don't think I could.

**RUSTLESS:**
Oh, she's definitely getting married, Bates – it's just a question of where.

**BATES:**
*(confused)* Who, milord?

**RUSTLESS:**
My niece. My sister thought it would be a damn good idea to have a wedding here, but naturally I said I'd have to ask you first. Quite a lot of work involved.

**BATES:**
*(embarrassed now)* Oh, I see, milord.

**RUSTLESS:**
Anyway, as I say, have a think about it.

**BATES:**
No, I think it would be a lovely idea.

**RUSTLESS:**
Oh, you do? I didn't think you seemed too sure about it.

**BATES:**
I'm sorry, milord, I got a bit confused. I understand now.

*(Tearfully)* Yes, I'm sure we can cope.

*(Badger enters)*

**BATES:**
*(starting to leave)* It will be nice. I shall look forward to it. *(Sobbing)* I love weddings! *(She rushes out.)*

**BADGER:**
Is Miss Bates all right, milord?

**RUSTLESS:**
What? Yes, she's fine, Badger. Funny how women get all emotional about weddings, isn't it? Anyone would think it was her own. Ha, ha. *(The phone rings.)* Answer that, would you, Badger. I've been trying to stick stamps on these blasted letters all morning. *(Picks up letters.)*

**BADGER:**
Certainly, milord. *(Into phone)* Hallo? Chrome Hall Hotel. Yes, Madame – Saturday? For how many?

**RUSTLESS:**
*(licking stamps)* We're fully booked.

**BADGER:**
I beg your pardon, milord?

**RUSTLESS:**
*(a stamp on his tongue)* We've got a wedding party. New booking. All rooms to be held in readiness. I'll tell you all about it in a minute. *(Stamp is now too wet to stick.)* Oh God! That's another three pee up the spout. *(Throws it away.)*

*(Fade out.)*

*(Fade in.)*

*(The hall: Friday afternoon.)*

*(Effie, the maid, is serving afternoon tea to the old lady guest who is sitting with the man with the hearing aid.)*

**OLD LADY:**
Thank you, my dear. Lovely. And I wonder if you could oblige Mr Williamson with one of your doughnuts? He had his eye on them at coffee time, but you moved away before he could get his hands on one.

*(Effie speaks, inaudibly, as usual, to Mr Williamson.)*

**WILLIAMSON:**
*(tapping hearing aid, stonily)* Damn batteries gone again. *(Twiddles with it, it emits loud high pitched squeak.)* What's she say?

**OLD LADY:**
I can't hear. Your thing's squeaking.

**WILL:**
What?

**OLD LADY:**
Your thing's squeaking!

*(Rustless enters.)*

**RUSTLESS:**
What the devil's going on? Sounds like a cat fight.

**OLD LADY:**
It's Mr Williamson. His equipment's falling to pieces. He'll have to go in for a service. *(To Effie)* Tell you what, just bring him a Danish pastry for the moment, he can make do with that.

**RUSTLESS:**
Mm – probably just as effective. How are the arrangements going for the wedding tomorrow, Effie old thing?

*(Effie speaks.)*

**RUSTLESS:**
Have you? Good. So they're all ship-shape and Bristol fashion, are they?

*(Effie speaks.)*

**RUSTLESS:**
Quite. Ever thought of getting married yourself?

*(Effie speaks.)*

**RUSTLESS:**
Oh did you. Pity. What sort of chap was he? A jockey – oh yes. Tried to what? Did he, by jove. What happened? Fell off the box, and got two black eyes. Yes, well he would; I mean to say, it sticks out a mile. Still, you haven't given up the idea, what?

*(Effie speaks, smiling.)*

**RUSTLESS:**
What? Putting things in your what?

*(Effie speaks.)*

**RUSTLESS:**
Oh, your bottom drawer. Yes – well, at least you've got something to fall back on. Right. Well, you'd better cut along Effie, there must be a lot to do. Take a deep breath, and keep it up!

*(Effie goes.)*

**RUSTLESS:**
*(to old lady)* How's your waterworks, by the way?

**OLD LADY:**
*(surprised)* Pardon?

**RUSTLESS:**
Has Dithers fixed your overflow yet?

**OLD LADY:**
Oh. Oh, no – I haven't seen him today.

*(Dithers enters, with large bird's nest.)*

**RUSTLESS:**
Ah, Dithers. Just talking about you. Where the devil have you been?

**DITHERS:**
Clearing out her guttering. The old crow's.

**RUSTLESS:**
What?

**DITHERS:**
Crow's nest. Bunging up the gutter.

**RUSTLESS:**
Oh I see. I say that's jolly interesting. My brother spent the war in one of those. You might take that down to Cook, she could make some soup out of it.

**DITHERS:**
No – that's the wrong sort. Can't make soup outta that.

**RUSTLESS:**
Nonsense. Since she's had that new liquidiser, she can make soup out of everything. Which reminds me, my tartan plus-fours have disappeared. I must have a word with her about those.

**DITHERS:**
You reckon she's liquidised them?

**RUSTLESS:**
I wouldn't put it past her. In any event, I shall keep an eye on the soup menu. If Cock-a-leekie comes up, she's for it.

*(The doors open and the wedding party arrives. Harriet, the mother – a large, county, horsey woman; Janet, her daughter, a pretty girl, about twenty; two bridesmaids fairly plain, about seventeen, one is large, the other small.)*

**MOTHER:**
Bonzo!

**RUSTLESS:**
Harriet, my dear old thing! How are you?

**MOTHER:**
Tophole, old sport. Frightful journey in that old banger that passes for a taxicab, but made it. This is my daughter, Janet – this is your Uncle Bonzo –

**RUSTLESS:**
How are you, my dear?

**MOTHER:**
Millicent and Alison – bridesmaids – the

groom's coming on later. He's up in town. *(Rustless is shaking hands. Dithers is hovering.)* Well! Saved us some decent rooms, I hope. What's the golf like here? Not that there'll be any time for that. Tea. Must have some tea. Gasping. Tea, girls?

**BRIDESMAIDS:**
*(mutter)* Yes.

**MOTHER:**
Fine. *(She removes her hat, places it on desk.)*

**RUSTLESS:**
Tea all round?

**MOTHER:**
Splendid. Must pay a call. Shan't be a jiffy. Which way, Bonzo?

**RUSTLESS:**
*(indicating)* Through there, old fruit.

**MOTHER:**
Fine. Wonderful to see you. See you in a minute. Coming, Janet? *(She sweeps out and Janet follows her.)*

**RUSTLESS:**
Right – Dithers – go and order tea for four, and then come back and show these young ladies to their rooms. No doubt they've all got bags they want to get rid of.

**DITHERS:**
Ar. *(He eyes the girls – then trots off.)*

**RUSTLESS:**
Well, nice to see you. Been to this part of the world before, have you?

**MILLICENT:**
No.

**ALISON:**
No.

**RUSTLESS:**
Oh, you'll like it. Pretty, isn't it?

**MILLICENT:**
Yes.

**ALISON:**
Yes.

**RUSTLESS:**
Mmm. Dashed pretty, round here. D'you play golf?

**MILLICENT:**
No.

**ALISON:**
No.

**RUSTLESS:**
Oh. Pity. Of course, golfers like it round here, because of the golf.

**MILLICENT:**
Yes.

**ALISON:**
Yes.

**RUSTLESS:**
Yes. Bit young for golf, I suppose. Ever thought of taking it up?

**MILLICENT:**
No.

**ALISON:**
No.

**RUSTLESS:**
No. No, well, if you don't play, you don't, and there's no point in talking about it – that's it.

**MILLICENT:**
No.

**ALISON:**
Yes.

**RUSTLESS:**
What? Er, sorry – didn't mean to start an argument about it. Perhaps I shouldn't have brought it up – always was a controversial subject.

*(Mother and Janet return)*

**MOTHER:**
Here we are again – getting on all right, are you?

**RUSTLESS:**
Yes – splendid. Just been having a chat about golf. Most informative.
*(Dithers has returned.)* Ah, there you are, Dithers. Perhaps you'd like to see your rooms?

**MOTHER:**
Right. We'll dump our stuff, have a sort out, and come down for that teaming dish of tea. Come on, girls. *(To Dithers)* You'd better carry the large one – got a bit of a bashing on the boat coming over.

**DITHERS:**
Righto. *(Attempts to pick up Millie, who squeaks.)*

**RUSTLESS:**
The suitcase, you old idiot!

**DITHERS:**
Oh, Ar. Beg pardon, Miss. *(Slaps her on the behind, good-naturedly and goes to pick up large suitcase.)*

**MOTHER:**
Be careful with it, it's got my wedding present in it.

**DITHERS:**
*(attempting to lift the case)* Lor! What you giving 'em, potatoes? *(He struggles off, followed by the women, all chattering.)*

*(Rustless notices mother's hat and picks it up.)*

**RUSTLESS:**
Dithers! You old ... *(but Dithers has gone)* Damned old fool. Leaving his birds' nests all over the hotel. *(He opens window, and slings the hat out.)*

*(Badger enters.)*

**RUSTLESS:**
Hello Badger – thought it was your half-day.

**BADGER:**
I'm just off, milord – er, Cook required a word.

**RUSTLESS:**
She certainly does. And I've just thought of a good one. Was going to use it on Dithers, but he'd gone. Where is she?

**BADGER:**
She's walking round from the kitchen, milord, through the garden.

*(Cook enters. She is wearing the hat which Rustless has just thrown out of the window.)*

**COOK:**
Oi!

**RUSTLESS:**
Ah, there you are, Cook. Why are you wearing that bird's nest?

**COOK:**
It's a hat. Just found it in the garden.

**RUSTLESS:**
I've just chucked it out of the window, man. It's a bird's nest.

**COOK:**
First bird's nest I've seen with a shot-silk lining. Anyway, I'm keeping it.

**BADGER:**
*(noticing birds next on a nearby table)* There's a bird's nest here, milord.

**RUSTLESS:**
Good grief – hang on. That must be Harriet's hat. Hand it over at once, Cook.

**COOK:**
Oh no. Finders keepers, losers weepers. It'll just do me a treat.

**RUSTLESS:**
My sister Harriet will do you a treat if she sees you wearing that. Come on.

**COOK:**
*(taking it off and slapping it on the counter)*

Well, tell her not to go dropping her garments in the garden – putting temptation in people's way, that is.

**RUSTLESS:**
Shut up. Why were you wandering about in the garden, anyway?

**COOK:**
I've got floury boots.

**RUSTLESS:**
Really? What were you doing, planting them out?

**COOK:**
*(to Badger)* He's a screw loose, if you ask me.

**RUSTLESS:**
No one's asking you, Cook. Now what do you want? Come on, state your case, and push off. Stand up, speak up, and shup up. Preferably in that order.

**COOK:**
It's this here wedding. Is it going to be sit down knife and fork, or standing up in your fingers?

**RUSTLESS:**
What? What the hell's she talking about, Badger?

**BADGER:**
Cook means is it to be a meal, or just a running buffet, milord.

**RUSTLESS:**
Oh. What do you think, Badger?

**BADGER:**
I think a proper breakfast is best, milord.

**RUSTLESS:**
Right, that's what we'll have. Let's see now – Bacon, sausages, eggs, kippers, toast and marmalade, coffee, tea, brandy; and plenty of toast.

**BADGER:**
With respect, milord – one wouldn't have

all that at a wedding-breakfast!

**RUSTLESS:**
Why ever not? Damned good breakfast, that. Sets you up for the day.

**BADGER:**
Yes milord, but this is in the evening.

**RUSTLESS:**
Breakfast in the evening? Whatever for? Are they going to be on night-work, or something?

**COOK:**
Well, you said it.

**BADGER:**
Perhaps it would be better, milord, if I took Cook away and sorted out the details. Come along Cook.

**RUSTLESS:**
Yes, damned good idea. Leave it to you entirely, Badger.

**COOK:**
What about the cake?

**RUSTLESS:**
Cake? For breakfast?

**BADGER:**
It's traditional, milord.

**RUSTLESS:**
Oh well, you know best. Off you go, the pair of you.

**COOK:**
Do you want it made in tiers?

**RUSTLESS:**
Look, damn it all, Cook. I don't give a monkey's raspberry whether you cry your eyes out or laugh your head off, just whizz off!

**COOK:**
He's round the twist!

*(She exits, followed by Badger, who is explaining as they go.)*

*(Rustless picks up the bird's nest – is about to throw it out of the open window, when the phone rings. He answers it, putting the nest down.)*

**RUSTLESS:**
Hello, are you there? Yes, this is me here, Rustless. Chrome Parva 3.6. Wrong number? No, no it's always been that. Must be at your end. Yes, don't mention it – nice to see you. 'Bye. *(To himself)* Now then, where was I? Oh yes. *(He picks up the hat, and throws it out of the window. Bates enters.)*

**RUSTLESS:**
Ah, Bates. *(Handing her the bird's nest)* I say, be a good chap and take this up to my sister Harriet's room, would you? She's probably worried about it.

**BATES:**
*(puzzled)* Very good, milord.

*(A young man enters – longish hair, about twenty-three.)*

**RUSTLESS:**
Good afternoon.

**YOUNG MAN:**
Good afternoon. Miss Janet Trevelyan, please?

**RUSTLESS:**
Ah, of course. Welcome. They're all here – upstairs, sorting themselves out. They'll be down in a tick.

**YOUNG MAN:**
I must see her at once, if possible. Er – alone.

**RUSTLESS:**
Yes – know how you feel. Was young meself, once. Look, I've put you in room sixteen – next to hers. So why not pop up and give her a knock?

**YOUNG MAN:**
Thanks – thanks very much – which way?

**RUSTLESS:**
Straight through. *(Indicates.)*

**YOUNG MAN:**
Thanks. *(He goes.)*

**RUSTLESS:**
Seems a nice enough chap. Bit eager, isn't he?

**BATES:**
I suppose on the day before his wedding he's entitled to be, milord.

**RUSTLESS:**
Oh, that reminds me – Badger has decided we're having breakfast instead of dinner tomorrow evening. He's just sorting Cook out at the moment.

**BATES:**
Yes – I met them on the way to the kitchen, milord.

**RUSTLESS:**
Good. You know, all that talk of food's made me feel quite peckish. Hold the fort here, Bates – I'm just going to see if Effie's got anything I can have a nibble at. *(He goes.)*

*(Bates stares at the bird's nest in her hand and puts it on the counter again. Starts to copy out bills into a ledger. A young man (Harcourt-Brown) enters – very grand and toffee nosed. He approaches the counter.)*

**HARCOURT-BROWN:**
*(pinging the bell)* A little service, please.

**BATES:**
*(looking up from ledger)* One moment, please.

**HARCOURT-BROWN:**
No moments, just a little attention, please. This is an hotel, isn't it?

**BATES:**
(*bristling rather*) This is Chrome Hall Hotel, yes sir.

**HARCOURT-BROWN:**
Good. Harcourt-Brown. I'd like my room number, key, and a porter. You won't be too long, will you, because I'm rather tired.

**BATES:**
Are you registered here, sir?

**HARCOURT-BROWN:**
Not yet, because you haven't given me the register to sign, but I presume you will, in the fullness of time.

**BATES:**
(*now very icy*) I'm afraid we are fully booked sir.

**HARCOURT-BROWN:**
Fully booked? This place, at this time of year?

**BATES:**
Yes sir.

**HARCOURT-BROWN:**
Rubbish. If you're fully booked, I'm a Dutchman.

**BATES:**
(*In Dutch tells him they are fully booked.*)

**HARCOURT-BROWN:**
What? What on earth's that?

**BATES:**
I'm sorry – you did say you were Dutch, sir? Perhaps my accent wasn't very good. I was explaining that we've no rooms. We are full.

**HARCOURT-BROWN:**
I think you will find that Mrs Trevelyan has reserved me a single room. If she hasn't I'll murder the old bitch. Dammit, I'm getting married from here tomorrow.

**BATES:**
(*amazed*) What?

(*Rustless enters, unseen by the others.*)

**HARCOURT-BROWN:**
God knows why – I could think of a few slightly more trendy places in which to tie the millstone. What a dump.

**BATES:**
You mean you're ...

**HARCOURT-BROWN:**
Look, I'm the groom, my good woman, so kindly uncross your legs and nip about a bit, would you. I need a bath.

(*Rustless approaches – Harcourt-Brown spots him.*)

**HARCOURT-BROWN:**
I say, porter! (*Rustless reacts.*) Take these cases upstairs would you.

**RUSTLESS:**
May I have the privilege of knowing who the hell you are sir?

**BATES:**
This is Lord Rustless, owner of the hotel.

**HARCOURT-BROWN:**
Oh – my mistake. How are you, old chap.

**RUSTLESS:**
Old enough to resent being called a porter in my own house by a chap with plastic luggage. (*Presses a buzzer on the desk.*)

**HARCOURT-BROWN:**
I say! Got out of the wrong side of the bed this morning, did we?

**RUSTLESS:**
My sleeping arrangements are entirely my own affair. Whether I choose to leave my bed in an Easterly or Westerly direction; cut my toenails on a Friday, or wear a bowler-hat in the shower is no concern of yours. Your room number is eleven. Dinner is at seven-thirty. (*Dithers enters.*)

No dogs in the lounge, and no biscuits in the bedrooms. And here is a man even older than me, to deal with your luggage. Now if you will excuse me, I have to go and clear out a drain. And I must say, I'm quite looking forward to it.

*(He stalks out, leaving Dithers and Harcourt-Brown to go off with the luggage. A close-up of Bates – proud of her beloved old earl.)*

*(Fade out.)*

*(Fade in.)*

*Scene – the tiny office adjoining the lounge hall. Bates, talking to Badger. He wears a raincoat and a trilby hat, which he hangs up on a coat rack.*

**BATES:**
So his Lordship really tore him off a most frightful strip. I wish you'd been here to see it. It was marvellous.

**BADGER:**
It seems I've been missing all the fun, Miss Bates.

**BATES:**
Oh, but he really is a most objectionable young man. And to think he's marrying that pretty young thing tomorrow. It's awful.

**BADGER:**
I haven't come into contact with any of the party yet.

**BATES:**
Oh, he's dreadful. The things he was doing with the bread rolls at dinner was nobody's business.

**BADGER:**
How do you mean, Miss Bates?

**BATES:**
Oh, I couldn't possibly go into details, Mr Badger, it's just that ... *(She stops, hearing a noise from the lounge ... )* I'll tell you later.

*(She goes through into the lounge. Mrs Trevelyan, the mother, is in there, smoking a cigar.)*

**MOTHER:**
Hello there!

**BATES:**
Good evening, Mrs Trevelyan. I trust you had a pleasant dinner.

**MOTHER:**
Very good. Though I thought my daughter's "intended" was behaving rather outrageously. God knows why she's marrying him at all. Extraordinary chap.

**BATES:**
As a matter of fact, we were just saying ... *(She decided perhaps she ought not to voice her thoughts ... )* We were just, er, saying we hadn't seen his Lordship *(Rustless enters.)* Oh, milord, I was just saying that we were just – saying ... Anyway, here you are.

**RUSTLESS:**
Quite. Well, Harriet, old socks? All set for tomorrow?

**MOTHER:**
Almost, Bonzo – one thing. Want you to give the bride away.

**RUSTLESS:**
Me?

**MOTHER:**
Why not. Nothing to it. Got a morning-suit?

**RUSTLESS:**
Certainly.

**MOTHER:**
Is it decent?

**RUSTLESS:**
Course it's decent. Damn good suit that. Worn it at three Coronations. Would have been four – had it cleaned and pressed all day for Edward the Eighth, but he backed down. I sent the cleaning bill to the

Duchess of Windsor, but she didn't reply.

**MOTHER:**
Good for you. Right. You game?

**RUSTLESS:**
Why not? I'll have a bash. I – er – hate to say this, Harriet old boots, but I wonder if you would excuse us for a minute or so – business, you understand. Why not stroll along to the billiard room? I'll be along in a few minutes, give you a quick three-hundred up.

**MOTHER:**
Splendid. Which way is it?

**RUSTLESS:**
Turn left outside, and keep heading north. *(She goes.)*

**RUSTLESS:**
*(as soon as she has gone)* Listen, Bates – Old Badger back yet?

**BATES:**
He's in the office, milord. *(Calling)* Mr Badger! *(Badger appears.)*

**BADGER:**
Good evening, milord.

**RUSTLESS:**
Hello, Badger. Enjoy the pictures?

**BADGER:**
It was a concert, milord. Stravinsky's *Rites of Spring*.

**RUSTLESS:**
Oh yes. Damn good, that. I think I've read the book. Now listen chaps – just been having a word with that young fellow-me-lad.

**BATES:**
The groom, milord?

**RUSTLESS:**
No, dammit, not that idiot – the other young fellow with the long hair. Nipped up to see the bride, in her room, and he

was in there. They were having a quiet game of Scrabble on the bed. Now, the point is this; after a lengthy chat with the two of them, I'm convinced that she doesn't want to marry the groom at all. It's this other young chap, Robin, she's really stuck on.

**BATES:**
Then whyever is she marrying the awful one?

**RUSTLESS:**
Ah. Well apparently, Robin's been a bit reticent about getting married – so she eventually got fed up, had a row with him, and took up with this other twirp, sort of on the recoil.

**BADGER:**
Rebound, milord.

**RUSTLESS:**
Yes – well I don't know the technical terms, but anyway, I think she's beginning to regret tomorrow already.

**BADGER:**
But she's going through with it

**RUSTLESS:**
Oh, she'll go through with it alright. Her mother will see to that. If the wedding fell through now, she'd never be able to hold up her head in Harrods again.

**BATES**
Oh dear. What a mess. Poor thing. What about the young man – Robin?

**RUSTLESS:**
I've told him to lie low in his room. Don't want the others to spot him – only make matters worse.

**BATES:**
Is it any good you saying anything to Mrs Trevelyan? As far as I could see, she's of the same opinion – that the groom is an awful bore.

**RUSTLESS:**
I know – but I also know my sister – the wedding must take place.

**BATES:**
Well, I think it's rotten.

**RUSTLESS:**
So do I, Bates old chap – so do I. As a matter of fact, I've got ideas about a way in which we might be able to put our spoke in – a few precautions we could take. Tell you what, Bates – go and make a large pot of coffee, and bring it back here. And a bottle of brandy. Might as well discuss things in comfort.

**BATES:**
Very good, milord. *(At door)* What fun! Like a midnight feast in the dorm. I'll bring some bikkies as well. *(She flutters off.)*

**RUSTLESS:**
Sit down, Badger, take the weight off. Now then. First of all – you're a church man – am I right in thinking that the vicar at St. Swithins plays the organ himself?

**BADGER:**
Yes milord – he goes in and has a practice for about an hour before each service. He's a brilliant musician. His recitals are a joy to listen to, milord.

**RUSTLESS:**
Good. I like a nice bit of good loud organ music. I think we'll make a point of getting there nice and early tomorrow, Badger.

*(Fade out.)*

*Cut to: film.*

*(Country road. Rustless and Badger, on bicycles, riding along.)*

*(The church. We hear the organ being played. Rustless and Badger ride into shot.)*

*(Closer shot as they dismount.)*

*(They enter the side door of the church. Close up, as they enter.)*

*(Long shot of the church. Suddenly, the music stops, after a great discord.)*

*(Flight of birds, rising from the trees, as they are scared by the noise.)*

*(Close up – Rustless emerges from side door – looks round. He mounts his bicycle, and pedals off.)*

*(The wedding cars leaving the hotel.)*

*(Close up bride, alone in Rolls Royce as it drives off.)*

*(Rustless approaching camera on bike. Wedding cars pass him.)*

*(Close up – he watches them go past.)*

*(The bride's car passes him – screeches to a halt, Rustless stops.)*

*(Close up – bride leaning out of window, beckoning him. Rustless runs up to car. He beams – throws his bike over the hedge, and approaches the car.)*

*(Shot of hedge where bike landed. A courting couple stand up behind the hedge, annoyed.)*

*(From inside the car – Rustless gets in, pats the bride's hand, as the car drives off.)*

*(The church. One or two locals watching as Rustless and bride get out of car, and go into church. "Here Comes the Bride" is struck up, played very badly, with lots of wrong notes. Locals react. Close up one aged local, amazed at the sound.)*

*(Stills sequence.)*

*(Another shot of church – colour. Fade to black and white.)*

*(Wedding group (we stay in black and white for rest of sequence).)*

*(Another.)*

*(Bride and groom walking down church yard path.)*

*(Another, further down.)*

*(Ditto – (the groom clowning, leaping in the air, camply).)*

*(Another, further down. (The groom flat on his back, sheepish).)*

*(Guests getting into cars.)*

*(Mother getting into car.)*

*(Film – (b & w) Rustless getting into car, with mother's behind in his face. Looks like a still photo but Rustless suddenly turns to camera and reacts (which should be a surprise!))*

*(Still photo of bride waving from car.)*

*(Cut to studio.)*

*(Another black and white still photo – the bride, waving from car, a little further away. Pull back to reveal that it is in Rustless's hand. The scene is the dining room, where the reception is already in progress.)*

**RUSTLESS:**
*(handing photo to photographer)* Yes, they're excellent, old chap. Quick work. Leave the lot, will you?

*(The photographer leaves the pile of photographs, and departs. The tables are in a 'T' shape. Everyone is seated, drinking and chattering. Dithers, now dressed as a waiter, is pouring champagne into the old lady's glass. He also fills a wine glass, and toasts the old lady, clinking glasses.)*

**DITHERS:**
Bottoms up! *(He drains the glass, and moves on.)*

*(Effie is bending over, serving the old lady with starters – her back to Mr Williamson.)*

**OLD LADY:**
Bottoms up, Mr Williamson!

**MR WILLIAMSON:**
*(leans closer to Effie's bottom, without looking)* What's that?

**OLD LADY:**
Bottoms up!

**MR WILLIAMSON:**
*(turns, facing Effie's knickers)* Oh yes, cheers. *(He nods at the knickers, turns away, and drinks. In the middle of the drink, he does a delayed choke on his drink. He looks round – Effie has gone, and the old lady is winking at him. He looks puzzled – he must be imagining things.)*

**BATES:**
*(at the head of the table somewhere)* Ladies and gentlemen! Ladies and gentlemen, could I have your attention please?

*(Mr Williamson turns up his hearing aid, which squeaks loudly.)*

**OLD LADY:**
*(who has had a few)* Oh, for heaven's sake, Mr Williamson!

*(She grabs a soda syphon and squirts the hearing aid into silence. General laughter.)*

**BATES:**
*(as the noise dies down)* Thank you. It is my great pleasure to call upon the Bridegroom to propose a toast to the Bridesmaids – I do hope that's the right way round. *(Applause from guests.)*

**HARCOURT-BROWN:**
*(rising to his feet)* Well, it's not actually, but who cares? A lot of nonsense, anyway, all this speechmaking. All I've got to say is, I hope you're all getting nicely drunk – I'm very pleased that all the fuss and bother is over – never did go much on tradition and all that jazz – and I'm glad Janet, my blushing bride ... was sensible enough to marry someone who's going to look after her, and not throw herself away on some

long-haired layabout without any ambition or business sense. She's a lovely girl, and personally, I can hardly wait. Roll on midnight! Oh – the bridesmaids. *(He raises his glass.)*

**ALL:**
*(rising, rather stunned.)* The Bridesmaids. *(They all drink, and sit. There is an awkward pause.)*

**BATES:**
Er – Pray silence now, for Lord Rustless, who will propose the toast to the bride and groom.

*(Rustless rises, to applause.)*

**RUSTLESS:**
Thank you. Janet – Jeremy – Ladies and gentlemen. The eloquence of the last speaker, has left me somewhat stunned. I am at a loss, very rarely does one hear such deep-rooted, heart-felt sentiments come pouring out from someone so young. He will obviously go far – sooner or later, and, in my opinion, the farther, the better, and, for Janet's sake, the sooner the better as well ... A young man with this sort of charm has the world at his feet, to tread on. He could charm the birds off the trees, and blood out of a stone. I am reminded of the late President Roosevelt's words to Winston Churchill in Ottawa. He turned to him and said.

**HARCOURT-BROWN:**
*(heckling)* Sit down, you old fool, you're drunk!

**JANET:**
Jeremy! Really!

**HARCOURT-BROWN:**
Well, how much longer? Let's have a drink, come on. Thank you milord!

**JANET:**
Jeremy – apologise immediately. How dare you.

**HARCOURT-BROWN:**
Now listen, my dear, don't start telling me what to do. We've only been married five minutes.

**JANET:**
*(bursting into tears)* Oh, Mummy! *(She turns to her mother.)*

**HARCOURT-BROWN:**
Oh, God! Now we're all going to have a cry. *(Gets up.)* I trust you'll excuse me, everyone. If anyone wants me, I'll be in the pub! *(He stalks out.)*

**MOTHER:**
How dare he be so rude!

*(Rustless is now on the other side of Janet. She turns to him.)*

**JANET:**
Oh, Uncle Bonzo! I – I wish I'd never married him!

**RUSTLESS:**
Do you? Well that's fine. Because you didn't.

**JANET:**
What?

**MOTHER:**
What do you mean, didn't marry him?

**RUSTLESS:**
*(picking up photos, and showing one to Janet)* See that chap?

**JANET:**
That's the vicar.

**RUSTLESS:**
I'm afraid not.

*(A close up of the photo in Rustless's hand. It is a picture of Badger, in clergyman's robes, with the bride and groom.)*

**RUSTLESS:**
That's Badger, my butler. *(calling)* Badger!

*(Badger enters, back in his butler's clothes.)*

**BADGER:**
Milord?

*(A general hubbub breaks out among the guests.)*

**RUSTLESS:**
*(banging on the table)* Ladies and gentlemen! A little explanation is called for. I'm afraid I'm guilty of a slight case of vicar-nobbling. This gentleman, my good and trusted Badger, temporarily replaced his reverence the Vicar at the service today. You may have noticed, (a) that the Wedding March was played somewhat approximately, that was Badger – and, (b) that the church bells were rung more than a little frantically. That was the Vicar, locked in the Belfry. However, he and I are now firm friends, and I've no doubt he is prepared to perform the ceremony properly tomorrow – provided we can find another bridegroom. *(Cheers from the guests.)* Any ideas, Janet?

**JANET:**
You mean, Robin? Where is he?

**RUSTLESS:**
He's waiting in the kitchen.

**JANET:**
What's he doing in there?

**RUSTLESS:**
I told you – waiting. I say, Waiter! *(Robin enters through the "out" door. He is dressed as a waiter.)* So, drink up, ladies and gentlemen – there's another wedding tomorrow.

*(Janet rushes over to robin, and hugs him. The "out" door hits them in the back, knocking them aside. Cook enters – the ruins of the wedding cake on a tray. She is covered in icing sugar.)*

**COOK:**
Anyone for cake?

*(As she dumps it on the table, the credits roll.)*

# EPISODE FOUR
*"A Man and a Woman and a Half"*

*Scene: The reception hall of the hotel. Rustless is on the phone. Bates is working at a ledger.*

**RUSTLESS:**
Ah, Ricketts, there you are old chap – your boy answered the phone, but I thought I'd better speak to you personally. No, that's quite alright, I've only been waiting a couple of minutes. In where? Oh, were you? Well, we all have to do that, don't we? ha, ha, yes. Yes, I'm always in there lately. *(To Bates)* He was washing up in the kitchen, Bates – yes, now, the point is, Ricketts, the order I phoned through yesterday. Yes – I ordered three medium sized lobster, and you sent me a rather smelly parcel of rock-salmon. Which has left me on the horns of a quandary. I can't really give the guests rock-salmon salad tonight. Supposed to be the dogs what? The dog's bits? Which dogs bits? Mrs Merton – oh, I see. Your boy got the deliveries mixed up. Which means, I presume, that her dachshund is tucking in to my lobster. Look, you'd better send the boy round at once to rescue them. What? Won't go in – afraid of the dog. Mmm. Bit nervous of the lobsters, as well. I should advise him to give up fishmongering, and take up something a little less hazardous. Well, it's not good enough, all this. Tell me, have you got a nice trout? You have. Well, I'd like you to stuff it – I say I'd like you to stuff it, and … Hello? Hah! He's rung off, Bates.

**BATES:**
I wonder why, milord?

**RUSTLESS:**
Can't think. Well. Looks like rock-salmon

and chips tonight, the guests aren't going to like that much.

**BATES:**
There are only two of them, at the moment milord, so perhaps it won't matter.

**RUSTLESS:**
Two? What happened to the couple with the three children?

**BATES:**
Checked out this morning, milord.

**RUSTLESS:**
Any new bookings? *(Picking up newspaper, glancing through it.)*

**BATES:**
No milord. Business isn't too good at the moment. It's rather disturbing. I do so want this venture to be a success.

**RUSTLESS:**
So it will be – we must look on the bright side, Bates old chap.

**BATES:**
I try to, milord – but I mean to say – eighteen rooms, and only two guests. I get goose-pimples sometimes. Still, it's probably the time of year. *(Writing in ledger.)*

**RUSTLESS:**
Why, do you always get goose-pimples at this time of year?

**BATES:**
No, no, milord – goose-pimples when I think about it.

**RUSTLESS:**
It?

**BATES:**
The business, milord.

**RUSTLESS:**
Oh I see. Well, it's no good you worrying your head about it.

**BATES:**
It's just that I'd hate it to drop off.

**RUSTLESS:**
What, your head?

**BATES:**
*(sighing)* Never mind, milord. *(Rustless reads the paper.)* Anything interesting in the newspaper, milord?

**RUSTLESS:**
No. Damn boring. I shall be jolly glad when I've finished it.

*(The old lady enters, and approaches desk.)*

**OLD LADY:**
*(to Rustless)* I'd like some tea, please.

**RUSTLESS:**
By jove, that's a damn good idea. Just what I could do with. Fancy some tea, Bates?

**BATES:**
Would be nice, milord.

**RUSTLESS:**
Right. Order a pot of tea for two, Bates. No, make it three – you could drink a cup of tea, couldn't you, Mrs Ringer?

**OLD LADY:**
Er – yes.

**RUSTLESS:**
Pot of tea for three. Get Dithers in here.

*(Bates presses buzzer.)*

**RUSTLESS:**
Sit down Mrs Ringer, take it easy. I expect you've been rushing around all day as usual?

**OLD LADY:**
I did venture as far as the lily-pond this morning.

**RUSTLESS:**
There you are you see. I'll order some

biscuits as well – I expect you're famished – you usually are. Had anything since lunch?

**OLD LADY:**
Only indigestion.

**RUSTLESS:**
Bolting your food again I expect. *(Returns to paper.)*

**BATES:**
Have you seen my pink sponge, milord?

**RUSTLESS:**
No, let's have a look! Oh, I see. Pink sponge.

**BATES:**
For the stamps. And I've lost my thick scissors as well.

**RUSTLESS:**
Thick scissors? These scissors, you mean?

**BATES:**
No.
The thick scissors.

**RUSTLESS:**
Thick scissors. *(Looking round)* Thick scissors.

*(Dithers enters.)*

**DITHERS:**
Were you buzzing?

**RUSTLESS:**
No, I was saying "Thick scissors". Oh, I see. Yes, we did buzz. Pot of tea for three, and some suggestive biscuits.

**DITHERS:**
Righto. *(He goes.)*

**BATES:**
Perhaps those scissors are in the office. *(She exits to the office.)*

**RUSTLESS:**
They were around here yesterday.

*(He gets down behind the counter, looking for them.)*

*(Miss Fifi de la Tour enters the room. She is a tall, ravishing brunette with a low-cut dress, revealing a very ample bosom. She slinks over to the desk, and leans her bosom on the counter. Rustless gets up and is presented with a very close view of them.)*

**RUSTLESS:**
*(amazed)* Good grief! I mean, good afternoon.

**FIFI:**
I'd like a room.

**RUSTLESS:**
*(rather mesmerised)* Yes. Quite. You'll want a pretty large one, I should imagine.

**FIFI:**
Please. *(She speaks with a French accent.)*

**RUSTLESS:**
Let's see now – there's number eight. That should suit you – it's got a bay window.

**FIFI:**
What is the view like?

**RUSTLESS:**
Wonderful. Er – rolling hills, and the, er the valley, with big er – you'll like it. If you'd care to sign the register. *(he pushes the register towards her – she leans over even further, to sign it)*. Can you see all right?

**FIFI:**
Voilà. *(She hands the register back.)*

**RUSTLESS:**
Oh. Pretty name. Oh, I see – Voilà! As in French. I'm sorry – Miss ...?

**FIFI:**
De la Tour. Fifi de la Tour.

**RUSTLESS:**
Ah. Well, on behalf of the Hotel may I welcome you and – er – and yours, to the, er – *(Bates enters from the office.)* Ah, Bates.

This is Miss Fifi de la Two. De la Tour, who has very kindly agreed to stay with us.

**BATES:**
(staring) Yes. I see, milord. Good afternoon.

**FIFI:**
Hello. One thing – has the room central heating?

**RUSTLESS:**
Oh yes.

**FIFI:**
Because I like to sleep in the nude.

**RUSTLESS:**
I see. Would you like early morning tea?

**FIFI:**
That would be nice. Two lumps.

**RUSTLESS:**
Naturally.

**FIFI:**
And of course, I shall need a bath. Will you see to that for me?

**RUSTLESS:**
I'd be delighted.

**FIFI:**
Has the bedroom got air conditioning?

**RUSTLESS:**
Ah, that I'm afraid we can't do. But I could always come and blow through the keyhole every quarter of an hour.

**FIFI:**
(laughing) You are very cute.

**RUSTLESS:**
Ha-ha. Well, damn civil of you to say so.

(Dithers enters, with tea tray. He sees Fifi, and starts to shake – the tray rattles.)

**BATES:**
Oh, thank you, Mr Dithers – put it on the

counter would you – (pointedly) If you can find room.

**RUSTLESS:**
Ah, tea. Care for a cup of tea, Miss de ...

**FIFI:**
Call me Fifi, please.

**RUSTLESS:**
Thank you. Yes. (As Dithers puts the tray down) "Miss de la Tour" is a bit of a mouthful.

**DITHERS:**
You're right there.

**RUSTLESS:**
Shut up Dithers. Now – tea? (Pouring) You can have Bates's cup. You don't really want tea, do you Bates old chap?

**BATES:**
Well – no, milord. (She is hurt.)

**FIFI:**
No, please – I would like to go to my room. My luggage is in the car. I am very tired.

**RUSTLESS:**
Come a long way, have you?

**FIFI:**
From Morocco.

**RUSTLESS:**
Oh – quite a long drive. Seeing the sights, were you?

**FIFI:**
No no. It was a film.

**RUSTLESS:**
I say, that's a damned long way to go to the pictures. You could have popped into our local. Get some good films there. Gold-diggers of 1937 next week.

**FIFI:**
I was making a film – starring in it. I was supported by an international cast.

**RUSTLESS:**
Yes, you'd have to be. Right, come on then Dithers – luggage.

*(Dithers still stares.)*

**OLD LADY:**
*(who has been sitting patiently throughout)*
Could I have my tea, please?

**RUSTLESS:**
Oh, sorry. Dithers – hand this to Mrs Ringer on your way out.

*(Hands him cup of tea.)*

**DITHERS:**
Righto. *(He walks over to Mrs Ringer, then turns and stares again at Fifi.)*

**RUSTLESS:**
Come on, man – luggage! Chop chop.

**DITHERS:**
Ar. *(He drinks Mrs Ringer's tea, hands her the empty cup, and goes out.)*

**BATES:**
*(briskly, to Fifi)* Here is the key, Madam. The door is a little stiff, I'm afraid – needs a good push. Still, I'm sure you'll be able to manage it.

**RUSTLESS:**
Right. All set, then?

**FIFI:**
You are most kind, monsieur – ?

**RUSTLESS:**
Rustless. Lord Rustless. Just call me George.

**FIFI:**
George.

**RUSTLESS:**
That's it – right – here we go then. *(Starts to go, picking up Fifi's bag.)*

**BATES:**
What about your tea, milord?

**RUSTLESS:**
No, never mind that, Bates – I'll take Miss Fifi to her room. *(To Fifi)* Stairs are a bit narrow. You've got a pretty big hold-all, you might overbalance. *(They go out.)*

**BATES:**
*(to herself)* Big hold-all! *(To Mrs Ringer)* Another cup of tea, Mrs Ringer?

**OLD LADY:**
*(meekly)* I haven't had one yet.

**BATES:**
Well, do have this one.

**OLD LADY:**
Don't you want it?

**BATES:**
No thank you. It would choke me.

**OLD LADY:**
Oh? What's wrong with it?

**BATES:**
Two lumps, that's what's wrong with it.

*(Badger enters.)*

**BADGER:**
Ah, Miss Bates – have you seen his Lordship?

**BATES:**
He's upstairs with a guest.

**BADGER:**
Oh, thank you. *(He starts to go.)*

**BATES:**
I wouldn't disturb him at the moment, Mr Badger – I don't think he would appreciate it.

**BADGER:**
Oh, I see.

*(Dithers enters, with two beautiful leather suitcases.)*

**OLD LADY:**
*(as he passes)* Do those belong to that lady?

**DITHERS:**
Ar.

**OLD LADY:**
She's got some beautiful things, hasn't she?

**DITHERS:**
Ar. Ha, ha. *(He chuckles his way off.)*

**BADGER:**
*(curious)* Who is this lady guest, Miss Bates?

**BATES:**
Calls herself Miss Fifi de la Tour.

**BADGER:**
Expensive luggage. Chauffeur?

**BATES:**
Not that I've seen. I would imagine she is the type that travels alone.

**BADGER:**
*(sensing Bates's jealousy)* I take it you don't really like her, Miss Bates?

**BATES:**
Not at all, Mr Badger – she's perfectly all right – if you like that sort of thing. His Lordship certainly seems to.

**BADGER:**
Oh dear. You don't mean he's fallen for her?

**BATES:**
Oh, I do hope not.

**BADGER:**
Yes. It's not often he's affected by the opposite, er, gender, but when he is, he really goes overboard. When was the last time?

**BATES:**
Just over four years ago, Mr Badger. Mrs

Eustasia Hornblower. The very name makes me shudder when I think of it. I would hate to live through that again ... Those terrible hunting breakfasts.

**BADGER:**
Not forgetting the thirty eight wasp stings I had to remove from his Lordship's person.

**BATES:**
I know. Fancy the two of them sitting down for a picnic in the middle of a wasp's nest.

**BADGER:**
I did mention that at the time, Miss Bates, but his Lordship's only remark was that no one's got eyes in the back of their head.

**BATES:**
The back of their head wasn't where they were stung.

**BATES:**
Quite. Mind you, his Lordship's stings wouldn't have been so bad if they had been treated at once. The trouble was he insisted on attending to Mrs Hornblower's injuries personally, there and then.

**BADGER:**
I had no idea, Miss Bates – I was looking the other way.

**BATES:**
Yes. Yes, it was a dreadful business.

**BATES:**
Still, Miss Bates – you got him out of that indiscretion – perhaps you can do the same this time.

**BATES:**
Oh, I hope so – you know what he's like when he's got something on his mind – everything else goes straight out of the window. And there's still so much to get sorted out – we really can't have him mooning about and letting the hotel go to pot.

**BADGER:**
Perhaps it's just a passing fancy.

**BATES:**
You haven't seen the lady. *(Hearing Rustless coming back.)* Cavee. Here he is.

*(Rustless appears.)*

**OLD LADY:**
*(to him, as he passes)* I was stung, once.

**RUSTLESS:**
Really? Where?

**OLD LADY:**
On my doorstep!

**RUSTLESS:**
*(looks, then goes to desk)* What the devil's she on about, Bates? Stung on the doorstep?

**BATES:**
I've no idea, milord.

**RUSTLESS:**
No. Don't suppose she has either. Now then. Badger, my dear old chap. I want you to call a staff meeting.

**BADGER:**
Oh. Very good milord. Now, milord?

**RUSTLESS:**
At once, Badger. Pronto. On the double. Cook, Effie and Dithers on the carpet as soon as possible.

**BADGER:**
Very good, milord. *(He starts to go.)*

**RUSTLESS:**
Run, Badger, run!

**BADGER:**
Er. *(Moves a couple of rapid steps.)* I'm not sure that I remember how to, milord.

**RUSTLESS:**
Well do your best.

**BADGER:**
Yes milord. *(He attempts a run out.)*

**RUSTLESS:**
Poor Old Badger. Getting past it. *(Sings)* "As I walked along the Bois de Boulogne, with an independent air, you can hear the girls declare ... "etc. *(He executes a few dance steps.)*

**BATES:**
Are you all right, milord?

**RUSTLESS:**
Never felt better, Bates. Rum tee tum tee tum tee tum ... Remember that one, Mrs Ringer? I bet you've been through a few sets of lancers in your time, what?

**OLD LADY:**
I was never allowed to go out with soldiers.

**RUSTLESS:**
Quite right. Devils with the women. I've never knew one I could trust.

**BATES:**
You were one yourself, milord.

**RUSTLESS:**
Precisely, Bates. *(He winks. Bates raises her eyes to heaven.)*

*(The staff – Effie, Cook, Dithers – enter hurriedly.)*

**RUSTLESS:**
Ah. Right. Attention. In a line over here. Now then. Oh, Mrs Ringer, I wonder if you'd mind clearing off for a bit? Sort of extraordinary general meeting. Staff only, that sort of caper.

**OLD LADY:**
Oh, very well. Sorry.

**RUSTLESS:**
Not at all. I won't charge you for those two cups of tea.

*(The old lady goes out.)*

**COOK:**
Is this going to take long? Only I was in the middle of a Madeira sandwich.

**RUSTLESS:**
Shut up, Cook and pay attention. Briefly: our latest guest, Miss de la Tour, has graciously consented to dine with me tonight. *(Badger and Bates exchange glances.)* As you may or may not know, she is an international star, and therefore expects the best. And, by the look of her, she frequently gets it. Therefore, I want the meal to be excellent, and everyone to be on their best behaviour. Dithers – no polishing the fish knives on your trousers, or joining the guests for a glass of brandy between courses. Effie – always serve from the left, and keep your knees together at all times. Badger, you will do your best as always, I'm sure.

**BADGER:**
Thank you, milord.

**EFFIE:**
*(Speaks, inaudibly.)*

**RUSTLESS:**
What? You're not on tonight?

**EFFIE:**
*(Speaks.)*

**RUSTLESS:**
You promised the butcher's boy?

**EFFIE:**
*(Speaks.)*

**RUSTLESS:**
Well, you should never go round promising things like that should you? I mean to say you're on early shift tomorrow, you'll be worn out. Can't he get someone else to do it for him?

**EFFIE:**
*(Speaks.)*

**RUSTLESS:**
Oh, I see. He prefers you, you've got a

longer reach, I see.

**EFFIE:**
*(Speaks.)*

**RUSTLESS:**
Does he. Bit of a fanatic, is he?

**EFFIE:**
*(Nods.)*

**RUSTLESS:**
All right, just this once, as you've promised him, but don't make a habit of it. *(To Badger)* Got to help the butcher's boy put up his aerial, Badger.

**COOK:**
Look, while I'm standing here me boiler's slowly going out.

**RUSTLESS:**
Ah yes, Cook. Now, menu. Beef and plenty of it – sole meuniere: and generous cheeseboard.

**COOK:**
You'll be lucky.

**RUSTLESS:**
What?

**COOK:**
The sole's rock-salmon for a start.

**RUSTLESS:**
Oh damn, yes. I'd forgotten.

**COOK:**
And the main course is breast of lamb, boiled or roast, and peas.

**RUSTLESS:**
Is that all? There's supposed to be a choice.

**COOK:**
There is. Eat it or leave it. Ta – ta. *(She starts to go.)*

**RUSTLESS:**
Come back here – look, I'm also sending

Dithers to the village for a couple of dozen oysters, and some Guinness.

**COOK:**
She can't eat rock-salmon and oysters!

**RUSTLESS:**
They're not for her, they're for me.

**COOK:**
Well don't blame me if you come over queer in the night. *(She goes.)*

**RUSTLESS:**
*(to himself)* What a dreadful thought. Right, Dithers – to the village for the oysters. Hold the fort, Bates – I'm going to my room for a little lie-down. I've a feeling I'd better conserve my strength. *(He goes off, humming to himself.)*

**BADGER:**
*(to Bates)* Oh dear. Oh dear, oh dear.

**BATES:**
All the symptoms. Every one. Mister Dithers?

**DITHERS:**
Ar?

**BATES:**
*(giving him some money)* While you are in the village, I'd like you to get something for me.

**DITHERS:**
Get what?

**BATES:**
Tights.

**DITHERS:**
Get tight?

**BATES:**
No, tights. You know, like stockings. I think they're all one size.

**DITHERS:**
Pair of stockings.

**BATES:**
No, not stockings. They're like stockings, only they are joined together at the top.

**DITHERS:**
Oh? How d'you get your leg in?

**BATES:**
No no, they're open at the top, but they're joined across the – look it doesn't matter, just get them, would you, please?

**DITHERS:**
Right. *(He goes.)*

**BADGER:**
*(looking at Bates)* You're up to something, Miss Bates.

**BATES:**
No, no, Mr Badger – it's just that tonight sounds as if it's going to be rather – special.

*(Fade out.)*

*(Fade in.)*

*(Dinner time.)*

*(We start on champagne, being poured out by Badger. Two glasses. Rustless enters.)*

**RUSTLESS:**
Ah good man, Badger. *(He is now dressed in tails, with stiff shirt, top hat and cloak. Badger registers surprise.)*

**BADGER:**
I didn't realise you were dressing, milord – I would have come up.

**RUSTLESS:**
Nonsense, Badger. Managed all right. Thought I'd better show the flag.

**BADGER:**
Yes, milord. If you'll excuse me, milord, you're also showing a cleaning ticket. *(Unpins a ticket from Rustless's tail.)*

573

**RUSTLESS:**
Oh am I? Ha. Long time since I've dressed for dinner – are these shoes on the right feet?

**BADGER:**
I'm – I'm not sure, milord. *(Looks at them.)*

**RUSTLESS:**
Tricky, isn't it? They don't feel too bad, but my legs tend to walk in opposite directions. Miss Fifi not down yet, I presume?

**BADGER:**
Oh, yes, milord – she is in the cloakroom.

**RUSTLESS:**
Oh, good. Titivating, eh?

**BADGER:**
Extremely, milord.

**RUSTLESS:**
What? No, I meant she's ...

*(He is interrupted by the arrival of Bates, who has transformed herself. She wears a violently coloured off-the-shoulder cocktail dress – shortish, with yards of net underskirt, etc. – Her hair is down, and she has heavy makeup on. She is obviously trying to compete for Rustless's affections.)*

**BATES:**
Good evening, milord.

**RUSTLESS:**
Good grief, Bates, what on earth have you come as?

**BATES:**
I thought I might dress for dinner, as it was a rather special evening, milord. *(She sits, revealing as much leg as possible – clad in Dithers' choice of tights – open-work, patterned affairs which don't go with the dress at all.)*

**RUSTLESS:**
But my dear old chap! You'll catch your death of cold like that. Shouldn't you have your woolly on?

**BATES:**
*(slightly put out)* No, milord. I'll be quite all right.

**BADGER:**
Champagne, Miss Bates?

**BATES:**
Ooh, lovely. *(He hands her a glass, which she drains at one gulp.)* Delicious. Aren't you going to sit down, milord? *(Indicates the settee on which she is sitting.)*

**RUSTLESS:**
Suppose I might as well. *(He sits beside her.)*

**BATES:**
Let me straighten your tie. *(She does so, trying to be sexy.)* There. That's better. Mm – you look very nice, milord – I love men in evening-dress.

**RUSTLESS:**
Really? Damned tight, I'll tell you that. *(Bates smiles at him.)* You all right, Bates? Not sickening for anything, are you?

*(Fifi enters – in a dress which is almost indescribable, with holes cut in it, all over.)*

**RUSTLESS:**
*(doing his best to leap up)* My dear Fifi. I say, you look magnificent, my dear. *(Kisses her hand.)*

**FIFI:**
Thank you – you're so sweet, Georgie. Oh, Champagne! *(Badger hands her a glass.)* It loosens me up.

**RUSTLESS:**
I say, does it really? Shall we sit. *(They turn – Bates is sprawled across the settee in what she thinks is a sexy attitude.)* Oh, Bates is having a lie-down – she's not feeling too good this evening. Over here.

*(Rustless indicates another small couch. They go to sit. A close up of Rustless's top hat and Fifi's bottom sitting on it – it collapses.)*

He gives a yelp!)

**FIFI:**
(retrieving hat from underneath her) Oh dear – have I squashed your little topper?

**RUSTLESS:**
No, it's all right – trousers a bit tight.

**FIFI:**
No – your hat! (She hands it to him.)

**RUSTLESS:**
Oh! No it's all right – it's meant to be collapsible. (He springs it back to shape.)

(Bates is lighting a cigarette, badly – Dithers, dressed as a waiter, enters – whispers to Badger, then catches sight of Bates. His eyes pop – he fancies her.)

**BADGER:**
Dinner is served, milord.

**RUSTLESS:**
Oh. Hungry, Fifi?

**FIFI:**
I could eat a horse.

**RUSTLESS:**
Really? Well, many a true word is spoken in jest. (Shot of Bates, coughing over her cigarette.) See you later, Bates. Nasty cough you've got there – told you you would catch cold without your woolly. Better get to bed old chap – get Dithers to give your chest a good rub.

(He and Fifi depart. Bates looks annoyed.)

**BATES:**
(to Dithers, who is staring at her) What are you looking at, Mr Dithers?

**DITHERS:**
You're pretty tonight. Want your chest rubbed?

**BATES:**
Certainly not. (She gets up to go.)

**DITHERS:**
What about the tights, then?

**BATES:**
What?

**DITHERS:**
You said you'd show me where you put your legs in.

**BATES:**
Not when I've got them on!

**DITHERS:**
Oh, come on! (He makes a grab at her skirts.)

**BATES:**
No – really, Mr Dithers – stop it! (She runs off, pursued by Dithers.)

(Fade out.)

(Fade in.)

(After dinner Badger is on the phone.)

**BADGER:**
I see, yes. So I take it she would be available for the twenty-third? Yes, thank you. I will phone you again and confirm the booking. Thank you, Mr Goodman.

(Bates enters from the office – she is now in her ordinary clothes again.)

**BADGER:**
Yes. I must apologise for ringing so late. Thank you. Goodbye. (Phone down.)

**BATES:**
Any luck?

**BADGER:**
(hands her paper) As we thought, Miss Bates. I've written it all down. Oh – you'd better return this note-paper to her room.

**BATES:**
So, she's obviously after his money.

**BADGER:**
Yes. And it's equally obvious that she's unaware that he has none.

**BATES:**
That's not the point, Mr Badger. We don't want His Lordship to get too deeper involved – it would break his spirit.

**BADGER:**
Quite. I doubt if it would do the rest of him much good, either.

**BATES:**
Mr Badger!

**BADGER:**
Sorry, Miss Bates. Did you manage to deal with Mr Dithers?

**BATES:**
Yes, he's locked in the scullery. I should think he's calmed down by now – it's fairly cold in there.

**BADGER:**
Good – we may need his help later. We will have to keep a constant watch on His Lordship's movements.

*(Rustless laughs, offstage.)*

**BATES:**
Oh. – They've finished dinner – they're coming out.

*(Rustless and Fifi enter – she is on his arm, very amorous.)*

**RUSTLESS:**
Hullo chaps – still up? Damned good dinner, wasn't it, Fifi?

**FIFI:**
Beautiful. Your choice of wines was excellent, darling Georgie.

**RUSTLESS:**
Thank you – what about the food?

**FIFI:**
Oh, did we have food too? I didn't notice.

*(Laughing.)*

**RUSTLESS:**
Bo – I can't remember much about it either. Well, I suppose you'll want to get to bed now, what?

**FIFI:**
Yes, I am a little tired. *(Winks at Rustless, unseen by the others)*

**RUSTLESS:**
Quite. *(Winks back.)* Well, I'll say goodnight, then. Our rooms are in opposite directions, you see. So I'll see you later – in the morning, that is.

**FIFI:**
Very well. *(She kisses him on the cheek and whispers)* – Don't be long.

**RUSTLESS:**
No. I won't be. Goodnight then, old thing! Goodnight, all. See you all in the morning. All of you. *(He goes.)*

**FIFI:**
*(To Bates and Badger)* Goodnight. *(She goes, in the opposite direction.)*

**BATES:**
Goodnight. *(Loudly, to Badger)* Well, we'll lock up and put the lights out, Mr Badger. *(Finger to lips – indicating that Rustless may be lurking outside.)*

**BADGER:**
*(loudly)* Very well, Miss Bates.

*(He bolts the front door while Bates puts out the desk lamps, etc. She then pushes him into the office, puts out the main lights, and hides behind the sofa. Silence. After a second or two, Rustless comes creeping back. Walks behind the sofa, falls over Bates. They both appear over back of the sofa.)*

**RUSTLESS:**
What the devil were you doing down there, Bates?

**BATES:**
I've – I've lost an ear-ring, milord.

**RUSTLESS:**
But you weren't wearing ear-rings, Bates.

**BATES:**
No milord – this was, er, last week. Did you come back for something, milord?

**RUSTLESS:**
My toothpaste. Left it in the other bathroom. Goodnight.

*(He goes. Bates hides again. After a moment, Rustless returns, crosses the hall, and goes off. Badger appears round the office door.)*

**BADGER:**
*(whispers)* All clear, Miss Bates?

**BATES:**
Shh! *(Badger disappears again. Bates crawls over to the main light switch. Rustless comes in again. Bates suddenly switches on the lights.)*

**BATES:**
Did you find your toothpaste, milord?

**RUSTLESS:**
Yes. Now I've lost my damned teeth.

*(He crosses, and goes off the other side again. Badger again emerges.)*

**BADGER:**
Where has he gone now?

**BATES:**
Gone to get his false teeth.

**BADGER:**
Oh. *(They wait for a few seconds.)*

**BATES:**
Just a minute.

**BADGER:**
What, Miss Bates?

**BATES:**
He hasn't got false teeth! *(They look at each other.)*

**BADGER:**
I'm afraid, Miss Bates, he has given us the slip.

**BATES:**
Come on – we'll get Dithers.

*Cut to: Fifi's bedroom*

*(A large double bed – perhaps a four-poster. She is lounging on the bed, still in her dinner-dress. The bedroom window is closed, but the curtains are open. Rustless enters, and closes the door quietly.)*

**RUSTLESS:**
Phew! Sorry to have kept you – bit tricky shaking off old Bates. Sticks like a limpet to a Bargee's bottom.

**FIFI:**
Darling! Come and sit down. *(She pats the bed.)*

**RUSTLESS:**
What, there?

**FIFI:**
Of course. You want to sit beside me, don't you?

**RUSTLESS:**
Oh, at least! Mind if I take my coat off?

**FIFI:**
Take off anything you want.

**RUSTLESS:**
Thanks. Damn civil. *(Sits on bed – she leans back.)* Well, now. *(A bit shy)* Pretty room, this. Pleasant aspect.

**FIFI:**
You think I will get a good night here?

**RUSTLESS:**
I certainly hope so. *(Backing away a little – turns, sees her alarm clock on the bedside*

*table)* This yours? *(Picks it up.)* That's jolly nice. *(Twiddles the hands round.)* What, er, what time do we – what time do you want to get up? In the morning?

**FIFI:**
Oh, not too early, eh? About eleven?

**RUSTLESS:**
Right. Eleven it is. *(Sets the alarm.)* Very nice. Yes. *(He turns to her – she is closer than he expected.)* I – er – I like your matching luggage, as well.

**FIFI:**
It's pigskin.

**RUSTLESS:**
Oh, I wouldn't say that. Er – well, tell me about yourself.

**FIFI:**
I've told you already, at dinner.

**RUSTLESS:**
Well, tell me again. I mean, I know you're an actress, and you've performed before all the crowned heads in Europe, but what sort of thing do you do? I mean, tell jokes, or what?

**FIFI:**
I dance.

**RUSTLESS:**
Oh, you dance? Oh, that must be nice. I – er – I expect the crowned heads go a bomb on that.

*(Cut to the window – the top of a ladder has appeared, leaning against the window. Dithers's head slowly appears. His eyes pop.)*

**RUSTLESS:**
What sort of dancing? Valeta, Military Two-Step, that sort of thing?

**FIFI:**
No no, you silly boy. Exotic dancing. *(She nestles next to him, her left bosom against the side of his head.)* Would you like me to show you?

**RUSTLESS:**
Pardon?

**FIFI:**
Shall I show you?

**RUSTLESS:**
I'm afraid you'll have to speak up, I seem to have gone deaf in the right ear.

**FIFI:**
I said, would you like to see me dance?

*(Quick shot of Dithers at the window.)*

**RUSTLESS:**
What, now?

**FIFI:**
Why not?

**RUSTLESS:**
But you haven't any music.

**FIFI:**
I have my record-player.

**RUSTLESS**
Oh. Alright then. Yes, grand.

**FIFI:**
I think you will like my dancing.

**RUSTLESS:**
Oh, I'm sure.

*(Fifi gets off the bed, and puts on the record player – a smoochy orchestration of an obscure number. Rustless sits up. She starts to remove a stocking.)*

**RUSTLESS:**
Have you started?

**FIFI:**
*(laughing)* No – I have to remove my stockings first.

**RUSTLESS:**
*(mesmerised)* I see. Er – do you mind if I open a window? It's all getting rather close in here.

*(He backs away to the window, still staring at her, fumbles for the window catch, and flings it open. It opens outwards and sideways, hitting Dithers on the side of the head, and knocking him off the ladder. There is a crash in the bushes below.)*

**RUSTLESS:**
Damned cats.

**FIFI:**
Now, sit down again.

**RUSTLESS:**
On the bed?

**FIFI:**
Of course. You can't watch me dance standing up.

**RUSTLESS:**
No. I don't think my knees will stand it. *(He climbs onto the bed again.)*

*(Fifi starts to dance – a sort of hip-swinging, slow, performance. Rustless follows her movements, occasionally choking a little over his cigar. Suddenly, the music changes to a more upbeat orchestration, and Fifi undoes a couple of buttons at the back of her dress, gives a heave, and the whole thing comes off, leaving her in a stripper's bra and pants.)*

**RUSTLESS:**
Good grief!

*(The music grinds away, and so does Fifi. The music builds to a crescendo, and Fifi approaches the bed. Just as she is about to remove her bra, the alarm clock goes off with a deafening buzz, right in Rustless's ear. He jumps about a foot in the air, makes a grab for the clock, and falls heavily off the bed.)*

**FIFI:**
*(running to him and kneeling by him)* Oh, Georgie, are you alright?

**RUSTLESS:**
Ooh – it's me back!

*(Fifi tries to get him onto the bed – she is just*

*about managing it, when the door bursts open and Bates appears, followed by Badger.)*

**BATES:**
*(outraged)* Miss de la Tour! What on earth are you doing to his Lordship?

**FIFI:**
He has hurt his back.

**BATES:**
I'm not surprised! What do you mean by having no clothes on? No-one is allowed in the bedrooms with no clothes on, it's a rule of the Hotel!

**FIFI:**
Not even when you're going to bed?

**BATES:**
Especially when you're going to bed! Mr Badger, help me with his Lordship. *(They pick him up.)*

**RUSTLESS:**
I'm alright Bates – I made a grab and misjudged the distance. I'd set the alarm twelve hours too soon.

**BATES:**
Don't try to talk milord. *(To Fifi)* I'm afraid I shall have to ask you to vacate this room by twelve noon tomorrow. This is a respectable house.

**FIFI:**
Don't worry – I'm going. You are all crazy.

**RUSTLESS:**
But look here ...

**BATES:**
Come along, milord, lean on me.

**RUSTLESS:**
Ow! It's gone right down me leg now.

**BATES:**
Don't worry, milord, you haven't got to walk far – I'm putting you in my bed for the night.

*(Fade out on Rustless's surprised expression.)*

*(Fade in – next morning. Rustless is lying on the sofa, in pyjamas and dressing-gown. Bates sits on the arm of the sofa.)*

**BATES:**
So we telephoned her agent – at least, Mr Badger did. He found the address on some notepaper in her room. And he confirmed our suspicions. She's just finished a tour of the clubs up North.

**RUSTLESS:**
You mean, she's a confounded stripper? But what was all that about appearing before the crowned heads of Europe?

**BATES:**
All lies. Just a big front.

**RUSTLESS:**
Yes, it was, wasn't it? Phew!

**BATES:**
Anyway, she's gone now milord. How are you feeling now, milord? Because you passed out as soon as I got you to my room. Was it the wine?

**RUSTLESS:**
No, the heat I should think. Damned stiff shirt of mine; far too tight.

**BATES:**
Yes, I know. I had a lot of trouble with it when I was putting you to bed.

**RUSTLESS:**
You put me to bed, Bates?

**BATES:**
Oh, don't worry milord – I looked the other way.

**RUSTLESS:**
Oh, that accounts for it. I wondered why my pyjama trousers were on back to front. Where is everybody?

**BATES:**
Mr Badger is still doing breakfasts, milord

– Mr Dithers is having a rest – he hurt himself as well last night.

**RUSTLESS:**
Really?

**BATES:**
Yes, he was, er, attending to the garden and he fell into a cold-frame milord.

**RUSTLESS:**
Oh dear. Any damage?

**BATES:**
Well, he apparently ruined his cucumbers. But he seems alright in himself this morning.

**RUSTLESS:**
Amazing resilience, that fellah.

**BATES:**
And Cook is on her way with one of her little delicacies for you, milord. You're being spoilt this morning.

*(Cook enters, with covered dish.)*

**BATES:**
Ah, here we are, here's Cook.

**COOK:**
And how's our old invalid this morning? *(Pronounced wrongly.)*

**RUSTLESS:**
Invalid, Cook, invalid! Invalid is something that's out of date, no longer any good. Oh well, perhaps you're right.

**BATES:**
Nonsense, milord. There's plenty of life in you yet. Perhaps Cook's little treat will brighten you up. What is it Cook?

**COOK:**
Well, seeing as how you're a bit dicky, you don't want nothing indigestible, so I made you a nice sandwich.

**RUSTLESS:**
Sandwich? What's in it?

**COOK:**
Some of that rock-salmon left over from last night.

*(She reveals a large doorstep sandwich under the dish cover. Rustless looks rather ill, as the credits roll.)*

# EPISODE FIVE

*"Up the Junction"*

*The reception hall. Evening. Rustless is on the phone.*

**RUSTLESS:**
When would this be for, Madam? The seventeenth. *(Looking at register)* I'm frightfully sorry, we seem to be completely booked up. Yes. Choc-a-bloc. Wait a minute, er, there's a very tiny attic room available. Yes, it is, very small yes. Well, how big are you, Madam? What? No, what I mean to say is, are you a large party? No, I wasn't meaning to be personal. What I'm trying to say is, if you were a single person, I wouldn't mind squeezing you in the attic. Oh, I see. You've got a husband. Yes, well it's only a single bed you see. I suppose you could both get in it. Oh, you don't fancy that. Bit too much on top of one another. Yes, quite. Well, other than that, the only thing I can offer you is, er, nothing, really. Yes, it is unusual at this time of year. Probably the motor racing at Brands Hatch. No, I know we're nowhere near Brands Hatch. I think that's why people come here, to get away from the noise. Anyway, if I do find a nice double bed, perhaps you'd like me to give you a tinkle? No, a tinkle. No? Oh, very well. Thank you Madam. 'Bye 'bye.

*(He puts down the phone, and pours himself a glass of whisky, adds soda, and goes and sits in armchair. Bates enters.)*

**BATES:**
Evening, milord. Enjoying a night cap?

**RUSTLESS:**
No, Bates.

**BATES:**
Oh – isn't it nice?

**RUSTLESS:**
Yes it's fine – it's just that I'm not going to bed yet.

**BATES:**
Oh, I see. Did you have a nice dinner, milord?

**RUSTLESS:**
I was called away to answer the phone – woman wanting rooms. I must say, it's a wonderful feeling, being completely full up.

**BATES:**
*(sitting)* Yes, it is. That apple crumble was scrumptious.

**RUSTLESS:**
No no, you're not getting my drift, old chap. I wasn't referring to the dinner – I meant the hotel. Full up.

**BATES:**
Oh, – yes milord – sorry.

**RUSTLESS:**
I noticed you were stuffing yourself rather in there. You put quite a bit away on the quiet, don't you Batesy, what?

**BATES:**
Well ...

**RUSTLESS:**
I was watching you last night, demolishing the roast potatoes. What did you get through, about nine or ten?

**BATES:**
Oh, no milord – I think it was five, actually. I can't resist them, all those crinkly bits.

**RUSTLESS:**
Yes, no doubt about it – you certainly love your tummy, Bates.

**BATES:**
Yes, I'm afraid I do.

**RUSTLESS:**
Hah. Well, I do, too, of course.

**BATES:**
*(blushing a little)* Oh – that's very nice of you, milord.

**RUSTLESS:**
Not your tummy, Bates. Never seen it, for one thing, except in that photo of you as a baby on a leopard skin rug.

**BATES:**
No no, milord, you couldn't have seen my tummy in that photo – I was lying on it.

**RUSTLESS:**
Well, I saw something.

**BATES:**
Yes, that would be my erm – well.

**RUSTLESS:**
Oh yes. Very sweet. Nice expression it had. I'd like to have another look at that sometime, when you've got a moment.

**BATES:**
*(suddenly giggles)* Perhaps we should change the subject, milord.

**RUSTLESS:**
You're a bit giggly tonight Bates – you been drinking?

**BATES:**
I did have a glass of wine with my meal, milord – I just felt like celebrating a little.

**RUSTLESS:**
Oh God – don't tell me I've missed your birthday again.

**RUSTLESS:**
No, milord – it's just that everything seems to be turning out so well suddenly. The hotel's absolutely full, things seem to be running smoothly – after all, it was a bit of a gamble – and I feel, well, you know, sort of pleased, and almost proud, that it's worked. You know.

**RUSTLESS:**
Beautifully put, Bates. Have a whisky.

**BATES:**
Oh, no thank you, milord. I mustn't.

**RUSTLESS:**
Why not? Just what you need to get the giggles out of your system. Couple of these, and you'd be laughing like a drain.

**BATES:**
Oh, that would never do.

**RUSTLESS:**
Never do what?

**BATES:**
Never do, for me.

**RUSTLESS:**
You sure.

**BATES:**
Alright then.

**RUSTLESS:**
Ah, good. Stout fellow. I'll join you. *(Pours out two whiskies – very little soda.)*

**BATES:**
Weren't you drinking gin before dinner milord?

**RUSTLESS:**
Yes.

**BATES:**
Is that alright?

**RUSTLESS:**
Oh yes. I'm not proud. I'll mix my drinks with anyone. Bottoms up.

**BATES:**
Cheers, milord.

**RUSTLESS:**
I must say, I hate turning away the customers though, you know Bates. Are you sure we haven't overlooked an odd room, here and there?

**BATES:**
Quite sure, milord. Everything occupied.

**RUSTLESS:**
Pity. It's just that I'd like a spare in case of emergencies.

*(The old lady enters.)*

**RUSTLESS:**
Ah, Mrs Ringer. Had your dinner?

**OLD LADY:**
Yes, thank you. Very nice.

**RUSTLESS:**
I suppose you'll be toddling off to bed then, what? Or are you staying up to watch the wrestling?

**OLD LADY:**
Oh, no – I think I'll go and sit in my room. It's pleasant up there.

**RUSTLESS:**
Yes. Nice big room, isn't it? You could actually get about three beds in there, you know, Bates.

**OLD LADY:**
I hope you're not going to ask me to share, milord?

**RUSTLESS:**
Well, it's just that I've got a Butchers Convention coming down next week, and it might solve the problem.

**OLD LADY:**
Oh, but I couldn't possibly ...

**RUSTLESS:**
No, what I meant was – couldn't your parents put you up for a week or two?

**OLD LADY:**
I have no parents!

**RUSTLESS:**
Oh dear – an orphan, are you?

**OLD LADY:**
My parents didn't die until I was over sixty.

**RUSTLESS:**
Oh dear, I'm sorry to hear that. Dreadful to become an orphan so late in life.

*(Bates suddenly bursts out laughing.)*

**RUSTLESS:**
Ah. I was waiting for that. Nothing personal, Mrs Ringer – Bates has had a few.

**BATES:**
So sorry, milord – I think I'd better go to bed as well.

**RUSTLESS:**
Righto Bates – sleep well, old fruit. Cheers!

**BATES:**
Bottoms up! Oh that reminds me milord – I'll look out that photo! *(She exits.)*

**RUSTLESS:**
Poor old Bates. She's very highly strung, you know, like an old violin.

**OLD LADY:**
Really?

**RUSTLESS:**
Oh yes. Can't blame her for getting a bit pizzicato once in a while *(He goes for another drink.)*

**OLD LADY:**
Well – I'm off. *(She toddles towards the exit.)*

**RUSTLESS:**
*(looking up from his drink)* Oh, you turning in?

583

**OLD LADY:**
*(without stopping)* No, it's these new shoes.
*(She is gone.)*

*(Rustless knocks back his drink.)*

**RUSTLESS:**
*(to himself)* Well, might as well lock up I
suppose. Lights out, lot to do in the
morning. *(Looks round)* Who the hell am I
talking to? No-one about. Must be getting
past it. Huh! I'm still doing it. *(He is at the
door.)* What's that? *(Looks on the floor.)* A
pin. "See a pin, pick it up, all the day
you'll have good luck." *(He bends to pick it
up, and is hit by the swing-door as Cook and
Dithers enter, both in their outdoor clothes.)*

**RUSTLESS:**
Good grief. *(He recovers.)* What the hell are
you two doing, out at this time of night?
Been to a dance?

**COOK:**
Pictures.

**DITHERS:**
Ar.

**RUSTLESS:**
Oh? What was on?

**COOK:**
*The Curse of the Mummy's Tummy.*

**RUSTLESS:**
The what?

**DITHERS:**
Tomb!

**RUSTLESS:**
Oh, really? I'm surprised they let you into
that – frighten the customers before they
start. What was it like anyway?

**COOK:**
Bit bloodthirsty.

**DITHERS:**
Ar. *(Chuckling)* It were good.

**COOK:**
It was all about this monster, cutting up
people – blood all over his hands. I kept
thinking of me beetroots.

**RUSTLESS:**
Yes, nasty. I can never understand why
people want to go and see those horror
films.

**COOK:**
Well, it's something a bit different, ain't
it? Something you don't see very often in
ordinary life.

**RUSTLESS:**
I should damn well hope not. You're both
fanatics, aren't you?

**COOK:**
He ain't. He just comes so he can have a
go at me fish and chips on the way home.

**RUSTLESS:**
Quite.

**COOK:**
Well, I'll say goodnight.

**RUSTLESS:**
Go on then.

**COOK:**
Goodnight.

**RUSTLESS:**
That's it. I'm off as well. Another busy day
tomorrow. *(Going to door)* Dithers – I
wonder if you could put that whisky away
before you come up?

**DITHERS:**
Righto.

*(Rustless and Cook have gone)*

**DITHERS:**
I'll have a go, anyway. *(He starts to drink
the Scotch from the bottle, as we:)*

*(Fade out.)*

*(Fade in.)*

*(Rustless's bedroom. Morning. A four-poster bed, low bedside table, window, door – perhaps a large stuffed bear, holding his clothes, in one corner. Rustless is asleep. An old-type alarm clock is suspended, by thin string, from an ornamental gas-bracket by the bed. Suddenly it rings, very loud. Rustless, half asleep, gropes for a pair of scissors on the bedside table, cuts the string, and the clock falls into a bucket of water on the floor. Silence. (There probably will be!) a loud knock on the door. Effie enters, with breakfast tray.)*

**RUSTLESS:**
*(sleepily)* Morning, Effie

**EFFIE:**
*(mouths silently)* – "Good morning milord."

*(She places the tray on the breakfast table. As she bends, we see that she has bright orange knickers.)*

**RUSTLESS:**
*(turning and blinking sleepily at the knickers)* Sun's a bit bright this morning.

**EFFIE:**
*(Standing up, mouthing inaudibly.)*

**RUSTLESS:**
Thank you. Oh – eggs again. Can't you get the hens to lay something else?

**EFFIE:**
*(Mouths.)*

**RUSTLESS:**
Yes, fine, thank you. How did you sleep?

**EFFIE:**
*(Mouths.)*

**RUSTLESS:**
Oh, downstairs, yes – because of the over-crowding. Yes, quite.

**EFFIE:**
*(Mouths.)*

**RUSTLESS:**
Really? Good gracious! Had you ever seen him before?

**EFFIE:**
*(Mouths.)*

**RUSTLESS:**
I see. Did he? On the billiard-table?

**EFFIE:**
*(Mouths.)*

**RUSTLESS:**
Yes. Well, that was quite uncalled for. *(She continues to mouth)* Sideways? Oh. Probably Chinese, I shouldn't wonder. I hope you didn't let him get away with it. Couldn't stop him – no, I suppose not. Still must have been dashed uncomfortable on the billiard-table. Did you – all night? Oh, that's too bad.

*(Badger, the butler, enters.)*

**BADGER:**
Good morning, milord. The morning papers, milord.

**RUSTLESS:**
Ah Badger! Just the chap. Effie here has been telling me she found a man sleeping on the billiard-table last night – sideways on. When she told him that she was supposed to be sleeping there, he refused to move. Poor girl had to sit up in a chair all night in the hall – she's stiff all over.

**BADGER:**
Oh, that would be Mr Noble, milord – he arrived quite late, and Miss Bates offered him the billiard-table, and he jumped at it.

**RUSTLESS:**
Did he? I hope he hasn't ripped the cloth. Well, never mind, Effie old thing – tell you what – take a couple of hours off. Pop into the shower-room and have a nice hot shower, and I'll join you later for a few exercises. *(Effie nods, and goes.)* Pretty little thing. Pity she doesn't speak up a bit.

**BADGER:**
Milord – may I draw your attention to page eight in the local paper. *(Hands him paper open at the page.)* I think you will find it of great interest.

**RUSTLESS:**
*(looking at paper)* What, "Man of eighty-seven injured on honeymoon – crashes through chemist's window on tricycle"?

**BADGER:**
No no milord – lower down – underneath the schoolgirls' orchestra.

**RUSTLESS:**
"Station to close down. Chrome Halt, once visited by Queen Victoria, is to be closed, British Rail announced today. It is one of the twenty-nine small branch line stations to be axed under the Authority's new 'cut out the dead wood' scheme. The station buildings will be demolished in order to make way for redevelopment. As from tomorrow, no more trains will stop at the station." Good grief!

**BADGER:**
Exactly, milord.

**RUSTLESS:**
But last time, when they were closing all the little stations, I was assured that Chrome Halt wouldn't be touched. Now the bounders have gone back on their word.

**BADGER:**
I presume it's since the Government changed, milord.

**RUSTLESS:**
What? Government changed? When?

**BADGER:**
There was a General Election a couple of years ago, milord.

**RUSTLESS:**
Was there? Conservatives are out, are they?

**BADGER:**
No, milord – they are in. The Labour people had been in for several years.

**RUSTLESS:**
The swine! Why wasn't I informed when I last went to the Lords?

**BADGER:**
When you last wen to the Lords, milord, the Liberals were in.

**RUSTLESS:**
Were they? How is old Asquith? – Still at the helm?

**BADGER:**
I'm afraid he's gone, milord – quite some time ago now.

**RUSTLESS:**
Thought so – knew he wouldn't stick it – flash in the pan. However, all that is beside the point, Badger. The point is, that they intend to close the Railway. You realise, of course, what this means?

**BADGER:**
Yes indeed milord – the Hotel business will be badly affected.

**RUSTLESS:**
Badly affected? It'll kill it stone dead, old fruit. It's unthinkable. There's not a decent trunk road for miles around – the railway is our only life-line. "Cut out the dead wood" indeed! They're cutting our throats. I mean the roads are so bad around here, some people have never been out of the village, you know.

**BADGER:**
Yes. Mr Dithers, for one, milord.

**RUSTLESS:**
Exactly. And it's never affected him. Something's affected him, but it's not that. But damn it all, when it comes to the railway, I mean, we need it. It's traditional. Been there since eighteen fifty-eight. It was one of the stopping places for Queen Victoria's long journey to Balmoral. Of

course, they didn't have corridors then. Had a special little throne-room built next to the waiting-room; velvet-covered seat and everything. It's still there to this day. Station-master keeps his ducks in it. No, it's impossible. They can't close it down.

**BADGER:**
Perhaps a petition, milord? Signed by the local people?

**RUSTLESS:**
Damned good idea Badger. Right – no time to be lost. Call a staff meeting at once, in the Hall.

**BADGER:**
Very good, milord. *(he starts to go, and turns at the door)* Shall I run your bath, milord?

**RUSTLESS:**
No, don't bother – I'll have one later.

*(He leaps out of bed, straight into the bucket of water.)*

*Cut to: the reception hall. (Cook, Dithers, and Badger wait. Bates enters.)*

**BADGER:**
Morning, Miss Bates. Sorry to hurry you – his Lordship wants a meeting.

**BATES:**
*(a little "hung-over")* That's quite alright, Mr Badger. I'm not quite myself this morning, I don't know why.

**DITHERS:**
*(offering her a hip flask)* Here you are. Hair of the dog.

**BATES:**
Oh, no thank you, Mr Dithers. *(Looks a bit green.)* Very sweet of you. *(Dithers take a swig himself.)*

*(Effie enters, draped in a bath towel, with shower cap on.)*

**BATES:**
Oh, Effie dear.

*(Dithers shows interest.)*

**BADGER:**
I had to drag her out of the shower, Miss Bates.

**DITHERS:**
Oh? *(Offers Effie hip flask, which she silently declines.)*

**COOK:**
*(impatiently)* Well, where is he then? I can't stand about for long. I've got a leg in the oven.

**BATES:**
I'm sure his Lordship won't be long, Cook dear.

*(Rustless enters – still in his night-shirt.)*

**COOK:**
Cor, he's undressed an' all! It's like the folly bergere.

**RUSTLESS:**
Right – everyone here?

**BADGER:**
Yes milord.

**RUSTLESS:**
You'll have to excuse my attire, but I've something important to tell you.

**COOK:**
Well make it snappy, else you'll finish up with soggy vol-au-vents.

**RUSTLESS:**
Shut up, Cook, and pay attention man. Briefly, I have just read, in the local paper, that British Rail is to close down Chrome Halt.

**BATES:**
Oh, no!

**RUSTLESS:**
Yes Bates, as from tomorrow, no trains will stop there. And the station itself is to be pulled down to make way for redevelopment.

**BATES:**
Oh, no!

**RUSTLESS:**
Oh yes. Now you all realise what this will do to the business here. It will close us within a month.

**BATES:**
Oh, no!

**RUSTLESS:**
You trying to start an argument, Bates? The facts are there. Now Badger, as always, has come up with a good idea. A petition – signed by as many people as possible. This is something we can all do, and this afternoon I propose we all go out and persuade everyone we know to sign it.

**BATES:**
Do you think that will amount to many, milord.

**RUSTLESS:**
Well, we must know quite a few people between us. Let's see – Dithers – how many people do you know?

**DITHERS:**
Two.

**RUSTLESS:**
Two?

**DITHERS:**
Ar. *(Pointing to Cook)* Me and her.

**RUSTLESS:**
Oh dear. Effie?

**EFFIE:**
*(Mouths.)*

**RUSTLESS:**
Thirty-four?

**EFFIE:**
*(Mouths.)*

**RUSTLESS:**
All men? What? Oh, I see. You help them out. Yes. *(To the others)* Effie sings with the local male voice choir. I should have thought your voice was a little light for that sort of thing – what position do you sing?

**EFFIE:**
*(Mouths.)*

**RUSTLESS:**
Oh, at the back, yes, very wise. Well you see, the figures are mounting already, Bates. I only hope it works.

**BATES:**
Oh, so do I milord – it would be a tragedy if they pulled down the station. I mean people come from miles away to have a look at Beavers Bump.

**RUSTLESS:**
Beavers Bump?

**BATES:**
It's a very well-known beauty spot, milord.

**RUSTLESS:**
Oh, so that's his name. D'you mean that wart on the side of his nose?

**BATES:**
Who milord.

**RUSTLESS:**
The station-master.

**BADGER:**
No no milord, Beavers Bump. The hill just beyond the station. Where the picnickers always go. It's beautiful.

**RUSTLESS:**
Oh, of course. Charming spot, yes.

**BATES:**
It means all those poor people will have to

do without their lovely picnics on Sundays. Oh no, it's outrageous. I think we should stage a protest march, milord.

**RUSTLESS:**
That's a damn good idea, Bates!

**BATES:**
With banners. I could paint some, milord.

**RUSTLESS:**
Excellent.

**COOK:**
I ain't carrying no banner.

**RUSTLESS:**
Shut up, Cook. You will carry the banner.

**COOK:**
Not tomorrow. I'll have a roast in the oven.

**RUSTLESS:**
I don't care if you've got a bun in the oven, you'll carry the banner; so shut up.

**COOK:**
Please yourself. Can I go now – me leg's burning. I don't want me crackling to go up in smoke.

**RUSTLESS:**
Yes, clear off. *(She goes.)* Now then, the rest of you – Badger, Bates, Effie – down to the village and get as many signatures as you can. Dithers can start making the banners. What's the best sort of stuff to make them out of, Bates?

**BATES:**
Oh, plain white cloth of some sort, milord, so that I can paint on it.

**RUSTLESS:**
Right. Dithers, you know where you can lay your hands on some?

**DITHERS:**
Ar. *(He makes a grab at Effie's towel.)*

**RUSTLESS:**
Stop that Dithers! Or at least give the girl a few yards start! *(Effie rushes off, pursued by Dithers. Rustless goes to the door, and watches the retreating figures.)* Hah! He'll never get that towel off her. She'll turn round suddenly and give him a smack in the eye. *(A yell from Dithers, off stage.)* Oh! He's got it!

**BATES:**
The towel, milord?

**RUSTLESS:**
No, the smack in the eye. I think I'd better go and lend a hand.

**BATES:**
Yes – do stop Mr Dithers, milord.

**RUSTLESS:**
Stop him? I'm going to help him. Even things up a bit.

**BATES:**
Milord?

**RUSTLESS:**
Yes – two against two. *(He nips off. Bates and Badger exchange glances.)*

**BADGER:**
Really, Miss Bates, I don't know where he gets the energy!

*(Fade out.)*

*(Fade in – the reception hall – afternoon. Rustless is sitting by a large transistor radio, at the counter. He is writing busily – he has four bottles of different coloured inks and four pens. The old lady and the deaf gent sit on the sofa – a tea tray in front of them.)*

**RADIO VOICE:**
*(an actor speaking)* So may we all, lady – and the bastard that even now kicks in your womb may taste the chill of steel ere it has found the legs to walk!

*Dramatic music, and announcer's voice over.*

**ANNOUNCER:**
That was the third episode in a new dramatisation of *The Rape of Mathilda* specially adapted for *Woman's Hour* by the Reverent Simon Tether. Those taking part were: Robert Hardy, Jeremy Clyde, Mark Dignam, Avis Bunnage, June Tobin and Michael Gambon. The play was produced by Maurice Murphy. *(Rustless is writing furiously throughout, using different pens.)* And now here is Eric Robinson with selections from the music of Johann Strauss. *(The music strikes up – Rustless switches off.)*

**OLD LADY:**
I did enjoy that play, didn't you Mr Williamson?

**DEAF GENT:**
Eh?

**OLD LADY:**
I say I enjoyed it, didn't you?

**DEAF GENT:**
Very good.

**OLD LADY:**
Wonderful acting.

**DEAF GENT:**
Yes, very nice.

**OLD LADY:**
Wonderfully high standard of acting.

**DEAF GENT:**
Eh?

**OLD LADY:**
Very high standard!

**DEAF GENT:**
Yes, yes. I always enjoy it. I think I'll have another cup.

**OLD LADY:**
Pardon?

**DEAF GENT:**
Eh?

*(Bates enters, with piece of paper.)*

**BATES:**
Hello milord.

*(Rustless quickly drops his pen, and comes from behind the desk.)*

**RUSTLESS:**
Ah, there you are Bates – how did you get on with the petition?

**BATES:**
Not too badly – sixteen. What about you, milord?

**RUSTLESS:**
*(reaching for his paper)* Er – not sure how many, Bates.

**BATES:**
*(taking paper)* Oh, you got quite a lot. Yes, ... Mrs Ringer, Mr Williamson – Mr and Mrs Smith, Mrs Jones, Mrs Brown, Mrs Green, Mrs Yellow?

**RUSTLESS:**
Yes. Odd name, isn't it?

**BATES:**
*(suspecting something)* The Reverend Simon Tether, Robert Hardy, Jeremy Clyde, Mark Dignam, Avis Bunny, June Tobin, Michael Gambon, Maurice Murphy, Eric Robinson? Johann Strauss? *(reproachful)* Oh, milord. You've been cheating.

**RUSTLESS:**
Well – only a bit, Bates. They're real people. Got them off the wireless. Damn good they were, too.

**BATES:**
But whoever reads them will know they're made up, milord.

**RUSTLESS:**
Nonsense, Bates – nobody reads them. They just put them on the scales – tot them up by the pound. That's why it's called the weight of public opinion. Ah,

Badger. *(Badger has entered, with his paper.)* Let's have a look.

**BADGER:**
*(handing over his paper)* Here you are, milord.

**RUSTLESS:**
*(staring at it)* What's this, Badger? Been doing your pools?

**BADGER:**
No, milord – I got quite a lot of people to sign, but they all seemed to be illiterate. They all put crosses.

**RUSTLESS:**
Oh, I thought your draws had come up. Let's see, how many ...

**BATES:**
Seventeen, milord.

**RUSTLESS:**
*(adding more crosses)* Just make it up to a round figure. There. Thirty. That's more like it. Right. Now, Bates – you'd better get on with your banners and placards for the march. I leave the wording to you.

**BATES:**
Very good, milord. I bought a lovely lot of paints and the grocer gave me some cardboard boxes to cut up. I can't wait – it's ages since I've done anything with a brush! *(She exits happily.)*

**RUSTLESS:**
That's true – it's about a month since she swept her room out. I could have written my name in the dust on her chest of drawers the other day.

**BADGER:**
I trust you didn't, milord.

**RUSTLESS:**
No no, that would be a bit of a give-away. I wrote yours instead.

**BADGER:**
Milord!

**RUSTLESS:**
No, don't worry, Badger – just one of my jokes. *(Thinking)* Huh!

**BADGER:**
What's the matter, milord?

**RUSTLESS:**
I was trying to think of the other one. Never mind. Now, we've got all these signatures – where do we take them?

**BADGER:**
It's usual to take them to Number Ten, milord.

**RUSTLESS:**
What, Downing Street you mean? We're not marching all the way up there. Anyway, I don't even know the fellow.

**RUSTLESS:**
Perhaps the police-station, milord?

**RUSTLESS:**
That's it. Damned good idea, Badger. The police station it is. Have the chaps ready to march at 09.30 hours precisely.

**BADGER:**
What time's that, milord?

**RUSTLESS:**
Er – about a quarter to ten. *(Goes to old lady and deaf gent.)* Exciting, isn't it? *(They are both asleep on each other's shoulders.)*

*Cut to: film.*

*(A village street, or country road.)*

*(Start on close up of Rustless poster – "A man must have his railway".)*

*(Pull back to see the procession. In front of Rustless is a Boys Brigade type bugle band, fairly tuneless but keen. We see the various placards and banners.)*

*(Effie and Badger – a banner, saying "We've got our rights".)*

*(Cook and Dithers – a banner saying "Don't let them take our station".)*

*(Then Bates – a placard, saying "They're letting our picknickers down".)*

*(Then the old lady saying "Join our campaign" and finally the deaf gent hobbling along with a placard which says "I need my MP's support".)*

*(Bates who is fourth in line, decides to move up a bit, and comes up between Dithers and Cook. Her placard gets partly obscured by Dithers's half of the banner, so that we read the two halves together, which now seem to say "don't let them take our nickers down".)*

*(Dithers notices this, and possibly an onlooker or two. Bates too, sees what has happened, and moves quickly away and joins Effie, who also has half of a banner (sharing with Badger). Bates looks rather relieved, and smiles at Effie. We pan up to the poster. The message now reads: "we've got our nickers down".)*

*(Dithers, by now, is swigging freely from his hip-flask, and has attracted a local tart, who is helping him out with the liquor.)*

*(Rustless, walking along, suddenly bangs his poster against a lamp post or overhanging branch of a tree. We see the bottom half of his poster fall off, revealing the grocer's carton underneath. The poster now reads.
"A man must have his oats – the way to health!")*

*(He carries on, ignorant of the new message.)*

*(Dithers is now weaving about a bit, causing the banner to keep collapsing (the banners are made of sheeting) and eventually – after draping itself round the old lady's head a couple of times – Dithers goes the wrong side of a lamp post, and it splits up the middle.)*

*(The procession reaches a sign on a fence saying "police station".)*

*(Rustless's face drops – and we see that the police station is a pile of bricks and rubble. A notice states that it has "been demolished to make way for redevelopment".)*

*(Rustless, Bates and Badger – looking determined.)*

*(The scene changes to the station itself – or at least, to the level-crossing close by.)*

*(A long shot as they approach the level-crossing gates.)*

*(Then a closer shot as Bates steps forward, and chains herself to the gates (on the level crossing side).)*

*(Close up as she tries to look like Mrs Pankhurst.)*

*(Close up of Rustless, looking at his pocket-watch.)*

*(Long shot – the others retreat, leaving Bates chained.)*

*(Close up of Bates – in background a train approaching behind her.)*

*(Reaction shot of the others, in a group.)*

*(Shot of signalman (close up) – train noise over.)*

*(Close up of his hand – presses a button.)*

*(The gates swing open, and Bates with them.)*

*(Close up of her in full swing. Terrified. She comes to a jerky stop. One of her stockings falls down. The train roars past. The gates open again, and she is once more across the line.)*

*(Disappointed reaction from the others.)*

*(Fade out and in – a long shot of the railway line – excluding the gates.)*

*(Everyone except Bates, is sitting on the line.)*

*(They are singing "we shall not be moved".)*

*(A couple of close ups – Dithers swigging his hip-flask.)*

*(Back to long-shot – a train is heard suddenly, as one, they leap up and run out of frame.)*

*(As soon as they are clear, the train thunders through.)*

*(As it disappears, the singing starts again.)*

*(Cut to them all, sitting on the station roof.)*

*(Cut to Bates's other stocking falling down as she crashes to a stop.)*

*(Fade out and in fast.)*

*(Long shot – train approaching.)*

*(Pull back to reveal the back of Effie, in a bikini, posing like a pin-up. As train approaches, we cut to her front – she is giving the hitch-hike gesture.)*

*(Train noise gets nearer.)*

Cut to: close-up of the driver's cabin.

*(The driver's face disappears. He is as queer as a coot. Train rushes by, disdainfully.)*

*(Bates swings out again and comes fact to face with a water-spraying lorry. As she swings back, the lorry moves forward, spraying her from the waist down.)*

*(The line again. Dithers is throwing chicken-meal on the line. He opens a basket, and takes chickens out (close up) a wider shot – the chickens are happily eating the chicken-food.)*

*(Another angle – a train approaching.)*

*(A shot of the others, watching. The train hurtles past them, and a chicken flies into shot near them.)*

*(Much clucking and squawking.)*

*(Cut to where the chickens were – the chickens have gone, and in their place are about a dozen new-laid eggs. Close up Dithers, looking surprised.)*

*(Shot of Cook as she gathers them up quickly, in her hat.)*

*(Fade out and in.)*

*(The whole group – Bates, bedraggled, has now joined them – sitting dejected on the platform.)*

*(A train is heard.)*

*(Nobody bothers to look up. Suddenly they realise that it is stopping.)*

*(They all leap up, delighted. A long shot of the train – they hurry towards it. Some doors open, and three policemen step out, grab everybody, and bundle them into the train. It pulls out of the station.)*

Cut to: studio.

*(A tiny cell in a police-station – the whole group are crammed into the cell.)*

**RUSTLESS:**
It's outrageous, Badger! Damned police. I'll have the bloody law on them.

**BADGER:**
I'm afraid they are the law, milord.

**RUSTLESS:**
What? Yes I know – but they might at least give us separate cells. I mean it's not decent. We can't all get in one bed.

**BATES:**
I don't expect they'll keep us here overnight, milord. They can't. I haven't got my nightie.

**RUSTLESS:**
Dammit all, Bates, if you're sharing a bed with three men, you won't need a damn nightie.

**BADGER:**
I wouldn't worry, milord – your solicitor is

bound to be here in a minute.

**BATES:**
How will he get us out, milord?

**RUSTLESS:**
With a shoe-horn, I should imagine, Bates.

*(A policeman arrives.)*

**PC:**
Your solicitor, your lordship. Shall I show him in?

**RUSTLESS:**
Show him in? It's so crushed in here it's affecting Effie's breathing.

*Cut to: shot of Effie, face to face with Dithers, squashed together. Dithers is breathing a bit heavy as well. (Solicitor approaches the cell.)*

**SOLICITOR:**
Afternoon, milord.

**RUSTLESS:**
Come on, Wainwright, we've been stuck here for ages.

**SOLICITOR:**
Sorry, milord. My partner rang me – I've just got back off holiday.

**RUSTLESS:**
Where have you been?

**SOLICITOR:**
Well we started off motoring through France, but the weather was so dreadful that we decided ...

**RUSTLESS:**
I'm not talking about your blasted holiday – don't want a damned travelogue. I mean, what took you so long?

**SOLICITOR:**
Oh – had to get you bailed. Of course, I went to the police station near Chrome Hall at first – but that's been pulled down, to make way for the new road.

**RUSTLESS:**
What? New road?

**SOLICITOR:**
Yes – didn't you know about that? New trunk road coming through the village. That's why the station is having to come down. To make room for it.

**BATES:**
But, milord – that's marvellous.

**RUSTLESS:**
What?

**BATES:**
We don't have to worry about the station, if there's going to be a decent road nearby.

**RUSTLESS:**
By jove, Bates, you're right. Solves our problem. The customers can still flow in. Splendid! I say, that's a relief. *(he sits on the bed)* Badger! This calls for a celebration. As soon as we get back, champagne all round. The best!

**BADGER:**
Very good, milord.

**RUSTLESS:**
Cook! A slap-up meal is indicated. Got anything in?

**COOK:**
No. You'll have to make do with scrambled eggs.

**RUSTLESS:**
Scrambled eggs?

**COOK:**
Well, I should think they will be by now – you've just sat on them.

**RUSTLESS:**
What?

*As he gets up slowly, revealing Cook's hat on the bed, the credits roll.*

# EPISODE SIX

*"Carnival Night"*

*The hall. Rustless is on the phone. Bates is arranging some flowers by the desk.*

**RUSTLESS:**
I see sir – yes, when will this be for? Next Friday night? Yes quite. It's a sort of trade convention is it? More of a conference. I see. And how many gentlemen will it be? Oh – fourteen single rooms. Must they be single? They must. Why is that? Aren't you speaking to one another? Yes, I suppose you've got a point. Talking to each other all day, you don't want to have to sleep with each other as well. Quite – I'm like that with Bates.

*(Bates reacts.)*

**RUSTLESS:**
Bates, my secretary. Anyway, look here, I think we can manage to fit you all in – some of you may have to sleep in double beds, on your own, but you won't mind that, will you? Well it costs a little bit more – it's a question of the maids getting done in the mornings. Still, give them five bob each and they're happy. Good, well, look forward to seeing you all on Friday night. Splendid. Ta-ta *(phone down.)*

**BATES:**
Large booking, milord?

**RUSTLESS:**
Yes – Convention, or conference, or something Bates. Jolly useful, what?

**BATES:**
Yes milord – where are they coming from?

**RUSTLESS:**
Blackpool – I suppose there's no room up there for conferences – always full of damn politicians.

**BATES:**
It must be a jolly good source of revenue milord – we ought to cultivate that sort of clientele.

**RUSTLESS:**
Yes, you're absolutely right – sort of make a special event of it – let the word get round that we give 'em a good time. Might get a lot more bookings.

**BATES:**
Yes. *(Uncertainly)* Do you think we do give people a good time here, milord?

**RUSTLESS:**
What?

**BATES:**
There's not really much in the way of entertainment, is there milord? Especially since Mr Dithers broke that croquet mallet.

**RUSTLESS:**
Yes – damn nuisance that. I'll have to get that crossed out of the AA book. Well, what do you suggest we do, Bates old thing? Invest in another snakes and ladders board.

**BATES:**
Well, it really needs to be something a bit more exciting, milord: something, oh I don't know, lively.

**RUSTLESS:**
You used to love it in the old days, Bates.

**BATES:**
I know milord, but people nowadays are more – *(She wriggles her shoulders and clicks her fingers.)* They want to – *(She sways from the hips and waves her arms about.)* – They want to sort of – move it about a bit.

*(Badger enters.)*

**RUSTLESS:**
Ah, Badger. It's alright. Bates is moving it about.

**BADGER:**
So I see milord.

**BATES:**
Sorry, milord. I just got carried away.

**RUSTLESS:**
You probably will be in you go on like that – in a plain van. Bates was just talking about entertainment, Badger. We've got a trade conference booked in for Friday. Fourteen of 'em.

**BADGER:**
Oh, splendid, milord.

**BATES:**
I was just saying Mr Badger, we really ought to try and provide something special in the way of amusement for the gentlemen. I mean, I don't know what men like to do.

**RUSTLESS:**
If you carry on dancing about like that, you'll pretty soon find out Bates.

**BADGER:**
Why not a dance, milord?

**RUSTLESS:**
What?

**BADGER:**
One could invite members of the public as well, milord – advertise it in the newspaper.

**RUSTLESS:**
Yes. Damn good publicity.

**BATES:**
Us? Do a cabaret milord?

**RUSTLESS:**
Why not? I've got a load of songs and comic patter upstairs – used to do it in the army. There's that marvellous take off of the Western Brothers I used to do with old Jimmy Snetterton. You and I could do that Bates.

**BATES:**
Oh. Yes milord.

**RUSTLESS:**
You're rather like old Jimmy, come to think of it Bates. Funny looking chap. Yes,

I've got loads of stuff – keep going for hours.

**BADGER:**
Er – might I suggest that we employ a speciality act of some sort as well, milord? To relieve the, er – to relieve the monotony of having to do it all?

**RUSTLESS:**
Speciality act? How d'you mean Badger?

**BADGER:**
Well, my brother in law at the Co-Op knows the name of an agency you can telephone, and they will provide an act, at a very reasonable fee.

**RUSTLESS:**
Really? Good, are they?

**BADGER:**
Oh yes milord. They sent an amazing gentleman contortionist to my brother in law's party. He came on in a sort of leotard and locked his elbows behind his head, and grabbed a foot in each hand. It was extraordinary.

**RUSTLESS:**
Must have been.

**BADGER:**
And do you know what he did then, milord?

**RUSTLESS:**
Fell over?

**BADGER:**
He rocked all around the room on his stomach.

**BATES:**
Golly – I would have loved to have seen him. *(She puts her arms behind her head, trying to get her elbows to meet.)*

**RUSTLESS:**
Now simmer down Bates – you're getting a bit physical this morning. You been eating those underdone steaks again?

**BATES:**
Sorry milord – it's just that I can't wait.

**BADGER:**
My brother in law would also oblige at the piano, milord – he's an excellent sight reader.

**RUSTLESS:**
Damn good idea, Badger. Tell you what, give him a ring, and ask him to book us a speciality act as well.

**BADGER:**
Very good milord.

**RUSTLESS:**
Better not get that contortionist though – I don't want Bates getting too worked up, she's liable to bust a suspender. *(Bates giggles excitedly.)* You see – she's giggling now. Ask Dithers to turn the central heating down in her room would you? Maybe that's what's causing it.

**BATES:**
No, honestly, milord, I'm quite alright. I do feel a bit excited though. I think I'll go and sit in a cold bath. That should damped my ardour!

*(She trips out, gaily, bumping into Cook, who is entering.)*

**BATES:**
*(giggling)* Sorry Cook, dear!

*(She exits.)*

**RUSTLESS:**
Ah, there you are, Cook.

**COOK:**
What's up with her? Sat on a feather?

**RUSTLESS:**
Now listen to me Cook–

**COOK:**
No, you listen to me. I've got a serious complaint.

**RUSTLESS:**
I know. Duck's disease.

**COOK:**
Look here, what's this I hear about a do next Friday?

**RUSTLESS:**
How can you have heard, we haven't told anyone yet. Have you been standing on tiptoe listening at the keyhole?

**COOK:**
I happened to be passing. These walls are very thin you know.

**RUSTLESS:**
Listen, Cook, you know the old saying "Thin walls need thick ears." And that's just what you'll get if I catch you listening at doors again. A thick ear.

**COOK:**
Never mind that – is there a do – or isn't there?

**RUSTLESS:**
We are considering holding a "do", as you put it, yes.

**COOK:**
Well how am I supposed to manage fourteen extra men? Me equipment's worn out.

**RUSTLESS:**
What?

**COOK:**
Falling to bits. Next time the dustman comes round, I'm going to stick it out the window.

**RUSTLESS:**
Stick what out the window?

**COOK:**
Everything. Mind you, I doubt if he'll touch it.

**RUSTLESS:**
Look here Cook, kindly stop rambling

and be more specific. Details man, details.

**COOK:**
Well for one thing, me carrot grater's on its last legs.

**RUSTLESS:**
Is it?

**COOK:**
Me gas pressure's uncontrollable; every time I light the gas it blows me hat off. And me pastry-sieve is full of holes.

**RUSTLESS:**
But dammit, a sieve is supposed to be full of holes.

**COOK:**
Big holes, I mean. Me dumplings drop straight through it into the sink. And all that marble.

**RUSTLESS:**
What's wrong with the marble? Damn good surface to work on.

**COOK:**
Treacherous, that's what it is. I'd like to see you take your puff pastry out of a hot over, and slap it on a cold marble slab. It's enough to give you pneumonia.

**RUSTLESS:**
Well, what do you want me to do about it?

**COOK:**
Come down to the kitchen and see for yourself. There's that old knife-grinder. That's another thing I'm up against.

**RUSTLESS:**
The whole thing sounds dangerous to me. Come on then. Badger! Where are you?

**BADGER:**
*(who has been in the office at the back)* I was just looking up that agent's number milord – for the speciality act.

**RUSTLESS:**
Good man. Get on with that – and ring the local rag, see if they can cover the event would you? Send someone up for an interview. We can't afford to hang about. There's a hell of a lot to do before Friday.

*(He and Cook exit.)*

**BADGER:**
Yes, milord. *(Looking in phone book and singing)* I could have danced all night –

*(Fade out.)*

*(Fade in.)*

*(It is the afternoon of the big day. Extra flowers in the hall, balloons hanging up. The deaf gent sits asleep in an armchair. The old lady is playing patience at a low coffee table. Rustless is talking to a callow youth – the reporter from the local rag.)*

**RUSTLESS:**
It's been a bit of a rush, but we've managed it.

**YOUTH:**
And you expect to be holding more of these Carnival nights, milord?

**RUSTLESS:**
If this one is a success, yes. And I don't see why it shouldn't be. In time, my intention is to make this place the playground of the Cotswolds.

**YOUTH:**
*(looking at deaf gent and old lady)* Pretty quiet at the moment, ain't it?

**RUSTLESS:**
Oh yes, but these good people are resident guests. Yes, it is quiet around these parts. That's why I want to get the place livened up a bit. I mean the nearest bit of excitement must be about ten miles from here.

**YOUTH:**
Oh, what's that?

**RUSTLESS:**
The Natural History Museum. Yes, we all need to *(wriggles his shoulders and snaps his fingers, as Bates did)* you know, get it all, I mean, move it up and down a bit. That's why I'm looking forward to tonight – all these bright young businessmen bursting, ready to paint the town, it'll bring a bit of life –

*(Two men have entered. They are dressed in dark suits, black ties, and both have glum, hard faces. They are about fifty years of age – they stare stonily about them, and approach the desk where Badger stands waiting.)*

**RUSTLESS:**
 –and er–I'm sure we'll all–er–have a damn good time. *(Staring at the two men.)*

**YOUTH:**
*(getting up)* Ah. Well, I wish you luck your Lordship – thanks for the interview. Cheerio.

**RUSTLESS:**
*(distracted)* Er – cheerio old fruit.

*(The youth passes the two men.)*

**YOUTH:**
Turned out nice again, hasn't it?

*(The two men stare at him, stonily. He exits.)*

**BATES:**
*(entering with gramophone)* Here we are milord. Mr Dithers got it working again.

**RUSTLESS:**
Oh good. What did he do?

**BATES:**
Oh. Nothing much milord – just removed one of your socks from the loudspeaker.

**RUSTLESS:**
Good grief, that's right. I remember now. I stuffed it in there during one of my first

wife's orgies. That was before the war. Should have stuffed it down her throat instead. Would have saved me a fortune in gin and orange.

*(Bates has put on a record – it plays "Keep Your Sunny Side Up" very scratchily. The two men pass by, on their way to their rooms.)*

**BATES:**
Pretty, isn't it?

**RUSTLESS:**
Charming Bates. *(Rushes over to Badger.)* Who in hell's name were those two, Badger?

**BADGER:**
Two of the party milord. Not very chatty gentlemen.

**RUSTLESS:**
Must be the firm's accountants. One the skids, the whole thing, I shouldn't wonder. *(To old lady)* How's the casino–paying out? *(He sits beside her, watching her play patience.)*

*(Effie enters, followed by Dithers. They both carry yellow dusters. Dithers also has a long feather duster. They start to dust. Bates is humming quietly to the music.)*

**RUSTLESS:**
*(pointing to cards)* Red eight on black queen.

**OLD LADY:**
You can't do that.

**RUSTLESS:**
I always do. Makes the game a lot quicker.

**OLD LADY:**
You can only put an eight on a nine.

**RUSTLESS:**
Oh well, of course, if you want to make it difficult for yourself.

*(Dithers aprroaches the deaf gent who is asleep. He dusts his chair, and then dusts the*

*deaf gent. Knees, shoulders, shoes – then takes off the deaf gent's glasses, polishes them and puts them back on. Finally removes his deaf aid, polishes the ear piece, blows into it and puts it back. Ambles off, dusting. Effie is leaning towards Rustless, dusting a low coffee table.)*

**OLD LADY:**
What goes on a red ace?

**RUSTLESS:**
*(staring at Effie – a close up of her bosom)* Er – pink two.

**OLD LADY:**
Pardon?

*(Effie turns away and bends over to pick up the ash tray, flowers etc. From the floor, where she had put them to dust the table.)*

**RUSTLESS:**
*(staring at her knickers)* Er – as you were – black two.

*(Dithers, with feather duster, is dusting a pair of large plant-stands or jardinieres. Having dusted one, he moves to the next one. Having dusted that, he moves on and dusts Effie's knickers. She straightens up and stalks out of the room.)*

**RUSTLESS:**
Play a lot of patience do you Mrs Ringer?

**OLD LADY:**
Since my husband passed on, yes.

*(Three men enter – all in dark suits, with black ties, and hatchet-faced. Rustless reacts.)*

**OLD LADY:**
He learnt to play cards in the army. He fought with Kitchener you know.

**RUSTLESS:**
Really? Who won? *(Distracted.)*

**OLD LADY:**
He loved cards. Unfortunately he was discharged from the army in 1916.

**RUSTLESS:**
What for? Cheating?

**OLD LADY:**
He was shot in the Dardanelles.

**RUSTLESS:**
*(staring at the men as they go upstairs)* Oh dear. Didn't interfere with your married life at all did it?

*(More men start to arrive, all solemn, and all soberly dressed. Bates, who has switched off the gramophone, sidles over to Rustless.)*

**BATES:**
Milord.

**RUSTLESS:**
What is it Bates?

**BATES:**
I do hope we've done the right thing. They don't exactly look as if they are bent on having a good time, do they?

**RUSTLESS:**
Not at the moment, Bates, no. Still, they'll probably loosen up later on – I mean, everybody likes a good laugh, don't they? I wonder what sort of business they're in?

*(We fade on his thoughtful face.)*

*(Fade up on the ballroom.)*

*(A small raised platform at one end of the room – chairs and wooden benches round the room. Various pathetic decorations hanging up. A piano – a low upright – on the platform. The gramophone is playing, the old lady is dancing with the deaf gent. A few people in fancy dress are dotted about. The fourteen men sit round the walls, solemnly.)*

*(We fade up on Rustless's face, talking to one of the men.)*

**RUSTLESS:**
Oh really? Undertakers? I say that's jolly interesting. How's business, alright?

**UNDERTAKER:**
Quite healthy, thank you. *(He speaks like he looks.)*

**RUSTLESS:**
Healthy is it? Ha ha! Still, I suppose this s a good time of year for you isn't it? Cold and wet. Dropping like nine-pins. What about wood? Alright for wood supplies are you?

**UNDERTAKER:**
Everything's going up.

**RUSTLESS:**
Oh, makes a change. I mean they usually go down don't they? *(Explains his joke)* You know. *(Indicates)* Down. Under the – *(the undertaker stares at him, po-faced.)* Enjoying yourself, are you?

**UNDERTAKER:**
Thank you.

**RUSTLESS:**
Oh splendid. Well, I must mingle. We must have a chat later – who knows. I might be able to put a little business your way one of these days.

**UNDERTAKER:**
*(sepulchrally)* I'm quite sure you will.

**RUSTLESS:**
Yes. *(Thinks about this)* Quite. Well – keep smiling.

*(He wanders off towards another group of guests. A woman in fancy dress enters – behind her comes Dithers, in his old boiler suit. The lady goes over to a group of people, including Mrs Featherstone, a large woman in fancy dress.)*

**MRS FEATHERSTONE:**
*(very frothy and country)*: Hello my dear Cynthia, so glad you could come. *(Shakes her hand.)* Good evening. *(Shakes Dithers's hand.)* Well I must say you've got splendid costumes. *(To Dithers)* I love the tramp costume – divine ! *(Dithers laughs and winks at her.)* I must say I've been longing

to meet you. Cynthia's told me so much about you. I'm so interested in psychiatry. *(closer to him, flirting)* I'd love to have a session with you sometime.

*(Dithers, not knowing quite what to do, gooses her firmly.)*

*Cut to: the hall.*

**RUSTLESS:**
*(hurrying in)* Bates! Bates, where are you?

*(Through the entrance comes a tall girl in a fur coat. Rustles approaches her.)*

**RUSTLESS:**
Oh, good evening. I'm Lord Rustless, may I take your coat?

*(Rustless removes the girl's coat. Underneath she wears only two tassels and a G string. Rustless puts the coat back round her quickly.)*

**RUSTLESS:**
I say, excuse me, you've forgotten to put any clothes on.

**GIRL:**
That's my costume.

**RUSTLESS:**
Really? What have you come as? A hot cross bun.

**GIRL:**
I'm the speciality act. I dance with a snake.

**RUSTLESS:**
*(reacts)* Ah – oh. Well. Er – I'm afraid it won't do.

**GIRL:**
Why not?

**RUSTLESS:**
Well – they're all vegetarians. They couldn't stand the sight of all that meat. The snake I mean.

*(He is still clutching the coat when Bates*

enters, dressed in a rather sad Greek-dancing costume. She stares, thinking Rustless is cuddling the girl.)

**BATES:**
Oh. Sorry to interrupt, milord.

**RUSTLESS:**
What? No, no Bates – the lady was just leaving. *(To girl)* Go into the office, and I'll give you the money in a minute. Then you can go home.

**GIRL:**
Oh right. *(To Bates)* That was the quickest twenty quid I've ever earned!

*(She goes.)*

**BATES:**
*(puzzled)* Hadn't you better sit down and rest milord.

**RUSTLESS:**
Rest? Why should I want to rest Bates? I've hardly started.

**BATES:**
Oh dear.

**RUSTLESS:**
By the by, Bates, I've just found out what our gentlemen do for a living.

**BATES:**
Oh? What milord?

**RUSTLESS:**
They're bally undertakers.

**BATES:**
They're what?

**RUSTLESS:**
Yes – the brass-handle brigade, Bates; the one-way ticket merchants.

**BATES:**
Oh golly gumdrops. Not exactly the ideal audience, milord.

**RUSTLESS:**
Quite. They'll not only kill the performance, they'll bury it as well. I say, it'll be time to start in a minute. Know your lines? For the song?

**BATES:**
Oh, yes milord. I've got my Greek dance first.

**RUSTLESS:**
Oh yes, of course. That might get 'em going.

*(Effie enters, with lots of balloons.)*

**RUSTLESS:**
Ah, Effie, old thing. How's the sale of balloons going?

*(Effie speaks silently.)*

**RUSTLESS:**
Do they? All want to buy the same ones? Which particular ones do they want?

*(Effie speaks.)*

**RUSTLESS:**
Oh, those ones. Yes. Rather embarrassing, what? *(She speaks.)* Quite. You can't let 'em have those, can you? They're not for sale. No. *(She speaks.)* A man keeps doing what? I should have thought they were ideal. You tell him to mind his own business. Right, off you go, there's a thing.

*(She goes.)*

**BATES:**
Trouble, milord?

**RUSTLESS:**
Everyone wants to buy the two big balloons over the door, Bates. People get very excited over nothing, don't they?

*(Badger's voice over a crackly microphone, is heard.)*

**BADGER:**
*(off)* Ladies and gentlemen – it's cabaret-

time! First of all I would like to present–
*(etc.)*

**RUSTLESS:**
*(over this)* Good grief, Badger's started!
Come on Bates, you're on! *(They rush out.)*

*Cut to: ballroom.*

*(Badger is at the mike.)*

**BADGER:**
–and here she is, dancing the Wind
Dance – Miss Mildred Bates!

*(Desultory clapping. Dithers is crouched at
the gramophone. Bates enters, and flits about
to the music. Reaction on the undertakers –
blank expressions.)*

*(Bates begins to flit about. The boards of the
platform are very hollow – they thud as Bates
dances. Dithers sits at the gramophone
swigging from his hip flask, happily. The
record runs down – Bates tries to do slower
and slower leaps in the air. Dithers winds it
up again. Bates increases speed. The record
sticks in the middle of a gesture. After about
eight or nine repeats, Bates gets upset and flits
off, near to tears. Badger leads polite
applause.)*

**BADGER:**
Well I'm sure we all enjoyed that flight
into fantasy.

*(Dithers burps.)*

**BADGER:**
And now, if I may, I would like to recite a
poem entitled "My Puppy".
I had a little puppy once
When I had just turned four
My mother bought it for me
From a gypsy at the door;
Oh how I loved that puppy,
The sweetest little thing
I used to take it for a walk
Upon a piece of string.
But soon my pup began to grow
It's face got quite distorted,
And when someone came to the door,

It didn't bark, it snorted.
It grew a little curly tail
And got so fat that one day
We realised it was a pig –
So we had it for lunch on Sunday!
Thank you.

*(Applause is getting thinner. More reactions
on the undertakers.)*

**BADGER:**
And now, Mr Nathaniel Dithers – with
song! And dance!

*(Dithers clambers up to the rostrum, and the
pianist plays the introduction to his song.)*

**DITHERS** *(sings freely)*:
I love the girls,
I take 'em behind the shed
I don't know what to say to 'em
'Cos I'm simple in the head.
But I've got a little trick
That pleases 'em I've found
I just lifts up me left leg
And thumps it on the ground.
*(thump thump – with foot)*
So if you're with a lady
And you don't know what to do,
Just remember this advice
What I am giving you,
If she's eighteen, or eighty
You'll please her I'll be bound
If you just lift your left leg up
And thump it on the ground.
*(Thump thump.)*

*(He executes four or eight bars of a curious
thumping dance.)*

**DITHERS** *(cont'd)*:
I met a girl in Aylesbury once,
And thought that I would try
To give her a quick *(thump thump)* me
dears
As she was passing by
I *(thump)* her once, I *(thump)* her twice
She stopped and gave a smile
We're married now and so I can
*(thump thump)* her all the while.

*(More thin applause, led heartily by Badger.*

*Behind the little door, Bates has changed into what is obviously one of Rustless's little dinner jackets. The coat isn't very much too big, but the trousers are enormous round the waist. She is made up like a western brother.)*

**RUSTLESS:**
It's us now, Bates old chap. *(Suddenly realising)* Good grief! Got the wrong tie on. Must have the old school tie. They always wore that. Where the hell is it Bates?

**BATES:**
Oh dear. I'm afraid I'm using it to keep these trousers up, milord. They're so enormous.

**RUSTLESS:**
Well, give it me man, for heaven's sake – quick, we're on.

**BATES:**
But, milord–

**RUSTLESS:**
No buts Bates, quick. *(He fumbles round her waist, pulls off the tie, and starts to put it on.)*

**BATES:**
But milord how am I going to manage – look!

*(She pulls out the waist, showing how big the trousers are.)*

**RUSTLESS:**
You'll have to hold them up with one hand, Bates – come on –

*(He grabs her arms, he grabs her trousers.)*

*Cut to: ballroom.*

**BADGER:**
Ladies and gentlemen – the Western Brothers, Kenneth and George!

*(Rustless enters, followed by Bates.)*

*(Standing together they begin to sing, or rather speak, in the manner of the Western Brothers.)*

**RUSTLESS:**
What's the world coming to? What's going on?

**BOTH:**
The end is in sight, the end is in sight.

**BATES:**
Dear old England is broke, to the dogs it has gone.

**BOTH:**
The end is in sight, the end is in sight.

**RUSTLESS:**
We can't afford whisky – it's ninepence a round –

**BATES:**
And with Income Tax up to three bob in the pound.

**RUSTLESS:**
We're really better off under the ground.

**BOTH:**
The end is in sight, the end is in sight.

*(Over this last line, reaction of disapproval from the undertakers.)*

**VERSE 2:**

**BATES:**
What's the world coming to? What's going on?

**BOTH:**
The end is in sight, the end is in sight.

**RUSTLESS:**
Now there's a woman in Parliament, all hope is gone.

**BOTH:**
The end is in sight, the end is in sight.

**BATES:**
We just can't compete with the feminine gender.

**RUSTLESS:**
When a short skirt goes up and we glimpse a suspender.

**BOTH:**
We might as well put up our hands and surrender.

*(They do so, and Bates's trousers fall down, leaving her in her "directoire" knickers.)*

**BOTH:**
The end is in sight, the end is in sight.

*Cut to: the Undertaker.*

*(He suddenly guffaws – so do all the others. Meanwhile, Rustless and Bates, the latter trying to retrieve her trousers, go into a simple dance to the same tune, played in tempo. The guffaws continue throughout. Rustless contrives to kick Bates in the dance, as she stoops to pick up her trousers again. At the end of the dance, which is short, they stagger off to thunderous applause.)*

**RUSTLESS:**
*(To Bates, as they arrive at the side of the rostrum.)* There you are Bates – told you they'd like the topical stuff. Always went well, that number.

**BATES:**
Oh, milord *(in tears)* I knew I'd make a mess of it!

**RUSTLESS:**
Nonsense old chap. It turned the tide – you'll never stop them now!

*Cut to: the rostrum. (The undertaker is up near the piano, whispering to the pianist. Badger is at the mike.)*

**BADGER:**
And now, it's talent-spotting time – and your own Mr Flint is going to lead you in some popular songs.

*(Loud applause and cheers. The pianist gives two bar intro and Mr Flint begins. He sings the first line, and everyone joins in with gusto.)*

**MR. FLINT:**
*(sings)*
Seated one day by the organ,
I was weary and ill at ease,

*He continues to sing "The Lost Chord" as balloons float down from the net on the ceiling and the credits roll.*

# EPISODE SEVEN

*"Full of Eastern Promise"*

*The reception hall. Rustless is on the phone*

**RUSTLESS:**
I see. Yes. Yes, that's rotten luck. Still, perhaps he can turn it into a short holiday. What? What? Oh, yes, it's very rural round here Oh yes, frightfully English. Yes, well it's rather short notice, but I'm sure we can accommodate His Excellency. Oh, His Serene Highness, I see. So how many will there be in the party? Ten. Yes, I think so, we're pretty empty at the moment. So I can expect them tonight? Fine, get the staff rushing about a bit. Thank you, Mr Salami, Malasi, sorry. Yes. About eight. Fine. 'Bye bye. Yes. May it shine on yours too. Ta – ta. *(Phone down.)*

*(The old lady totters in – passing through the hall.)*

**RUSTLESS:**
Morning, Mrs Ringer – how was breakfast?

**OLD LADY:**
I haven't had breakfast yet.

**RUSTLESS:**
I see. Old Bates isn't in there, is she? *(Bates enters.)* Ah, there you are, Bates old chap.

*(The old lady goes.)*

**BATES:**
Morning, milord. I'm looking for Mr Dithers, milord.

**RUSTLESS:**
Funny you should say that, Bates. So am I. In fact, I'm looking for everybody.

**BATES:**
Everybody, milord? What's happened?

**RUSTLESS:**
Bit of a panic on, Bates. Got a large party arriving at eight tonight. Lot to do. Get Badger on the blower, would you?

**BATES:**
Yes milord. *(Picks up internal phone, dials.)* What sort of party milord?

**RUSTLESS:**
An eastern Sheikh, complete with eight wives and a bodyguard,

**BATES:**
Golly Moses! *(Into phone)* Mr Badger? Could you round everyone up and come up to the hall? His Lordship wants a word. Thank you. *(Phone down.)* They're on their way, milord.

**RUSTLESS:**
Splendid.

**BATES:**
Did you say eight wives, milord?

**RUSTLESS:**
And a bodyguard. I should think he'd need one. Eight on to one's pretty frightening odds.

**BATES:**
Oh no, milord – it's the other way round. The bodyguard is to protect the wives, usually. These Eastern potentates are very jealous men. No one is allowed near their women, milord,

**RUSTLESS:**
Of course, you'd know about all this, wouldn't you, Bates?

You were brought up out East.

**BATES:**
Well, India mostly, milord. But I did spend quite a time in Turkey. My father worked in Constantinople, with an attaché.

**RUSTLESS:**
What, sort of door-to-door salesman you mean?

**BATES:**
No, not an attaché case, milord – he worked for the government.

**RUSTLESS:**
I see.

**BATES:**
The bodyguards are usually eunuchs, milord.

**RUSTLESS:**
I beg your pardon? What's a eunuch?

**BATES:**
*(embarassed)* Well, milord – it's a man with erm, you know, milord.

**RUSTLESS:**
Oh, hang on – it's that politician chap, isn't it?

**BATES:**
No, milord, that's "Enoch". A eunuch is a man without any feminine interests.

**RUSTLESS:**
Really? Must be a queer sort of chap.

**BATES:**
Anyway – er – what I was going to say, milord, is, what about sleeping arrangements?

**RUSTLESS:**
Ah. Now, I thought we'd put them in the west wing. There are four rooms in a row there.

**BATES:**
You mean that the wives could double up, milord?

**RUSTLESS:**
Let's face it, they'd have to, in these rooms They're so tiny, even a single person has to double up. The point is he'll want to be near his wives. And there's a bathroom at the other end of the corridor.

**BATES:**
I think he'll want to be nearer than that, milord.

**RUSTLESS:**
Really? In case he has to get up in the night, you mean?

**BATES:**
Not nearer the bathroom, milord – nearer his wives.

**RUSTLESS:**
Oh I see.

**BATES:**
I think he'll want them all in the same room with him.

**RUSTLESS:**
Good grief! What a terrifying thought. Imagine having breakfast in bed with that lot. One's elbows would never be out of someone else's porridge.

*(Enter Badger, followed by Cook, Effie and Dithers.)*

**BADGER:**
Here we are, milord, sorry to keep you waiting.

**RUSTLESS:**
Ah, there you are everyone. Now then.

**COOK:**
Oi!

**RUSTLESS:**
What is it, Cook?

**COOK:**
Is this going to be a long session? Only my meat puddings need seeing to.

**RUSTLESS:**
What?

**COOK:**
I don't want 'em hanging about and going limp.

**RUSTLESS:**
All right, Cook, all right. I'll be as brief as possible. Shut up and pin your ears back. Tonight, a large party is arriving to stay here; namely, a sheikh and his eight wives.

**DITHERS:**
*(interested)* Oh, ar?

**RUSTLESS:**
Yes, I thought that would interest you. Now the point is we are at the moment discussing where to sleep them.

**DITHERS:**
Two of the wives can sleep in my room.

**RUSTLESS:**
And where are you going to sleep?

**DITHERS:**
In my room.

**RUSTLESS:**
I was afraid you'd say that. No, they've all got to be together.

**BADGER:**
In one room, milord? We haven't got one big enough.

**BATES:**
Cook's room is very large, milord, we could get quite a few beds in there.

**RUSTLESS:**
No, that's no good either, Bates – then Cook's got nowhere to sleep.

**COOK:**
Don't worry about me. I could sleep on a clothes-line.

**DITHERS:**
Clothes-line's broke.

**RUSTLESS:**
Oh, pity.

**COOK:**
*(to Rustless)* What about your room?

**RUSTLESS:**
If you think I'm sharing my bed with you, Cook, you've got another think coming. Anyway, if it got around the village, people might begin to doubt your maidenly innocence.

**BATES:**
I don't mind giving mine up if it's going to help the situation, milord.

**RUSTLESS:**
That's awfully sweet of you, Bates. But I don't quite see how you giving up your maidenly innocence is going to help the situation.

**BATES:**
Oh no – my room, milord.

**RUSTLESS:**
Oh I see. I thought you were sticking your neck out a bit there,

**BADGER:**
If I may say so, milord, I think we are getting a little confused.

**RUSTLESS:**
You're quite right Badger. Now, let's start again. Dithers, you're a practical chap. What have you got to say?

**DITHERS:**
Hammocks!

**RUSTLESS:**
How dare you! There are ladies present.

**DITHERS:**
Hammocks – from the ceiling.

**RUSTLESS:**
Oh, my apologies.

**BATES:**
That's a good idea, milord.

**RUSTLESS:**
What, in my bedroom ceiling? Have you ever laid there and looked at it, Bates.

**BATES:**
No, of course not, milord.

**RUSTLESS:**
No – well if you had, you'd realise that it wouldn't take the weight of a drawing-pin: let alone three or four hammocks, filled with hefty young ladies. Matter of fact, a rather overweight bluebottle landed on it last night, and I got a bit worried. No, I should think His Serene Highness has enough trouble with his wives as it is; wouldn't want him to wake up with three or four of them on top of him. Would only increase his predicament.

**BADGER:**
Milord, I think the only answer is the billiard-room.

**RUSTLESS:**
The billiard-room?

**BADGER:**
There's ample room in there, milord – I'm sure we could organise it.

**RUSTLESS:**
I say, it's not a bad thought, Badger. And there's that downstairs bathroom next to it. What do you think, Bates?

**BATES:**
Well yes, milord, if Mr Badger thinks we can get it ready in time.

**BADGER:**
It's just a question of beds – I've got Mr

Dithers to help. We'd better start at once. *(He starts to go.)*

**DITHERS:**
It's my day off.

**RUSTLESS:**
Not any more, Dithers. The day off's off. Today, you are definitely on. So clear off, and get on.

**BATES:**
I'll go with them, milord – organise the linen with Effie. *(She goes.)*

**COOK:**
I'll get me puddings moving then. *(She starts to go.)*

**RUSTLESS:**
No, hang on, Cook, I we must have a chat about food. We've got to decide what to give them.

**COOK:**
Give 'em same as we're having. Irish stew.

**RUSTLESS:**
Stew? You can't give a Turkish nobleman Irish stew,

**COOK:**
Why not? An Irishman eats Turkish delight, doesn't he?

**RUSTLESS:**
Yes but not with carrots and onions in it. They like things like sheep's eyeballs, that sort of thing.

**COOK:**
Sheep's eyeballs? Where am I going to get sheep's eyeballs from?

**RUSTLESS:**
Sheep, I suppose. Ring the butcher.

**COOK:**
What shall I serve with 'em? A few chips?

**RUSTLESS:**
Look, I don't know what to serve 'em

with. Look in that Fanny Craddock annual I bought you for Christmas.

**COOK:**
I reckon he'd rather have traditional English food.

**RUSTLESS:**
Yes. You're probably right – well all right then, but for God's sake make it look a bit exotic. Now get cracking, there's a good chap, before we know where we are, the place will be full of dancing girls.

*(Fade out.)*

*(Fade in.)*

*(The same evening. Reception hall.)*

*(Bates is behind the reception desk. Rustless stands beside it. Badger waits at the door. A close up of the grandfather clock. It says half past four. It strikes three.)*

**RUSTLESS:**
Hmm. Quarter past eight. He's late.

**BADGER:**
*(looking out of door)* Here he is, milord.

*(A large Middle-Eastern man enters – bald, with dark glasses. He is dressed in a European suit.)*

**RUSTLESS:**
Your Serene Highness – welcome to our humble three-star hotel.

**MAN:**
I am Bagdore, His Serene Highness's bodyguard. I will sign register, please.

**BATES:**
Oh, certainly. *(Hands him register, he signs.)*

**BODYGUARD:**
His Serene Highness wishes to retire immediately.

**RUSTLESS:**
I see very well. Everything's prepared. I've

put you all in the billiard-room.

**BODYGUARD:**
Me also?

**RUSTLESS:**
Yes. That all right? You're not averse to billiard-rooms, are you?

**BODYGUARD:**
I not know anything about them.

**RUSTLESS:**
No, I suppose you wouldn't. Anyway, I hope you'll find it comfortable.

**BODYGUARD:**
Thank you. *(He goes to the door, and claps his hands, and beckons.)*

*(The wives enter in single file. Eight of them, all covered from head to foot in black loose costumes, just one eye showing. They line up in a row. The Sheikh enters – tinted glasses, bearded, head-dress, and European suit. He passes the line, bows to Rustless, who bows back, and follows the bodyguard, who is following Badger, towards the exit to the billiard-room. The wives trot along behind, still in single file.)*

**RUSTLESS:**
*(after they have gone)* Good gracious. Fancy being married to that lot. Like living with a lot of ball-point pens. Do they always dress like that Bates?

**BATES:**
Only in public, milord – in the harem they dress in much flimsier, lighter clothes. But that's only for the Sheikh himself, unless he cares to invite a close friend into the harem.

**RUSTLESS:**
Oh, they do that occasionally, do they?

**BATES:**
Sometimes, milord. It's considered a great honour.

**RUSTLESS:**
Yes, naturally. Might be a mixed blessing, though – I mean they're probably all shapes and sizes under that lot. Well. So much for this evening. Bit of an anticlimax. You'd better tell Cook to put her delicacies in the fridge.

**BATES:**
Very good, milord.

*(She goes towards the exit – the bodyguard appears suddenly, almost bumping into her.)*

**BATES:**
Oh! So sorry. You made me jump! *(She sidles off.)*

**BODYGUARD:**
I have a message from His Serene Highness.

**RUSTLESS:**
Oh yes?

**BODYGUARD:**
He wishes to tell you that he finds the room satisfactory.

**RUSTLESS:**
Oh, good.

**BODYGUARD:**
None of your servants must disturb him tonight. He is settling in with his wives.

**RUSTLESS:**
Quite.

**BODYGUARD:**
He will probably sleep until dinner-time tomorrow.

**RUSTLESS:**
I'm not surprised.

**BODYGUARD:**
Also he wishes to have word with you in his room regarding certain minor alterations to the amenities of the hotel.

**RUSTLESS:**
Ah. What, now?

**BODYGUARD:**
If you please. Will you come?

**RUSTLESS:**
Certainly. I shall be honoured. I've never seen the inside of a sheikh's billiard-room.

*(As they go, we fade out.)*

*Cut to: film.*

*(A corridor in the house. Low wide shot. Then close up of clock on the wall near a door. The time is eight o'clock. A cock crows. The clock begins to strike eight. When it has struck three, the door is thrown open, swinging back and hitting the clock.)*

*(It gives a fourth strangled, quivering note, followed by a cuckoo, and is silent. It is Dithers who has opened the door. He ambles along the corridor. He stops at a door. Close up of the door – marked "billiard room". He looks down. We cut to shot of the Sheikh's shoes outside his door, together with eight pairs of ladies' shoes. Snoring is heard from within. Dithers looks round, sees no-one about and peers through the keyhole. He straightens up – and opens the door a fraction.)*

*(From the other side of the door, we see his head slowly appear and react.)*

*(Then we cut to a wide shot of what he sees – the Sheikh, asleep on the billiard-table, which is piled up with cushions and mattresses.)*

*(A close up of him here, to establish.)*

*(All around – his wives, on mattresses and cushions on the floor. Dithers gulps, and starts to creep a little closer.)*

*(The camera tracks along a couple of sleeping girls, and we intercut close ups of girls with shots of Dithers's face.)*

*(The girls should appear semi-nude, without actually seeing too many vital statistics. They are Eastern, Arabic and Negro girls, no Europeans.)*

*(We hear Eastern music from the time the door opens. We see one of the girls stirring and waking up.)*

*(Cut to Dithers's reaction – petrified. Then, in slow motion, the girl gets up, and comes towards Dithers. She wears something floating and flimsy. She beckons Dithers, he reacts – they both float back to her bed by now, other girls have awoken and float round towards the bed. The first girl jumps up and down on the bed. Dithers, enchanted by it all, starts to do the same.)*

*(A couple of low shots of Dithers, on a trampoline which we don't see. He gets off the bed, leaps round the room. Reactions of delight from girls. He floats, in close up, and we pan him right into the arms of a bodyguard. Slow motion stops. The bodyguard hauls him off into the adjoining room, struggling. The girls all rush in after him.)*

*(The bodyguard comes out again, stands by the door, grinning. After a second or two, the girls come out. The first girl comes out last, wearing only Dithers's bib and brace overalls. On her it looks good. The girls clear and Dithers emerges in his shirt tails. He backs away and runs out of the door, the girls giggling.)*

*(A final close up of the Sheikh, still sleeping through it all.)*

*Cut to: the reception hall.*

*(It is now bereft of any sort of furniture which could be sat on – settees, chairs, stools etc., all removed. In their place, mattresses covered with curtains, and, or rugs, and cushions and pillows scattered everywhere. An enormous gong stands in a prominent position.)*

*(The old lady enters, takes a magazine from a low table, walks to where the settee was, and goes to sit down. Halfway through the sit, she stops, and realises the settee has gone.)*

*(She is still stooping when Rustless appears from the office.)*

**RUSTLESS:**
Careful, Mrs Ringer – we've moved it.

**OLD LADY:**
Yes, so I see. What's happening, have you gone bankrupt?

**RUSTLESS:**
No, nothing like that it's on account of His Serene Highness – they never sit down on chairs out there, you see ...

**OLD LADY:**
Oh dear. They must get awfully tired.

**RUSTLESS:**
Not at all – they lie about on cushions all the time. Very relaxing – why don't you try it?

**OLD LADY:**
Oh I couldn't. I'm not used to lying down in mixed company.

*(Bates enters.)*

**BATES:**
Phew! It's very hot in here, milord.

**RUSTLESS:**
Ah. Got the central heating up, Bates, helps create the middle-east atmosphere.

**OLD LADY:**
Oh, that's what it is, I thought I was sickening for something.

**RUSTLESS:**
No, no – got old Dithers down in the cellar, stoking away for all he's worth. Standing there in his shirt-tails, shovelling it on.

**BATES:**
In his shirt-tails, milord?

**RUSTLESS:**
Yes. Odd, isn't it? Says he had his boiler-suit pinched. He'll get something else

pinched if Cook catches him like that

**OLD LADY:**
I don't think I can stand this heat I've got too many clothes on.

**RUSTLESS:**
I'll nip up and turn your radiator off in your bedroom if you like, you can go up there.

**OLD LADY:**
Oh, would you?

**RUSTLESS:**
Certainly. You go up and take your things off and lie on the bed. I'll be up in a minute.

**OLD LADY:**
Oh. *(She goes.)*

*(Dithers enters with wheelbarrow full of cushions. He stops at mattresses and begins to throw cushions on with a garden fork.)*

**RUSTLESS:**
Ah, good man Dithers. Where did you get these?

**DITHERS:**
Summer house.

**RUSTLESS:**
Oh yes, never thought of that. I hope they're not damp.

**DITHERS:**
Oh no, not damp. Did my courting in there.

**RUSTLESS:**
Really? You mean to say you can actually remember going courting?

**DITHERS:**
Oh ar. It was last night.

**RUSTLESS:**
Last night? You told me you were going to watch television. You said I'm just going off to see *Elizabeth R.*

**DITHERS:**
No, no, not gonna see Elizabeth R, gonna see Elizabeth – Arrrr!

**RUSTLESS:**
Oh, I see. It wasn't Elizabeth the First.

**DITHERS:**
No – and it won't be the last either.

*(He exits, as Bates enters down the stairs.)*

**RUSTLESS:**
Ah there you are Bates.

**BATES:**
Sorry to be so long milord – I wasn't sure what to wear. Will this be alright?

**RUSTLESS:**
I don't see why not Bates – it's fairly plain, not likely to offend anyone.

**BATES:**
You were telling me about the Sheikh, milord. When did he ask for all these alterations?

**RUSTLESS:**
Last night – I was invited into his harem. It was just after we were talking about it – remember? You saying it was a great honour.

**BATES:**
Oh yes, it is, milord.

**RUSTLESS:**
Yes, it's also highly embarrassing, Bates old chap. I mean, all those wives, standing about. Amazing, some of them you know.

**BATES:**
I presume they'd taken off their black robes and changed into something more comfortable, had they?

**RUSTLESS:**
Well, yes and no Bates. They'd taken off their black robes, but they hadn't changed into something more comfortable.

**BATES:**
Oh dear, you mean they didn't have anything, milord?

**RUSTLESS:**
Oh I wouldn't say that – quite the reverse, some of them. I mean, you can imagine. Well, I didn't know where to look for the best. Now then, Bates, are we all set for the Dinner?

**BATES:**
Yes milord – ooh! Gramophone. I thought perhaps some suitable music – I've sorted out a few records from upstairs that might do. I'll just get them.

*(Effie enters with Dithers's boiler suit.)*

**RUSTLESS:**
Ah there you are, Effie old thing – how are you both? I say, are they Dithers's overalls?

**EFFIE:**
*(Speaks silently.)*

**RUSTLESS:**
Did you? In the Sheikh's room? What were they doing in there, what?

**EFFIE:**
*(Speaks.)*

**RUSTLESS:**
Oh, he called you in. Wanted his what dusted? Oh his legs? Oh the legs of the billiard table, yes, he's using it as a bed.

**EFFIE:**
*(Speaks.)*

**RUSTLESS:**
Did he? Laid hands on you. Oh dear. Chucked you under the what? Oh chin. I see. What did you think of him? Sharp elbows. Yes, well, you'd notice that. Yes, the room is somewhat crowded. Lying about all over the place were they? No, couldn't really dust round them. Oh yes, Sheikhs always have lots of them, it's the custom: They use the big ones to sit on

you know, and put their feet on the little ones.

*(Enter Dithers, now in his page-boy suit and hat.)*

**RUSTLESS:**
Ah, Dithers, Effie's retrieved your boiler-suit. *(Sniffs at it.)* Reeks of perfume – you'd better get it laundered, Effie. *(Gives it back to her.)* Otherwise he'll be getting a bad name in the village.

*(Effie goes.)*

*(The deaf gent enters and stares round at the room.)*

**RUSTLESS:**
Evening, Mr Blunt.

*(Badger enters.)*

**BADGER:**
Cook says she is ready to serve dinner, milord. Is His Highness down yet?

**RUSTLESS:**
My orders are to strike the gong, Badger, and he will then grace us with his presence. Dithers, clout the gong will you?

**DITHERS:**
Righto. *(He goes to the gong, and gives it a great swipe. The noise is deafening. The deaf gent, on his way out, is passing the grandfather clock. He takes out his pocket-watch, and alters it, staring at the grandfather clock.)*

**DEAF GENT:**
Bloody thing's fast. *(He exits.)*

*(Bates rushes in, now dressed in unsuitable cocktail dress.)*

**RUSTLESS:**
Ah Bates, you heard the gong?

**BATES:**
Oh yes milord – it shook the whole room

– three of my hair-pins fell out. I just came to put the gramophone on. *(At gramophone)* Oh blow! It's not wound up.

*(She is busy winding it, when the bodyguard appears, followed by the Sheikh, dressed this time in gorgeous Eastern robes.)*

**SHEIKH:**
May the sun shine on your grandchildren.

*(The record on the gramophone starts to play a ragtime vocal version of "The Sheikh of Araby". The Sheikh stops and stares, haughtily. Bates, flustered, removes it and puts on another.)*

**RUSTLESS:**
*(during the pause)* Welcome, Your Serene Highness, to our humble table. Er. Floor.

*(The gramophone now plays "Scheherazade". The Sheikh claps his hands twice, and the line of wives appear, this time in flimsy, belly dancer type costumes. They are indeed, all shapes and sizes, most young and pretty but also two or three older, fatter ladies.)*

**SHEIKH:**
My wives – as token of my esteem – wear private garments.

**RUSTLESS:**
I say, my dear old Highness – I am honoured. Pray pull up a mattress and sit down.

*(The Sheikh sits, the wives then sit round him.)*

**RUSTLESS:**
Bates! *(Bates joins Rustless.)* Bates too wears traditional indoor clobber. Be seated Bates. *(Bates sits, leaving a space between the sheikh and herself for Rustless.)* Badger – tell Cook to bring on the repast.

*(He attempts to sit cross legged like the others – and falls on Bates, but recovers quickly.)*

**SHEIKH:**
May I, before we take food with each other – may I utter a prayer to almighty Allah?

**RUSTLESS:**
Well, with Cook in charge. It's probably a wise move. Carry on.

**SHEIKH:**
Allah! *(Kneels up. Raises his hands then puts his head on the floor. The wives do likewise.)*

**BATES:**
*(whispers)* Milord! *(She indicates that they should do the same.)*

**RUSTLESS:**
Oh. *(He attempts to get his head on the floor – can't quite do it.)*

**SHEIKH:**
You will repeat please *(they repeat each phrase after him)* Almighty Allah, bringer of the rain, and sender of the wind; Give us strength from this food to bear many lusty sons, and make our bodies able to bear the pain of life on earth. We kiss the ground. *(Rustless says "we nearly kiss the ground".)* In praise of thee, Allah be praised.

**RUSTLESS:**
Thank God.

*(They all sit up – Rustless is stuck. Bates taps him.)*

**BATES:**
We've finished, milord.

**RUSTLESS:**
I know that dammit. I can't get up. Do something Bates.

*(Bates thumps him in the back – he jumps up with a yell.)*

**RUSTLESS:**
Ooh! Thank you Bates.

*(Cook enters, with trolley, laden with food.)*

**COOK:**
Right! Grub's up!

*(Badger hands champagne from a tray to sheikh, Rustless, Bates etc)*

**SHEIKH:**
Ah! I have travelled all over the world, sampling the foods of many nations. Nightingales' tongues in Persia, sheeps' eyeballs in Egypt, frogs' legs in France.

**COOK:**
Well, this is Britain's contribution.

**SHEIKH:**
What is it?

**COOK:**
Fish fingers.

*(She starts dishing some onto a plate as we fade out.)*

*(Fade in – the meal is over – everyone is lounging back on the cushions – Badger is absent, as is Cook. The Sheikh is slightly tipsy from champagne. Rustless and Bates are similarly affected.)*

**SHEIKH:**
In the past, I've had dealings with many women.

**RUSTLESS:**
Naturally, still got quite a few on your books at the moment. *(Rustless looks around, sees Dithers lounging on the ground with a couple of wives and a bottle.)* Dithers! What the devil are you doing? Go and see where Badger is with that champagne. *(Dithers staggers off.)* Sorry, Your Highness, old fruit – I interrupted.

**SHEIKH:**
Many women – of all nations and beliefs. But your English rose, I have never plucked.

**RUSTLESS:**
Really?

**SHEIKH:**
I have been looking at your boots.

**RUSTLESS:**
My boots?

**SHEIKH:**
Your lady, Boots. *(Points to Bates.)*

**RUSTLESS:**
Oh Bates. Yes?

**SHEIKH:**
She is very desirable.

**BATES:**
Oh, Your Highness! *(She is flattered, but embarrassed.)*

**SHEIKH:**
To me, sitting there she seems to have got what my wives haven't got.

**RUSTLESS:**
*(peering at Bates)* No, no – must be a trick of the light.

**SHEIKH:**
Behind that flat bosom, beats a brain.

**RUSTLESS:**
Ah. Little higher up, actually, but I see what you're getting at.

**SHEIKH:**
Is she one of your wives?

**RUSTLESS:**
What, Bates? Dear me, no – she's just a chap who helps me out.

**SHEIKH:**
But she is your servant.

**RUSTLESS:**
Er – I employ here, yes.

**SHEIKH:**
Good. Boots!

**RUSTLESS:**
Bates.

**SHEIKH:**
Bates! Will you become my ninth wife?

**BATES:**
Oh! Oh no, I couldn't Your Highness. Honestly.

**SHEIKH:**
Why? Am I not rich and handsome.

**BATES:**
Oh yes, yes, you're very pretty, very charming, Your Highness – but, well – my place is here with his Lordship. I have all the accounts to do, and the flowers, and anyway, I don't know you.

**SHEIKH:**
You refuse?

**BATES:**
I'm – I'm afraid so Your Highness. But thanks very much for asking. *(She is very embarrassed.)*

**SHEIKH:**
So be it. We will speak of it no more. Come now, what masques, what dances shall we have, to wear away this long age of three hours, between our after supper and bed time?

**RUSTLESS:**
I say, you Eastern chaps have certainly got a wonderful way of putting things.

**SHEIKH:**
That was William Shakespeare.

**RUSTLESS:**
Was it by jove? Never heard that bit.

**SHEIKH:**
Do you not understand the writings of your great masters and doctors?

**RUSTLESS:**
We certainly don't understand the writings of our doctors. Damned prescriptions. I nearly got treated for rabies once. However. Entertainment. What d'you fancy? Game of cards?

**SHEIKH:**
Excellent. We will wager.

**RUSTLESS:**
Yes, alright – I like a bit of a gamble. Get the cards, Bates.

*(Bates gets up and find cards in reception desk.)*

**RUSTLESS:**
What shall if be? Halfpenny pontoon?

**SHEIKH:**
We cut one card.

**RUSTLESS:**
Oh, I see. Sudden death. Alright, I'm game. *(Takes cards from Bates.)*

**SHEIKH:**
You first. *(Rustless cuts, and then the Sheikh.)* Now your wager.

**RUSTLESS:**
Er, sixpence.

**SHEIKH:**
One pound.

**RUSTLESS:**
Your pound, and up a pound.

**SHEIKH:**
Your two pounds and up five pounds.

**RUSTLESS:**
I say – I'll see you.

*Sheikh throws down his card.*

**RUSTLESS:**
Ah! Beat you! Jolly exciting wasn't it? Shall we have another go?

**SHEIKH:**
Don't you find money tedious?

**RUSTLESS:**
Er – well, I haven't done up to now, no. I rather like it.

**SHEIKH:**
Would it not be more interesting to play with possessions? Trinkets, baubles – things more precious to us?

**RUSTLESS:**
Oh – very well. *(To Bates)* Better get some of the insurance policies out, Bates.

**SHEIKH:**
No, no- I merely mean, things we have about us at the moment.

**RUSTLESS:**
Oh I see! Sort of strip poker with your clothes on.

**SHEIKH:**
Precisely. Pray cut. And may the sun shine on your forehead and out of your mouth to bring you fortune.

**RUSTLESS:**
Thank you – may it shine out of yours too. I cut. *(He cuts – the Sheikh cuts.)*

**SHEIKH:**
I wager – my jewelled pin. *(Throws pin down.)*

**RUSTLESS:**
Your jewelled pin – and up my gold watch.

**BATES:**
Milord!

**RUSTLESS:**
Quiet Bates, this is man's work.

**SHEIKH:**
Your gold watch – and my ceremonial dagger.

**RUSTLESS:**
Ah. Er- your dagger – and up my pearl handled penknife.

**BATES:**
Oh do "see" him, milord!

**RUSTLESS:**
What, and lose my gold watch. Certainly

not Bates.

**SHEIKH:**
*(considers for a moment, then)* Your penknife and – and my fourth wife, Selima.

*(Reactions of wives, then Rustless.)*

**RUSTLESS:**
*(stares at him)* Your fourth wife – and up Bates.

**BATES:**
*(astounded)* Milord! No!

**SHEIKH:**
*(quickly)* I'll see you. *(Rustless drops his card.)* I win! I win!

**BATES:**
No milord, I refuse – you can't.

**SHEIKH:**
Silence! Badger – take her to my quarters. *(Badger grabs Bates.)*

**RUSTLESS:**
I say, hang on – I thought we were just playing "lendums".

**SHEIKH:**
Don't worry, my friend – I will return her in the morning. But tonight, she is mine. Take her away!

*(Badger picks up Bates, who stars to yell and kick, and carries her off, followed by the giggling wives.)*

**RUSTLESS:**
*(shouting to Bates, as the Sheikh bows and strides off)* Hang on Bates, remember you're British! I'll – I'll bring you some tea in the morning!

*(Fade out on the chaos.)*

*(Fade in – next morning.)*

*(Camera starts on tray of tea, cup being stirred. Pull back – it is Rustless, at desk. He downs tea. Badger enters.)*

**BADGER:**
Anything happened yet, milord?

**RUSTLESS:**
That damned bodyguard – Backdoor, or whatever his name is, has just been down and paid the bill.

**BADGER:**
They're leaving?

**RUSTLESS:**
Apparently. His Serene Highness appears to be displeased with the way last night turned out.

**BADGER:**
Oh dear.

**RUSTLESS:**
Well I mean it's only natural isn't it? I mean to say he's used to all those lumpy looking belly dancers. You can't expect poor old Bates to compete with that lot. Poor thing, she can't even do the fox-trot.

**BADGER:**
I doubt if the fox-trot was what he had in mind, milord.

**RUSTLESS:**
I know – exactly.

**BADGER:**
I take it you haven't seen her yet.

**RUSTLESS:**
No, he hasn't returned her yet, Badger. Still, there's one consolation – I got my gold watch back.

*(Badger reacts to this and then, bedraggled and covered in powder, in comes poor old Bates. Her hair is awry, her hair is all crumpled.)*

**RUSTLESS:**
Bates! My dear old chap! *(He goes to her, as does Badger.)*

**BATES:**
*(exhausted, and trying not to cry)* Oh milord!

**RUSTLESS:**
There, there, come and sit down.

**BATES:**
Oh milord – I've had such a terrible night. I didn't get a wink of sleep!

**RUSTLESS:**
Yes – it must have been hell Bates.

**BATES:**
I'm black and blue all over.

**RUSTLESS:**
Badger – pour her a cup of tea. Do you want to talk about it?

**BATES:**
Oh yes please milord. Do you mind?

**RUSTLESS:**
No, not at all Bates – Badger here's a man of the world. What's happened to your clothes Bates?

**BATES:**
*(tearfully)* Those wretched girls took them all off and put them in the rubbish bin. I still can't find my vest.

**RUSTLESS:**
Never mind old chap – I'll buy you another. It's your birthday soon. What's all this talcum powder all over you?

**BATES:**
That's not talcum powder milord – it's chalk – from the billiard cues. That's why I'm black and blue.

**RUSTLESS:**
You don't mean to say they knocked you about with billiard cues Bates? The blackguard!

**BATES:**
No, milord – they shut me in the cupboard. That's where I spent the night – standing up. It was a terrible squash.

**RUSTLESS:**
You mean you didn't have to – with the –

he didn't–

**BATES:**
No milord.

**RUSTLESS:**
Oh, what a relief. Why not?

**BATES:**
I refused to go through a ceremony of marriage with him milord – some strange Eastern rites – and I just couldn't. I'm strict Church of England milord, and I always promised Mummy I'd be married in church. *(She bursts into tears.)*

**BADGER:**
*(deeply moved)* Well done Miss Bates. You are a credit to your sex. *(He puts his arm round her.)*

*(Suddenly the bodyguard, followed by the Sheikh and the line of wives enter and cross past Rustless, Bates and Badger. Nothing is said. The Sheikh bows slightly and Rustless stares at him. The party exits.)*

**RUSTLESS:**
And good riddance. Well Bates old thing, you better go and lie down. At least your courage and fortitude have saved you from a fate worse that death.

**BATES:**
*(at the door)* I wouldn't have minded that so much – I was quite looking forward to it.

**RUSTLESS:**
What?

**BATES:**
It's just jolly upsetting for a girl to expect a night of bliss, and finish up spending it bolt upright in a cupboard.

*(She goes – and, on Rustless's astounded face, the credits roll.)*

# CLARENCE

The character of Clarence Seal, the myopic removals man, actually began life back in a 1971 episode of *Six Dates With Barker*, entitled "The Removals Man" and written by Hugh Leonard. Ronnie kept the character with him for a further two decades before Clarence got his own series, a series that was to prove to be Ronnie Barker's final work for television.

Ronnie had decided to retire a full two years before actually doing so and it's easy to see how that bitter-sweet knowledge informs Clarence, written during this period. It was credited to Bob Ferris, probably an unconscious nod to writers Dick Clement and Ian LaFrenais, who had given Ronnie one of his biggest successes with their *Porridge*. (Bob Ferris was the name of one of the principal characters in Clement/LaFrenais' *The Likely Lads*.) Ronnie chose to set his final series in the Oxfordshire countryside, where he now made his home, and to work once again with one of his most trusted collaborators, Josephine Tewson, who co-starred as Travers.

*Clarence* debuted on BBC 2 in January 1988, just a few days after Ronnie Barker left the following message on his answer phone: "As of January 1, I am retiring from public and professional life so I am unable to undertake any more commitments. To those people with whom I have worked, I would like to express my gratitude and good wishes. So it's a big thank you from me and it's goodbye from him. Goodbye."

# EPISODE ONE

*Scene 1: Coronation procession of 1937 (stock film).*

*Coronation procession of King George VI and Queen Elizabeth.*

*Over this we superimpose the title : "Coronation Day. May 12th, 1837."*

*Scene 2: Ext. Belgravia Street. Day.*

*Preparations are being made to celebrate the Coronation. Domestic staff from the big houses are listening to a BBC radio commentary of the procession while they decorate the exteriors of the houses. Flags and bunting adorn the terrace. Children are building a bonfire from old boxes and scrap timber.*

*The radio is relaying a live commentary. A flag is being lifted by a maid and handed to a man standing on step ladders. A lady passes by. A child is skipping in the foreground. Through the railings we see a delivery boy on his bicycle riding by. In the background children are piling wood onto the beginnings of a bonfire. The delivery boy stops outside a house.*

*Our attention is taken by two children carrying a packing case for the bonfire. They pass child skipping. The two children carry the box to the bonfire joined by two already there. In the background another child is helping put up bunting.*

*A furniture van approaches the terrace. Two men are wedged in the driver's cab. Albert is a callow youth of 24 – Clarence, our hero, is 50. he wears thick pebble glasses and a flat cap. As the van stops he peers myopically ahead, seeing the children piling up wood for the bonfire.*

**CLARENCE:**
Traffic Jam, is it?

**ALBERT:**
No, we're here. No. 16A, first floor.

**CLARENCE:**
Right.

**ALBERT:**
Mind your door. (*Albert gets out.*)

(*Clarence takes a careful look to the rear, through the mirror, before opening the door.*)

(*We see the world through his eyes: it is an opaque blur. He grunts in satisfaction and flings the door open.*)

(*A passing cyclist swerves wildly, screams, and goes out of shot.*)

(*Clarence climbs out of the cab oblivious to the clatter of pulverised hardware, off. He gives a friendly nod to a pillar box.*)

**CLARENCE:**
'Morning, Sir. Nice day for the Coronation. (*To Travers:*) I love to see them old Chelsea Pensioners, don't you? Well, come on let's get started.

**ALBERT:**
Clarence …

**CLARENCE:**
Who's there?

**ALBERT:**
I thought I might nip off for an hour and have a look at the Procession.

**CLARENCE:**
You what?

**ALBERT:**
I'll be back before you have time to brew up. You get started with the packing. I'll take over with the heavy stuff.

**CLARENCE:**
You rotten lead-swinging skiver – you're going to leave me here to –

**ALBERT:**
Clarence, face up to it. Where's the sense in you going to look at their Majesties? You can't even see past the far side of your specs.

**CLARENCE:**
*(blasting off)* There ain't nothing the
matter with my eyesight

**ALBERT:**
No, Clarence. *(He walks back to the van and
gets in.)*

**CLARENCE:**
*(still addressing the spot where Albert was)* I
got the eyesight of an eagle, and I'll have
you know these glasses are for reading.

*(The sound of the van moving off. Clarence
continues to address Albert who isn't there,
and an old lady who is.)*

**CLARENCE:**
We're going to move the furniture out of
that house and get it to Southampton like
we agreed, and you try walking off the
job, you lazy skiver and I'll knock yer
block off? Got that? I said have you got
that? Ha-ha! That's right, go on sulk!

*(The old lady looks puzzled.)*

*Scene 3: Interior. Drawing room. Day.*

*The maid – Travers – struggles in with several
heavy pieces of luggage.*

**MRS VAILE:**
Anyone would think you were the only
girl in the world with a broken
engagement. *(As Angela sniffs.)* And don't
be emotional when there's a servant
present. *(She crosses to mirror.)*

**ANGELA:**
Oh, mother, really!

**MRS VAILE:**
Bad business, showing one's feelings in
front of servants. I remember when poor
Deidre Playfair's husband hanged himself.
He got his valet to hold the ladder. Of
course none of us went to the funeral.
Never mind, seeing the Coronation will
cheer you up. Are you looking forward to
it, Travers? After all, it is a holiday for the
working class people as well, isn't it? Not
that you've got a holiday, of course, but
that can't be helped, can it?

**TRAVERS:**
Yes ma'am. I mean no ma'am. That is, I
mean no it can't be helped, and yes I am
looking forward to it. The street looks
lovely all decorated.

**MRS VAILE:**
Yes don't go on about it Travers. That's the
trouble with servants. Give them half a
chance they'll stand and gossip all day.
Personally I think the decorations
frightfully vulgar. The colours are
dreadful.

**ANGELA:**
You can't choose colours for a Coronation
mother. They have to be red white and
blue. *(She crosses to window.)*

**MRS VAILE:**
I still think it would have been possible
occasionally to veer towards the violet
and the cerise. However, as the servants
were responsible for putting them up, one
could hardly expect anything
approaching taste.

**ANGELA:**
*(looking out of the window)* Who are those
ragged-looking children building the
bonfire?

**MRS VAILE:**
Yes, that's another thing I don't approve
of. Allowing the servant's children to
build that monstrosity. If the wind
changes, we shall all be burned in our
beds.

**ANGELA:**
We won't be in our beds tonight, Mother.
They will all be in the furniture van.

**MRS VAILE:**
Don't be so pedantic, Angela. It's an
expression, like "Love makes the world go
round". Which reminds me. Travers – no
followers while we are out.

**TRAVERS:**
No, ma'am.

*(A ring at the door.)*

**MRS VAILE:**
That will be the removers at last. Answer it, Travers.

**TRAVERS:**
Yes. ma'am. *(Travers walks to hall. She opens the door. Clarence is there). (To Clarence)* Are you the removals?

**CLARENCE:**
Yes, madam. Which way?

**TRAVERS:**
I'm not Madam; I'm Travers. Do come in; they've been waiting for you.

*(She leads Clarence into the flat. Mrs Vaile is having words with Angela.)*

**MRS VAILE:**
Not coming to the Coronation, are you mad?

**ANGELA:**
I'm going to stay here in case Geoffrey telephones.

**MRS VAILE:**
If you miss the Procession, how will you dare to face your grandchildren?

**ANGELA:**
If Geoffrey doesn't telephone me I'm not likely to have any grandchildren. *(Angela exits.)*

**CLARENCE:**
*(peering around the room)* Hello!

**MRS VAILE:**
Oh, the removal persons Where are the others?

**CLARENCE:**
He's uh, in the van.

**MRS VAILE:**
I trust you know what you have to do. Everything in this flat must be in Southampton by midnight.

**CLARENCE**
I'll drive it there meself.

**MRS VAILE:**
We shall return here at six for our personal effects. Travers will point them out to you, and they are not to be removed.

**CLARENCE:**
Leave it to me, madam.

**MRS VAILE:**
And take particular care of my porcelain.

**CLARENCE**
Treat 'em like me own, madam.

**MRS VAILE:**
Some of it was once owned by the Duke of Wellington.

**CLARENCE:**
Oh, and you bought it when they pulled it down.

**MRS VAILE:**
*(distantly)* They didn't pull down the Duke of Wellington. They buried him.

**CLARENCE:**
Oh. I thought you meant the pub.

**MRS VAILE:**
Pub?

**TRAVERS:**
Public House, ma'am.

**MRS VAILE:**
I know what a "pub" is, thank you, Travers. I'm not entirely ignorant of working-class phraseology. I hope you're not a frequenter of "pubs", my good man.

**CLARENCE:**
Who me? No mum.

**MRS VAILE:**
Because I don't want a disappearing act at lunchtime for an hour and a half, and coming back the worse for drink.

**CLARENCE:**
Don't worry mum, I'm never the worse for drink. I'm sometimes the better for it. Drink makes me amorous.

**MRS VAILE:**
Precisely. Travers, I hope you're taking note or all this.

**TRAVERS:**
Oh yes Ma'am.

**MRS VAILE:**
I'm leaving you alone with this person, and I expect you to behave in a lady-like manner, even though you're not one. If there is the slightest hint of any nonsense, you will be severely reprimanded. I never stand, for nonsense.

**CLARENCE:**
Oh. What do you do, lie down?

*(Travers hides a giggle behind her hand.)*

**MRS VAILE:**
What did you say?

**CLARENCE:**
I said there's a box or two to tie down. Up, I mean. I'll need some rope from the van.

**MRS VAILE:**
And I want the flat left spotlessly clean for the incoming tenant. Now, Angela?

**ANGELA:**
I'm going to wait a bit to see if Geoffrey telephones.

**MRS VAILE:**
*(tight-lipped)* Well if you miss the procession, it's your own funeral.

**CLARENCE:**
She won't miss that! *(He laughs at his own joke.)*

*(Mrs Vaile goes out. Clarence removes his jacket.)*

**TRAVERS:**
The suitcases and the trunk will be going with the master and mistress to Rangoon. They aren't to be touched.

**CLARENCE:**
Right. I'll just move this lamp standard out of me way.

*(He picks up Angela, who objects strenuously.)*

**ANGELA:**
What are you doing? Put me down.

**CLARENCE:**
*(peering into her face)* Who's that then?

**TRAVERS:**
It's Miss Angela do please put her down: she's going through an unhappy time.

**CLARENCE:**
Oh. *(Putting her down)* No harm done, just trying to guess your weight. Nine stone five. I'm never wrong used to lifting wardrobes.

**ANGELA:**
*(on her dignity)* Travers, if the telephone rings I shall be locked in my bedroom. *(She goes to bedroom.)*

**TRAVERS:**
Yes miss.

*(Angela goes out.)*

**CLARENCE:**
Anyone else here?

**TRAVERS:**
Just us.

**CLARENCE:**
That's good. People hide, you know … get dug in behind curtains and under sofas, come up behind you, think it's funny. You still there?

**TRAVERS:**
Yes.

**CLARENCE:**
Quite a nice little room, this I've seen worse. If there's one thing I'm partial to, it's a bit of Chippendale. *(He runs his hand over a packing case.)* Yes lovely.

**TRAVERS:**
Shouldn't there be others here to help you?

**CLARENCE:**
Albert and me got an arrangement: I do the packing, he does the heavy lifting. My trouble is, I'm too strong for lifting ... give me a billiard table to carry and I'll knock chips off your ceiling. Built like a Brahma bull. Feel them thighs go on. *(She puts her hand hesitantly on his thigh.)* Is that you?

**TRAVERS:**
Yes.

*(He looks into her face. We see her from his point of view: her face is a featureless blur.)*

**CLARENCE:**
I like the look of you. I don't hold much with women they're too – what's the word? – female. But you got strong lines on your face all over it. You married?

**TRAVERS:**
Why, no.

**CLARENCE:**
Keep it that way. You don't want to go making some bloke's life hell. I can respect a woman what dies single and miserable.

**TRAVERS:**
I was engaged once.

**CLARENCE:**
Yecch! What did he do – run off with another woman? *(He cackles.)*

**TRAVERS:**
You won't laugh when I tell you. He ran off with another man!

*(This really breaks Clarence up. His cackling turns into a wheezing paroxysm. Travers is offended.)*

**TRAVERS:**
Well, that's a nice way to go on.

**CLARENCE:**
Excuse me, I always cough when I laugh ... I was gassed in the war. Oh. Dear me!

**TRAVERS:**
Don't you think you had better get on with your work?

**CLARENCE:**
Yes, but don't go away you cheer me up. Ran off with another man. Oh dear ... Which way is the porcelain?

**TRAVERS:**
Over there.

*(She points. Clarence clutches and explores her arm to ascertain in which direction it is pointing. He gets to the mantelpiece on which the collection of porcelain is arrayed. He runs his hand along the shelf dangerously. Travers looks worried. Clarence knocks off a piece. Travers catches it.)*

**TRAVERS:**
You will be careful. Won't you?

**CLARENCE:**
Me? I got hands like a surgeon.

**TRAVERS:**
*(noticing sticking plaster on his finger)*
What's that?

**CLARENCE:**
Cut meself. Porcelain, eh? Don't fancy it much meself a bit too namby-pamby.

*(He begins to spread out newspapers on floor.)*

**TRAVERS:**
Oh you mustn't say that – according to Madam, it's "very choice". It's alright for her, she doesn't have to dust it.

**CLARENCE:**
Well it's all according to what you like, isn't it? I nearly went in the quality china business once. *(He stands.)*

**TRAVERS:**
Oh, are you interested in good china?

**CLARENCE:**
No, that's why I never went into it.

**TRAVERS:**
Oh I see.

*(She watches as with great care he places a piece of porcelain on a newspaper which is laid out on the floor. He proceeds to wrap up the sheet of newspaper next to it.)*

**CLARENCE:**
There! That's got the job started. *(He steps on the piece of porcelain, which disappears into powder with a crunching noise.)* Dry rot in them floorboards. I bet they're glad to be moving.

**TRAVERS:**
*(desperately)* Won't you please let me help you?

**CLARENCE:**
Ha-ha! I was waiting for that. Women is always making up to me. Once I start a job they're at me ... "Please let me help you!" I know what happens when you let a woman do you a favour she wants tit for tat. Sews a button on your front, takes her a couple of ticks, only she calls it the best years of her life. Well, come on then, if you're going to help. Get some more paper. *(Clarence wraps the porcelain, and also the telephone, and begins to fill the first crate.)* Women will chase any old thing what's single. That's why I got to be double careful, on account of my looks. It's ain't no fun being the spittin' image of him.

**TRAVERS:**
Who?

**CLARENCE:**
Come off it you know who I look like. Funny, you know I never noticed it meself until I heard a woman on the bus saying "Cor, look at Spencer Tracy".

**TRAVERS:**
Spencer Tracy?

**CLARENCE:**
*(smugly)* You see it too, do you?

**TRAVERS:**
No, I don't.

**CLARENCE:**
I can see you're one of the cunning ones. You want to intrigue me, don't yer?

**TRAVERS:**
Certainly not. *(Goes to mantel.)*

*(Clarence has found a solar topee which he puts on.)*

**CLARENCE:**
What about this, then?

**TRAVERS:**
What about it?

**CLARENCE:**
Spencer Tracy – "Dr. Livingstone, I presume". See the likeness?

**TRAVERS:**
No.

**CLARENCE:**
Hang on. *(He shoves a comb under his nose.)* What about Ronald Colman, then?

**TRAVERS:**
Oh I do like him!

**CLARENCE:**
So who do I remind you of?

**TRAVERS:**
Charles Laughton. *(She leans over to place an ornament into a tea chest.)*

**CLARENCE:**
*(talking to her rear)* If you're trying to
infatuate me, you're going the wrong way
about it. *(He sits.)* So where is this
employer of yours going to then?

**TRAVERS:**
Rangoon.

**CLARENCE:**
Where's that then? Is that abroad is it?

**TRAVERS:**
It's in the mystical East.

**CLARENCE:**
Oh is it. You going too and all are you?

**TRAVERS:**
No, I finish today. I was only temporary.
I'm out of work at 5 o'clock.

**CLARENCE:**
Ordinarily, I wouldn't work on
Coronation Day, not even on a rush job
like this is. But when it comes to the
upper classes, God bless them, I'm their
man. *(Clarence stands.)* We got to treat 'em
right ... backbone of the country. Right –
now then. You watch me ... half an hour's
time, you're going to see an empty room.

*(He is about to drop a goldfish bowl, and its
contents, into the crate.)*

**TRAVERS:**
Stop. Those are goldfish.

**CLARENCE:**
Where? That's another thing I hate about
women when it comes to animals you're
all soft. Here – put 'em down the lav.

**TRAVERS:**
I most certainly will not put them –

*(Ringing is heard.)*

**CLARENCE:**
Ah, that's me mate. *(He goes to the door,
opens it and stares into the empty hall.)* And
about time. I have been doing all the

packing on me own ... and stop ringing
that bell?

**TRAVERS:**
It's the telephone.

**CLARENCE:**
It's not, it's him.

*(He jabs a finger at the hall. Angela hears this
in the bedroom.)*

**ANGELA:**
*(delirious)* It's him? Oh, it's Geoffrey! I'm
coming, darling, I'm coming. Where is it?

**TRAVERS:**
Where's what, Miss?

**ANGELA:**
The telephone you fool ... what have you
done with it?

**TRAVERS:**
Well, it was here a – here's the string, it ...
*(To Clarence)* You've packed the telephone.

**CLARENCE:**
Eh?

**TRAVERS:**
*(pointing at the packing case)* It's in there.

**ANGELA:**
Get it out now!

**CLARENCE:**
Women! They can't make up their ruddy
minds. First it's pack, then it's unpack.
*(Delving into the packing case)* What's the
good of being systematic I say, what's it all
for? *(As he removes packages, Travers and he
place them in the other case.)*

**ANGELA:**
Will you hurry! Hold on Geoffrey.

**CLARENCE:**
Hang on Geoffrey. What did it look like?
Ah! *(He attempts to retrieve the telephone
which is still ringing, but the flex is caught
under some of the other objects in the packing*

627

*case.)* Hang on. It's caught round some rope. *(He jerks the flex hard – the handset comes away, the cord snapped off from the earpiece. He hands it to her.)*

**ANGELA:**
Geoffrey, Geoffrey ... I can' t hear you.

**CLARENCE:**
Oh, here's the other bit. *(he hands her both pieces)*

**ANGELA:**
Oh, my God. *(Into the mouthpiece)* I think I'll kill myself. *(She hands Clarence the bits and rushes back into the bedroom.)*

**CLARENCE:**
There you are! She disrupts me day and never even says thanks.

*(He replaces the telephone into the packing case. He walks to cardboard box, lifts it up, leaving the contents on the ground, which he walks over, breaking them. Travers reacts.)*

**CLARENCE:**
Right. Glassware next – which way is the pantry?

*(Travers looks horrified.)*

*Scene 4: Int. Drawing room. Day.*

*Thirties-style picture: close up of tea tray.*

*Music over: "Tea for Two" (vocal).*

*We become live action.*

*(Travers enters with teapot.)*

**TRAVERS:**
*(she sees Clarence)* What on earth are you doing? *(We see that Clarence, with an armchair on his head, is in difficulties.)* You said you were only going to do the packing!

**CLARENCE:**
Well, he ain't here, is he? Good-for-nothing basket, he swore on his mother's knickers he'd be back, so where is he? Someone's got to move the stuff. Where's the door gone?

**TRAVERS:**
*(taking his arm)* It's this way.

**CLARENCE:**
Here give over. I ain't blind, and you ain't an Alsatian. Just point me.

*(She does so.)*

**TRAVERS:**
Straight ahead ... right ... right.

*(He staggers towards the door and goes out. Travers sits and begins to pour tea. Without her noticing, her reactions coincide with a series of terrible bumps and bangs off as Clarence gets the chair downstairs. She finally puts in two sugars. Then has second thoughts and adds another. Coinciding with a final bump she pours her own.)*

**CLARENCE:**
We're getting on.

**TRAVERS:**
Don't you think you'd better wait for your friend?

*(He picks up another armchair.)*

**CLARENCE:**
Wait? How can I wait? You think this rubbish is going to walk to Southampton?

**TRAVERS:**
But you can't do it on your own. When your friend comes back ...

**CLARENCE:**
That rotten layabout ain't no friend of mine. And when he comes back it'll be because the boozers is shut. It's no joke, see? Let poor old Clarence do it. He takes advantage of me, 'cause he knows I'm one of them what-you-may-call it, perfectionists.

*(He blunders into a stool and boots it savagely out of the way.)*

**TRAVERS:**
Look why don't you sit down and have some tea? There's no van to put the furniture in, anyway.

**CLARENCE:**
That ain't my fault. I'm going to leave it all outside the front door, then I'm going home to my hobby.

**TRAVERS:**
Your hobby? What's that?

**CLARENCE:**
Watch repairing Is that tea, did you say? *(He puts down chair and sits in it.)*

**TRAVERS:**
You really do deserve it. I've never seen a man work so hard. *(As he raises the teapot to his lips)* That's the teapot.

**CLARENCE:**
Just examining a crack in the spout. Oh, there isn't one. 'Cor, I don't envy his poor Majesty. Look at the country he's getting … nothing in it but leadswingers and women. *(Grudgingly)* You ain't so bad .

**TRAVERS:**
*(blushing)* Thank you.

**CLARENCE:**
You going to Hong Kong too, then?

**TRAVERS:**
Rangoon. No, I told you, I've had give notice. As of this evening I shall have to find a new position.

**CLARENCE:**
*(his kind of joke)* Try standing up in a 'ammock. *(he laughs wheezily)*

**TRAVERS:**
*(giggling)* Oh, you are coarse.

**CLARENCE:**
Or hanging upside down from a street lamp.

**TRAVERS:**
Oh, go on with you! *(She gives a high-pitched shriek of laughter which stops abruptly.)* No, we shouldn't … not on Coronation Day.

**CLARENCE:**
I don't often come over funny … think I've done meself a mischief.

**TRAVERS:**
Perhaps it was that heavy chair?

**CLARENCE.**
*(looking into her eyes)* You make lovely tea.

**TRAVERS:**
Do I?

**CLARENCE.**
So you ain't going with them, then?

**TRAVERS:**
They asked me to. Do you think I was wrong to refuse?

**CLARENCE:**
Nah you don't want to go into the jungle.

**TRAVERS:**
Don't I?

**CLARENCE:**
Nothing out there but monkeys and coconuts. Girl the other day said I look like Tarzan you know, Johnny Weismuller – him in the little skirt, at the Odeon.

**TRAVERS:**
*(now anxious to please)* There is a resemblance.

**CLARENCE:**
Think so? Funny how many people I look like. It's even more striking when I take me clothes off.

**TRAVERS:**
I'm sure.

**CLARENCE:**
What's your name, then?

**TRAVERS:**
Travers.

**CLARENCE:**
No, I mean your first name.

**TRAVERS:**
Jane.

**CLARENCE:**
Struth!

**TRAVERS:**
What?

**CLARENCE:**
There we are then. You Jane, me Tarzan! Proves it. doesn't it?

**TRAVERS:**
Oh very good.

**CLARENCE:**
I just come to one of my decisions. For you I'm going to break the rule of a lifetime. You can help me.

**TRAVERS:**
With the packing? It's all done.

**CLARENCE:**
Nah, I mean with the lifting.

**TRAVERS**
Oh, I don't think I –

**CLARENCE:**
And afterwards we'll go and look at the Coronation bonfires. They got a big one up in Highgate.

**TRAVERS:**
You'll take me?

**CLARENCE:**
Last time I went out to a bonfire with a woman was Armistice Day. Nice girl we use to call her Dirty Daphne.

**TRAVERS:**
What happened to her?

**CLARENCE:**
Well, I took her down Putney, but er –

**TRAVERS:**
I mean afterwards.

**CLARENCE:**
It was about that time I got some new glasses. Took one good look at her, and God, she was fat. All of her even her hair was fat. Never changed me glasses no more after that.

**TRAVERS:**
That's sad. *(She stands.)*

**CLARENCE:**
You ain't fat, are you? *(Sudden doubt assails him on this point. He puts a hand on each side of her as if measuring the girth of a fat person; then with growing relief he moves his hands inwards until they touch her. Trying to conceal his surprise)* You're a bit thin.

**TRAVERS:**
Is that good?

**CLARENCE:**
*(stoutly)* It's the next best thing to slender.

**TRAVERS:**
*(pleased)* Let's get going. Where shall we start?

**CLARENCE:**
Bedroom ...

*(Travers reacts.)*

**TRAVERS:**
I'll put the tea things away.

**CLARENCE:**
Where is the bedroom?

**TRAVERS:**
That way. *(She points.)*

*Scene 5: Int. Bedroom. Day*

*Angela, bent on ending it all, has just turned on the gas fire. She lies down beside it and puts her head on a cushion. Clarence comes in. He trips over her …*

**CLARENCE:**
Rotten tiger-skin rugs!

*(He kicks Angela. She yelps in pain.)*

**ANGELA:**
Oh you coarse, awful man you've hurt me.

**CLARENCE:**
Who's there?

**ANGELA:**
*(getting up)* I shall be bruised for days. It's come to a pretty pass when a person cannot do away with herself in the privacy of her own home. I might just as well throw myself under some vulgar motor car. Yes, I think I will! *(she exits)*

*(Clarence gropes his way towards the sound of her voice. He comes up against a radio set which he identifies by touch.)*

**CLARENCE:**
*(to the radio)* Well, go on what happens next? Wouldn't you know they always break down at the exciting part.

*(He lifts the radio and bangs it down heavily. There is the sound of jangling valves. He nods.)*

**CLARENCE:**
Bust. Never mind, first things first. Put the rugs in the wardrobe, save a journey.

*(He picks up a couple of rugs, looks around for the wardrobe, sees the French windows opening on the balcony. He throws the rugs out.)*

*(Travers enters.)*

**TRAVERS:**
Well, I'm ready.

**CLARENCE:**
Get hold of the other end. *(She takes up one end of the sofa.)* Right, you go first.

*(She takes the lead and heads out of the door. He follows her out.)*

*(Fade in music: "The Grasshopper's dance" – non-vocal.)*

*Scene 6: Ext. Front of house. Day*

*Clarence and Travers come out carrying the sofa. They put it down on the footpath just outside the front door. The gang of street urchins building their bonfire regard them with curiosity.*

**CLARENCE:**
Come on. Right, wardrobe next.

**TRAVERS:**
Give us a chance.

*(It is too late. Already he is heading back into the house.)*

*(We go to a montage, never changing our point of view. Almost before our eyes, a pile of furniture appears on the footpath. Then the pile turns into a mountain: chairs, tables, sofas, bric-à-brac, beds, mattresses, dressing tables, radio set, kitchen ware: all magically appear until the mountain becomes a veritable Everest of household furniture. The urchins come into shot, stare at furniture, then begin to play on it.)*

*Scene 7: Int. Drawing room. Day*

*Thirties style picture of the elegant drawing room now empty.*

*Music: "A Room with a View" (vocal.)*

*It becomes live action. Pull out to wide shot.*

*(Clarence and Travers are sitting on the floor in an absolutely empty flat. They are in a state of utter exhaustion.)*

**TRAVERS:**
Well, we did it.

**CLARENCE:**
I told you – nothing to it.

**TRAVERS:**
You were wonderful.

**CLARENCE:**
Not many people would see that on a short acquaintance.

**TRAVERS:**
How long have you had your own removals business?

**CLARENCE:**
Ever since I gave up my other and bought the van – twenty-three years ago.

**TRAVERS:**
What was your other profession?

**CLARENCE:**
Demolitions. Do you like the name of the firm – "Get a Move On"?

**TRAVERS:**
Yes, well, it's different.

**CLARENCE:**
Named after what me Mum used to say to Dad. Good en it ?

**TRAVERS:**
(not sure) Yes – why didn't you call it by your own name?

**CLARENCE:**
Well, me second name is Sale. S.A.L.E, and with the first name Clarence, it looked like "Clearance Sale" on the side of the van. As soon as I started to unload, people tried to buy everything. I thought of going in for that for a while, you know, totting. Buying and selling. That's a great cockney tradition, buying and selling. Was any of your family in trade?

**TRAVERS:**
Some of my ancestors were gypsies.

**CLARENCE:**
Go on!

**TRAVERS:**
Quite a long way back – and I've got Irish blood in me as well.

**CLARENCE:**
Well well, the old "gypos", eh? I ought to take you on as a partner.

**TRAVERS:**
How do you mean?

**CLARENCE:**
A bit of gypsy blood would be very suitable in my business. I mean, they like to keep moving don't they?

**TRAVERS:**
Oh, I see. (She giggles) You're quite humorous, aren't you?

**CLARENCE:**
You're a bit of a laugh yourself. That's the Irish in you They like to laugh at themselves don't they? Well, I suppose everybody else laughs at them, so they might as well join in.

**TRAVERS:**
My uncle Dick, he was Irish. He used to mend kettles on the side of the road.

**CLARENCE:**
I bet he was a little tinker. (He wheezes) Uncle Dick – that's rhyming slang that is. Uncle Dick – sick. Not ill, like – just, like, when you've had a few pints and you start throwing it all about.

**TRAVERS:**
Oh dear, do you have to? Not a very nice subject.

**CLARENCE:**
No it's not. is it? Sorry about that. (Puts out cigarette.) Not used to female company, got to watch me mouth, mind me manners. Got nothing to eat, have you? I'm starving. Me stomach thinks me throat's been cut.

**TRAVERS:**
No, not really. All I've got is a cheese and pickle sandwich I made for meself for later on.

**CLARENCE:**
Yeah. that'll do. Anything.

**TRAVERS:**
*(taken aback)* Oh. Alright then. It's in my handbag. *(She gives it to him, wrapped in a brown paper bag.)*

**CLARENCE:**
*(taking it)* Ta..*(He takes a bite)* Cor. Tastes of perfume. You're not the sort that tarts herself up with perfume are you?

**TRAVERS:**
I like to smell nice.

**CLARENCE:**
Ruins the taste of the pickled onion.

**TRAVERS:**
Well I'd rather smell of perfume than pickled onions, thank you very much. You don't have to eat it.

**CLARENCE:**
No, I'll manage. I'll have another fag in a minute to take the taste out. So you got no traders in your family then? Just as well. They're a mad lot, usually. There's a bloke lives down the road from me. Barmy. Harold, his name is. He had this old car. 1929 Morris. He sold it to a pal of his for twenty quid. Then about a fortnight later, he bought it back off him for thirty. Then the bloke bought it back again for forty. This went on for about three months back and forward, back and forward, buying it from each other. Then suddenly, this other bloke sold it to a London dealer. My mate Harold was livid. "What the flaming hell did you want to do that for?" he said. "We was both making a good living out of that!" See? Barmy. Well, this won't get the baby washed will it. Look, why don't you get your hat on, and we'll go to Highgate and see the bonfire.

**TRAVERS:**
I can't wait. It won't take me a minute. Don't go away

*(Clarence puts the sandwich back in her handbag and lights another cigarette. Angela comes in. She is wearing her hat and coat. She bumps into Clarence.)*

**CLARENCE:**
Hello, that was quick and that's another thing I like about you, my girl.

**ANGELA:**
*(blankly)* What?

**CLARENCE:**
I been thinking about you. You're a good sort, and you've been crossed in love.

**ANGELA:**
What?

**CLARENCE:**
Hold on. Normal like, I don't hold with women. But you're different, you carry your weight, you don't go yack-yack-yack, and I like the looks of you. *(We see Angela's face as Clarence sees it.)* So how about It?

**ANGELA:**
*(baffled)* What?

**CLARENCE:**
Us. You and me. Getting spliced.

**ANGELA:**
Oh! Oh! *(She slaps his face.)*

**CLARENCE:**
That, I take it, is in the nature of a refusal. In which case, I'll just take my leave of you … you daft-looking rotten female!

*(Very much on his dignity, he walks into the hall.)*

*(Angela reacts.)*

*Scene 8. Int. Outside drawing room. Evening.*
*(We see Clarence standing in the lavatory.)*

**CLARENCE:**
What's the matter with this bleeding lift?

*Scene 9. Int. Drawing room. Evening.*

*(Angela is sobbing.)*

*(Enter Travers by another door.)*

**TRAVERS:**
Well, I'm ready Where is he? Is something wrong miss?

**ANGELA:**
Wrong? That … that manual labourer has had the effrontery to ask me to marry him.

**TRAVERS:**
He what?

**ANGELA:**
He said I was the . .. girl for him. If he hadn't packed our telephone I should certainly ring up his employers.

**TRAVERS:**
He asked you to marry him miss?

**ANGELA:**
The very idea! I should have thought you would have been more his mark. If mother comes back, tell her I've gone to have a nervous breakdown.

*(She goes.)*

**TRAVERS:**
He asked her to … he meant me. *(Dawning realisation.)* He meant me.

*(She rushes out.)*

*Scene 10. Front of house. Dusk.*

*The mountain of furniture has now almost disappeared.*

*(Travers comes out of the house. She looks wildly around for Clarence.)*

**TRAVERS:**
Where's all the furniture gone? Oh no – I …

*(She spots him. He is lighting a cigarette. We reveal that he is standing next to a bonfire containing items of furniture.*
*Music: "I Don't Want to Set the World on Fire")*

**CLARENCE:**
*(to the bonfire)* Thanks, mate, much obliged. Turned warmer, en it? Night.

*The end music starts.*

*(Clarence sets off down the road.)*

*(Travers smiles and follows him, and the credits roll.*
*During the credits, we see Travers explaining out of our earshot, what happened. When all but the director's credits are over, we cut close for the final dialogue …)*

**CLARENCE:**
Oh. Well, good riddance to her then, I say. Are we still going up to see the bonfire?

**TRAVERS:**
'Course. I'd love to.

**CLARENCE:**
Good. Then we'll pick up the van at the pub, kick me mate out, and drive back to my place for some fish and chips.

**TRAVERS:**
Ohh! Where do you live?

**CLARENCE:**
Peckham.

**TRAVERS:**
Peckham? They'll be cold by the time we get them home.

**CLARENCE:**
No they won't – I solved that years ago.

**TRAVERS:**
How?

**CLARENCE:**
I live over the chip shop. Come on.

*(They wander off, arm in arm. We freeze frame, the music swells up, and the picture becomes a poster-style painting again, as the final credits appear.)*

# EPISODE TWO

*Titles.*

*Scene 1: Live action resume of Episode One.*

**TRAVERS' VOICE OVER:**
He's a funny bloke, Clarence. A removals man. Not at all suited to his job. For a start, he's as blind as a bat. Can't see beyond his own pebble glasses.

Won't admit it mind you. Very proud of his skill and his strength, and at the same time, the clumsiest man I ever met. He's ever so nice though. I only met him last week, but I do like him. On Coronation Day. He came to move madam out – and we got on ever so well. He proposed before the day was out. Not to me; but he thought he was proposing to me.

So I ran after him and told him I'd think it over.
Then he suggested we go up to see the Coronation bonfires …

*From here on we repeat the full version. The end of Episode One, starting with Travers's line, "I'd love to". Obviously excluding the end credits to episode one. We mix through to the next scene.*

*Scene 2: Int. Clarence's flat above the chip shop. Night.*

*(Clarence and Travers are sitting at the table, consuming fish and chips. She has hers on a plate, but he is eating from the newspaper, although there is a plate underneath that.)*

**CLARENCE:**
Does a nice bit of fish downstairs doesn't he?

**TRAVERS:**
Lovely.

**CLARENCE:**
Good fat chips an' all. I like 'em better out of the paper. Do you know what is the largest selling newspaper in the Welsh Mining Villages? The Times. Thicker, see. Makes better tablecloths. That's true, that is. They can't afford no tablecloth, so they use *The Times*.

*(He rises, and goes to a shelf which is cluttered with oddments. He gropes around and picks up a torch battery.)*

**CLARENCE:**
Want some salt?

**TRAVERS:**
No thanks.

*(Clarence shakes the battery over his chips. He puts his hand underneath it; obviously nothing is coming out.)*

**CLARENCE:**
Hmph! Must be damp.

*(Travers reacts. Getting up and finding the real salt shaker.)*

**TRAVERS:**
Try this one.

*(She sits.)*

**CLARENCE:**
Ah, that's better. What was that other one, pepper was it?

**TRAVERS:**
It's a torch battery.

**CLARENCE:**
Oh, that's good, en it? Not a salt and pepper, a salt and battery.

*(He wheezes at his joke.)*

**CLARENCE:**
That's good that is, assault and battery. What do you think of the old place then eh? It's not much, but it's home.

**TRAVERS:**
Did you decorate it yourself?

*(She is looking at the wallpaper – a large patterned affair. One vertical strip is upside down. Clarence stands.)*

**CLARENCE:**
Yeah, did it all myself. I'm quite handy at decorating. I did the bedroom at the same time.

*(We see the other wall. One strip is of a completely different pattern – a pale blue and white stripe.)*

**TRAVERS:**
What colour is the bedroom, blue and white?

**CLARENCE:**
Yeah. How did you know that?

**TRAVERS:**
I just guessed. I like blue and white in a bedroom. A lot of people have blue and white bedrooms.

*(Clarence returns and sits.)*

**CLARENCE:**
Oh, been in a lot of bedrooms have yer? Naughty girl, you told me you was a good girl.

**TRAVERS:**
In my job, silly. I see a lot in my job.

**CLARENCE:**
Oh, yeah, course. Yeah, it's blue with a white stripe; well, either that or it's white with a blue stripe. It's hard to tell with stripes, isn't it? Which is the stripe and which is the other bit? *(he stands)* Want a cup of tea?

*(He picks up her handbag, which does, it must be said, have a handle not unlike a kettle, and puts it on the gas stove, and prepares to put a match under it.)*

**TRAVERS:**
*(darting up)* I'll make it. You sit down and put your feet up.

*(She fills the kettle.)*

**CLARENCE:**
I'll get the cups.

**TRAVERS:**
No, no – You sit down. I'll do all that. *(Clarence reacts.)* Where are the cups?

**CLARENCE:**
Use these over here – these. Next to that picture of me Dad. *(He points. Travers goes uncertainly in the direction of his finger and arrives at a wall cupboard. Next to a wooden framed mirror. She stares at the mirror.)*

**TRAVERS:**
This one? This the picture you mean?

*(we see her reflection, puzzled)*

**CLARENCE:**
*(moving over towards her.)* Yeah. *(She moves out of his way as he arrives at the mirror, and stares into it.)* That's him. Funny-looking bloke, wasn't he? *(We see his blurred version of the mirror refelcting his own face.)* People say I'm like him, but I can't see it myself.

**TRAVERS:**
I thought you were going to sit down and let me do this.

**CLARENCE:**
Oh, yeah, righto. Take the weight off. I'm a bit excited, I suppose. I don't get many people come here.

**TRAVERS:**
Do you like living on your own?

**CLARENCE:**
I'm used to it. How about you?

**TRAVERS:**
I hate it. That's why I went into service.
It's so lonely. I've only got one real friend
in the world – my guinea pig.

**CLARENCE:**
Well, isn't that enough?

**TRAVERS:**
*(sighing)* No. *(She returns to cooker.)*

**CLARENCE:**
Why don't you get another guinea pig?

**TRAVERS:**
Listen Clarence whatever-your-name-is,
you made a proposal of marriage to me
earlier on. Well, after a manner of
speaking, anyway.

**CLARENCE:**
It wasn't you I asked, it was that other
hoity toity bit of crumpet.

**TRAVERS:**
Yes, but you thought it was me, and I'm
considering your offer.

*(She goes for the sugar.)*

**CLARENCE:**
You slapped my face.

**TRAVERS:**
No, that was her.

**CLARENCE:**
Was it? Confusing en it? Well? Trying to
back out now are you? Now you see the
way I live?

**TRAVERS:**
I got nothing to back out of. I'm still
considering. I've been thinking. I think
maybe we should have a trial period.

**CLARENCE:**
Yeah, suits me. You can stay tonight if you
like. I'll show you me blue stripes in me
bedroom.

**TRAVERS:**
I don't mean that! I mean separately. Live
together, but sleep separately.

**CLARENCE:**
What, take it in turns, you mean? Like the
Navy, one on and one off?

**TRAVERS:**
Now just listen a minute. Sit down, finish
your chips and listen.

**CLARENCE:**
Very good madam. Your word is my
command. *(He sits on a non-existent chair
and disappears with a crash behind the table.)*

**TRAVERS:**
Oh, God, are you alright?

**CLARENCE:**
*(getting up)* Did you move that chair?

**TRAVERS:**
Sorry, I must have done. You alright?

**CLARENCE:**
Right as ninepence. Well, eightpence
anyhow. You were saying?

**TRAVERS:**
What I'm saying is, I'm not just going to
straightaway start living with you. Like –
in sin. Like some tuppenny hapenny tart.
I'm not going to live with you like that. A
lot of women have done that, and
regretted it.

**CLARENCE:**
What do you mean, a lot? There's only
ever been two in my life, and neither of
them were tuppenny hapenny tarts. Well,
one of 'em was, but that didn't last long.
*(He combs his hair back into place with a
pocket comb, which he puts down on the
table.)*

**TRAVERS:**
Why not?

**CLARENCE:**
She put the price up to threepence.

**TRAVERS:**
No, look that's not what I mean. I mean I've met women who have been talked into this sort of arrangement, and have finished up on the scrap heap. Nobody wants other people's left offs.

**CLARENCE:**
Left offs, scrap heap Look, I'm a removals man, not a rag and bone man. Anyhow, I'm not like that. Once I get used to things, I don't part with them. I stick to them. These socks for instance. And this watch. See this watch? *(He shows old silver pocket watch.)* My Grandad's watch. He gave me that in his will.

**TRAVERS:**
He left it.

**CLARENCE:**
Well, of course he did. You have to don't you. And do you know, ever since he died, I've wound that watch, and looked after it, and it's never stopped ticking from that day to this.

**TRAVERS:**
Does it keep good time?

**CLARENCE:**
Probably

**TRAVERS:**
Well, what time is it now?

**CLARENCE:**
*(peers at it)* I don't know, the hands have fallen off.

**TRAVERS:**
Well. It's no good then, is it?

**CLARENCE:**
It is to me. I love that old watch.

**TRAVERS:**
It doesn't go.

**CLARENCE:**
It does. It goes everywhere I go. It's an old friend. It wouldn't do to abandon an old friend, would it?

**TRAVERS:**
What about new friends?

**CLARENCE:**
Them neither.

**TRAVERS:**
I hope you mean it.

**CLARENCE:**
I do. *(Puts sugar in tea.)*

**TRAVERS:**
Cos I'm going to tell you something now. *(Taking a deep breath, and delivering her important announcement)* I had a stroke of luck recently. My auntie died of a heart attack.

**CLARENCE:**
Oh. Wasn't a stroke of luck for her. Just a stroke.

**TRAVERS:**
Well, really! That's not very nice.

**CLARENCE:**
No, sorry. Spoke without thinking. *(He stirs tea with comb.)*

**TRAVERS:**
What I'm trying to say is, she left this little cottage in the country. To me. And two hundred pounds.

**CLARENCE:**
Blimey! Good old Auntie. What's this got to do with you and me sleeping together? I've got no objection to hob-nobbing with the landed gentry.

**TRAVERS:**
What I was going to suggest is – why can't we go for a trial period there? There's two bedrooms.

**CLARENCE:**
What, live there? What about my job?

**TRAVERS:**
You're your own master. It's your own van. You can do removals and odd jobs in the country the same as up here.

**CLARENCE:**
What about me contacts.

**TRAVERS:**
Have you got any contacts?

**CLARENCE:**
No.

**TRAVERS:**
It would be nice, in the country.

**CLARENCE:**
I don't know about that. I haven't even seen the place. I'd have to have a good look at the place, close to.

**TRAVERS:**
I could take you down there – or at least, you could take me, in the van.

**CLARENCE:**
Yeah. *(Thinking)* What would we live on?

**TRAVERS:**
The two hundred pounds to start with – 'til you got some work.

**CLARENCE:**
I'd have to sell up here.

**TRAVERS:**
So we'd have that money too.

**CLARENCE:**
Give me the weekend to think it over.

**TRAVERS:**
Alright. *(A pause – they drink tea.)* I'd better go soon. Paddy will wonder where I am.

**CLARENCE:**
Paddy? *(Stands.)*

**TRAVERS:**
My guinea pig.

**CLARENCE:**
Oh yeah. I had visions of some big hairy Irishman I'd have to fight with to get you.

**TRAVERS:**
No. No-one to fight. I think you're ever so nice. *(A moment.)* Right, I'm going now. *(She gets up and puts on her coat. Clarence approaches her.)*

**CLARENCE:**
Right. Well give us a nice kiss to be going on with then.

**TRAVERS:**
No – I mustn't. I've got scruples.

**CLARENCE:**
That's all right – I've had them when I was a kid. *(He kisses her – she reacts, flustered, but he holds her by the arms. We see his misty view of her.)* You look lovely. Let's go to the pictures tomorrow, eh?

**TRAVERS:**
Yes, alright. Which one?

**CLARENCE:**
The Electric, Walham Green. There's a good juicy one on there they say. About a man who kills everybody, including his mother, and drives his best girl mad.

**TRAVERS:**
Oh, I know the one, yes.

**CLARENCE:**
What's it called?

**TRAVERS:**
Well last time I saw it, it was called *Hamlet*.

*Scene 3. Int. Cinema foyer and entrance. Night. The cinema entrance.*

*The foyer is empty, except for a scruffy manager in mangy dinner-jacket talking to an usherette. The strains of "God Save the King" are heard. Seats tip up. Two youths shoot out of the exit doors, to the disgust of the manager, who is standing to attention.*

*He snarls under his breath.*

**MANAGER:**
Hooligans!

*(As the anthem finishes, the doors open and the audience begins to leave. Clarence and Travers are among the first few out.)*

**TRAVERS:**
Good, wasn't it?

**CLARENCE:**
Yeah. I still think you can see better from the front row.

**TRAVERS:**
That was the front row. *(They stop outside by the entrance.)* So the decision is yes then?

**CLARENCE:**
Yeah, we'll give it a go. See you Monday, with the van. *(He kisses her. The manager looks out of the door.)*

**MANAGER:**
Hey! Go and do that at home, not outside my cinema. Old married couple like you ought to have got over all that by now.

*(He goes. Clarence turns and addresses a pillar, on which is pasted a poster photograph of Boris Karloff in* The Mummy.*)*

**CLARENCE:**
You better watch what you're saying, mate. You're no spring chicken yourself.

*Scene 4: Exterior. Country road. Day. Cut to: thirties-style graphic of english country road, sunny and beautiful.*
*Music: "Who's Been Polishing the Sun" (Vocal)*

*Mix to live action of the actual pretty country road. The van comes into view, in the far distance. It weaves along the road erratically, and quite slowly. Inside the van, Travers sits on the edge of her seat, terrified. Clarence peers ahead. The sky is a beautiful blue.*

**CLARENCE:**
Pity this fog had to come down, wasn't it?

*(A wide shot, to see the complete absence of fog. Then back to Travers, who says)*

**TRAVERS:**
Yes, you better go careful.

**CLARENCE:**
I always go careful. How do you think I'm still in the land of the living? *(He chuckles.)*

**TRAVERS:**
Yes, it's a question that crossed my mind.

*(A shot of a signpost in the middle distance.)*

**TRAVERS:**
Ah, we turn left here.

**CLARENCE:**
Turn left. Righto.

*(He immediately turns the wheel to the right. In long shot, we see the van heading into the right-hand hedge. As it mounts the grass verge and enters the hedge, a cow looks up in surprise. Back to the van, Clarence is pretending nothing has happened.)*

**TRAVERS:**
I didn't mean straight away. I meant at the next turning.

**CLARENCE:**
*(covering up)* I know you did. I thought this would be a good place to have the sandwiches.

*(Travers fishes into her wicker basket for the flask and sandwiches, and Clarence opens the door of the van.)*

**CLARENCE:**
What's that funny smell?

**TRAVERS:**
That's the countryside.

**CLARENCE:**
Oooh! *(Sniffs again.)* Bit strong, en it.

**TRAVERS:**
It's lovely. That's the hay and the earth, and the – well, the *(lost for words)* the cows and that.

**CLARENCE:**
Oh, cows, is it. *(points)* That's a cow, isn't it? *(The same cow looks up disdainfully.)*

**TRAVERS:**
Course it is! Don't tell me you've never seen a cow before.

**CLARENCE:**
Only on the pictures. They don't bite, do they?

**TRAVERS:**
No. They just chew the cud.

**CLARENCE:**
Oh. Thanks for the warning. I must remember to keep mine well out of the way.

**TRAVERS:**
*(giggles)* You are daft.

**CLARENCE:**
Yeah! Pleasant, though en I?

**TRAVERS:**
You'll do, until my belted Earl comes along.

**CLARENCE:**
If he does, I'll belt him.

**TRAVERS:**
*(tentatively)* Listen, you must teach me to drive the van.

**CLARENCE:**
Yeah, easy. Learn you in half-an-hour. Nothing to it.

**TRAVERS:**
*(relieved)* Good. Well, we've allowed half-an-hour to eat our sandwiches and they won't take that long to eat. You can teach me now. Here – get those down your neck quick.

*(On his surprised face, as he accepts his packet of sandwiches, we mix to)*

Scene 5: Ext. The road. Day.

*The van, in long-shot, now going even slower, but straight. In the distance we can see a little tin bungalow nestling by the side of the road. This is Travers's auntie's cottage.*
*A shot of Travers, driving with Clarence by her side, peering into space.*

**TRAVERS:**
There it is! That's it! *(she points)*

**CLARENCE:**
Oh yeah! *(he looks in the opposite direction)* Home at last.

*(The tin bungalow in foreground; they emerge from the cab, and approach. Travers has taken Clarence's arm, and guides him to the little front gate. She opens it, and passes through. Clarence closes the gate, and, unnoticed by Travers, veers off to the left and out of frame. A close up of his myopic face as he enters frame.)*

**CLARENCE:**
Nice, en it?

*(We see that he is contemplating an old garden shed.)*

**TRAVERS:**
*(by the house)* That's the shed.

**CLARENCE:**
I meant, it's nice for a shed.

*(He makes his way across to where Travers stands by the front door. He arrives and peers closely at the house, reaching out and touches the wall.)*

**CLARENCE:**
It's tin.

**TRAVERS:**
Corrugated iron. Lots of little places used to be built like it. *(She is struggling with the big old key.)*

**CLARENCE:**
Be alright if you lose your key, won't it?
All you need is a tin-opener.

*(They go in.)*

*Scene 6: Inside the cottage. Day.*

*As they come through the front door and move slowly into the living room, Travers stares about her, her face dropping a little as she contemplates the dilapidated state of the place. Cobwebs, dustsheets over the main pieces of furniture, peeling wallpaper, sooty chimney, curtains half-fallen from the windows, dark damp-stains here and there, and places where pictures once hung.*

**CLARENCE:**
Well, she kept it nice, anyhow.

**TRAVERS:**
Fair bit of work to do on it, though. Lot of decorating, wallpapering.

**CLARENCE:**
That's alright. I can do that. I'm good at decorating. Mind you, I ain't never put paper up on corrugated iron. Be alright in the bathroom. Put my blue stripe up. It'll look like the tide coming in won't it? *(He wheezes.)*

**TRAVERS:**
The walls aren't wavy inside – they been plastered.

**CLARENCE:**
Oh, yes, so they have. Yeah, now I look closer. *(He rubs his hand over a large overmantel mirror.)* Made a good job of that, an all. Smooth as a baby's bottom lip. Shouldn't be no trouble. *(His hand has left dust marks on the mirror.)*

**TRAVERS:**
God, look at the dust. *(She goes to bedroom.)*

**CLARENCE:**
Well, what's a bit of dust matter. You women are all the same, bit of dust drives you dotty. I never notice it. *(He sits heavily in an armchair and clouds of dust arise around him.)* What's happened, you lit the fire?

*Cut to: A bedroom.*

**TRAVERS:**
Gawd, every room's the same. What a state! Still, nothing that a bit of elbow-grease can't cure. *(She looks round.)* This will be my bedroom. *(She leaves.)*

**CLARENCE:**
Suit yourself. I don't mind where I doss down.

*(He goes to window. The light streams through the thin material of the closed curtains, which are of an undulating, multi-coloured pattern.)*

**CLARENCE:**
Nice view from here – is that the sea?

**TRAVERS:**
What? *(She is just outside the door, exploring.)*

**CLARENCE:**
*(calls)* You can see the sea from here.

**TRAVERS:**
What, in Oxfordshire?

**CLARENCE:**
Oh is that where we are. *(Turns to go.)* I ain't got no sense of direction. *(He enters living room.)* I once went to night classes to learn map reading but I couldn't find me way back home.

**TRAVERS:**
Well. What do you think?

**CLARENCE:**
What?

**TRAVERS:**
This place. Shall we move in? *(Clarence joins her.)* Do you reckon we can make it habitable?

**CLARENCE:**
Yeah. Yeah, it's not too bad, what I've seen of it. You game?

**TRAVERS:**
I am if you are.

**CLARENCE:**
Well, I am if you are.

**TRAVERS:**
*(her eyes shining)* Right then.

**CLARENCE:**
Right then. Saturday?

**TRAVERS:**
Let's make it Sunday. No traffic on the road. We'll pack your furniture in the van, and just come here.

**CLARENCE:**
That's it. Pack up all our cares and woe, here we go, singing low, bye bye Peckham.

*Scene 7: Ext. The cottage. Day.*

*The music of "Bye Bye Blackbird" fades in as we see them leave the cottage. The gate sticks again. Clarence peers at it.*

**CLARENCE:**
That'll need fixing, for a start. *(He slams it. A low shot, gate in foreground, as they clamber into the van. Clarence slams the van door, and the garden gate falls flat. The music continues, swelling up as they drive away.)*

*Scene 8: The van. Day.*

*Voices over as the van moves through a sunny wide shot. A dot in the distance.*

**CLARENCE:**
I hope we're doing right.

**TRAVERS:**
Not in the eyes of the church, we're not.

**CLARENCE:**
I don't mean that. Anyhow, the eyes of the church ain't gonna be looking through the key-hole all the time, are they?

**TRAVERS:**
They're very nosy in these little villages. They frown on people cohabiting.

**CLARENCE:**
We're not going to be cohabiting, are we? Just living together.

**TRAVERS:**
I can't see the difference.

**CLARENCE:**
Can't you? Blimey, you're just the girl I been looking for! Whey-hey!

*(The van swerves momentarily.)*

**TRAVERS:**
Hey! Stop that! Don't you dare when I'm driving. You know I can't drive without both hands on the wheel.

**CLARENCE:**
I know. That's why I did it.

**TRAVERS:**
Clarence! I'm warning you. You do that once more, I'm off home.

**CLARENCE:**
Oh, right.

**TRAVERS:**
I mean it.

**CLARENCE:**
Yeah, I can see. Sorry. Cross me heart.

**TRAVERS:**
Alright. *(A pause.)*

**TRAVERS:**
*(primly)* Would you mind putting my dress back down over my knees, please.

**CLARENCE:**
Of course. Nothing would give me greater disappointment. There.

643

**TRAVERS:**
Thank you.

**CLARENCE:**
Nice dress that. Lovely colour.

**TRAVERS:**
I had this for my fortieth birthday.

**CLARENCE:**
Blimey! It has worn well. *(A slap is heard.)* Ow! You took your hand off the wheel to do that, didn't you? Dear, dear ...

*Scene 9: Ext. The cottage. Day.*

*The van approaches the cottage. Clarence and Travers get out. Cut in close.*

**TRAVERS:**
Well, here we are.

**CLARENCE:**
*(peers at it, then agrees)* Yep.

**TRAVERS:**
*(Stares at him, smiles – then snaps into action.)* Well you open up the back of the van, and we can start unloading. *(Clarence gets out of van.)*

**CLARENCE:**
Righto Sergeant.

**TRAVERS:**
I'll unlock the door now I've found the key. *(She gets out of the van and goes towards the house.)*

*(Clarence gropes his way to the back of the van, opens the doors, and takes out a pine kitchen table, about 4' by 2'. He carries it towards the house, but connects with a clothesline post, which spins him round.)*

**CLARENCE:**
Windy, en it.

*(He carries on walking; he is now heading away from the house.)*

**TRAVERS:**
*(emerging, and seeing him)* Oi! Round this way.

**CLARENCE:**
*(turns)* Just looking round the garden. *(He regards a pile of old paint tins.)* Nice lot of dahlias coming up.

**TRAVERS:**
*(now in the van)* Pooh! Terrible smell of fish and chips on these cushions. *(Talking to herself.)* Better leave them outside to air. *(She bends over, unloading small objects out of a tea-chest. Clarence approaches, and sees her rear view.)*

**CLARENCE:**
Blimey. That old sofa needs re-stuffing.

*(He feels the upholstery of Travers's behind.)*

**TRAVERS:**
*(leaping up)* Hey!

**CLARENCE:**
Oh sorry.

**TRAVERS:**
You kindly keep your hands to yourself. We're not married yet you know.

**CLARENCE:**
Sorry, I didn't know it was you. *(A smile)* I do now though.

**TRAVERS:**
*(pointing a finger)* That's enough!

**CLARENCE:**
Yes. Plenty.

**TRAVERS:**
Now listen!

**CLARENCE:**
Yes, sorry, I'll behave meself. Work to be done. Let's take this first. *(They pick up a piece of tatty furniture, and begin to manoeuvre it into the house.)*

*Scene 9a. Int. The cottage. Day.*

*They enter, carrying the furniture, and set it down inthe centre of the room. Travers stares at it. It is a strange lopsided rectangular object, made of wood. As Travers lets go it flops.*

**TRAVERS:**
What is it?

**CLARENCE:**
 It's a cupboard. Solid oak. I made it out of me own head.

**TRAVERS:**
Did you? It's unusual for a cupboard.

**CLARENCE:**
You're wondering why there's no back in it, ain't you? Well, it goes against the wall, see? I realised, you don't need a back when you've got doors.

**TRAVERS:**
It hasn't got no doors.

**CLARENCE:**
No, I took 'em off to put on my wardrobe.

**TRAVERS:**
What happened to your wardrobe doors?

**CLARENCE:**
I had to cut 'em up to make the sides of this cupboard. And the shelf.

**TRAVERS:**
Oh, well, now it's becoming clear. What shelf?

**CLARENCE:**
Ah, well, I had to use the shelf at the bottom, 'cos the bottom fell out. Pity, 'cos I used to keep me book on that shelf.

**TRAVERS:**
What book?

**CLARENCE:**
The book I had, for reading.

**TRAVERS:**
Oh? What sort of book was it?

**CLARENCE:**
A green one.

**TRAVERS:**
Did it have a title?

**CLARENCE:**
Yes, it was called *The Wide Wide World Volume Two*. Have you read it?

**TRAVERS:**
No, can't say I have. Not Volume Two.

**CLARENCE:**
I learnt a lot from that book. You could ask me anything about the world, and I could tell you. Providing it begins with C or D.

**TRAVERS:**
Where's the kettle?

**CLARENCE:**
Kettle doesn't begin with C. Begins with K.

**TRAVERS:**
I want to make some tea, stupid.

**CLARENCE:**
Oh, I see. It'll be on the gas, I expect.

**TRAVERS:**
There isn't no gas.

**CLARENCE:**
No gas?

**TRAVERS:**
Not in the country. Never is. Can't lay gas pipes right out here.

**CLARENCE:**
How do we go on then?

**TRAVERS:**
Everything has to be heated on the fire. The range.

**CLARENCE:**
What, no electric either?

**TRAVERS:**
Nope.

**CLARENCE:**
What do we do when it gets dark I hope.

**TRAVERS:**
Light the oil lamps. And candles at bedtime.

**CLARENCE:**
I always have cocoa.

**TRAVERS:**
*(laughing)* Well, I might manage some of that.

**CLARENCE:**
Oh, lovely. Anything else you might manage? *(Travers raises an admonishing finger.)*

**TRAVERS:**
Listen my lad, it's still broad daylight. We've still got half a van-load to shift. Come on.

**CLARENCE:**
Alright. Just give us a hand with this then.

*(They manoeuvre thing to the wall.)*

**CLARENCE:**
Have we got any candles?

**TRAVERS:**
Dozens. *(Travers leaves.)*

**CLARENCE:**
Pity. *(He ambles out, standing the cupboard against the wall. It immediately sags in towards the room again, as he exits.)*

*Scene 10. Int. The cottage. Day.*

*Travers is seated at an ancient fretted-front pianola, playing "Just A Song At Twilight". The pianola is terribly out of tune and tinny. Clarence appears in the doorway.*

**CLARENCE:**
Got the wireless working then?

**TRAVERS:**
Auntie's favourite tune, this was. *(She continues to play.)* It's funny to think how often this tune must have been played on this old pianola over the years. She used to sing it to me when I was little.

**CLARENCE:**
*(the conversationalist)* Her favourite, was it?

**TRAVERS:**
Yeah. Beautiful isn't it?

**CLARENCE:**
Yeah. "Any Old Iron", isn't it?

*(Music stops.)*

**TRAVERS:**
Not "Any Old Iron". "Loves Old Sweet Song".

**CLARENCE:**
Oh yes. I always mix them two up.

**TRAVERS:**
I know every note of it. Makes Auntie seem so close. You almost feel she might be with us here, in this very room. *(She notices a small framed photo on the wall.)* There she is, look!

**CLARENCE:**
*(alarmed)* Where! Where!

**TRAVERS:**
That photo, look. That's her.

**CLARENCE:**
Gawd, you gave me a turn there for a minute. Oh that's her is it? Was it. Looks a chirpy old soul don't she. Well, let's not hang about – what's next?

**TRAVERS:**
Well we ought to get the bedrooms in some sort of order *(She gets up and joins him.)* Good fun isn't it?

**CLARENCE:**
Yeah. I'm enjoying meself. Makes a change for us, doesn't it? Me moving furniture and you cleaning the house.

**TRAVERS:**
Ah, but it's different when it's your own place. Are you going to put my bed up for me, while I sort out the kitchen things?

**CLARENCE:**
Yeah. Got to get you to bed tonight somehow, haven't I?

*(Clarence goes into a built-in cupboard. He shuts the door. Travers gives a knowing look. He reappears – brooms fall out.)*

**CLARENCE:**
That's the broom cupboard.

*(He exits – Travers shakes her head, smiling.)*

*Music:- "When We Build Our Little Home"* *(vocal)*

*Mix to:*

*Scene 11: Int. The bedroom. Day.*

*Clarence has just finished putting together the single bed – the mattress leans against the wall. There are several tea-chests to hand. He sits on the bed-spring, and reaches for something in the chest with which to mop his brow. We see, but he doesnt of course, that it is a pair of "directoire" knickers. He mops away, and Travers enters.*

**TRAVERS:**
How's it going? Oh, you got it put together.

**CLARENCE:**
Yep. Solid as a rock. Heavy, this bed is. Not to me, of course, but to a normal bloke.

**TRAVERS:**
Oh, well, I'm glad you're feeling strong, 'cos I've got *(She suddenly shrieks)* Oh gawd, a mouse!! *(She leaps on Clarence's lap.)* Ooh, dear, I hate mice. Get it!

**CLARENCE:**
How can I with you on top of me.

**TRAVERS:**
Where's it gone? We must get rid of them.

**CLARENCE:**
If you're going to behave like this, I'll get some more in.

**TRAVERS:**
*(still on his lap)* Here! *(Noting "directoires" in his hand)* What are you doing with my knickers?

**CLARENCE:**
I never touched you.

**TRAVERS:**
No these! *(Taking them.)* Thank you very much. They're my unmentionables.

**CLARENCE:**
Don't mention it.

**TRAVERS:**
What you doing with 'em?

**CLARENCE:**
Just mopping me brow – I thought they was a bit smooth for a duster.

**TRAVERS:**
Now don't get personal again. *(Peering over the edge of the bed)* I wonder where that mouse went.

**CLARENCE:**
Look, I got some mousetraps in my crate in the kitchen – got any cheese?

**TRAVERS:**
Yes, a bit – I'll get some. *(Gingerly putting her feet down.)*

**CLARENCE:**
These floorboards are very creaky. Might be a touch of dry rot here.

**TRAVERS:**
That's bad, isn't it?

**CLARENCE:**
Depends how rotten it is. And how dry it is. I'll investigate it. Get me claw hammer out. Getting a bit nippy in here.

**TRAVERS:**
I know. I'm going to clear out the grate in the other room and light the fire. Oh, and see if you can find any mouseholes and bung them up.

*(She goes, and immediately returns.)*

**TRAVERS:**
On second thoughts, I'll do that. You'll probably bung up the fireplace by mistake. *(He looks puzzled.)*

*Scene 12: Int. The living room. Evening.*

*Travers is kneeling at the grate. She has just lit the fire. Smoke billows out, engulfing her. She takes the broom, and pushes it up the chimney. There is a loud crash off. She stops, looks round. Clarence enters, still clutching his claw hammer, covered in dust.*

**CLARENCE:**
Listen. Will you marry me or not? Yes or No?

**TRAVERS:**
Yes!

**CLARENCE:**
Good. 'Cos the floor's just fell through in your bedroom. *(He walks towards her, the mousetrap snaps shut on his foot.)*

*Closing song: "Keep Your Sunny Side Up".*

*The credits roll during which Travers helps to extricate Clarence from the mousetrap. She then tells him, in dumb-show, that the chimney is blocked. He takes the broom and shoves it up the chimney. As the main credits finish, a load of soot descends, covering them.*

**CLARENCE:**
*(sings)* Oh de camp-town races sing this song, doo dah, doo dah.

*(The picture freezes, turns into a thirties poster, like blacked up-minstrels – and the music continues to play "Kemp-Town Races")*

# EPISODE THREE

*Scene 1: A resume, in live action, of the story so far. Travers's voice over.*

**TRAVERS:**
*(v/o)* He's a funny bloke, Clarence. Blind as a bat and the clumsiest man I ever met. We met when he was doing removals where I worked. I fell for him straight away. I told him of my recent windfall – my Auntie's cottage in the country. The long and the short of it was, we decided to move down here. Well, of course, the place is in a right state, but we'll manage. He has proposed to me, and I told him we would have a trial period, in separate bedrooms. Unfortunately, circumstances caused the trial period to be shorter than I had expected.

*From here on we repeat the scene from the end of the previous episode, starting with the loud crash off, and Clarence entering, covered in dust.*

**CLARENCE:**
Listen – will you marry me or not? Yes or No?

**TRAVERS:**
Yes!

**CLARENCE:**
Good. 'Cos the floor's just fell through in your bedroom.

*(He walks toward her – the mousetrap snaps shut on his foot.)*

*Scene 2: Int. Bedroom. Night.*

*Link tune – "Goodnight Sweetheart" (vocal) actual 1930s recording.*

*The other bedroom, small, but with an ancient double bed. Against one wall. At the foot of this bed, Travers is busy making up a bed on a mattress on the floor.*

*(Clarence enters, peers around myopically. He listens. Then he calls out.)*

**CLARENCE:**
Travers! I can still hear mice in here!

**TRAVERS:**
It's me, dopey.

**CLARENCE:**
Oh, sorry, didn't see you down there. What you doing, lost something?

**TRAVERS:**
I'm making up an extra bed. *(She stands.)*

**CLARENCE:**
Why? We expecting visitors?

**TRAVERS:**
It's for you.

**CLARENCE:**
Eh? But I thought you said you'd marry me.

**TRAVERS:**
I know what I said. And I know what you thought. You thought we was going to share the same bed. But now I've had a think, and I think easy does it. Let's not rush into anything too hasty.

**CLARENCE:**
No, alright – you're the boss. *(He sits.)*

**TRAVERS:**
You do understand, don't you Clarence?

**CLARENCE:**
Yes, of course. Easy does it. Anyway, you're the woman, ain't you? It's always up to the woman, en it.

*(Travers goes and sits on bed.)*

**TRAVERS:**
I mean, you realise how I must have felt. I was lonely – I've been lonely all my life, really – then suddenly, I meet this man. He's lonely too – older than me, set in his ways – but nice. 'Course I'm going to be eager – only natural. But then I said to myself "hold on – don't go leaping into marriage before you know what he's really like."

**CLARENCE:**
Yeah. Well, just as well you didn't marry him, the silly old buffer, 'cos now I've come along.

**TRAVERS:**
It's you I'm talking about.

**CLARENCE:**
Me? Oh, I see. Set in my ways, am I?

**TRAVERS:**
Well, you are a bit.

**CLARENCE:**
Like what, for instance?

**TRAVERS:**
Well, you always wear your cap in the house.

**CLARENCE:**
There's a reason for that, and I'll tell you why. If I put it down, I can never find it again, that's why.

**TRAVERS:**
Well you must take it off sometimes.

**CLARENCE:**
No. Only to scratch me head.

**TRAVERS:**
You don't sleep with it, do you?

**CLARENCE:**
Yes. Not on me head, of course. I tuck it in me vest.

**TRAVERS:**
Vest? I can see there's a lot I've got

649

to teach you my lad.

**CLARENCE:**
Ooh. I hope so. *(He grabs her.)*

**TRAVERS:**
Behave! *(But she stays in his arms.)* You shouldn't wear your vest in bed!

**CLARENCE:**
I ain't got no night clothes.

**TRAVERS:**
Come to think of it, neither have I – haven't had time to get them sorted out. Well, it'll have to be underwear tonight. I'll get organised in the morning.

**CLARENCE:**
Righto. We turning in now then?

**TRAVERS:**
Yes – I'm absolutely exhausted. I'll go outside and undress while you get into bed – then you blow out the candle, and give me a shout, alright?

**CLARENCE:**
Yes – please your joyful.

*(She starts to go – then, as an afterthought.)*

**TRAVERS:**
You don't snore, do you?

**CLARENCE:**
How do I know? Do you?

**TRAVERS:**
I don't know. *(A depressing thought.)*

**CLARENCE:**
There you are, you see. Tell you what, we'll both know by tomorrow morning, won't we?

**TRAVERS:**
*(brightening up)* Yes, that's true.

**CLARENCE:**
When I was a kid I used to mutter. P'raps I still do.

**TRAVERS:**
Mutter?

**CLARENCE:**
Yeah – just mutter things. I hope I don't keep you awake.

**TRAVERS:**
Don't worry – just you go off to sleep.

**CLARENCE:**
Oh, I will. Never have no trouble sleeping. Soon as me head touches the pillow.

**TRAVERS:**
I'm afraid you haven't got a pillow.

**CLARENCE:**
Well, as soon as it touches the floorboards then.

*(She smiles, and goes – taking the oil lamp with her. He is left with the candlelight. He removes his trousers, then his longjohns, but leaves on his shirt – the shirttails cover his embarrassment as he goes to blow out the candle. At first he tries several times to blow out its reflection in the mirror, but eventually realises and finds the real one. In the ensuing darkness, we see him, by moonlight, slip into the made-up floor bed. He calls out.)*

**CLARENCE:**
Ready! *(The door opens a crack. Travers's head appears.)*

**TRAVERS:**
Are you in?

**CLARENCE:**
Yes – snug as a bug in a rug.

*(She opens the door wider – we see her silhouette – vest and bloomers – as she flits into the big double bed.)*

**TRAVERS:**
Night, night.

**CLARENCE:**
Night. Sleep well.

**TRAVERS:**
And you – God bless.

*(A pause. We see Clarence's eyes close. We see Travers's eyes open. Clarence starts to mutter.)*

**CLARENCE:**
*(muttering)* Listen my girl I like the look of you will you marry me? I think you're lovely *(Travers's face, smiling – she snuggles down and turns on her side to sleep. A shot of Clarence's face. Still muttering.)* I'm sure we'd be happy together *(His eyes open, and we realise he's shamming.)* We could settle down in the cottage I could look after you *(He pauses, listening and smiling. A loud snore from Travers. He reacts, as we mix to:)*

*Scene 3: Ext. The cottage. Morning.*

*A wide shot of the countryside – the cottage is sunlit. A cock crows in the distance. Sheep are bleating.*

*Scene 4: Int. The bedroom. Morning.*

*Travers's face. She opens her eyes. Clarence's snoring is heard. She frowns, looks sideways. We cut wider to show that Clarence is now in bed with her. He wears his cap. She is shocked, and sits up, clutching the bedclothes to her. Clarence stirs in his sleep, and opens his eyes.*

**TRAVERS:**
Here!

**CLARENCE:**
Oo-er. Morning. Sleep alright did you?

**TRAVERS:**
What the devil do you think you're doing in here?

**CLARENCE:**
I dunno. I got out in the night to go to the lavvy. I must have got back in here without thinking.

**TRAVERS:**
Well you better get out again, quick! No! Wait a minute – what have you got on?

**TRAVERS:**
Just me shirt.

**TRAVERS:**
You stay where you are. But keep well over that side, please. *(A pause)* I hope you're not going to make a habit of it.

**CLARENCE:**
So do I! No joke having an outside lavatory. I had to grope around in the pitch dark, get dressed and find me way out in the garden. So I don't need moaning at by you an all.

**TRAVERS:**
No, no, you're right. Sorry. It must have been very difficult for you.

**CLARENCE:**
It was. I had me trousers on back to front.

**TRAVERS:**
Oh dear! I hope you lifted the seat.

**CLARENCE:**
I lifted the lid of the chicken-run to start with.

**TRAVERS:**
*(beginning to see the funny side)* Good job there were no chickens in there. They'll have a peck at anything. *(She giggles.)*

**CLARENCE:**
You can laugh, my girl.

**TRAVERS:**
Thanks, I will. *(She has a good guffaw.)*

**CLARENCE:**
Listen, are you going to get us a cup of tea?

**TRAVERS:**
Yes. No! I'm not getting out in front of you. I'm not decent.

**CLARENCE:**
Well, if I can't get out in front of you, and you can't get out in front of me, we're going to be stuck here all day, ain't we?

**TRAVERS:**
Looks like it.

**CLARENCE:**
Suits me. Give us a cuddle. *(He makes a move.)*

**TRAVERS:**
Stay where you are! I know. *(She leans across and removes his glasses.)* There. That'll solve it. I'll bring 'em back when I've got the tea. *(She gets out of bed in vest and "directoires".)*

**CLARENCE:**
Coo! That's funny. I can see a lot better without them glasses!

*(She shoots out of the door, then puts her head back round.)*

**TRAVERS:**
You lying devil. How many fingers am I holding up?

**CLARENCE:**
I dunno, but I can guess. *(Of course it's two.)*

**TRAVERS:**
You're rotten.

**CLARENCE:**
*(his turn to laugh)* Got you going for a minute, though, didn't it?

*(Travers reacts.)*

*Scene 5: Int. The kitchen. Morning.*

*Music: – "I Like a Nice Cup of Tea in the Morning" (vocal)*

*A kettle, boiling on the crackling fire in the old kitchen range. Travers fills the teapot, and we widen to see Clarence seated at the kitchen table, devouring bacon and eggs. Travers joins him, putting the teapot on the scrubbed table, and continues with her breakfast.*

**CLARENCE:**
I'll say this for you, Travers, you can cook. Well, bacon and eggs, any road. Dunno

about anything else.

**TRAVERS:**
There's a lot of things you don't know about me. You haven't sampled my fluffy dumplings.

**CLARENCE:**
Not for want of trying, is it?

**TRAVERS:**
Now don't get smutty. Why do men always get smutty?

**CLARENCE:**
Well, it's on account of a woman's mind is cleaner than a man's. Know why? 'Cos she changes it more often. *(He gives his wheezy laugh.)*

**TRAVERS:**
Oh, dear, where did you read that, in a comic?

**CLARENCE:**
Certainly not. I don't read comics. It was *Tit-Bits*. Either that or the *Financial Times*. I know I was wrapping up stuff when we moved that big bug in the City, so it was probably *Tit-Bits*. I got all my wit off Comic Postcards – my uncle Norman used to have an Album with 'em all in, when we used to stay with him. They was funny, some of them. A woman goes into an ironmongers and says, "Could I have a mousetrap quickly please, I want to catch a train.." Good, en it? And a newly-wed girl in the shop says, "Have you got a dish two foot long by three inches wide?" And the man says, "What for?" and she says, "I want to make a rhubarb pie."

**TRAVERS:**
Oh, that reminds me. There's some rhubarb in the garden. Do you like it stewed?

**CLARENCE:**
Yes. Talking of stewed, how's the tea?

**TRAVERS:**
Oh sorry! *(She pours the milk.)* Sorry it's

only condensed milk. The milk we brought has gone off. I must get down to the village today, shopping. See if I can find out whether there's a milkman comes round.

**CLARENCE:**
I shouldn't think so, he wouldn't come round here. Miles from anywhere, en it?

*(She pours tea.)*

**TRAVERS:**
Tell you what, there's a nice friendly looking cow in the field out there. I might have a go milking it.

**CLARENCE:**
Make sure it is a cow. You go milking a bull you're asking for trouble.

**TRAVERS:**
I know the difference, silly! You keep forgetting I used to come here for me school holidays. I'll teach you to milk it if you like.

**CLARENCE:**
Nah. Don't fancy it. Don't reckon the cow does much, either. I mean how would you like it if you was standing in a field and someone came up and started doing it to you?

**TRAVERS:**
It's different – they're used to it. *(She stands.)* Look, let me teach you, go on, please.

**CLARENCE:**
Oh, please is it? What will you give me if I do then, eh?

**TRAVERS:**
*(smiles teasingly, then gets up and whispers in his ear)* A nice big pat on the back.

**CLARENCE:**
Yeah, that's probably what I'll get from the cow, an' all. *(He stirs the can of condensed milk instead of his tea, and takes a gulp – surprised reaction.)*

*Scene 6: Ext. The garden. Day.*

*Music – "The Sun has got his Hat On" – vocal. 1930s-style graphic picture of the privy at the bottom of the garden; becomes live action – then reverse to show Travers coming out of the back door. She carries a wicker shopping basket, and wears a black or navy-blue raincoat, nanny-style, and a blouse with a white collar. She approaches the privy.*

**TRAVERS:**
Are you in there?

**CLARENCE:**
Yes, you want to come in?

**TRAVERS:**
No thank you! I'm going down to the village to see what shops there are.

**CLARENCE:**
Righto, I'll still be here when you get back.

**TRAVERS:**
I hope not. Are you reading the paper in there?

**CLARENCE:**
Yes. It says, "ISAL Medicated. Now wash your hands".

*(Travers reacts, and leaves.)*

*Scene 7: Ext. The countryside. Day.*

*A wide, pretty shot of the countryside – the road winding up towards us. Travers is a dot, briskly stepping out towards the village. A close up of her as she looks around. A shot of a pretty grey donkey, looking over a low hedge. She smiles, goes to it.*

**TRAVERS:**
Hello, dearie. You are a pretty boy, aren't you?

*(A fearsome looking young yokel, ugly in the extreme, pops his head up beside the donkey, his face cracks into a toothless grin. Travers hurries away, and up the hill.)*

653

*Scene 8: Int. The cottage. Day.*

*In the parlour, a load of piled-up furniture, and a lot of tea chests dotted about. Clarence is sorting through one of these. He brings out a German World War I helmet, an elaborate thing with a big spike on top.*

**CLARENCE:**
Cor, me old German trophy! Must hang that up somewhere. I'd better put some of these pictures up an' all, make the place cosy. *(He goes to kitchen.)* Talking to yourself again, Clarence. One day someone will hear you, and then where will you be? Talking to someone else, that's right.

*(He picks up hammer and nail, and goes to upstage left wall. The wall he is considering already has a large hook for a picture but Clarence cannot, of course, see this. He bangs in his nail a foot or so away from it. He then picks up his picture, and hangs it on the original hook. He stands back to admire his work. We now see that the picture is backwards, facing the wall with a yellow circular framer's label on the back. Satisfied, he exits.)*

*(Parlour.)*

*(He enters and sets about moving furniture. He takes a dining chair from the pile – we see that the seat has fallen out. He puts it down. He moves the table and then attempts to pick up a heavy chair. He manages to get it on his head but then slowly sinks to the ground, disappearing from view beneath it. He crawls out from the back, and peers round.)*

**CLARENCE:**
Dear dear. Everything went dark. Phew! That's an 'eavy piece.

*(He takes out his handkerchief, mops his brow, and sits on the dining chair which has no seat. As he sits, we see that he has placed it over the german spiked helmet. The spike connects, and he leaps into the air with a yell, clutching his backside.)*

**CLARENCE:**
Ow! Flaming wasps. Ooh, blimey, what a place to get you. Might be a bee. They leave their stings in.

*(He is still wincing in pain when a knock is heard at the front door. He staggers over to open it.)*

*Scene 8a: Ext. The cottage. Day.*

*Vicar's wife approaches the front door.*

*Scene 9: Ext. The cottage. Day.*

*At the door stands a large woman, with a gushing smile, which very soon freezes on her face as Clarence speaks.*

**CLARENCE:**
Blimey, that was quick. Listen, you're just in time. I just been bitten by a bee or a wasp on the backside. Will you have a look? *(He turns his back on her.)*

**VICAR'S WIFE:**
*(for that is who it is)* Pardon?

**CLARENCE:**
Only if it's a bee you have to pull it out quick.

*(He starts to undo his belt.)*

**VICAR'S WIFE:**
Stop! I think you must be mistaking me for someone else!

**CLARENCE:**
Eh? *(Peers at her)* Oh, do beg pardon. I thought you was another lady. Don't worry, it was probably a wasp. I was just shifting some furniture in the front room, and it got me. Don't half hurt when they sting you there. Have you ever been stung there?

**VICAR'S WIFE:**
In the front room, no I haven't.

**CLARENCE:**
Ooh. It's going off a bit now.

**VICAR'S WIFE:**
I saw the van. You, I take it, are the removals man.

**CLARENCE:**
Yeah, that's me.

**VICAR'S WIFE:**
And where is the lady of the house?

**CLARENCE:**
She's gone out.

**VICAR'S WIFE:**
And left you here on your own?

**CLARENCE:**
That's alright, I live with her.

**VICAR'S WIFE:**
I beg your pardon?

**CLARENCE:**
We're man and – er – man and er woman. So to speak.

**VICAR'S WIFE:**
Oh, you're married – why didn't you say so?

**CLARENCE:**
I didn't say so.

**VICAR'S WIFE:**
No – now I understand. Well, I'll come straight to the point – are you willing to move from room to room? It's worth ten shillings to me.

**CLARENCE:**
Eh?

**VICAR'S WIFE:**
I have a very large chiffonier.

**CLARENCE:**
*(peering at her)* Oh, I wouldn't say that.

**VICAR'S WIFE:**
My husband can't manage it on his own. It needs another man's strength behind it.

**CLARENCE:**
Ah, well, I'm just the bloke. Built like a brick outhouse. Feel them thighs.

**VICAR'S WIFE:**
I'd rather not, thank you. So I take it you would be willing to come to the house and give me the benefit of your muscle?

**CLARENCE:**
Put like that, I can't refuse, can I.

**VICAR'S WIFE:**
I would like it in the dining room.

**CLARENCE:**
You can have it where you like, madam. Same difference to me.

**VICAR'S WIFE:**
Shall we say tomorrow morning then? The Vicarage.

**CLARENCE:**
Oh – you look after the Vicar, do you?

**VICAR'S WIFE:**
Of course not. I'm his wife.

*(Clarence looks over her shoulder.)*

**CLARENCE:**
Well well!

*(We see Travers coming in through the garden gate.)*

**CLARENCE:**
Here is the Vicar himself – talk of the Devil. Morning Vicar. Got your missus in here. Co-inky dinky en it?

**TRAVERS:**
*(sotto)* It's me, you daft ha'pporth.

**CLARENCE:**
Oh. The Vicar's wife has been a-visiting.

**TRAVERS:**
Oh. *(They exchange distant smiles.)* Good morning.

**VICAR'S WIFE:**
Good morning. *(To Clarence.)* Tomorrow morning, then?

*(She sweeps out of the front gate. Travers and Clarence go into the house and close the door.)*

*Scene 10: Int. Parlour / kitchen. Day.*

**TRAVERS:**
What did she want?

**CLARENCE:**
She just made me a proposition.

**TRAVERS:**
What sort of proposition?

**CLARENCE:**
I'm not sure. What's a chiffonier?

**TRAVERS:**
*(indicates width with hands)* It's a big thing, with drawers.

**CLARENCE:**
That's what I was afraid of.

**TRAVERS:**
A sort of sideboard.

**CLARENCE:**
Oh! Oh, well, that's all right then. She wants it shifted to the dining room.

**TRAVERS:**
Oh, that's good. Your first little job! It's a start isn't it? When have you got to go?

**CLARENCE:**
In the morning.

**TRAVERS:**
Oh, good – I can drive you up there in the van.

**CLARENCE:**
*(he goes to poke fire)* I can drive the van. Been driving it for twenty years.

*(She comes out of larder and sees picture.)*

**TRAVERS:**
I know, and it's time you stopped.

**CLARENCE:**
Why?

**TRAVERS:**
*(a difficult subject)* I don't think your eyesight's what it was.

**CLARENCE:**
Rubbish! People been saying that to me all me life.

*(Travers is looking at the picture he hung up backwards.)*

**TRAVERS:**
Did you put that picture up?

**CLARENCE:**
Yeah. Nice en it? I like sunsets.

**TRAVERS:**
It's back to front.

*(She turns it over.)*

**CLARENCE:**
That must have been the wind. *(She reacts as she is about to turn it over.)* I tell you my eyesight is as good as the next man's.

*(We pan off Clarence, to the picture, as it is turned over. It is Nelson complete with eye-patch.)*

**TRAVERS:**
Well, if you say so. But I'll still drive. I want to see the Vicarage.

*(Clarence peers round at the picture.)*

*(Music under – "If I had a Talking Picture of You" – (vocal)*

*Scene 11: Ext. The Vicarage. Day*

*1930s graphics-style picture of the Vicarage, wide and pretty. Becomes a wide shot, as the van drives up. Clarence and Travers get out of the van. Close up finger on doorbell. The door*

*is opened by the vicar's wife. Back to the wide
shot as they enter the house.*

*Now a montage of shots, as we hear bangs
and crashes as Clarence gets to work.
Chickens react, birds fly away in flocks, ducks
run for it, as each bump is worse than the
last.*

*We start a slow ease in from a very wide shot,
and we home in on the dining room window.
As we get nearer, the distant, muffled voices
become clearer. We hear Clarence's voice say
"Up your end, madam", and Travers's
"Careful". Clarence again. "No up your end,
madam." By now we have a medium wide
shot of the dining room window. The leg of a
sideboard shatters the glass and pokes
through. General groans as it is withdrawn.*

**CLARENCE:**
*(off)* I did say Up your end, madam.

**VICAR'S WIFE:**
*(off)* It should have been up yours!

**CLARENCE:**
*off)* No no, up yours!

*(They continue to argue.)*

*Scene 12: Int. The kitchen. Evening.*

*Music over link – "'Little Man You've Had a
Busy Day" – (vocal)*

*Clarence, head in hands, is sitting glumly in
front of his supper. Travers is opposite,
enjoying hers.*

**TRAVERS:**
Come on, eat up. Don't you like
shepherds' pie?

**CLARENCE:**
Yes, it's very nice.

**TRAVERS:**
Well, eat it then, and stop moping. The
day turned out very well really.

**CLARENCE:**
Oh yes. Earned ten bob for doing the job,
paid out seven and six for the window
glass, two bob for the putty, and
twopence for the nails. So I finished up
with fourpence. That's a good day's work,
isn't it, fourpence.

**TRAVERS:**
I'm not talking about that. That was
unfortunate. What I'm talking about is
the fact that she offered me the job of
domestic. I think it was on account of
how quickly I tidied up the mess that you
– the mess that was made. That's why I
got the job.

**CLARENCE:**
There was one condition, though, wasn't
there? That I never went near the place
again.

**TRAVERS:**
Oh, she'll come round later on.

**CLARENCE:**
Not round here she won't. Fat old faggot.

**TRAVERS:**
No, I mean she'll relent when I tell her
how nice you are really.

**CLARENCE:**
Am I?

**TRAVERS:**
You're lovely.

**CLARENCE:**
Well when we going to get married and
live together as man and wife, eh?

**TRAVERS:**
Is marriage so important to you?

**CLARENCE:**
Not marriage itself, no – it's the other bit.

**TRAVERS:**
The other bit?

**CLARENCE:**
Yes, a bit of the other.

**TRAVERS:**
Now I've told you – there's to be none of that till after we've tied the knot.

**CLARENCE:**
Yes, that seems to be the answer.

**TRAVERS:**
What.

**CLARENCE:**
Tie a knot. Can't wait for ever though. I'm warning you.

**TRAVERS:**
You talk as though you've never like, well – been with a woman.

**CLARENCE:**
I haven't.

**TRAVERS:**
Eh?

**CLARENCE:**
Not for months. Last August Bank Holiday it was, up the Embankment. She was a big girl.

**TRAVERS:**
I don't want to know the sordid details, thanks very much.

**CLARENCE:**
She had an embankment of her own.

*(Travers fetches the dish from the oven.)*

**TRAVERS:**
Do you want some more of this, there's plenty left.

**CLARENCE:**
That's what she said.

**TRAVERS:**
You're incorrigible, you are!

**CLARENCE:**
Yes, I know I am. What is it?

*(He rises, but she pushes him back onto his chair.)*

**TRAVERS:**
It means you shouldn't be encouraged.

**CLARENCE:**
*(wincing)* Ow!

**TRAVERS:**
What's the matter?

**CLARENCE:**
Damn wasp sting. When I was shifting furniture while you was out, I sat on it in the front room. It's probably squashed on the chair in there.

**TRAVERS:**
Oh dear, can't have that. *(She exits, finds helmet and returns almost immediately with the German spiked helmet.)* This was underneath the chair. And the chair had no seat in it.

**CLARENCE:**
*(taking it)* Blimey. I should have hung it up straight away when I said I would. *(Examining it lovingly)* That's my German trophy, that is. One of the spoils of war. Got that on the Somme.

**TRAVERS:**
*(impressed)* Coo dear. Did you actually take it off a dead German?

**CLARENCE:**
No, I pinched it from under a tart's bed in the village. She used it to keep it under there for emergencies. Only up the other way it was. Stuck in the floorboards.

**TRAVERS:**
*(sarcastically)* Quite a colourful life you've led, haven't you, really, one way and another?

**CLARENCE:**
Yes – s'pose I have. I lived with a woman

once. That was during my drinking period. It was a bit of a stormy passage with her. We used to have terrible rows when I used to stagger home at two in the morning. I used to crash about in the bedroom getting undressed. It used to wake her up, see.

**TRAVERS:**
It would. I mean you're bad enough sober.

**CLARENCE:**
So this drinking pal of mine, Harry, he said to me once , "Look, what you do is you take all our clothes off before you go up the stairs, and your shoes, and carry em up with you. Then you just got to put em down and creep into bed." So one night I said goodnight to Harry, and we was both pie-eyed – absolutely rat faced we was – so I though I'd try it. I took of all me clothes and put em over me arm, picked up me boots, and tip-toed up the stairs. When I got up to the top I found it was Baker Street Station.

*(Travers reacts, then starts to giggle. They both enjoy the moment.)*

**TRAVERS:**
Well, I sincerely hope you won't get up to that sort of thing here.

**CLARENCE:**
I can't, can I? It's a bungalow, isn't it? Trains don't run through here.

*Scene 13: Int. The bedroom. Night.*

*Travers is putting the bolster down the middle of the bed. Clarence enters.*

**CLARENCE:**
Oooh, it's cold down in that lavvy tonight. Freeze the brass buttons off a flunkey. Be careful, you'll get frozen to the seat.

**TRAVERS:**
Yes, I know, it is cold. And – listen to me – for that reason, and that reason only, we're going to sleep in the same bed. But

before you get too interested – I've put a bolster down the middle.

**CLARENCE:**
Oh dear – that means there's bee three of us in there.

**TRAVERS:**
I feel I must also insist that you wear something in bed. Now I've got two nighties – they're both floor length, and very voluminous.

**CLARENCE:**
Voluminous?

**TRAVERS:**
You can wear one, and I can wear the other.

**CLARENCE:**
Oh I see, volume one and volume two is it? *(She hands him one.)* I can't wear this. I'd look ridiculous.

**TRAVERS:**
Who's going to see you?

**CLARENCE:**
Well you are, for a start.

**TRAVERS:**
Look, it's either that or back on the floor again. Go on, go outside and put it on while I change.

**CLARENCE:**
Alright – gawd, the things I do for England!

*(He exits. Travers starts to undress, slowly and methodically folding her cardigan, skirt and blouse. She is now in vest and bloomers. The door rattles. She shrieks. When the door opens and a vision of loveliness in a flat cap enters. She shrieks, and hides behind her own nightdress, clutched to her.)*

**CLARENCE:**
I mean, look at this. It's too tight, anyhow. I wouldn't get a wink of sleep.

**TRAVERS:**
No, you're right. Nor would I, for laughing!

**CLARENCE:**
I knew you'd laugh at me.

**TRAVERS:**
Go on then, put your shirt back on. But remember – behave yourself.

*(He goes. She now puts on her nightie. Clarence returns, once more in his shirt.)*

**TRAVERS:**
Right – into bed – I'm just going to put the lamps out. It's been a hard day. *(She gives him a peck – he rests his arms on her shoulders.)* By the way – I meant to say you put that glass back in that window very nicely. You're very good at close work, aren't you?

**CLARENCE:**
If you'd let me get close enough I'd show you how good.

**TRAVERS:**
Yes, now that's enough of that. Do you realise there's nothing but your shirt between me and dishonour? I must remember to wash that in cold water – I don't want it shrinking. *(she goes)*

**CLARENCE:**
That makes two of us.

*(He gets into bed – then lifts up the clothes and looks underneath the bed, on the floor. We see the German helmet, spike sticking into the floor. Clarence nods in satisfaction, and snuggles down to sleep.)*

*(Closing song begins.)*

*(During the credits, Travers in the kitchen – puts out the oil lamps or gas lamps, brings the candle into the bedroom, creeps into bed and settles down. At end of credits, she looks at Clarence, already asleep. Gently she removes his glasses, and puts them on to the bolster - –and then removes his cap, and places that,*

*too, on the bolster. She smiles, and gives the bolster a goodnight kiss.)*

*(She blows out candle.)*

*(Last credit appears.)*

# EPISODE FOUR

*Titles:*
*Scene 1: A resume, in live action of the story so far.*

**TRAVERS'S VOICE OVER:**
He's a funny bloke, Clarence. Blind as a bat for a start, and him a removals man. Me and him sort of hit it off right away, though. He's very kind and gentle in a clumsy sort of way. Me and him moved down to this cottage me old Auntie left me, and we're still not straight. We're still not straight about the sleeping arrangements, either – he wants me to marry him, but I've said I want a trial period first – and that means without any hanky-panky either. And as there's only one bed, that's not easy …

*We now pick up last week's episode from Travers saying –*

**TRAVERS:**
… I meant to say. You put that glass back in the window very nicely. You're good at close work, aren't you?

**CLARENCE:**
If you'd let me get enough I'd show you how good.

**TRAVERS:**
Yes now that's enough of that. Do you realise there's nothing but your shirt between me and dishonour. I must remember to wash that in cold water, don't want it shrinking.

**CLARENCE:**
That makes two of us.

*Scene 2: Int. The cottage. Day.*

*The parlour. More or less straight now – a few tea-chests and orange boxes of the period still dotted about.*
*Clarence enters, and peers about in his pebble glasses. On the settee a large rug is rolled up, leaning in an upright position. He wanders to the window and stares into the net curtains.*

**CLARENCE:**
Looks like a bit of a mist this morning.

*(He yawns, and wanders over to a picture of a pretty little dog which hangs on the wall.)*

**CLARENCE:**
Cor dear, I must get a shave before I do anything else.

*(He sits down next to the rug, and addresses it conversationally.)*

**CLARENCE:**
So what's next on the agenda then my dear? *(He pats the rug.)*

*(Travers enters. She wears a black choker of jet beads.)*

**TRAVERS:**
What you say?

**CLARENCE:**
(realising) I was just asking this – I was just asking what's next on the agenda?

**TRAVERS:**
You'll go blind drinking all tea.

**CLARENCE:**
You can't go blind drinking tea.

**TRAVERS:**
You can if you leave the spoon in the cup. *(Clarence reacts.)* Here, look what I've just found – Auntie's jet beads.

**CLARENCE:**
Where? *(He gets up.)*

**TRAVERS:**
*(hands to throat)* Here round me neck – they're a choker.

**CLARENCE:**
Are they working?

**TRAVERS:**
What?

**CLARENCE:**
Choking you.

**TRAVERS:**
They are, as a matter or fact – could you undo them for me, I can't get them off.

*(Clarence gropes his way to behind her, and fumbles with the clasp.)*

**CLARENCE:**
I thought you hadn't washed your neck.

*(they laugh – he tugs at the clasp and the string breaks, scattering the beads everywhere)*

**TRAVERS:**
Well, that's got them off alright.

**CLARENCE:**
Sorry about that. I I'm not used t' women's things. If that had been a bicycle chain, I could have managed it.

**TRAVERS:**
Oh, p'raps I'll wear a nice bicycle chain instead then.

**CLARENCE:**
I'll help you look for 'em.

**TRAVERS:**
No, don't bother, I'll find them.

**CLARENCE:**
There's one here, look.

**TRAVERS:**
No, that's a beetle. I must get some stuff for them.

**CLARENCE:**
Stuff?

**TRAVERS:**
Stuff you put down for them. They eat it.

**CLARENCE:**
No, don't encourage them, let 'em find their own food. You'll have 'em coming in from the garden if it gets around.

*(Travers puts beads on table.)*

**TRAVERS:**
*(eyes to heaven)* Dear Lord! Listen, talking of gardens, that's the next job. Organising that. It's only May, still time to plant some runner beans, put some dahlias and chrysanths in. There's a place in the village got some plants and seeds for sale, there's a notice. I'm going to take a walk up there this morning. I'll see what there is in. Look you have a go at clearing a vegetable patch. Pick somewhere nice and sunny, not too near the hedge.

**CLARENCE:**
What about tools?

**TRAVERS:**
Must be some in the shed. Have a look.

**CLARENCE:**
Righto, sergeant. *(Goes to bedroom.)* I reckon this country air agrees with me. I feel like doing a hundred press-ups again today.

**TRAVERS:**
Again?!

**CLARENCE:**
Yeah. I felt like it yesterday an' all. (I didn't do it.)

*(He lies on bed.)*

*Scene 3: Ext. Garden shed. Day.*

*Graphic of garden and shed. Mix into live action.*

*Link music – "Knee deep in daisies. Head over heels in Love".*
*The garden shed. Clarence is rattling around inside it – a clatter of garden implements. He emerges with an old rusty spade. He peers around, and selects a spot. He sticks the spade into the ground, rams it in with boot, and lifts. The head of the spade stays in the ground, and the handle comes away. Clarence carries the handle a few feet away, and tips the imaginary earth off it, still unaware.*

**CLARENCE:**
Very light soil round here. Oops! Talking to yourself again, Clarence.

*(He returns, attempts to put the spade into the earth again, but gropes around in the air with his foot, trying to find the place to push. He finally picks up the handle and peers at the broken end.)*

*Scene 4: Int. The cottage. Day.*

*(Meanwhile, Travers has collected the jet beads into an envelope, and is writing "beads" on it in pencil. She seals it and puts it on the mantelpiece, then puts on her hat and picks up her coat.)*

*Scene 5: Ext. The garden. Day.*

*Clarence emerges with another spade from the shed.*

**CLARENCE:**
I better pace out a square before I start. *(He strides out, the spade over his shoulder.)* One, two, three, four, five, six.

*(He turns, repeats this three more times. His turns, of course are not at right angles, however. Travers emerges from the back door, and watches as his irregular square eventually takes him round the corner of the cottage. She moves off to investigate. We find Clarence coming to rest very near the corner, close to the cottage wall. As he prepares to dig, Travers pops her head round the corner.)*

**TRAVERS:**
*(a discreet clearing of the throat)* Ahem!

**CLARENCE:**
*(starts, then peers round)* Oh, Hello, Vicar. Out on your round are you?

**TRAVERS:**
I think you're a bit near the house.

**CLARENCE:**
Eh? I thought I'd just have a look at the drains first.

**TRAVERS:**
No, don't bother digging up the drains, let's get the vegetable patch right first. I'm going down to the village, alright? Do be careful.

*(She goes. Clarence gropes his way round the wall, back towards the garden. A shot of him spade over shoulder, crossing the garden.)*

*(Music – "Hi-h hi-ho, it's off to work we go" – vocal)*

*Scene 6: Int. The kitchen. Night.*

*The oil lamps are burning. Travers and Clarence are consuming a simple supper of bread, cheese, and pickles.*

**TRAVERS:**
Well, you have worked hard. I'll bet you'll be stiff in the morning.

**CLARENCE:**
Eh? Oh, yes. Still, job well done, isn't it.

**TRAVERS:**
Well, a good start, anyhow. Tomorrow you can put in the runner beans and the dahlias. Pass your cup.

**CLARENCE:**
No. I think I'll have that bottle of beer you brought me. *(He stands.)* This country air gives you a thirst, doesn't it. I reckon we're settling in very nice here, don't you? *(He goes to scullery.)* I like it in the country. No traffic. Nice open spaces and green fields. *(He returns.)* If you go up the back of the garden and into the field, you can see for miles.

**TRAVERS:**
*(giving him an old-fashioned look)* Can you?

**CLARENCE:**
Yeah, the postman told me. Very friendly he was.

**TRAVERS:**
What did he come here for? Can't have been any post for us. No one knows we're here.

**CLARENCE:**
No, he said he was just passing, and had this postcard, and he couldn't read the address on it so he asked if we'd like it. Nice of him, wasn't it? Here it is, look.

*(He locates it on the mantelpiece and hands it to her.)*

**TRAVERS:**
Let's have a look. *(She tries to read it.)*

**CLARENCE:**
What's it say?

**TRAVERS:**
I think it says – "Wish you were here."

**CLARENCE:**
Oh. What's the picture, Dartmoor prison? *(He wheezes.)*

**TRAVERS:**
*(turns the card over, it is a Donald McGill-type comic card)* It's er … *(we see a closeup of the card, and can easily read its risque caption)* It's a picture of St. Paul's Cathedral.

**CLARENCE:**
Oh, nice. Our first bit of mail. We ought to frame it and put it on the piano, for when the Vicar comes.

**TRAVERS:**
Yes, well – we'll see.

**CLARENCE:**
Nice drop of beer, this. Do you know what would go down well with this? A few

radishes. I'm going to sow some in the garden. I love radishes, eat 'em like sweets.

**TRAVERS:**
Don't you get troubled with wind?

**CLARENCE:**
Not if you hold the seed packet close to the ground.

**TRAVERS:**
I don't mean that sort of wind – I mean "the wind".

**CLARENCE:**
 Oh, the wind. No, never get that trouble.

**TRAVERS:**
Oh, that's a relief.

**CLARENCE:**
No – I just belch a lot.

**TRAVERS:**
Not in the house you won't. I'm not having that. It's not – well, it's not lady-like.

**CLARENCE:**
No – funny you should say that – 'cos I do try not to be too lady-like; I learnt that in the Army. Our PT instructor frowned on all that. A man had to be a man. He used to say "A man is a man", and he should live up to his name. He certainly lived up to his.

**TRAVERS:**
What was his name?

**CLARENCE:**
Flossie Merryweather.

**TRAVERS:**
Eh?

**CLARENCE:**
Nah, that's only what we called him. Merryfield his name was. Merryfield by name and a pain in the Aston Villa by nature. We used to be glad to get up to the front line for a rest.

**TRAVERS:**
Was it terrible – the front line?

**CLARENCE:**
Well it wasn't exactly the Savoy Hotel.

**TRAVERS:**
Did you see much fighting?

**CLARENCE:**
No; there was a lot going, on, but I couldn't see it. That was before I had glasses. I could hear it, and smell it mind you. The horses were the worst – cor dear! I tell you something though – things didn't half grow well there.

**TRAVERS:**
Because of the ...

**CLARENCE:**
The horses, yeah. That's when I developed my taste for radishes. Me mum sent me a packet of seeds through the post from Blighty, and I planted them all along the top of the trenches. I used to pop me head up to see if there was any Germans about, and pick a couple of radishes at the same time. Lovely, it was. Then we had to retreat. It used to make me really browned off to think of some ruddy Jerry sitting there eating 'em.

**TRAVERS:**
So you never saw them again.

**CLARENCE:**
I did. About three weeks later we we're ordered to counter-attack. Wasn't half a fight, an' all. But we got there. Do you know, I reckon the only reason we won was the fact that we were all determined to recapture my bleedin' radishes.

**TRAVERS:**
Must have been a marvellous lot of lads.

**CLARENCE:**
They was. England's finest. A wonderful bunch.

**TRAVERS:**
*(teasing)* I'm talking about the soldiers, not the radishes.

**CLARENCE:**
I know you was. Got any more of your home-made chutney?

**TRAVERS:**
Some in the larder. Do you like it that much then?

**CLARENCE:**
It's just like my old grandma used to make.

**TRAVERS:**
Is it?

**CLARENCE:**
That's why me granddad left her.

*(Travers reacts.)*

*Scene 7: Ext. Road outside cottage. Day.*

*1930s-style poster-like graphic of an old milk cart, pulled by a horse. It becomes live action, we see it approach the cottage. The milkman gets off but the horse doesn't stop. The milkman delivers a pint of milk and the horse strolls leisurely on. The milkman catches it up, and climbs aboard. They plod on to their next customer.*

*Music: "Blue Skies are round the Corner" (vocal)*

*Scene 8: Int. Kitchen / parlour. Day.*

*Clarence is making toast. Travers enters, in her coat and hat from garden.*

**TRAVERS:**
Listen, I been outside having a think ...

**CLARENCE:**
Yeah I thought you had, your dress is tucked in your knickers.

**TRAVERS:**
No listen. If I could produce eggs, we could sell them outside the gate.

**CLARENCE:**
*(after a beat)* If you could produce eggs you'd be the talk of Harley Street.

**TRAVERS:**
Not me personally, you dopey. We could get some chickens. We've got that old chicken-run out there, we could patch it up. I'd look after them, you wouldn't have to trouble with them. They'd be my pets. I could give 'em all names and that.

**CLARENCE:**
All? How many you reckoning on having then? *(He sits.)*

**TRAVERS:**
Six. Go up to the market in Woodstock, they're not very dear.

**CLARENCE:**
Would be nice to have our own eggs, yes.

**TRAVERS:**
Tell you what, when you've set the runner beans, see if you can fix up the chicken-run. There's some bits of wood in the shed. I'll see you dinner time.

**CLARENCE:**
Oh yes, your first day working up the Vicarage, en it. Give my love to Big Bertha.

**TRAVERS:**
You mustn't call her that. She'd have a blue fit if she heard you.

**CLARENCE:**
Not much chance of her hearing me, is there? I've been forbidden the place.

**TRAVERS:**
Ta-ta then, don't get into trouble. *(Gives him a peck on the cheek.)*

**CLARENCE:**
Oh, ta. Things are looking up.

**TRAVERS:**
It was only a friendly peck.

**CLARENCE:**
I should leave that to the chickens my dear. You shouldn't be pecking at your age.

**TRAVERS:**
What d'you mean?

**CLARENCE:**
Well, you're no chicken, are you?

*(She puts her bag down and playfully slaps his face.)*

**TRAVERS:**
You just watch it!

*(She points a finger at him, and leaves. He smiles, then suddenly realises the slap was quite painful.)*

**CLARENCE:**
Ow! *(calling after her)* Hey! Where's them plants and things?

**TRAVERS:**
*(Off)* Dahlias by the back door – runner beans in a packet in the parlour. Tara! Oh I say – take this milk in. *(We hear the front door slam.)*

**CLARENCE:**
Where in the parlour? What milk? Blimey, talk about gone with the wind.

*(He gropes his way into the parlour, and peers round the room. He gravitates towards the mantelpiece, and his fingers make contact with the envelope containing the jet beads. He places it up against his nose and squints at it.)*

**CLARENCE:**
B.E.A. … Beans, there they are. *(He shakes them, reassured.)* Right. I'll get these in now – oops milk.

*(He wanders out. In foreground, on the table, lie a packet of runner-bean seeds.)*

*Scene 9: Ext. The cottage. Day.*

*The front doorstep.*

*A pint of milk. Next to it, a little grey stone garden gnome. Clarence opens the door and takes them both inside.*

*Music: – "Tip-toe thru' the Tulips" (vocal)*

*Scene 10: Ext. The garden. Day.*

*A string tied across the vegetable patch. Clarence, using the string as a guide, is making holes with a "dibber" and dropping a large black bead into each hole, taking them from the envelope. He is approaching the camera as he does so. When he reaches the end of the row, he rams a stick into the ground, and thrusts the envelope, clearly marked "beads" onto the stick, as gardeners do to mark the row. Satisfied, he walks out of shot.*

*We see the old, dilapidated chicken run. Then a shot of Clarence, coming out of the shed, clutching some wooden battens – old pieces of three-by-one, etc. Now we have a montage of shots and slow mixes, as Clarence rebuilds the chicken run, during which time he nails his coat to it, etc.*

*At the end of the montage, we see, in a wide shot, the very patched-up look which his work has managed to impart to the chicken-run.*

**CLARENCE:**
*(to himself)* That's a good job done Clarence. Now, just give them a drop of water.

*(He wanders off towards the house. Now we see a close up of a stand-pipe with a brass tap, near the kitchen wall. Clarence arrives with an enamel washing up bowl. He tries to turn the tap with one hand – it is too stiff. He puts down the bowl, and with two hands manages to wrench the bowl into action. He gropes around for the bowl, picks up instead a rusty old sieve that lies near the tap. He places it beneath the tap, and the water lands in it and seeps away. After a few seconds, he wrenches*

the tap closed again, and carefully transports the empty sieve over to the beans, where he flings the imaginary water over them. He is puzzled that he hears no sound of water splashing.)

(He returns. "Refills" the sieve and then picks it up, and turns it over. No sound again. He holds up the sieve and peers myopically at it.)

**CLARENCE:**
Must be a hole in this somewhere.

*Scene 11: Ext. The cottage. Day.*

*The furniture van pulling up outside the gate. Travers and Clarence get out, each carrying baskets of chickens, six in all. Travers looks very pleased with life, as they approach the chicken run. Clarence opens the top – a sort of hinged lid – and they eventually manage to get all six chickens inside. The chickens flutter about – or whatever they decide to do – and Travers gets a paper bag from a large carrier bag she is carrying, and sprinkles corn into the chicken-run. The chickens peck around happily.*

**TRAVERS:**
There. Isn't that lovely? Look, they're eating it.

**CLARENCE:**
Well, they will, won't they? It's food to them, isn't it? It's what they live on. I'm the same.

**TRAVERS:**
But you'd think they'd want to sort of see where they were first.

**CLARENCE:**
Nah. If someone puts a plate of fish and chips in front of me, I don't look round the walls, I get stuck in.

**TRAVERS:**
True. Come on let go and get some tea.

*(She links arms happily with him, steers him round several hazards and into the house.)*

*Scene 12: Int. The kitchen. Day.*

*Tea, bread and butter, jam and fruitcake on the table, plus Clarence's elbows. A peaceful, contented scene.*

**TRAVERS:**
Nice market, wasn't it? Nice fresh vegetables and stuff, we must go there again. That's what I like about the country, plenty of fresh vegetables.

**CLARENCE:**
Have our own soon. Beans, anyhow. You can't never buy runner beans that taste like the ones you pick yourself out of your own garden.

**TRAVERS:**
You better get planting them then.

**CLARENCE:**
I have planted 'em today.

**TRAVERS:**
No you didn't, they're still on the parlour table.

**CLARENCE:**
I got them off the mantelpiece.

**TRAVERS:**
Oh! You know what you've done, don't you? Were they in a brown envelope?

**CLARENCE:**
In a packet, yes. "Beans" written on it.

**TRAVERS:**
In pencil. You've planted me Auntie's beads.

**CLARENCE:**
Yeah?

**TRAVERS:**
Auntie's jet beads.

**CLARENCE:**
Oh, dear. That's your writing again.

667

**TRAVERS:**
*(seeing his despair)* Yes, my fault – don't worry about it.

**CLARENCE:**
All that watering was a waste of time, then.

**TRAVERS:**
*(playfully)* Oh, I don't know – they might come up.

**CLARENCE:**
They will – don't you worry. Tomorrow morning, first thing.

**TRAVERS:**
Yes, look never mind that. *(She unwraps some objects.)* Look what I bought us down the market. *(She unwraps an egg-timer from her bag.)*

*(It is a figurine of a lady's maid.)*

**CLARENCE:**
More ornaments? *(Peers at it closely.)* Looks like you in your uniform.

**TRAVERS:**
It's an egg-timer. For when we get our first egg. Pretty. isn't it? I couldn't resist it – two and eleven. *(Puts egg-timer on mantel-shelf.)*

**CLARENCE:**
Yeah lovely, yeah. You thought of a name for these chickens then? It's a pity you didn't get one more, then they could have been Monday, Tuesday, Wednesday, Thursday, Friday, Saturday. Sunday, couldn't they?

**TRAVERS:**
No, they're going to be named after that new film that's coming out – it's in my *Woman's Own* here. *(She goes to get it from the parlour.)* It's a big new cartoon film, you know the man that does Mickey Mouse. It's called – here we are – *Snow White and the Seven Dwarfs.* Look, there they all are, aren't they funny?

*(Clarence peers at the magazine.)*

**CLARENCE:**
Don't look much like chickens to me.

**TRAVERS:**
No. it's their names. Look. Happy, Grumpy, Sneezy, Sleepy, Bashful, Dopey and Doc.

**CLARENCE:**
That's seven.

**TRAVERS:**
Well, seven pets; six chickens and you. *(She gives him a squeeze.)*

**CLARENCE:**
Oh. That's nice. Which one am I?

**TRAVERS:**
Dopey.

**CLARENCE:**
Yes, I saw that coming.

**TRAVERS:**
*(She giggles, kisses his forehead.)* So tomorrow, first thing, I shall go out and name them. *(She sits.)*

**CLARENCE:**
I was thinking, shouldn't we get a cockerel?

**TRAVERS:**
No – what for? I don't need one.

**CLARENCE:**
You don't, no – I was thinking about the poor old hens.

**TRAVERS:**
How do you mean?

**CLARENCE:**
Well, how would you like it, six women all cooped up, and no man about the place? I mean they are condemned to a life of complete celebration.

**TRAVERS:**
Celibacy.

**CLARENCE:**
Yes, all that sort of thing. I mean. it's not much of a life they've got anyway is it, just scratching about and laying eggs and that. Without a bloke around they'll get bored out of their brains, won't they? They're only human, after all.

**TRAVERS:**
They're not human, that's just it. And they haven't got much of a brain to get bored out of. They're used to just eating, sleeping and laying. That's their life.

**CLARENCE:**
Yes, I suppose so. Seems to work for Errol Flynn.

**TRAVERS:**
There's a lady present.

**CLARENCE:**
*(looks round, startled)* Where? Where?

**TRAVERS:**
Me, Dopey!

**CLARENCE:**
That was no lady. That was my wife-to-be. We hope. When you think about it, you're a bit like the chickens, ain't you? Just eating, sleeping, and laying the table. You seem to manage without a man's company.

**TRAVERS:**
Don't be daft, I've got you. You're a man aren't you.

**CLARENCE:**
It's been so long I can't remember.

**TRAVERS:**
*(taking his hand)* I know. I know. *(Gently)* I am making up my mind, and I will tell you as soon as I'm sure, I promise. I know it's difficult for you, but it's all working out so well, and I'm sure that in the end, you'll have no cause to worry. I can't really say more than that at present.

**CLARENCE:**
No, fair enough me old dear. I can wait. Is there any more Rosie in the pot?

**TRAVERS:**
I'll just get some more milk. *(She moves towards the larder.)*

**CLARENCE:**
I expect it's because you think I'm a bit eccentric, don't you? Odd little habits and ways?

**TRAVERS:**
I love your odd little habits and ways. Everybody is different, aren't they? Wouldn't do for us to be all the same, would it? But no, I certainly wouldn't call you eccentric. *(She opens the larder door, stops, and looks.)* What's this garden gnome doing in the larder?

*Scene 13: Ext. The garden. Day.*

*1930s-style graphics picture of the cottage and back garden. It becomes live action as Travers comes out of the back door. It is early morning.*

*Music: – "Get up, Get out, and Meet the Sun Halfway" (vocal)*

*A close up of Travers's happy face, which changes into alarm. A shot of the chicken-run. Empty.*

**TRAVERS:**
Oh, gawd, where have they gone?

*(She rushes over to the chicken-run, and starts to feel along it, examining it for a hole. All seems secure, until she reaches the other end. The other end is not, and never was, there.)*

**TRAVERS:**
Oh, for heaven's sake: why didn't I check it?

*(She looks wildly around, and spots a chicken some way off, apparently asleep, and another one in the far corner, happily strutting around. Of the rest, no sign. She rushes back*

*to the house and meets Clarence as he comes out of the back door.)*

**TRAVERS:**
*(angrily)* They're gone. All got out.

**CLARENCE:**
Eh? How?

**TRAVERS:**
You'd forgotten to put the end on.

**CLARENCE:**
Put the end on? Where?

**TRAVERS:**
On the end, of course! Gawd knows where they are, they could be miles away. There's two of them over there *(points)* but the other four are nowhere in sight.

**CLARENCE:**
Well, at least there' two. She's happy, and she's sleepy.

**TRAVERS:**
And you're Dopey!

**CLARENCE:**
And you're Grumpy!

**TRAVERS:**
I'm going to find them. *(She marches off.)*

**CLARENCE:**
Have your breakfast first, woman!

**TRAVERS:**
Breakfast will have to wait! *(She is gone.)*

*(Clarence wanders disconsolately to the end of the run, staring at the place where the end should be. Suddenly he reacts. Through his eyes, we see a misty oval object nestling in the straw. He carefully picks it up. It is an egg.)*

**CLARENCE:**
*(staring at it joyfully)* Cor, look at that. *(He carefully carries it inside.)*

Scene 14: Int. The kitchen. Day.

*A saucepan, bubbling on the old kitchen range.*

Music: – "Chick-chick-chick-chicken, Lay a Little Egg for Me" (vocal)

*Clarence puts the egg onto a large spoon, and lowers it into the water. He then gropes around and finds the little ornamental egg timer, and places it on the table. He sets it in motion by turning it upside down, then glues his eye to it for a second or two, to see that it is working. He then attempts to set the table for breakfast. He cuts some bread and places it on a dinner plate – the wrong way up – hurries back and glues his eye again to the egg timer.*

Scene 15: Ext. The garden. Day.

*The chicken run. Travers approaches it, a chicken under each arm. She pushes them in, and we see two more are already in. She looks across at the lone chicken still strutting in the corner of the garden. She throws some corn into the run, and we see that the missing end is covered by the old tin bath taken down from the wall. She sighs, and goes indoors.*

Scene 16: Int. The kitchen. Day.

*The table, looking fairly chaotic. Clarence is just collecting an egg cup from the dresser.*

*(Travers enters.)*

**TRAVERS:**
I got them all, except one. They were over the next field. Four of 'em are in, and the other one in still lurking about in the corner.

**CLARENCE:**
I expect she's bashful.

**TRAVERS:**
Yeah, that's who she'd better be. Five out of six isn't bad I suppose.

**CLARENCE:**
Yes. We can do without Grumpy, can't we?

**TRAVERS:**
*(taking the point)* I know, I'm sorry I shouted at you, I thought they was gone for good.

**CLARENCE:**
Now, you sit down. Ready for your breakfast are you?

**TRAVERS:**
Yes, I could eat a horse.

**CLARENCE:**
No, I haven't got one of those, but what I have got is – *(he turns round, the egg on the spoon)* our first egg! For you, timed to perfection with your new timer.

*(He gingerly picks it up and steers it into the egg-cup in front of her.)*

**TRAVERS:**
*(staring)* Where did you find that?

**CLARENCE:**
*(happily)* In the run!

**TRAVERS:**
*(not knowing whether to laugh or cry)* They gave me that to encourage them to lay – it's a china one!

*(The credits roll.)*

*(During the credits, Clarence's incredulous expression, and Travers explaining the china egg. She gets a sheet of instructions, or a booklet on keeping chickens, and shows him the illustrations. Then attempts to sort out the breakfast table. When all but the last credits are gone, a shot of Clarence, disconsolately staring at the egg in the egg-cup.)*

**CLARENCE:**
Well, that's knocked that on the head then hasn't it.

*(He strikes the egg with a spoon. The shell cracks. They both stare and Clarence is triumphant. They laugh, and he scoops out the top of the egg.)*

*Fade out.*

# EPISODE FIVE

*Scene 1: A resume, in live action, of the story so far.*

**TRAVERS:**
*(voice over)* He's a funny bloke, Clarence. Blind as a bat for a start – and him a removals man. We hit it off right away though. He asked me to marry him and I said I wanted a trial period first and it has been quite a trial, one way and another. We've been living in the cottage that used to belong to my old Auntie – in the country. Of course, we not cohabiting, as they say. We're sleeping together; we have to, there's only one bed – but we're sharing it with a bolster, Clarence can't find any work, but I've got a job as a daily up at the Vicarage – so on the strength of that, we bought some chickens. Mind you, him being so short sighted caused trouble even with them.

*We now pick up last week's episode from the point where Clarence says:*

**CLARENCE:**
Our first egg! For you – timed to perfection with your new timer.

**TRAVERS:**
Where did you find that?

**CLARENCE:**
*(happily)* In the run.

**TRAVERS:**
*(not knowing whether to laugh or cry)* They gave me that to encourage them to lay – it's a china one.

*Scene 2: The kitchen.*

*Clarence is in the kitchen, gropes his way to the sink, puts the kettle in and turns on the tap, stands it in the sink and waits. The tap*

*fills up a saucepan standing in the sink. He
gropes for the kettle lid on the drainer, places it
on the empty kettle, and places it on the
range. He returns, peers about, finds a packet
of soap flakes, and empties some into his
breakfast bowl on the table. Adds milk, then
sugar, and stirs it into a nice froth.*

*(Travers enters. She spots the situation
immediately and whisks the bowl away.)*

**CLARENCE:**
What you doing?

**TRAVERS:**
We said we'd have eggs for breakfast.

*(She hides the bowl among other washing up.)*

**CLARENCE:**
Oh yeah. That's where you've been. Our
own hens. Good, 'en it. How many did
they lay?

**TRAVERS:**
None. You'll have to have toast and
marmalade.

*(She goes to larder.)*

**CLARENCE:**
I don't follow that. Not really hungry
anyhow. I'll just have a cuppa ta and a fag.

*(Travers returns to table.)*

**TRAVERS:**
You smoke too much you do.

**CLARENCE:**
I have to. I'm collecting the fag cards.
Smoking can't kill you.

**TRAVERS:**
Oh yes it can. It killed my cousin Harry at
the age of thirty-four.

**CLARENCE:**
Go on?

**TRAVERS:**
He was coming out of a tobacconist's and

got run over by a tram.

**CLARENCE:**
That's nothing to do with it. He could
have been coming out of his own house,
couldn't he?

**TRAVERS:**
No he couldn't.

**CLARENCE:**
Yes he could.

**TRAVERS:**
No he couldn't. Trams don't run by his
house.

**CLARENCE:**
Well, anyhow, it won't get me before I get
the set I'm collecting. I'm collecting radio
celebrities. I only need two – H. S. Pepper
and Stainless Stevens. Have you seen my
collection of fag cards? They're in there.

*(He exits to fetch them. Travers hears the
kettle sizzle, and finding no water in it,
hurriedly fills it and returns it to the hob, as
Clarence re-enters, clutching several cigarette
card albums.)*

**CLARENCE:**
Here you are, look. Lovely, aren't they?
These are my favourites. Kings and
Queens of England.

**TRAVERS:**
*(looking through the album)* Yes, lovely.
When was he King of England?

**CLARENCE:**
*(peering)* Who?

**TRAVERS:**
Don Bradman.

*(We see close up of the cricketer among the
royalty in the book.)*

**CLARENCE:**
How did he get in there? Must have been
his fancy cap – looked like a crown. Who
does it say underneath? Who's it

supposed to be?

**TRAVERS:**
Queen Anne.

**CLARENCE:**
She's probably in the other book, wicket keeper for Gloucestershire.

**TRAVERS:**
You are an idiot.

**CLARENCE:**
Takes one to know one. Has that kettle boiled yet?

**TRAVERS:**
Won't be long. I've got plenty of time, don't have to be at work for another hour. Which reminds me, we've got to find you a job. I thought we'd put a card in the post office window.

**CLARENCE:**
Doubt if I'll get many removal jobs. I mean there's nowhere to move from round here, is there? Hardly any houses.

**TRAVERS:**
It doesn't have to be removals. Strong bloke like you could do anything.

**CLARENCE:**
There was an advert in the local paper for a watch-mender.

**TRAVERS:**
Yes ... You have to have ever such good eyesight with a job like that.

**CLARENCE:**
Nothing wrong with my eyesight. I only wear these for reading and seeing things. When I was younger I once worked in a chemist, making up prescriptions.

**TRAVERS:**
Really.

**CLARENCE:**
Didn't last long though.

**TRAVERS:**
You surprise me. Why not?

**CLARENCE:**
The business closed down. Owner poisoned himself.

**TRAVERS:**
Poisoned himself. Was that proved?

**CLARENCE:**
*(realising)* Wasn't nothing to do with me! He was dead before I started there. His missus decided she would try to carry on.

**TRAVERS:**
And didn't she?

**CLARENCE:**
Oh yes. She carried on with the bloke next door for about a month, then they got married and she closed the business. Big, generous woman she was. She liked me. I was never in need of a hot water bottle or talcum powder. And she was the one woman I've ever known who never had a headache.

*(Travers takes her toast to the table.)*

**TRAVERS:**
Sounds highly suspicious to me. Are you sure it was the man next door she was carrying on with?

**CLARENCE:**
You're jealous, aren't you? I can see it in your face.

*(Travers is at that moment bending over getting the tea from the dresser.)*

**TRAVERS:**
Not a bit! But I don't somehow think you're going to find that sort of job round here.

**CLARENCE:**
Well we can still put a card in the post office – "Man needs odd job."

**TRAVERS:**
Yeah. But we can't rely on that alone. There's only one thing for it – it's the Labour Exchange for you my lad.

**CLARENCE:**
Labour Exchange? But I'm me own boss with me own business. I'm a self employed man.

**TRAVERS:**
You're a self unemployed man at the moment. My bit of savings won't last forever – and what I'm earning won't keep us. It certainly won't keep you in fags. How you going to get the last two cigarette cards to make up the set?

**CLARENCE:**
I'll say this for you girl – you know how to spot a man's weak spot, don't you? His athlete's foot.

**TRAVERS:**
Achilles heel.

**CLARENCE:**
Yeah, that. Alright then, you win. I'll go down to the Labour tomorrow. See if they've got a job suitable to my special condition.

**TRAVERS:**
What special condition?

**CLARENCE:**
Skint. P'raps I will have a bit of toast.

*Music – "We're in the Money" – vocal version, 1930s record.*

*Scene 3: Int. The cottage. Day.*

*Graphic of cottage exterior at sunrise. Slow mix to: the bedroom. Next morning – Clarence, the bolster and Travers lie in bed.*

*(Clarence snores lightly. Travers, already awake, leans over and tickles his ear, hoping to make him move, and therefore stop snoring. He moves, but turns towards the bolster, and finishes up almost on top of it. This alarms Travers, who slips out of bed, in her decorous nightie, and is just about to put on her dressing gown, when Clarence squeezes the bolster affectionately and mutters half in his sleep.)*

**CLARENCE:**
Cuddly ain't you? What made you decide to get rid of the bolster?

*(She tip toes out of the room. Clarence continues to roll with the bolster.)*

*(The kitchen. Two mugs of steaming tea. Pull back to see Travers as she takes them into the bedroom. She nudges Clarence, who rolls over, but takes the bolster with him, so that he is now on Travers's side of the bed. She therefore, hops into the other side, so that the bolster is still between them.)*

**TRAVERS:**
Tea!

*(Clarence wakes, mutters.)*

**CLARENCE:**
I was just dreaming about you.

**TRAVERS:**
Oh? What was happening?

**CLARENCE:**
I was climbing a tree.

**TRAVERS:**
Oh, that's a relief. Where was I?

**CLARENCE:**
You were up it. The chickens were up there an' all. I was trying to reach you. I said "What are you doing up there?" And you said "I'm collecting eggs." And I said "I'm collecting cigarette cards. Got any swaps?" And you swapped me a hard boiled egg for Don Bradman. Do you think dreams mean anything?

**TRAVERS:**
Oh yes, certainly.

**CLARENCE:**
What did that one mean?

**TRAVERS:**
It meant you ate too much cheese for supper last night. Drink your tea.

**CLARENCE:**
Oh ta. Here! We've changed sides. You're on my side of the bed. Why did you do that?

**TRAVERS:**
Cos you were rolling around climbing the tree.

**CLARENCE:**
Sorry. Was I misbehaving?

**TRAVERS:**
Only with the bolster. Now – Labour Exchange this morning. I do hope they can find something suitable for you.

**CLARENCE:**
Well, we shall see what we shall see, shan't we?

**TRAVERS:**
That's what I'm worried about.

*Scene 4: Ext. The cottage. Day.*

*Clarence's old van stands beside the road. Clarence and Travers leave the cottage, both dressed for work.*

**TRAVERS:**
Good luck. Sure you'll be alright driving?

**CLARENCE:**
I've been driving this van twenty years woman – course I'll be alright. (He gropes around for the driver's door.)

**TRAVERS:**
(turning him round) Steering wheel's at the other end.

*(She points him in the right direction and he finds the door. A wide shot as the van drives away, and Travers starts to trudge up the hill.) Music: "My Blue Heaven"– vocal, 1930s version.*

*Scene 5: Int. The parlour. Evening.*

*Clarence is painting the fireplace surround. A nice pale blue. It is the old fashioned kind with small shelf below the main mantelpiece, containing little ornaments and photos in standing frames. All these have been painted blue as well.*

*(The door of the cottage is heard to open and close.)*

**CLARENCE:**
(calling out) I'm in the parlour.

*(Travers enters from work. She stares at the mantelpiece and drops her bag.)*

**CLARENCE:**
Thought I'd brighten up the old place a bit. Nice colour isn't it?

**TRAVERS:**
(dazed) Lovely.

**CLARENCE:**
Show off the ornaments, won't it? They'll stand out, won't they?

**TRAVERS:**
Not now. You've painted them blue as well.

**CLARENCE:**
Have I? I thought that bit felt a bit strange. I thought the paint was lumpy.

**TRAVERS:**
(pointing at painted photograph) Auntie's under there somewhere.

**CLARENCE:**
Oh dear, is she?

**TRAVERS:**
I'd better make some tea.

**CLARENCE:**
I put the kettle on.

**TRAVERS:**
Lovely. I'll just go and put some water in.

*(She is gone.)*

*(Clarence walks downstage. He puts his paint brush in a jam jar full of water and picks up a cloth to clean the photograph.)*

**CLARENCE:**
Sorry Auntie. Never mind, I'll give you a good scrub down with turps, and you'll feel like a new woman. Well, as new as you can feel when you're dead.

*(He wipes away the paint, Auntie peers out from the photograph.)*

**CLARENCE:**
Just as well you was a Conservative, 'en it?

*(He places the photo on newspaper on the table and calls out to Travers.)*

**CLARENCE:**
Did you put that advert in the post office window?

**TRAVERS:**
*(off)* Yes. One and sixpence for a week.

**CLARENCE:**
Well you've wasted your money.

**TRAVERS:**
Oh why?

**CLARENCE:**
Aren't you going to ask me how I got on down the Labour?

**TRAVERS:**
Course I am.

**CLARENCE:**
Well go on, ask me then.

*(Travis enters.)*

**TRAVERS:**
Well? How did you get on down the Labour? *(She puts tray on table.)*

**CLARENCE:**
I got a job.

**TRAVERS:**
You never!

**CLARENCE:**
I did.

**TRAVERS:**
You didn't.

**CLARENCE:**
Alright, I didn't, but in spite of the fact I didn't, I start on Monday.

**TRAVERS:**
Oh that's lovely! *(She give him a hug.)*

**CLARENCE:**
Mind the paint.

**TRAVERS:**
Where?

**CLARENCE:**
Working for the council.

**TRAVERS:**
Oh. Doing what?

**CLARENCE:**
They didn't say – they just said turn up on Monday. The bloke there seemed very impressed with my knowledge of the removals business and cigarette cards. So I should think I'll be some sort of executive.

**TRAVERS:**
Er – well, we'll have to wait and see, won't we?

**CLARENCE:**
Well, it must be quite important, 'cos they're gonna give me me own overalls.

**TRAVERS:**
Oh, well there you are the! Well, that's good. I'm ever so glad. Maybe things are going to work out well for us. *(She sits on his lap.)*

**CLARENCE:**
Yes. Then perhaps we can get married, eh? Live as man and wife, instead of man and

friend. A man's best friend is supposed to be a dog, not a lady's maid.

**TRAVERS:**
Yes, well for the moment, you must treat me as your lap-dog. I'll be a faithful friend and fetch your slippers for you.

**CLARENCE:**
Yes, alright, but I'm more interested in when you're going to start wagging your tail.

**TRAVERS:**
*(getting off his lap, in mock outrage)* Now that's enough of that my lad!

**CLARENCE:**
Oh, that's frightened her off.

**TRAVERS:**
Tell you what, I'll nip to the pub and get us a bottle of Guinness each to go with our supper tonight – we'll have a celebration.

**CLARENCE:**
Yes, that'll be nice. I've forgotten what the taste of Guinness looks like. It's good living here, isn't it? It's lovely to get up in the morning and hear the birds singing and the cuckoos cucking and all the bleating sheep.

**TRAVERS:**
Hey! No swearing.

**CLARENCE:**
Bleating sheep I said. Sheep, that's what they do, bleat.

**TRAVERS:**
Oh sorry. Yes. I love the sounds of the countryside.

**CLARENCE:**
In Peckham, all you get is the sparrows coughing their little lungs out round the glue factory. Do you know what they make glue out of? Horses.

**TRAVERS:**
Horses' what?

**CLARENCE:**
Horses. They make glue out of horses. "Horse's what?" They just melt down old horses to make glue out of. Smells terrible that glue factory. Glad to be out of that lot.

**TRAVERS:**
Don't you miss your mates and the pub and all that?

**CLARENCE:**
Never had any mates. Always been a bit of a loner – prefer me own company.

**TRAVERS:**
How about your fish and chips then – I bet you miss them – living above the chip shop.

**CLARENCE:**
Funny enough, that's the only smell I do miss, the old chish and phipps. Still, you can fry chips can't yer. And I can go and catch some fish in the river, can't I?

**TRAVERS:**
*(doubtfully)* Do you know how to fish?

**CLARENCE:**
Yeah, nothing to it. You just get your rod, "tackle up" and chuck it in.

**TRAVERS:**
Tackle up?

**CLARENCE:**
You take this very fine line, you wind it onto your reel – then you thread it through the little screw-eyes on the road, then you attach a float, and these little tiny lead weights, then tie the hook on the end through the little eye, fix on your bait, and throw it in.

**TRAVERS:**
I see, yes. Perhaps there's a nice fish shop in the village.

**CLARENCE:**
Why, don't you think there's any fish in the river then?

677

**TRAVERS:**
I've a feeling we shall never know.

**CLARENCE:**
How do you mean?

**TRAVERS:**
Never mind – anyway, you won't have much time for fishing now you've got this job. You'll be off every morning earning us a crust. One thing though – you're not going to work in the van.

**CLARENCE:**
Why not? *(picking up his paint brush.)*

**TRAVERS:**
Cos I'm not having it that's why. There's a perfectly good bus service every hour on the hour. Give or take ten minutes. I shall feel easier in me mind, alright?

**CLARENCE:**
*(starting to paint)* Whatever you say, Fido.

*(Travers swipes at his head, boxing his ears.)*

**CLARENCE:**
Hey, watch the paint.

*(She picks up tray.)*

**TRAVERS:**
You haven't finished your tea. *(Places his mug on table.)* I'm going to get changed and go and get the Guinness.

*(She goes.)*

**CLARENCE:**
I'll paint your ornaments if you're not careful.

*(He puts his brush into his mug of tea, picks up the jam jar and takes a swig.)*

**CLARENCE:**
Eeurggh! There's no sugar in this.
Scene 6: Ext. Council gates. Day.

*Graphics picture, 1930s poster-style of wide shot of rural council gates: become live action film. Music: "Grasshopper's Dance" (non-vocal).*

*(Clarence emerges from the council gates and we cut closer to see the sign on the gate as he passes through. It says "Oxfordshire County Council sewage works". He wears brand new overalls, which are filthy, especially from the knees downwards. A close up of his feet, surrounded by a cloud of flies. A wide shot as he walks away from camera. The sun is shining brightly.)*

*(A country bus stop.)*

*(Four people waiting for the bus. Clarence arrives and stands with them. They all move away. A wide shot to show the separation. Clarence stands alone. A bus arrives. The people hurry past Clarence and board the bus. Clarence tries to get on. The conductor reacts and rushes forward, stopping Clarence from getting on. He waves Clarence away – a close up of the bell being pressed twice. Wide shot as the bus moves off, the conductor still gesturing from the back. Clarence turns and starts to trudge home.)*

*(A country pub on the roadside.)*

*(Clarence approaches and enters. A wide shot, as seven people quickly emerge. The last one is a dog, whining. Eventually Clarence comes out with a bottle of beer and a pie, and sets off down the road.)*

*(Mix to: his face, sweating. He takes a swig of beer. A wide shot, to see him sitting by the side of the road. A cyclist is seen approaching. A change of angle and we see the cyclist suddenly swerve to the other side of the road, passing Clarence in a wide arc. A close up of the cyclist's face with wrinkled nose. A close up of Clarence, oblivious. Just behind him, a field gate. A pig approaches, snorts and walks away. Wide shot as it runs off across the field.)*

*Scene 7: Int. The cottage. Evening.*

*Travers sitting on the sofa. Supper stands ready. She knits. Suddenly she raises her head and sniffs. Turns her head and sniffs again. Puzzled.*

*Scene 8: Ext. The cottage. Evening.*

*A shot of Clarence, walking, approaching the cottage.*

*Scene 9: Int. The cottage. Evening.*

*Travers again – she lifts the lid of the cheese dish, sniffs and replaces it. Clarence gets nearer. Travers goes into the hallway, still sniffing. The smell is obviously getting nearer. She lifts a pair of wellington boots and sniffs the soles. Clarence approaches front door. She is drawn by the smell to the front door. She opens it and screams.*
*Clarence stands there, quite oblivious of the situation. Travers gasps, backs away and disappears into the parlour, closing the door.*

**CLARENCE:**
I'm working in the sewage works.

**TRAVERS:**
Well! I'd never have guessed.

**CLARENCE:**
Why won't you let me in? You got nothing on?

**TRAVERS:**
*(backs away towards kitchen)* It's not what I've got on, it's what you've got on! You can't come in, you smell dreadful! You'll have to have a bath quick, before I suffocate.

*(She turns as Clarence appears behind her.)*

**CLARENCE:**
I'll have a scrub down in the kitchen.

**TRAVERS:**
*(alarmed)* You can't wash in here?

**CLARENCE:**
Where then? I can't strip off in the garden can I?

**TRAVERS:**
*(desperate)* Look –it's a fine evening – go

for a walk for half an hour – I'll think of something.

**CLARENCE:**
Listen – I don't want – I've walked all the way home.

**TRAVERS:**
Go on, for gawd's sake – you'll turn the milk sour.

**CLARENCE:**
They wouldn't let me on the bus.

*(He goes, reluctantly.)*

*Scene 10: Ext. Garden shed. Evening.*

*Poster-style graphic of shed, becomes live action film as usual.*
*Music: "Tiptoe through the Tulips" (vocal).*

*Travers is approaching the shed, carrying an ancient tin bath. With difficulty, she gets it inside. We hear a crash or two. She emerges, a little dishevelled, and heads back towards the house.*

*Scene 11: Int. The cottage. Evening.*

**CLARENCE:**
*(through the front window)* I'm back.

**TRAVERS:**
*(opening the kitchen door a crack)* I know you are! I put the tin bath in the shed. There's a big towel in there, and some soap.

**CLARENCE:**
I can't get in that bath, it's too small.

**TRAVERS:**
It isn't. Throw out all your clothes and I'll put 'em into soak, if I can get near 'em.

**CLARENCE:**
Here!

**TRAVERS:**
What?

**CLARENCE:**
When I'm in there I don't want you peering through the keyhole at my naked person.

**TRAVERS:**
Listen, if you're worried I might see something I shouldn't, hang your cap over it.

**CLARENCE:**
I beg your pardon?

**TRAVERS:**
The keyhole, stupid!

**CLARENCE:**
Oh right. Here goes then.

*Scene 12: Int. The shed.*

*Evening sunlight streams through the one window. The tin bath in foreground – a low angle. The door opens, Clarence gropes his way in, peering round. He steps on a rake, which misses him, but dislodges a pile of flower pots.*

**CLARENCE:**
Who's there? Damn rats, I shouldn't wonder. Very heavy footed ones, I'll say that. Talking to yourself again, Clarence. Well, I have to talk to meself – there's no one else here. Don't much like the idea of taking me clothes off with rats about. They say the big ones go for your throat. I wonder what the little ones go for?

*(He gropes around, finds the edge of the bath.)*

**CLARENCE:**
I think I'll just try it for size before I strip off – no point in filling it all up with water, then finding I can't get in it. *(He sits down in the bath.)* Oh gawd!

*(We now discover, as he does, that it is already filled with water. He stands up dripping wet.)*

*Scene 13: Int. The kitchen. Evening.*

*Travers by the range. Clarence appears at the window, and taps on it.*

**TRAVERS:**
Oh dear, what now?

**CLARENCE:**
You never told me it was full of water.

**TRAVERS:**
Well of course it's full of water. What do you expect, dry cleaning or what?

**CLARENCE:**
I got in to test the size, with me clothes on.

**TRAVERS:**
Only a man would get into a bath with his clothes on.

**CLARENCE:**
I'm soaking wet.

**TRAVERS:**
Yes, you would be. Look, I can't stand anymore of this, now listen to me. Take off all your clothes in the garden, come in here and I'll scrub you down meself.

**CLARENCE:**
Take me clothes off in the garden? Suppose someone sees me and the Vicar's wife gets wind of it?

**TRAVERS:**
The whole village has gone wind of it by now I should think. Listen, I've got an enormous bottle of Paris toilet water I got last Christmas, we'll smother you in that.

**CLARENCE:**
Is that strong enough to kill it?

**TRAVERS:**
It's strong enough to kill sheep. Come on, let's get it over with. Dump your clothes in the garden, we'll leave them out to air.

**CLARENCE:**
I'll drop'em on the rhubarb, might do it some good.

*Scene 14: Int. Bedroom. Night.*

*They both sit in bed, the bolster, as usual, between them. Clarence is without his cap this time. They are sipping mugs of cocoa.*

**CLARENCE:**
Well, how do I smell now?

**TRAVERS:**
Lovely. I told you that Paris toilet water would do the trick.

**CLARENCE:**
Yes. I smell like a Paris toilet.

**TRAVERS:**
Well at least you're clean.

**CLARENCE:**
Thanks to you.

**TRAVERS:**
I reek of it as well.

**CLARENCE:**
You're a bit rough with the scrubbing brush, mind you.

**TRAVERS:**
Do you good. Stimulates the blood vessels.

**CLARENCE:**
Yes. I enjoyed it!

**TRAVERS:**
I'm sure you did.

**CLARENCE:**
Well at least you know what you're getting when we get married.

**TRAVERS:**
Now don't get coarse please. And it's still if we get married.

**CLARENCE:**
Oh dear. Something put you off? Wasn't

me muscles was it? I got them through me job.

**TRAVERS:**
No, your muscles are alright. For a man of your age.

**CLARENCE:**
Oh, thanks very much.

**TRAVERS:**
You're alright. I think we might make a go of it. On conditions.

**CLARENCE:**
Conditions? What?

**TRAVERS:**
I can't have you working at that sewage works. You're on a daily basis – you hand in your notice tomorrow.

**CLARENCE:**
Course I will. So you'll marry me will you?

**TRAVERS:**
Alright *(She leans over, kisses his forehead.)*

**CLARENCE:**
Oh good. Can we move the bolster tonight then?

**TRAVERS:**
No we can not! And don't dare touch anything connected with sewage tomorrow – otherwise, I'm warning you, you won't touch anything connected with me. Night night.

*(She snuggles down. Clarence puts down his cocoa and lies down. A pause.)*

**CLARENCE:**
Do you mind if I open a window? This perfume is making me dizzy.

*(He gets out of bed. He wears a night shirt, and opens the window and takes a deep breath.)*

**CLARENCE:**
Oh dear me! *(He closes it again.)* I forgot – the rhubarb's right under the window.

*(He gets into bed and blows out the candle.)*

*Scene 15: Bus stop. Day.*

*Clarence at the bus stop: ordinary work clothes, no overalls. A middle aged man of uncertain sexual preferences, clutching a bunch of flowers, joins Clarence waiting for the bus. After a second or two the man sniffs the air and looks at Clarence. He smiles, then sniffs his flowers, shakes his head and sniffs. Clarence again, sidling closer. Clarence is oblivious of all this. The man makes eyes at Clarence and finally clears his throat genteelly, and speaks in a light tenor.*

**MAN:**
Excuse me.

**CLARENCE:**
*(turns and peers at him)* Yes? What is it Madam?

**MAN:**
*(giggling)* I was, er, just wondering –

*Mix to:*

*Scene 16: Ext. The cottage. Day.*

*Music: "Lavender Blue, Dilly Dilly" (vocal). 1930s graphic of Scene, into live action.*

*Travers is feeding the chickens. She stops, sniffs, and smiles, she hurries in through the back door.*

*Scene 17: Int. The hall. Day.*

*Clarence enters front door. Travers runs in to greet him, she flings her arms round his neck.*

**CLARENCE:**
Ah well, that's more like it.

**TRAVERS:**
Your tea's ready. Did you give your notice in?

**CLARENCE:**
Yes, I've finished. The foreman was a bit put out. He said with work being difficult

to find, it wasn't the sort of job to turn your nose up at. I said "Well that's just what my missus did anyhow, so I'm leaving."

**TRAVERS:**
Your missus? Who's she when she's at home?

**CLARENCE:**
You of course. I mean you're married, but not churched as they say.

**TRAVERS:**
I'm not anything yet I'll have you know. *(she is still holding him).* Cor this perfume isn't half strong. Clings doesn't it?

**CLARENCE:**
So do you – what you so happy about?

*(She releases him and they enter the kitchen.)*

**TRAVERS:**
I got the sack from the Vicarage.

**CLARENCE:**
You what?

**TRAVERS:**
His wife accused me of being a tart.

**CLARENCE:**
You? A tart.

**TRAVERS:**
She said she couldn't have a smell as strong as this lingering around the Vicarage, people would talk. So I told her what I thought of her.

**CLARENCE:**
What happened?

**TRAVERS:**
She nearly bust her corset.

**CLARENCE:**
Good for you. You should have told her what I thought of her, she'd have split her knickers as well. So she sent you packing.

**TRAVERS:**
She practically threw me out bodily. Ooh but it was worth it, great fat lummox.

**CLARENCE:**
Still, wasn't very clever was it? Now we've got no money coming in.

**TRAVERS:**
We will have. On the way in this morning I called in this morning at the Post Office to see if there was an answer to your advert, and the woman in there said there was an old lady in the village wants looking after.

**CLARENCE:**
I can't do that.

**TRAVERS:**
No, I've taken the job. I popped up to see her – sweet old thing she is – only got one leg.

**CLARENCE:**
Oh, cuts down on the shoe cleaning then.

**TRAVERS:**
Don't be awful. She's looking for a part-time gardener, too, so you could do a bit of that. She's redoing her garden – says she wants things in it to attract the butterflies.

**CLARENCE:**
Well, smelling like this, I should be just right.

**TRAVERS:**
What d'you reckon then?

**CLARENCE:**
I might consider it – along with my other offer.

**TRAVERS:**
What other offer?

**CLARENCE:**
All due to your perfume again. A bloke at the bus stop offered me a job as a window dresser. How about giving me another

bath to get the smell off.

*(Travers reacts.)*

*(The credits roll.)*

*(Closing sequence: Travers fills saucepan and takes it to the range. She returns with another one. Clarence struggles in with bath and puts it in front of the fire.*
*Travers fills kettles and joins him.)*

*(As credits end, Clarence starts to undo his shirt.)*

**TRAVERS:**
Listen – I don't want any hanky-panky while I'm scrubbing your back. Just because I smell like a tart it doesn't mean I am one.

**CLARENCE:**
I know you're not.

**TRAVERS:**
Promise.

**CLARENCE:**
I promise. I won't think of you as a tart. I shall just think of you as a scrubber.

*(She takes off his cap, drops it into the empty bath, and pours the kettle of water over it. He reacts.)*

*(The final credit appears.)*

*(Fade out.)*

# EPISODE SIX

*Scene 1: (VT compilation)*

*A resume in live action, of the story so far. We hear Travers's voice.*

**TRAVERS:**
*(voice over)* He's a funny bloke, Clarence. Blind as a bat, and clumsy as a bull in a

china shop. And him a removals man. At least he used to be a removals man until I started living with him. When I say living with him, we don't sleep together, but we do have to spend the night in the same bed, but with a bolster down the middle to stop any untoward rolling by mistake – or in his case, on purpose. Anyway, all that will change soon, 'cos we're getting married. We like it here in the old cottage in the country, and decided to try to make a go of it. He's ever so nice really, and I already feel very close to him. Except last week, of course, when he got a job at the sewage works. Then I couldn't get within a mile of him. He soon packed that job in – but it took ages to get the smell off him. I had to smother him in a big bottle of Paris toilet water I had for Christmas.

*Cut to: live action from previous episode.*

**CLARENCE:**
I smell like a Paris toilet.

**TRAVERS:**
Well, at least you're clean.

**CLARENCE:**
Thanks to you.

**TRAVERS:**
I reek of it as well.

*Travers v/o continues.*

**TRAVERS:**
In fact, I reeked so strong I got the sack at the Vicarage. The Vicar's wife said I smelled like a tart, and if it lingered around the Vicarage, it would play havoc with the confirmation classes.

*We now pick up last week's episode from the point where Clarence says:*

**CLARENCE:**
Still, wasn't very clever, was it? Now we've got no money coming in.

**TRAVERS:**
We will have. On the way in this morning

I called in at the Post Office, and there was an answer to the advert. An old lady in the village wants looking after. So I've taken the job. I popped up to see her. Sweet old thing she is – only got one leg.

**CLARENCE:**
Oh, cuts down on the shoe-cleaning then.

**TRAVERS:**
Don't be awful. She's looking for a part-time gardener, too, so you could do a bit of that. She's re-doing her garden – she says she wants things in it to attract the butterflies.

**CLARENCE:**
Well, smelling like this I should be just right.

*Music – (to be added in sypher) vocal 1930s version of "It's Love makes the World go Round" as we mix to Scene 2.*

*Scene 2. Int. The kitchen. Night.*

*Travers selects a jar of pickle from the larder.*

**CLARENCE:**
Any more tea in the pot?

**TRAVERS:**
It'll need some more water in.

*(Clarence goes to the kitchen range, and picks up a flat iron next to the kettle, and approaches the table.)*

**TRAVERS:**
What you going to do with that, iron the corned beef?

**CLARENCE:**
Oh silly me – not looking what I'm doing.

*(He returns it and gropes around for the kettle. Returns to table and attempts to pour water into milk jug. Travers swaps it for teapot.)*

**TRAVERS:**
Do you think you're going to be able to cope with this gardening job?

*(He takes kettle back to range.)*

**CLARENCE:**
Well, apart from not knowing one flower from another. Being a London lad, we only saw 'em in the graveyard. For years I thought they only grew in little circles. *(He sits.)*

**TRAVERS:**
I don't think old Mrs Titheridge will expect you to know much about all that. It's more tidying, and weeding and that.

**CLARENCE:**
Oh, well, I can't see the weeds being a problem.

**TRAVERS:**
Yes, that's what I think will be the problem an' all.

**CLARENCE:**
Eh?

**TRAVERS:**
I reckon I'll have to pinch her glasses, then she won't see them either.

**CLARENCE:**
You'll have to keep coming out and pointing them out for me.

**TRAVERS:**
I'll have to keep coming out and pulling 'em out for you, I shouldn't wonder. Never mind, we'll manage. It'll be nice to be working together, won't it. And the banns are being called at the Church. In three weeks we'll be married.

**CLARENCE:**
Yeah. We'll be living without that flaming bolster down the middle. I can't wait, meself. Give us a kiss. *(He stands.)* You ain't never kissed me properly. *(They kiss.)*

**TRAVERS:**
*(looking into his eyes)* There's more tongue if you want it.

**CLARENCE:**
Pardon?

**TRAVERS:**
*(flustered now)* Cold tongue. Look, there's a bit left – do you want it?

**CLARENCE:**
No, that kiss has put me off me food.

**TRAVERS:**
Well that's nice, I must say.

**CLARENCE:**
No, I mean you're lovely you are. I feel I've known you all me life.

**TRAVERS:**
You couldn't have done – you're older than me. Much older.

**CLARENCE:**
How old are you?

**TRAVERS:**
How old are you?

**CLARENCE:**
Fifty-five.

**TRAVERS:**
Well, there you are then, that proves it. If you're that much older than me, I must be that much younger than you.

**CLARENCE:**
*(puzzled)* I can't work that out.

**TRAVERS:**
No. I know. That's what I mean.

**CLARENCE:**
What does that mean?

**TRAVERS:**
It means I'm not going to tell you.

**CLARENCE:**
Oh, alright, please your joyful. Don't make no difference. I don't have to know everything about you in order to love you – in order to marry you.

**TRAVERS:**
I don't know who I'm marrying, do I?

**CLARENCE:**
You're marrying me.

**TRAVERS:**
Yes, but who are you?

**CLARENCE:**
Me? *(Looking round.)* I'm the bloke sitting here having supper with you. I'm the bloke you're sleeping with.

**TRAVERS:**
Please! Someone might hear you.

**CLARENCE:**
Who? There's nobody about.

**TRAVERS:**
There's the chickens.

**CLARENCE:**
That's alright. Get 'em excited, they might lay a few more eggs.

**TRAVERS:**
No, I mean I don't know nothing about you, do I? Your early life, and that.

**CLARENCE:**
Not much to know really. Left school when I was fourteen, worked for me Dad for a bit, but we never did see eye to eye – even after I got me glasses. So I was a boxer for awhile, at Billingsgate.

**TRAVERS:**
A boxer? Isn't that dangerous?

**CLARENCE:**
Not boxing kippers isn't. Bit smelly. Worked for a bloke called Boswell. We never got on. Only lasted about three months, then I walked out.

**TRAVERS:**
Why?

**CLARENCE:**
On account of a remark he made.

**TRAVERS:**
What did he say?

**CLARENCE:**
"You're sacked." So then I went into a job with a demolition firm. It was either that or working in a glass factory.

**TRAVERS:**
I think you made a wise choice.

**CLARENCE:**
Course, then the War came. Not much difference really – just carried on demolishing things. Got gassed in Belgium, plastered in Paris and wounded in the Dardanelles. Do you want to see the scar?

**TRAVERS:**
Not if it's in the Dardanelles, thank you.

**CLARENCE:**
*(grinning)* The Dardanelles is a place.

**TRAVERS:**
I know. I'm just pulling your leg.

**CLARENCE:**
Well be careful, it might affect the Dardanelles.

**TRAVERS:**
*(She stands.)* Time for bed – come on. We start work tomorrow, both of us. Got to be up with the lark.

**CLARENCE:**
How about going to bed with one? *(He gooses her.)*

**TRAVERS:**
Can't you wait three weeks? *(She goes to sink.)*

**CLARENCE:**
Just about. Who is this old bird we're going to look after. Do I know her? *(Travers goes back to table.)*

**TRAVERS:**
Old Mrs Titheridge. You must have seen

her round the village. Big old wheelchair. Sort of vague face and fuzzy hair.

**CLARENCE:**
*(shaking his head)* Everybody looks like that to me.

*Cut to Sequence 1*

*Scene 3: Ext. Mrs Titheridge's garden. Day.*

*1930s-style graphic of country garden. Becomes live action. Music – vocal version of "It's a lovely day Tomorrow". The garden of Mrs Titheridge's country house. Sunny and pretty. Mrs Titheridge, a jolly old soul, is seated in her old-fashioned bath chair, wearing a big "picture" hat of straw, or something similar. Peace reigns.*

*Clarence, against a wall on which are affixed two taps for hosepipes. One is attached to a rolled-up hose on a reel, the other attached to a hose which lies in a heap. Clarence is unravelling its coils, and soon leaves frame with nozzle end.*

*A wide shot as he drags the hose across the lawn. He is heading for Mrs Titheridge. As he arrives, she sees him, and gives a discreet cough.*

**CLARENCE:**
Oh it's you. What are you doing out here, have you finished? What's the old bird up to?

**MRS TITHERIDGE:**
Which old bird is that, Mr Sale.

**CLARENCE:**
Oh, it's you, madam. I thought it was Travers.

**MRS TITHERIDGE:**
I see.

**CLARENCE:**
*(embarrassed)* I was talking about her old parrot. She loves the old bird. Polly, her name is. Well, they're all called that, ain't they?

**MRS TITHERIDGE:**
The lady parrots usually are, yes.

**CLARENCE:**
Yeah. My Travers loves her. She's a funny old thing – very affectionate. Loves lying on her back with her legs in the air.

**MRS TITHERIDGE:**
I take it we are still talking about the parrot.

**CLARENCE:**
Oh yes, not, er – no, hardly! Not that she's, well, but, you know. Mind if I smoke?

**MRS TITHERIDGE:**
Not at all.

**CLARENCE:**
Do you smoke?

**MRS TITHERIDGE:**
I'd love one.

**CLARENCE:**
*(takes out packet)* They're only Woodbines.

**MRS TITHERIDGE:**
I love Woodbines.

**CLARENCE:**
*(opens packet)* Oh. I've only got one.
*(Shows packet.)*

**MRS TITHERIDGE:**
One's plenty, thank you. *(Takes it.)*

**CLARENCE:**
I ain't got no matches.

**MRS TITHERIDGE:**
Oh, well, I'll smoke it later, thank you.
*(Hides it away.)* What are you up to at the moment?

**CLARENCE:**
I was just going to water your roses.
*(Indicates a patch of lilies.)*

**MRS TITHERIDGE:**
They're lilies.

**CLARENCE:**
Oh. Well I'll water Lily's roses then.

*(Mrs Titheridge laughs – something she does quite often.)*

**MRS TITHERIDGE:**
Here – what do you think of this. *(Shows her embroidery.)*

*(Clarence puts down the hose behind her chair, and peers at it.)*

**CLARENCE:**
Knitting, is it?

**MRS TITHERIDGE:**
Knitting? Don't you know embroidery when you see it?

**CLARENCE:**
Oh, when I see it, yes. *(peering)* What is it?

**MRS TITHERIDGE:**
Queen Mary.

*(We see, through Clarence's eyes – a complete fuzz of colour.)*

**CLARENCE:**
Delicate work, isn't it? Yes, very nice. I love the funnels.

*(He moves away, and we see Mrs Titheridge's reaction – and then a close up of her petit-point, with Queen Mary staring regally at us from beneath her tiara.)*

*(Clarence is meanwhile finding his way back to the tap, using the hosepipe as a guide, and hitting a tree round which the pipe is wrapped, etc.)*

*(He arrives back at the taps on the wall. He is bending down, trying to unravel the knotted hosepipe, when we hear Travers's voice near at hand.)*

**TRAVERS:**
*(off)* How you getting on?

*(Clarence looks up, and we see Travers wave to him, and start to approach. She carries the broom.)*

**CLARENCE:**
Alright – just watering.

*(He bends again to unravel the pipe, and gooses himself on the handle of a rake leaning against a wheelbarrow. He straightens up with a whoop.)*

**CLARENCE:**
*(addressing Travers)* Hey, don't do that, someone might see you.

**TRAVERS:**
What?

**CLARENCE:**
Dangerous, that is. Specially to your future husband.

**TRAVERS:**
I don't know what you're talking about. I was only wondering how things were.

**CLARENCE:**
Things are fine, thank you. At least they were 'til you did that with your broom handle.

*(He gropes around the taps, and turns on the wrong one. We see the water shoot from the coiled hose hanging on the wall, straight up into the air in an arc. Clarence sets off along the pipe, but after a few feet walks into the shower caused by the hose. He puts out his hand, looking up.)*

**CLARENCE:**
Typical, en it? As soon as you start watering it comes on to rain.

*(Travers, meanwhile, seeing the problem, moves to the taps and switches off. He arrives back at the taps.)*

**CLARENCE:**
It's raining. Better get the old lady in.

**TRAVERS:**
It was only a shower. It's stopped again then.

**CLARENCE:**
Changeable, isn't it? Start again then.

*(He gropes around, this time finding the other tap. Travers, in horror, sees where the hose lies under Mrs Titheridge's chair. She stays his hand.)*

**TRAVERS:**
Look, leave that for now, time for a cup of tea in the kitchen.

**CLARENCE:**
Oh, right. (*As they go, he looks back towards the old lady.*) Is it safe to leave Mrs Titheridge out there when I'm not out there?

**TRAVERS:**
Safer, if anything.

**CLARENCE:**
We don't want her to get soaked.

**TRAVERS:**
No, that's what I mean.

*(Clarence looks puzzled.)*

*Scene 4: Int. The bedroom. Night.*

*Music link – vocal version "Isn't it a lovely Day to be caught in the Rain".*

*Travers is taking her dressing gown off. Bolster in place down the middle of the bed. Clarence enters. He wears nightshirt, but underneath still has his trousers on. He carries two mugs of cocoa.*

**CLARENCE:**
Cocoa, madam. What time would you like to be woken in the morning, Madam?

**TRAVERS:**
Seven-thirty please, waiter.

**CLARENCE:**
Very good, madam. I'll give you a nudge.

*(He crosses behind the foot of the bed, trips over his own feet and his cocoa shoots out of his mug, straight through the open window. We hear a cat screech outside.)*

**CLARENCE:**
Crikey – lucky the window was open, wasn't it. Not so lucky for the cat mind you. That was boiling hot, that cocoa.

**TRAVERS:**
Couldn't have been a cat – there's no cats round here.

**CLARENCE:**
Oh. Must have been a squirrel that does cat impressions.

**TRAVERS:**
Would it be wild?

**CLARENCE:**
I should think it'd be furious, wouldn't you.

**TRAVERS:**
Are you alright? Look don't worry about the cocoa – I'll make you some more.

**CLARENCE:**
No, you can have mine. (*He gives it to her.*) Can I have a sip?

**TRAVERS:**
Course you can.

**CLARENCE:**
Ta.

*(He takes her cup and sits on her side of the bed.)*

**TRAVERS:**
Here, steady – you're on the wrong side of the bed.

**CLARENCE:**
It's alright, I've still got me trousers on. *(Sits in chair.)*

**TRAVERS:**
Talking of trousers, what are you wearing for the wedding?

**CLARENCE:**
Me best suit.

**TRAVERS:**
I didn't know you'd got a best suit.

**CLARENCE:**
Course I have, everyone's got a best suit. It's in me trunk. I used to have three. All made by the same bloke at the same time, about twelve years ago.

**TRAVERS:**
Tailor-made eh? Bit expensive.

**CLARENCE:**
No – this pal of mine made them for thirty-five bob each. Cheaper than the 50 bob tailors.

**TRAVERS:**
Why three?

**CLARENCE:**
Last longer in the long run – keep chopping and changing, none of 'em wear out so quick, see. Mind you, two of 'em did. Only got one now.

**TRAVERS:**
What colour is it?

**CLARENCE:**
Well, it's sort of a grey-ee bluee brownee sort of colour. I'm not very good on colours.

**TRAVERS:**
Well, I'll have to give it a good press if it's been in that trunk. It'll be like a rag.

**CLARENCE:**
(Stands and joins her.) I'll do it. Used to press all me own clothes in the Army. Anyway, it's bad luck to see the bridegroom in his wedding dress before the day, en it?

**TRAVERS:**
That's the bride, stupid. Come on, get to bed.

**CLARENCE:**
Dangerous words!

**TRAVERS:**
Less than three weeks to go, lovey.

**CLARENCE:**
Yes. Then goodbye to the bolster forever. I'll have me own real bolster. (He kisses her forehead.)

**TRAVERS:**
Hey, none of that, come on. (She pushes him away, and he stands up.) Listen, Clarence. When the time comes – you know, the honeymoon, like – well, you'll have to take things, well – slowly. Do you know what I mean? I've never had much to do with men, and I don't want to be rushed. We've got all the time in the world, haven't we?

**CLARENCE:**
I know. I know what you mean. I know I'm a bit clumsy, bump into things a lot and that, but when I try I can be very controlled. You're all that matters to me, and I just want you to know that I shall be doing my very best to be gentle, patient, and caring towards you. For always.

**TRAVERS:**
(visibly moved) I know. I know you will.

**CLARENCE:**
Don't worry. I won't put a foot wrong.

(He removes his trousers, gets his leg caught, and overbalances, grabbing at a shelf on the wall as he goes. The shelf collapses at one end, and all the ornaments slide off gradually, each one smashing as it hits the floor. Clarence, on the floor, watches helpless. Finally, the shelf collapses completely, landing on his head.)

**TRAVERS:**
(shaking her head in dismay) Heaven help me three weeks from now.

690

*Mix to Sequence 2*

*Scene 5: Ext. The cottage. Day.*

*The van – exterior.*

*(Clarence has the bonnet up, working on the engine. Travers approaches, and peers over his shoulder.)*

**TRAVERS:**
I've been meaning to say.

**CLARENCE:**
*(preoccupied)* What's that?

**TRAVERS:**
How are we getting to the church for the wedding?

**CLARENCE:**
In this.

**TRAVERS:**
I was afraid you were going to say that. Won't it look a bit funny, the bride turning up driving a removal lorry?

**CLARENCE:**
Well you won't let me drive it, will you?

**TRAVERS:**
No I will not.

**CLARENCE:**
We'll park it round the back, then walk round. No-one will see us. It's not as if there'll be a crowd of people, we're not inviting anybody.

**TRAVERS:**
Couldn't we walk?

**CLARENCE:**
It's a mile.

**TRAVERS:**
I'd rather do that than take this old thing.

**CLARENCE:**
Old thing? This is my only pride and joy, this is.

**TRAVERS:**
I thought I was.

**CLARENCE:**
Well, this is my other only pride and joy.

**TRAVERS:**
If it's so precious, supposing someone pinches it while we're in church?

**CLARENCE:**
Simple. I take this bit out. Rotor arm, see? *(He shows her the rotor arm.)* Put this in me pocket, no-one can move it. Old trick, that.

**TRAVERS:**
Well, I'd honestly much rather walk.

**CLARENCE:**
Look, let's not fight about it. We're going in the van, O.K.?

**TRAVERS:**
We'll see. *(As she leaves)* Your tea's on the table.

*Music – vocal version, 1930s "Tea for Two" or "Everything stops for Tea", as we mix to:*

*Scene 6: Ext. Mrs Titheridge's garden. Day.*

*A close up of tea being poured into a fine china cup. Pull or cut back to reveal Mrs Titheridge pouring.*

**MRS TITHERIDGE:**
How many lumps in your tea, Mr Sale?

**CLARENCE:**
I prefer it all smooth, thank you.

**MRS TITHERIDGE:**
*(with a laugh)* You're a card, and no mistake.

**CLARENCE:**
Well, you have to laugh don't you?

**MRS TITHERIDGE:**
You do. There you are. *(Hands him teacup.)*

**CLARENCE:**
Ta. Very good of you. I should be getting on, really.

**MRS TITHERIDGE:**
Nonsense. Sit down and tell me about yourself. You're really a removals man, aren't you?

**CLARENCE:**
Well, was. Travers doesn't like me to drive the van anymore – says me eyes aren't good enough. I been driving motor cars for twenty years, but that don't seem to count.

**MRS TITHERIDGE:**
Did it take you long to learn?

**CLARENCE:**
Oh, three or four.

**MRS TITHERIDGE:**
Months?

**CLARENCE:**
No, motor cars.

*(Mrs Titheridge roars with laughter.)*

**MRS TITHERIDGE:**
Dear dear! You'll have to learn to ride a horse.

**CLARENCE:**
I can ride a bit.

**MRS TITHERIDGE:**
I love horses. Ever since I was a gel, when I saw them at the circus. Wonderful riders, these circus people. There was a man at the circus who jumped onto the horse's back, slid underneath, caught hold of its tail, and finished up being dragged along.

**CLARENCE:**
That's easy – I did that the first time I got on a horse. *(Mrs Titheridge laughs again.)* It was the coalman's horse. His yard was at the top of our street. He let me have a go on him after work. Big black horse it was. Well, it would be. He wouldn't have a

white horse, would he? Not for long, anyhow.

**MRS TITHERIDGE:**
No, quite. How do you like the garden? *(She waves her parasol in the direction of the flower-beds.)*

**CLARENCE:**
Lovely. *(Pointing to a flowering bush near the house.)* They're pretty, aren't they.

**MRS TITHERIDGE:**
Mm. Prolific bloomers.

**CLARENCE:**
Oh are they? Sorry, I thought they was flowers. Good drying day for washing.

*(Mrs Titheridge: smiles to herself, but decides to leave well alone.)*

**CLARENCE:**
Fancy going for a walk?

**MRS TITHERIDGE:**
A walk? I've only got one leg, you know. This one's only for show. I can take it off – like Long John Silver in the play. *(With a chuckle.)* I ought to borrow your parrot!

**CLARENCE:**
Parrot?

**MRS TITHERIDGE:**
You said Travers had a parrot.

**CLARENCE:**
Oh, that parrot, oh yes.

**MRS TITHERIDGE:**
No, I can hobble about a bit, but not enough to go striding round the countryside.

**CLARENCE:**
No, I meant I would push you, go for a walk. Me walking, you riding.

**MRS TITHERIDGE:**
I think that would be most charming. Let's go.

**CLARENCE:**
Lovely. Anything you want before we go?

**MRS TITHERIDGE:**
You'll have to lift my leg up, and put it onto the chair if you would.

**CLARENCE:**
*(hurries to oblige)* Like that?

**MRS TITHERIDGE:**
Fine. Thank you.

**CLARENCE:**
Very life-like, isn't it? It actually comes right off, does it?

**MRS TITHERIDGE:**
Certainly. I take myself to bits every night.

**CLARENCE:**
I tell you what. Next Saturday I could take you down to the local Hop.

*(Mrs Titheridge roars with laughter, as they set off, heading for the gate. She carries her rolled-up parasol across her lap.)*

*Scene 7: Ext. Country road. Day.*

*Cut to 1930s poster-type caption – a winding road in beautiful hilly countryside. It becomes live action as Clarence, with Mrs Titheridge enter from behind camera and walk up the road. They are chatting and laughing. A slow mix to another location – mid shot as we track with them, or they approach camera in a static shot. We begin to hear what they are saying.*

**MRS TITHERIDGE:**
I used to visit the Opera a lot. Do you like Opera?

**CLARENCE:**
It depends. Long as there's not too much singing.

**MRS TITHERIDGE:**
Quartettes are my favourites. I think quartettes are lovely, don't you?

**CLARENCE:**
Well, they're quicker than four solos.

**MRS TITHERIDGE:**
*(laughing loudly at this)* Oh Clarence! You are what I believe is popularly known as a caution!

*(They leave frame, chuckling.)*

*Mix to:*

*Scene 8: Ext. Country pub. Day.*

*They approach, and pull up outside the door. We clearly see a pictorial painted sign – "The Fiddler's Arms".*

**CLARENCE:**
Sure you won't come in?

**MRS TITHERIDGE:**
No, just bring me a packet of crisps. Must be Smiths, with the little blue packet of salt.

**CLARENCE:**
I'll down a swift half, and be out before you can say Jack Robinson.

**MRS TITHERIDGE:**
Jack Robinson?

**CLARENCE:**
No, hang on, give us a chance – not 'til I'm in there.

*(He goes. She laughs – then spies an outhouse door marked "ladies". She manages to get to her feet, sticks her parasol down the side of the chair, and, removing her hat, hangs it on the parasol handle, and hobbles off to the toilet. A shot of the picture hat, balanced on the parasol.)*

*(Clarence comes out of the pub, without the crisps.)*

**CLARENCE:**
They hadn't got no Smiths crisps – there's another pub down the road, I'll have me half in there.

693

*(He sets off with the empty chair – his myopic eyes mistaking the hat for Mrs Titheridge.)*

*Mix to:*

*Scene 9: Ext. Country road (2). Day.*

*The pretty country road. Clarence is pushing the empty chair, chatting away to it.*

**CLARENCE:**
Yes, I've always loved chocolate. Chocolate drops, chocolate fudge – Black Magic – anything. I've always been the same, ever since I can remember.

*(A fat country woman approaches from the opposite direction, and registers Clarence's odd behaviour.)*

**CLARENCE:**
I just can't seem to get enough of it. I crave it all the time. It's like a disease with me almost. I go made if I can't get it.

*(The fat woman looks alarmed as she hears only the second half of the conversation and gets the wrong idea. Clarence stops as they are about to pass, and speaks to her.)*

**CLARENCE:**
Excuse me, I wonder if you could oblige me. Have you got the time?

**COUNTRYWOMAN:**
No I haven't, it's one o'clock, my husband will be home. He's a big man. He'll be wanting me for his dinner. He eats a lot of meat.

*(She hurries away as fast as she can. Clarence stares after her.)*

*Scene 10: Ext. Second pub. Day.*

*(Clarence parks the chair, and enters the pub. An old-fashioned optical wipe – a clock wipe, possibly – and out he comes again, clutching the familiar bag of crisps.)*

**CLARENCE:**
*(to chair)* Here we are. I'll open 'em for

you. *(He does so.)* There you are – don't eat the blue one.

*(He tries to hand the crisps to Mrs Titheridge and realises, for the first time, that she is not there. He gropes around where she should be – then straightens up.)*

**CLARENCE:**
Oh, I know – she's gone to the toilet.

*(We see Clarence come round the corner to where, behind the pub, there are toilets – one marked "ladies". He is wheeling the chair.)*

**CLARENCE:**
*(calling through the door)* Hallo – it's only me. I guessed you were in there. Take your time.

*(Inside the toilet sits a middle-aged woman. She looks apprehensive.)*

**CLARENCE:**
I'll wait around in case you want me to lift your leg up.

*(The woman looks terrified, and calls out to him.)*

**LADY IN LOO:**
Go away, or I'll call the police!

**CLARENCE:**
*(off)* Is that you, Mrs Titheridge?

**LADY IN LOO:**
No, it's Miss Hardacre.

**CLARENCE:**
Oh, I'm sorry to hear that. I'll leave you to it.

*(The woman reacts. Outside, Clarence is beginning to panic.)*

**CLARENCE:**
*(to himself)* She must have fallen out the chair somewhere along the road. No wonder she was quiet. I thought she was asleep.

*(He moves off round the corner.)*

**CLARENCE:**
She hadn't dropped off, she'd dropped out.

*(He sets off down the road again, agitated.)*

*Scene 11: Int. Mrs Titheridge's house. Day.*

*A close up of Travers.*

**TRAVERS:**
But that was an hour ago.

**CLARENCE:**
I know, I been looking in all the ditches all along the road. No sign of her.

**TRAVERS:**
There's only one explanation. She's been run over. She'll be in the hospital. I'll have to telephone them up.

**CLARENCE:**
Yeah.

**TRAVERS:**
You do it.

**CLARENCE:**
Eh?

**TRAVERS:**
Go on – then you can break the news to me gently.

**CLARENCE:**
I can't do that. I can't see good enough.

**TRAVERS:**
You don't have to see, you dopey, you have to hear.

**CLARENCE:**
Well, me earsight's not too good either. You do it.

**TRAVERS:**
Don't be so daft – get on with it.

**CLARENCE:**
Well, what do I do?

**TRAVERS:**
Just pick it up and wind its handle, and it rings.

*(Clarence gingerly approaches the telephone. As he is about to pick it up, it rings stridently, frightening him.)*

**CLARENCE:**
*(jumping)* I never touched it! How's it do that?

**TRAVERS:**
It's someone ringing up us. It'll be the hospital. *(Taking phone)* Is that the hospital, how is she? She's what? Oh dear. Is she conscious? I'll come straight away. *(She puts phone down.)*

**CLARENCE:**
Hospital, was it?

**TRAVERS:**
*(putting down phone)* No, it was the "Fiddler's Arms". Would I collect Mrs Titheridge, as she's rather the worse for wear.

*(Travers leaves.)*

**CLARENCE:**
That's where she went.

*Cut to Sequence 3*

*Scene 12: Ext. Country road (3). Evening.*

*Mix to: a wide shot of the country road. Across the horizon comes Travers, pushing Mrs Titheridge in her chair. Mrs Titheridge is singing lustily "Knees up Mother Brown". After a few moments, we cut to a closer shot.*

**MRS TITHERIDGE:**
*(sings)* "Ei-ei-ei-o, if I catch you bending, I'll saw your leg right off". Whee! *(At this point she waves her artificial leg in the air, which by now is resting on her lap.)*

"Knees up, knees up, don't get the breeze up" –

*(As she uses the leg for simulated high kicks, we cut to Travers's long-suffering face. Then wide again for the end of the chorus.)*

**MRS TITHERIDGE** *(cont'd)*:
"Knees up Mother Brown. Oh! Knees up Mother Brown" – *(in the same key, the 1930s record takes up the tune as we mix to Scene 13.)*

*Mix to Sequence 4*

*Scene 13: Ext. The cottage. Day.*

*Graphic of exterior of cottage – morning. Birds warbling. Animates.*

*Scene 14: Int. The parlour. Day.*

*Inside the parlour, Travers in her dressing-gown, but is putting the finishing touches to her hair and make-up – an important occasion. She is singing quietly to herself, slowly, disjointedly, as people do when occupied.*

**TRAVERS:**
There was I ... waiting at the church, waiting at the church (lipstick) waiting at the church ... then I found he'd left me in the lurch ... oh how it did upset me ... set me.

**CLARENCE:**
It's the grey one. Isn't it? *(He picks up the lapel and places it to his eye.)* Yes. I got the carnation out the garden.

**TRAVERS:**
*(looking at the daisy, and warming to his eagerness to please)* It's lovely. You look grand.

**CLARENCE:**
I'm going out to warm up the van. You've come round about going in the van, haven't you? Don't mind any more, do you?

**TRAVERS:**
You just go and get it started.

*(He goes. She moves towards the mantelpiece, and takes something from a tobacco jar then leaves the room.)*

*Cut to Sequence 5*

*Clarence enters. He has a dog daisy in the buttonhole of his jacket. He wears his "best suit" which consists of a grey herringbone jacket, brown herringbone trousers and a grey-blue waistcoat.*

**CLARENCE:**
How do I look?

*(Travers stares at him, not knowing what to say.)*

**TRAVERS:**
Fine. Fine. Yes. Is that one of the three suits your friend made for you?

**CLARENCE:**
Yes. The other two wore out. This is the only one left. I had a blue one, a grey one, and a brown one.

**TRAVERS:**
And which one is that?

*Scene 15: Ext. The cottage + van. Day.*

*Clarence is trying to start the van. It won't start.*

*A shot of Travers looking through the bungalow's bedroom window.*

*Scene 16: Int. The bedroom. Day.*

*Inside the bedroom, she takes off her dressing gown. From the pocket she takes the van's rotor arm. We see it in close up as she closes her hand over it. As the spluttering of the van's engine continues, she tucks the rotor arm into the back of her "directoire" knickers. We see her face, a faint smile of satisfaction as she watches Clarence's doomed efforts. She starts to put on her best dress.*

*Scene 17: Int. The parlour. Day.*

*Travers is dressed, primping at the mirror.*

*(Clarence enters, annoyed.)*

**CLARENCE:**
Someone's pinched the rotor arm.

**TRAVERS:**
*(without looking round)* Oh dear! Must have been those boys I saw playing round the van yesterday.

**CLARENCE:**
Why? Why would they do it?

**TRAVERS:**
Just for mischief. You know what boys are.

**CLARENCE:**
Yeah. They're little swine, that's what they are. Probably slung it over the field. It's lying somewhere in the undergrowth at the back of beyond.

*(Travers puts her hand to where it is hidden behind her.)*

**TRAVERS:**
Never mind. We'll walk up to the church. Cheer up. *(She goes to him.)* It's our Wedding Day.

**CLARENCE:**
I know. But it's always been my first love, that van.

**TRAVERS:**
Well, now I'm your second love.

**CLARENCE:**
Yeah. *(He takes her in his arms.)* I've got you now, haven't I? *(He stops, puzzled.)* What's that?

*(His hand has encountered the rotor arm through her dress.)*

**TRAVERS:**
*(flustered)* Never you mind. That's part of my underpinning.

**CLARENCE:**
Underpinning? You're not going to collapse when you take your corset off, are you?

**TRAVERS:**
Course not. Anyway, you'll find out later, won't you? Come on, we'll be late.

*(She picks up bouquet on table.)*

*Cut to Sequence 6.*

*Scene 18: Ext. The cottage. Day.*

*They come out hand in hand. The sun shines down. They reach the gates and pass through.*

**TRAVERS:**
*(tenderly)* Are you ready for this? This is for good, you know. For ever.

**CLARENCE:**
Yes, it's a turning point in my life, this is. Now I can see me way clear.

*(They set off, Clarence in competely the wrong direction. She corrects him, and arm in arm, they go up the hill. The live action becomes a poster-style graphic as the music swells up into the vocal, and the credits roll.)*

*Scene 19: Ext. The church. Day.*

*During the credits, the film resolves into black and white photograph. The two of them, the vicar, and single photographs of each. Clarence, the sun reflecting on his pebble glasses, looking completely the wrong way, etc.*

*Scene 20: Ext. The cottage. Night.*

*Scene 21: Int. The cottage. Night.*

*Cottage interior. A shot of the closed bedroom door. Outside it, in an upright position, the bolster leans against the wall, resting on Clarence's shoes, and wearing Clarence's cap.*

*(The final – director's – credit appears.)*

*(Fade sound and vision.)*

# THE PLAYS

## RUB A DUB DUB

*Rub A Dub Dub* (as in Two Men in a Pub) was written in 1998 as a curtain raiser for Ronnie's play, *Mum*. However, in the initial run of that play due to time constraints this vignette was never performed and appears here for the first time.

*A spotlit round pub table, with two chairs. On one of them sits Brian, a pint beside him on the table. His face is hidden by his tabloid newspaper as he reads. He lowers it, and sips his pint. He is forty-six or so. A Cockney.*

*A jukebox is heard in the background from time to time.*

*After a moment, Alec, another Cockney enters, carrying a pint – he is about twenty-eight. He looks at the empty chair next to Brian.*

**ALEC:**
Anybody sitting here is there?

**BRIAN:**
*(looking at chair briefly)* No.

*(Alec sits. A pause)*

**ALEC:**
Funny how people say that, "Anybody sitting here?" You can see there's no-one sitting there.

**BRIAN:**
*(putting down his newspaper)* It's just an expression.

**ALEC:**
Stupid though isn't it.

**BRIAN:**
'Course, if someone had come along five minutes later, it would have been true.

**ALEC:**
What would?

**BRIAN:**
There would have been someone sitting there.

**ALEC:**
Who?

**BRIAN:**
You.

**ALEC:**
Oh yes, see what you mean, yes.
*(He removes his jacket and hangs it over the back of his chair as he speaks.)*

**ALEC:**
'Course, they wouldn't bloody say it then, 'cos they could see me sitting there. Bloody stands to reason.

**BRIAN:**
I do hope, if you are going to continue to sit there, you will refrain from swearing.

**ALEC:**
Who?

**BRIAN:**
You. You swore twice in that last remark.

**ALEC:**
I never noticed.

**BRIAN:**
Well you did.

**ALEC:**
Anyhow, why should you want me to stop swearing?

**BRIAN:**
I don't bleedin' like it.

**ALEC:**
*(incredulously)* You don't bleedin' like me swearing?

**BRIAN:**
There you go again.

**ALEC:**
That's what you said! You don't bleedin' like it.

**BRIAN:**
I never said any such thing.

**ALEC:**
You bloody did.

**BRIAN:**
I bloody didn't!

**ALEC:**
There you go again.

**BRIAN:**
Alright, alright. My wife's trying to stop me swearing, so if I can't, I thought I'd ask other people to stop an' all. Might make it easier.

**ALEC:**
Well, doubt it. It's not like smoking, is it? You don't sort of smell the whiff of swearing in your nostrils, do you. Not like cigarette smoke. *(He takes out packet of cigarettes and a lighter.)* In a place like this, giving up smoking must be impossible.

**BRIAN:**
I've given that up, as well.

**ALEC:**
Smoking?

**BRIAN:**
The wife insisted.

**ALEC:**
So you don't swear or smoke now?

**BRIAN:**
Definitely not. *(A pause.)* Oh bugger it, give us a fag will you?

**ALEC:**
Certainly. *(He hands him the packet. Brian takes one, puts it behind his ear.)*

**BRIAN:**
Save it for later.

**ALEC:**
Later? How much later?

**BRIAN:**
Mind your own bleedin' business!

**ALEC:**
You're swearing again.

**BRIAN:**
Oh gawd, so I am. Give us a light will you? *(Alec lights his cigarette.)* Ah! That's better.

**ALEC:**
Of course it is. Bound to be. So you're going to forget the idea of giving up, are you?

**BRIAN:**
Certainly not. I shall give up again just before I go home.

**ALEC:**
Won't she smell it on your breath?

**BRIAN:**
No. I intend to drink enough beer to hide the smell of smoke. I shall just reek of beer.

**ALEC:**
That'll be nice for her.

**BRIAN:**
She doesn't mind the smell of beer.

**ALEC:**
Does she ever come to the pub with you?

**BRIAN:**
No, no. Wouldn't be seen dead in a pub, her. No – against her upbringing.

**ALEC:**
But she doesn't mind you going in pubs.

**BRIAN:**
No. "You go on and enjoy yourself" she says. So off I go.

**ALEC:**
So what does she do while you're at the pub?

**BRIAN:**
She gets drunk at home.

**ALEC:**
Oh, she's not a teetotaller then?

**BRIAN:**
No, she likes a drop of gin. So I arrive home full of ale, and she sits there full of gin, and we're both ready for a drop of the other.

**ALEC:**
Really.

**BRIAN:**
Nice drop of brandy.

**ALEC:**
Oh.

**BRIAN:**
You know what they say – "Ale makes you pale, Stout blows you out, Gin makes you thin, Brandy makes you randy" –

**ALEC:**
What about rum?

**BRIAN:**
We won't go into that. So we has a nip of brandy, then she nips into bed. I hop into the bathroom, sort myself out, hop out again, and hop into bed.

**ALEC:**
She nips, and you hop.

**BRIAN:**
That's right yes.

**ALEC:**
If she's nipping, why are you hopping?

**BRIAN:**
I lost one of me bedroom slippers. It's cold that lino. So there she is, sitting up in bed in her see-through nightie.

**ALEC:**
See-through, eh?

**BRIAN:**
Yeah. She loves see-through things. She's got a see-through duffel-coat. My trouble is, I'm asleep as soon as my head touches the pillow. Then I start snoring, and she kicks me out of the room. I have to go and sleep somewhere else.

**ALEC:**
So you don't get a very good night, then.

**BRIAN:**
I sleep like a log.

**ALEC:**
Where?

**BRIAN:**
The wood shed. I've tried other places in the garden, but they're not as good. How anyone says they can sleep on a clothes line, it's impossible.

*(A pause.)*

**ALEC:**
*(Staring at him.)* You're making all this up, aren't you.

**BRIAN:**
Yes I am. I like to fantasise. My wife's nothing like that.

**ALEC:**
But she really made you give up swearing and smoking.

**BRIAN:**
Oh yes, that bit's true. She's my second wife, you see. "If at first you don't succeed, try, try again." On the other hand, though, they say "Once bitten, twice shy."

**ALEC:**
There's a lot of sayings like that. That contradict each other. "Many hands make light work" but "Too many cooks spoil the broth."

**BRIAN:**
Exactly. "Look before you leap."

**ALEC:**
"He who hesitates is lost."

**BRIAN:**
"The more the merrier", but "Two's company, three's a crowd."

**ALEC:**
"You can drive a horse to water, but a pencil must be lead."

**BRIAN:**
That's not an old saying.

**ALEC:**
It is partly. Partly it's out of a Christmas cracker.

**BRIAN:**
I wonder when these old mottoes started?

**ALEC:**
Back in the middle ages I expect. Most things did.

**BRIAN:**
I wonder who made them all up. Why were they all so clever in the middle ages?

**ALEC:**
Well they were all monks then weren't they.

**BRIAN:**
They can't all have been monks, otherwise they wouldn't have been able to keep the human race going, would they.

**ALEC:**
Perhaps some of them cheated. With the nuns, like.

**BRIAN:**
Thank God for that.

**ALEC:**
Yes, they probably did.

*(A pause. They drink.)*

**BRIAN:**
You married at all?

**ALEC:**
No. not at all. Not one little bit.

**BRIAN:**
Why not?

**ALEC:**
Don't want to tie myself down. I'm wary. "Fools rush in where angels fear to tread."

**BRIAN:**
"Nothing ventured, nothing gained."

**ALEC:**
"There is no rose without a thorn."

**BRIAN:**
Gawd, don't let's start all that again for Christ's sake.

**ALEC:**
Here! What's all this swearing?

**BRIAN:**
Oh yes, I forgot. Give us a fag, will you?

**ALEC:**
You've given up! You don't smoke, and also you've just put one out.

**BRIAN:**
I can't give up. I shall never conquer the craving. It'll drive me to drink.

**ALEC:**
You're drinking now!

**BRIAN:**
No I'm not.

**ALEC:**
*(indicating pint mug)* What do you call that then?

**BRIAN:**
An empty mug.

**ALEC:**
Gordon Bennett. *(He stands up.)* What are you having?

**BRIAN:**
Is it your round?

**ALEC:**
It's nobody's round, is it – we bought our own.

**BRIAN:**
Oh that's very kind, I'll have the same again.

**ALEC:**
What was it?

**BRIAN:**
A pint of Boddingtons Superbrew No.3 real ale from the wood, please. If you can't remember that I'll have a double brandy.

**ALEC:**
I'll remember it, don't worry. Cheeky git!

*(He goes. Brian looks around the pub. He raises his hand to an unseen drinker)*

**BRIAN:**
Evening vicar!

*(He opens his wallet, counts his money. He takes cigarettes out of Alec's coat pocket hanging on the back of the chair. Searches for lighter, lights cigarette. Takes another cigarette, tucks it into his top pocket. He leans back and enjoys the cigarette. Alec returns with two more pints, and sits.)*

**ALEC:**
There you go.

**BRIAN:**
Ta. Cheers, all the best.

**ALEC:**
Cheers. *(They drink.)*

**BRIAN:**
So you're not married then.

**ALEC:**
Not me, no. I like to feel free I do. Go where I like, do what I like, when I like.

**BRIAN:**
And who you like.

**ALEC:**
Exactly.

**BRIAN:**
You don't agree with marriage then?

**ALEC:**
Oh I agree with the idea of it. As an

institution. Just don't think I need to go into a institution at my age.

**BRIAN:**
Oh I see. You're not that way inclined.

**ALEC:**
What?

**BRIAN:**
You don't like women.

**ALEC:**
Who doesn't? I love 'em. I worship 'em.

**BRIAN:**
Well that's what you're supposed to do. So my wife says anyhow.

**ALEC:**
I look up to 'em.

**BRIAN:**
Well that's one way of going about it, yes. But not married.

**ALEC:**
Certainly married.

**BRIAN:**
You said you wasn't married.

**ALEC:**
I'm not married. They're married.

**BRIAN:**
You like married women?

**ALEC:**
The best kind, believe you me. Takes all the hassle out of it. More comfortable. Nice little house, warm and cosy. Proper bed. Always the spare room, of course. Not in her bed, not her husband's bed. I draw the line at that.

**BRIAN:**
Nice to know you've got some sense of decency.

**ALEC:**
Oh yes, spare room. Guest room. Usually

more comfortable than the main bedroom anyhow. Little table lamps with fringes round, that sort of thing.

**BRIAN:**
Oh, you prefer to have it in artistic surroundings do you?

**ALEC:**
Just comfortable that's all. Beats lying in the wet grass embankment or trying to manage in a car. You ever tried the back of a Ford Cortina?

**BRIAN:**
What's wrong with a Ford Cortina. I've got a Ford Cortina. Reliable.

**ALEC:**
A nice soft bed's better.

**BRIAN:**
Not in traffic it's not.

**ALEC:**
Well 'course it's not. I'm not talking about driving down the high street. I'm saying a nice soft bed in a nice spare room is better than a railway embankment or the back of a car.

**BRIAN:**
I once made love on the railway embankment. Express went by and blew me shirt up. Excuse me for asking, but where's this woman's husband all the time?

**ALEC:**
He's at work.

**BRIAN:**
Well why aren't you at work?

**ALEC:**
I work nights. Royal Mail sorting office. Finish at four in the morning, go home, sleep till twelve, get up and go round to her place for me dinner, lovely.

**BRIAN:**
Oh very nice. Cooks for you as well

does she?

**ALEC:**
That's another advantage with married women. They've already learned how to cook. You don't have to eat the failures and pretend to enjoy them.

**BRIAN:**
Sounds ideal.

**ALEC:**
So you have your dinner, up to the spare bedroom –

**BRIAN:**
With the lampshades –

**ALEC:**
Right. Then down for a nice hot cup of tea and leave just before he gets home from work at half past four. Works out perfect. My only worry is that he'll come home and feel the tea-pot, it would still be warm.

**BRIAN:**
Or anything else for that matter.

**ALEC:**
Exactly. The great thing about it is that she doesn't have any hang-ups you see.

**BRIAN:**
Oh dear. So what do you do – put your trousers over the back of a chair, or what?

**ALEC:**
No I mean no pressure – she's not possessive, or anything. And she don't cost me nothing – don't have to take her out for a meal or the pictures, or anything. Whichever way you look at it, she's cheap.

**BRIAN:**
That's the name I'd give her I think, yes. So how many times in your life have you had this arrangement?

**ALEC:**
How many women, you mean? Ooh, lots.

**BRIAN:**
How many on the go at the moment, like?

**ALEC:**
Oh only one at once, come off it. Would never be unfaithful.

**BRIAN:**
Oh you don't call this unfaithful then.

**ALEC:**
I'm not being unfaithful. She's being unfaithful. That's her look-out.

**BRIAN:**
True.

**ALEC:**
Don't get me wrong, I'm very fond of her. We're very romantic.

**BRIAN:**
Oh well that's nice. Do you take her flowers and things?

**ALEC:**
Yeah. Well not exactly flowers. Her old man would wonder where they came from. I take her vegetables.

**BRIAN:**
Vegetables? That's novel.

**ALEC:**
Then we eat 'em for dinner, you see. Destroy the evidence. Vegetables or fruit.

**BRIAN:**
Yes, good idea. I can just see you turning up on the door-step in your best suit with a bunch of carrots in your hand and a banana in your pocket for later. Is she local this girl? Where does she live?

**ALEC:**
Ah, that'd be telling, wouldn't it? I don't want you going round there, trying your luck.

**BRIAN:**
Me? I'm not interested, mate. Anyway I

don't work nights.

**ALEC:**
That's a point.

**BRIAN:**
I'm not interested in other women. One's quite enough to be going on with. Nuisance, women are, most of the time. Mine is. No smoking, no swearing, no snoring, your life ain't your own. Still, she does the washing and gets the meals and keeps the place tidy. Where would I be without her?

**ALEC:**
Single. Like me.

**BRIAN:**
Yes, well. I've been everything, you see. Single, married, divorced, married again. There's no other category left, is there? Except dead. So I've seen it all. On the whole, I think, of the four, marriage is the best state to be in. With a wife. Mind you, I'm in more of a state than she is. She's younger, looks after herself.

**ALEC:**
Yes – does she look after you though?

**BRIAN:**
Oh yeah. Well, she tries. No smoking, no snoring –

**BOTH:**
No swearing!

**BRIAN:**
Yeah. Bleedin' hard work that is.

**ALEC:**
Still, you're managing it. Have a fag.

**BRIAN:**
No thanks, just put one out.

**ALEC:**
*(laughing)* You're hopeless, aren't you.

**BRIAN:**
Not entirely. I haven't snored once since

you arrived. Incidentally, why aren't you at work tonight?

**ALEC:**
Eh?

**BRIAN:**
You said you work nights – why aren't you at work tonight?

**ALEC:**
It's me night off. Friday, isn't it.

**BRIAN:**
Don't you work Fridays?

**ALEC:**
No. Sunday, Monday, Tuesday, Wednesday, Thursday. We have to work Sunday nights so you get your post Monday morning.

**BRIAN:**
Oh right. Do you ever read the postcards when you're sorting?

**ALEC:**
No, don't get time.

**BRIAN:**
Do you ever nick anything out of the registered letters?

**ALEC:**
Me? Course I don't. I'm as honest as the day is long, me.

**BRIAN:**
Yeah. You work nights don't you?

**ALEC:**
Cheeky git.

*(He drinks. A pause.)*

**BRIAN:**
Full in here tonight.

**ALEC:**
Is this your local? I've never seen you in here before.

**BRIAN:**
That's 'cos you've never been in here before. I'm here every night. It's not your local, is it?

**ALEC:**
No. I live three miles from here.

**BRIAN:**
What are you doing round here then?

**ALEC:**
She lives round here. I've been to see her.

**BRIAN:**
What, in the evening? Where's her husband then?

**ALEC:**
He's out. Always goes out Friday nights.

**BRIAN:**
So why aren't you round there now then? With her?

**ALEC:**
'Cos he comes home, doesn't he? No point in risking it, not when you've got all day. I leave early. Anything else you want to know?

**BRIAN:**
No, I'm not interested.

**ALEC:**
Good. Nosey git.

**BRIAN:**
She must be quite well off living round here. Very nice houses round here. Front gardens and everything. Her husband must have a decent job.

**ALEC:**
Not especially I don't think. He bought the house years ago when they were cheap.

**BRIAN:**
They were cheap by today's standards, but I only earned about ten pounds a week when I bought ours. I had a mortgage of

four pounds ten a week, I thought that was terrible. We had to live on what was left over. About a fiver. We had two pounds a week for food. Two pounds! Your bunch of carrots and a banana must cost that much. Of course, we wouldn't buy them in those days. We'd grow our own.

**ALEC:**
What, bananas?

**BRIAN:**
Carrots, you twit. I used to like gardening. Still do. You fond of it?

**ALEC:**
No, not me. I suppose vegetables are alright, but all these flower-beds and fancy pots and hanging baskets and stuff – people overdo it. Her husband's gone mad with all these garden gnomes all over the front garden. All digging and smoking pipes, looks like Snow White and the seven idiots. One of these gnomes is supposed to be fishing in the little pond, but someone has pinched his fishing rod, he's sitting there like this. (He demonstrates, his fists between his legs.)

**BRIAN:**
Steady on don't sit like that.

*(Alec removes his hands.)*

The barmaid saw you, she thinks she's on a promise.

**ALEC:**
I'd chuck 'em all out if they were mine, stupid they look.

**BRIAN:**
Oh, I quite like 'em. They're worth something now, those old ones. You can't get 'em now.

**ALEC:**
She hates 'em an' all.

**BRIAN:**
There was a time, you'd walk up a street which had front gardens, it was like walking through Munchkin Land. But they've nearly all disappeared. They're an endangered species. Like men's caps.

**ALEC:**
You want to get David Attenborough on it. Get some stickers in car windows – "Save the Gnome".

**BRIAN:**
And "Save the Cap". There's lots of things. "Save the Bedsock". Mind you. I wouldn't lose no sleep if the bedsock became extinct. But I wouldn't like my garden gnomes to die out.

**ALEC:**
Oh, you've got some yourself, have you?

**BRIAN:**
Had 'em for years. They were my Dad's.

**ALEC:**
Where do you live then?

**BRIAN:**
Just round the corner from here. Rosemary Avenue. Number 22.

*(Alec is rather taken aback, but tries to hide it.)*

**ALEC:**
Oh. Do you?

**BRIAN:**
Yes. I've never seen no other gnomes round here though. You say her garden's full of them? Where's that then?

**ALEC:**
Streatham.

**BRIAN:**
Streatham? That's bleeding miles away. You said she lived round here.

**ALEC:**
I was lying. Something to do. Giving the story local colour, like.

**BRIAN:**
You wasn't lying. You are now, but you

wasn't. What would you be doing round here if you'd just been to see her in Streatham? It's twenty-two Rosemary Avenue isn't it?

**ALEC:**
No it's not.

**BRIAN:**
Little blonde about five foot three, fat legs and a mole on her chin. I'm the man who comes home at half past four to a warm tea-pot. Pity I never thought to go and feel the bedclothes in the spare room.

**ALEC:**
*(With a laugh)* Oh, well, you've caught me out.

**BRIAN:**
Oh you admit it?

**ALEC:**
No you've caught me out fantasising. Like you do. Fantasise. You said you did. I do it all the time. I made it all up.

**BRIAN:**
Go on. What you doing round here then?

**ALEC:**
I sell double-glazing in my spare time.

**BRIAN:**
Oh dear. A liar and a double-glazing salesman. Things are getting worse.

**ALEC:**
I know your house with the gnomes –and I met your wife, nice respectable woman. I knocked on the door with me brochures, but she wasn't having any.

**BRIAN:**
Not double-glazing, no. What about your vegetables?

**ALEC:**
Look, that's all rubbish. I've never had an affair with a married woman. I live with my mother.

**BRIAN:**
And you've never lived with a married woman?

**ALEC:**
No.

**BRIAN:**
Is your mother married?

**ALEC:**
Was.

**BRIAN:**
There you are then.

**ALEC:**
Look, you know what I mean – it's all made up. Sounds good, makes me look macho. It's all fantasising, out of me head.

**BRIAN:**
You must be. Dangerous game though, isn't it? I could have thought you really was having it away with my wife couldn't I? I could have knocked your block off.

**ALEC:**
*(looking at him)* I doubt that.

**BRIAN:**
Well — I could have knocked your beer over. A man could get nasty you know, someone going around making free with his wife, insulting his gnomes. I could have seen red, gone berserk, if I really had been her husband.

**ALEC:**
*(amazed)* You what!

**BRIAN:**
Got you worried, though, didn't I?

**ALEC:**
You're not her husband?

**BRIAN:**
No – I live opposite. Number 25. Mr and Mrs Elphinstone their name is.

**ALEC:**
You sod, you was having me on weren't
you!

**BRIAN:**
Just fantasising – two can play at that
game. No, I just see her going in and out
the house. Snappy little dresser, she is. Bit
of alright.

**ALEC:**
What's he like, the husband?

**BRIAN:**
Looks very ordinary. Can't see what she
sees in him. But I bet with the right bloke
she'd be a right little goer.

**ALEC:**
She is, I'm telling you. Like a train.

**BRIAN:**
You what? I thought so. You're a crafty so-
and-so aren't you. It's true, isn't it!
*(He chuckles to himself)* I thought it was too
good a story. You and your double-glazing.

**ALEC:**
Well I panicked. I suddenly thought,
Christ, I'm sitting here with her husband
telling him all about it. So I just said
anything that came into me head. If you'd
kept it up I'd have got in a terrible mess.

**BRIAN:**
I didn't have the heart.

*(They both laugh.)*

**BRIAN:**
Well this calls for another pint. My round,
I'll get 'em.

*He half rises picking up the glasses. He looks
towards the bar, Then suddenly sits
again and quickly opens his newspaper and
hides behind it.)*

Oops! Look out, it's her.

**ALEC:**
Who?

**BRIAN:**
Your Mrs Elphinstone. She mustn't see me
with you, she knows I'm a neighbour –
her game would be up.

**ALEC:**
*(looking across)* Yes, it's her all right. She
ever been in here before?

**BRIAN:**
Never.

**ALEC:**
She's talking to the barmaid. She must be
looking for me. I'd better go. Been nice
talking to you mate.

**BRIAN:**
Yes, very pleasant evening. Mind how you
go.

**ALEC:**
Yeah. I think I'll keep me mouth shut
from now on. Ta-ta. *(He calls)* Jenny!

*(He exits.)*

*(Brian peers cautiously from his paper.)*

**BRIAN:**
*(to himself)* Two-timing bitch. So that's
why we've been getting so many bleedin'
vegetables.

*Black out.*

# MUM

*A play in two acts*

Having retired at the dawn of 1988, Ronnie was surprised to find himself putting pen to paper once more a decade later, writing his first stage play. The result was even more surprising, *Mum* being a poignant tragi-comedy, quite unlike anything else in his back catalogue. The play was written for Ronnie's actress daughter Charlotte. "Must put her on the map somehow I thought" Ronnie explained to the *Daily Telegraph* at the time. "And it was within my power to write something and probably get it put on."
The play (originally credited to "Richard Mervyn" although Ronnie did allow it ultimately to bear his name) had its debut run at the King's Head theatre in London in November 1998.

*Characters:*
*Alison*
*Dad*
*Bob*

# ACT ONE

The sitting-room of a two-room flat in the suburbs of London. A small dining-table, two chairs. At the back, a sideboard. At the front of the stage, the back of a gas fire. Down left, a wing armchair, facing obliquely upstage. Dressings and props as necessary. The whole effect is drab but tidy. Around this lit area, the stage is in darkness.

*(At the start of the play, the stage is empty. A distant train is heard briefly. A voice, offstage.)*

**ALISON:**
Mum! Mum! I'm back!

*(Then a door slams, offstage, and Alison enters.)*

*(She is twenty-eight, she wears jeans, and sweater underneath her top coat, which she removes during her first few lines.)*

I wasn't long was I? God, it's cold up there. I tell you, you're a lot better off here than up in that old cemetery. I changed your flowers. They look nice. Weeded round a bit.

*(A pause. She rubs her hands and warms them in front of the gas-fire.)*

Well Mum, it's a year ago today since the funeral. Doesn't seem anywhere near that long, does it? I'm glad I never went. Then I can always think of you still here with me, like you've always been. I don't like funerals, anyway. Vicar droning on about you as if he's known you all his life – most of the people he buries he's never seen upright. Such a sham, it strikes me. Complete sham. Anyway, enough of that. I'll go again next month as usual.

I thought I'd get down to sorting out all those papers and photos and things at long last. This drawer's stuffed full. You can't open it. *(She does, with difficulty.)*

Look at 'em! Not exactly a very efficient filing system is it. What would old Mr Farnley say about this lot. Bald-headed old twit. Young Mr Farnley's no better. He's nearly as bald as his Dad now Mum. He's only my age. Do you remember him at the office when you were there? Doubt if you would, eight years ago. He was just starting. A kid.

*(She comes across a photograph.)*

God, look at that. What do we look like?

*(She giggles and finds another, which makes her laugh louder.)*

Three of us on one donkey. No wonder the buggers sag in the middle.

*(Another photo.)*

I hate that one of me. Uncle Joe took that – Isle of Wight, wasn't it. Yes, he took that. Typical of him, that one is. As soon as any of us girls got into a bathing costume, out would come his camera. Snapping away when you weren't looking. Dirty old devil.

*(Another photograph.)*

Aah! There's poor old Fluffy. I do miss him. I cried for a week when he had to be put to sleep. Couldn't have kept him here. Not in an upstairs flat. Anyway, he wouldn't have liked coming to a town after living all his life in the country. House with a proper garden and a field right next door. He'd have hated this tatty place. For a start, there aren't forty-seven types of wild-life for him to chase. This place has got nothing. Nothing. It's a pity we ever moved. I know we had to, but still … *(a heavy sigh)* I don't know.

*(She rummages deeper.)*

A lot of this stuff can go. You were always a hoarder, Mum. The amount of paper bags I turned out of the larder before we moved. I mean, look *(holds up a piece of paper)* why you needed to keep a receipt for a bottle of Jeyes fluid from Boots. Oh, hold on, there's a message on the back.

Two pints please. *(She screws it up, fetches a waste paper basket, places it near her, dropping the paper in to it, speaking while she does so.)* Right. That's made a start. *(A newspaper.)* Queen's Jubilee. That'll never be missed *(into bin)*. Twelve sepia views of the Isle of Wight *(into bin)*. Insurance policies. Better have a look at these. Might be sitting on a fortune *(she looks at the first one)*. Oh no, this is Great Grandma's. "Paid in full to defray funeral expenses, thirty three pounds seventeen shillings and sixpence". You wouldn't get much of a send-off for that nowadays. I'll keep this. Great Grandma was always talking about this policy. She used to pay twopence a week all her life just so as she could be buried. Bit pointless I'd have thought. I mean they're going to have to bury you anyway aren't they? They wouldn't just leave you lying about. The man used to come to the door every week just for tuppence. Tuppence! I should have thought he spent more than that in shoe leather. Especially when people were out. Or hiding behind the door because they hadn't got the tuppence. Can't believe it, can you? Still, money's changed so much – men get three hundred pounds a week now. Ordinary working men. Funnily enough I was just reading about old Mr Churchill – they reckon that's about what he got when he saw England through the War. Mind you, they also said whisky was fifty p. a bottle, and them big cigars he smoked about ten p. a time. He could have a good night out for a pound. Anyway *(discarding the policy)* there's no hidden treasure there then. What's this. Ration book. God, what must it have been like? Here Mum, you didn't use all your clothing coupons. *(Turns pages.)* These would be meat coupon pages. They're all crossed out. Stamped "Astons", I remember that butcher, he was still there when I was a girl. No good now.

*(She throws the ration book into bin.)*

Oh, here's a guarantee. It's for my Trudy-doll. Well, that's for the twelve months ending October 1974. Do you remember my Trudy-doll? I had it for my birthday. You fed it with water in a tiny milk bottle and then it wetted itself *(she discards it)*. What's this doing in here? *(She holds a photo. She stares at it for a second.)* Photo of Bob. I thought I'd got all his photos in my room. In his uniform. *(tenderly)* Bless him. *(A pause.)* Bastard. Getting himself killed. Stupid, the way it happened Mum. I know you said get out and meet some body else, but you can't, you don't feel like it, not when something like that happens to someone dear to you. You just drift on, from day to day, hoping you'll get over it, but you don't. Then suddenly years have gone by, and you think – I'm over it. And by then it's too late. You've forgotten what it's like to go out with a man. You don't meet many, either, as an office cleaner, let's face it. They've nearly all gone home by the time I get there; and those that haven't look right through you. They think of you as just another attachment to the hoover. There was Nigel in dispatch; he was alright. Sort of. But he moved away before I finished the sweater I was knitting for him. I hope he got the parcel, he hasn't replied.

My trouble was, when you broke your hip, Mum, I shouldn't have let that stop me going out and meeting people. Boys. I shouldn't have stayed in with you all the time, I should have got on with my life. You were always very possessive, didn't like me bringing anyone home – jealousy. I suppose. You thought one of them was going to take me away from you. I didn't need to stay in. I should have been firmer. My own silly fault. So naturally, boys stopped asking me. All except Trevor. The missing link. My god, talk about Neanderthal. When he said to me if we had children the first thing he would do was build them a tree-house, I thought that's it! I couldn't ditch him fast enough.

But then that was seven years ago. Now I'm twenty-eight, Mum. And twenty-eight's not twenty-one. I ask myself, what is the future? Have I got a future? Or is it just going to be an endless repetition of the present? Drawing the dole once a fortnight, cleaning the offices of Messrs Redditch and Farnley three times a week, casual work, cash in the hand, no questions asked? Sitting in this God-forsaken flat, in this God-forsaken town, day in, day out, with nothing to look forward to but a fish and chip supper Friday night and the *Daily Mail* crossword? I know I've always got you to talk to, Mum, just like before you died, but although you're perfectly real to me, and I can see you so clearly, other people, well, they just can't, Mum.

And you know that as well as I do. You know we can't go out in the shops or anything, 'cos I'd just look as if I were talking to myself, they'd think who's that loony. You know I love you and am glad of your company, but I do so wish you were still properly alive. I miss our outings. Before you broke your hip we had some good times together. Our trips on the river; Longleat; even the bus rides. Then when you broke your hip, all that stopped. The money got tight, you couldn't move out of the house, so I had to take over your cleaner's job. Then, on top of it all, eighteen months ago, you got cancer. Everybody dies of cancer, don't they? Sooner or later. I expect I shall. It's such a terrible thing. You would have thought the hip would have been enough suffering for one person. Some people don't get anything. Just pop off, merry as a cricket, quick heart-attack, wallop, gone, no trouble. But not you. They decided you had to suffer. And so you did. And so did I, because of it.

*(She sighs. Stares at a scrap of paper, tears it up.)*

We don't know anybody here. I haven't got a single friend. No one. Days go by when I don't speak to a single soul all day. Except you of course, Mum. But nobody in the outside world, in the real world even notices that I exist. I'm so lonely, Mum. I'm lonely.

*(She breaks down into tears. Sobbing, she gets up and wanders over to the wind-up gramophone. She winds it, starts the record. It plays "The Sun Has Got His Hat On" in a cheery manner. She blows her nose violently, and returns to her seat. She picks from the pile of paper two comic postcards. She looks at the caption and chuckles in spite of herself. The next card makes her giggle even more. She shouts "FILTH" and tears them up and throws them into the bin, smiling. The music plays merrily on. She sings with it. She picks up a floppy hat and puts it on. She executes a few simple tap-dancing steps.)*

I should have kept up my tap lessons. Never fails to cheer me up, that old gramophone, best two pounds fifty I ever spent. I must go to the boot sale again. See if I can find another record.

*(She sits again. A distant train is heard.)*

Sorry about my little emotional outburst Mum. I'm all right really. I'm up and down. Mustn't give way to it though. That's what I tell myself. "Come on girl, put a sock in it". *(Throws away more papers.)* Do you know where that expression, put a sock in it, comes from? It's from the old gramophones, like that one *(indicates it)*. You couldn't control the volume, so if they were too loud people used to shove an old sock or duster or a pair of underpants in the soundbox to deaden it. A man's sock was the best. So when someone kept on talking about something, people would say "Put a sock in it" to shut 'em up. That's how the expression caught on. Just as well the sock worked best. Wouldn't sound the same saying put a pair of underpants in it. I read that in the doctor's. He said there's absolutely nothing wrong with me.

*(She looks up.)*

Mum? Mum, are you there? Mum? *(She gets up and looks at the chair)*
You are there. Sometimes. *(Hesitantly)* Sometimes I can't always see you. It worries me. You sort of fade. I wonder

whether it's something to do with me. My feelings about you. Don't ever leave me for good, will you. I don't want you to go. Don't think ever that I'd be better on my own, because I wouldn't. I need you here with me. *(She turns away from chair)* Well, you know that.

*(She goes to her handbag, takes out cigarettes and lights one. A distant train is heard.)*

I don't suppose you realise this is the first cigarette I've smoked since I came in. I'm trying to give them up. So far, completely unsuccessfully. Trouble is, I like smoking. I actually enjoy it. I mean, people who hate the fact that they smoke, it's easier for them. They say "God, I hate this filthy habit, it makes my hair smell, it makes me cough and wheeze in the morning, makes my breath smell – if only I could give it up – it's repulsive!" Well it's easier for them, isn't it? They've got the best reason in the world for packing it in. Also it's considered very anti-social nowadays. Even the tobacco companies try to put you off. In the old days they used to advertise on the packet how lovely they were. Now it just says "these are cigarettes – they'll kill you". But I love it. First cup of tea in the morning, the end of a good meal, it just rounds it off . I'd miss it so much. Life would be very grey without it. Mind you, it's not exactly Technicolour at the moment; but it would be a lot worse without a cigarette. So why am I giving them up, Mum? Do you know? I'd put on weight, which I don't need; I'd be tense, and nervy, more than I am now even; I'd be denying myself one of life's pleasures, which aren't too thick on the ground at this moment in time; so, all things considered my decision is *(she considers for a moment longer, then)* I shall smoke more. Which means I shall be less tense, I shan't put on more weight, and I shall carry on coughing. I know it's bad for my health Mum so I must make sure I keep up my exercises *(She starts to exercise her upper body, saying a rhyme as she does so.)*

Stand straight, upright pose. One of these

and one of those. *(Repeats this action)* Stretch up, touch toes. Two of these and one of those.

*(She repeats the touching toes once or twice. She suddenly stops at the "touch toe" position.)*

What's that under there?

*(She has caught sight of something under the sideboard. She crawls and retrieves a pound coin.)*

Oh, a pound. That was worth the effort. I wonder how long that's been there. That'll come in very handy. Every pound counts at the moment. And it's going to get worse, Mum. *(She sits.)* That thirteen hundred pounds is nearly gone, you know. I don't know how you did it. Week after week, year after year, sneaking a little bit of the housekeeping, keeping it secret from Dad, so that he wouldn't drink it all away. All that effort, all those lies, all that scrimping and saving. Thank god you did, it's been a godsend to us these last few years.

But now it's nearly gone, used up. A pound here, a pound there, you can't say I've been extravagant with it, but it's gone. We'll have to just manage on my dole money, and the cleaning wage. At least that's in the hand, no PAYE to eat a hole in it. God knows what would happen if the dole people found out. We shall just have to see, that's all. The phone sales thing is more or less a waste of time, just based on commission, because you hardly ever make a sale, and if you do it's such a piddling amount they pay you. Hardly pays for your damn phone bill. We may have to give up the phone Mum; if I give up doing the phone sales we don't need the expense of it.

What I should really be doing is getting myself a proper job. Nine to five in some big office. I can type. Or a big shop. The Co-op's always advertising for sales staff. I could do the job just as well as the bimbos you see in there. The trouble is I haven't done a real job for so long. Since you first broke your hip I've always stayed home to look after you. Then when you got cancer you were a full-time job. Now you are through all that, and you don't need my help any more, I've sort of got out of the habit of going out to work. I just don't really feel inclined. I don't feel up to it. I'm not sure I could face it. *(She sighs. She picks up phone book, which has a bookmark in it, opens it at the page and picks up the phone and dials.)* I won't get any sales if I don't dial any numbers. Hello. Mrs Dillinger? Good-day to you, I wonder if you can help me, I'm carrying out a survey. Well yes, it does have to do with making the most of insulation certainly, it's – Pardon? Oh, you have double-glazing, yes, I see. Sorry to have bothered you Mrs, er – yes, thank you. Bye.

*(She dials again.)*

They're mostly on to this survey lark nowadays *(she waits)*. Nobody in. Hello? Mrs Dimchurch? Good-day to you. I wonder if you can help me, I'm carrying out a survey on heating in the home, I wonder if I … *(puts down phone)* Yes, they spot it a mile off.

*(Picks up and dials next number.)*

They'll have to think of another method. *(She waits)* Hello? Mrs Dinitrioskova? Dinitrioskova, sorry. Good-day, Mrs Dinitrioskova I wonder if you can help me. Help. Assist me. I'm carrying out a survey *(speaks slowly and clearly)* carrying out, carrying out a survey. Survey. Is there someone there who speaks English? Yes, I know you do – is there someone there who speaks more English? No, I think I've got the wrong number. The wrong number. Wrong, Oh, forget it. (puts down phone) I'd have never got past "efficient insulation" with her. *(Dials again)* This is a soul-destroying job, Mum, it really is. Hello? Mrs Dipstaff? Oh, Mr Dipstaff. Is your wife there? She's not. No, she doesn't know me, no. I'm carrying out a survey, and *(she reacts)* you're what? Am I what?

*(shocked, she slams down the phone)* Disgusting. Well, that's it. I'm finished with this bloody job once and for all. Sorry Mum, but it makes you swear, it's so futile. I'm finished with it. I don't have to put up with that sort of treatment for three pounds a sale. We'll have the 'phone taken out. No one phones us up anyway. I'll get on to British Telecom in the morning. *(She is sitting down again, sorting the papers.)* I'd better keep this one Mum. *(She reads)* "Grand Thanksgiving Dance, Base Camp U.S. Air Force, KETTERING." That was nineteen forty-four. I remember you telling me about this. Do you remember telling me about this dance? Your first date with a G.I. you were eighteen, you met him on the bus coming home from work. He must have been a fast worker, you only used to travel five stops. They were fast though, these boys, so I've heard. Elsie, that girl at school said her mother got pregnant by one of them. Mind you, her bus ride was more than five stops. She must have gone all the way. They used to look very smart though, didn't they? In their uniforms. Made our lot look scruffy, by the looks of the photos. Look at your cousin Walter here, in his army greatcoat. It looks too big for him. He'd slip through that if you hung him up. Very rough material, as well. Big rough uniforms, with little weak men inside 'em. I'm surprised we won the war at all in those clothes. You can see why the girls preferred the G.I's – they had nice well-cut smooth uniforms. Plus all the nylons and chocolate and chewing gum they used to hand out – I don't blame you for falling for all that. The pity is you didn't hang on to one of them, instead of finishing up with Dad. That's where you made your mistake Mum – you could have spent your life on a ranch in Arizona or somewhere. And I would have been called Betty Mae and worn a cowboy hat and rode my horse all day.

Bit different from this. Eh Mum? Bit different.

*(Picks up soiled packet containing ordinary*

*playing cards.)*

These cards are the ones we used to tell our fortunes with. With the adverts on the back.

*(She clears a space on the table)*

I can't remember how we used to set them out. Oh, that's it. *(She lays out cards)* That goes in the middle. Deal them out round there. Now, that's my card, and these influence that one. One at the head, one each side, one at the foot. Turn my card up. Seven of hearts. Middling sort of person. That's about right. Count seven in *(counts out seven, turns up the seventh card).* Jack. A man in my life. Tall dark stranger? Card at the head of the circle – spade, but only a four. Short dark stranger. Card at the foot? *(Turns it.)* Club, short dark stranger with a club foot. I'm not doing this right. *(She collects up the cards.)* Anyway. I'm not sure I want to know the future, particularly. Perhaps I do. It would have been nice to have something to look forward to. You might find, when you know the future, that there wasn't anything to look forward to. Then, it would be better not to know.

*(A train is heard.)*

I wonder where that train's going to? I used to love going on a train. I haven't been on one for years. They're so expensive. I don't mean the Underground. Real trains, that go through the countryside, with the fields on either side, I love the fields, Mum. I miss them. The autumn trees. Leaves blowing up the road. And here we are in sunny Dalston. Beer cans blowing up the road. *(A pause.)* Some of the men round here are repulsive. Ones you see in the street. Scruffy, dirty. I see some of them hanging about doing damn-all, and I think "Why don't you get a flaming job." Hard work never killed anybody. It certainly never killed my father. He never did any. God! What a waster he was Mum. He wasted his own life and he wasted

yours. Oh, I know why you married him. He was charming. He was also a drunk, a gambler and a liar. From the first moment he met you he lied to you. About how much money he'd got, about his qualifications as a skilled engineer and lathe operator. He could no more operate a lathe than fly in the air. But he talked you into marrying him and from then on he made your life a misery. Never gave you enough money – staggered in every Friday night, leaving half his pay packet at the pub on the way home. Then by Tuesday he was trying to borrow the rest of it back from you to put on some horse or chat up some tart in the Fox and Hounds. I hated the way he treated you. I hated his snide remarks, the way he talked to you as if you knew nothing and he knew everything, the smart-arse. Most of all I hated the way he ignored me. No interest in anything I had to say. "Done your homework dear? Off to bed then, your mother's tired." "Tired of you you dosey layabout," I wanted to say, but I daren't, for fear of his temper. He could be vicious when his temper was up. I used to lie in bed and think, why doesn't she leave him? But you never did. You just got more and more desperate, until you were at the end of your tether.

And then, suddenly, as if by magic – suddenly, we were on our own, Mum. He was gone. That was the best, best feeling I ever remember, realising we were rid of him. He'd gone! It was like some great wound suddenly healing up.

*(A figure has appeared in the shadows at the back of the stage. It is Dad. He is wearing rather down-at-heel clothes – jacket and flat cap. He looks rather old-fashioned with a moustache and rather outdated long sideburns. She has not yet seen him.)*

It was like some great weight had been lifted from our lives. Do you remember that feeling Mum? *(She suddenly realises something)* Mum? Mum, where have you gone? *(She is panicky now.)* Mum, don't go! Where are you?

**DAD:**
*(still in shadow)* Ali. It's me.

**ALISON:**
*(turning, shocked to see him)* What do you want?

**DAD:**
Ali, it's your dad.

**ALISON:**
I know who you are. I said what do you want?

**DAD:**
Somebody was talking about me.

**ALISON:**
Me and Mum were.

**DAD:**
I thought so. My ears were burning.

**ALISON:**
I should have thought everything was burning where you came from.

**DAD:**
Ah, don't be like that …

**ALISON:**
The name's Alison.

**DAD:**
Where is your mother?

**ALISON:**
She's gone – you've frightened her off. She sensed you before I did. If you've upset her I'll never forgive you. I'll never forgive you anyway, the way you treated her.

**DAD:**
Now, there's two sides to this, Ali, be fair.

**ALISON:**
Alison! It's bloody Alison! God knows, you ought to know, you gave it me. "What's your favourite name, Jack?" Says my mother. You looked up from your newspaper and said "Alison", so Mum thought she'd call me Alison. She found

out later it was a name you'd just read in the *News of the World*. You'd no interest in naming me, or anything else about me ever since I was born. Mum told me.

**DAD:**
And you'd believe her instead of me?

**ALISON:**
You're joking! You wouldn't know that it was like to tell the truth. You were always a liar. A drunk, and a waster, and a liar.

**DAD:**
Now hold on …

**ALISON:**
We don't want you here. We never did. We were glad to see the back of you when you went. What are you doing here?

**DAD:**
I don't know. I seemed to just arrive here. You must have sent for me.

**ALISON:**
Don't talk so daft. I can't send for you. How can I send for you? Where from?

**DAD:**
I don't know where from. I've no recollection of things like that.

**ALISON:**
You must have some idea where you are. Are you in heaven or hell? Is it cool and sunny or hot and smoky?

**DAD:**
It's not like that at all

**ALISON:**
Well, wherever it is just go back to it. We're better off on our own thank you. We don't need you. When you went out of our lives it was a joyous moment. We were overjoyed to get rid of you.

**DAD:**
That hurts me to hear you say that Alison.

**ALISON:**
Good.

**DAD:**
Matter of fact I don't remember walking out on you and your mother, you know.

**ALISON:**
Twenty-second of October 1986. That date is engraved on my memory.

**DAD:**
Was that when it was? I remember coming home one night from the Fox, I'd had a few.

**ALISON:**
You'd had several more than a few, Dad, you'd had a lot.

**DAD:**
Well. Anyway, I got to the front door, and it was locked. So I knocked the door.

**ALISON:**
You banged on the door. You thumped the door and shouted.

**DAD:**
And you opened it, and I came in, and you were there, your mother was nowhere in sight, and you tore into me – I've never heard you talk like that in your life, not to me, any road. And I followed you down the hall …

**ALISON:**
You pushed me down the hall.

**DAD:**
And then, suddenly there was a blinding light, like a searchlight switched on. Bright, bright light.

*(A pause.)*

And then I don't remember anything else. My mind's a blank. I have no memories at all. Not yesterday, or the day before, or last week, or anything. Its all a grey mist. What happened that night? Did I sober up?

**ALISON:**
You just walked out. You eventually left the house.

**DAD:**
What, just went?

**ALISON:**
Without a word. And we rejoiced, Mum and I. We clung to each other and laughed and jumped all around the kitchen.

**DAD:**
Funny, I don't remember anything about it.

**ALISON:**
I do. It was the happiest moment of my life.

**DAD:**
Alison, don't. *(He goes to sit.)*

**ALISON:**
Don't sit there! That's Mum's chair!

*(He stands again.)*

I've told you, we don't want you here. Go back to where you came from. Mum hates you, and so do I. You rotten bastard.

**DAD:**
Alison, I'm your father.

**ALISON:**
You were never a father to me. I don't know how you can say you were ever a father to me. I had a mother, and I loved her. That's all I had. We were a one-parent family. I had no father.

**DAD:**
Listen, I've had enough of this. You watch it, my girl.

**ALISON:**
I'm not your girl. You never had a girl, Jack! *(She spits out the name. Then, suddenly weary, she sighs.)*

Just go. Go on, get out. I've had enough of this.

**DAD:**
I don't know how you can talk to me like this.

**ALISON:**
Well I can. I can say anything I like. Not when you were alive, I had to keep it all bottled up, for fear you took it out on Mum. But you can't touch either of us now. You're dead.

**DAD:**
How do you know I'm dead?

**ALISON:**
Because you couldn't just appear in this room, just appear from nowhere, without remembering a thing, could you? You'd have had to have taken a train and two buses to get here.

**ALISON:**
You're sober aren't you.

**DAD:**
Yes.

**ALISON:**
Well that never happened when you were alive did it? You didn't know the meaning of the word.

**DAD:**
Now listen. It's about time you learnt a few home truths. Do you know why I was never at home? Because there was no life at home. There was no life in your mother. There wasn't one jot of affection, or friendliness, or interest in anything I had to say. She would drear around the house, never a smile, never a word, except to nag me about some bloody trivial thing or other. At least in the pub there was a barmaid who'd give you a few laughs.

**ALISON:**
And anything else you asked for probably.

**DAD:**
Sex, you mean? S.E.X.? Your mother couldn't even spell it. From the moment we got married not a thought of it ever crossed her mind. I did my duty by her, I stood by her, married her, and that's what I got! Nothing.

**ALISON:**
What do you mean "Stood by her"?

**DAD:**
When she got pregnant with you. We weren't married.

**ALISON:**
You weren't? *(She is taken aback, shocked)*

**DAD:**
So just be careful who you're calling a bastard in future. You could have been one yourself, if it hadn't been for me. And for doing the decent thing, all I got from your mother was the cold shoulder. She didn't have an ounce of feeling, of love for me ever.

**ALISON:**
Did it ever occur to you that you didn't deserve any love? You have to earn it, you know, love and affection, you can't just assume its your right just because you put a wedding ring on her finger.

**DAD:**
She loved you. She was always cuddling and fussing over you, and you didn't seem to be doing much in the way of earning it – just bawling your head off most of the time. You were a miserable baby and you've turned out to be a miserable woman, by the look of it. Just like your mother.

**ALISON:**
She might not have been so miserable if you'd tried a bit. If you'd sacrificed a few of you're little pleasures, like boozing and gambling, in order to give her enough money every week to scrape by on. Gambling is a bloody fool's game.

**DAD:**
I had some bad luck on the horses.

**ALISON:**
Did you ever see a poor book-maker? Have you ever known Mr Littlewood down to his last penny?

**DAD:**
Horses got me into trouble once.

**ALISON:**
Once? Every week.

**DAD:**
I mean serious trouble. Your mother never knew about it. At least I was decent enough to keep it from her.

**ALISON:**
Like the housekeeping money.

**DAD:**
Are you going to listen?

**ALISON:**
Go on then, tell us about this trouble. I'm looking forward to hearing about it.

**DAD:**
Well, as I said, I'd been very unlucky with the horses for months, and eventually I was owing the bookie nearly £250, and one day he said he wanted it. It had gone on long enough, he said, and if I didn't pay up in a week he might have to send some friends of his round to see that I did. I knew he meant business because there'd been a previous incident involving one of his clients a few months earlier. The man was in hospital for a fortnight. Well, I hadn't got any money, so I had to go out and get some. I broke into the back of Travers the Jewellers. I didn't take any goods, just what was in the till. It was on a Friday, two weeks before Christmas, so I netted about three hundred quid. I thought I'd cut the burglar alarm, but it was one of those ones that phone up the police when you cut the wire, so when I came out there were two policemen who offered me a lift to the station. Up before the beak, fined four hundred pounds with two weeks to pay. Otherwise three months in jail. I'd got away with nothing, and still owed the bookie.

**ALISON:**
I never noticed you absent from home for three months. Godsend.

**DAD:**
No. I paid the fine.

**ALISON:**
Where did you get the money?

**DAD:**
I stole it.

**ALISON:**
Oh my god.

**DAD:**
I made sure I chose somewhere without a burglar alarm. I got away with it an' all. Posh dress shop it was. Nearly seven hundred quid. Paid the fine, paid the bookie, and put the rest on a horse. It lost.

**ALISON:**
*(She stares at him.)* And I suppose you're proud of that little escapade, aren't you? You arrogant sod.

**DAD:**
Hey! Less of that.

**ALISON:**
I hate you. I loathe you.

**DAD:**
I'm not bothered.

**ALISON:**
You've frightened Mum away. I don't know if she'll come back. I'm sick of looking at your stupid ugly face, just go back to where you came from and leave me in peace.

**DAD:**
*(Walks a little way off, stands in the shadows.)* I don't know where I'm

supposed to go.

**ALISON:**
Out of my life.

**DAD:**
*(He turns, walks disconsolately away.)* 'Bye
Alison. *(She doesn't reply; just watches him
as he disappears into the gloom. She turns
away.)*

**ALISON:**
Mum? He's gone Mum. You can come
back now. I don't think we'll see any more
of him. Do come back Mum, don't let
him drive you away for good, I couldn't
bear it.

*(She takes the chair from behind the table,
draws it near to her mothe'rs chair, and sits,
watching it, anxiously. After a long moment,
she looks relieved.)*

Oh Mum. I'm beginning to see you again.
Oh I'm so glad! *(Tears come to her eyes.)* I'm
sorry to cry, Mum, but you're everything
to me, I'm terrified of losing you. Tears of
happiness, really, that's all. *(She smiles.)*
Now, I promise I'll cheer up. *(She goes to
table, replaces her chair.)* I don't seem to be
getting very far with this load of junk do
I? I expect it will all finish up back in the
drawer. *(Picks up bundle of papers.)* Look,
here's all my drawings you kept when I
first went to school. I used to love
drawing. Later on, in senior school that
art teacher said I ought to go to art school,
do you remember? I'd have loved that. I
used to see them coming out of the
college, and they'd come upstairs on the
bus, and I used to think I'd love to be one
of them. They all looked so interesting, so
lively with their long straggly hair and
scarves and those big portfolios they were
carrying. Imagine spending all day
drawing, I used to think. But, of course,
we had no money for that sort of lovely
life. I could have won a scholarship, but
there's all the paper and paints and art
books and drawing books and easels and
all those beautiful things you have to
provide. There wasn't a hope in hell of

you finding that sort of money out of the
miserable pittance he gave you. So I just
had to leave school and start work at
Hellermans.

*(A pause as she thinks about the dreary office
she worked in.)*

Still, at least I learned to type. Which
reminds me, where's Friday's local paper?

*(She goes and finds it.)*

I said I'd look for a proper job didn't I.
Now then, let's see.

*(She reads for a few seconds, silent except for
the occasional grunt at something she reads.)*

Waitress. Can't do waitress, 'cos of the
cleaning job. Anyway, it's not a proper
job, I want full-time. I might give up the
cleaning if I can find a day job. I might be
able to afford a T.V. again – rented. Be nice
to sit and watch television, not have to go
out in the evenings working, 'specially on
these cold nights. It seems to be winter
nearly all the time here.

*(She reads.)*

No Co-op job. They know when they're
on to a good thing, those girls. Cushy. Do
you remember when I worked at that
warehouse for a week? United Dairies,
wasn't it. I think it's gone now. Groceries
warehouse, tinned and bottled goods.
There was one man there, loader, big
hairy fat man he was, always looked dirty.
I saw him sitting on a packing case, and
he turned round, reached into a case of
marmalade, took out a jar, unscrewed it,
stuck his finger in it, dug out a big lump
of marmalade and ate it. Then he screwed
the lid back and put it back where it came
from. Nobody said anything, just carried
on talking about football or whatever. I
just walked out, never went back, and
never ever again bought a jar of Golden
Shred. It does make you wonder how
people can go through life being so filthy,
and uncaring. He'd no thought for the

721

person who bought that jar. He couldn't give a bugger. There's a lot of repulsive people in this world, Mum. Ugh. Makes me sick to think of it.

*(She shivers at the thought. She reads, then looks up from the newspaper.)*

You know where I'd like to work Mum? Bread shop. The smell of all that new crusty bread is so wonderful. And all those fancy cakes and sticky buns. Women who work in bread shops always look contented.

*(She is reading again.)*

"Assistant required for chemists. Messrs Reed and Co. 41 King Street. Hours 9.15 to 5.30, half day Saturday. Experience not necessary, but knowledge of cosmetics an advantage." Well, I know what they are. They're paints for your face. What else is there to know? You're not going to put eye shadow on your mouth or lipstick on your eyelids are you? Mind you, some of them look as if they have. All colours of the rainbow. I can paint, and I'm not colour-blind. I'll phone up.

*(She goes and dials, speaking aloud for the last four numbers.)*

… 7-6-6-8 *(she waits.)*

I expect it's gone. *(She waits.)*

Hello? I'm ringing to enquire about the job as assistant. Has it gone? Oh, good, I … Twenty-eight. Just. No, haven't got one at the moment. Yes, cosmetics would be fine, I-er-studied them at Art College.

*(Cups hands over phone, and raises eyes to Heaven.)*

God forgive me. Hello? Yes, still here, sorry. Do I what? Yes, I do smoke, actually, but … No, well naturally I understand I couldn't smoke at work, I wouldn't expect … well, why is that?

*(She listens for a few seconds.)*

But … *(she listens again.)*

I see. Well, that's that then isn't it? Thank you. Goodbye. *(She puts down phone.)* That's ridiculous. They insist on employing only non-smokers.

*(She slumps down in her chair.)*

This smoking thing's going a bit too far. They'll be making it illegal soon. All this business about the rights of the individual, in the name of democracy. It strikes me the more democracy we get, the less freedom we have. You can't smoke on the underground, you can't smoke in hotels, in cinemas, in taxi-cabs, in shops, some restaurants don't allow smoking! I ask you, if you can't have a cigarette after a meal out, what are things coming to? Notices everywhere "Thank you for not smoking". I'm just waiting to see one on the door of a tobacconist's.

*(A pause.)*

If the Government want to stop people smoking, I've always thought that they should put up the age limit by one year, every year. So next year it would be seventeen, then eighteen, and so on. This means that if you're fifteen you'd never be allowed to – you'd never catch up. But that's alright, what you've never had, you'll never miss. But all the people who were already smokers could always keep ahead, because they get older each year, and keep pace with the age limit. They'd be O.K. until they died. Or smoking killed them. It's foolproof. It'll never happen though. It's too easy. No, they'll just keep on making more and more places where you can't smoke, till eventually smokers will become a minority group. Then someone will take up their cause, all right. It's all mental. The world's gone mad. I wonder what they'll try to stop next. Sex, probably. All the places where they've got "Thank you for not smoking" signs they'd have "Thank you for not having sex" signs as well. There'd be a few complaints about that. You couldn't have sex in hotels, in cinemas, in taxi-cabs ...

*(She puts the newspaper aside.)*

There's nothing in there. Waste of time looking. Just have to keep on with the cleaning job. It's so dreary, though. I sit here all day, bored, waiting to go to the office, then when I get there it's more boring than here, I can't wait to get home. I'd rather be bored here than there any day.

It wouldn't be so bad if I had a husband to come home to. "Nice day at the office, dear? Tell me all about it." "Well, I emptied all the waste-paper baskets, cleaned the wash-basins, that's always exciting. Then I hoovered round Mr Farnley's desk, then I hoovered round Mr Braithwaite, 'cos he's always still sitting at his desk. Then I dusted round and finished by sweeping the front step. Then I came home, where's my Martini?"

Old Braithwaite had nodded off the other day, Mum. The hoover woke him up, and he didn't quite know where he was. He said "Morning Mrs Ferguson, you're early" then he realised I wasn't Mrs Ferguson, and he was so embarrassed, he went to the toilet. What I mean is he went to the gentlemen's toilet.

*(She sighs, picks up some mending, and works on it. A train is heard.)*

I wish there were some men there. They're all ancient since Nigel left before I'd finished knitting his sweater. He's only been gone a month, it seems like a year. I hope he likes it. He might give me a ring. Perhaps I'll leave the phone for another week or so before I have it disconnected. It would be nice if he took me out for a meal. Wouldn't have to be anywhere fancy. It's not the actual food that you go for, it's the company. Auntie Doris used to say that when we went there. Mind you, with her food she had to. And when you

think about it, her company wasn't up to much, either. Dull. Dreary. When you look around you. Most people are dull, leading drab dreary lives, and yet they seem content. Content to make a little nest for themselves, and settle down and bring up two or three kids, all dreary. Why don't you ever meet exciting people, like you read about in the papers, or see on television? Or used to, rather, when we had one. People like Robert Redford or Michael Heseltine or Noel Edmunds? Well, perhaps not Noel Edmunds, but the other two. You never see anyone like Robert Redford walking down the High Street do you Mum? Plenty who look like Lenny Henry – but no glamorous exciting people. The answer I suppose is that Dalston High Street is a dump, and no glamorous people would be seen dead within a mile of it. Chelsea would be another story. Couldn't walk ten yards without tripping over some celebrity or other down there. But not where we live Mum. Your life was always dreary and drab wasn't it? Even when we lived in the country. You had a rough time of it. He gave you such a rough time. Every day I saw it in your face.

*(A pause – she continues to sew.)*

It was a bit of a shock earlier on when he turned up. I don't blame you for making yourself scarce. Bastard! I don't know what brought him here but I'll tell you what – he hasn't changed. He's still as smarmy and cocky as ever. Only thing different about him was he was sober. Well I suppose he would be. They wouldn't have any pubs where he is – up or down.

*(She indicates Heaven and Hell with a pointing finger.)*

I don't suppose you knew anything about him getting caught breaking and entering did you. He managed to wriggle his way out of that. Luck was always on his side – but then it often is with villains.

*(She rummages through the documents.)*

There's something else he told me as well. I saw it here somewhere *(she finds document)*. Yes, here we are. Your marriage certificate.

*(She reads it.)*

Yes, he was telling the truth for once. Married May 17th 1967. I was born four months later. I wonder why you never told me I was nearly illegitimate. Not that it matters a hoot these days. These days family's more important than the wedding. Quite right too, I say. I wish I could have a family. If Bob hadn't got himself killed I could have a child of school age by now. It was so unnecessary, his death. If it wasn't so tragic it would be laughable. I mean, joining the army as a career, well you expect one day you might have to fight for your country, and you would have to prepare yourself to be killed, if the worst came to the worst. But to get run over by a bus coming out of the barrack gates is ludicrous. I shall never forget his Grandma at the funeral "Well, thank god he was wearing his uniform, his mother will get his pension" she said. "Every cloud has a silver lining" she said. Not for me it hasn't, I thought. What I thanked God for was the few precious times we'd had together. And we did have some lovely times. I've never really told you everything about me and Bob, Mum. I used to be embarrassed, I suppose. Also I didn't want to share everything with you, not all my secrets. But now it doesn't matter any more. I can tell you things now. More things. Things I couldn't tell you when you could question me, and get things out of me. And Bob's dead and gone, it doesn't matter anymore. I'm not embarrassed any more.

*(She settles her chair nearer to her mother's.)* I'm going to tell you something now that I've never told a soul. Only me and Bob ever knew about it. Oh God!

*(She jumps up, looks at her watch.)*

Sorry, Mum, it will have to wait a while. I must get those library books back before they shut, or I'll get a fine. Can't afford fines at the free library, otherwise it's not free, is it?

*(She puts on her coat.)*

I might get a bit of something for my tea while I'm at it. Ten to five. I shan't be long.

*(She grabs two library books from the sideboard.)*

I'll see you in about quarter of an hour, alright? Ta-ta. *(She is gone.)*

# ACT TWO

*The same, fifteen minutes later. She enters, shivering. She carries two different books, a newspaper and a small carrier bag containing food for her tea.*

**ALISON:**
God, do you know inside that library it's actually much colder than it is in the street. You go in out of the freezing weather and you notice a distinct chill. It's as cold as charity it really is. That librarian woman – I think she's actually frozen to the chair. I've never seen her standing up. And that poor little thin girl who puts the books away looks absolutely perished. Pretty little thing she is – blonde hair, blue eyes, blue hands, blue face. I can't see her surviving the winter. She's got a terrible cough. She keeps trying to stifle it 'cos of the silence rule in there.

*(She has taken off her coat and is warming her hands by the gas fire.)*

I wonder why you always have to be quiet in a library, it's as if people can't read unless everywhere's silent. People read on trains, on buses. It's not quiet on a bus. Or a tube train. Terrible racket. Yet you see all these men sitting reading the *Sun*, or the

*Daily Mail.* Usually the Sun, all hurrying past page three. Saving it for later. And yet in these libraries you're all creeping about, frightened to clear your throat. Anyway. Got two more books. The new Kingsley Amis and this one by Andrea Bates, called *Shout It Aloud.* I'm surprised they even let that in the library. Now then. Tea.

*(She goes offstage. We hear a crash of saucepans. She shouts out.)*

God! I must clean out these damn cupboards!

*(We hear kettle being filled, gas lights. She returns carrying packet of sliced bread and butter dish.)*

No room to swing a cat in that kitchen. I suppose I shouldn't say that, being a member of the R.S.P.C.A.

*(Gets teapot out of the sideboard. Also plate and knife, cup and saucer.)*

Got myself a bit of ham *(she unwraps it, regards it).* They could have cut that thinner. If they'd tried very, very hard.

*(She sits, begins to make herself a sandwich.)*

I was going to tell you about me and Bob, Mum. As I say, I've never told you before because I was embarrassed. But you might as well know the truth. Then perhaps you'll realise why I couldn't just go out and find someone else. The fact is, Mum, we were much closer than you ever knew. I mean, I know you guessed I was in love with him, but I think you thought it would blow over. Because you weren't that keen on him from the start. I knew that. But you didn't know him like I did. He was so kind. Not only to me, but to other people who he didn't need to be kind to, just little things. But I noticed them. And he was funny, and quite sort of light-hearted all the time. He cheered me up so every time I went out with him. Well, you knew that. You could tell when I came home at night.

What you didn't know – what I never dared tell you, was that we had a relationship. We actually made love. But only once. It was the time when you went over to see your sister, and you stayed the night. Bob came over to the house, and I cooked him a meal, and he brought a bottle of white wine. I think we both knew what was going to happen, but neither of us mentioned it. But of course it did happen. In our house. In your bed Mum. My parent's double bed. And from that moment we both knew we'd marry. He was just as mad about me as I was about him. We were never apart. It was so – smashing *(she sighs).* But it wasn't long before we were brought down to earth. I missed my monthly period. Oh dear God I was terrified. Bob was a bit taken aback, but he said Well, look on the bright side, now we'll have to get married soon. It wasn't anything nowadays, he said, getting married with a child on the way. But I wasn't worried what other people would say, I was worried what you would say. I felt I'd really let you down, ever since I was thirteen you'd kept on to me about not letting a man touch me, and now this. I couldn't face it. I said to Bob "I can't face it, I'll have to have an abortion." This made him cross, and we argued for three or four weeks and then guess what? I got my period. Oh! Boy! I was so relieved.

*(The kettle is heard to whistle.)*

I went round singing the whole day.

*(She goes off, and as the kettle's whistle dies away, we hear her singing to the tune "The Sun Has Got His Hat On".)*

"Oh, I'm not really pregnant, shout hip hip hooray, I'm not really pregnant so I'm coming out to play."
*(She returns with teapot and jug of milk.)*

So of course, we didn't have to rush into marriage. It's a pity we didn't. Of course, we weren't to know he was going to go and get himself killed. Anyway, I put my foot down after that. I said never again, until after we're married. I wasn't risking the worry of that again. It used to drive him mad every time he came home on leave. He used to get lot of leave. Well, he was only at Basingstoke. He used to ring up and say "I'm getting leave next week" and I used to say "Yes and that's all you're getting." He used to get annoyed, but he knew I was right. He respected me. He was so good. So nice.

*(She pulls herself together with an effort, pours tea for herself.)*

No good crying over spilt milk. Bloody stupid expression that is. Now, let's see what we're missing on television because we haven't got a television.

*(Reads newspaper.)*

*Blind Date.* Repeat. *You've Been Framed.* Clive Anderson interviews Tony Slattery. Oh well, things could be worse. We could be watching television.

*(Turns page.)*

Horoscopes. Let's see. Sagittarius.

*(She takes a large bite of her sandwich, and reads aloud with her mouth full, so that we cannot decipher what she says.)*

"With Saturn rising in conjunction with Venus, tomorrow is not a day to be reckless in decisions involving the heart or pocket book. Keep spending to an absolute minimum, and be wary of strangers of the opposite sex. Avoid evening invitations."

*(She swallows her mouthful so that we don't hear "avoid evening invitations".)*

I didn't understand a word of that.

*(Reads again – this time audibly, the end of paragraph.)*

"Avoid evening invitations". Humph. Pub will be empty tomorrow then. It's so

stupid – these things can't be correct for everybody, stands to reason. At the bottom here there's one for everybody, look. "On a general level, the presence of Venus rising indicates a meeting with a person or persons of particular interest in work and/or romance." Well I never. The world's going to be full of fascinating people tomorrow Mum. Make a change, won't it? God, what rubbish.

*(She discards paper, and sips her tea.)*

They'll all be just as dull. Dull to me, anyway. Thinking about Bob makes you realise what you're missing. Not that he was God's gift to Woman or anything like that. He never thought he was. But he was kind and polite and he cared for me. And he looked nice in his uniform.

*(Bob appears in the shadows. He is in army uniform. He stays in partial darkness for a while, as she continues.)*

Whatever possessed him to join the army in the first place? He said it was to get away from his previous girlfriend, that Wendy. I'm not sure I ever believed him though.

**BOB:**
*(speaking from the shadows)* Excuse me.

*(She rises, shocked to see him.)*

**ALISON:**
Bob! Oh my God, Bob!

**BOB:**
I'm sorry to intrude. *(He approaches into the light.)*

**ALISON:**
Oh Bob. *(She slumps down and covers her face with her hands for a moment, then looks again at him.)*

It's really you. I can't believe it.

**BOB:**
Do you know me? You seem to know me.

**ALISON:**
Bob it's me. Alison. Alison, Bob. *(She rises.)*

**BOB:**
Alison. That's right – Alison. And I'm Bob. Sorry, I'm confused. I can't seem to remember anything.

**ALISON:**
What's happening? My father was here. I was talking to Mum about him. And now, we were just talking about you, and here you are.

**BOB:**
Yes.

*(He nods smiling, but confused.)*

**ALISON:**
It's been such a long time Bob. How – how have you been?

**BOB:**
I – well, I honestly don't know.

**ALISON:**
It's so wonderful to see you. I'd better sit down.

**BOB:**
Yes. Yes, it's coming back. A minute or two ago I'd had no idea who I was or where I was. Alison, my dearest, I'm beginning to remember.

**ALISON:**
I've missed you so much.

**BOB:**
We were going to be married. Where has all my memory gone. We were going to get married, and then –

**ALISON:**
And then you got yourself killed Bob.

**BOB:**
That's it. That's right. That's why I can't seem to remember. Nothing since then. Not a thing. But before that, yes things are coming back.

*(He points at her, remembering.)*

I was in the army.

*(He looks at his outstretched sleeve, then looks at his uniform.)*

It looks as if I still am.

**ALISON:**
Oh I've missed you so much. It's seven years, you know.

**BOB:**
Is it? Seven years? It seems like yesterday. That's because there's been nothing in between. You'll have to help me remember things Alison, it's all very hazy. What's been happening to you?

**ALISON:**
Nothing. Nothing to speak of.

**BOB:**
We never got married, did we?

**ALISON:**
No. If only we had, I was just saying to Mum, it's something I've regretted ever since. Not only because I could have had a child, but I would have felt respectable, somehow. A married woman, with a family to bring up. A respectable woman.

**BOB:**
My dear, you would have been a widow.

**ALISON:**
*(with spirit)* I could have been a merry widow instead of an old maid!

**BOB:**
You're not an old maid. You're only twenty-nine.

**ALISON:**
*(with a look)* Twenty-eight.

**BOB:**
Sorry. Yes, well. Plenty of time. What about the fellas at work?

**ALISON:**
What work?

**BOB:**
You have got a job, haven't you?

**ALISON:**
No, Bob. Haven't had a job for years. Didn't you know that?

**BOB:**
No. How would I know that?

**ALISON:**
I just thought. I'm obviously wrong, but I had thought you'd be – sort of watching. Over me, like. I've always thought of you as watching over me. I pray to you sometimes. Not that I believe in God, but I still pray to you. Don't you ever hear me praying to you?

**BOB:**
No. No, I've told you. I haven't even been aware I existed. Nothing. Now I suddenly find myself here, with only half a memory.

**ALISON:**
I wish you could stay here, Bob. I do miss you. Can I touch you?

**BOB:**
I don't know.

*(She reaches out and touches him.)*

**ALISON:**
Yes, I can.

*(She hugs him to her.)*

Oh Bob I do love you. This is so weird. Do you love me?

**BOB:**
This feels very odd.

**ALISON:**
Do you Bob? Love me?

**BOB:**
I ... well, I used to. I know I used to.

*(She looks at him, then breaks away.)*

**ALISON:**
It's hopeless. Did you even feel me holding you just then?

**BOB:**
I'm not sure.

**ALISON:**
It's hopeless. Why did you have to die? Why did you have to get run over?

**BOB:**
Run over?

**ALISON:**
Don't you even remember that?

**BOB:**
Alison, look. You'll have to be patient with me. Things are gradually coming back. Just take it easy.

**ALISON:**
I'm sorry. It's so hard to understand.

**BOB:**
Well, let's just take it easy. I don't remember my death. I do remember you. It's beginning to happen.

**ALISON:**
Do you remember the baby?

**BOB:**
*(shocked)* Was there a baby?

**ALISON:**
No, there wasn't, but we thought there was going to be.

**BOB:**
*(shaking his head)* There's so many gaps.

**ALISON:**
Well let's go slowly. You want to know all about you and me? Then I'll tell you. Sit down, you're making the place

look untidy. *(He sits.)*

You and I were in love, Bob. I'll tell you how we met.

**BOB:**
It was raining.

**ALISON:**
Yes! Yes it was. It was soon after Mum and I moved to London. It was a very romantic meeting too.

**BOB:**
Outside the Wet Fish Shop.

**ALISON:**
*(Laughing)* That's it. It was pouring with rain and I'd just run across the road, dodging the traffic and one of my shoes came off right in the middle of the road.

**BOB:**
And I picked it up.

**ALISON:**
I was sitting on the shop step, and I saw you dash across the road and pick it up. And there you were, dressed in your uniform, like Prince Charming carrying the Glass Slipper. Without looking to right or left, you came straight over and offered to see if it fitted. "My guess is, it will" you said. I think you knew it was fairly safe to assume that.

**BOB:**
Well you were the only girl in the street with only one shoe on.

**ALISON:**
You put it on me, and I thanked you, and we went in opposite directions.

**BOB:**
I turned and watched you go. About ten yards down the road your heel broke off.

**ALISON:**
Absolutely right. You caught me up, and we limped down to the bus stop. Well, you remembered quite a lot of that.

**BOB:**
Yes – it's all coming back. Thank god, it's flooding back now. After that we started seeing each other.

**ALISON:**
We were in love.

**BOB:**
We were.

**ALISON:**
And then you were killed by that stupid bus.

**BOB:**
Was that it? A bus.

**ALISON:**
Run over by a bus. A stupid bloody double decker. What galled me was that you were buried with full military honours.

**BOB:**
*(Laughing at this)* I wasn't.

**ALISON:**
You were. Coffin draped with a flag, and your flat hat, your dress uniform cap lying on top. I'm surprised they didn't put the bus-driver's cap next to it.

*(He laughs again.)*

**ALISON:**
You can laugh. I didn't find it in the least bit funny at the time. I still don't.

**BOB:**
Come on love, you used to like to have a laugh.

**ALISON:**
I still do. But not when your life's ruined. There aren't many who'd laugh at that. Are there, be honest.

**BOB:**
Look, Alison it was nobody's fault, it happened. It was an accident.

**ALISON:**
Yes, but you still died though, didn't you. You still died. You still left me on my own – you still denied me a life with you. A family with you. You still did all that.

**BOB:**
I didn't do anything. It was done to me. I was the one who suffered.

**ALISON:**
No, I was the one that suffered. You were gone, out of it, I was the one that had my future crushed and torn away in one single tragic stupid moment of time, I've suffered every day since that moment.

**BOB:**
I think I'd better go away.

**ALISON:**
No! No, don't go.

*(She is suddenly scared of losing him again.)*

Please stay, Bob. I love you. I know it's not your fault. I'm sorry I went on, but it's only natural. I was just letting off steam I suppose. Let's talk about something else. Let's talk about when we were together. The nice days, the special times. Is the old memory-bank beginning to sort itself out yet?

**BOB:**
Yes, I think it is.

**ALISON:**
Fog clearing?

**BOB:**
Definitely. It was MacFisheries.

**ALISON:**
You what?

**BOB:**
The fish shop. We met outside MacFisheries.

**ALISON:**
That's right.

**BOB:**
And I was stationed near Basingstoke. And I was a corporal. And we used to go the Odeon together, and your favourite film star was Sean Connery because he was so butch, and my favourite was Glenda Jackson because she was so butch –

*(Alison laughs.)*

and we loved each other very much, and – and my god we nearly had a baby.

**ALISON:**
Yes we did. Yes, your memory is flooding back now. We did nearly have a baby. I was so scared. And then that all blew over, and it was all fine again.

**BOB:**
Except you wouldn't let me make love to you.

**ALISON:**
No. I wasn't risking it a second time. You used to be hopping mad.

**BOB:**
I was.

**ALISON:**
I don't know why – it was your fault it happened in the first place.

**BOB:**
But it didn't happen, did it. We only thought it happened.

**ALISON:**
Well it was your fault we thought it happened then. Not using any protection.

**BOB:**
I thought you'd taken care of that.

**ALISON:**
Well you could have asked.

**BOB:**
I was embarrassed to.

**ALISON:**
Then you should have worn one.

**BOB:**
I was embarrassed to.

**ALISON:**
Oh god!

**BOB:**
You look so silly in one of those.

**ALISON:**
Well you had socks on your feet, what's the difference?

*(Bob laughs and Alison giggles at him.)*

**BOB:**
I had exactly the same trouble with Wendy.

**ALISON:**
Wendy?

**BOB:**
Yes. You know Wendy. The girl who I knew before.

**ALISON:**
Before me, you mean.

**BOB:**
Yes – I was embarrassed with her as well. Trouble was she did get pregnant. It was just the same, I thought she'd taken a pill, she thought I was going to bring something, and I hadn't. Well it's a bit late then, isn't it? You get carried away, don't you.

**ALISON:**
Yes – well, we certainly did.

**BOB:**
That's why I joined the army, to get away from her.

**ALISON:**
Didn't you like her?

**BOB:**
Oh, I liked her well enough, but not enough to marry her.

**ALISON:**
So you left her with the baby.

**BOB:**
She had it adopted. I regretted the whole thing, all due to my not thinking ahead. I should have learned my lesson with Deidre.

**ALISON:**
Deidre??

**BOB:**
She was before Wendy.

**ALISON:**
God, your memory's working overtime now isn't it. You never told me there was any Deidre. She's new on the horizon.

**BOB:**
I didn't tell you years ago, Alison because there seemed no point in giving you too many girls to think about. But now – well, there's no point in not telling you everything is there.

**ALISON:**
You obviously don't think so. So who are the others, then Bob? Who else is listed in your little black book?

**BOB:**
Not many. No others to speak of really – except Zoe.

**ALISON:**
Zoe. Was she before Deidre?

**BOB:**
No, she was actually at the same time as you.

*(This is a great shock to Alison. She is for the moment stunned into silence.)*

She lived in Basingstoke, near the army camp.

**ALISON:**
(*quietly*) You were seeing her at the same time as me?

**BOB:**
Yes, I was.

**ALISON:**
Why?

**BOB:**
I just was lonely. I fell for her. She was blonde.

**ALISON:**
(*still dazed*) And did you make love to this blonde called Zoe?

**BOB:**
Well, yes of course.

**ALISON:**
And did you get her pregnant?

**BOB:**
No, of course not. I'd learnt my lesson.

**ALISON:**
I should think you had. Bob –

**BOB:**
Yes?

**ALISON:**
Bob. Just tell me one thing. Why? Why did you have to tell me this? Why could you not have kept this to yourself. Why cause me more pain? Why, if you have any feelings for me at all, do you do this?

**BOB:**
Alison. Try to understand. I'm not the Bob you knew. There is nothing left of the person of flesh and blood who once loved you. All love, all tenderness is part of the physical side of life. It's to do with looking and feeling and touching. And when the physical side no longer exists – when "Bob" becomes just a shade, a spiritual presence if you like, then there is no more love, no more tenderness, no feeling for you, as you put it. It's gone. All gone.

(*She is sobbing quietly.*)

**BOB:**
I feel nothing now.

**ALISON:**
Nothing.

**BOB:**
No, nothing at all. I expect that hurts you.

**ALISON:**
Yes, it does. It does hurt.

**BOB:**
And I know I should feel sorry about that. But I ... I feel ... nothing.

(*A pause. She looks at him, then says calmly*)

**ALISON:**
Then I don't know who or what you are, but you are not my Bob.

**BOB:**
I am Bob. Alison.

**ALISON:**
You are not my Bob. Go back to where you came from. I want nothing more to do with you.

(*She turns away. He takes a step towards her.*)

**BOB:**
Thank you for these few moments. It was like living again.

(*She sits, still looking away from him.*)

**BOB:**
Goodbye Alison.

(*He walks towards the darkness, and is gone. A moment. Then, with a sob, she jumps up and runs to where he has disappeared.*)

**ALISON:**
Bob! Come back! I love you Bob!

(*She waits sobbing, for him to return, but he doesn't. She goes and sits down again.*)

He's gone, Mum. I shan't ever see him again. All those years, each night I've been praying to him, talking to him, thinking he is somewhere watching over me, and he's nowhere. He's nothing.

*(She sighs, and dries her tears.)*

I only knew him about eighteen months. If only you knew when someone was going to die. You always think you've got forever. I missed out. It was because of you Mum. I should have had a baby. I missed out because of you. I should have had a baby and got married. But I didn't, because of you. You never liked him, and I didn't want to upset you, I didn't want to hurt you. But I was wrong. I should have upset you, I should have risked it, risked hurting you. It was my life, it was my young life – you'd had yours. But I didn't want to hurt you, so I finish up the one being hurt. It was all your fault Mum. Your fault!

*(A pause. She sits, stares at the fire.)*

But I forgive you *(she sighs)*. After all, you were the cause of us coming to London. I would never have even met Bob if we'd stayed in that little house in the country. I wouldn't have had that eighteen months with him at all. So it was good that you did what you did when you did it. And Dad was giving you a terrible, miserable time. You were at the end of your rope, I could see that. I'm surprised you stuck it that long.

God, what an extraordinary night that was. He'd been worse than ever the few days previous – drunk in the middle of the day, coming home from the pub and demanding his dinner, swearing and cursing if the food was too cold or too hot, then if you dared answer back he'd throw his plate at the wall. That very day he struck you across the face, and I thought "you pig, I hate your guts". What a terrible way to think of your father – but I did, that's what I thought, and I meant it. Off he went, back to the pub at half past five, and when he came home and banged on the door at eleven o'clock I thought "Christ he's had a skinful". I let him in the front door and I said to him "you don't need to bang on the door like that" and he swore at me, and pushed me down the hall way and starts using the filthiest language about me, and about you Mum, he said some terrible, awful things about you that I couldn't believe anyone could say to their daughter about her mother, and then I saw you. You came out of the front room behind him. And you had that big heavy polished steel poker from the fireplace in your hand. I shall never forget the look on your face. Almost a peaceful look, as if you knew that troubles were finally at an end. I can still hear his neck snapping. But you didn't stop, you kept hitting his head and face, still with that calm smiling look. Blood was going everywhere, but I didn't try to stop you. I was enjoying it too much to stop you. And when you'd finally exhausted yourself and his head was practically a pulp, you looked at me, and gave such a great sigh, and we clung to each other and you started to laugh with the pure relief of it. I don't know how long we stood there laughing and clutching each other, and then you suddenly said –

*(She shakes her head and laughs)*

You suddenly said "Well I think it's time for a nice cup of tea, don't you?" And then the hard work started. We sat in the kitchen, drank tea, and planned what to do next. The body had to be buried first. And it had to be buried there and then, while it was dark. The field behind the house was the obvious place. We were very isolated where we were, so there wasn't much chance we would be seen. God, it took a long time though, didn't it? The hardest part was getting him out there. I've never seen you like you were that night, though. You seemed to have the strength of ten men. You amazed me. You set about cleaning up the blood and mess just as if you were doing a bit of spring-cleaning. I wouldn't swear to it, but I actually think you were humming to yourself. Do you remember telling people he'd gone off and left you? You actually went into the "Fox and Hounds" and asked the barmaid if he'd been in lately. I don't know how you had the nerve Mum, I honestly don't. Even when we put the house up for sale, you were still going round asking if anyone had seen him. What a strange few months it was. It doesn't seem like eight years ago, but it is. We've been in London eight years. I remember walking in this room, and sitting down and saying to myself this is the future from now on, is it.

*(She looks around her.)*

And eight years later, here I am, still sitting here. Nothing important happened in my life in those years. Just getting up in the morning, and going to bed at night. I sit here, every day, talking to myself. I pretend I'm talking to you Mum, but I know you're not really there. It's just an empty chair I'm talking to. You're dead and gone. I'm completely on my own. Alone. With nothing to look forward to.

*(There is a knock at the door offstage. She goes off to answer it. An indistinct male voice is heard, and she replies "Thank you. Thank you very much". We hear the door close off.)*

*(She re-enters, carrying a large parcel.)*

**ALISON:**
Mr Jackson from downstairs. Parcel post he says. *(Tears open parcel.)* Wonder who it's from? *(A man's sweater is revealed, and a note.)* It's Nigel's sweater I knitted. *(She reads the note, briefly.)* It's too SMALL! *(She moans)* I never do ANYTHING RIGHT!

*(She bursts into tears.)*

Well, that's it. That's the finish. I can't bear it.

*(The telephone rings. Still weeping, she moves to answer it.)*

Hello. Yes, speaking. Who? … Oh. What's the trouble? Oh. Oh. Oh dear. Er, yes, I can do. Tomorrow you mean. Ten o'clock, yes, that's fine. Thank you. Goodbye.

*(She puts the phone down.)*

Mum. I'm sorry about those things I said just now. I know you're with me, and always will be. Mum, on the phone just now.

*(She now appears quite calm.)*

That was the police. They want me to go down to the station tomorrow. They've found Dad's body. A farmer ploughing.

*(She has started to clear up documents, etc, on table. She returns them to sideboard as she speaks.)*

**ALISON:**
I have to be there at ten o'clock in the morning.

*(She puts papers back in to sideboard.)*

I'll leave those for a stranger to do. So Mum. I've got about seventy pounds here.

*(Takes money out of tobacco jar.)*

I shall go to the railway station, and buy a first-class ticket as far as the money will take me. Then I shall just step off.
*(She puts on her coat.)*

You're coming too, Mum. You'll always be with me. You'll be with me until the minute I die.

*(She goes towards the darkness.)*

After that, we'll see, won't we?

*(She goes. We hear the train, but this time much closer. The sound builds to a crescendo. Then suddenly, it cuts off.)*

# EDITOR'S ACKNOWLEDGEMENTS

The editor would like to thank Glenn and Vicky Archibald, without whose much-valued assistance the book you are currently holding would probably have been rendered in crayon.

Also, for invaluable technical aid in the field, much thanks to Dave and Joyce Wilson.

Finally, for peace, love and understanding I am so deeply indebted as always to Lucy Merritt, Jessie McCabe and, now, Jack!

Bob McCabe
April 1998